Fundamentals of Insurance Planning

Huebner School Series

H. King McGlaughon, Jr., Editor

Huebner School Series

Fundamentals of Insurance Planning

*Burton T. Beam, Jr., Eric A. Wiening,
and David L. Bickelhaupt*

The American College Press/*Bryn Mawr, Pennsylvania*

This publication is designed to provide accurate and authoritative information about the subject covered. While every precaution has been taken in the preparation of this material, the authors and The American College assume no liability for damages resulting from the use of the information contained in this publication. The American College is not engaged in rendering legal, accounting, or other professional advice. If legal or other expert advice is required, the services of an appropriate professional should be sought.

Library of Congress Control Number 2005920480
ISBN 1932819185

Printed in the United States of America

To
Lindsay, Chris, and Jan
BTB

To Betsy, Don, Jon, and Mark
EAW

Contents

Preface

This book is a basic text in insurance. Like most other "fundamentals" or "principles" books, it covers risk and insurance theory as well as current products and practices. Many basic insurance books are written for college students who will become insurance consumers, risk managers, or insurance company employees. We took a different approach and emphasized what we feel a financial services professional must know about insurance in order to serve clients most effectively. Client service can involve either product sales or the analysis and evaluation of existing insurance programs. We set out to cover all the insurance topics a financial planner must master to become a Certified Financial Planner (CFP™) or a Chartered Financial Consultant (ChFC®). We also designed this text to provide a solid foundation for a life insurance professional who will pursue further insurance studies to become a Chartered Life Underwriter (CLU®).

Following introductory chapters on risk, insurance, the insurance business, and basic legal principles and contract analysis, the book describes Social Security, Medicare, and other government programs. For most clients, these and employer-provided benefits form the foundation on which an individual insurance program is built. The foundation topics are followed by an in-depth discussion of life insurance, annuities, medical expense insurance, disability income insurance, long-term care insurance, homeowners insurance, auto insurance, and other property and liability insurance coverages. Both the personal and business needs of clients are addressed.

This book is a substantially revised version of an earlier publication, the fourth edition of *Fundamentals of Insurance for Financial Planning,* published in 2003. We updated material where necessary, corrected a few errors that had crept into the predecessors of this textbook, and rewrote some sections to improve clarity. The most significant changes include the following:

- Mini-cases and more examples were added to many chapters.
- Chapter 7 was updated and revised to include the changes to Medicare as a result of the Medicare Prescription Drug, Improvement, and Modernization Act.
- Chapters 12, 13, and 15 were updated to reflect the many changes that have recently occurred in the health insurance marketplace.

- Chapters 16, 17, 18, and 19 were heavily revised to focus more on property-liability insurance principles and less on fine coverage details.

Chapters 7 and 12–15 have been the primary responsibility of Burton T. Beam, Jr., since the inception of the original book. He was also responsible for chapters 16–19 in the earlier publications.

Chapters 1–6, 8–11, and 16–20 in this edition were revised by Eric A. Wiening. Chapters 1–6 and 8–11 were originally written by the late Robert M. Crowe.

We continue to include two special features from the predecessors to this book that have been of value to students. The first is a series of checklists for evaluating and comparing insurance products. The second is a list of up-to-date sources for further in-depth study. This is not a traditional bibliography that identifies other sources that cover essentially the same material as the text. Rather, the sources listed enable a financial services professional to obtain a much more comprehensive understanding of a topic than we can cover in one book.

Writing a book of this nature and length requires a lot of hard work by a lot of people. However, we as authors have the ultimate responsibility for providing you with the best book possible. It would be foolish to believe that any book is the perfect book. Please take some time to give us your constructive comments on how we can better improve future editions. Also, if this book contains any errors, we apologize, and each of the authors acknowledges that the errors are the fault of the other author.

Burton T. Beam, Jr.
Eric A. Wiening

Acknowledgments

The American College wishes to acknowledge the following people for their contributions to *Fundamentals of Insurance Planning*. With the possible exception of the authors, no one else has spent more time working on this book than Lynn Hayes, editorial director, and Evelyn Rice, production assistant. We owe them a debt of gratitude for putting up with frequent manuscript revisions and the usual annoyances of dealing with authors and deadlines.

We gratefully thank other members of The American College's editorial, production, and graphics departments who have worked on some aspects of this text.

We thank Virginia Webb, librarian at The American College's Knowledge Center, and her staff for their support in finding all the information we have requested.

We owe a special thanks to our colleagues at The American College who have assisted us when we have had questions about their areas of expertise. We particularly want to acknowledge Ed Graves, the Charles J. Zimmerman chairholder, for his assistance with the life insurance and annuity chapters.

Finally, we must recognize the past students who asked questions and gave feedback about earlier versions of this book. Their input has provided guidance for many of the latest changes.

Burton T. Beam, Jr.
Eric A. Wiening

About the Authors

Burton T. Beam, Jr., CLU, ChFC, CPCU, CSA, is associate professor of insurance at The American College. Mr. Beam did his undergraduate work at the University of Oregon and holds graduate degrees from that institution and the University of Pennsylvania. Prior to joining The American College, Mr. Beam was on the faculties of the University of Florida and the University of Connecticut. He has written extensively in the areas of group and health insurance and has had articles published in several professional journals. He is the author of *Group Benefits: Basic Concepts and Alternatives.* He is also coauthor of *Fundamentals of Insurance for Financial Planning, Meeting the Financial Need of Long-Term Care, Health and Long-Term Care Financing for Seniors*, and *Employee Benefits,* a textbook used at many colleges and universities. Mr. Beam is an assistant editor of the *Journal of Financial Service Professionals.* He is a member of the National Association of Health Underwriters, the Financial Planning Association, the CPCU Society, the Society of Financial Service Professionals, and the Society of Certified Senior Advisors.

Eric A. Wiening, CPCU, ARM, AU, AAI, API, is adjunct professor of insurance at The American College. An insurance educator since 1975, he previously authored or co-authored a number of textbooks dealing with insurance principles and coverages. Before retiring to form his own consulting business, Mr. Wiening was assistant vice president and ethics counsel at the American Institute for CPCU. During his 26 years with the American Institute, an estimated 250,000 students of insurance took exams based on the following eight textbooks he authored or co-authored: *Personal Insurance, Foundations of Risk Management and Insurance, How Insurance Works: An Introduction to Property and Liability Insurance, Property and Liability Insurance Principles, Insurance Contract Analysis, Commercial Property Risk Management and Insurance, Commercial Liability Risk Management and Insurance,* and *Commentary on the CPCU Code of Professional Ethics.* Most of these books have been or are being translated into Chinese, Japanese, Portuguese, or Russian. He was coordinating author of *Personal Risk Management and Insurance.* Mr. Wiening is an active member of the Society of Insurance Trainers and Educators, currently serves on the Ethics Committee of the CPCU Society, and was appointed as a charter member of the

National Underwriter's FC&S Editorial Advisory Board. He has an MS degree from Temple University where he majored in insurance and risk management. Mr. Wiening served as a reviewer for the four editions of the prior publications of this text.

David L. Bickelhaupt, CLU, ChFC, CPCU, ARM, is professor emeritus of insurance and finance, College of Business, Ohio State University. He is the author of *General Insurance*—from which the roots of this textbook stem. Through its 11 editions, more than one million students of insurance in 300 colleges and many professional insurance courses have used this book. Among numerous articles he has written are those appearing annually in the *Encyclopaedia Britannica*. Over the course of his career as a leading insurance educator, Dr. Bickelhaupt has been a member of the Insurance Institute of America's National Examination Committee, president of the American Risk and Insurance Association, executive director of the Griffith Foundation for Insurance Education, and on the boards of State Auto Insurance Companies, the International Insurance Seminars, and the Insurance Hall of Fame.

Fundamentals of Insurance Planning

1

Basic Concepts of Risk and Insurance

Learning Objectives

An understanding of the material in this chapter should enable the student to

---

1-1. Define risk, loss, uncertainty, and risk-related terms.

1-2. Describe the measurement and classification of risks.

1-3. Compare insurable and uninsurable risks.

1-4. Describe how individuals may respond to risk.

1-5. Explain the costs of pure risks.

1-6. Explain how insurance can treat pure risks.

1-7. Describe the benefits and costs of insurance.

1-8. List and describe the major categories of insurance.

1-9. Define key terms in insurance terminology.

Chapter Outline

Financial planning involves three coordinated components:

- insurance planning
- investment planning
- tax planning

As its name implies, this text, *Fundamentals of Insurance Planning,* deals with the first of these components. Because appropriate insurance planning should precede investment planning and tax planning, the Chartered Life Underwriter (CLU)®, Chartered Financial Consultant (ChFC)®, and Certified Financial Planner (CFP)® programs all recommend an early course that focuses on the subject of insurance.

Both single-purpose financial planners who specialize in insurance and comprehensive financial planners recognize that insurance provides an important tool to deal with many of the risks their clients face. In order to discuss risk exposures with their clients, these financial planners, for whom this book was written, need to have a sound understanding of risk and related concepts. Accordingly, we will begin this book with two chapters that review basic concepts associated with risk. Later chapters will provide more detail regarding specific risks and how they are managed

RISK AND RELATED TERMS

Risk

Although we will attempt to define most terms used in this text as precisely as possible, "risk" presents some difficult challenges. Insurance scholars argue at length over the definition of risk. Some insurance textbooks evade the issue by omitting a definition on the basis that the meaning of risk is usually clear from its context.

risk

For purposes of this book, we will define *risk* as the *possibility of loss*. Note that this definition of risk refers to the *possibility*, not the probability or chance, of loss. Possibility means that something could occur, whether or not the chances of the occurrence can be measured or estimated. As shown later in this chapter, insurance is concerned primarily with risks that can be measured, at least in a rudimentary fashion.

Risks are everywhere, ranging from unavoidable risks to those assumed by choice. Examples of risks often assumed by choice include crossing the street when the light is red, starting a family, or buying a house. Anyone who owns property faces risks from perils such as fire, windstorm, or theft, as well as the possibility of liability lawsuits from persons who might be injured on the property.

Insurance practitioners often use risk to describe the object of potential loss or the person or object insured. An applicant for auto insurance may be referred to as a "risk." Likewise, the building to be covered by fire insurance may be referred to as "the risk." A healthy applicant or an auto insurance policyowner with a good driving record might be a "preferred risk." Chapters 1 and 2 do not use "risk" in this sense.

Loss

loss

The undesirable end result of risk is *loss*—a decline in value, usually in an unexpectedly or relatively unpredictable manner. However, losses are not always related to risk. A person giving property to a friend or a relative as a gift loses the value of that property, but this planned and intentional loss is not the result of a risk. Likewise, declines in value are often predictable. Examples include the depreciation of property or the depletion of resources as they are consumed.

loss exposure

A client's cost of risk includes not only the cost of actual losses but also the cost of dealing with losses that might occur. Losses that might occur are often called *loss exposures* and include, for example, financial losses that would arise if a fire or a death were to occur. Because only some loss exposures result in loss, loss exposures are much more numerous than actual losses.

direct loss

Losses may be direct or indirect. *Direct losses* are the first or immediate losses that arise from an event. To illustrate, if a client is found guilty of

indirect (consequential) loss

negligently driving an auto and causing bodily injury to another, the direct loss is the damages award levied against the client. An *indirect loss*, sometimes called a *consequential* loss, is a loss that occurs only as a secondary result following the occurrence of a peril. An indirect loss may be the income the client loses while attending court proceedings resulting from a liability claim.

As another example, if a client's home is severely damaged by fire from defective wiring, the direct loss is the cost to repair the damage to the home. The client and his or her family will also experience an indirect loss if they must incur extra living expenses to stay in a motel and eat meals in restaurants while their home is being repaired.

Indirect loss may result for a client even when there is no direct loss for that client. For example, many residents of lower Manhattan whose apartments escaped direct damage were not permitted to return to them for some period of time following the September 11, 2001, terrorist attack on the World Trade Center.

Uncertainty

uncertainty

While *risk* is related to "uncertainty," we believe that risk and uncertainty are separate but often related concepts. *Uncertainty* is a state of mind, typified by lack of sureness about something. Uncertainty is subjective and experienced differently by each individual, despite the same set of facts, objective reality, or risk. For example, one client may refuse to ride in a glass-enclosed elevator on the outside of a high-rise hotel, while another may be perfectly comfortable doing so. The risk—the possibility of loss in the form of bodily injury—is the same for both clients, but the two clients' uncertainty (doubt, worry, fear) differs greatly.

Uncertainty is often the result of risk. For example, a client may be highly uncertain because of the risk that his or her dependent parent may someday have to be confined to a nursing home for an extended period. On the other hand, uncertainty is also often unrelated to risk. One may be present while the other is absent, and one may be great while the other is small. An ill-mannered client may be oblivious (no uncertainty) to the possibility (a very real risk) that a lewd remark to a colleague will lead to a suit for sexual harassment. Conversely, a timid client may be terrified (highly uncertain) of flying commercially because of the possibility (but low risk) of a crash. Uncertainty is not necessarily bad. An effective financial planner can play a very important role in helping his or her client develop a healthy sense of uncertainty by pointing out risks that the client has not recognized or cannot realistically estimate. One important function of a financial planner is to achieve some balance between a client's risks and uncertainties. Although irrational phobias are hard to overcome, a planner can do a great deal to address the client's financial risk, thereby reducing the client's uncertainty.

> ***Example:*** A client with an irrational fear of contracting cancer expresses an interest in specific disease insurance (discussed in chapter 13). A financial planner can help the client recognize that he or she also faces an exposure to other health risks. The planner can then explain how adequate insurance against all health risks, not only those involving a specific disease, will address the client's uncertainties

Perils and Hazards

peril

The word *peril* refers to a cause of loss. Perils are commonplace and include unemployment, illness, old age, death, forgery, theft, fire, earthquake, windstorm, flood, and hundreds of other causes of loss.

hazard

A *hazard* is an act or condition that increases the likelihood of the occurrence of a loss and/or increases the severity of a loss if a peril does occur. Ordinarily, any particular person or object is exposed to many separate hazards. Hazards fall into three major categories:

- physical hazards
- moral hazards
- attitudinal hazards

Physical Hazards

physical hazard

The first category of hazards is *physical hazards*. These are physical conditions relating to location, structure, occupancy, exposure, and the like. Insurance underwriting requires an evaluation of all physical hazards. The following are a few examples of physical hazards: high blood pressure, a dangerous hobby, newspapers piled on a staircase, gasoline stored on the premises, weak construction that may fail in a heavy wind, unsafe brakes on a car, holes in a sidewalk, and improper water drainage systems. Each of these conditions, as well as many others, increases the chance of a loss occurring, or perhaps the magnitude of the loss if one does occur, in regard to a specific peril such as illness, accident, fire, windstorm, or theft.

Moral Hazards

moral hazard

The second category of hazards consists of *moral hazards*. These are dishonest tendencies, often due to an insured's weakened financial condition, that are likely to increase loss frequency and/or severity. Examples include tendencies to cause deliberate damage in order to collect insurance proceeds or to intentionally inflate claims for insurance proceeds beyond the actual size of the sustained loss.

Recognizing moral hazard requires studying the client's character and reputation. Evidence that an applicant ever defrauded another person, has a bankruptcy record, or has a poor credit reputation can indicate possible moral hazard with regard to insurance. Investigators also scrutinize insurance applicants' reputations in trade, their ratings with banks, their standings with competitors, and the regard in which they are held by those with whom they transact business. Individuals who have a reputation for taking unfair advantage of legal technicalities or people who have repudiated contracts in the face of possible financial loss are generally regarded as likely to resort to other unethical actions.

Financial planners need to understand the concept of moral hazard, a technical term well understood and often used among insurance professionals. This technical term is best avoided, however, when dealing with clients who understand "moral" in a different sense. A client whose financial condition is questionable is not likely to welcome any implication that somebody questions his or her morality.

Attitudinal Hazards

attitudinal hazard

The third category of hazards consists of *attitudinal hazards*, evidenced by carelessness or indifference as to whether a loss occurs or the size of a loss if it does occur. For example, laziness, disorderliness, poor dental hygiene, and lack of concern for others are termed attitudinal hazards rather than moral hazards, which are more likely to involve dishonesty. Leaving car doors unlocked increases auto thefts, and heavy smoking increases health risks. Underwriting and rating of applicants based on apparent attitudinal hazards are important to the successful operation of the insurance mechanism, as is consideration of physical and moral hazards.

Example:	A client, Mr. Rich, is purchasing a large yacht. Mr. Rich faces loss exposures because various perils could damage or destroy the yacht or result in a liability claim as a result of the yacht's use. Mr. Rich therefore applies for yacht insurance. In evaluating Mr. Rich's application, the insurer will assess the physical, moral, and attitudinal hazards associated with this particular yacht. For example, the insurance underwriter will consider the yacht's age and condition (physical hazard), any indications of negligence in the care of the boat (attitudinal hazard), and Mr. Rich's financial stability or lack of stability (moral hazard). Financial stability is relevant because a policyowner who

finds himself or herself in financial difficulty might be tempted to sink the boat and file an insurance claim to raise cash. Financial instability might result from high-stakes gambling or other questionable practices, or it might involve speculative and risky business ventures.

MEASUREMENT OF RISKS

In some cases, the probability of a loss can be measured, often precisely. In these cases, we can refer to the chance of loss, or the probability of loss, rather than merely to the possibility of loss. For example, if you enter a wager that, on the first draw from a fair deck of playing cards, you will not draw the ace of clubs, you know that the probability or chance of loss is one in 52.

In other cases, it is not possible to measure the probability of a loss. This is particularly true of unique or highly unusual risks. Consider the case of a healthy 42-year-old male client. Is it possible that he will die this year? Of course. Can we measure the probability in any meaningful way? No. Although we may learn from statistical studies that the probability of death within one year for a 42-year-old male is, say, 1.8 in 1,000, that is no help in measuring this particular client's likelihood of dying this year. He is one person, not a group of statistical persons. Either he will die or he won't die in the coming year, but certainly 1.8 one-thousandths of him will not die in the coming year. Statistical probabilities cannot be meaningfully applied in this case.

In what ways can some risks be measured? Basically, there are two ways: through *deductive* reasoning, sometimes called *a priori* reasoning, and through *inductive* reasoning, which is reasoning based on statistical analysis.

Measurement of Risks

- Deductive (a priori) reasoning: Risk is measured by physical examination before any losses occur.
- Inductive reasoning: Risk is measured by statistical analysis of past loss experience.

In the deductive approach to risk measurement, we can physically examine in advance all the possible outcomes associated with a risk and calculate the chance of loss. For example, we can examine a fresh and shuffled deck of playing cards and note that it contains 52 different cards, of which only one is the ace of clubs. We can thus deduce that, in the absence of cheating, the probability of selecting the ace of clubs on the first draw from the deck is one in 52. Similarly, we can measure the odds of heads being the result in a coin flip, the odds of rolling a seven with a pair of dice, or the odds of losing in Russian roulette.

It is important to remember that, in a small number of trials, the actual results may differ from the underlying probability. For example, 10 flips of a coin may produce seven heads and three tails. As the number of trials increases, however, the actual results will gradually come closer to the underlying 50-50 probability.

Of course, in the insurance business, the probabilities of loss cannot be derived a priori, or deductively. For example, it would be fallacious to conclude that because a 42-year-old male client will either die or not die in the coming year, the probability of his death is 50 percent.

Insurers measure risk through inductive reasoning based on statistical analysis. To illustrate, assume that an insurance company observes the loss experience on 10,000 single-family brick homes in a particular city for one year. Assume that nine of these homes experience a fire during that period. The insurer could then conclude, at least tentatively, that the probability of fire loss for single-family brick homes in that city during a one-year period is nine per 10,000, or .9 per 1,000 homes. The insurer could then develop a premium for fire insurance based on, among other things, that probability of loss.[1] However, as with the coin-flipping example, in order for the insurer to measure the odds accurately and to achieve the expected results, certain practices must be observed. The group under analysis must have both mass and homogeneity.

Mass

mass

law of large numbers

First, the statistical group that is observed for purposes of measuring the probability must have *mass*—that is, the sample must be large enough to allow the true underlying probability to emerge. As with coin flipping, if there are only a few trials, we will not be able to discern inductively the true probability. The *law of large numbers*, expressed simply, states that as the size of the sample or insured population (such as houses vulnerable to fire loss) increases, the actual loss experience will more closely approximate the true underlying probability. This means not only that the insurer's statistical group must be large enough to produce reliable results, but also that the group actually insured must be large enough to produce results that are consistent with the underlying probability.

Homogeneity

homogeneity

Second, the statistical group that is observed for purposes of measuring the probability must have *homogeneity*—that is, it must include exposure units that have similar characteristics in order for the true underlying probability to emerge. Note that the probability of .9 fire losses per 1,000 homes referred to earlier emerged from a fairly homogeneous group of exposure units: single-family brick homes in a particular city. A different probability would have emerged if apartment buildings, motels, frame-constructed homes, and homes in rural locations had been included.

In addition to homogeneity, the statistical group actually insured must have homogeneous characteristics. Moreover, the characteristics of the homogeneous group actually insured must be similar to those of the homogeneous statistical group; otherwise, actual loss experience may depart substantially from expected experience. To take an extreme case, the loss probability derived from a statistical study of single-family brick homes in a particular city is unlikely to be the same as the loss probability for a homogeneous group of oil refineries in Texas.

CLASSIFICATIONS OF RISKS

Risks can be classified in several ways. At least five of these classifications are all-inclusive and overlapping in the sense that any single risk fits into all five classifications. These classifications are as follows:

- financial versus nonfinancial
- particular versus fundamental
- static versus dynamic
- pure versus speculative
- insurable versus uninsurable

Financial versus Nonfinancial Risks

financial risk

Risks can be *financial risks* in the sense that they involve a loss of money, or they can be nonfinancial. Clearly, the possibility that a client may be faced with mountainous medical bills and lost earnings following a severe stroke is a financial risk. Various *nonfinancial risks* also involve losses associated with a severe stroke: pain and suffering, paralysis, and loss of memory for the stroke victim; loss of consortium for the victim and his or her spouse; worry and distress on the part of the stroke victim's loved ones; and so on.

nonfinancial risk

Insurance is primarily designed to treat financial risks through the payment of money as compensation in some way for monetary loss. However, insurance also frequently "compensates" for nonmonetary loss. For example, liability insurance often provides the funds to pay damages to individuals who have endured pain and suffering, emotional distress, or some other nonmonetary loss because of a policyowner's negligence. Although the insurer's payment provides compensation for a nonfinancial loss, the possibility of such a liability claim against a client involves a financial risk the client faces.

Particular versus Fundamental Risks

particular risk

Risks can also be classified as particular or fundamental. *Particular risks* are loss possibilities that affect only individuals or small groups of individuals at the same time, rather than a large segment of society. Losses from events such as embezzlement, lightning, disability, and retirement are examples that result from particular risks.

fundamental risk

Fundamental risks, in contrast, are loss possibilities that can affect large segments of a society at the same time. Examples include possibilities of widespread unemployment in an economic downturn, lost purchasing power due to runaway inflation, and massive destruction due to a nuclear accident.

Dealing with particular risks is generally thought to be the responsibility of the individuals who are exposed to them. Some social insurance programs, however, also deal with particular risks. Fundamental risks, on the other hand, are not directly related to any specific individual, and dealing with them is generally thought to be the responsibility of society as a whole through government action.

Static versus Dynamic Risks

static risk

Static risks exist apart from changes in society or the economy and include such risks as death or fire damage to a client's home.

dynamic risk

Dynamic risks are possibilities of loss resulting directly from changes in society or in the economy. Changes in consumer tastes can cause losses to some businesses. For example, the low-carbohydrate diet fad caused a noteworthy drop in income for some business firms that produce high-carbohydrate food. Changes in technology cause losses to other businesses that fail to adapt as their technology becomes obsolete. In recent years, for example, traditional film-based photography has given way to digital photography for many purposes. These changes also affect the risks of individual clients. Dietary changes, for example, affect individuals' health, and changes in photographic equipment create changes in the types of equipment various clients own and insure. Although they tend to be unpredictable, dynamic risks often involve scientific advances that improve our society. Static risks generally do not benefit society over the long run. However, because static risks are usually fairly predictable, insurance can readily treat many of them.

Pure versus Speculative Risks

Risks can be pure or speculative. Pure risks involve only the chance of loss or no loss, whereas speculative risks involve the chance of loss, no loss/no gain, or gain.

pure risk

Pure risks are "pure" in the sense that they do not mix both profits and losses. Insurance is concerned mainly with the economic problems created by pure risks. Risk aversion applies to pure risks, in which the prospect of loss only is the cause of concern. The ownership of property involves a pure risk. In regard to a peril such as a windstorm, the owner may either suffer a loss or not suffer a loss. There cannot be a gain from having the loss as long as it is assumed that an insurance payment is not for more than the actual loss. On the other hand, risk seeking—for example, by businesspersons whose purpose is the realization of gain if the business venture is successful—applies to *speculative risks*.

speculative risk

Pure vs. Speculative Risks

- Pure—possibility of loss or no loss
- Speculative—possibility of loss, no loss/no gain, or gain

Many activities involve both pure risks and speculative risks. For example, a client who purchases a house faces pure risks because a fire or other peril could damage the house, reducing its value. The client also faces speculative risks, because the market value of the house might either increase or decrease depending on the general real estate market or other local factors. Most of the pure risks can be insured, but the speculative risks are not insurable.

Because speculative risks involve an element of both profit and loss, they may sometimes be nullified by a process known as *hedging*. Hedging is a procedure by which two compensating or offsetting transactions are used to ensure at least breaking even.

hedging

Example: Sam Farmer has a crop of corn that he will harvest and sell at the end of the season. He is concerned that the price of corn will decline and he will have difficulty recovering his cost of production. If his cost of production was $250 per bushel, and at the time of harvest the market price is $300, he will have a $50 profit. If the market price at the time of harvest is $225, he will have a $25 loss. He currently has a *speculative* or *unhedged* position, where he has unlimited upside potential if the market price increases, but he also can lose up to his full investment if the market price declines.

Sam might hedge his position by selling a contract now that is binding on both sides, guaranteeing a sale price of $290. At the time of harvest, regardless of the market price, he must sell at the contract price of $290 and realize a $40 profit. Thus, in a hedged position, both the upside potential and the downside loss are limited.

The hedging process is not always available because it depends on the existence of an active futures market. The futures market is well developed for some goods and financial instruments within certain time limits, but it does not exist for many others.

Subcontracting can involve a form of hedging. In subcontracting, for example, a general contractor obtains contracts at fixed prices for parts of the total job to be completed in the future.

gambling

Gambling, which is a special type of speculation, shares many of the attributes of insurance. Perhaps this is the reason so many uninformed persons think of insurance as gambling and sometimes even feel that they have "lost the bet" if they fail to have a loss equal to the cost of insurance. The methods of operation may appear similar, but insurance is concerned with an existing risk. Insurance does not create risk; it transfers and reduces a risk that already exists. Contrast this to a bet: No risk exists before the bet is made, but one is created at the time of the gambling transaction, thereby putting values in jeopardy that were not in jeopardy before the bet.

Personal, Property, and Liability Risks

The pure risks confronting individuals and businesses are ordinarily divided into three categories. The first of these categories of risks is ordinarily termed *personal risks* and is concerned with death, injury, illness, old age, and unemployment.

personal risk

The second category of risks arises from the destruction or loss of property and is referred to as *property risks*. Direct losses from fire, lightning, windstorm, flood, and other forces of nature, and from man-made perils like vandalism, theft, collision, and terrorism offer a constant threat of loss to real estate, as well as to all kinds of personal property. Indirect losses also may occur, including the loss of profits, rents, or favorable leases.

property risk

Finally, *liability risks* involve the operation of the law of liability. An individual may be legally liable for an injury to another—for instance, through an auto accident where the driver is negligent and injures a pedestrian. Liability risks are termed third-party risks because, when insurance is used to shift the burden of responsibility, the insurer and the policyowner have agreed that a third party, the injured person, will be paid for injuries for which an insured is legally liable.[2] The liability risk mainly includes both bodily injury and property damage and also includes various other types of risks. For example, the potential responsibility to pay personal injury damages for such offenses as libel, slander, trespass, invasion of privacy, or wrongful eviction is also a liability risk.

liability risk

Insurable versus Uninsurable Risks

insurable risk

An *insurable risk* has certain characteristics that can effectively be addressed with private insurance—that is, insurance from privately owned insurance companies. As we will explain elsewhere in this text, government insurance programs and other forms of social insurance do not necessarily meet the same criteria. Insurable risks are usually financial, particular, static, and pure risks involving losses that meet these five requirements:

- The amount of the loss must be important.
- The loss must be of an accidental nature.
- Future losses must be calculable.
- The loss must be definite.
- The loss cannot be excessively catastrophic.

Many insured risks do not meet each of the requirements perfectly, but when considered as a whole, they must meet the requisites to the satisfaction of an insurer.

Importance

Insurance functions most efficiently and effectively to treat substantial risks for which the major component in the insurer's premium is expected claims rather than the insurer's administrative expenses. The insurer's expense of selling and administering insurance for small claims is too high to make insurance efficient for small claims. Risks that involve a threat of no great consequence are best handled by other means.

For example, a client's favorite pen might be lost or eyeglasses broken. These are loss exposures. But the financial, particular, static, and pure risks they involve are not significant enough to warrant the use of insurance. The client can treat these losses as current expenses, to be paid out of pocket.

Some commonly insured losses violate the principle that insurance should be used for important losses. For example, many auto insurance policies cover towing costs for nominal amounts such as $25. This practice apparently developed years ago because a benefit offered by the American Automobile Association or other auto clubs prompted a demand for a similar benefit from auto insurers. Similarly, group health insurance often covers relatively minor medical expenses, partly because the costs are subsidized by the client's employer. The financial planning process often involves identifying unimportant insurance coverages that might represent an inefficient use of the client's financial resources.

Accidental Nature

Insurable risks normally must be of an accidental nature. Insurance is intended to cover fortuitous or unexpected losses. The loss need be accidental only from the insured's standpoint. The loss could, for example, be intentionally caused by someone else such as a thief or a vandal. Intentional losses caused by the insured are usually uninsurable because the insurer cannot reasonably predict them, and payment for them would violate public policy by encouraging such actions as fraud or arson. Other losses are so common as to be expected rather than unexpected. Wear and tear and depreciation are examples of expected losses that normally are not insurable.

Calculability

A third requisite of an insurable risk is that the chance, size, and variability of future losses should be reasonably calculable. Losses may be unpredictable for any one individual, but an insurer should be able to obtain reasonable projections of future losses if it covers a sufficiently large number of homogeneous (similar) loss exposures.

Insurers occasionally cover isolated loss exposures for which there is no previous experience. For example, aviation insurers must provide insurance that will keep pace with the rapid advances in the industry. The advent of space travel created a need for large amounts of insurance in a field where statistical data once were entirely lacking. Most insurance is written, however, to cover risks where losses may reasonably be expected and where mathematical treatment or judgment based on experience permits a sufficiently exact estimate of losses to project the aggregate probable cost. When experience extends over a period of years, the number of exposure units is great enough, and underlying conditions have not changed, a premium can be computed that will reasonably ensure a sum sufficient to pay losses, compensate the insurer, and provide stability and permanence in the business. When new insurance forms are instituted, it becomes necessary to make rates that depend on "underwriting judgment." In some instances, this is nothing more than an approximation or guess that is adjusted with the accumulation of experience. A good example is long-term care insurance, a relatively new product that began to appear in the early 1980s. Insurance rates were initially based on underwriters' judgment, but rates have been refined over the years as premium and loss experience accumulates.

The need for large numbers applies not only to the total business an insurer accepts but also to each class of business. In addition, the exposures must be independent of one another so that reasonable estimates of loss can be made.

Definiteness of Loss

Losses should be definite; otherwise estimates of possible loss are difficult. Many insurance contract provisions have the objective of making the determination and measurement of insured losses as clear and definite as possible. The contract must clarify the perils as well as the losses. Whether or not the loss actually occurred and, if so, when, where, and why it occurred, as well as how many dollars of loss are involved, all usually must be discernible. A loss due to lightning meets the definiteness criterion rather well, whereas a loss due to sickness may not meet it as well.

Example:	Ted is a salesman of beachfront homes in Destin, Florida. His income is entirely in the form of commissions, almost all of which he earns during the spring and fall months. In December, Ted becomes ill with a case of the flu and is unable to work for 7 weeks. Ted's loss is not very definite. Was he really ill or just taking a vacation from work? When did the illness begin and end; was he really laid up for the full 7 weeks? How much income would he have earned during the period of his illness?

No Excessively Catastrophic Loss

Ordinarily, no excessive catastrophic possibility of loss should be associated with an insurable risk. A single large loss or the simultaneous occurrence of many smaller ones could destroy an insurer's financial stability. A geographic concentration of many small loss possibilities, such as insuring most of the houses in the same small town, can be potentially catastrophic for an insurer. The size of loss deemed catastrophic depends on the financial resources available to the insurer.

Summary

The requirements for an insurable risk are not absolute. Insurability is best described as a relative matter in which the insurable quality of the risk is determined by appraisal of all the requirements together. The size and ability of the insurer are also important. Many common kinds of insurance do not meet each of the requirements perfectly. Consider, for example, the following: Is a theft loss definite (that is, was the item really stolen or just lost)? Are all drivers similar in regard to the risk of auto accidents? Obviously not, although they may be relatively similar within age, type of car, and other classifications. Is a fire caused by carelessness always accidental? Aren't windstorms such as hurricanes and tornadoes catastrophic in nature?

Careful analysis in applying each of the requirements for an insurable risk to a particular peril shows that few, if any, are perfect insurable risks. Most are only relatively good ones, and some are fine examples of bad ones. Many insurance contract and insurer underwriting restrictions deal with this problem, trying to improve the insurability of a risk by such methods as limitations on the amount of coverage and locations, prohibited types of activities, specific contract definitions, deductibles, and reinsurance. What is insurable may change over time and with the use of such limitations. Long-term care, for example, was considered uninsurable for many years, but the costs of long-term care are now commonly insured.

Example: Shem is a client who owns a vacation home on the lakeshore. In addition to perils such as fire and vandalism, Shem is concerned about the possibility of flood damage to this property. Is flood damage to a lakeshore home an insurable risk? Consider the criteria:

- Unless Shem's vacation home is a shack, the amount of the loss appears to be important.
- Unless the water level in Shem's lake is controlled by a dam, a flood loss would almost always be of an accidental nature.
- Unless conditions have changed, the frequency of flood losses on Shem's lake can probably be calculated based on historical records and a flood map available from the Federal Emergency Management Agency (FEMA). which, in March 2003, became part of the Office of Homeland Security (see www.fema.gov). Unless Shem's land washes away or is permanently buried under rising water, the value of any flood loss should readily be calculable.
- Any flood loss will be definite. Nobody is likely to question whether a flood has occurred.
- The loss might, however, be excessively catastrophic from the viewpoint of any private insurer. A localized flood will probably affect many homes on the same lake. A widespread flood will result in losses not only at Shem's lake but also throughout the region.

Flood damage to real property meets most of the requirements to qualify as an insurable risk. However, the catastrophic loss potential is so great that private insurers are generally not willing to bear the risks of selling flood insurance. As noted later in this book, a government insurance program enables private insurers to offer this coverage.

DIFFERENT REACTIONS TO RISK

Risk may result in substantial losses, worry, and inefficiency. It can also lead to great reward and satisfaction.

Linus, in the famous *Peanuts* comic strip, enters the risky world reluctantly. He drags his security blanket around continually in order to have the comfort of familiarity to buffer the unknown. His friend Charlie Brown deals with unpredictable risk as he attempts to kick off the new football season, because he never knows whether Lucy will pull the ball away from him. This example illustrates the undesirable features of risk: unpredictability or not knowing, insecurity, and some resulting discomfort.

Risk is desirable to those who believe "nothing ventured, nothing gained." Entrepreneurs invest time, effort, and money for the uncertain profits that may result. Businesspersons conduct their operations with the hope of profit and the threat of loss in mind. The skydiver, the astronaut, and the drag racer also are risk takers. Sir Walter Scott valued risk taking, too, when he said, "One hour of life . . . filled with noble risks is worth whole years of paltry decorum."[3]

risk-tolerance level

Each person's reaction to risks depends on his or her *risk-tolerance level*. A person's risk-tolerance level is the degree to which that individual is attracted to or adverse to the possibility of loss. Risk tolerance clearly differs widely from person to person, situation to situation, and risk to risk. Although it is extremely difficult to measure risk tolerance accurately, it is also extremely important that a financial planner recognize each client's risk-tolerance level in order to tailor a financial plan that includes appropriate levels of risk.

Behavioral psychologists who examine individuals' risk tolerance have reached the following conclusions:

- Most people are more risk averse than they are risk tolerant.
- Risk taking in physical or social activities (for example, race car driving or marital infidelity) is not correlated with financial risk taking.
- The way in which questions about a risk are worded or posed to a person can influence the person's expressed attitude toward that risk.
- Emotions can severely limit a person's ability to make rational decisions about a risk.
- People tend to overestimate low-probability risks (for example, the risk of having one's child kidnapped) and to underestimate higher-probability risks (for example, disability).
- People are more likely to be risk averse if the major effect of a possible loss will fall on them or their loved ones, rather than mainly on strangers.
- Most people have a greater fear about risks with which they are inexperienced (for example, skydiving) than about risks with which they are experienced (for example, driving on an interstate highway).

COSTS OF PURE RISKS

Because pure risks generally produce either losses or no losses, they represent potential costs with few or no offsetting benefits. The costs of pure risks include not only actual losses that occur and associated expenses, but also worry and fear, less-than-optimum use of resources, and the expense of managing risks.

Costs of Pure Risks

- Actual losses that occur
- Worry and fear about possible losses
- Less-than-optimal use of resources
- Costs of managing the risks

Actual Losses

Actual losses may be serious, crippling a business or causing an individual or family great financial hardship. Direct physical loss, such as fire damage, causes several billion dollars of property loss each year in the United States. The cost of indirect loss, such as lost profits following a direct loss, is also considerable. Billions of dollars are lost, too, because of the loss of human life values due to such perils as death and disability. It is no wonder that most people prefer to do something about pure risks rather than merely to accept them.

Fear and Worry

Fear and worry are costly. Valuable time is spent thinking about real or imagined chances of loss. The opportunity cost of worry, time, and effort is probably staggering when we consider the many other things that we could do if there were no fear of loss. "If only we could work as hard as we worry" expresses the cost of lost peace of mind.

Less-than-Optimal Use of Resources

Pure risk leads to a less-than-optimal use of resources, the third factor that contributes to the cost of pure risks. Most people do not predict the chance of loss correctly. Some are pessimistic and overestimate; others are optimistic and underestimate. The result is either wasteful preparation for losses that are not as likely as expected or lack of preparation for unexpected losses that may have serious financial consequences.

Investments are frequently influenced by the exposures to loss with which they are associated. Sometimes activities or investments are completely avoided because the exposure to loss is high in spite of excellent earnings potential. Too much money "put away for a rainy day" may be in very safe liquid investments to be readily available if and when it does rain or some other peril causes loss. Without such risk and uncertainty, the money could be invested in a much more productive capacity with potential for greater return. Returns in relation to true loss exposures are often less than optimal, and these reduced earnings are an additional cost of risk.

Because of loss exposures, there is also a tendency to concentrate planning on the near future rather than on the significant benefits of long-range planning. The cost of risk increases to the extent that exposures to loss cause this error in planning.

Cost of Managing Risks

The third type of cost that society experiences because of the presence of pure risks is the cost of managing pure risks. There are numerous ways to treat pure risks. For example, a sprinkler system can be installed in a factory to minimize the size of a loss if a fire occurs. An alarm system can be installed in a jewelry store to reduce the likelihood of a burglary loss. An annual mammogram or PSA test can help in the early detection of cancer. Insurance can be purchased to cover the possible legal liability for negligently driving an auto. However, all of these ways cost money, and these expenditures thus represent an added burden for society directly resulting from the presence of pure risks.

RISK EXAMPLE

Don and Andrea Green, a married couple in their early 30s, own a small home in a suburban community that borders on a large lake. They park their two cars in the driveway when they are not at work. Don, who has a masters degree, works as a bank loan officer. Andrea, who has a high school diploma, works as a supervisor in a local pet shop. The Greens have no children yet, but they have two dogs and many other pets. Both Don and Andrea are covered by the group medical expense plan available through Don's employer. Andrea has no employee benefits other than a one-week annual vacation.

Risk is the possibility of *loss*. Don and Andrea face many risks. To name just three of them, their home could be damaged by the *peril* of flood, resulting in a loss of value of this asset; one of the dogs could bite a neighbor's child, resulting in a liability lawsuit against the Greens; and Don could lose his job, resulting in a loss of income. They address the *uncertainty* associated with these risks, at least in part, by purchasing homeowners insurance that provides both property coverage and liability coverage and by establishing a small emergency fund. For Don and Andrea, the insurance and the emergency fund are some of the *costs of risk*—costs they must incur because of the risks they face.

The *physical hazards* Don and Andrea face include the potential of flood damage because they live near a lake, plus any conditions that might cause one of their dogs to leave the yard and attack a child, such as a defective fence or leash. Because they are careful with the dogs, the situation does not present an *attitudinal* hazard that would be of special concern to an underwriter, and the Greens' sound financial and personal situation does not suggest a *moral* hazard.

Death and sickness rates can be computed for people their age, but general statistics do little good in evaluating the likelihood that either Don or Andrea will die or face a serious health problem in the coming year. The *law of large numbers* simply does not apply to only two people. This is true even though Andrea has a minor heart condition that puts her in a slightly higher-than-average risk category that might cause an insurer, applying the law of large numbers to its entire insured population, to charge a higher premium for any individual life or health insurance she might purchase.

Don and Andrea face *financial risks,* including the possibility of medical bills and a loss of income resulting from disability. They also face *nonfinancial risks*, such as the pain and suffering that could result from an auto accident.

The possibility that Don, the primary breadwinner, could lose his job because the bank that employs him is acquired by another bank presents a *particular risk*. The possibility that the bank could reduce its workforce due to a general decline in the overall economy presents a *fundamental risk.*

The risk that fire might damage their big-screen TV is a *static risk.* The risk that the TV becomes worthless because new high-definition TV technology makes it obsolete presents a *dynamic risk.* In any case, the TV presents a *pure risk* rather than a *speculative risk*; the TV might lose value if it is damaged or becomes obsolete, or its value might hold fairly constant, subject only to depreciation; it is not likely the TV will increase in value.

Don and Andrea's *personal risks* include the risks of unemployment, injury, illness, disability, and death. Their *property risks* include the risks of damage to their home, cars, big-screen TV, or pets. Their *liability risks* include not only the possibility of a dog-bite claim against them, but also the possibility of an auto accident or other incident that might result in a claim for damages.

Insurance can address many of Don and Andrea's risks. Auto liability risks, for example, can be insured because the amount of a potential loss is important, any insured loss would be accidental, future losses are calculable, any loss would be definite, and the loss is not excessively catastrophic.

INSURANCE AS A TECHNIQUE TO TREAT PURE RISKS

In this section, we will examine insurance as a means of treating pure risks. For now, we will consider only what insurance is, the benefits and costs it creates for society, and the major categories of insurance.

What Insurance Is

Insurance, like risk, is difficult to define succinctly, and different definitions are used when insurance is examined from different viewpoints. For example, insurance may be viewed as

- an economic system that reduces financial risks through a transfer and combination (pooling) of losses
- a binding legal contract that transfers risks to an insurer
- a contract that meets specific legal or regulatory definitions
- a business institution that provides many jobs in a free enterprise economy
- a social device through which the losses of few are paid by many
- an actuarial system of applied mathematics
- a risk management technique for financing insurable risks

Defined As an Economic System

insurance

Insurance has been defined as an economic system that reduces financial risks when a policyowner transfers risks to an insurer, which combines the potential losses. Perhaps this is the most common definition, but it is not the only one, and it is far from perfect. For example, insurers sometimes cover unique situations that do not combine the losses of similar policyowners. And various loss-financing techniques, such as pooling (various parties agree to share their losses), can combine potential losses without transferring them to an insurer.

The insurance system responds to the economic law of supply and demand. Ideally, insurance increases value for the insured by reducing the insured's cost of risk while, at the same time, enabling the insurer to earn a profit. This win-win situation occurs when the cost of insurance is both low enough to appeal to insurance buyers and high enough to produce a profit for the insurer.

Defined As a Legal Contract

An insurance policy, also known as a contract, is a legal document used to transfer financial risk for a premium (price) from one party, known as the *insured* or the *policyowner,* to another party, known as the *insurer.* Through a legally binding contract, the possibility of an unknown large financial loss is exchanged for the certainty of a comparatively small premium payment. The insurance contract does not guarantee losses will not occur, but it provides a method of insuring repayment, or indemnity, if any loss occurs that is within the scope of the contract.

Legal or Regulatory Definitions

Because many types of regulation and taxation apply specifically to insurance, it is often critical to determine whether a given plan or contract qualifies as insurance under the relevant definition. Various state and federal laws and regulations define insurance for regulatory and tax purposes, and the definitions are not necessarily concise or consistent. The National Association of Insurance Commissioners, for example, has drafted a 12-page definition of insurance.[4] Readers might be grateful that we will not attempt to summarize that document here.

Situations in which a legal or regulatory definition of insurance can be critical include the following:

- Product warranties on new homes, autos, tires, and appliances are sometimes referred to as insurance, but they are not generally recognized by law as insurance. The companies that offer these products need not therefore organize an insurance company, hold reserves, or pay state insurance premium taxes.
- Variable annuity contracts, which are not defined by the courts as exclusively insurance contracts, are subject not only to state insurance laws but also to the federal regulation of the Securities and Exchange Commission.
- Employee benefit plans, including hospital and medical benefit plans, have been subject to many legal decisions that affect their status as insurance contracts.

Business Institution

Insurance companies are financial institutions—often very large financial institutions—that specialize in the treatment of risks. As a business, an insurance company performs various functions that include marketing, underwriting, and claims, all of which will be discussed in more detail in a later chapter.

Social Institution

Insurance has also been defined as a social device by which the risks of many individuals are transferred to a group of persons who, in effect, agree to pool their losses. All members of the group contribute to a common fund, administered by an insurer, and payments are made from this fund to those who have a loss. Contributions to a fund are not essential. Groups may rely instead on assessments collected from the various participants after each loss.

Mathematical Sense

In a mathematical sense, insurance merely applies certain actuarial principles, such as laws of probability and statistical techniques, to achieve predictable results.

Risk Management Technique

Insurance can be viewed as one of many techniques used to manage risks. Specifically, insurance can be viewed as a risk-financing technique that transfers the financial consequences of covered losses to an insurance company. Losses can be transferred to other individuals or organizations, but unless an insurance company is involved, the technique does not qualify as insurance.

Benefits and Costs of Insurance

In a society without insurance, would banks lend money on homes or businesses if they were uncertain as to whether the collateral value could be lost due to fire, windstorm, or other perils? Would finance companies approve installment loans for autos or other household goods? Would anyone want to drive an auto if liability for losses caused to others could not be insured? Would anyone want to own a home that could be destroyed in a few hours without any way to recover the loss? Would workers choose hazardous but important occupations if they were uncertain whether employers would pay for work injuries? How would a young family man or woman provide an income for dependent children without life insurance? How would a person provide for payment of large medical bills? Insurance provides protection regarded as essential throughout the economic and business environment.

Clearly, insurance provides many benefits. But these benefits are not cost-free. In this section of the chapter we will discuss the benefits and costs associated with insurance.

Benefits of Insurance

We have already presented some examples of the wide scope and benefits of insurance. A summary of the most important benefits of insurance includes all the concepts discussed in the following paragraphs.

The most obvious benefit of insurance is that it pays claims when losses occur. Additional benefits, some of them more subtle, include that insurance

- encourages peace of mind
- provides a basis for credit
- stimulates saving
- provides investment capital
- offers advantages of specialization
- fosters loss prevention

We will briefly examine each of these benefits.

Pay Losses. Insurance supplies the financial resources that often permit a family or an organization to continue despite serious losses. The death or disability of a breadwinner can bring financial disaster to a family. With family income stopped, the spouse and/or children might have to give up their home and accept undesirable alternatives such as foster homes, living with relatives, or relief payments. A fire or a liability suit can wipe out a family's assets. These perils can be met through insurance, which provides indemnification or repayment at the time of need in order to keep a family or business intact.

Encourages Peace of Mind. Uncertainty is a state of mind that leads to anxiety. To the extent that insurance improves policyowners' ability to predict their financial futures, it reduces uncertainty and improves peace of mind. Although this psychological benefit is hard to measure, peace of mind adds to the quality of everyday life.

Provides a Basis for Credit. Commercial lenders naturally want assurances that their loans will be repaid. Loans are available—often at a favorable interest rate—when insurance provides these assurances. Money is often borrowed to finance the purchase of property, such as an auto or a home, that could be destroyed or seriously damaged before the loan is paid off. Lenders routinely require debtors to purchase auto physical damage insurance, homeowners insurance, or other appropriate insurance to protect the lenders' interests in property used as collateral for a loan. Similarly, life insurance—either face values or cash values—is used to guarantee that a loan will be repaid despite the borrower's death. Other forms of insurance may protect the lender in the event the borrower's disability reduces his or her ability to make payments on the loan.

Stimulates Saving. Many kinds of insurance encourage thrift. An insurance premium, although small in relation to the possible loss it protects against, is basically a prepayment of a potential loss. All the payments are combined in a fund from which those few who do suffer losses are paid. In essence, insurance encourages all to save so that the few who are unfortunate can be repaid for their losses. In addition, life insurance has special advantages in stimulating savings. The long-term contracts, often over an insured's entire lifetime, build substantial loan, emergency, or retirement values. Policyowners treat their regular premium payments as an obligation to their families or beneficiaries; greater savings result than with other well-intentioned but less regular savings programs.

Provides Investment Capital. Insurers are required to hold huge amounts of money in reserve to pay future losses and expenses. This money is invested in government and corporate bonds, stocks, and other assets. Because insurers' assets are huge, their investments provide a gigantic source of capital for the economy—hundreds of billions of dollars to governments and business organizations. Property and liability insurers invest a smaller, but very significant nonetheless, amount.

Offers Advantages of Specialization. Insurers specialize in handling risk, and they can often handle risks more efficiently than individuals or businesses can. By transferring its financial risks to an insurer, insurance buyers say, in effect, "Here, you take care of these bothersome, unpredictable risks for us, and we will concentrate on our primary goals." Insurance can help a married couple, for example, to focus their retirement planning on positive lifestyle goals rather than on building a large emergency fund to deal with unpredictable health care expenses.

Fosters Loss Prevention. Insurance benefits society by fostering considerable effort to prevent losses. Loss prevention is a secondary goal for most kinds of insurance, but undoubtedly more loss prevention work occurs because of insurance than would occur without it. The net effect is advantageous, as lives are saved and property values preserved. Examples are fire prevention campaigns, motor vehicle safety research, education by health insurers, and elevator and boiler inspections. Also important in this work are associations such as Underwriters Laboratories Inc. and the Insurance Institute for Highway Safety.

Costs of Insurance

The costs of insurance include

- operating costs
- profits
- opportunity costs
- increased losses
- adverse selection

Policyowners fund these costs by paying premiums.

Operation Costs. Operating expenses that enable insurers to do business account for approximately one-fourth of each dollar that insurers take in. The proportion varies by type of insurance. Operating expenses include agents' commissions, home office and field administrative expenses, loss adjustment expenses, and taxes. The costs of operating insurers, their agency systems, and other services must be balanced against the benefits of insurance, enumerated earlier.

Profits. Insurers must earn profits to increase their surplus positions and reward investors. Profit margins are small, perhaps less than 5 percent on average, in relation to the total premium dollar. Profits are necessary, however, because insurers would not otherwise attract the necessary operating capital.

Opportunity Costs. Opportunity cost is defined as the cost of pursuing one alternative versus another. The insurance business requires financial capital, personnel, and materials that could make other valuable contributions to the economy and to society if they were not devoted to the insurance business. For example, people not employed in the insurance business, a service business, might instead work in a factory and produce tangible products. These opportunity costs represent one of the costs of insurance.

Increased Losses. Increased losses result because insurance sometimes stimulates moral and attitudinal hazards. The existence of insurance can encourage fraud to collect losses that insureds cause intentionally and to exaggerate claims beyond actual losses. The greater carelessness that occurs when people feel completely insured is another cost of insurance. These effects tend to be relatively minor and rare, but some, such as fires caused by arson, are a major and growing problem. Although the costs are difficult to measure precisely, constant effort to control these possible costs is necessary.

adverse selection

Adverse Selection. *Adverse selection* is the natural tendency for those who know they are highly vulnerable to loss from a specific risk to be most inclined to acquire and retain insurance to cover that loss. For example, a person who has just been diagnosed as a diabetic is likely to be highly desirous of obtaining and/or retaining medical expense insurance. A family with a 16-year-old son who has just acquired a driver's license will probably want full-coverage auto insurance on the car. And a homeowner living in California will be especially interested in obtaining earthquake coverage.

Adverse selection simply reflects a rational emphasis on the applicant's own self-interest. In any case, however, adverse selection produces poorer loss experience among those who are insured than among those who are not insured.

Table 1-1 summarizes the benefits and costs associated with insurance.

TABLE 1-1
Benefits and Costs of Insurance

Benefits of Insurance	Costs of Insurance
Pays for losses Provides a basis for credit Encourages peace of mind Stimulates saving Provides investment capital Offers the advantages of specialization Fosters loss prevention	Operating costs Insurer profits Opportunity costs Increased losses Adverse selection

Major Categories of Insurance

Many types of insurance are available to households and organizations. Several overlapping ways of grouping these types are as follows:

- life and health insurance versus property and liability insurance
- personal insurance versus business insurance
- private insurance versus government insurance
- individual insurance versus group insurance

Each of these pairs is described below.

Life and Health versus Property and Liability

The life and health category of insurance includes various types of insurance that deal with personal risks related to death, medical care costs, disability, and old age. Examples in this category are life insurance, medical expense insurance, disability income insurance, and long-term care insurance.

The property and liability category of insurance includes coverages that provide reimbursement for direct and indirect losses to property. It also includes types of insurance that cover the possibility of being held legally responsible for damages to someone else. Examples in the property and liability category include auto insurance, homeowners insurance, aviation insurance, marine insurance, and surety bonds.

Personal versus Business

Personal insurance is the category of insurance used by individuals and families. Examples in this category are homeowners insurance, personal auto insurance, life insurance, and disability income insurance.

Business insurance is the category of insurance used by businesses and other organizations. Examples include key employee life insurance, commercial liability insurance, business overhead expense insurance, workers' compensation and employers liability insurance, commercial auto insurance, commercial property insurance, business income insurance, and disability income insurance to fund a disability buy-sell agreement.

Private versus Government

Private insurance includes all forms of insurance that privately owned insurers provide. Government insurance consists of various types of insurance programs that the state or federal governments operate. Government insurance programs can be divided into social insurance programs, such as Medicare, and other government insurance programs such as flood insurance and crop insurance. However, the distinction between social insurance programs and other government insurance programs is not always clear-cut.

social insurance   *Social insurance* consists of various government programs in which the elements of the insurance technique are present. These programs are designed to help solve the major social problems that affect a large portion of society. Social insurance programs are of several types: Social Security, Medicare, unemployment insurance, temporary disability insurance, and workers' compensation insurance. These major insurance programs are described in chapter 7.

Even though there are variations in social insurance programs, and exceptions to the rule always exist, social insurance programs tend to have the following distinguishing characteristics:

- compulsory employment-related coverage
- partial or total employer financing
- benefits prescribed by law
- benefits as a right
- emphasis on social adequacy

Compulsory Employment-Related Coverage. Most social insurance programs are compulsory and require that the persons covered be attached—either presently or by past service—to the labor force.

Partial or Total Employer Financing. Although there are significant variations in social insurance programs, most require that the employers of the covered persons fully or at least partially bear the cost of the program. The remaining cost of most social insurance programs is paid primarily by the persons covered under programs. With the exception of Medicare and certain unemployment benefits, the general revenues of the federal government and state governments finance only a small portion of social insurance benefits.

Benefits Prescribed by Law. Although benefit amounts and the eligibility requirements for social insurance benefits are prescribed by law, benefits are not necessarily uniform for everyone. Benefits may vary by such factors as wage level, length of covered employment, or family status. However, these factors are incorporated into the benefit formulas specified by law, and covered persons cannot choose an increased or decreased level of benefits.

Benefits As a Right. Social insurance benefits are paid as a right. The need for benefits is presumed. This feature distinguishes social insurance programs from public assistance or welfare programs under which applicants, in order to qualify for benefits, must meet a needs test by demonstrating that their income or assets are below some specified level.

social adequacy

Emphasis on Social Adequacy. Benefits under social insurance programs are based more on social adequacy than on individual equity. Under the principle of *social adequacy*, benefits are designed to provide a minimum floor of benefits to all beneficiaries under the program, regardless of their economic status. Above this floor of benefits, persons are expected to provide additional resources from their own savings, employment, or private insurance programs. Within certain maximum and minimum amounts, benefits are a function of a person's covered earnings under social insurance programs. The main emphasis, however, is on social adequacy. An emphasis on social adequacy results in disproportionately large benefits in relation to contributions for some groups of beneficiaries. For some programs, high-income persons, single persons, small families, and the young are subsidizing low-income persons, large families, and the retired.

individual equity

In contrast, private insurance programs are based on *individual equity*. Each individual's contributions to the program, in the form of insurance premium payments, are based on an actuarial analysis that reflects the insurer's cost of providing insurance benefits for the risks that individual face.

Individual versus Group

Private insurance can be written on either a group basis or an individual basis. Most auto and homeowners insurance is individual insurance, whereas most medical expense insurance is group insurance provided through an employer. More persons have life insurance through group plans than under individual policies, but the premium volume and amount of coverage in force are greater for individual policies. People who buy individual life insurance often purchase substantial amounts of insurance as part of a financial plan that reflects the extent of their life insurance needs, while group life insurance usually covers most or all employees for more nominal amounts set by the employer.

individual insurance

Individual insurance is usually owned by the person or entity who is the insured or who owns the insured property, but there are some cases where the policy may be owned by a third party. Examples include life and health insurance purchased by individuals on their family members and by businesses on key employees. The acceptability for coverage and the premium charged are usually determined by the characteristics of the person, entity, or property insured.

group insurance

master contract

In contrast to most individual insurance contracts, *group insurance* provides coverage to more than one person under a single contract issued to someone other than the persons insured. The contract, referred to as a *master contract*, provides benefits to a group of individuals who have a specific relationship to the policyowner. Group contracts usually cover full-time employees, and the policyowner is either their employer or a trust established to provide benefits for the employees. However, the policyowner can also be a union, association, fraternal group, or other organization.

Example: Darrel and Sally Lewis, a married couple in their late 50s, are covered by both individual insurance and group insurance. Darrel's employer provides group health insurance that covers both Darrel and Sally, as well as group long-term and short-term disability and group term life insurance on Darrel's life amounting to two times his salary. Darrel pays part of the cost of his life insurance, which is deducted from his paycheck; his employer pays the other costs of his group insurance. Sally's employer provides $25,000 of group term life insurance covering Sally's life, which is paid entirely by her employer.

     Their individual insurance includes auto insurance, homeowners insurance, and long-term care insurance policies. In addition, Darrel and Sally have both purchased individual whole life insurance policies.

certificate of insurance

     Employees covered under the group insurance contract receive *certificates of insurance* as evidence of their coverage. A certificate is merely a description of the coverage provided and is not part of the master contract. In general, a certificate of insurance is not even considered to be a contract and usually contains a disclaimer to that effect. However, some courts have treated it as a contract when the provisions of the certificate or even of the explanatory booklet of a group insurance plan vary materially from the master contract.

Individual vs. Group Coverage

Individual	Group
• Mostly property and liability insurance	• Mainly life and health insurance
• Policyowner is usually the insured	• Policyowner is usually the sponsor of the group
• Only one or a few people are insured under one contract	• Many people are insured under one master contract
• Insured is usually the policyowner and receives the policy	• Insured is usually not the policyowner and receives a certificate of insurance
• Coverage begins at the inception of the policy	• Many people's coverage begins long after inception of the policy
• Individual evidence of insurability required	• Usually no individual evidence of insurability required
• Class rating often used to set rates	• Experience rating often used to set rates

In individual insurance, the coverage of the insured normally begins with the inception of the insurance contract and ceases with its termination. However, in group insurance, individual members of the group may become eligible for coverage long after the inception of the group contract, or they may lose their eligibility status long before the contract terminates.

evidence of insurability

For group insurance, individual members of the group are usually not required to show *evidence of insurability* when initially eligible for coverage. Evidence of insurability is the documentation or other evidence submitted to the insurance company regarding the physical condition, financial condition, driving records, or other attributes of the applicant for insurance coverage. This evidence will be taken into account when the insurer determines whether or not to accept the risk.

This is not to say that group insurers neglect to underwrite group members, but rather that they focus on the characteristics of the group (such as its prior claims experience, size, composition, geographic location, and stability) instead of the insurability of individual members of the group. As with individual insurance, the underwriter must appraise the risk, decide on the conditions of the group's acceptability, and establish a rating basis. Underwriting is discussed in further detail in chapter 4.

A final distinguishing characteristic of group insurance is the use of experience rating. If a group is sufficiently large, the past loss experience of that particular group will be a factor in determining the current premium the policyowner is charged.

OTHER INSURANCE TERMINOLOGY

Insurance is a large and diverse business, and its discussion requires the use of many terms that have specific insurance meanings. Some terms such as risk, hazard, peril, and loss exposure are defined earlier in this chapter. At this point, however, we should mention a few additional terms that are used throughout this book.

applicant
policyowner

An *applicant* is a person or organization that applies for insurance coverage. If an insurance contract comes into effect, the applicant becomes a *policyowner* or policyholder. Traditionally, the common insurance usage was policyholder. However, over time and for many types of insurance, the term policyowner has become increasingly common, and, for the sake of consistency, this is the term the authors of this book have decided to use.

insured

An *insured* under a policy can be, but is not necessarily, the policyowner. In individual life insurance, for example, the person on whose life a policy is issued is always the insured and is often but not necessarily the policyowner. A policyowner may own a policy on the life of another person, the insured. Typically, the policyowner determines the beneficiary of the coverage for future death claims and has the rights to change, renew, or cancel the policy and the obligations to comply with policy conditions such as the payment of premiums.

In most types of individual insurance other than life insurance, an insured can best be defined as a party to whom, or on whose behalf, benefits may be payable. The policyowner (often referred to as the named insured) is usually an insured but so can many others be such as family members or employees of the policyowner, or other drivers of a covered auto.

In group insurance, the policyowner is usually a business or some other type of organization. The insureds are the persons who have coverage under the group, and, in most cases, the policyowner is not an insured. The varying definitions of who is insured is discussed in later chapters for specific types of insurance.

Example:	Nathan purchases a life insurance policy that will pay $100,000 to his wife, Jane, if Nathan dies. Nathan is the policyowner and the insured; Jane is the beneficiary.
	Nathan also purchases a life insurance policy that will pay Nathan $50,000 upon Jane's death. In this case, Nathan is the policyowner and the beneficiary, but Jane is the insured.
	Nathan's father, Walter, purchased a $200,000 life insurance policy on Nathan's life to provide funding for the college education of Nathan's daughter, Lauren. In this policy, Walter is the policyowner, Nathan is the insured, and Lauren is the beneficiary.
	Nathan also owns an auto insurance policy that covers the liability of family members and others using his car with permission. Nathan is the policyowner; Nathan, Jane, Lauren, and other drivers are insureds. No beneficiary is involved in an auto insurance policy.

line of insurance

In insurance terminology, *line of insurance* usually means a type of insurance. Regulators are specific about what constitutes a line from a regulatory standpoint because detailed statistics must be reported by line. For example, some lines of insurance for property and liability insurance companies include homeowners, ocean marine, workers' compensation, private passenger auto liability, and surety bonds. Lines of life and health insurance companies include ordinary life, credit life, individual annuities, and group accident and health. The functional operations of a specific insurer may or may not be broken down along these same regulatory lines, and an insurer may use the term line for nonregulatory purposes to describe its business from a functional standpoint. For example, all private passenger auto insurance may be handled by one department and be referred to as a line, while regulators consider this insurance two lines—private passenger auto liability and private passenger auto physical damage. Types of insurance for individuals and businesses are often referred to as personal lines and commercial lines, respectively.

PLAN OF THIS BOOK

Chapter 2 of this book further examines pure risks, particularly the process for managing pure risks. The chapter describes various techniques for identifying these risks, as well as techniques, in addition to insurance, that can be used to treat them.

Thereafter, the focus of the book is on insurance. The insurance industry and its marketing and other functions are discussed, along with its regulation. Then the basic legal principles that underlie insurance contracts and insurance contract analysis are examined.

Chapter 7 deals with the principal social insurance programs noted earlier in this chapter. Individual life insurance and annuities for individuals, families, and businesses are the focus of chapters 8 to 11.

Health insurance—medical expense coverages, disability income insurance, and long-term care insurance—is discussed in chapters 12 to 15. Then attention is turned to several major personal property and liability coverages in chapters 16 to 19, including auto and homeowners and concluding with a review of certain types of business property and liability coverages.

MINI-CASE: AMY AND JOHN SCHULTZ

This mini-case introduces Amy and John Schultz, who are the basis for several mini-cases throughout this text. Chapter 1 introduces basic information regarding Amy and John. Later chapters provide more information as additional topics are discussed.

Amy Schultz, aged 28, and her husband, John, aged 33, are both engineers employed by SKH, Inc. John, a product manager, has a masters degree and an annual salary of $95,000. Amy has a bachelors degree and a current salary of $55,000. They met at work and moved into Amy's small apartment when they were married 2 years ago and began saving money for a house. They currently have $60,000 in a money market account.

SKH provides group benefits that include life insurance of two times their salaries, medical expense insurance, short-term disability insurance, and long-term disability insurance. SKH also offers a 401(k) plan, but Amy and John have never participated.

Amy and John have just purchased their first house which is across the street from an elementary school. The location is especially desirable because they plan to have children in the near future.

Both Amy and John own and drive late-model compact cars, purchased before they were married, and both cars are now completely paid for. They carry separate auto insurance policies, partly because of John's bad driving record, with the minimum coverages required by law.

They purchased their 80-year-old home for $240,000 with 20 percent down and a 15-year mortgage at an interest rate of 5 percent. They also purchased a homeowners insurance policy to satisfy one of the conditions of their mortgage. Amy and John plan to invest a great deal of time and effort during the next few years to repair, redecorate, and maintain the home.

Amy and John own no individual insurance policies except the auto and homeowners insurance policies mentioned above.

a. Identify one peril and one hazard John and Amy face.

b. Identify one risk that Amy and John face in each of the following categories:

- financial
- nonfinancial
- particular
- fundamental
- static
- dynamic
- pure
- speculative
- insurable
- uninsurable

c. Based on the case facts, how do Amy and John appear to react to risk?

d. Give one example of each of the following types of insurance that currently protects Amy and John, or if they have no insurance of that type, cite one example they could consider:

- life and health insurance
- property and liability insurance
- individual insurance
- group insurance

e. What benefits are associated with Amy and John's current insurance? f. What costs are associated with Amy and John's current insurance?

(See answer section for answers to mini-case.)

SOURCES FOR FURTHER IN-DEPTH STUDY

Many books include a bibliography of other material on the subjects covered. Unfortunately, many of these sources cover the material at a similar level and in similar detail. The authors of this book have instead decided to include a selected list of sources that go into more detail for those readers who desire further in-depth study. Each of the sources includes a phone number and/or Web site from which you can obtain ordering information.

•   •   •

- For more on the topic of client risk tolerance, Taylor, Don. A., and Worsham, C. Bruce, *Financial Planning: Process and Environment,* chapter 4, Bryn Mawr, PA: The American College Press, 2005. Phone 888-263-7265. Web site address www.theamericancollege.edu
- For a detailed discussion of group insurance, Beam, Burton T., Jr., *Group Benefits: Basic Concepts and Alternatives,* 10th ed., Bryn Mawr, PA: The American College Press, 2004. Phone 888-263-7265. Web site address www.theamericancollege.edu
- For a surprisingly interesting book on risk, Bernstein, Peter L., *Against the Gods: The Remarkable Story of Risk,* New York: John Wiley & Sons, Inc., 1996. Phone 877-762-2974. Web site address www.wiley.com
- For a more detailed discussion of risk and its relationship to insurance concepts, Wiening, Eric A., *Foundations of Risk Management and Insurance,* chapter 1, 1st ed., Malvern, PA: The American Institute for Chartered Property Casualty Underwriters, 2002. Phone 800-644-2100. Web site address www.aicpcu.org

CHAPTER REVIEW

Answers to mini-case, review questions, and self-test questions start on page 793.

Key Terms

risk	physical hazard
loss	moral hazard
loss exposure	attitudinal hazard
direct loss	mass
indirect (consequential) loss	law of large numbers
uncertainty	homogeneity
peril	financial risk
hazard	nonfinancial risk

particular risk	adverse selection
fundamental risk	social insurance
static risk	social adequacy
dynamic risk	individual equity
pure risk	individual insurance
speculative risk	group insurance
hedging	master contract
gambling	certificate of insurance
personal risk	evidence of insurability
property risk	applicant
liability risk	policyowner
insurable risk	insured
risk-tolerance level	line of insurance
insurance	

Review Questions

1-1. What is the difference between risk and uncertainty?

1-2. Your client Jim owns a printing business but rents the premises where the business is conducted. What types of losses might a fire cause to Jim's business?

1-3. Sally, a single working mother with two young children, recently learned that her stress at work is giving her high blood pressure. Sally is concerned that if she were to die, her children would no longer have her income to support them until they are grown. In this case, specify what the following factors represent for Sally:
   a. risk
   b. peril
   c. hazard

1-4. Your client Al is applying for auto insurance to cover Al and his wife, Anne. For each of the following conditions identified in the underwriting process, indicate the type of hazard involved:
   a. Anne is blind in one eye and has had two heart attacks recently.
   b. Al recently received two speeding tickets.
   c. There have been several instances in the past where Al submitted inflated claims for property damage under his homeowners insurance coverage.

1-5. Your client Janet Jones is 29 years old and works full-time to support her two small children and her husband, who was disabled in an auto accident last year. Although money is tight, you suggest that she consider the purchase of life insurance to provide support for the children and her disabled husband if she were to die. How would you respond to the following questions posed by Janet:

    a. She first asks, "With the probability of death so small for a woman aged 29, there's very little chance that I'll die in the near future. So why do I really need to buy life insurance?"

    b. After you respond, she asks, "If life insurance companies can use probabilities to determine the likelihood that a woman aged 29 will die, why can't I use them to determine the likelihood that I will die?"

1-6. Distinguish between fundamental and particular risks with respect to
    a. whom they affect
    b. who is generally thought to be responsible for dealing with them

1-7. Give an example of how ownership of a home can provide a client with each of the following types of risk:
    a. pure risk
    b. speculative risk

1-8. Describe the types of risks with which insurance commonly deals.

1-9. Your client believes that insurance is just a form of gambling and would prefer to gamble her money in Las Vegas rather than make bets with an insurance company. Explain why insurance is not a form of gambling.

1-10. List the five requirements that must be met substantially in order for a risk to be considered insurable.

1-11. Explain why the various clients you encounter will react to risk differently.

1-12. What costs are experienced by society as a result of pure risks?

1-13. Define insurance from the following viewpoints:
    a. economic
    b. legal
    c. business
    d. social
    e. mathematical

1-14. Describe the benefits and costs of insurance.

1-15. Identify the distinguishing characteristics of social insurance programs.

1-16. Explain how group insurance differs from individual insurance.

Self-Test Questions

T   F   1-1. Risk is the reason that insurance exists.

T   F   1-2. As defined in this course, risk is the probability or chance of loss.

T   F   1-3. The extra expense a client incurs by living in a hotel after a fire has damaged his home is an example of a direct loss.

T   F   1-4. Because uncertainty is a state of mind, two clients facing the same risk situation can have varying degrees of uncertainty.

T   F   1-5. Hazards are causes of loss such as death, fire, or legal liability.

T   F   1-6. Moral hazards are evidenced by carelessness or indifference.

T   F   1-7. Hazards are important in underwriting and rating applicants for insurance.

T   F   1-8. A client can use the probability of a loss to measure the risk he or she faces.

T   F   1-9. If an insurer observes a large number of similar exposures in estimating the probability of loss, it is very likely that the actual loss experience for its own insureds will closely approximate the expected loss experience from its observations even though the number of its own insureds is very small.

T   F   1-10. Because fundamental risks are not the fault of any specific individual and affect large segments of the population at the same time, they are generally thought to be the responsibility of society as a whole through government action.

T   F   1-11. Because pure risks involve a possibility of gain as well as loss, they can be handled effectively with hedging.

T   F   1-12. Insurance is essentially a form of gambling risk because the policyowner pays a relatively small premium to protect against a relatively large loss.

T   F   1-13. To be insurable, a risk must substantially meet the requirements of importance, accidental nature, calculability, definiteness of loss, and no excessively catastrophic loss.

T   F   1-14. The only cost associated with pure risk is the actual loss that takes place.

T   F   1-15. One of the several ways in which insurance can be defined is as an economic system that reduces financial risk through a transfer and combination of losses.

T   F   1-16. Adverse selection refers to some people's attempt to take unfair advantage of insurance.

T   F   1-17. There are a variety of benefits as well as costs associated with insurance as a technique for handling risk.

T   F   1-18. Depending on their characteristics, government insurance programs may or may not be social insurance.

T   F   1-19. Unlike welfare programs, social insurance emphasizes individual equity rather than social adequacy.

T   F   1-20. Employees covered under group insurance receive a certificate of insurance as evidence of their coverage.

NOTES

1. Among the other factors on which the premium would be based are the average size of the losses experienced, a margin for contingencies, a loading to cover the insurer's expenses, a margin for profit or addition to the insurer's surplus, and perhaps the investment earnings the insurer could realize from the time the premiums are collected until the losses must be paid.
2. If the first party is the insured policyowner and the third party is the claimant, readers might be wondering, "Who is the second party?" The second party to the insurance contract is the insurer. However, the term "second party" is rarely used in practice.
3. Sir Walter Scott, *Count Robert of Paris*, chapter 25.
4. National Association of Insurance Commissioners, *Definition of Insurance* (Kansas City: NAIC, draft: August 4, 2000).

2

Managing Risks

Learning Objectives

An understanding of the material in this chapter should enable the student to

2-1. Describe the nature and scope of risk management.

2-2. Describe the basic methods of treating risks.

2-3. Describe the objectives of risk management and the role of the risk manager.

2-4. Explain how insurance works.

2-5. List and describe the four steps in the risk management process.

2-6. Describe various forms of employer-sponsored insurance.

Chapter Outline

Chapter 1 discussed the costs of pure risk. Those costs include (1) the actual losses that occur from various perils, (2) fear and worry because of possible losses from those perils, and (3) the less-than-optimal use of resources because of the difficulty of estimating the probability of loss. Because these costs are not accompanied by corresponding benefits, most people want to do something **risk management** about the pure risks they confront. *Risk management* is the term commonly used to describe a systematic process for dealing with these risks. The need for risk management, in turn, gives rise to a fourth cost of pure risks—the expenses that must be incurred to treat them.

Financial planners must help their clients identify risks and alternatives for managing those risks. This chapter begins by looking at the nature, scope, and objectives of risk management as well as the role of the risk manager. Next, it describes the basic methods of treating risks, because the major goal of risk management is the coordination of these various alternatives. Then it discusses the individual steps in the process of risk management in more detail. Finally, the entire risk management process is reviewed in a few brief case studies that illustrate risk management decision making.

NATURE AND SCOPE OF RISK MANAGEMENT

The key steps in the risk management process are[1]

- identification. The process begins with the recognition and classification of various risks.
- measurement. The next step is the analysis and evaluation of risks in terms of frequency, severity, and variability.
- choice and use of methods to treat each identified risk. Some risks can be avoided, some controlled, some retained under planned programs, and some transferred by a method such as insurance.
- administration. Once the methods of treatment are chosen, plans for administration of the program must be instituted. This last step includes both implementing the methods selected and monitoring the choices to see that they are effective.

The details involved in these steps are described later in this chapter.

Insurance is the principal method of treating the pure risks of many businesses and households. But without careful study of all the risk management alternatives in a coordinated decision-making process, insurance may be used inappropriately, or not used where it is appropriate.

OBJECTIVES OF RISK MANAGEMENT

The objective of risk management is to preserve the assets and income of the organization or household against the possibility of accidental loss. Implicit is the idea that preservation concerns all assets—those of property and of people. Also, the idea of protection encompasses many different methods of treating pure risks.

More specific risk management goals might be the following:

- survival
- peace of mind
- lower costs or higher net income
- stable earnings
- minimal interruption of business operations or personal life
- continued growth
- satisfaction of social responsibility with a good public image

Some of these are pre-loss objectives, meaningful before a loss has occurred. Some are post-loss objectives, and several are significant both before and after a loss.

Example:	Karen and Joel Wolf are empty nesters in their late 50s who are considering an early retirement. They are not yet eligible to receive Social Security benefits, and retirement will eliminate the flow of earned income. However, Karen and Joel believe they can support themselves on income from their investments and their employers' retirement benefits. Karen and Joel's risk management goals are likely to focus on survival, peace of mind, reduced costs, stable cash flows from their retirement plans and investments, minimal interruption of their personal life, and maintaining their public image. Meeting these goals requires attention to preserving their assets and their retirement income, using both insurance and other risk management techniques.

ROLE OF THE RISK MANAGER

Many business firms and other organizations employ a full-time risk manager. The risk manager of a larger firm has, in a majority of cases, full responsibility in the property and liability area for (1) identifying and evaluating risks, (2) selecting insurers, (3) approving insurance renewals and amounts, (4) negotiating insurance rates, (5) seeking competitive insurance bids, (6) keeping insurance records, (7) choosing deductibles, and (8) handling insurance claims. The risk manager usually shares authority for (1) deciding whether to insure or retain (including self-insuring) financial risks, (2) selecting insurance agents and brokers, (3) instituting safety programs, and (4) reviewing contracts other than insurance. In some organizations, the risk manager also has some responsibility for life and health insurance programs, while in others these programs fall within the scope of the human resources or personnel department.

Sometimes, particularly in small- and medium-size firms, an insurance agent, broker, or consultant serves as the risk manager, because the organization has no one person assigned to these responsibilities. Larger agencies and brokerages, especially, offer to serve in this capacity. Care must be taken to see (1) that the services are much broader than mere insurance coverages and include loss prevention and other risk treatment alternatives and (2) that the insurance agency or brokerage representative or consultant knows the firm's special individual needs.

Risk management is not only a business concept. Individuals and families can apply the same risk management principles a business uses, usually on a smaller scale. Like a business, almost every individual or household uses various techniques, including insurance, for treating pure risks. Few, if any, families employ a full-time risk manager. Like small- or medium-sized businesses, individuals and families often draw on the advice and services of an insurance agent or broker in addressing some of their risk management needs. Many also benefit from the services of a financial planner.

BASIC METHODS OF TREATING RISKS

It is said that, if the only tool in your toolbox is a hammer, then every problem will look like a nail. The point, of course, is that no single tool adequately addresses all needs. By the same token, any single risk management tool does not provide an adequate solution to deal with all pure risks. In practice, usually all, or at least several, techniques are used together to provide the best answers for meeting the financial problems of risk. Two basic methods of treating risks are risk control to minimize losses and risk financing to pay for those losses that do occur.

Risk Control Methods

risk control

Different ways of subdividing the major methods of *risk control* for clients are possible. The emphasis of each of the following four risk control methods is on minimizing losses that might occur to assets and income:

- risk avoidance
- loss prevention
- loss reduction
- noninsurance transfers

Risk Avoidance

risk avoidance

One of the most obvious methods of handling risks is *risk avoidance*. Risk avoidance, the most extreme form of risk control, is used when a party decides not to incur a loss exposure or to eliminate one that already exists. For example, a family might avoid some specific liability loss exposures by deciding not to place a trampoline in its back yard or removing a trampoline that is already there. A family can decide to rent rather than buy a home, avoiding the possibility of losing the home's value through the peril of fire. A manufacturer may decide not to produce a chemical that could generate products liability claims. People who worry about poisonous snakebites or heat exhaustion can live in the Arctic, or at least locate in an area with a minimum exposure to these perils. People who want to avoid the risk of airplane accidents, drownings, and sports injuries can do so largely by keeping away from airplanes, water, and sports activities, respectively.

Example:	Jack and Jean Hill have recently relocated to Naples, Florida, with their three young children. They have instructed their realtor that they do not wish to consider any home that has a swimming pool. Thus, they wish to use avoidance to treat the risk of a child's drowning in their pool.

Avoidance is not a practical solution to many risks inherent to normal activities. True, some unusual risks with a high chance of loss can be avoided, but realistically, risk avoidance is only an alternative for a limited number of risks. Some risks may be impossible to avoid; others may not be economically desirable to avoid because of the high costs of doing so or because avoiding one risk may create another. For unavoidable risks, other solutions must be considered.

Loss Prevention and Reduction

loss prevention
loss reduction

Two methods of risk control, loss prevention and loss reduction, are closely related.

Loss prevention is directed at lowering the probability of loss. The goal of *loss reduction* is to reduce the severity of loss, and it includes steps taken either before or after the loss occurs.

Example:	Marie's doctor has urged her to obtain a flu shot in November. He points out that the shot will lower the likelihood that she will contract the flu in the ensuing months (loss prevention) and may speed up her recovery time if she does contract the flu (loss reduction).

Some loss prevention and loss reduction measures available to families and organizations are as follows:

- building fire-resistant structures
- installing security devices in homes
- scheduling annual physical examinations and mammograms
- using auto seatbelts
- introducing wellness programs into workplaces
- using safety devices to guard against injuries from lawn mowers and other machinery

Loss prevention measures, which attempt to keep losses from occurring, are obviously used before any loss occurs. Loss reduction measures apply when a loss occurs and attempt to limit its severity. However, many loss reduction measures must be put into place before losses occur. A fire extinguisher, for example, can limit the damage done by a wastebasket fire. But the fire extinguisher—a loss reduction measure—must be purchased before the fire occurs.

Noninsurance Transfers

noninsurance
transfer

The final method of risk control includes some *noninsurance transfers*. These transfers are effected by a contract other than an insurance contract, in which one party transfers legal responsibility for a specific activity and any resulting losses to another party. A later section of this chapter discusses other noninsurance transfers that are methods of risk financing rather than risk control, because they transfer financial risk but not ultimate legal responsibility.

Subcontracting is one example of a noninsurance transfer as a means of risk control. To illustrate, a contractor may wish to transfer the possibility of injury to employees in a particularly dangerous part of a construction project to someone else. Subcontracting thus eliminates the original contractor's exposure to these losses.

Likewise, a homeowner might hire a pest control company rather than using a do-it-yourself approach that might subject the homeowner, family members, or neighbors to the improper application or use of poisonous chemicals.

Risk Financing Methods

risk financing

In most cases, the methods of risk control previously discussed reduce the possibility of losses. The one exception is risk avoidance, which eliminates the possibility of loss. Under the other risk control techniques, losses can still occur—and some additional choices are necessary when deciding how to pay for those losses. The alternative methods of *risk financing* may be divided into two major types:

- risk retention
- risk transfer

Risk Retention

risk retention

If a risk has not been avoided, the exposed person or organization may choose to keep, or retain, the financial burden of any resulting losses by *risk retention. Planned risk retention* is the result of purposeful, conscious, intentional, and active behavior. For example, a household or firm may evaluate some of its risks as having high frequency but low severity and deliberately decide to retain them. However, many pure risks are retained due to lack of planning or failure to recognize the risk rather than from a rational planning process. *Unplanned risk retention* is also common. Some risks are retained because the existence or significance of the risks is not known. Lack of knowledge or inability to reach the right decision, even with adequate knowledge, may result in unplanned risk retention. Information may be available and not used, or perhaps the necessary information is unavailable. Consider the long-term care loss exposure. Retention here is often the result of (1) not knowing the probability or possibility of the need for and costs of long-term care, or (2) not knowing that insurance can be obtained for such a loss exposure.

Unplanned risk retention can also result from unintentional or irrational action or from passive behavior due to laziness or lack of interest in discovering possibilities of loss. Many young married people, for example, carry little or no life insurance because they view death as a problem for much later or a subject they don't want to discuss.

Unimportant risks may be intentionally retained due to (1) necessity, when other alternatives are not possible, (2) control or convenience, or (3) the cost of insuring. The first reason demands that risk retention be used; the second and third result from a conscious effort to analyze the benefits of retention in terms of control, convenience, or cost, and the ability of individuals or business firms to handle their own risks effectively.

Some important pure risks must be retained because transferring them is not possible. For example, a self-employed person with a long history of heart disease may be uninsurable for life and health insurance, so retention of the loss possibilities associated with further heart disease may be the only available option. Sometimes markets for insurance are temporarily unavailable, and retention is necessary until the competitive world markets make adjustments that permit risk transfer. For example, political risk insurance is sometimes unavailable to cover property loss exposures in certain foreign countries.

Organizations often practice risk retention because they wish to have the control or convenience of paying for their own losses. An employer may pay employees' hospital expenses directly, for example, to improve cash flow by handling expenses when they occur rather than paying a premium in advance. A manufacturer in a competitive technical field might decide to retain both property and products liability loss exposures in connection with a research laboratory's highly secret inventions. Individuals or families who have accumulated an adequate emergency fund might also choose to retain certain exposures, often by purchasing insurance with a substantial deductible.

deductible   A *deductible* is a portion of a covered loss that is not paid by the insurer. Deductibles are a form of partial risk retention. Having the insured receive payment only for losses over a stated amount or duration has been accepted for many years in most types of medical expense, disability income, and property insurance. Deductibles are also found in some types of liability insurance policies. Deductibles lower insurance premiums by eliminating the relatively high claims costs associated with small losses. From the insurer's perspective, deductibles also minimize moral/attitudinal hazards by leaving an insured responsible for a portion of any loss.

Some insurance policies require deductibles. In most cases, however, any required deductible is a relatively modest amount. Optionally higher deductibles are usually available, often at significant premium savings.

Example:	Tom Burton has a homeowners deductible of $1,000 rather than his insurer's standard amount of $250. The annual premium saving is $200. In other words, by decreasing his loss recovery by $750, he saves $200 per year. Inasmuch as the average policyowner has a homeowners loss only once every 15 to 20 years, the long-run savings could be substantial.

The appropriate deductible for a given situation varies, based on several factors. Among these factors are the nature of the perils, including the frequency and severity of loss patterns; the client's financial ability to withstand losses; the existence of reserves or funds to help finance the deductible portion of losses; the policyowner's or the insurer's desire for claims handling; the need for loss prevention services; and the client's degree of risk aversion. Another important consideration is the premium reduction associated with any deductible. One fundamental risk management principle is, "Don't risk a lot to save a little." Suppose $500 deductible collision coverage on an auto costs only $10 more than $1,000 deductible coverage. Even if a client is able to retain a $1,000 loss, the added retained risk of the higher deductible might not be worth the savings.

The relative costs of alternative risk treatment methods are a major consideration in most decisions to retain a risk. A comparison of the cost involved in each alternative method of financing losses is necessary. If insurance against earthquake damage is available, how much will it cost? If earthquake damage could be prevented by extra-strong building construction, how much would this cost? Would a self-insurance program with a reserve fund be feasible for a business, and what would its cost be? In each of these comparisons, the need for complete evaluation is obvious. Not only must loss frequency and severity be considered, but also all costs of the various alternatives, including indirect as well as direct costs, must be evaluated for fair comparisons. Another significant cost factor that must be evaluated is the cost of funds, which can make risk retention plans more desirable because assets are held until losses actually occur. Tax-related issues must also be considered.

Risks that a business client or a family retains must be financed in some way. The more common methods are described below.

Absorption in Current Operating Expenses. The most common method of risk financing for retained risk is to absorb losses out of regular operating expenses or family budgets. Large organizations often generate sufficient cash inflow to absorb costs, but smaller firms are less likely to be equipped to withstand ongoing losses. Businesses might consider treating glass breakage, transportation shipment damage, and auto physical damage as current operating expenses. For individuals and families, the budget usually provides even less room for absorbing unexpected losses. However, dental bills, eyeglasses, and auto towing expenses can be among the possible candidates for this type of treatment.

Funding and Reserves. For an organization, a fund of actual segregated assets or a reserve may be used to offset losses that are too large to absorb in current operating expenses but small enough that the entity can reasonably retain the risk. For a family, an emergency fund might serve the same role.

The major disadvantage of many reserve accounts is that they do not guarantee that cash will be available to meet losses. Problems with segregated funds include (1) how large the fund should be, (2) how it can be accumulated in spite of intervening losses that might be disastrous, and (3) how the fund can be maintained without raiding it for other emergencies or in the organization's or household's regular operations.

Many individuals and families have savings and liquid investments that serve a similar role, whether or not they are set aside as a segregated emergency fund. Within limits, these resources can enable a family to retain the financial consequences of a loss that is too large to assume out of the monthly budget. A good example of this type of loss is short-term disability or limited periods of unemployment.

self-insurance

Self-Insurance. Although the term *self-insurance* is often applied to any retention of financial risks, the proper use of the term applies to formal programs of risk retention. Self-insurance is generally appropriate only for a large business in which the business acts like an insurance company for its own risks. This involves having a large number of similar potential losses, the ability to predict overall losses with some degree of accuracy, and the establishment of a formal fund for future losses and their possible fluctuations.

captive insurer

Captive Insurers. Another risk financing method—the use of a *captive insurer*—is closely related to self-insurance. In this risk-financing method, a large organization establishes a separate subsidiary insurance company to write its own insurance. Today, many captive insurers also write insurance for unrelated outside firms as well as for their own parent companies or groups.

Risk Transfer

Some of the most important risks that individuals and organizations must finance cannot reasonably be retained. Often, these risks have low loss frequency but high loss severity. Then the sole risk financing method left for consideration is *risk transfer*, which involves shifting as much as possible of the financial consequence associated with the risk to someone else. The risk itself will still exist, but another party will largely bear the financial consequences. Three methods of risk transfers are possible: (1) credit arrangements, (2) other noninsurance transfers, and (3) insurance.

risk transfer

Credit Arrangements. The use of credit contracts to pay for losses may be considered a method of risk transfer. However, borrowing money usually has other primary purposes such as home financing or business expansion. Because credit is always limited, depending on the borrower's financial situation and capabilities ("All you have to do to get credit is to prove you don't need it"), it seems generally unwise to rely overly on credit for relatively unpredictable needs. Pure risks, especially for large and infrequent types of losses, are difficult to handle by borrowing after the need arises. Therefore, the household or organization that relies on credit should make prior arrangements to obtain these funds, such as establishing a line of credit, in case a loss occurs.

Other Noninsurance Transfers. Risks may also be shifted by several other types of noninsurance transfers. When noninsurance transfer is used as a risk financing method, the financial burden of losses, rather than the ultimate legal responsibility, is transferred. For example, purchasing an extended warranty on an auto or an air conditioning system is a common noninsurance transfer method that individuals and households can use to handle the financial consequences of pure risks. Likewise, businesses and organizations often use hold-harmless agreements to transfer the financial consequences of some of their pure risks.

hold-harmless agreement

Most noninsurance transfers to finance risk deal with liability risks. In a *hold-harmless agreement,* the transferee agrees to hold the transferor harmless in case of legal liability to others. The transferee agrees to pay claimants or the defense costs of claims or lawsuits, or to repay these losses if they fall on the transferor. If the transferee is unable to pay the losses, the ultimate responsibility remains with the transferor.

Several types of legal contracts commonly include hold-harmless agreements. In lease contracts, a variety of legal responsibilities are transferred from one party to another in this manner. A sample hold-harmless agreement appears in figure 2-1. This particular agreement is between a catering company and a property owner, Tucson Activities Center, Inc. The catering company wants to hold functions on this property, and the property owner wants to protect itself in the event the catering company does anything, such as injuring a guest or serving liquor to a minor, for which the property owner could be sued. A similar agreement might be signed by a couple or a family renting the facility for a wedding reception or a graduation party. For example, a lease often states that property maintenance is the responsibility of the transferee (lessee) who rents the property from the owner. Homes, apartments, autos, and many other types of property are often leased or rented subject to hold-harmless agreements.

Insurance. Among the methods of risk transfer, insurance is by far the most common. Chapter 1 described the nature of this risk transfer method. The next section of this chapter describes briefly how insurance works.

HOW INSURANCE WORKS

How can an insurance company assume a large risk for a comparatively small premium and soon thereafter make a large loss payment? For example, life insurance pays some death claims on policies issued and in force for less than

FIGURE 2-1
Hold Harmless Agreement—Example Document

HOLD HARMLESS AGREEMENT

This Hold Harmless and Indemnification Agreement ("Agreement") is entered into by and between First Class Catering, a Partnership, hereinafter "Promisor," and Tuscon Activities Center, Inc., a Corporation, hereinafter "Promisee," on this _____ day of _____, 20__, in Tuscon, Arizona.

Recitals

Promisor desires to rent Promisee's premises and building, located at 300 Party Lane, Tuscon, Arizona, for an event to be held on <date>, and at other times as mutually agreed upon between the parties. The intent of this Agreement is to indemnify Promisee from any claims arising from and related to Promisor's use and rental of these premises.

Agreement

FOR VALUABLE CONSIDERATION, the receipt of which is hereby acknowledged, Promisor and Promisee agree as follows:

Promisor will indemnify and hold harmless Promisee from any and all claims, actions, and judgments, including all costs of defense and attorney's fees incurred in defending against same, arising from and related to Promisor's use and rental of the premises located at 300 Party Lane, Tuscon, Arizona. Promisor's actions include the acts of Promisor's agents and employees.

Promisee shall be entitled, in its reasonable discretion, to settle claims prior to suit or judgment, and in such event Promisor shall indemnify and hold harmless Promisee for any such claims paid, including Promisee's reasonable attorney's fees incurred resulting from such claim.

In the event any claim or suit is brought against Promisee within the scope of this Agreement, Promisor shall pay for legal counsel chosen by Promisee to defend against same.

This Agreement shall encompass claims resulting from (i) the furnishing of alcoholic beverages, and (ii) valet parking services hired by Promisor as independent contractors.

In the event either party files suit in a court of law to interpret or to enforce the terms of this Agreement, the party prevailing in such action shall be entitled, in addition to any legal fees incurred in defending against any thirty party claim, to its reasonable legal fees and costs incurred in such action to interpret or to enforce the terms of this Agreement.

This Agreement shall be interpreted under the laws of the state of Arizona.

Tuscon Activities Center, Inc.

_____
by Louise K. Russel, President

First Class Catering

_____
by: Manfred O. Gerzabek, General Partner

Source: www.legaldocs.com/htsgif.d/xholdhar.mv 3/11/04. Used with permission.

a year. Fire insurance on a building may require an insurer to pay thousands of dollars in return for the payment of a few dollars in premiums. The following four concepts help explain how insurance works:

- the insurance equation
- probability and uncertainty
- the law of large numbers
- adequate statistical data

The Insurance Equation

insurance equation

The equality between the receipts taken in and amounts paid out constitutes the *insurance equation*. The receipts include (1) premium payments from policyowners, (2) investment earnings, and (3) other income. The cost factors include (1) the cost of losses, (2) the cost of doing business, or expenses, and (3) the cost of capital, or profits. Figures 2-2 and 2-3 explain each of these cost factors.

Losses

Insurers deal with groups. A life insurance company is not concerned with when one person will die but with how many will die each year out of a large group. Knowing this within reasonable limits, the life insurer sets its rates so

---

FIGURE 2-2
The Insurance Equation

Amounts Paid In	Equal	Amount Paid Out
Premiums from policyowners + Investment earnings + Other Income	=	Cost of losses + Cost of doing business + Cost of capital, profits

---

FIGURE 2-3
Insurance Equation Illustrated
Life Insurance Company Annual Statement of Operations

Premiums	$267,775,200	Cost of losses	$269,314,100
Investment earnings	$303,452,600	Cost of doing business	$268,276,800
Other income	$ 10,659,000	Cost of capital, profits	$ 44,295,900
Totals	$581,886,800 =		$581,886,800

that it will take in enough money to be able to pay all expected losses. With other forms of insurance, the procedure is the same, although the result might be less predictable. The fire insurer is interested not in whether specific buildings will burn but in what the ratio of losses to premiums is likely to be when a large group of buildings is insured.

The percentage of the premium paid in the form of losses varies with the line of insurance written. The losses per premium dollar may be 80 percent or more for group health insurance or less than 50 percent for lines such as surety bonds and equipment breakdown insurance.

Margins are included in the rates that insurers charge. These margins are required by state law to cover specific loss reserves for some lines of insurance. Insurance rates also sometimes include margins to cover possible future catastrophic losses. For example, fires have destroyed large sections in major cities, windstorms have damaged wide areas, and accidents have caused the deaths of a vast number of people at one time. Insurers must take catastrophes into consideration when computing premiums.

Expenses

In addition to securing sufficient funds to meet all covered losses, insurers must collect enough money to pay business expenses such as salaries, rents, supplies, taxes, and agents' commissions. Some insurers also provide special engineering and loss prevention services that are designed to save property or to promote healthy lifestyles. An insurer's cost of doing business is affected greatly by the marketing system it uses and the services its agents render to policyowners.

Profits

Premiums must also be sufficient to generate profits. Profits are the amounts left after all losses and expenses have been paid out. In a stock company, insurers usually retain some profits to increase surplus, and the remainder is distributed to shareowners. Mutual insurance companies may return some of their profit to policyowners as policy dividends, with the remainder added to surplus for purposes of growth and financial stability.

The insurance equation is an adaptation of the basic accounting concept that total income must equal total outgo plus profits. As explained earlier, total income in the insurance equation consists of premiums plus investment earnings and any miscellaneous income. Unless the insurer is operating at a loss, this total income must equal the total outgo, which, as mentioned above, consists of incurred losses, expenses, and profits. Insurers sometimes operate at a loss for a period of one or more years. But this condition obviously cannot continue indefinitely. Profits are essential if an insurance company is to survive in the long run.

Probability and Uncertainty

Insurers try to avoid operating at a loss by applying the concepts of probability and uncertainty. Within calculable limits, the insurer can foresee the normal losses and can also estimate losses from catastrophes in order to compute the premium necessary to pay all losses, as well as to cover expenses and profits.

The ability to use probabilities gives the insurer a different perspective from the policyowner's. Without this ability, insurance would be nothing more than the accumulation of many small risks and accompanying uncertainties into one enormous risk and accompanying uncertainty. By using probabilities, even though the element of uncertainty is extreme for each individual insured, the insurer can predict a reasonably definite loss for its entire group of insured persons. The uncertainty element is not entirely eliminated, and some insurers are more successful than others in their predictions. Every insurance company endeavors to achieve reasonable predictability, but some companies do suffer losses and expenses beyond what they take in.

Law of Large Numbers

The *law of large numbers*, a principle referred to in chapter 1, is especially important to insurance. Also known as the law of averages, this principle states that as the number of independent events increases, the likelihood increases that the actual results will be close to the expected results.

Insurance is concerned with the number of times an event, or loss, can be expected to occur over a series of occasions. Certain events occur with surprising regularity when a large number of instances are observed. The regularity of the events increases as the observed instances become more numerous. The concept is that of *credibility*, which indicates the degree of reliability placed on past experience to predict what will happen in the future.

credibility

Applying these conclusions to insurance in a hypothetical case, assume that we are considering the predictability of auto accidents in a given city. We have gathered data on two different classes of drivers, under age 25 and age 25 or older, in the city over the past several years. The data are shown in table 2-1.

It is perhaps not surprising that, on average, a higher percentage of young drivers were involved in auto accidents during a year than older drivers. In addition, however, note that as a smaller group, the younger drivers showed a wider relative variation around their average from year to year than did the older, considerably larger group. If we were to use these data to predict future accident rates, we could predict only within a wide range of percentages for the younger drivers compared with the older group. As a result, there would be a rather low probability of actual experience equaling expected experience for the under-age-25 group. The relative variation in results for the 25-and-over group is smaller, so we could make predictions for the future more accurately. This is the "magic" of insurance—increasing predictability and reducing uncertainty by applying the law of large numbers.

TABLE 2-1
Data on Two Different Classes of Drivers

	Under Age 25	Age 25 or Over
Average annual number of drivers	2,000	25,000
Average annual percentage involved in an auto accident	20%	12%
Range of annual percentages involved in an auto accident during the period	9%–31%	8%–16%

Adequate Statistical Data

mortality

morbidity

Use of the mathematical laws of probability and large numbers requires adequate statistical data. Predictions in the form of probabilities must be based on adequate and accurate statistical information. For each line of insurance, insurers carefully compile statistics to accumulate experience as a basis for rate making. Important life insurance statistical data deal with *mortality,* defined as the relative incidence of death. The statistical data used in estimating the number of deaths for life insurance purposes are arranged in a mortality table that shows how many persons alive at different ages are expected to die during the coming year. Likewise, health insurers are concerned about statistics regarding *morbidity,* the relative incidence of disease. The number of individuals exposed to the risk of illness and disease at each age is shown in a morbidity table. In commercial property insurance, statistics are developed for such factors as construction, occupancy, fire protection, and location pertaining to different types of buildings. For auto insurance, data for many classifications of type and use of car, territory, age of driver, and other factors are collected. These classifications help to achieve equity in the rates charged to many policyowners with different loss probabilities.

The insurer's goal is to reduce judgment factors to a minimum and to set premium rates scientifically. Insurance applies mathematical tools to statistical data on groups to achieve better predictions than individuals can make.

STEPS IN RISK MANAGEMENT

The first part of this chapter presents the background of the basic methods of treating pure risks. The following pages explain the steps in risk management:

- risk identification
- risk measurement

- choice and use of alternative methods of treatment
- risk administration

Risk Identification

risk identification   The process of risk management begins with *risk identification*, the careful and systematic discovery of all risks that confront a household or an organization. Often, a risk and insurance survey form, sometimes called a loss exposure audit or fact finder, is used to organize this information. Several other effective methods of risk identification for households or small businesses are financial statement analysis, personal inspections, and contract analysis.

Survey Forms

Survey forms, questionnaires, and checklists are often used as one tool to identify the loss exposures of a business or nonprofit organization. Similar forms are also available for use with individuals and families. Survey forms, questionnaires, and checklists have been prepared by insurers, financial planners, and insurance agencies. A brief exposure checklist that might be used with a family appears in table 2-2.[2]

Risk and insurance survey forms involve risk detection, identification, and classification. Sometimes they also include estimates of the possible loss values, which are part of risk measurement. Survey forms may be brief or lengthy, depending on whether they are for a household or a business and on the complexity of the case under consideration.

Financial Statement Analysis

Businesses routinely prepare a balance sheet, an income statement, and other financial statements. Although most families' accounting practices are much more informal, individuals and families who are serious about their financial planning and have not already done so are often advised to prepare a balance sheet, an income statement, and a budget. These documents can be useful in risk identification and risk measurement.

In financial statement analysis, each account on the balance sheet, the income statement, and other financial statements is listed and analyzed to determine the potential perils that might result in losses. For example, the tangible assets listed (house, autos, jewelry, and other items) raise questions regarding the perils that could cause loss or damage to those assets, as well as liability that might result from their ownership or use. The items on the income statement and budget pinpoint the sources of income and profits subject to indirect loss when perils occur. A comprehensive analysis of financial statements thus becomes a very useful method for identifying both direct and indirect losses.

TABLE 2-2
Identification of Household/Family Loss Exposures

Types of Loss Exposure	Consequences

Property
• Real property
  – Unimproved land
  – Residence premises
  – Other structures
  – Fixtures
• Personal property
  – Tangible
    ▪ At residence premises
    ▪ Elsewhere
  – Intangible
  – Property held as bailee
	Property
	• Reduction in value
	• Loss of use

Liability
• Premises liability
• Libel, slander, and other
    intentional torts
• Employment of domestics
• Autos
• Recreational vehicles
• Watercraft
• Business-related liability
• Personal activities (for example,
    hobbies, baby-sitting, serving
    alcohol, keeping pets)
	Liability
	• Damages awards
	• Specific performance
	• Injunction
	• Fines
	• Costs of defense
	• Court costs

Illness and Injury • Related to employment • Not related to employment	Illness and Injury • Medical care expenses • Lost income • Extra expenses and loss of services • Long-term care

Death	Death
	• Costs associated with death (for
	    example, funeral, taxes, estate
	    administration fees)
	• Lost income for dependents
	• Lost employee benefits for
	    dependents

Retirement	Retirement • Lost income
Unemployment	Unemployment • Lost income • Extra expenses (for example, relocation, job hunting)

Personal Inspections

Although many methods of risk identification are valuable as checks against possible sources of loss, none of them can replace the technical knowledge that consultants or agents provide. Personal inspections of a business operation or a household remain a significant source of information about possible losses.

Contract Analysis

Almost every person or organization has contractual agreements. Hold-harmless agreements, mentioned earlier in this chapter, can mean liability exposures are transferred to the client—or from the client to others. Other relevant contracts with both financial planning and insurance implications involve short-term auto rental agreements, auto lease agreements, apartment rental agreements, and agreements for the purchase or sale of a house, and the master deed or declarations of a condominium complex. Legal expertise is often necessary to interpret contractual agreements.

Techniques for Risk Identification

- Survey forms
- Financial statement analysis
- Personal inspections
- Contract analysis

Risk Measurement

Risk measurement is the second step in risk management. Each risk can be measured in three basic ways: (1) loss frequency, (2) loss severity, and (3) variation. Business risk managers often estimate expected losses on the basis of past loss experience or judgment. Risk managers also try to predict variations in future losses, in both frequency and severity. Because the law of large numbers cannot apply, past loss experience is of limited value in evaluating many of the risks facing individuals and families. Many families go 20 years or more without a homeowners insurance claim, but the risk of a serious house fire still exists. Past loss experience can be useful in predicting some expenses, such as the cost of prescription drugs for blood pressure or for a chronic illness.

Some potential losses can be so infrequent that it would be impractical to try to deal with them. Flood damage to property high on a mountain is an example of this type of loss probability. At the other extreme, some losses may be so frequent as to be regularly anticipated. If the losses are small relative to a family's or business firm's assets or income, retaining these risks by absorbing the losses in normal expenses or by reserving for the losses as they occur would be effective. For this sort of retention to work, however, not only must the frequency of loss be high and the severity low, but the variation of losses must also be regular and predictable within ranges that the household or firm can handle. We will discuss this approach further in connection with the next step in the risk management process, choice and use of methods of risk treatment.

If complete data are lacking, or if the cost of making more precise estimates is too high, other methods of measuring risks may be advisable. For example, a client might divide potential losses into various categories such as losses that are of high, moderate, or slight importance. Estimates of *maximum possible loss*, the worst that could happen, and *maximum probable loss*, the worst that is likely to happen, can also be valuable.

maximum possible loss

maximum probable loss

Several dimensions of maximum probable loss are pertinent. To determine the effect of losses on a household or organization, it is worthwhile to estimate the maximum probable loss not only for a single item or life exposed to loss (such as one building or one person), but also for multiple losses that could occur together (such as a windstorm over a large area or the death or disability of both parents in an accident). In addition, the risk manager should evaluate the maximum probable loss per year in terms of its financial effect on the household's or organization's resources, budget planning, and taxes.

Choice and Use of Methods of Risk Treatment

The third step in risk management is to evaluate both the suitability and the cost of various methods of treating pure risks. Sound risk management considers all methods of dealing with risks. Even considering one peril, such as fire, usually requires a risk manager to integrate the two basic methods of risk control and risk financing.

To choose among alternatives, the risk manager must understand each alternative, the conditions under which it should be considered, its advantages, and its limitations. Can the risk be avoided, or can it be controlled by other means such as loss prevention or reduction? Can some or all of the risk be financed by risk retention or risk transfer? More important, if several methods are feasible, which one method or combination of methods will provide the most desirable result?

Factors to Consider

Elaborate mathematical models have been designed to compare the benefits and costs of the various methods, and combinations of methods, to treat various pure risks. However, these models are probably not very helpful when risk management is practiced at the level of the household or small business organization. At that level, the choice of the best technique or combination of techniques is likely to be determined by factors such as the following:[3]

- the maximum probable loss associated with a particular risk in comparison to the household's or firm's financial and other capacities to bear risk

- the legal restrictions that may impose or preclude the use of one or more of the available techniques
- the extent to which the household or firm is able to exert control over the loss frequency or severity associated with the risk
- the loading fees (expense charges) associated with the available risk management techniques
- the value of ancillary services that may be provided as part of the risk treatment technique, especially the insurance technique
- the time value of investable funds that may be gained or lost by using certain of the available techniques
- the federal income tax treatment of losses under the various techniques
- the possible unavailability of certain techniques for dealing with some pure risks

Reviewing Insurance Priorities

Reviewing insurance priorities is one of the simplest approaches to choosing a technique or combination of techniques for a household or small business. Assume that insurance will be used, if available, for each of the pure risks that have been identified and measured in the risk management process. The most suitable policy and its cost are listed for each risk as a benchmark against which to evaluate other possible techniques. Listing insurance coverages also clarifies which risks must be treated by means other than insurance—that is, the risks for which no insurance is available.

Next, insurance coverages are grouped into priority categories such as

- essential (for example, insurance required by law or losses of possibly disastrous results for the household or business)
- desirable (for example, losses that would seriously impair but not totally wipe out the financial position of the household or business)
- available (all other types of insurance coverage)

Finally, each insurance coverage is compared with the other available techniques for treating the particular risk. For example, can some of the risks in the "essential" category be avoided? Reduced? Transferred? Can some of the risks in the "desirable" category be less expensively addressed through loss prevention and reduction? Can some of the risks in the "available" category be retained, at least partially?

Grouping by Frequency and Severity

A different approach to selecting the most appropriate technique, although it might lead to the same conclusion as the review of insurance priorities, is grouping the most logical techniques based on the probable frequency and severity of the losses associated with each pure risk.

- For risks that involve both high loss frequency and high loss severity, the most suitable technique is avoidance. Retention is not realistic, and insurance is too costly, assuming it is even available. If avoidance is not possible, loss prevention or loss reduction measures might to reduce frequency and/or severity to a more manageable level.
- For risks that involve high loss frequency and low loss severity, the most suitable technique is usually retention. Where possible, loss prevention measures might be employed to reduce loss frequency.
- For risks that involve low loss frequency and high loss severity, insurance is often the most suitable technique. Retention is not appropriate for one individual's or business's high-severity losses, but the cost of insurance should be manageable because the insurer covers the risks of many insurance buyers and utilizes the law of large numbers.
- For risks that involve both low loss frequency and low loss severity, the most suitable technique is usually retention. Losses don't happen very often, and when they do, the consequences are not major.

The simplicity of this approach is somewhat misleading, because it implies that risks can easily be placed into one of the four categories shown in the matrix below. In reality, risks are just not that simple. The approach is especially instructive for this book on insurance planning, however, because it calls attention to the types of risks for which insurance is suited. Clearly, insurance is best suited for low-frequency, high-severity risks. Insurance is not likely to be available for high-frequency, high-severity risks, and it probably is not economically feasible for low-severity risks.

Risk Administration

The fourth step in the risk management process is risk administration. Actually, risk administration must be carried out in conjunction with each of the first

Appropriate Risk Management Techniques

Expected Frequency	Expected Loss Severity	
	High	Low
High	Avoidance	Retention
Low	Insurance	Retention

three steps of risk management. New risks must be continually identified, and all risks must be frequently remeasured. Treatment alternatives, too, must be reconsidered and reviewed for their effectiveness and their actual and potential costs.

binder

Arranging for the actual issuance of the contracts of protection is an important part of risk administration. Sometimes insurers issue binders for temporary coverage, particularly in property and liability insurance. A *binder* makes insurance effective immediately, even though the complete written contract might not be delivered until weeks later. The client must have a clear understanding of when the protection is effective and what the scope of the coverage will be when the completed contract is written. Binders can be given orally, but the best practice is to document these agreements in writing as soon as possible.

Often the process of initiating and reviewing insurance coverages for a household or small business involves shopping around for the best coverage. Agents, brokers, or financial planners are helpful in searching the available markets. Lowest costs are not the only factor to consider; the insurer's quality of service, financial strength, reputation, claims services, loss prevention, and other business with that insurer are also important. Shopping around may be a useful way to compare markets periodically, but it is not practical to do so every year because there is value in continued services, and there are costs involved in shopping around.

The administration of existing insurance coverages is another part of risk management. Renewal and expiration records are essential to prevent any unplanned lapse in coverage. Amounts of coverage must be kept up-to-date through frequent appraisals. Rate classifications and costs must be checked.

If methods of risk treatment other than insurance have been chosen, risk administration includes additional procedures and review. For example, if the client is relying on an emergency fund or on other liquid assets to cover deductibles and other retained losses, it is important to review periodically whether these assets remain both adequate and available.

EXAMPLES OF RISK MANAGEMENT DECISION MAKING

Two brief case studies serve as a review of the steps in risk management and risk treatment techniques. The first case involves a small business firm, with emphasis on its property loss exposures. The second case involves a family, with emphasis on its life and health loss exposures.

Small Business Case

This case concerns a small manufacturer of specialty plastic goods. The risk manager or consultant for the firm might assemble a risk management package as described below.

Step 1—Risk Identification

Fire and products liability are relatively obvious as two major possible sources of potential loss. The risk manager or consultant also identifies and classifies other sources of loss by using a survey form covering perils or loss exposures and comparing these with financial statement accounts.

Step 2—Risk Measurement

Using past company records, the risk manager or consultant finds out that there has been extreme variation in both the number and amount of losses during the past 20 years. The degree of uncertainty and maximum probable loss are therefore high. Industry loss probability is also found to be higher than that for most manufacturers. Values of buildings, machinery, inventory, and other property are appraised.

Step 3—Choice and Use of Methods of Treatment

Risk control methods for this small manufacturer include

- avoiding some risks. To conserve working capital and avoid risks, the firm leases three trucks, with the rental company taking care of the fire, theft, and collision coverage. The manufacturer chooses the same risk management technique by leasing a new computer to replace an outdated one.
- adopting an intensive loss prevention and loss reduction program against the perils of fire and explosion. The firm installs an automatic sprinkler system, hires night security guards, trains employees in fire prevention habits and the use of extinguishers, and conducts regular inspections.
- using noninsurance transfer of risk. The manufacturer subcontracts with another firm to produce one of the more toxic plastics necessary for the company's research department.

Risk financing methods include

- retaining some risks by
  - setting up a reserve in the corporate accounts to cover small losses up to $5,000. Alternatively, the operating expense accounts might simply absorb these losses.
  - selecting a deductible of $5,000 in connection with the fire insurance contract. Making the supervisors aware of the deductible may encourage loss prevention.
- transferring some risks by
  - insuring the building and its contents, including fire and explosion coverage, for $1 million with a $5,000 deductible. Consultation

with several insurers and agents will help determine the proper perils and the amount of coverage.

– making a noninsurance transfer of risk through a hold-harmless agreement with the firm's major sales distributor. In the agreement, the distributor agrees to pay for any product liability losses caused by negligence in the distribution process.

Step 4—Risk Administration

The manufacturer implements the risk treatment alternatives in step 3 through the following procedures: communication and discussion with other departments of the firm, rental of the trucks through the purchasing department, sale of the unneeded computer through the accounting and property departments, establishment of reserve accounts with the accounting department and the treasurer's office, explanation of deductibles to the supervisors of various departments, and coordination of the loss prevention program with the safety and security department. The manufacturer also purchases fire insurance through a carefully selected agent or broker who will provide appraisal services for property values at stated time intervals.

Finally, the manufacturer schedules annual reviews of all risk management methods and property values, with the option to conduct more frequent reviews if necessary. The firm also hires a consultant to evaluate the risk management decisions and to arrange for the reevaluation of prices for the insurance at 5-year intervals.

Family Case

Now consider how the risk management process might be applied in a family situation—in this case, to the applicable life and health pure risks. Assume that Travis and Ruth Jordan, a husband and wife, have two children: Edward and Penny. Edward is aged 17 and will begin college as a full-time student in a few months. Penny is aged 13 and in the eighth grade. Travis is 42, and he is an executive for a chain of grocery stores. He earns about $120,000 per year. Ruth, aged 39, works part-time for an orthodontist and earns about $15,000 per year. Risk management as it relates to the family's life and health pure risks might be applied in this situation as shown below.

Step 1—Risk Identification

The Jordan family faces the following risks:

* The death or disability of Travis might cause a major loss of earnings for the support of Ruth, Edward, and Penny.
* Travis's death would result in some costs, perhaps significant, to clear his estate (funeral, probate, taxes, last illness, and so on).

- Travis's disability could cause extremely high medical bills and other costs (rehabilitation therapy, long-term care, and so on).
- Travis's unemployment could result in lost income for the support of Ruth and the children, as well as some direct costs to obtain another job.
- Several years from now, Travis's retirement from his job will cause a significant loss of income for his and Ruth's support.
- Ruth's death, disability, unemployment, or retirement would cause the same types of losses as described for Travis. The size of the income losses (and some of the estate clearance costs) would be less than for Travis, but the out-of-pocket expenses if Ruth becomes disabled could be fully as large as if Travis were disabled.
- The death of Edward or Penny would cause a loss of their future earning power, some of which might be needed eventually for the support of their parent(s). There would also be some out-of-pocket costs immediately if Edward or Penny were to die.
- The disability of Edward or Penny could lead to very high costs for medical and other types of care.

Step 2—Risk Measurement

Measurement of the death, disability, unemployment, and retirement risks for family members is extremely difficult. Except for short-term disabilities and periods of unemployment, loss frequency rates are meaningless for individuals. For example, although it is possible to calculate the odds of death, long-term disability, or long-term confinement in a nursing home within one year for a 42-year-old male, those odds mean nothing to Travis. The only safe assumption he can make is that, in fact, he will die, experience a long-term disability, or be confined in a nursing home within the next year—that is, that the odds are 100 percent against him. The risk of long-term unemployment may be slightly more measurable, based on Travis's informed judgment about the likelihood of being terminated by his employer. The retirement risk is reasonably measurable, because it is likely that Travis has a planned retirement date and a desired income level if he survives to that date.

Measuring the loss severity of most risks to a family is more meaningful than measuring loss frequency. Therefore, the family's loss exposures can be subjectively grouped into three broad categories based on maximum possible or maximum probable loss, as follows:

- Calamitous losses include income loss due to Travis's death, medical bills and other expenses due to his or any other family member's serious disability, income loss due to his long-term disability or unemployment, and Travis's income loss due to his retirement.
- Serious losses include income loss due to Ruth's death or long-term disability, income loss due to Travis's short-term unemployment,

income loss due to Ruth's retirement, estate clearance costs due to Travis's death, and medical bills due to routine accidents or illnesses of Travis, Ruth, Edward, or Penny.

- Bearable losses include estate clearance costs due to the death of Ruth, Edward, or Penny and lost income for possible support of Travis or Ruth due to the death of Edward or Penny.

At this point, dollar values are not assigned to each of the potential losses in each category. Several later chapters, which deal with life insurance, annuities, medical expense insurance, disability income insurance, and long-term care insurance, offer guidance in assigning dollar values to all the Jordans' losses except the unemployment peril.

Step 3—Choice and Use of Methods of Treatment

The Jordan family can undertake some risk control techniques, particularly in the areas of loss prevention and loss reduction. For example, family members can schedule periodic medical checkups and take preventive measures to lower the likelihood of death or disability and so reduce the lost income and out-of-pocket costs associated with those two perils.

The family can also undertake some risk financing. For example, they can retain the losses listed in the "bearable" category, perhaps through the accumulation of an emergency fund and through absorption as part of normal operating expenses. The Jordans can partially retain some of the losses in the "serious" and "calamitous" categories through the use of deductibles and waiting periods in insurance policies. The household can also transfer some of these losses, perhaps through prearranged, guaranteed sources of credit in times of emergency (for example, a home equity line of credit from a bank). Of course, the best way for the Jordans to transfer the losses they cannot control or fully retain is through insurance. The family should give the highest priority to coverage of potentially calamitous losses through life insurance on Travis, major medical expense insurance on all four family members, long-term disability income coverage on Travis, and some type of retirement plan for Travis. The Jordans should also consider long-term care insurance, especially for Travis and Ruth. Life insurance and, if available, disability income coverage for Ruth are a somewhat lower priority, as is some type of retirement plan for her. The Jordans might also consider dental expense coverage for all family members.

Step 4—Risk Administration

Most of the Jordans' risk administration activities, of course, involve arranging and coordinating various forms of insurance coverage in proper amounts and with appropriate deductibles or waiting periods. They should consider three broad categories of insurance in this process: social insurance, employer-sponsored insurance, and individual insurance. These are the three building blocks that the Jordans can use to construct a program of economic security from the perils of death, disability, unemployment, and old age.

Social Insurance. The first building block for the Jordans is several social insurance programs, each of which is designed to provide a safety net of protection against certain perils. We will discuss the benefits under these programs in detail in chapter 7. One of these programs is Social Security, which will provide a basic level of retirement income for Travis and Ruth. Social Security will also replace a portion of the income lost following the death of Travis or Ruth and, in certain cases, will replace some of the income lost if either of them becomes disabled.

Under certain circumstances, social insurance benefits may also be available under workers' compensation insurance, unemployment insurance, or temporary disability insurance programs.

Employer-Sponsored Insurance. The second building block for the Jordans is various insurance programs made available where Travis and Ruth work—both group insurance plans and voluntary benefit plans. Because Ruth works part-time, she may not be eligible for employee benefits. Group insurance programs—which may either be insured or self-funded by an employer—can provide specified types of coverage such as group life insurance, group medical expense insurance, and a pension plan. In some cases, coverage is automatically given to all employees at no cost; in other cases, an employee must elect coverage and pay a portion of the cost. However, the employer often pays a significant amount of the cost, and only in rare circumstances is the cost more than that of comparable coverage in the individual marketplace.

voluntary benefits

Employers are increasingly making *voluntary benefits* available to employees. Under these plans, which are referred to by various names such as worksite products or mass-marketed insurance plans, the employer makes the plan available but does not share in the premium cost. Voluntary benefit plans have some of the characteristics of group insurance and some of individual insurance. As in individual insurance, each employee decides whether to purchase the coverage. Individual underwriting of applicants is frequently used, although sometimes the underwriting standards are less stringent than for individual insurance. Voluntary

---

Building Blocks for Economic Security

- Social insurance
- Employer-sponsored insurance
- Individual insurance

benefit products also have some of the convenience of group insurance, particularly premium payment by payroll deduction.

The most common products offered as voluntary benefits are various forms of life insurance, short-term and long-term disability income insurance, dental insurance, vision insurance, and more recently, long-term care insurance. Some insurers also offer auto and homeowners insurance as voluntary benefits, although these are not a concern of the Jordan family in this case study. Employees should pay attention to the cost of voluntary products. In some cases, the cost of coverage may exceed the cost of comparable coverage in the individual marketplace, particularly if an employee is in good health has a good driving record.

cafeteria plan

Cafeteria plans, also referred to as flexible benefit plans, allow employees to choose among several different types of benefits options. In its purest sense, a cafeteria plan gives employees a specified amount of employer-provided dollars, and the employees can choose from among the available benefits, and possibly even cash. The plan generates no taxable income when an employee chooses the types of benefits that are normally nontaxable. However, the choice of cash or normally taxable benefits, such as life insurance in excess of $50,000, will result in taxable income. Cafeteria plans can also be designed so that employees can obtain additional benefits with optional payroll or salary deductions.

premium-conversion plan

Various cafeteria plan options can enable employees to elect a before-tax salary reduction to pay for their contributions to any employer-sponsored health plan or certain other types of employee benefits. This option, called a *premium-conversion plan*, may be part of a broader cafeteria plan or may stand alone.

flexible spending account (FSA)

In addition, a cafeteria plan may allow *flexible spending accounts (FSAs)*, under which an employee can fund certain types of expenses other than insurance premiums on a before-tax basis. FSAs are used almost exclusively for medical and dental expenses not covered by an employer's plan and for dependent care expenses. FSAs and premium-conversion plans are covered in more detail in chapter 12.

Cafeteria plans are subject to complex government rules, and an in-depth discussion is beyond the scope of this book. However, they do offer many employees a cost-effective way to meet some of their personal insurance needs.

Forms of Employer-Sponsored Insurance

- Group insurance plans
- Voluntary benefit plans
- Cafeteria plans

Individual Insurance. After the Jordans have met their economic security needs to the greatest extent possible through the first two building blocks—social insurance and employer-sponsored benefit plans—they should turn to the third building block, individual insurance. Here, the Jordans should make purchases to fill in coverage gaps left by social insurance and employer-sponsored insurance and to increase total coverage amounts to the necessary levels.

Auto insurance, homeowners insurance, umbrella liability insurance, and other forms of property-liability insurance not typically available through an employer fall in this area, together with individually purchased life insurance that provides higher limits and more permanent protection than that offered by an employer-sponsored plan. Long-term care insurance is also commonly purchased on an individual basis.

Monitoring the Risk Program. Once the Jordans have implemented each of the risk treatment methods, including the insurance method, administration of the risk management process requires ongoing monitoring of the choices and coverages by the Jordans and their financial consultant. New risks must be identified as they arise. The Jordans' insurance coverages and other risk treatment methods must also be reviewed periodically in light of their costs and their effectiveness in meeting the Jordans' needs.

MINI-CASE: AMY AND JOHN SCHULTZ

Amy and John Schultz, introduced in chapter 1, form the basis for a series of mini-cases throughout this text. Basic information regarding Amy and John is introduced in chapter 1. More information is provided in later chapters, as additional topics are discussed.

Recall that Amy Schultz, aged 28 and her husband John, aged 33, are engineers at SKH, Inc., which provides group benefits that include life insurance of two times their salary, medical expense insurance, short-term disability insurance, and long-term disability insurance. They just purchased their first house, which is across the street from an elementary school, and are planning to have children soon.

Amy and John both own and drive late-model compact cars, for which they carry separate auto insurance policies, partly because of John's bad driving record, with the minimum coverages required by law.

a.   Describe three systems Amy and John can use to identify the risks they face.
b.   Explain one specific way in which Amy and John can use each of the following risk management techniques to address the risks they face:

- risk avoidance
- loss prevention
- loss reduction
- noninsurance transfer
- risk retention

c. Categorize each of the following risks Amy and John face in terms of its expected loss frequency and expected loss severity, and suggest an appropriate way of addressing the risk:

- damage to John's car, which has a current market value of $12,000
- liability claim against Amy and John because a guest is injured on their property
- the necessity of surgery for Amy
- a cavity in one of John's teeth that needs to be filled

(See answer section for answers to mini-case.)

SOURCES FOR FURTHER IN-DEPTH STUDY

- Relating to property and liability exposures, a detailed personal exposure survey (including recommendations) and coverage checklists for personal auto, homeowners, personal umbrella, and personal inland marine may be found in *Personal Risk Management and Insurance,* International Risk Management Institute, Dallas, TX. Phone 800-827-4242. Web site address: www.irmi.com
- For a detailed discussion of business risk management, see the textbooks for the three-course Associate in Risk Management Program of the Insurance Institute of America. Phone 610-644-2100. Web site address: www.aicpcu.org.
- An alternative discussion of risk management and the insurance equation appears in Wiening, Eric A., *Foundations of Risk Management and Insurance,* chapters 2–7, 1st ed., Malvern, PA: The American Institute for Chartered Property Casualty Underwriters, 2002. Phone 800-644-2100. Web site address www.aicpcu.org.
- For a detailed discussion of cafeteria plans:
  - Beam, Burton T., Jr., *Group Benefits*: *Basic Concepts and Alternatives*, 10th ed., chapter 19, Bryn Mawr, PA: The American College Press, 2004. Phone 888-263-7265. Web site address www.theamericancollege.edu
  - Johnson, Richard E., *Flexible Benefits—A How-To-Guide*, 6th ed., Brookfield, WI: International Foundation of Employee Benefit Plans, 2002. Phone 888-334-3324 option 4. Web site address www.ifebp.org
- For a detailed discussion of voluntary benefit plans, Podgurski, Walter B., *From Worksite Marketing to Website Marketing*, 4th ed., Erlanger, KY: National Underwriter Company, 2000. Phone 800-543-0874. Web site address www.nuco.com

CHAPTER REVIEW

Answers to mini-case, review questions, and self-test questions start on page 793.

Key Terms

risk management	insurance equation
risk control	credibility
risk avoidance	mortality
loss prevention	morbidity
loss reduction	risk identification
noninsurance transfer	maximum possible loss
risk financing	maximum probable loss
risk retention	binder
deductible	voluntary benefits
self-insurance	cafeteria plan
captive insurer	premium-conversion plan
risk transfer	flexible spending account (FSA)
hold-harmless agreement	

Review Questions

2-1. List the four steps a client might use in applying the risk management process.

2-2. List the objectives of risk management.

2-3. Explain how the risk manager's role is carried out differently in large organizations as opposed to small- and medium-size firms.

2-4. Explain how the two basic methods of treating risk—risk control and risk financing—differ from one another.

2-5. Explain why risk avoidance is not a practical solution to many risks.

2-6. Why might inadequate planning cause a client to retain pure risks?

2-7. Why do planners often suggest that clients use higher insurance deductibles?

2-8. Your client Sam Jones feels that if he is going to buy insurance, it should pay whenever he has a loss. As a result, his insurance program includes coverage for high-frequency, low-severity losses. For example, his health insurance program includes basic medical expense coverage that pays from the first dollar of expense when he or his family goes to the doctor or the hospital. What could you recommend to Sam that would treat his risks involving high-frequency, low-severity losses more efficiently than using first-dollar insurance?

2-9. List the ways that risks a family or business retains are commonly financed.

2-10.   Four key concepts help explain how insurance works—(a) the insurance equation, (b) probability and uncertainty, (c) the law of large numbers, and (d) adequate statistical data. Explain each concept and its importance to the operation of the insurance mechanism.

2-11.   Describe four methods of risk identification that a planner can use with households or businesses.

2-12.   What factors should a client consider in choosing the best technique(s) for dealing with a risk situation, especially for a household or small business?

2-13.   Describe two approaches a client can use in deciding which technique or combination of techniques would best handle the risks households and small businesses face.

2-14.   Describe the three "building blocks" that can be used to form an insurance program to protect a client from the perils of death, disability, unemployment, and old age.

2-15.   Norma and Sidney took an early retirement from their jobs in a northern state and purchased a condominium in the sunbelt. Norma expects to remain involved in cultural and social activities while Sidney pursues his dream of writing the great American novel. They leased a convertible to enjoy the year-round sunny climate in their new area, and they also plan to travel abroad and to travel north frequently to visit their children and grandchildren.

Briefly summarize the risk management process Norma, Sidney, and their financial planner might use to identify and address the risks associated with this major change in Norma's and Sidney's lives.

Self-Test Questions

T   F   2-1.   Risk management is a systematic process for dealing with risks, usually pure risks.

T   F   2-2.   A weakness of using the risk management process is that only insurance products are considered for treating risks.

T   F   2-3.   While loss prevention involves reducing the probability of loss, loss reduction involves lessening its severity.

T   F   2-4.   Deductibles are a form of partial risk retention that can often be used to handle high-frequency, low-severity losses efficiently.

T   F   2-5.   Self-insurance is an especially appropriate technique for small businesses and families to use in dealing with risks.

T   F   2-6.   Although a variety of noninsurance risk transfer methods are available, insurance is the only risk transfer technique that can be used to handle pure risks.

T   F   2-7.   For an insurance business to operate in the long run, premiums must equal losses, expenses, and profits.

T   F   2-8.   The law of large numbers states that as the number of independent events increases, there is a greater chance that the actual results will be close to the expected results.

T   F   2-9.   The first step in the risk management process is risk measurement.

T   F   2-10.   In risk management, each risk can be measured in terms of frequency, severity, and variation.

T   F   2-11.   Risk management involves, among other things, a careful evaluation of the suitability and cost of various alternative methods to treat pure risks, and the choice of the method or combination of methods that provides the most desirable result.

NOTES

1. Some textbooks break the risk management process into six steps: identifying loss exposures, analyzing loss exposures, examining the feasibility of risk management alternatives, selecting the best risk management techniques, implementing risk management techniques, and monitoring results. See, for example, Wiening, Eric A., *Foundations of Risk Management and Insurance,* 1st ed., chapter 1, Malvern, PA: The American Institute for Chartered Property Casualty Underwriters, 2002, p. 3.7. Others combine identification and analysis, and list five steps.
2. Table 2-2 was created from materials in Hamilton, Karen L., and Malecki, Donald S., *Personal Insurance: Property and Liability,* 2d ed., chapter 1. Malvern, PA: American Institute for CPCU, 1999.
3. For a fuller discussion of these factors, see Williams, C.A., Jr., Smith, M.L., and Young, P. C., *Risk Management and Insurance*, 8th ed., pp. 280–286. New York: Irwin McGraw-Hill, 1998.

3

Types of Insurers and Their Marketing Systems

Learning Objectives

An understanding of the material in this chapter should enable the student to

3-1. Distinguish among the ways private insurers may be classified by line of business and by domicile.

3-2. Compare stock and mutual insurance companies.

3-3. Explain why many mutual insurance companies are converting to stock companies.

3-4. Identify the key characteristics of reciprocal exchanges, captives, health associations, Lloyd's associations, and banks' insurance operations.

3-5. Briefly describe the insurance market.

3-6. Describe the types of marketing representatives used by property-liability insurers and life insurers.

3-7. Explain an insurance agent's legal duties to an insurer and an insurer's duties to the agent.

3-8. Compare and contrast the marketing systems used in insurance.

Chapter Outline

Financial planners play an important role in identifying their clients' risks and assisting their clients in risk management. A financial planner cannot function effectively without understanding one of the major tools of financial planning: insurance. The balance of this book deals primarily with insurance, which is, as we noted in chapter 2, a technique for financing pure risks. This chapter and the next two examine the structure of the business that produces and/or sells the insurance products individuals, families, and businesses need. Financial planners who wish to serve their clients effectively must understand not only insurance products and services but also the structure and organization of the business that delivers them.

TYPES OF PRIVATE INSURERS

The following pages summarize the characteristics of the major types of insurers that make up the United States insurance business. Throughout this book, the terms "insurer," "insurance company," and, often, "company" are used to identify the business or government organization that issues insurance "contracts" or "policies." Although the first three terms and the last two terms are generally interchangeable, the choice of words often depends on the context. This book generally uses the first three terms and the last two terms interchangeably, an approach that follows the practice of the business and enhances the readability of this text.

As explained in this section, any private insurer—as opposed to a government insurer—can be classified according to the lines of business it writes, according to its state or country of domicile, and according to its form of organization.

Insurance companies can also be categorized in a variety of other ways not specifically discussed here. For example, a given insurer may write business within one county, within a state, within a region, or nationally. An insurer may focus on providing insurance for a particular market segment, such as farmers or teachers, or it might market its products broadly. Some insurers are very selective in their underwriting and provide low-cost insurance to applicants who qualify as preferred risks; other insurers concentrate on the high-risk or substandard-risk market. Some provide an elite set of products designed for wealthy clients, while others market heavily to wage earners. To the client, all insurance companies may seem alike. Experienced financial planners, however, discover that each insurance company has its own personality or flavor, and they often become adept at helping clients find the insurer that best matches their specific needs. One especially important distinguishing characteristic of any given insurer is its marketing system or systems. Insurer marketing systems are discussed in a later section of this chapter,

Classification by Line of Business

Private insurers can be classified according to the lines of insurance they write. Any given insurer might, for example, be categorized in one of the following ways:

- a life and health insurer
- a property and liability insurer
- an all-lines insurer (writing life, health, property, and liability insurance)
- a monoline specialty insurer (specializing in one line of coverage, such as medical professional liability insurance)

Many insurers have groups of affiliated companies, often with a common field force, that write and sell all lines of insurance.

Classification by Domicile

These classifications are used to classify insurers operating in the United States:

domestic insurer
- A *domestic insurer* is one doing business in the state where it is incorprated. For example, New York Life Insurance Company is classified as a domestic insurer when it does business in New York.

foreign insurer
- A *foreign insurer* is one doing business in a state other than its state of incorporation. Hartford Fire Insurance Company, domiciled in Connecticut, is a foreign insurer doing business in New York. New York Life Insurance Company is a foreign insurer when it does business in Connecticut.

alien insurer
- An *alien insurer* is incorporated in another country but doing business in the United States. Munich Reinsurance Company (domiciled in Germany) is an alien company when it does business in New York.

Classification by Form of Organization

Private insurers can be divided into three major groups, according to their legal form of organization:

- stock
- mutual
- other

Ways to Classify Private Insurers

- By lines of insurance written—for example, life and health, property and liability, monoline, all lines
- By domicile—for example, domestic, foreign, alien
- By legal form of organization—for example, stock, mutual, and so on
- By marketing system

"Other" insurers include reciprocal exchanges, captive insurers, fraternal societies, banks, health associations, and Lloyd's associations.

Stock Companies

stock insurance company

A *stock insurance company* is a corporation organized as a profit-seeking venture owned by stockholders. The stockholders elect the members of the company's board of directors and vote on other major issues facing the company such as mergers or acquisitions. As with other types of insurers, insurance laws enacted by the various states govern the company's operations. To be licensed, stock insurers must have at least a specified amount of capital and surplus. The contracts stock companies issue are usually written for a definitely stated consideration or premium. As will be explained later, however, a significant portion of the company's life insurance may be written on a flexible-premium basis. The policyowner usually receives no benefit in the form of dividends from the company's earnings, and policies are nonassessable. Nonassessable policies charge no additional premium if losses for a class of policies exceed income. Except for participating policies (those with dividends) issued by some stock life insurers, the policyowner's first cost is usually the final cost.[1]

Shareholder equity serves as an extra amount, in addition to premium payments and retained earnings, out of which losses can be paid. Stockholders are entitled to any of the residual profits declared by the board as dividends after losses and expenses have been paid and proper reserves established.

Stock insurance companies thus have the following basic legal characteristics:

- They are incorporated and owned by stockholders who supply capital funds that serve as part of the financial security for the firm's operations.
- Except for flexible-premium contracts, they usually issue contracts for a fixed cost. The contracts are usually nonparticipating and non-assessable.
- They can pay residual profits to the stockholders.

Mutual Companies

mutual insurance company

A *mutual insurance company* is a corporation owned by its policyowners. The policyowners also participate in the operations of the company, at least through voting rights, and they share in the company's financial successes and, sometimes, its failure. The company is organized primarily to provide insurance for its policyowners, rather than to seek a profit. Every policyowner is an owner of the company. There are no stockholders. The mutual policyowners elect the board of directors, and the board elects the executive officers who actually manage the company. The mutual corporation assumes the risks of its policyowners. When the premiums in a given period are more than adequate to meet losses and expenses, part or all of the excess may be returned to the policyowners as a dividend. When premiums are inadequate, dividends may be omitted and, in a few cases, assessments can be levied on policyowners.

There are several different kinds of mutual insurers. These include (1) advance-premium mutuals, (2) assessment mutuals, and (3) fraternal insurers.

advance-premium mutual

Advance-Premium Mutuals. Advance-premium mutuals write all but a small percentage of total mutual insurance. The operations of *advance-premium mutuals* closely resemble those of stock companies. Legally, advance-premium mutuals are different because they are owned by the policyowners, have no stockholders, and may pay policyowner dividends.

Advance-premium mutuals issue nonassessable contracts in which the cost of the insurance is set when the policy begins. Legal requirements for writing nonassessable policies require these mutuals to possess specified amounts of surplus to ensure the company's financial solvency in case of temporary periods of heavier-than-normal losses or expenses.

Advance-premium mutuals may issue dividends to policyowners. At the end of the policy period, a return may be made as a dividend for any amount beyond the company's losses, expenses, and reasonable contributions to reserves and surplus. The actual amount of the return is unknown to the policyowner until after the insurance contract expires, and it depends on the company's experience for that policyowner classification. The actual net cost (original premium less dividend) to the policyowner is thus uncertain until the dividend is paid.

In most states, advance-premium mutuals must comply with the same reserve, investment, policy form, and regulatory laws as stock companies. Organizational requirements are somewhat different, in that a minimum number of policyowners is required to start a company, and the board of directors must be subject to the control of policyowners, rather than stockholders.

assessment mutual

Assessment Mutuals. Some small mutual companies are called *assessment mutuals*. Policyowners may or may not pay an advance premium, but they can be assessed for a portion of the company's losses and expenses at the end of the policy period. The policyowner's liability for the assessment may be limited or unlimited.

fraternal insurer

  Fraternal Insurers. The *fraternal insurer* is another type of mutual insuring organization. A fraternal is a special type of insurer providing insurance benefits, particularly life insurance, for its members. The operations of the fraternal are closely related to and controlled by the bylaws of a lodge or a nonprofit social organization. Many fraternals are church oriented.[2]

Choosing between the Stock and Mutual Form

  Stock companies are far more numerous in life and health insurance than are mutuals. Also, the bulk of life insurance is written by stock companies. Their share is increasing, due in part to the conversion of many mutual life insurers to the stock form of organization. In property and liability insurance, stock companies again are more numerous than mutuals, stock companies write most of the business, and many mutuals have demutualized and become stock companies.

  From the standpoint of the insurance consumer, which type of insurer is better—a stock company or a mutual company? Neither type is inherently superior. The stock form of organization may entail lower initial premiums than the mutual form, and a stock company may be better equipped to raise the capital needed for insuring, both initially and subsequently. The mutual form, on the other hand, may charge lower premiums net of dividends because of its nonprofit status. The real issue for the consumer of insurance, then, is which specific insurer and which specific insurance contract to select, not which type of insurer to select. Chapter 5 deals with this issue.

  From the standpoint of the insuring organization itself, which form is better—stock or mutual? Again, there is no definitive answer. New insurers are usually formed as stock companies because it is very difficult to form a mutual by persuading would-be policyowners to put up capital before the insurer can come into existence.

demutualization

  On balance, the number of mutual insurers in the United States is on the decline due to mergers, insolvencies, and intentional shifting of mutual companies to the stock form of organization—a process called *demutualization*. Probably the most important reason for demutualization is to enable the insurer to raise capital quickly. A stock company, of course, can raise new capital by issuing stock, bonds, warrants, and other types of debt instruments, as well as by earning profits. Mutual insurers have only their profits and borrowings to provide additional capital for expansion, acquisition, or other purposes.

  A second and often related reason for demutualization is to enable the insurance company to diversify its activities by acquiring other insurers or other types of financial institutions through the issuance or exchange of stock. Mutual insurers, having no stock, are less able to diversify in this way. Also, stock

---

Reasons for Demutualizing

- Raising new capital
- Insurer diversification
- Noncash executive compensation
- Federal income tax savings

---

insurers, having no stock, are less able to diversify in this way. Also, stock insurers can create upstream holding companies to facilitate diversification. Until recently, this avenue was not open to mutual insurers, and in many states it still is not available.

A third reason for demutualization is to facilitate payment of certain types of noncash compensation to the insurance company's key executives and board members. Compensation through tax-advantaged stock options and stock-ownership plans is not available in a mutual company, because they have no stock.

A fourth reason for demutualization is to gain federal income tax savings. The Internal Revenue Code, for example, limits the amount of dividends to policyowners that a mutual company may deduct for federal income tax purposes.

Nevertheless, the process of demutualization has certain significant disadvantages. The time, cost, and complexity may be enormous because of regulatory, tax, legal, and accounting requirements. Of particular importance is the regulatory requirement that the policyowners of the company seeking to demutualize be compensated adequately for loss of their ownership rights. A second disadvantage of demutualization is that, as a stock company, the insurer might become vulnerable to a hostile takeover. Third, as a stock insurer, the company would have to meet SEC and state rules relating to its equity securities. Fourth, demutualization represents a major change in corporate philosophy with the introduction of an explicit profit motive, a change that may be very difficult for senior executives and other long-standing employees of the former mutual company to accept.

mutual holding company

Several states allow mutual insurers to create a hybrid form of organization—the *mutual holding company*—to overcome some of the disadvantages of either remaining a mutual or demutualizing. In this circumstance, the mutual insurer creates an upstream holding company controlled by the policyowners. The holding company then acquires at least 51 percent of the stock of a newly created stock insurance company that takes over the business of the former mutual insurer. The remaining stock can be sold to outsiders to raise new capital for the insurance company.

Other Types of Insuring Organizations

Most of the private insurance in the United States is written by stock companies and advance-premium mutual companies. There are, however, several other legal types of insurers that merit discussion because they represent the wide variety of insurers in the market or because they are relatively significant in particular types of insurance or certain areas of the country.

reciprocal exchange

Reciprocal Exchanges. In the property and liability insurance field, another type of insurer includes many characteristics of a mutual insurer, which is owned by its policyowners. The *reciprocal exchange*, often called an interinsurance exchange, is an unincorporated association. In a reciprocal exchange's original and purest form, each policyowner is insured by all the others. Thus, each policyowner is also an insurer because contracts are exchanged on a reciprocal basis. In its now more popular modified form, a reciprocal exchange operates without individual accounts for its subscribers, and it closely resembles a conventional mutual insurer.

A reciprocal exchange is not a mutual insurer in the legal sense because the individual subscribers assume liability as individuals, not as a group as a whole. Another basic difference from mutual insurers is that reciprocal exchanges are not incorporated but are formed under separate laws as associations under the direction of an attorney-in-fact.

The funds held by a pure reciprocal exchange are the total of individual credits held for the accounts of individual subscribers. These subscribers are required to accumulate reserves representing a multiple ranging from two to five annual premiums before underwriting earnings, if any, are returned in cash. A separate account is maintained for each subscriber, and a proportional share of each loss and expense is paid out of each subscriber's account. Beyond that, the reciprocal exchange can usually levy an assessment of up to some multiple of premiums paid, such as 10 times, but each subscriber's liability is definitely limited.

Reciprocal exchanges are few in number, but in certain areas and for personal lines of insurance, they have some significance. Although many are small, a few reciprocal exchanges have grown to substantial size.

Captives. Captive insurance companies are hard to classify. As we suggested in chapter 2, a captive insurer is sometimes considered a sophisticated form of self-insurance or retention. We mention captives again here because, like a mutual insurance company, a captive insurance company is an insurance company owned by the organization or organizations it insures. In that sense, a captive insurance company resembles a mutual insurance company.

A single-parent captive is an insurance company organized for the sole purpose of insuring the "parent" company that formed it. A group captive, also known as an association captive, provides insurance to a group of corporations (often members of a trade association) that also own the captive. A risk retention group is a special type of group or association captive formed under the Risk Retention Act of 1986 to provide liability insurance subject to limited state regulation. Captive insurers are increasingly important as a source of business insurance, but they are of little, if any, relevance in personal lines insurance.

Banks. In recent years, the entry of banks into the business of insurance has been characterized by a considerable amount of publicity, controversy, and legal jousting. However, one particular type of bank—the mutual savings bank—has been providing life insurance for many years in a few states.

Laws in these states authorize mutual savings banks to write life insurance on residents of the state and on persons regularly employed there. The amounts that may be issued are limited. Because the coverage is written without a commissioned agent as an intermediary, premium rates for savings bank life insurance usually compare favorably with those charged by other insurers. Nevertheless, the amount of savings bank life insurance represents only a small percentage of the total amount of life insurance sold in the three states. Perhaps this is attributable to the absence of an aggressive, commission-based sales force in savings bank life insurance.

The past few years have also seen the gradual entry of other types of banks in other states into the insurance business, particularly in such lines as fixed and variable annuities, homeowners insurance, auto insurance, and life insurance. Initially, the majority of these banks created entirely new insurance operations from scratch. Later entrants to the field, however, have tended to form alliances with existing insurers and their insurance agencies, thus becoming, rather than insurers, marketing channels for insurance "manufactured" by others.

Health Associations. Blue Cross and Blue Shield organizations and health maintenance organizations (HMOs) play a particularly important role in the field of medical expense insurance. Detailed information about health maintenance organizations and other managed care organizations is contained in chapter 12. Chapter 3 simply summarizes the basic characteristics of the "Blues."

Blue Cross organizations have historically provided hospital care in member hospitals on a service basis, rather than on a cash reimbursement basis. Blue Shield organizations have covered the costs of member physicians and surgeons, also on a service basis. Under the service-benefit concept, benefits are expressed in terms of the services that the hospitals or physicians who participate in the plan will provide, rather than in terms of dollar maximums. For example, a Blue Cross plan might provide hospitalization in semiprivate accommodations. In contrast, an insurance company might provide reimbursement for hospital charges subject to a dollar limitation such as $600 per day.

While Blue Cross and Blue Shield plans have traditionally operated separately in limited geographic areas, most Blue Cross and Blue Shield plans in each area have now merged into a single entity. Blue Cross and Blue Shield plans must be members of the National Blue Cross and Blue Shield Association, which sets certain standards for the local organizations. Among these standards are requirements that the local organizations have boards of directors, the majority of whom are not health care providers, and that the organizations participate in national plans that offer portability of coverage and benefit availability for insureds outside their home service areas.

Although the Blues and insurance companies were once quite different, they have evolved over the years so that they now probably have more similarities than differences. The Blues tend to exist under special enabling legislation, which gives them some advantages, such as favorable state taxation, but also limits their underwriting and rating flexibility. The majority of plans are structured as not-for-profit organizations, making them similar to mutual insurance companies. Profits are not distributed to shareholders or policyowners, but some of the Blues have accumulated a rather substantial surplus despite their nonprofit status. However, several have converted to the traditional forms of stock or mutual companies.

Lloyd's association

Lloyd's Associations. In contrast to stock and mutual insurers, which are corporations, *Lloyd's associations* are groups of individual insurers. Insurance written by Lloyd's associations accounts for only a small percentage of the total insurance sales in the United States. However, Lloyd's organizations are significant from a historical standpoint, and in the world market, they are very important for reinsurance and for insuring unusual and difficult risks. There are two types of Lloyd's associations: Lloyd's of London, which is by far the more important, and the American Lloyd's associations, which are small and few in number.

Lloyd's of London, one of the most famous institutions for the insurance of loss exposures, bears the name of the coffeehouse where it originated more than 300 years ago as a center of shipping news and financial information. Lloyd's itself does not directly issue insurance policies; rather, insurance is written by underwriting members who sign "each for himself and not for another." The insurer, then, is not Lloyd's but the underwriters at Lloyd's. A policyowner insures *at* Lloyd's but not *with* Lloyd's.

Underwriting members, also called *names*, from around the world supply capital but do not work at Lloyd's. These members are organized into syndicates, with membership varying from a few to more than 1,000 in each. Each syndicate is operated by an underwriting agent, who commits the members of that syndicate to the risks from the business written. There are firms consisting of authorized Lloyd's brokers. With an adequate description of the property, life, or activity to be insured, the broker offers the insurance to the underwriters. Each underwriter who accepts signs a slip—underwriting his or her name to it, hence the term underwriter—indicating the amount of insurance accepted. When the broker has obtained enough signers so that the amounts the broker assumes total the required insurance, the Lloyd's Policy Signing Office draws up the policy and affixes its official seal. The document, however, is not signed by the corporation but by members, who must themselves pay their proportional share in the event of a loss. The function of the corporation of Lloyd's is purely to supervise transactions and to guard the institution's reputation.

The fame of Lloyd's of London is heightened by the unusual loss exposures that have been insured. Practically any large loss in the world, such as a multimillion-dollar fire, the crash of a huge ship or airplane, or a major hurricane, involves Lloyd's of London.

Lloyd's of London is licensed directly in only two states, Illinois and Kentucky, although Lloyd's brokers and agents operate throughout the United States and the rest of the world. In the United States, state excess and surplus line laws allow coverage to be placed at any nonadmitted insurer, such as Lloyd's, if the desired coverage is not available from licensed insurers. Although the usual household or small business would have little need for insuring at Lloyd's of London, businesses can insure at Lloyd's to obtain needed high liability limits, special coverages such as worldwide package policies, or difficult-to-obtain protection for unusual perils or very large amounts of insurance.

There are a few American Lloyd's associations, including several in Texas. These associations write primarily fire and allied lines and auto physical damage insurance. In the American Lloyd's associations, each member is ordinarily liable for only a specified maximum, and the strict regulations of Lloyd's of London that govern membership, deposits, and audits are not present. Each American Lloyd's organization depends on the financial strength of its individual members within their limited liability. The American Lloyd's and the original London organization have no connection, and the American Lloyd's associations play a relatively small role in United States insurance.

THE MARKETING PROCESS

With this background of the types of organizations that provide insurance to individuals, households, and businesses, we now turn to the process by which organizations market their insurance. Why do financial planners need to understand how the insurance business markets its contracts and services? First, financial planners are in many cases active participants in the marketing process, deriving some of their compensation from being participants. Second, working with consumers of insurance, financial planners need to understand the choices among insurers and agents that clients must make in buying insurance. Finally, financial planners need to recognize that the methods companies use to sell and service insurance contracts are significant in determining their costs and usefulness.

Marketing the Insurance Product

Figure 3-1 shows the relationship of marketing to the product design, underwriting, and loss payment functions as insurance is distributed from insurers to policyowners. The other functions and insurance regulation are described in later chapters.

FIGURE 3-1
Functional Viewpoint of Insurance

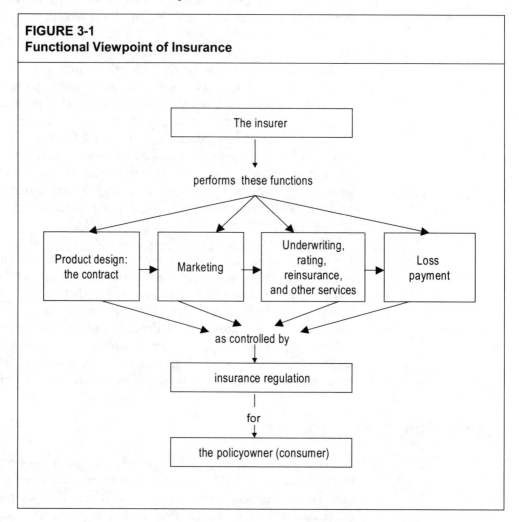

Marketing, or directing the flow of goods and services from the insurer to the consumer or user, is a particularly important business activity for insurance companies. The insurance product consists of a written legal contract, plus a bundle of services. An insurer's representative may provide motivation, education, and advice both before and after an insurance policy is issued. In some ways, at least, this bundle of services distinguishes insurance from tangible goods for which service often begins and ends with the sale.

The Insurance Market

In one sense, a market is a meeting place for people who wish to transact business. The term can mean either the region in which a product or service is sold, the group of persons who might be expected to purchase it, or the place of purchase. As examples, there are, respectively, the West Coast market, the young marrieds market, the local supermarket, and Internet markets such as eBay. Financial planners might refer to their target audience as the middle-income market or the affluent market.

Insurance practitioners use the term market to indicate both the area of distribution and the available sources of the different coverages. For example, persons in the middle salary brackets might be referred to as a market for retirement annuities, or small business organizations as a market for key employee life insurance or business overhead expense coverage. The second use of the term applies to the place or source for the purchase of different forms of coverage. One might refer, for example, to the aviation, disability income, substandard life, fire, or marine insurance markets.

Insurance buyers or their agents usually have little difficulty in placing insurance—that is, in finding a market—for most clients. Every insurance company selects applicants on the basis of underwriting judgment, and there are many classes that one company or another will not write at all. For example, some commercial property insurers will not insure restaurants. Many companies will not provide motorcycle insurance. In life and health insurance, some insurers will not write insurance on sky divers, test pilots, or juvenile diabetics.

Some insurance agents limit their business to selling either life insurance or property-liability insurance. Some specialize in personal lines insurance, while others handle only business insurance. Many are all-lines agencies that embrace all forms of the insurance business. An insurance agency represents insurance companies that provide a market for most of the classes of business its customers need. When a local agent does not have a market for a specific coverage, the agent may "broker the line," in whole or in part, by obtaining the coverage through another agent.

A financial planner must be familiar with the insurance market and its limits. The usual coverages, such as life, homeowners, and auto insurance, are obtainable in every community through a local agency. For more hazardous lines, such as professional liability, the market is more limited.

Types of Marketing Representatives

Insurance buyers care more about the person with whom they deal, who represents one or more insurance companies, than they do about the insurer itself. A typical client is much less concerned whether the insurer is organized as a stock insurer, a mutual insurer, or in some other form. Most are not even aware what marketing system the insurer uses. However, financial planners need to understand the distinctions among the types of insurer representatives with whom a client must deal. The applicant for insurance makes contact with the insurer through one or more of the following: (1) agents, (2) brokers, (3) insurance consultants and financial planners, and (4) service representatives.

Agents

agent

An insurance *agent* is often referred to as a producer because he or she produces business for the insurance company or companies that he or she represents. Legally, any agent represents a principal; an insurance agent's principal is an insurance company. Insurance companies appoint agents to solicit prospects for insurance, to negotiate with these prospects, and, in some cases, to put contracts of insurance into effect. Agents are typically compensated by a commission that is a percentage of a policy premium.

The agent's powers are defined by his or her agency contract with the insurer. The agency contract spells out the agent's express authority. The agent also has implied or incidental authority to carry out those acts needed to exercise his or her express authority. An agent's acts may bind the principal even if those acts are outside the scope of the agent's express or implied authority, provided the acts are within the agent's apparent authority. Apparent authority arises when the agent, without contrary action by the principal, performs an act that appears to a reasonable person to be within the agent's express or implied authority. For example, if a life insurance agent waives a policy provision for a policyowner relating to the grace period for payment of renewal premiums, the insurance company might, if silent on the matter, be bound by the apparent authority of the agent. To prevent this from happening, the insurer normally includes a provision in the policy stating that only specified home office personnel have the authority to waive or modify a policy provision.

A principal may instead ratify an agent's actions that are outside the scope of the agent's authority, and as a result be bound by those actions. For example, if an insurance contract states that renewal premiums must be sent to the insurer's home office, but the company routinely accepts premiums sent to its local agent, in the event of a dispute, the insurer would probably be found to have ratified the agent's collection of renewal premiums.

An agent owes the following legal duties to his or her principal:

- Exercise reasonable care.
- Obey the principal's instructions.
- Maintain accurate accounting records.
- Keep the principal informed.
- Comply with the agency contract.

The principal, in this case the insurance company, also owes certain duties to its agents:

- Pay for the agent's services.
- Maintain accurate accounting records.
- Reimburse the agent for expenses incurred as an agent.
- Reimburse the agent for liability incurred as an agent without the agent's fault.
- Comply with the agency contract.

Both the agent and the insurer are responsible for maintaining accounting records. The agent is responsible for properly handling any funds that belong to the insurer such as premiums collected by the agent. The insurer, of course, is obligated to maintain accurate accounting records and to pay the agent commissions and, if applicable, other expenses provided for in the agency contract.

The liability that an agent may incur requires a comment. A customer who receives inappropriate advice, inadequate service, or incomplete coverage from an insurance agent who was allegedly negligent may bring a liability claim against that agent. These are referred to as errors and omissions claims. Insurance professionals and financial planners strive to serve their clients faithfully and avoid errors and omissions claims.

Errors and omissions can take many forms, and a detailed discussion is beyond the scope of this chapter. In discussing the principal-agent relationship, perhaps we should note that an error or omission on behalf of an agent sometimes obligates the insurer to pay a claim that should not have been covered. For example, the agent might bind coverage for which the agency contract does not provide binding authority. When the agent acted with apparent authority as an agent of the insurance company, the insurer will typically pay the claim and then seek reimbursement from the agent. Insurance agents, like other professionals, need to protect themselves against these and other claims with errors and omissions (E&O) professional liability insurance. Because E&O insurance usually includes a large deductible, even an agent who is insured faces a substantial loss in the event of an error or omission.

The terms general agent, local agent, and special agent, among others, are frequently used in the insurance business. All of these terms have a specialized significance within the business and may represent the nature of the agent's position with the company or the commission arrangement. Legally, regardless of terminology, an agent is either a general agent or a limited agent. A *general agent* can bind insurance for a client, making insurance effective immediately and prior to the actual issuance of the policy. A *limited agent* has limited or restricted powers. The scope of the delegated authority determines what the

general agent

limited agent

agent may or may not do. However, the principal may still be bound by any action within the limited agent's express, implied, or apparent authority.

Life insurance companies customarily limit the authority to issue or modify life insurance contracts to salaried company officers. Life insurance agents, even those called general agents, are thus limited agents. Generally speaking, life insurance agents are authorized to solicit, receive, and forward applications for the contracts their companies write. Agents are authorized to receive the first premiums due on applications but not subsequent premiums. The life insurance agent's authority to accept business or bind coverage is also limited. The life insurer issues the contract only after receiving the written, signed application and, often, a medical examination report. The agent may not cover the policyowner immediately, nor may contract modifications be made later without the insurance company's approval.

Agents appointed to represent property and liability insurers are often granted the powers of a general agent. The limitations on their authority are set forth in the agency agreement. General agents may bind their companies for a client's coverage in certain cases. An oral or written binder is temporary evidence of coverage until the insurance company issues the full insurance policy. Among their other responsibilities, these agents may inspect and collect initial and sometimes renewal premiums. Some general agents even issue contracts in their own offices for auto or homeowners policies. Contracts for other lines of insurance may have to be issued by the insurer in the home office or a branch office.

Brokers

broker

Brokers legally represent the policyowner rather than the insurer. With widespread contacts and knowledge of many fields of insurance, brokers can offer significant advice and counsel to their clients. The larger insurance brokerage firms are especially well equipped to handle the problems of insurance for a buyer with individual and specialized requirements.

A broker is an independent contractor. The broker assists the applicant for insurance by finding coverage, but the broker is usually paid by the insurer. The duties of a broker are similar to those of an agent as described earlier, except that the broker's legal duties pertain more directly to the applicant or policyowner whom he or she represents.

Policyowners sometimes do not differentiate between an insurance broker and an agent. As explained above, the insurance agent is acting under specific and delegated authority from the insurer and is sometimes authorized to bind coverage within specific limits. The broker, on the other hand, has no such authority. Because the broker represents the applicant or policyowner, the applicant or policyowner is bound by the broker's acts. For example, any misrepresentation, mistake, breach of warranty, or fraud perpetrated by the broker on a policyowner's behalf makes the policyowner responsible as if the policyowner had committed the act. Furthermore, a statement by an applicant to a broker is not presumed to be known to an insurance company, whereas a statement by an applicant to an agent is presumed to be known by the company.

Some insurance agents are licensed as both agents and brokers. For example, a producer may act as an agent who commits the insurer for a part of a desired amount of coverage and as a broker in placing any excess coverage.

Example:	Ripley is an agent for the XYZ Insurance Company, which specializes in preferred auto insurance. Ripley also has a broker's license that includes auto insurance. Ripley may have authority to bind coverage for an applicant in XYZ, but Ripley has no authority to bind coverage that he wishes to place with another insurer for which he acts a broker.

surplus lines broker

A special type of broker called an excess lines broker or *surplus lines broker* places coverage for which there is no available market in the state, such as exposures that have a high loss frequency or severity. Examples of business that surplus lines brokers place are liability insurance for amusement parks and ski resorts and many product liability situations. Usually, the coverage is placed with companies that have not been licensed to do business in the particular state and are therefore known as *nonadmitted insurers*. The surplus lines broker may not always deal with the policyowner directly but may be sought out by the policyowner's broker. Many states require special licenses for surplus lines brokers.

nonadmitted insurer

Insurance Consultants and Financial Planners

Financial planners, who help clients protect their income and assets, play a major role in the personal insurance marketing system. Financial planners are among the various other types of insurance and risk management consultants that may serve as intermediaries between insurance companies and their customers. Insurance consultants are usually compensated by the policyowner on a fee basis. Financial planners may be paid a fee by the policyowner, a commission from the insurer if they are also agents or brokers, or some combination of a fee and a commission.

Salaried Specialists

Many insurers, as well as some large insurance agencies, employ salaried service representatives to help agents sell or service the more complex lines of insurance. State insurance regulations usually do not require service representatives to be licensed.

Life insurance service representatives include advanced underwriting specialists who aid the life insurance agent in estate planning and pension or tax planning. General agents use salaried training specialists to recruit, supervise, and assist new life insurance agents. Most companies that write group life and health coverages have salaried company representatives who assist the life insurance agent with writing group contracts. Many property and liability insurance companies use special agents to initiate agency contracts, help agents with special sales problems, and keep agents informed of the insurer's new contracts and services. Engineering, appraisal, and loss prevention services are often provided by company specialists in conjunction with local agents. In addition, company claims adjusters work in cooperation with agents on many losses involving large amounts or special problems.

Marketing Systems Used in Insurance

Agency versus Direct-Response Marketing Systems

The complex and intangible nature of insurance and its significance to the policyowner make personal contact through an intermediary essential to the sale of most insurance.

direct-response marketing

Direct-response marketing provides the exception to the general rule that insurance is sold through agents. Under a direct-response marketing system, the insurer deals directly with the applicant, without agents, through employees of the insurer. In specialized lines in certain market segments of insurance, these systems assume some importance. Dread disease insurers or hospital indemnity health insurers who use direct mail or television advertising are common examples. All correspondence circulates directly between the company and the prospect, and the insurance contract is written and serviced by mail or telephone without an agent.

As another example of direct-response marketing, some insurers sell such coverages as annuities and life, health, auto, homeowners, and long-term care insurance over the Internet. A few auto insurers have applied the direct response approach successfully in writing auto insurance. Some life insurance sales are also accomplished in this way.

Mixed marketing systems are becoming increasingly common. For example, some insurance agencies market insurance through the Internet. Some insurance companies market through agents and also market directly to consumers through the Internet or through the mail. With group life and health insurance, it is increasingly common for salaried employees to assist commissioned agents.

Life Insurance Agency Systems

general agency system

Many life insurance companies use a *general agency system*, although as discussed earlier, an insurance general agent is not a general agent in the legal sense. Historically, a general insurance agent was an individual entrepreneur granted a franchise by an insurer to market the insurer's products in a specified geographic area. The general agent represented only that one insurer- and was responsible for hiring, training, motivating, and supervising agents. The general agent was compensated solely by commissions on business the agency produced and was fully responsible for all expenses of operating the agency. More recently, however, insurance companies typically provide some form of financial assistance to the general agent, perhaps paying some of the costs involved in hiring and training new agents and/or providing an allowance to cover some of the operating agency's expenses.

branch office system

In contrast with the general agency system, many life insurance companies use a *branch office system*, also referred to as a managerial system. Here, the insurer establishes branch offices in the areas where it writes business, with each branch headed by a manager who is a salaried employee of the insurance company. Again, the manager is responsible for hiring, training, motivating, and supervising agents for the company, but the insurer bears all costs of operating the branch. The branch manager may also receive a bonus as part of his or her compensation, depending on the quantity and quality of business the branch writes. Payment of bonuses to branch managers, together with coverage of some general agency operating expenses, has tended to blur somewhat the historical distinctions between the two agency systems.

personal producing general agent (PPGA)

A variation of the general agency system that has become significant in some life insurance companies is the *personal producing general agent (PPGA)* system. In this system, the insurer hires an experienced agent with a proven record of sales success as its general agent in a given territory. Unlike a traditional general agent, however, the PPGA's main responsibility is to sell the insurer's products, rather than to build an agency force for the company. The PPGA often receives higher commissions than other agents to help cover operating expenses. The PPGA may be expected to meet certain sales quotas for the company but may also be allowed to represent other insurers.

Property and Liability Insurance Agency Systems

independent agency system

The two main agency systems that insurers use in the property and liability field are the independent agency system and the exclusive agency system sometimes referred to as the captive agent system. In the *independent agency system*, the insurance agency is an independent business organization that usually represents several insurance companies or groups of companies. The head of the agency pays all his or her own operating expenses and is compensated mainly through commissions on the business the agency writes. Some independent agencies are paid fees by the insurer for settling small claims or by the policyowner for providing risk management services.

The independent agent usually has some authority to bind the insurer for a client's coverage, to collect the initial premium and in some cases the renewal premiums, to submit the application to the insurer, and to deliver the policy to the policyowner. The policyowner is, by contract, the customer of the agent. The independent agent owns the policyowner's business and is free to place it with a different insurer when the policy comes up for renewal, unless the policyowner objects. One of the results of this ownership status is that commission rates tend to be the same for renewal policies as for new policies. If renewal commissions were lower, the independent agent might be inclined to place the business with a different insurer at each renewal date to earn the higher first-year commission. Another result of ownership of the customer's business is that when the independent agent elects to retire or leave the business, he or she can sell the book of business to another agent. The insurer may not interfere with the agent's ownership rights.

One of the main advantages of the independent agency system is that the agent who represents several insurers can place business with the company that offers the best coverage at the best price for each applicant. One of the disadvantages is that a conflict of interest may exist when the agent is free to place business with any of several companies that pay different commission rates.

exclusive agency system

In the *exclusive agency system*, the agent usually represents only one company or group of affiliated companies. Compensation comes mainly from commissions on the sale of new business, with lower commission rates on renewals. The insurer may cover some of the agent's operating expenses, particularly for new agents. The agency contract typically gives the agent either limited or no ownership, use, and control of policy and expiration data while the contract is in force. The agent has no control over what happens to the business when he or she retires or leaves the insurance field.

In the exclusive agency system, billing and collection of renewal premiums are almost always the insurer's responsibility, not the agent's. The agent may have the power, within limits, to bind the insurer on a client's coverage. The agent may also have the authority to settle small claims.

Although a clear distinction between independent agencies and exclusive agencies once existed, the lines today are blurring. Many exclusive agents

---

Main Agency Systems in Insurance

- Life insurance
  - General agent system
  - Branch office system
  - PPGA system
- Property/liability insurance
  - Independent agent system
  - Exclusive agent system

have reportedly found ways to establish related independent agencies, often operated by a family member, or to participate in broker arrangements with independent agents.[3]

On the property-liability side of the business, the current trend is toward increased growth in the use of independent agents. Although the number of independent agencies is shrinking, the average agency continues to grow in size. According to a recent study, independent agents and brokers wrote nearly 79 percent of commercial lines business. In personal lines, independent agents and brokers had a 36 percent share.[4] On the life side, a recent census from LIMRA International put the number of affiliated career producers at about 179,000 and the number of independent brokers and personal producing agents at about 161,000.[5]

Group Insurance Systems

Marketing to consumers in the group insurance system is usually done through the employer. Payroll deductions are a convenient method of premium payment. Labor unions, credit unions, finance companies, professional associations, and other groups may also sponsor group insurance programs to lower insurance costs to the members of the group.

Group life insurance has been expanding since such plans began many years ago. Health insurance has used the group method of marketing even more extensively, especially in medical expense insurance. Annuities or insured pensions, too, have used the group system widely.

Group plans in property and liability insurance are much less established and differ from group life and health insurance in some respects. Most of these plans have individual selection, rating, and contracts instead of group underwriting, master contracts, and certificates. However, employer participation is involved in the arrangements for the plans, premiums are collected through payroll deductions, and the objectives of the plans are similar to those of group life and health insurance. Auto and homeowners policies are the principal fields in which mass merchandising of quasi-group property and liability insurance has been tried.

SOURCES FOR FURTHER IN-DEPTH STUDY

- For detailed information on banks in insurance:
  - American Bankers Insurance Association, 1120 Connecticut Ave. NW, Washington, DC 20036. Phone 202-663-5163. Web site address www.aba.com/
  - Bank Insurance and Securities Association, ABIA, 303 W. Lancaster Ave. Suite 1C, Wayne, PA 19087. Phone 610-989-9047. Web site address www.bisanet.org

- For a thorough treatment of the subject of agency law, especially in life insurance, Graves, Edward E., and Christensen, Burke A., editors, *McGill's Legal Aspects of Life Insurance,* 4th ed., chapter 16, Bryn Mawr, PA: The American College Press, 2004. Phone 888-263-7265. Web site address www.theamericancollege.edu

CHAPTER REVIEW

Answers to review questions and self-test questions start on page 793.

Key Terms

domestic insurer	general agent
foreign insurer	limited agent
alien insurer	broker
stock insurance company	surplus lines broker
mutual insurance company	nonadmitted insurer
advance-premium mutual	direct-response marketing
assessment mutual	general agency system
fraternal insurer	branch office system
demutualization	personal producing general
mutual holding company	agent (PPGA)
reciprocal exchange	independent agency system
Lloyd's association	exclusive agency system
agent	

Review Questions

3-1. Compare the features of stock and mutual insurance companies as to form of business, ownership, voters for the board of directors, and recipients of dividends.

3-2. In recent years, numerous mutual insurance companies have shifted to the stock form through the process of demutualization.
    a. Why do companies demutualize?
    b. What are the potential disadvantages associated with demutualizing?

3-3. Explain how reciprocal exchanges differ from mutual insurance.

3-4. With regard to Lloyd's of London, who provides the insurance (who is the insurer)?

3-5. After you discuss an insurance policy available from a mutual insurance company, your client, Sara Lott, asks whether mutual insurance companies always provide lower-priced coverage because they do not need to earn a profit for stockholders. How would you respond?

3-6.   Why does a financial planner need to understand how the insurance business markets its contracts and services?

3-7.   Describe the three powers held by an agent and the legal duties an agent and principal owe each other.

3-8.   Legally, an agent is either a general agent or a limited agent. Indicate which legal type each of the following insurance agents typically is and what authority is generally given to them by their insurers:
   a.   life insurance agents
   b.   property-liability insurance agents

3-9.   At the advice of his financial planner, Tom Johnson meets with an agent at an all-lines agency to discuss obtaining coverage to meet his various protection needs. In each of the following cases, indicate whether or not Tom has coverage immediately and why.
   a.   After gathering information about Tom's new home and its contents, the agent recommends a homeowners policy with XYZ Insurance Company. After getting satisfactory answers to questions regarding price and the claims service offered by the company, Tom tells the agent he wants the policy from XYZ. The agent tells Tom he's covered.
   b.   After gathering information about the needs of Tom's family in the event of his death and about Tom's existing group life coverage at work, the agent recommends a $500,000 variable universal life policy from ABC Life to meet Tom's additional needs. The agent points out the flexibility of the policy both in terms of premium payments and investment choices. Tom fills out the application and gives the agent the minimum first premium. The agent tells Tom, "You're going to like the flexibility and performance of your new policy."

3-10.   Explain the difference between insurance agents and brokers in terms of
   a.   whom they represent
   b.   their power to bind the insurance company

3-11.   Describe the key features of the following agency systems used to market life insurance:
   a.   general agent
   b.   branch office or managerial system
   c.   personal producing general agent (PPGA)

3-12.   Compare the key features of the two main agency systems, the independent agency system and the exclusive agency system, used to market property-liability insurance.
   a.   How many companies or groups of companies are represented?
   b.   Who pays operating expenses?
   c.   How are agents compensated?

    d.   What is the relative size of renewal versus initial commissions?

    e.   Who generally has ownership, use, and control of policy and expiration data?

    f.   Who generally collects premiums and settles claims?

3-13.   Your client, Bill Johnson, asks your advice as a financial planner about whether it is better to purchase homeowners insurance from an independent insurance agency, which represents several insurers, or an exclusive agent, who represents only one insurance company. How would you respond?

3-14.   Mark and Liz Olson have an individual life insurance policy issued by a mutual insurance company that has its corporate headquarters in their state, a homeowners policy issued by a stock insurance company based in another state, and an auto insurance policy issued by a reciprocal exchange. They also have medical expense protection through a Blue Cross/Blue Shield plan provided by their employer. Last year when their auto insurance premium increased, they decided to do some comparison shopping and were surprised to discover that some insurance agents represent may different companies while others represent only one insurance company.

    a.   Explain the different types of insurers with which the Olsons are dealing.

    b.   Explain the different types of marketing representatives with whom the Olsons are dealing.

Self-Test Questions

T   F   3-1.   On the basis of where they are domiciled, insurers are considered foreign if incorporated in another country.

T   F   3-2.   Stock and mutual insurers are both owned by stockholders, who elect the board of directors.

T   F   3-3.   Stock and mutual insurers may both pay dividends—stock companies to their stockholders and mutual companies to their policyowners.

T   F   3-4.   Because mutuals are owned by their policyowners, they are usually better than stocks from a consumer's standpoint.

T   F   3-5.   To facilitate access to capital markets and diversification of activities, there is currently a trend for stock companies to convert to mutual companies.

T   F   3-6.   In Lloyd's of London, insurance is written by the corporation of Lloyd's.

T   F   3-7.   Because a reciprocal is an unincorporated association, each insured is also an insurer.

T   F   3-8.   Although reciprocals are usually small, a few exchanges that write auto insurance have grown to substantial size.

T   F   3-9.   Because Lloyd's of London is not licensed directly in most of the United States, the insurance coverage provided by Lloyd's underwriters in most states is the same as that permitted under state excess and surplus lines laws.

T   F   3-10.   When representing an insurance company, an insurance agent has only the express authority spelled out in the agency contract.

T   F   3-11.   From a legal standpoint, nearly all life insurance agents are granted the powers of a general agent.

T   F   3-12.   A broker represents the policyowner, unlike an agent who is a legal representative of the insurance company.

T   F   3-13.   Key life insurance marketing systems include general agents, branch offices managed by company employees, and personal producing general agents (PPGAs).

T   F   3-14.   In property and liability insurance, an independent agent can represent several insurers or groups of companies, whereas an exclusive agent typically represents only one company or group of affiliated companies.

T   F   3-15.   Exclusive agents generally receive the same commission rate for renewing a policy as for initially selling the policy, whereas independent agents have traditionally received renewal commissions that are considerably smaller than their initial commissions.

NOTES

1. In some commercial lines, such as workers' compensation insurance, the insured's first cost takes the form of a tentative deposit premium that is subject to adjustment after an audit at the end of the period of protection. Large commercial insureds might also have loss-sensitive insurance programs in which the ultimate premium is based in part on the insured's losses during the current policy term.
2. The Association of America's Fraternal Benefit Societies maintains an informative web page at http://www.nfanet.org.
3. Barbara Bowers, "Easy Pass," *Best's Review*, March 2004, pp. 51–52.
4. Independent Agents & Brokers of America, "Independent Agents & Brokers Show Impressive Gains in Personal, Commercial Lines" (Alexandria Virginia, press release, March 17, 2004).
5. Barbara Bowers, "Easy Pass," *Best's Review*, March 2004, pp. 51–52.

4

Insurance Company Operations

Learning Objectives

An understanding of the material in this chapter should enable the student to

4-1. Describe the purpose of underwriting and the selection of applicants.

4-2. Explain the purposes of reinsurance.

4-3. Explain the purpose of claims adjustment, the types of claims adjusters, and procedures for claims adjustment.

4-4. Describe factors involved in insurance rate making.

4-5. Explain the investment function and other functions of an insurance company.

Chapter Outline

In the previous chapter, we discussed the various classifications of private insurers and how they market their products to the public. Now we turn our attention to insurers' internal operations. The principal areas described are underwriting, reinsurance, claims adjusting, rate making, and investing. Financial planners need to understand the basic operation of these functions in order to help their clients make the most effective use of insurance, which is invariably a part of any sound financial plan.

UNDERWRITING

Insurers are not usually required to sell insurance to every person who applies for it.[1] This fact puzzles many people. Something seems wrong with a business that can refuse to sell its product or service to the people who need and want it most. In the case of insurance, these are the people most likely to have losses. Insurers are more interested in finding and accepting the clients who are least likely to have losses.

Insurance is legally viewed as a "business affected with the public interest."[2] Insurers serve the public interest not only by providing a wide variety of coverages to most applicants, but also by remaining, or at least attempting to remain, financially solvent so that they can deliver on the promises made in the insurance contracts they sell. Financial planners need to recognize and appreciate the delicate balancing act insurers face in meeting these sometimes conflicting objectives.

Purpose

underwriting

Underwriting is simply the selection and pricing of insurance applications that are offered to an insurer. The insurer attempts to accept only applicants who, on average, will have actual loss experience comparable to the expected loss experience for which the company has set its premium rates. Selection implies that there are some acceptances and some rejections, or that not all applicants will be accepted for insurance. Most other businesses welcome virtually all paying customers and do not attempt to screen them. However, banks and other institutions that lend money practice a selection process that resembles insurance underwriting. The selection process lenders use is, in fact, referred to as credit underwriting or loan underwriting.

Most insurance prices are based on an average rate for an entire class or group such as 30-year-old female nonsmokers or owners of 2004 Buick Park Avenues in Philadelphia with no youthful drivers. Some applicants within each class will be better than average and some worse than average. Which type of policyowners will an insurer that does no selection tend to have? Those persons who are better than average are most likely not to want or need the insurance at the price quoted for the class, and conversely, those persons who know they are worse than average will be most likely to desire the insurance contract at that price. This result is obvious: The bad applicants at the average rate would be getting a bargain.

Adverse selection is found throughout the field of insurance. As mentioned in chapter 1, adverse selection refers to the natural tendency for those who know they are highly vulnerable to loss from a specific risk to be most likely to acquire and retain insurance that covers those risks. Insurers, on the other hand, are most eager to sell insurance to the people least likely to suffer a covered loss. Insurers attempt to avoid adverse selection in order to prevent the financial disaster that results when an insurer ends up with a customer base of worse-than-average applicants, who will have worse-than-average losses, but collects premiums based on applicants whose loss experience would be average. Underwriters attempt to avoid adverse selection by selecting a large, safely diversified, profitable group of applicants.

The major need for insurance underwriting stems from this tendency toward adverse selection, which, without underwriting, would ruin insurers. An insurer can be profitable only by exercising careful selection that reasonably offsets the natural economic forces that lead to adverse selection in insurance applications. The insurer needs adequate and accurate information about its applicants to determine fair classifications and to charge sufficient prices

Underwriting is the process by which the insurer evaluates the applicants it has been asked to accept. A compromise is often necessary between two objectives: (1) to obtain a large number of individual insureds within each classification so that reasonable predictability of losses is possible and (2) to obtain a homogeneity of insureds within each classification so that reasonable equity between the better and poorer individual insureds is achieved. The care with which an insurer combines these objectives is vital to its underwriting success and thus to its entire operations.

Underwriters are the backbone of the insurance business. They must decline many applications, but they are also often able to help consumers become insurable and thereby have their applications accepted. Proper rate classes and prices, with good loss prevention practices, can help make insurance available to most people who need it.

Selection of Applicants

The selection of applicants and the pricing of insurance contracts are closely related. If an adequate price for a class of insureds has been established, the insurer must underwrite to secure at least an average group of insureds within that class. Otherwise, the insurer's losses will exceed the premium income available to pay those losses. If the pricing for an insurance contract is inadequate, even reasonably careful selection can fail to produce a profitable group of applicants. The alternative in such a case is to underwrite strictly, accepting only the very best applicants in each rate class. Pricing, or rate making, is discussed later in this chapter.

The Agent and Insurer As Underwriters

field underwriting

For most insurers and most lines of insurance, the choice of applicants begins with the underwriting done by the agent, sometimes referred to as *field underwriting*. Each time an agent prepares a prospect list or, for example, telephones Mr. White instead of Mr. Green to sell insurance, the agent is performing the first step in underwriting. If an insurer appoints well-qualified agents, they will usually try to choose clients that meet the insurer's underwriting rules. Even though the agent does some underwriting for the insurer, most of the underwriting is an insurance company function, performed by salaried employees in the home office or branch office.

Underwriting does not involve rejecting all difficult or doubtful applications. Both the agent and the insurer frequently explain how a borderline applicant can become acceptable through loss prevention or other methods. Good judgment and good information are needed in this process. For example, an auto insurance underwriter whose company rules do not permit him or her to write a teenaged driver with a high-performance sports car might suggest that the parents purchase a more conservative vehicle that would meet underwriting standards at a standard rate. Or the underwriter might suggest that an applicant for disability income insurance, whose type of work occasionally involves minor injuries, would be acceptable for coverage with a waiting period longer than the one indicated on the original application.

Generally, the insurer determines the underwriting rules to be carried out by its agents and its company personnel in the underwriting department. Agents receive instructions on what types of applicants are unacceptable, as well as encouragement through directives and sales contests that specify what types of contracts and what kinds of business the company particularly desires. Other

---

Types of Underwriting

- Field underwriting
- Initial home office or branch office underwriting
- Renewal underwriting

types of applicants may be specified as insurable only after the insurer has detailed information.

The authority that many agents have to put the contract into effect immediately through the use of a binder, or temporary contract, is a good example of the importance of field underwriting. Many property insurance contracts, for example, go into effect immediately when the agent issues a binder that provides temporary coverage until the actual contract is written. The insurer can decide not to write the contract or can cancel the contract written by the agent, but this is unusual. Even in somewhat doubtful cases, the insurer is more likely to continue the protection and perhaps ask for additional information before renewing the contract.

Underwriting by the insurer and the agent takes place not only at the time of the original application but also at each renewal of the insurance contract. During renewal underwriting, loss experience and other new information are considered in most insurance lines.

Sources of Underwriting Information

The sources of underwriting information on which insurers rely, depending on the line of insurance, include (1) the applicant, (2) the agent, (3) the insurer's own inspection or claims department, (4) insurer bureaus and associations, and (5) outside agencies.

The applicant for an insurance contract often makes both written and oral statements. Signed written statements are standard in life and health insurance, and the application becomes a part of the contract. Auto and business insurance applicants also frequently complete written application forms that give the insurer basic underwriting details. Agents in many kinds of insurance give their companies reports, opinions, and recommendations that are valuable aids in selecting or rejecting applications. Many insurers maintain separate inspection departments to give the underwriters physical inspection and engineering reports on applicants' properties. The insurer's claims department, too, can be a source of important underwriting data for renewal decisions.

Insurers also combine efforts to maintain bureau or association lists of insurance applicants. For example, MIB, Inc., formerly the Medical Information Bureau, offers a centralized source of information about medical and other impairments of individual applicants for life insurance. Other service organizations provide regular inspection and rating services in regard to property insurance.

Insurance companies often use outside agencies to supplement the information gathered from the applicants, agents, and other insurer representatives. For example, physicians supply life insurance companies with medical reports after physical examination of the applicants. Standard financial rating services such as Dun & Bradstreet (D&B) are used for many insurance applications from businesses. Life insurers have used credit investigations by outside firms for many years. Auto insurers have used external agencies to check motor vehicle reports and court records of new applicants, especially for younger drivers.

Agencies such as Fair Isaac and ChoicePoint that develop a credit score or an insurance score have become increasingly important sources of information in several other personal lines of property and liability insurance as well.

Inspection agencies are valuable for gathering factual data and for identifying a prospect's poor habits or moral problems through such sources as employers, neighbors, or associates. The evaluation of moral and attitudinal hazards is crucial, yet difficult, for many kinds of insurance. The moral and attitudinal hazards that cause increased losses are discussed in chapter 1. The aim of these investigations is not only to gather negative information but also to obtain positive character reports that will permit insurance to be written. The independent investigative companies must comply with federal legislation that deals with credit reporting and privacy. Insurers must also meet these requirements, as well as laws on the state level, such as the NAIC (National Association of Insurance Commissioners) Health Information Privacy Protection Model Act, adopted by many states.

REINSURANCE

reinsurance

Financial planners must recognize how underwriters' ability to accept applications is both broadened and limited by reinsurance available to the insurer. *Reinsurance* is insurance an insurer purchases. In reinsurance, one insurer, the primary insurer or ceding company that issued the policy, transfers all or part of the risk to another insurer, the reinsurer.

Purposes

How can an insurer accept large loss exposures that sometimes exceed many millions of dollars in a single building, a ship, or an airplane? How can liability contracts for business firms have policy limits of $100 million or more? How can a person obtain in excess of $10 million of life insurance? When hurricanes affect many policyowners at one time, how can insurers survive the concentration of loss that occurs? Gigantic losses do not occur frequently, but when they do occur, they illustrate the real reason for insurance—protection against losses that perhaps only the insurance system can provide.

Catastrophes illustrate the most important purpose of reinsurance: the spread or diversification of losses. One insurer can write large amounts of insurance on a single life or property or in a concentrated area, then use reinsurance to shift part of the loss exposure to perhaps several other insurance companies. Large losses are thus shared, and excessive losses in one occurrence are less likely to cause financial instability for individual insurers. Without reinsurance, each insurer would be limited to its own financial ability to pay losses. Reinsurance enhances financial strength by spreading losses throughout the insurance business.

Reinsurance also has other purposes. Mandatory reserve requirements drain surplus and restrict growth, a particularly severe problem for newer or smaller companies. These companies can achieve more rapid growth by transferring part of the responsibility for maintaining reserves from the insurer to a reinsurer, permitting the insurer to increase its writing of new business. Reinsurers also offer many technical advisory services to new insurers or those expanding to new types of insurance or territories.

Significance to Financial Planners

Insurance companies usually obtain reinsurance from two basic types of organizations: (1) professional reinsurers, which sell only reinsurance, and (2) other insurance companies that write some reinsurance in addition to issuing policies directly to consumers. The financial planner should recognize that the policyowner is not a party to a reinsurance agreement. Reinsurance is usually transparent to the policyowners. Neither the policyowner nor the financial planner is usually aware of the primary insurer's specific reinsurance arrangements. Reinsurance operates in the background as a separate contract between the primary insurer and the reinsurer. The policyowner or other claimant looks to the primary insurer that wrote the policy for claims payment. This primary insurer is responsible for paying the entire claim and is then reimbursed by the reinsurer, if reinsurance applies.

Reinsurance agreements are often highly complex, and the typical financial planner does not need to understand the many types of such agreements. However, the planner should at least be aware of the difference between treaty, or automatic, reinsurance agreements and facultative agreements.

treaty (automatic) reinsurance

Treaty (automatic) reinsurance exists when the primary insurer agrees in advance to transfer, or cede, some types of loss exposures and the reinsurer agrees to accept them. The reinsurer agrees to insure an amount or a proportionate part of a designated class of past or future business written by the primary insurer. The reinsurer is liable as soon as the primary insurer accepts the loss exposure. Automatic protection is thus ensured for the primary insurer because the reinsurer has agreed beforehand to accept all loss exposures with the terms of the treaty. Usually, the policyowner will not even be aware of the existence of this type of reinsurance.

facultative reinsurance

Facultative reinsurance, on the other hand, is optional for both the insurer and the reinsurer. Each facultative reinsurance contract is written on its own merits and is a matter of individual bargaining between the primary insurer and the reinsurer. The primary insurer may or may not offer part of a loss exposure to the reinsurer. The reinsurer is under no obligation to accept the loss exposure if it is offered. Each party thus retains the "faculty" or privilege of accepting or rejecting the reinsurance agreement. For large or unusual cases, the availability of facultative reinsurance may be the deciding factor in the underwriting process as to whether an application for insurance is acceptable to the primary insurer. Delays in obtaining coverage for a client often result from the primary insurer's need to obtain a reinsurance commitment.

CLAIMS ADJUSTING

Payment of losses is certainly the most obvious function of insurance. Without claims that culminate in loss payments, there would be no insurance business. This section of the chapter gives a broad picture of insurance in action, explaining who pays insurance losses and how.

claims adjusting

The basic function of loss payment is commonly referred to as *claims adjusting*. The term is not very satisfactory, but it has become well fixed in the business of insurance. "Adjustment" suggests a compromise or change before settlement is reached. A better term might be claims payment, with the persons who do this work referred to as claims persons or claims representatives. However, because the more common reference is to adjusting and adjusters, these terms will be used here.

Claims adjustments are a daily routine of the insurance business. Thousands of claim checks are routinely delivered to insureds, third-party claimants, or beneficiaries every day. Sometimes, however, the routine becomes the spectacular. Even single-building fires can be devastating. Losses from hurricanes can affect hundreds of thousands of persons. Tornadoes, earthquakes, floods, explosions, and other natural catastrophes can destroy property values and cause deaths or injuries. Large losses attributable to human failures can also result in multimillion-dollar liability lawsuits.

When policyowners receive payment for values that have been lost, they often realize why they purchased insurance contracts. Up to that time, they might only have had a feeling that there were some vague reasons why they purchased the protection. When they actually receive a loss check that makes it possible for them to rebuild their homes, to replace lost income, or to pay nursing home expenses, they fully realize the value of their insurance.

Purpose

Insureds and beneficiaries who have honestly suffered loss or damage need not approach the insurance company apologetically. They have a legally enforceable contractual right to seek payment for a covered claim. It should be the objective of both insurers and claimants to arrive at a fair and equitable measure of the loss. There are sometimes areas of disagreement, but if both parties resolve to reach an equitable adjustment, disagreements will usually be reconciled readily.

Insurance adjusters link the insurer and the policyowner. The adjusters deliver the goods that the agent has sold. Insurers recognize that years of insurance programming and planning will mean nothing if the policyowner faces difficulties following a loss. New adjusters are taught that their responsibility is to settle claims equitably and not, as is sometimes believed, to pay the smallest dollar amount to which claimants will agree. Adjusters are also advised to give reasonable assistance to claimants during the traumatic days immediately following a serious loss—for example, helping the family relocate to temporary housing following a fire or providing names of reputable repair shops after an auto accident. Adjusters are further instructed, when claimants do not know what is due them under their contracts, to fully explain what amounts should be included in their claims. In the interest of equity, adjusters are also trained to recognize unethical practices and to resist padded claims or fraudulent demands. Fairness to uninformed claimants and resistance to wrongful claims benefit both the insurance business and the policyowners, who in the long run must pay premiums based on loss experience.

From the insurer's point of view, claims adjustments afford an attractive area of competition, especially in those types of insurance where premium rates are relatively similar. Although only a minority of all insureds have a loss in a given year, the insurer's reputation rests not only on how satisfied the claimants are but also on how many other persons the claimants tell about their losses and payments. Dissatisfied policyowners tell everyone why they believe they were unfairly treated, whereas satisfied claimants take their payments as a matter of course. If the insurer fails to effect a prompt and equitable adjustment following a loss, it will have failed in the most crucial of all competitive areas.

Loss adjustments are set in motion when a notice of loss is filed with an insurer. The purpose of the adjustment process is to confirm the insurer's liability for a given loss and to reach an agreement on the amount of loss or damage payable under the insurance contract. In paying losses, adjusters have been advised to follow the "4F rules": Be fair, frank, friendly, and firm.

Insurance Adjusters: Types and Organization

There are four categories of adjusters:

- insurance agents
- staff adjusters
- independent adjusters
- public adjusters

Agents As Adjusters

Many insurers allow the insurance agent, whenever possible, to settle claims that involve small losses to policyowners. After all, the agent is usually closest to the client, is familiar with the policyowner's insurance contracts, and usually has the earliest facts on the occurrence of the loss. The agent also has a prime interest in seeing that the consumer receives prompt and fair treatment in the claims adjustment process. The policyowner's satisfaction is important to the agent in terms of goodwill and continued business with the policyowner and the policyowner's friends.

Some property insurance agents have their insurance companies' authority to settle small claims with policyowners immediately by issuing a check in the name of the company. This is often the most expedient way to handle smaller and uncomplicated claims. For agents, the authority to settle a claim with policyowners immediately is a valuable right that enables the agents to render prompt service with a minimum of paperwork. This practice is common for fire, windstorm, and medical payments under homeowners and auto insurance contracts. For larger losses or losses that involve more complex adjusting methods, such as in liability insurance, the insurer must provide specialized help to the agent and the insured. Staff or independent adjusters are used in these cases.

In life insurance, the agent is often involved in loss payment as an intermediary but not as an adjuster. The claims procedure for smaller contracts is simple. Notice to the company and a death certificate are often all that is required before the policy's death benefit can be paid. The life insurance agent usually forwards the death notice and certificate to the insurer. In some cases, especially those involving smaller amounts, the insurer may issue a check for the agent to deliver to the beneficiary, or the company may simply mail the check. When larger amounts are involved, instead of issuing a check, the company will usually open a money market account, funded with policy proceeds, and provide the beneficiary with a checkbook on that account. Unlike property insurers, life insurers do not usually have the problem of determining the extent of loss payment because the contract itself states the amount to be paid upon loss. For larger policies, the agent may need to explain various installment payment options in place of a lump-sum cash payment. In health insurance loss payments, the agent can often use special personnel from the insurer's claims department.

Financial planners discover that claims provide an extremely rewarding opportunity to see insurance in action. Tremendous personal satisfaction results when a family receives steady income during a long period when the primary breadwinner cannot work, because the family took the planner's advice and purchased disability income protection. It is highly gratifying to see a dream home rebuilt, with homeowners insurance proceeds, on the ashes of a fire that otherwise would have caused a loss of a lifetime of savings. Experienced financial planners point with quiet pride to families whose sons and daughters have been able to attend college without financial hardship, despite the unexpected early death of family breadwinners. Because experienced financial planners and insurance agents have seen firsthand the value of insurance, it is easy to understand their missionary zeal in urging clients to have adequate coverage.

Staff Adjusters

staff adjuster

Many insurance claims are settled by *staff adjusters* who are employees of the insurer. Staff adjusters are the primary type of adjuster for life and health insurance claims. In property and liability insurance, staff adjusters are usually employees who devote their entire time to handling loss settlements. Some auto insurers in larger cities have drive-in claims locations where immediate estimates and payments for covered damage to autos are made by staff adjusters known as physical damage appraisers.

The use of staff adjusters depends on the volume and kinds of business written in the territory in which the loss occurs. To support a full-time staff adjuster in a given area, the insurer must have enough claims to be adjusted. Some companies use staff adjusters almost exclusively, while others are more apt to use the services of independent adjusters.

Independent Adjusters

Insurance companies often use independent adjusters to settle claims. Independent adjusters are experts who have made loss adjusting a business. Some have specialized in particular fields. Others have a general knowledge and understanding of adjustment procedures and handle losses whenever it is impossible or inconvenient for the staff or other types of adjusters to do so.

independent adjuster *Independent adjusters* include both individuals and adjusting firms that are in the business of providing claims adjusting services. National adjusting firms include rather sizable organizations.

Independent adjusters work on a fee basis for the insurers who request their services. A typical use is in auto insurance when the insurer has only a small volume of business in an area. Independent adjusters are also used frequently to supplement staff adjusters when catastrophic events, such as a major hurricane, give rise to a large number of separate claims. Independent adjusters can also be used by insurers to settle claims in highly technical areas in which the staff adjusters lack the necessary skills or expertise. Independent adjusters often develop continuing working relationships with particular insurers, in addition to accepting infrequent adjusting assignments from other insurers.

Public Adjusters

public adjuster As the name implies, *public adjusters* represent the public, in contrast to adjusters who represent insurers. Sometimes the insured retains a public adjuster to negotiate the loss settlement. Policyowners sometimes assume that a staff adjuster is biased and will make borderline decisions to the insurer's advantage. These situations are the exception, however; most insurers strive toward fair loss payments. Claimants who feel the need to have someone represent their interests can turn the claim over to a public adjuster. Sometimes claimants retain attorneys to perform a similar function.

Public adjusters offer their services, usually on a fee basis, using their expert insurance knowledge to estimate damages and effect loss settlements. In some states, public adjusters are required to obtain a license from that state's insurance department. This is important because public adjusters act as agents for the insureds within the scope of their employment. If a public adjuster perpetrates a fraud in an attempt to obtain a generous adjustment, the policy may be voided as if the insured perpetrated the fraud.

Claims Adjustment Procedures

The process by which claims are settled varies by line of insurance. Each policy spells out the steps that the policyowner or other claimant must follow, as well as his or her responsibilities following a loss. Those steps and responsibilities are described in other chapters in this book as they relate to certain specific types of insurance. In general, however, there are four main steps in the claims adjustment process: (1) The policyowner furnishes a notice of loss to the insurer, (2) the insurer investigates the claim, (3) the policyowner files a proof of loss with the insurer, and (4) the insurer pays or denies the claim, sometimes after negotiating the amount to be paid.

Notification to the insurer must be provided as spelled out in the policy. Often, the time frame is specified as "immediately," "promptly," or "as soon as practicable." A few types of policies may be more specific such as "within 30 days after the occurrence of a loss."

Claims investigation determines whether a loss occurred and, if so, whether the policy covers it. In life insurance, this process is usually quite simple, but complicating factors can arise in some cases. For example, what if the insured has mysteriously disappeared, so that at best it can only be presumed that he or she is dead? What if there is evidence that the insured died by his or her own hand, in which case the policy's suicide clause might come into play? What if there was a material misrepresentation in the application for the coverage, in which case the incontestable clause may be applicable? Several of these and other clauses that may affect claims settlement are discussed in later chapters.

In other lines of insurance, the investigation phase can be more complex. Some of the questions that may have to be resolved include the following:

- Did a loss actually take place?
- Did the loss occur while the policy was in force?
- Did the loss occur at a location covered by the policy?
- Was the loss caused by a covered peril or activity?
- Do any policy exclusions apply to the loss?
- Do any exceptions to policy exclusions apply to the loss?
- Has the policyowner fulfilled all necessary conditions?
- Is there any evidence of fraud?
- Is the claimant entitled to recover under the policy?
- Does the policy cover the particular type of loss consequence?

The third step in the process of adjusting a claim is filing a proof of loss. In life insurance, the proof of loss may be a death certificate. In other lines, a written and sworn statement may be required that details all the specifics of the loss.

Finally, the amount to be paid must be determined in one of three ways: (1) denial of the claim, (2) payment of the claim in full, or (3) payment of a different amount than the claimant initially seeks. Life insurance claims are usually simple because there are no partial losses. Complicating factors, however, can affect the amount to be paid, including an accidental death benefit provision, a misstatement-of-age clause, or a settlement option the policyowner or the beneficiary selects. Various provisions that affect the amount to be paid are discussed, where appropriate, in later chapters.

In other lines of insurance, the amount to be paid, if any, can involve complex issues. Numerous policy provisions may be applicable. These include provisions that

- deal with other insurance covering the same loss
- provide for a deductible
- specify that recovery will be affected by the amount of insurance carried relative to the value of the covered property
- give the insurer the choice of two or three methods of calculating the amount of the loss
- stipulate the use of appraisers to establish the amount of the loss
- impose a specific limit on the insurer's liability for certain types of losses

These types of policy provisions are described in later chapters that deal with specific lines of insurance.

RATE MAKING

rate making

Insurance rate making, or establishing the price to be charged for insurance, is based on the costs of providing the product, plus a margin for profit. The task is complicated in insurance, however, because the insurer does not know the amount or timing of the largest cost element—the claims to be paid—in advance. Claims can only be estimated. Predicting future loss costs—and in long-term contracts such as life insurance, their timing—and adding necessary margins for expenses and profit to those predictions is called *rate making*. Rate making is carried out by actuaries, who are specialists in the mathematics of insurance.

Components of the Insurance Premium

rate

The insurance *rate* is the price charged for each unit of coverage, called an exposure unit, the policy provides. Units of coverage are not the same for different lines of insurance. For example, in life insurance, the unit of coverage is $1,000 of face amount. For long-term disability income insurance, it is usually $100 of monthly income. For medical expense insurance, it is an individual or family. For most property insurance, it is $100 of value. For auto liability insurance, it is one covered vehicle.

premium

The insurance *premium* is the price charged for the amount of coverage the policy provides. The premium is the rate multiplied by the number of units of coverage. For example, in life insurance, the rate for a particular category of insureds might be $30 per $1,000 of face amount per year. The annual premium for a $50,000 policy, then, is $30 x 50 units, or $1,500. In fire insurance, the annual rate might be $.25 per $100 of coverage. Therefore, the annual premium for coverage of a $200,000 building is $.25 x 2,000 units of coverage, or $500.

How, then, is an insurance rate derived? Usually, the rate is developed by the pure premium method, which first requires an estimate of the future loss costs per unit of coverage during the policy period. That portion of the rate is called the

pure (net) rate

pure or *net rate*. Then a factor, called a *loading*, is added to cover the insurer's

loading

anticipated expenses and to provide a margin for profit and contingencies. The

gross rate

sum of the pure (net) rate and the loading is called the *gross rate*.

This leads to the next logical question: How is the pure (net) rate derived? Most lines of insurance use a statistical analysis of past loss data for each class of insureds and a projection of that loss experience into the future time period during which the rate to be charged for each class will be in effect.

The rate-making task is complicated in some lines of insurance by a scarcity of data on past loss experience. This scarcity of data can exist either for all insureds, as in a newer line of coverage such as long-term care insurance, or for particular classifications of insureds such as very elderly auto drivers. In most lines of insurance, such as homeowners coverage or disability income insurance, loss data must also be sufficient to allow accurate predictions of both loss frequency and loss severity. An explanation of how actuaries deal with these and other rate-making complexities is well beyond the scope of this introductory text.

Property Insurance As an Example

advisory organization

Property insurance offers insight into the many rate-making factors. Here, insurance advisory organizations play a key role. An insurance *advisory organization* is an organization that assists insurers by collecting and furnishing loss statistics or by submitting rating recommendations. These advisory organizations, such as the Insurance Services Office (ISO), are permitted under state statutes in order to allow cooperation for property and liability insurance, subject to state regulation of their activities. Reasonable competition is achieved by permitting individual insurers to file separate rates or to add separate loadings to published loss costs or net rates.

A property insurance contract usually covers more than just the fire peril. The advisory organization develops separate prices for such allied perils as windstorm, hail, smoke, explosion, riot, and others; loss of income, rents, and extra expenses; water damage and sprinkler leakage; and earthquake.

The price of property insurance also varies with the location or territory of the property, the construction of the building, the use or occupancy of the property, the loss prevention or protection facilities, and the proximity or exposure to other properties from which a peril might spread. The advisory organizations carefully define standards for the classes, so there is a higher rate for a frame building than for a brick or a fire-resistant building.

Two types of property insurance rates are set: (1) class rates for groups of similar properties and (2) specific rates for individual properties. Having some rates for groups of applicants with similar characteristics and separate individual rates for applicants that differ widely in their specific characteristics is common to many types of insurance.

Class Rates

class rates   As explained earlier, *class rates* are group rates with an average price that applies to each category or classification of similar insureds. A common example is class rating of separate dwellings or residential homes. Class-rated dwellings are subdivided into groups according to their construction, and a rate is assigned to such classes as frame or brick and to combustible or noncombustible roofs. The rate also varies as to the fire protection classification of the city or town and the number of families that occupy the property. In addition, many jurisdictions apply class rates to commercial buildings when the elements of construction and occupancy are similar enough to permit a ready grouping into rate classes. ISO filings expand class rating to most smaller buildings in general classes such as mercantile, churches, schools, warehouses, and offices, and to habitational classes such as apartments, motels, and boardinghouses. Class rates must be used for properties to which the rates apply.

Class rates provide not only economy and simplicity but also reasonable equity, provided that the individual properties within a given class do not vary too much with regard to potential loss-causing characteristics. Thus, for example, all one-family brick dwellings in a midwestern town of 200,000 in population and with fire hydrants within 1,000 feet might have a one-year fire insurance rate of $.30 per $100 of insurance.

Specific or Schedule Rates

specific rate   When class rates do not apply, the rate is said to be specific. *Specific rates* are set for larger mercantile and manufacturing properties, educational institutions, public buildings, and many types of business establishments. Specific rates are determined by applying a schedule that measures the relative quantity of fire hazard to the particular loss exposure. Most larger buildings use specific rates developed after a physical inspection of the individual property. These include manufacturing, hotel, restaurant, and other properties.

The process of developing a specific rate considers differences in hazards for different properties. This process takes into consideration the various items that contribute to the insured perils, including the construction of the building, its occupancy or use, its protection, and its exposure to nearby buildings. Credits and charges that represent departures from standard conditions for each of these items are incorporated into the rate.

Life Insurance As Another Example

Life insurers collect voluminous amounts of data on mortality rates. The most important basis for classifying these data are the age and gender of insureds and whether they are smokers or nonsmokers.

A large percentage of life insurance is sold on a level-premium basis. Death rates, on the other hand, rise with increasing age. Most claims on these policies occur years after the policies are issued. To deal with the imbalance of level premiums in traditional life insurance products and rising claim costs, life insurers first compute a *net single premium* per $1,000 of face amount for the policy. This net single premium is an amount that the insurer would need today from each insured in a classification, together with future investment earnings, to pay all claims within that class of insureds as those claims arise. The net single premium per $1,000 of face amount is then spread or leveled over the policy's premium-paying period on an actuarial basis to produce a *net level annual premium* per $1,000. Finally, a level annual amount of loading is added to cover such insurer expenses as commissions, premium taxes, general administrative expenses, and an allowance for contingencies and profit.

net single premium

net level annual premium

The establishment of rates for nontraditional life insurance products, such as universal life insurance and variable life insurance (see chapter 8), is considerably more complex. A detailed description is well beyond the scope of this book.

Loss Ratio Method for Adjusting Rates

We previously described the pure premium method, which entails development of a pure or net rate plus a loading. For many property and liability insurance lines in which rate changes upward or downward are common, the loss ratio method of rate making is used to adjust rates. Emphasis in the loss ratio method is not on calculating a new rate directly but on determining the necessary change to an existing rate.

loss ratio

Loss ratios can be calculated in various ways, but the most common way is to divide losses incurred plus loss adjustment expenses incurred by earned premiums. The needed change from an existing insurance rate is found by comparing the actual loss ratio experienced with the expected (or desired) loss ratio. The difference is then divided by the expected or desired loss ratio.

Example: The present rate in a particular auto liability insurance classification is $700 per year. The insurer's expected loss ratio in that classification is 75 percent. During the latest experience period, that classification generated $4.5 million of incurred losses, $400,000 of expenses allocated to settle specific claims, and $7 million of earned premiums. The actual loss ratio was, therefore, 70 percent:

$$\left(\frac{\text{Incurred losses} + \text{Loss adjustment expenses}}{\text{Earned premiums}} \right) \times 100 =$$

$$\left(\frac{\$4,500,000 + \$400,000}{\$7,000,000} \right) \times 100 = 70\%$$

The needed rate change, then, is a reduction of 7.1 percent, determined as follows:

$$\left(\frac{\text{Actual loss ratio} - \text{Expected loss ratio}}{\text{Expected loss ratio}} \right) \times 100 =$$

$$\left(\frac{70 - 75}{70} \right) \times 100 = \left(\frac{-5}{70} \right) \times 100 = -7.1\%$$

Therefore, the indicated new rate will be $650, determined as follows:

$$\$700 \times (1 - .071) = \$700 \times .929 = \$650$$

Note, however, that because of expected inflation in the future and other variables. the rate might not be lowered by the full 7.1 percent.

Rate Classifications

The previous discussion implied the use of different rate classifications. Not all applicants for any type of insurance will be charged the same rate. Insurers must establish overall rates so that they have sufficient funds to pay losses and expenses. At the same time, they must provide reasonable equity among policyowners and charge rates that reflect quantifiable characteristics that affect losses. For example, because smokers have shorter life expectancies than nonsmokers, most life insurers have both smoker and nonsmoker rates. Life insurance rates also vary by age and gender. At the opposite extreme is auto insurance, where rate classifications reflect many factors, including age, gender, marital status, geographic location, miles driven, vehicle use, and driving record. In a given state, an insurance company may have more than a thousand classifications when all combinations of these factors are considered.

The degree to which rate classifications are refined depends on available and reliable statistics, the administrative costs of establishing classifications, and government regulations. For example, some states require the use of unisex rates for certain types of insurance even though loss statistics can justify gender-specific rates. The number of exposure units to be insured is also highly relevant in determining how many rating classifications to use. It would be possible to develop a classification plan so detailed that each insured was in his or her own rating category. This would obviously defeat the purpose of having a large number of similar exposure units in each class so that an average rate for that class can be developed. Auto insurance classification plans can be highly refined because each rating territory contains many insured drivers.

INVESTING

Insurers accumulate huge amounts of capital, most of it through policyowner premiums. Except for amounts needed for the insurer's operating expenses, those funds will be used primarily to pay claims. Funds not immediately needed are invested, both as a means of lowering the cost of insurance and as a source of profit for the insurer.

As explained in the next chapter, the ways an insurer can invest the funds it holds are closely regulated by state laws. Emphasis is on safety, both of principal and of income.[3] An additional objective is an adequate yield, or rate of return. Life insurers guarantee a minimum rate of return to policyowners in many of their products, so they must earn at least that much. Perhaps more important, a life insurance company's rate of investment earnings must be high enough to enable its insurance contracts to be priced at a competitive level. Even though in most states, property and liability insurers are not required by law to build investment income into their rate making, investment income still is essential. In many years and for lines of insurance in which loss experience is unfavorable, investment income is the insurer's only source of profit.

Life Insurer Investments

Because life insurance claims are usually paid many years after the policy is put into force, life insurers tend to invest heavily in long-term securities, for which yields tend to be better, all other things being equal. Liquidity of the investments, or the ability to convert them into cash quickly without loss of value, is not a major consideration.

Table 4-1 shows the latest data available as this text was being prepared. As indicated, United States life insurers had over $3.2 trillion of invested funds. About 58 percent of it was invested in government and corporate bonds. A much smaller percentage was invested in corporate stocks. Other investment assets took the form of cash equivalents, real estate mortgage loans, policy loans, and miscellaneous assets.

TABLE 4-1
Insurance Company Investments

	Life Insurers	Non-life Insurers
Total amount of invested assets (in billions)	$3,264	$848.0
Distribution of invested assets		
Cash and cash equivalents	1.1%	8.5%
Bonds		
Government	14.2	23.0
Corporate	43.6	22.9
Stocks	23.4	18.1
Mortgages	7.4	0.3
Policy Loans	3.1	0
Other	3.7	5.7

All percentages rounded to nearest decimal place. Does not add up to 100 percent due to rounding.

Sources: *Life Insurers Fact Book 2003*, American Council of Life Insurers, Washington, DC, pp. 17–19, and *The Fact Book 2004*, Insurance Information Institute, New York, p. 21.

Non-Life-Insurer Investments

United States non-life insurers' invested assets show a somewhat different pattern. The aggregate amount invested, $848 billion, is much smaller than for life insurers because property and liability contracts are of short duration and do not build up a savings element. Moreover, in many property and liability policies, large reserves are not needed because claims are settled not long after they arise.[4] As with life insurers, the invested assets of property and liability insurers heavily emphasize bonds and common stocks, vehicles that are attractive because of their usually generous yields. Government bonds constitute a larger holding, percentagewise, for property and liability insurers than for life insurers.

OTHER FUNCTIONS OF INSURERS

Auxiliary departments of insurers perform numerous other functions. The word auxiliary does not mean that these functions are unimportant. In fact, many insurers' success can be traced to the excellent support these departments give to the primary operating functions of marketing, underwriting, reinsuring, adjusting claims, and investing.

The legal department, for example, often works closely with the property and liability insurers' underwriting and claims departments. The legal department is generally also responsible for meeting general incorporation, licensing, and taxation requirements of the many states in which insurers do business. Often, the legal department helps design insurance contracts, drafts agency agreements, and provides general legal counsel for the insurer. In life insurance, the department offers substantial aid to the sales and underwriting departments by reviewing cases that involve complex tax problems.

The actuarial department is most closely related to insurers' rating and underwriting departments. Life insurance companies need a separate actuarial staff to diagnose mortality trends, determine costs for various contracts, and provide research for many phases of their activities. Although separate research departments are not common for most insurers, companies are increasingly realizing the need for economic and social research. Many insurers also maintain public relations departments. Education and training is another important area for insurance companies.

Other functional areas within an insurance company are also critical to the organization's success. The accounting department prepares the insurer's financial statements, both for regulators and for the general public. Accountants also prepare various internal financial reports for managers and in preparation of the company's state and federal tax returns. The information technology department is responsible for automating many of the formerly manual tasks in policy issuance, premium billing, and claims payment, to mention just a few. Loss control departments in property and liability insurance companies provide advice and inspection services in many areas of loss prevention and minimization. Finally, many general administrative functions are performed within an insurance company such as personnel management and purchasing.

MINI-CASE: AMY AND JOHN SCHULTZ

As explained in chapter 1, Amy Schultz, aged 28 and her husband John, aged 33, are both engineers employed by SKH, Inc. John earns an annual salary of $95,000; Amy's annual salary is $55,000. SKH provides group benefits that include life insurance of two times their salary.

Amy's and John's late-model compact cars, which they purchased before they were married, are completely paid for. They carry separate auto insurance policies, partly because of John's bad driving record, with the minimum coverages required by law. They also purchased a homeowners insurance policy to satisfy one of the conditions of their mortgage.

a. After reading a magazine article, Amy and John decided to upgrade their insurance by buying a $100,000 whole life insurance policy on John and to increase the $50,000 limits of liability coverage on their auto insurance policies to $300,000. Explain why they were able to buy more than $100,000 in auto insurance coverage by telephone, but they could not purchase $100,000 in life insurance without answering a number of questions and undergoing physical exams.

b. Two months after they moved into their house, the fuel oil tank for their furnace ran dry while they were at work, and cold temperatures in the house caused a pipe to freeze and burst with resulting water damage. Describe in general terms the process Amy and John and their insurance company will follow in pursuing a homeowners insurance claim.

(See answer section for answers to mini-case.)

SOURCES FOR FURTHER IN-DEPTH STUDY

- For details of the underwriting process and the investing function:
  - Graves, Edward E., editor, *McGill's Life Insurance*, 4th ed., chapters 17–19 (underwriting), chapter 26 (investing), Bryn Mawr, PA: The American College Press, 2004. Phone 888-263-7265. Web site address www.theamericancollege.edu
- For details on the underwriting process, rate making, and investment with emphasis on property and liability insurance:
  - Myhr, Ann E., and Markham, James J., *Insurance Operations, Regulation, and Statutory Accounting*, chapters 4–6 (underwriting), chapter 7 (rate making), and chapter 14 (investing), Malvern PA: American Institute for Chartered Property Casualty Underwriters, 2003. Phone 800-644-2101. Web site address www.aicpcu.org

CHAPTER REVIEW

Answers to mini-case, review questions, and self-test questions start on page 793.

Key Terms

underwriting	premium
field underwriting	pure (net) rate
reinsurance	loading
treaty (automatic) reinsurance	gross rate
facultative reinsurance	advisory organization
claims adjusting	class rates
staff adjuster	specific rate
independent adjuster	net single premium
public adjuster	net level annual premium
rate making	loss ratio
rate	

Review Questions

4-1.   As a financial planner, you are working with a client, Bill Jackson, on meeting his various protection needs. Answer the following questions asked by Bill:
   a.   Bill asks, "Why can't insurance companies insure every applicant since they seem to charge pretty high premiums?"
   b.   After you answer that question, Bill asks, "Even if you qualify for insurance, sometimes companies charge a much higher rate than they charge other similar insureds. Why?"

4-2.   Your client, Nancy Hall, asks how an underwriter obtains the information necessary to evaluate her insurance application. Briefly explain the sources of underwriting information insurers typically use.

4-3.   Although reinsurance is transparent to the client, it is often helpful to explain the extra security it provides. What are the key purposes of reinsurance?

4-4.   Explain the difference between facultative and treaty reinsurance.

4-5.   Contrary to the opinion of some clients, it is *not* the purpose of the claims department to minimize claims payments. What is the purpose of the claims (loss) adjustment process?

4-6.   Compare the role of the agent in property insurance with that of the life insurance agent regarding the claims adjustment process.

4-7.   List the four main steps in the claims adjustment process, and explain how their implementation differs in life insurance versus other lines of insurance.

4-8.   During a discussion of insurance needs with a financial planning client, Sally Johnson, she asks the following questions:
   a.   What's the difference between an insurance rate and an insurance premium?
   b.   How is an insurance rate derived?

Self-Test Questions

T   F   4-1.   The general purpose of underwriting is to select only those insureds who are expected to have no losses.

T   F   4-2.   Among other things, reinsurance can help insurers spread large losses and reduce the surplus drain associated with writing new business.

T   F   4-3.   Under facultative reinsurance, the insurer agrees in advance to transfer some types of risks, and the reinsurer agrees to accept those risks.

T   F   4-4.   The purpose of the claims adjustment process is to determine the insurer's liability for a given loss and to reach agreement with respect to the amount of loss or damage payable under the insurance contract.

T   F   4-5.   Most life insurance agents have their companies' authority to settle claims.

T   F   4-6.   Independent adjusters usually represent the public, in contrast to staff adjusters, who represent insurers.

T   F   4-7.   In calculating the insurance premium, the pure (net) rate is multiplied by the number of units of coverage.

T   F   4-8.   Under the loss ratio method of rate making, the actual loss ratio experienced is compared with the expected (or desired) loss ratio to determine the needed change in the existing insurance rate.

T   F   4-9.   Both life and property-liability insurers invest more heavily in bonds than in stocks.

NOTES

1. Exceptions apply in some cases. For example, insurers are required in some states to provide an insurance policy to all applicants for auto insurance. However, behind the scenes, the insurer can transfer an undesirable risk to a residual market facility.
2. See *German Alliance Insurance Co. v. Lewis*, 233 U.S. 389 (1914).
3. These regulations apply to the insurer's general investment account. Life insurers also have substantial amounts of funds in separate accounts, in cases where insureds choose more aggressive investment goals. Examples of separate accounts are those that underlie a life insurer's variable life insurance business, variable annuities, and much of its pension business.
4. An important exception to this general rule exists in some liability lines, such as products liability insurance, where claims may not even arise until long after the period of coverage has expired and ensuing claim payments may be spread over many years.

Regulation and Evaluation of Insurers

Learning Objectives

An understanding of the material in this chapter should enable the student to

5-1.   Explain why insurance regulation is needed.

5-2.   Describe the methods of insurance regulation.

5-3.   Describe the kinds of insurance regulation by the states, and explain the issue of state vs. federal regulation.

5-4.   Discuss the criteria for selecting an insurer and agent or broker.

Chapter Outline

Financial planners clearly need to understand insurance regulation in order to understand the regulatory environment in which they work. Insurance is a highly regulated business, and insurance regulation is subject to frequent change. This chapter explains why and how the business of insurance is regulated. It also describes factors a client should consider in evaluating and selecting an insurance company, as well as an agent or broker.

WHY INSURANCE REGULATION IS NEEDED

The general purpose of insurance regulation is to protect the public against insurer insolvency or unfair treatment by insurers. From the state's viewpoint, regulation is also important because state taxes on insurance premiums are a substantial source of revenue.

As mentioned earlier, the insurance business is generally considered to be "affected with a public interest." This characteristic explains why many types of government supervision of insurance are deemed necessary. Uncontrolled competition in insurance could impose a hardship on insurance buyers and insurance claimants or beneficiaries, who do not understand insurance contracts. The value of insurance contracts depends on the insurer's ability to fulfill these policies' promises to the public, sometimes many years after the policies are issued. Ability to carry out contract provisions depends on many factors, including the efficient operation of the insurer, satisfactory underwriting, proper premium rates, and wise investment of adequate reserves. Consequently, the need for insurers to show long-range financial stability renders government regulation of insurance appropriate.

METHODS OF INSURANCE REGULATION

State governments undoubtedly play the most important role in regulating insurance. Before we consider this and other phases of government insurance regulation, however, we will summarize insurance self-regulation.

Self-Regulation of Insurance

After explaining the general concept of self-regulation, we will examine some of the ways this concept is currently applied within the insurance business. The concept of self-regulation in general is clearly described in the following excerpt from remarks made in 1998 by Robert Pitofsky, chairman, Federal Trade Commission:[1]

The public and private benefits of industry self-regulation are many. First, self-regulatory groups may establish product standards that often assure safety. The private standards "industry," with groups such as the American National Standards Institute (ANSI) and the American Society of Mechanical Engineers (ASME), promulgates tens of thousands of voluntary standards to promote safety or quality. In turn these standards may facilitate the emergence of markets by establishing minimum levels of product quality, and improving consumers' understanding and trust of new products.

Standard setting also can lower the cost of production. For example, a standard can be established to assist manufacturers in producing interconnecting or interchangeable parts. Especially in high-tech industries, standards assure a manufacturer that if its product conforms, the product will interconnect with complementary or rival products of similar specifications.

Industry self-regulation also helps consumers evaluate products and services by providing information about the qualities and characteristics of the seller's products. As then-Circuit Judge Breyer explained, the promulgation of standards "provide[s] information to makers and to buyers less expensively and more effectively than without the standard."[2] Testing organizations that grade products, such as Underwriters' Laboratories or Consumer Reports, can provide these benefits.

An industry group may engage in self-regulation to enhance its reputation for fair and honest service by establishing ethical standards and disciplining those who do not abide by the standards. Professional associations, for example, often exclude unqualified applicants to assure the public that practitioners possess a minimum level of competence and to protect the associations' reputations as well. Self-regulation often may deter conduct that would be universally considered undesirable, but that the civil or criminal law does not prohibit. For example, cheating in sporting contests may not violate the law because the improper conduct is not considered sufficiently serious or because no injured party is likely to appear to bring suit. As a result, industry self-regulation may provide the only meaningful deterrent to would-be cross checkers and bean ball artists.

From a public policy perspective, self-regulation can offer several advantages over government regulation or legislation. It often is more prompt, flexible, and effective than government regulation. Self-regulation can bring the accumulated judgment and experience of an industry to bear on issues that are sometimes difficult for the government to define with bright line rules. Finally, government resources are limited and unlikely to grow in the future. Thus, many government agencies, like the FTC, have sought to leverage their limited resources by promoting and encouraging self-regulation.

Of course, self-regulation can be anticompetitive. Competitors may use the self-regulatory process to disadvantage new rivals or new forms of competition. When that happens, enforcement must be forceful and firm. As the Supreme Court has observed in connection with standard setting:

"There is no doubt that the members of [private standard-setting] associations often have economic incentives to restrain competition and that the product standards set by such associations have a serious potential for anticompetitive harm. Agreement on a product standard is, after all, implicitly an agreement not to manufacture, distribute, or purchase certain types of products. Accordingly, private standard-setting associations have traditionally been objects of antitrust scrutiny."[3]

And of course, government regulation has advantages of its own, such as the increased chance that a point of view other than the industry's will be considered in developing and applying the standards.

Cooperation by insurers to regulate themselves is permitted by law and is practiced extensively. Many insurers and trade association groups exercise considerable control or provide advice with regard to each of the major functions of insurance. For example, the Insurance Services Office (ISO) drafts and files forms and compiles loss data for many property and liability types of insurance on behalf of individual insurers for approval by the state insurance departments, saving duplication of effort and reducing costs. In claims administration, independent adjusting firms handle some losses involving several insurers, so that several insurers involved in the same losses do not need to provide separate loss investigation and payment services. Many insurers cooperate with one another to coordinate loss prevention. Examples include the Insurance Institute for Highway Safety and the National Fire Protection Association. MIB, Inc., gathers information needed in life insurance and disability income insurance underwriting. Rules that apply to members of numerous organizations of insurance agents, brokers, and companies regulate marketing activities. Insurers' joint efforts with LIMRA International and the Society of Insurance Research (SIR) enhance research. The American Council of Life Insurers (ACLI), the Insurance Information Institute, and the Risk and Insurance Management Society (RIMS) promote better public relations and legislation. To improve insurance education and set standards for professional courses and designations, the following organizations are important: the American Academy of Actuaries, The American College (and the related LUTC), the American Institute for CPCU (and the related Insurance Institute of America), and LOMA (Life Office Management Association). Professors of insurance and other industry personnel exchange much valuable information through conferences and publications of the American Risk and Insurance Association (ARIA). Many insurers and these types of organizations supply representatives directly to industry committees that work in conjunction with government regulatory bodies to draft legislation, coordinate programs, and improve both self-regulation and public regulation of insurance. For example, the National Association of Insurance and Financial Advisors (NAIFA) has encouraged much legislation for implementation in state legislative bodies.

Self-regulation works extremely well in some aspects of insurance, while in others it is disappointingly ineffective. Difficult areas for self-regulation include competitive practices that involve such factors as production costs, commissions, advertising, selling practices, and rates.

As a review of this section on self-regulation and as an introduction to the next section on government regulation, see figure 5-1, which summarizes the methods of insurance regulation.

Government Regulation of Insurance

Three basic methods of insurance regulation are available to government: (1) legislative action, (2) administrative action, and (3) court action. Corresponding to the three main branches of the government, each of these methods

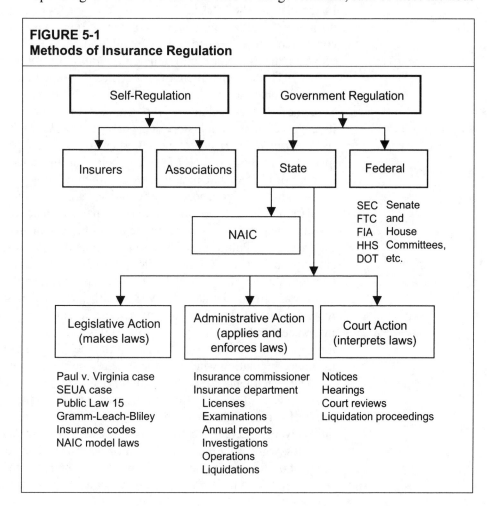

FIGURE 5-1
Methods of Insurance Regulation

is significant in the supervision of insurance. Legislation is the foundation of insurance regulation because it creates the insurance laws. The insurance laws of each state are often combined in what is known as an insurance code,[4] and these codes are of primary importance. Administrative action is also very important because the application and enforcement of insurance laws are left in the hands of the insurance commissioner in each state. Court action has great value in regulation because of its effect in providing detailed interpretations of troublesome parts of the law.

Legislative Action

State regulation of the insurance business was well established by the late 1800s and continues today as the predominant form of regulation. The practice is based on a series of court decisions, and it has been continued despite some contention that insurance might better be regulated by the federal government. In the classic 1868 case *Paul v. Virginia*, the Supreme Court decided that insurance "is not a transaction of commerce" and thus can be neither interstate commerce nor subject to federal regulation.[5] Until 1944, a period of about 75 years, the Supreme Court upheld the *Paul v. Virginia* decision.

In 1941, the Department of Justice heard complaints that certain insurance company practices violated the Sherman Antitrust Act. In 1944, the U.S. Supreme Court handed down a momentous four-to-three decision before one of its largest audiences in history. This case, *U.S. v. South-Eastern Underwriters Association (SEUA) et al,*[6] now known to the legal profession and to the insurance business as the *SEUA* case, held that insurance is commerce. Thus, because of its interstate nature, it would often be subject to federal regulation.

As a matter of practice, because of delegation of authority by Congress, the regulation of the business of insurance remains primarily a state function. The specific delegation to the states of the power to regulate insurance occurred with the passage of Public Law 15, also known as the McCarran-Ferguson Act or simply the McCarran Act, in 1945.[7] Congress made the Sherman Act, the Clayton Act, and the Federal Trade Commission Act applicable to the business of insurance after January 1, 1948, "to the extent that such business is not regulated by state law." In other words, the jurisdiction for regulating interstate insurance was left with the individual states as it had been for many years, but the important proviso was added permitting the federal government to take over insurance regulation whenever the state regulation became inadequate.

The enactment of the Financial Services Modernization Act, also referred to as the Gramm-Leach-Bliley Act, again addressed the regulation issue as a result of a growing number of affiliations between banks and insurance. Traditionally, the federal government and, in some cases, the states regulated banking activities, while only the states regulated insurance. The act indicated that each segment of the financial services business is to be regulated separately and that states continue to have primary regulatory authority for all insurance activities.

Today, most insurance regulation remains with the states. However, federal legislators, consumer advocates, and various insurance industry associations frequently question whether all or some of these regulatory activities should instead take place at the federal level, reducing the challenges and inefficiencies both U.S. and alien insurers currently face in attempts to meet the requirements of more than 50 jurisdictions. Issues recently discussed at the federal level include such diverse topics as the role of banks in insurance, terrorism coverage, and underwriters' use of credit scoring.

Today, most insurance regulation takes place at the state level. However, the role of federal insurance regulation has been gradually expanding, as noted later in this chapter.

Landmark Events in the History of Insurance Regulation

- U.S. Supreme Court decision in the case of *Paul v. Virginia*, 1868
- U.S. Supreme Court decision in the case of *U.S. v. South-Eastern Underwriters Association*, 1944
- Public Law 15 (McCarran-Ferguson Act), 1945
- Financial Services Modernization Act's reaffirmation of states' primary role in insurance regulation, 1999

Administrative Action

The insurance commissioner[8] of each state has broad powers. The commissioner's wide authority extends to licensing insurers and agents, requiring annual reports from the insurers, approving forms and rates in some, but not all, lines of insurance, and investigating complaints of many kinds.

In most states, the insurance commissioner is appointed by the governor and is a member of the governor's cabinet. The rationale behind this method of choosing the head insurance regulatory official is that the governor is ultimately responsible for the business success of his or her term of office and therefore should be able to appoint a person to carry out this responsibility. In about 10 states, insurance commissioners are elected by voters in a general election. Recent history has not demonstrated that either voters or governors have done a better job of selecting commissioners of high caliber and integrity. Both methods of selecting and retaining insurance commissioners clearly involve a political process.

The insurance department within which insurance commissioners carry out their duties may vary from a few persons in some of the smaller states to several hundred employees in a state such as New York. Many departments have existed for a century or more. Some states have relied on New York as their guide for insurance legislation and administrative action. Some New York laws apply to all insurers licensed there, wherever they do business, a provision called extraterritoriality. This provision has played an important role in creating a degree of uniformity in practice among many states.

The insurance commissioner's major powers involve licensing, examination, and investigation. In addition to following the required incorporation procedure for domestic organizations, each insurer that wishes to do business in the state must be licensed for the lines of business it plans to write. The commissioner has broad interpretive powers to decide whether an insurer is qualified, financially and otherwise, to operate in the state. Licenses are usually renewable on an annual basis. The insurance commissioner has considerable power to refuse to issue a renewal license, as well as the power of suspension or revocation. Tests are also administered that determine licensing of insurance agents or brokers.

On-site examination of insurers once they have been licensed is also an important responsibility of the commissioner. Insurers' continued solvency is the major objective of detailed examinations that are conducted according to law, at intervals usually of from 3 to 5 years. Checking assets, liabilities, and reserves is part of this procedure, as is reviewing the insurer's underwriting, investment, and claims practices. A regional zone system is used in cooperation with the National Association of Insurance Commissioners to avoid unnecessary redundant examination of multistate insurers by many states. In this way, the examination of insurers licensed in many states is standardized and simplified, and all states in which the insurer does business accept the results of the regular zone examination. In the intervening years between complete examinations of insurers, every state requires the filing of an Annual Statement with the insurance commissioner. This filing reports current financial conditions and changes that have occurred during the year. A standard NAIC form is used that, for most details, provides uniformity of the information the statement requests. These Annual Statements are available to the public in the state insurance department offices.

National Association of Insurance Commissioners (NAIC)

The *National Association of Insurance Commissioners (NAIC)* is a voluntary nonprofit association of state insurance administrators. The NAIC itself has no regulatory authority. It is important, however, not only for the zone examination procedures but also for its influence through the commissioners on uniformity of insurance laws in the various states. The NAIC assists state insurance departments by developing model laws and regulations. A *model law* is a draft bill—the suggested wording of a new law—for consideration by state legislators. Any state may choose to adopt the model bill or adopt it with modifications. A *model regulation* is a draft regulation that may be implemented by a state insurance department if the model law is passed. The insurance laws and regulations of many states incorporate at least the primary concepts of NAIC model laws, resulting in some degree of uniformity among the states.

The NAIC has been criticized for its inability to bring about greater uniformity in state insurance legislation. A highly controversial program under which the NAIC accredits state insurance regulatory bodies, based largely on the extent to which the state has adopted certain of the NAIC's model laws and regulations, has been developed to counter some of this criticism. The NAIC has recommended many model laws and regulations for such areas as holding companies, variable contracts, guaranty funds, life insurance replacement, and unfair advertising. In addition, the NAIC has been instrumental in developing risk-based capital requirements. These requirements call for differing minimum amounts of capital that insurers must maintain, based on the riskiness of their insurance and investment operations. Other NAIC model laws or regulations deal with unfair claims practices, privacy protection, unfair sex discrimination, and long-term care policies, among numerous other topics. Major research projects have covered such topics as auto insurance, premium taxation, competitive rating, credit life and health insurance, and mass marketing. Statistical reporting systems both for testing company solidity and for measuring profitability have been operational for several years.

In most states, several of the insurance commissioner's investigative powers help determine whether insurers and their representatives meet statutory requirements. Open access to insurers' records and books and hearings on such matters as rate violations and unfair trade practices are examples of this authority. As a result of such procedures, which are often informal, the commissioner may issue administrative rulings or advisory opinions with regard to the business conduct of insurers or their agents. In extreme cases, the commissioner can declare an insurer insolvent and order its liquidation. All these investigative powers have as their major goal the protection of insurance policyowners and claimants. Financial planners must realize that insurance regulation does not serve as a guarantee against any and all possible insolvencies and abuses, but the commissioner's insurance regulatory powers do serve as an important means of reducing insolvencies and abuses.

Court Action

The extremely broad authority of insurance commissioners is subject to some measures of review and interpretation by the courts. To determine whether the commissioner's duties conform with state statutes, the courts may review the notice and hearing procedures that commissioners conduct to arrive at official rulings. Examples are actions to compel the commissioner to issue a license to an insurer or to prevent its cancellation, and court review of decisions to permit or refuse rate increases. Not only may the courts be used in private actions, or by the attorney general of the state against an insurance commissioner, but the commissioner may also, for example, petition the courts to enforce compliance with laws or rulings. Courts also resolve disputes between insurers and policyowners or claimants.

KINDS OF INSURANCE REGULATION BY THE STATES

The insurance codes, as well as the general business laws, vary among the 50 states. For specific insurance laws, administrative practices, and court decisions, the lawyer and the student of insurance must refer to the regulatory activities in a particular state, district, and territory. This section of the chapter summarizes the regulation usually found in the more important insurance jurisdictions such as New York state.

Insurance regulation by each state is largely aimed at the insurers that conduct an insurance business within the state's jurisdiction. Some regulation is also provided for agents, brokers, and other persons who are part of the marketing of insurance contracts and provide certain other services to insurance policyowners. The regulation of insurers falls into the following categories: (1) formation and licensing requirements, (2) supervision of operations, and (3) liquidation procedures. The second category includes a wide variety of regulatory controls, some extensive and some slight, over such activities as contract forms, rates, reserves, assets, and trade practices. Truly, the birth, life, and death of an insurance company are in the hands of the state regulators.

Formation and Licensing of Insurers

Insurance companies are required to meet specific standards that are often higher than those set for general business organizations. The rationale for such high standards is discussed earlier in this chapter. Standards that ensure the solvency, competence, and integrity of the insuring organization are necessary. The first step is incorporation,[9] an introductory process in which the state recognizes and approves the existence of a new legal identity.

The next step, licensing, is a check on the insurer's financial condition to ascertain that it has the required initial capital and surplus for the kinds of insurance permitted in the license. Domestic, foreign, and alien insurers that wish to become "admitted" insurers in the state must meet the statutory requirements for licensing. (The subject of nonadmitted insurers is referred to briefly in chapter 3.) The requirements to be admitted, or licensed, as an insurer sometimes vary among these three types of insurers, but the laws usually specify at least as high standards for foreign and alien insurers as for domestic insurers. Standards vary by legal type of insurer, with requirements for mutual insurers somewhat different from those for stock insurers. These standards also vary widely in the different states.

The licensing procedure is not dependent on financial requirements alone. Many states give the insurance commissioner leeway to apply considerable judgment in acting, or refusing to act, on a license application. The objective of licensing is to provide a preliminary method to lessen the chance of the insurer's financial insolvency, particularly during the difficult formative years. A license may be denied for many other reasons, including the bad faith or reputation of the proposed incorporators or management of an insurer. General managerial ability is undoubtedly as important as capital and surplus requirements for an insurer to achieve sustained financial stability. For that reason, the insurer's license is no more a guarantee against failure than an auto driver's license is a guarantee against an accident.

Insurer Operations

As a protection against insolvency and unfair treatment of policyowners, insurance regulation continues after the formation and licensing of an insurer. The states exercise some control over many phases of insurer operations. Continual regulation is needed because most insurer obligations extend years into the future, and the state should provide supervision so that the contractual promises are fulfilled. The ways in which insurer operations are supervised are strikingly different among the states and among the various kinds of insurance. Most states provide some regulation of the following types: contracts and forms, rates, reserves, asset and surplus values, investments, agents' licensing and trade practices, claims practices, and taxation.

Contracts and Forms

Because insurance policies are complex legal documents that consumers often do not fully understand, they could be used to mislead or unfairly treat policyowners. Consequently, in many lines of insurance, policy forms must be approved by, or at least filed with, the insurance commissioner. The task of gaining approval is simplified if an insurer uses a standard policy form developed by an insurance advisory organization such as ISO or the American Association of Insurance Services (AAIS). Independent insurers may have individualized contracts that vary significantly.

Life and health insurance contracts are not standard contracts in the sense that similar forms or benefits are required. Most states do, however, impose some uniformity by requiring standard provisions in life and health contracts pertaining to such items as the grace period and loan and surrender values.

Many insurance forms are subjected to little or no regulatory review. One example is transportation insurance. The contracts that cover property in transit are not at all uniform, and policyowners should review their benefits, conditions, and exclusions carefully.

Rates

The regulation of insurance pricing varies by line of business. In some lines of insurance, such as aviation insurance, practically no state regulation exists. In life insurance, regulation involves maintaining minimum reserves, rather than setting prices. Most other major kinds of insurance are subject to some direct rate regulation.

Insurance rating laws usually require that rates be

- *adequate.* Rates are considered adequate when, along with investment income, they are expected to produce sufficient revenue to pay all losses and expenses of doing business along with a reasonable profit.

- *not excessive.* Rates are considered nonexcessive if they do not generate an unreasonably high profit for the insurer. This, however, does not guarantee that rates will be affordable to consumers.
- *not unfairly discriminatory.* Rates are considered not unfairly discriminatory if they reflect the expected loss costs and expenses of the homogeneous group of insureds to whom they apply.

Discrimination and Insurance

It is important to distinguish between discrimination and unfair discrimination.

For example, in the United States, age discrimination is considered inappropriate for many business purposes. However, age discrimination is commonly practiced in insurance rates, especially with regard to life insurance. Age discrimination in life insurance rates is not *unfair* discrimination, because it reflects the differing mortality rates of people of different ages and enables insurers to charge equitable premiums.

Many of the states passed rating laws some 50 years ago, which followed a model bill the NAIC developed. In these states, the laws provide specifically that there is no intent to prohibit or discourage reasonable price competition, and they do not prohibit or discourage price uniformity. The laws permit, but do not require, concerted rate making. The state insurance department passes on the reasonableness of the rules and regulations of rating advisory organizations that furnish insurers with loss statistics and other material for rate making. An advisory organization may not exclude or withhold its facilities from any insurers, each of which has the statutory right to become a subscriber by paying reasonable fees.

Any rebate of the insurance premium to an insured, other than dividends to a class of policyowners, is considered discriminatory. A rebate is usually contrary to the law, whether it is made in the form of a direct payment or a credit against the premium or by means of any subterfuge. The statutes do not, however, prohibit the payment by one broker or agent of a part of his or her commission or other compensation to other licensed agents or brokers.

Proposed rates for property and liability insurance are often based on loss data accumulated by advisory organizations, formerly called rating bureaus. Subscribing insurers add loss data to margins for covering expenses, contingency reserves, and desired profits. Some large insurers do not subscribe to these organizations' services and instead base rates on their own independent loss and expense data. Individual insurer rate making has increased in recent decades and has become an important factor in auto insurance and homeowners contracts.

Several different types of rating laws are used in different states and lines of insurance. The most common types are (1) prior approval laws, (2) file-and-use laws, (3) open competition laws, (4) use-and-file laws, and (5) flex-rating laws.

prior approval law

A *prior approval law* requires that the proposed rates be filed with the insurance commissioner. The rates may not be used unless and until the commissioner approves them. With increased competition, potentially lower rates, and deregulation of insurance, prior approval laws have come under heavy fire. Although some states have adopted other types, regulation through prior approval laws remains predominant.

file-and-use law

Several states employ a *file-and-use law*, which permits the immediate use of filed rates without the insurance commissioner's affirmative approval. The commissioner, however, may disapprove the rates within a certain time period such as 30 or 60 days. Some states use this method for one type of insurance while retaining the prior approval rule for other kinds of insurance.

open competition

From time to time for some lines, some states have also adopted *open competition*, which was pioneered in California. Open competition, which relies on competition to set rates, actually represents the absence of government regulation. A broader movement toward open rate competition for selected commercial insurance has begun in recent years.

use-and-file law

Numerous states have a *use-and-file law*. Rates are filed with the insurance commissioner within a specified time after they are first used. The rates may be disapproved if not in compliance with the law.

flex-rating law

A few states have enacted *flex-rating laws* for some lines of insurance. Under these laws, no prior approval is needed if a proposed new rate represents a change of less than 5 or 10 percent of the existing rate. Other rate changes require prior approval.

Instead of direct regulation of insurance prices by required rate approval, some state laws supervise the cost of life insurance by limiting the portion of the premium that can be used for expenses other than claims. The New York law applicable to life insurance is most influential in this regard because, under the extraterritoriality provision, all insurers that do business in that state must conform to its regulations for all insurance contracts, regardless of where they are written.

Types of State Laws Affecting Insurance Rates

- Prior approval laws
- File-and-use laws
- Open competition
- Use-and-file laws
- Flex-rating laws
- Expense limitation laws

Reserves

The states require insurers to maintain, as a liability on their balance sheets, a minimum reserve considered adequate to meet policy obligations as they mature. In life insurance, the *legal reserve* is an amount that, augmented by

legal reserve

premium payments under outstanding contracts and interest earnings, is sufficient to enable the life insurer to meet its expected policy obligations. These include death benefits and nonforfeiture benefits such as policy loans and surrender values. These minimum reserve requirements also indirectly regulate life insurance rates, at least by reducing the likelihood of inadequate rates.

unearned premium reserve

In property and liability insurance, the *unearned premium reserve* must always be adequate to pay a return premium to policyowners if their policies are canceled prior to expiration. The unearned premium reserves the proportion of the written premium that the insurer has not earned by providing protection for the full policy period. The purpose of this reserve is to meet all liabilities under the contract and to pay expenses in the future. At the same time, it accounts for income the insurer has received but not yet fully earned.

Example: Assume that an insurer issues a one-year homeowners policy on October 31 of a particular year. On December 31 of that year, the insurer has an unearned premium equal to five-sixths of the annual premium for the policy. This and the unearned premiums for other unexpired policies make up the unearned premium reserve shown as a liability on the insurer's balance sheet.

loss reserve

A second type of reserve required of property and liability insurers is the *loss reserve*. Because many claims do not result in immediate payment of all incurred losses, the insurer must set up a reserve to ensure their payment. For example, a workers' compensation or disability income claim may be made against the insurer today. In many cases, the loss payments are made gradually over a long future period of disability. In auto liability cases, several years may elapse after a loss before a court decides who is liable and for how much. In these cases, an estimate of the reserve that will be needed to pay the insurer's obligation is made and carried on its books as a loss reserve. In this way, losses and loss expenses for claims that are known but not yet paid are provided for by the insurer under the loss-reserve laws of the states.

Assets and Surplus Values

The value of assets that appear on insurers' balance sheets must be correct and conservative in order for liabilities, other reserves, and residual surplus items to be meaningful. Securities insurers hold are valued according to practices adopted by a committee of the NAIC. Stocks are usually given year-end market values, while most bonds are carried at amortized values. The valuations are only advisory to the states, but the result is a good example of voluntary and state regulation working together. For some insurers, such as mutual insurers, both surplus accumulation and distribution are subject to regulation aimed at providing equitable treatment for all policyowners.

nonadmitted asset

Insurance companies are not allowed to carry some assets on their balance sheets as assets. These assets, called *nonadmitted assets*, are thought to be of marginal quality or of little liquidity for policyowners if their insurers should get into financial difficulty. Examples of nonadmitted assets are most office furniture and supplies, as well as premiums that are 90 days or more past due.

Investments

To protect insurer solvency most states have laws that govern the types of securities that may be purchased for investment. The strictest regulations apply to life insurers because they retain many billions of dollars of assets for many years for their policyowners.

Life insurers' investment portfolios are subject to rigorous supervision. Each Annual Statement filed with the insurance department lists every individual investment with detailed information about its date of acquisition, costs, values, and earnings. As noted in chapter 4, bonds and common stocks are the prime investments in life insurers' portfolios, involving a large majority of total assets. Most states grant some limited permission for certain investments. Stocks may be limited, for example, to a stated percentage of assets or to 100 percent of surplus. Real estate holdings, especially commercial properties and housing projects, are also limited to a maximum in various states. The legality of all the insurer's holdings is checked carefully in periodic audits of the insurer's portfolio.

Property and liability insurers' investment of assets is also supervised, although the laws are more lenient and vary greatly among the states. The laws of each state specify the investment restrictions. The general practice aims at requiring the safest types of investments for all assets held as reserves, both for unearned premiums and losses, and for other liabilities. Cash, high-grade bonds, and perhaps preferred stocks of proven quality may be permitted for such assets. The remainder of assets (representing capital and surplus) may be invested in a wider range of securities, including common stocks that meet certain standards. Limitations on real estate holdings, the size of single investments in relation to total assets or surplus, and investments in foreign companies, as well as many other restrictions, are also common.

Agents' Licensing and Trade Practices

Laws in all states require insurance producers to be licensed. The insurance departments usually administer these laws; the objective is insurer representation that is competent and trustworthy. All states require a comprehensive written examination before licensing. The examinations are often divided into separate tests for different lines of insurance. Some adjusters and consultants also must be licensed in a few states. All states now require continuing education as a condition for license renewal.

Unfair trade practices in insurance are illegal in all states under laws similar to the Federal Trade Commission Act. Under the provisions of Public Law 15, these laws aim at retaining jurisdiction for the states to prevent fraudulent and unethical acts of agents and brokers. They provide fines and, more important, suspension or revocation of licenses as penalties for violations. Examples of such unfair practices in insurance include the following:

rebating

- *rebating,* the return of any part of the premium, except in the form of dividends, to the policyowner by the insurer or agent as a price-cutting sales inducement[10]

twisting

- *twisting,* a special form of misrepresentation in which an agent may induce the policyowner to cancel disadvantageously the contract of another insurer in order to take out a new contract

misappropriation

- *misappropriation,* an agent's unlawful keeping of funds belonging to others

commingling of funds

- *commingling of funds,* prevented in some states by requiring a separate bank account for the agent's premium funds held in trust for the insurer

misleading advertising

- *misleading advertising,* restrained by many regulations that require full and fair information in advertisements by insurance companies and agents

The insurance commissioner has broad powers to prevent unfair practices and exercises this authority by investigating complaints, as well as by initiating investigations of any questionable acts of insurance companies or their representatives.

Licensed insurance agents are responsible for ascertaining that the carriers for which they are selling are approved by the department of insurance in that state. Any agent who sells coverage from an unauthorized entity faces the risk of regulatory penalties, liability for unpaid claims, and imprisonment on a felony charge. An *unauthorized entity* is an insurance company (or other organization either real or fictitious) that has not gained approval to place insurance business from a department of insurance in the jurisdiction where it or a producer wants to sell insurance.

unauthorized entity

Claims Practices

An insurer's practices in adjusting claims represent a major source of possible mistreatment of insureds and other claimants. Most states now have enacted laws patterned after the NAIC's model laws and regulations pertaining to unfair claim settlement practices. Some of the practices that are regarded as unfair are the following:

- failing to investigate claims promptly
- failing to communicate with or acknowledge communications from clients on a timely basis
- failing to provide a reasonable explanation as to why a claim was denied
- failing to maintain procedures for handling complaints about claims
- misrepresenting pertinent policy provisions that affect claims
- failing to try to settle a claim once the insurer's liability becomes clear
- attempting to settle a claim for far less than a reasonable person would expect based on the insurer's advertising material

Other Areas of Consumer Protection

In some lines of insurance, insurers are required to use policies that meet specified readability standards. These standards relate not just to the size of the print font used but also to expressing policy provisions in terms that a typical high school graduate should understand. Some states require that insurance consumers be given shopper's guide booklets for certain lines of insurance. These booklets help consumers make comparisons of the costs and benefits of different policies.

Taxation

Revenue for the states has become an important reason for insurance regulation. In addition to federal income taxes, insurers pay to the state what resembles a sales tax on gross premiums received from all of their policyowners. This premium tax is usually about 2 percent of premiums. Although insurers pay the tax, its cost, of course, is built into in the price of insurance and thus is paid by the policyowners.

The taxes are primarily to generate revenue for the state, rather than to pay for the cost of insurance regulation. The state premium tax usually goes into the state's general revenue fund, with insurance department expenses being based on separate appropriations from that fund. Only a small percentage of the total tax revenue and fees is used to operate the state insurance departments.

Rehabilitation and Liquidation of Insurers

The insurance commissioner of a state not only officiates at the birth and oversees the ongoing operation of an insurer but also presides over its demise if necessary. An insurer may be liquidated for numerous reasons, including financial insolvency.

rehabilitation   The insurance commissioner acts under the insurance laws as the official in charge of supervising *rehabilitation* if the insurer can be restored to financial

liquidation

stability through reorganization, or *liquidation* if the insurer is dissolved. The purpose of both actions is to conserve as much of the insurer's assets as possible for fair distribution to claimants, policyowners, and investors. Sometimes an insurer's license is suspended temporarily for not meeting financial solvency standards or for other noncompliance with department rulings on rates, advertising, and so on. This suspension may be a prelude to liquidation proceedings or may be a temporary action to force changes in the insurer's operations.

Some insurers suffer liquidation because of financial difficulty. In some cases in the 1980s and 1990s, the failed insurers were large and highly regarded companies. In other cases, the infusion of major amounts of outside capital or mergers rescued insurers with serious financial problems from near insolvency. The result has been some support for a federal guaranty fund for insurers that would operate somewhat as the Federal Deposit Insurance Corporation (FDIC) does for banks. State deposit laws and several special state workers' compensation security funds are already in use that are similar in principle.

guaranty fund

In recent years, all 50 states have adopted insurance *guaranty fund* plans to at least partially protect consumers against insurer insolvency. Model legislation promulgated by the NAIC encouraged states to adopt these laws. A "guaranty" is an agreement by which one party assumes another's debts. Guaranty funds should not be confused with guarantees, which assure the performance of a product or a service. Guaranty plans, administered on a state-by-state basis, usually assess solvent insurers in order to pay an insolvent company's unpaid claims and to return unearned premiums to its policyowners. Insurers each pay a proportional share of the losses, based on their premium volume in the state.

The guaranty funds appear to be doing a reasonably good job of protecting the consumer, and some states have adopted several improvements. These improvements concern (1) giving the guaranty funds immediate access to the insolvent insurer's assets, rather than waiting until liquidation proceedings are complete, (2) giving the guaranty funds priority over general creditors to obtain the insolvent insurer's assets, and (3) permitting a tax offset against premium taxes to solvent insurers for money paid into the guaranty funds. Even with these improvements, however, some problems remain, including lengthy delays before consumers receive their money and dollar limits on some types of claims.

Guaranty funds do not guarantee that an insurer will be able to pay its claims. A system to pay for insolvencies does not completely protect insurance buyers against insurer insolvencies. Detecting troubled insurers in advance of insolvency proceedings is an important goal. The NAIC has developed an "early warning system" based on a series of financial ratio tests. These tests have dealt mainly with the adequacy of the insurer's reserves, changes in its surplus, its rate of growth, and the adequacy of its prices. Other tools for the early detection of insurer financial difficulty include the risk-based capital standards and the on-site examination system developed by the NAIC, noted earlier in this chapter.

Federal versus State Regulation

This chapter emphasizes regulation of insurance by the states because most government legislation, administrative action, and court decisions that pertain to insurance have been at the state level. The McCarran-Ferguson Act reaffirmed the states' predominant role in insurance regulation. This role still continues because the law conditionally exempts insurance from major federal statutes such as the Sherman Act (except for boycotts, coercion, or intimidation), Clayton Act, Robinson-Patman Act, and other laws. Federal laws apply only to the extent that state legislation is inadequate.

The federal government has increased its regulation of insurance in some specific and limited, but nonetheless important, areas of insurance. For example, federal agencies have regulated some aspects of interstate advertising and mergers through the Federal Trade Commission (FTC), variable life insurance and annuities through the Securities and Exchange Commission (SEC), occupational safety under various rules of the Occupational Safety and Health Administration (OSHA), and pensions and other employee benefits under the Employee Retirement Income Security Act (ERISA) administered mainly by the U.S. Department of Labor.

The Financial Services Modernization Act, also referred to as the Gramm-Leach-Bliley Act, which, as mentioned earlier, addressed the role of banks in insurance, is a relatively recent example of federal legislation that directly affects the insurance and other financial services organizations. This act makes it clear that banking regulators regulate banking activities, but states continue to have primary regulatory authority for banks' insurance activities.

Why should regulation of insurance be performed mainly by the states? Advocates of state regulation have pointed out such reasons as (1) the local nature of many insurance transactions, for which any difficulties can best be resolved on a state basis, (2) the reasonable success of state regulation for many years, during which insurance has become an important and sound business, (3) the value of regulation on a state-by-state basis, which permits gradual changes and innovations in regulation without applying them to the entire country all at once, and (4) the NAIC's help in recommending model legislation to the states to achieve some uniformity in insurance regulation. While supporters recognize that state regulation is not perfect, they claim that federal regulation would be much worse. It would, they argue, be cumbersome, expensive, less effective, and fragmented among dozens of agencies.

Conversely, the proponents of federal regulation of insurance have criticized state regulation on many points, emphasizing (1) inconsistencies and lack of uniformity in regulation of insurers, (2) inadequate funding for the important tasks of the insurance commissioners, and the short-term and political aspects of their terms of office, (3) the need for greater standardization in insurance contracts to cover many interstate exposures, and (4) the desire for increased competition to ensure availability and lower and fairer insurance prices. The threat of federal regulation wherever the states fail to perform adequately is a constant incentive to improve state insurance regulation.

EVALUATING INSURERS

The second major topic in this chapter is the evaluation of insurers for possible inclusion in a client's insurance program. That evaluation may be needed with respect to the insuring organization itself, the sales personnel who represent it, or both.

Criteria for Selecting an Insurer

A financial planner may assist the client in the selection of insurers. The choice of a competent and reliable insurance agent or broker is likely to be a part of this responsibility. Of course, the financial planner may himself or herself be the client's insurance agent or broker. If he or she represents only one insurer, the issue may be moot. Often, however, choices with respect to insurers must be made, and the question is what criteria should be used in making these choices.

Probably the single most important criterion is the insurer's financial strength. Because an insurer's basic function of is to pay claims, care must be taken to select only those insurers that are most likely to be able to do so if the need arises. In light of the number of insolvencies and near insolvencies among insurers in recent decades, and the limitations of state insurance guaranty funds noted earlier, an insurer's claims-paying ability cannot simply be taken for granted.

The size of an insurer is not always the most relevant factor, as financial strength and size are not necessarily equivalents. Growth over a period of years is significant. State insurance departments can provide some current information about insurers, including records about consumer complaints against specific insurers, risk-based capital compliance, and early warning financial ratios noted earlier. Many states make this information available through the Internet. A link to state insurance department Web sites appears at the NAIC Web site.

Several rating organizations publish the financial history, ratings, and analyses of individual insurers. These organizations include A.M. Best Company, Fitch Ratings (formed by a merger of Duff & Phelps and Fitch IBCA), Moody's Investors Service, Standard & Poor's, and Weiss Ratings. A few words of caution are in order with respect to reliance on ratings assigned by these organizations, however. First, the criteria and methodology differ among the rating organizations, so an insurer may receive different ratings from different organizations. Second, a rating of A, which many people associate with excellence, may not be the highest possible rating. For example, Best's has two ratings higher than A, and Standard & Poor's has five ratings higher than A. Third, some rating agencies seem to be more generous in their ratings than others. Fourth, not all insurers are assigned ratings by all of the rating organizations. In light of all of these differences, it is probably wise advice to choose insurers that have very high ratings from at least two or three of the rating organizations. It is important also to remember, however, that financial ratings are based on past performance. A good rating does not ensure that an insurer will remain solvent for years to come, and a poor rating does not always mean that the insurer is about to become insolvent.

Selecting an insurer should be based on willingness and ability to pay claims. Companies' attitudes toward claims may differ, and the applicant should be concerned with the company's viewpoint on technicalities, as well as the claims department's reputation for satisfactory dealings with insureds. Consumer complaint files that state insurance departments maintain can be helpful.

Service is another criterion that should be used in evaluating insurers. The insurer must be able to provide proper protection for the applicant. Does the insurer specialize in a few lines of insurance, or does it sell all coverages that the purchaser may need and want? Is the insurer experienced in offering all the contracts it will write? Will the insurer individualize contracts to meet the insurance buyer's particular needs? Does it have capacity and adequate reinsurance for the amount of insurance the buyer may require? Is it licensed in all of the states where the buyer needs coverage? In addition to indemnification for losses, can the insurer provide any engineering and loss prevention services that the purchaser may need? And again, what is the insurer's general attitude and reputation with regard to prompt and fair settlement of all reasonable claims?

As part of the evaluation of an insurer's service, the applicant should be interested in knowing whether or not the insurer is liberal with respect to underwriting. A company that is selective in underwriting may prove unsatisfactory when a consumer has a difficult situation such as poor health or extremely hazardous business activities. Conversely, a consumer with very favorable risk characteristics may benefit by dealing with a highly selective insurer.

Another important criterion in the evaluation of an insurer, of course, is the cost of its products. Cost should usually be considered and compared only after the above criteria are analyzed. Exorbitant rates are obviously undesirable. Lower rates are beneficial to the purchaser; however, rates that are too low could reflect an unduly strict attitude toward claims payment, inadequate financial reserves, restrictive policy provisions, or minimal services.

Criteria for Selecting an Insurance Company

- Financial strength
- Attitude concerning claims payment
- Lines of coverage offered
- Service before and after a claim
- Underwriting standards
- Cost of the coverage

Initial costs are only part of the necessary analysis; final costs over a longer period of protection must be considered, including possible rate changes, dividends, assessments, or premium adjustments under some types of rating plans. In life insurance, net cost comparisons over a period such as 20 or more years, considering dividends, cash values, and interest factors, may be appropriate. Also, all insurance costs should be analyzed along with other risk management costs such as those of loss prevention.

Criteria for Choosing an Agent or Broker

Because most insurance is written through the agency system, the choice of a competent and reliable insurance agent is often an important decision for the insurance buyer. If an exclusive agent who represents one insurer only is chosen, this selection also determines the insurer with which business is conducted. If an independent agent is chosen, the insurance buyer often leaves the selection of the insurer up to the agent, or at least relies heavily on the agent's recommendations.

Part of the insurance premium represents commission or salary to the agent or broker. If no service or inadequate service is rendered for this part of the premium, the policyowner is paying for something he or she did not receive. The purchaser of insurance must determine whether the agent or broker is only an order taker. If so, the policyowner is getting less than full value.

Some applicants place insurance with numerous agents. Frequently, this distribution is made to create goodwill or to distribute business among a number of friends. Sound practice suggests selecting one agent or broker, or as few as possible, to handle an entire insurance account. Both the insurance buyer and the agent should prefer this practice. Most agents would rather have fewer accounts for which they are fully responsible than to participate in many accounts to which they contribute little service. Sometimes an account may be split so that one agent handles the property and liability lines and another agent the life, health, and annuity business. Regardless of the number of agents, the more information that an agent has about the client's total insurance account, the better he or she may be able to analyze the risks and recommend coordinated protection for the client's needs.

The insurance consumer or financial planner who allows friendship to govern the selection of an agent may receive inadequate protection or pay an exorbitant amount for excessive or duplicate coverages. Placing insurance only on the basis of personal friendship is as foolish as selecting a doctor, lawyer, or a architect on that basis. Because of the complex nature of various risks, insurance coverages, and rates, the insurance agent or broker should be selected with the same care and discrimination used to choose other professional advisors.

Choosing an agent or a broker is an essential step toward a sound insurance and risk management program. Some of the criteria that might be used to evaluate insurance agents and brokers include knowledge and ability, willingness, integrity, and character.

Knowledge and Ability

The agent or broker must learn about the client's insurance needs and help the client understand the value of the services rendered. The agent must have the background and experience necessary to identify, analyze, and treat risk properly. One method to evaluate the agent's knowledge and ability is to ask questions such as, "Are you a CFP, ChFC, CLU, or CPCU? If not, are you working toward these or other educational objectives on a regular basis?" "Are you a full-time agent?" Some part-time agents and some agents who have not earned professional designations are still competent. However, agents who are fully committed to the insurance business are more likely to do a really successful job for their clients by developing their professional skills and keeping abreast of rapidly changing knowledge requirements.

The insurance consumer needs a technically competent agent who performs the wide variety of services essential to proper insurance protection. These services may include understanding needs, analyzing significant possibilities of loss, finding markets, comparing alternative coverages and contracts, arranging for credit or installment payments, checking on the accuracy of classifications and rates charged, providing loss prevention or engineering services, making evaluation appraisals, seeing that claims payments are made promptly, reviewing changing needs frequently, and many other important duties.

Willingness

Is the agent willing to take the time to apply his or her knowledge conscientiously and fully evaluate all the client's needs and alternatives? If not, the client won't receive the benefit of that knowledge and ability. The agent must be able and willing to take the time to see that services, including those of agency staff and insurance companies, are performed as effectively as possible.

The agent should recommend additional legal, accounting, or consulting services as needed. Loss prevention suggestions and help with filing claims are also important services provided to the insurance buyer. The best qualified agent who is too busy is of no value to the client. The time and desire to perform these services regularly must be present when the client needs them.

Integrity and Character

Even willing and able agents or brokers lack an important requirement if they are unable to command the policyowner's confidence and trust. An insurance purchaser who cannot trust recommendations is not receiving full value for the insurance dollar.

Because insurance is purchased to reduce uncertainty, agents or brokers must be able to give their clients both psychological and actual security. Consumers need someone with whom they can identify closely in discussing their financial needs and goals. The values of agent and client, if similar, can help them establish a good rapport. The agent's age in relation to the policyowner's can be a factor in this regard, but differences in age are probably less important than differences in philosophy and lifestyle. Confidential information from the purchaser is often required to provide good insurance counseling services. Thus, the agent or broker must respect the buyer's trust with complete honesty as would a doctor, a lawyer, or an accountant.

Representation

Good agents generally do not represent weak insurers. They must represent or have contacts with one or many insurers that can provide the required protection and services for the policyowner. Ideally, all necessary coverages, including even special or unusual ones, should be available through the agent(s) at a reasonable cost. The insurer or insurers represented should be capable of writing many different kinds of insurance with a progressive attitude toward newer coverages and forms designed to meet individual buyers' particular needs.

Insurance agencies and brokerage firms vary from the individual agent to organizations that have large staffs and offer a wide range of specializations. Some agencies consist of one person, others have a half-dozen agents and office personnel, while still others have 100 or more employees and operate much like a small insurance company. These organizations differ in the services they are able to offer, their methods of doing business, and the types and kinds of insurance they handle. Frequently, the members of an agency who handle life insurance limit their activities to this field. Also, in a large agency certain persons become recognized experts in such lines as pensions, liability, workers' compensation, or surety coverages. When selecting the agent or broker, the insurance consumer should consider whether the particular agent and agency office have the needed experience and service facilities.

Some buyers solicit competitive bids on an annual basis for their property and liability insurance or their group employee benefits. Lower costs for insurance may come at the price of less satisfactory service from the agent, who may not regard the policyowner as a permanent client. Policyowners have found the competitive approach detrimental because in a period of losses, a business firm may have no assurance of continued coverage and competing insurers will be reluctant to participate. Thus, insurance buyers who shop too aggressively may seriously limit their market. This is less likely to occur if an insurer may expect to recoup over a period of years losses incurred in an unfavorable year. From the buyer's standpoint, as well as the agent's, a long-term relationship on a professional basis seems to work best in the long run.

SOURCES FOR FURTHER IN-DEPTH STUDY

- For more detail on insurance regulation:
    - Myhr, Ann E. and Markham, James J., *Insurance Operations, Regulation, and Statutory Accounting*, chapter 2, Malvern PA: American Institute for Chartered Property Casualty Underwriters, 2003. Phone 800-644-2101. Web site address www.aicpcu.org
    - The National Association of Insurance Commissioners maintains a Web site, which also has links to state insurance departments, at www.naic.org
- For more on insurance guaranty funds:
    - The National Conference of Insurance Guaranty Funds maintains an informative Web site at www.ncigf.org
- For more on insurance company financial ratings:
    - A. M. Best Company publishes insurer financial ratings on the Internet at ambest.com
    - Standard and Poor's insurance company ratings are available on the Internet at www.standardandpoors.com/RatingsActions/RatingsLists/Insurance/InsuranceStrengthRatings.html
    - Weiss Ratings maintains a Web site at www.weissratings.com
    - Fitch Ratings maintains a Web site at www.fitchratings.com
    - Demotech maintains a Web site at www.demotech.com

CHAPTER REVIEW

Answers to review questions and self-test questions start on page 793.

Key Terms

National Association of Insurance Commissioners (NAIC)	nonadmitted asset
prior approval law	rebating
file-and-use law	twisting
open competition	misappropriation
use-and-file law	commingling of funds
flex-rating law	misleading advertising
legal reserve	unauthorized entity
unearned premium reserve	rehabilitation
loss reserve	liquidation
	guaranty fund

Review Questions

5-1.   Your financial planning client asks why insurance seems to be so highly regulated. How would you explain the general purpose of insurance regulation to this client?

5-2.   Insurers participate in many activities that are forms of self-regulation. Describe two ways that insurers engage in self-regulation.

5-3.   Explain the three basic approaches to insurance regulation.

5-4.   Briefly describe the three key categories of state regulation of insurance.

5-5.   Explain how each of the following aspects of insurer operations tends to be regulated, pointing out any differences between regulation applying to life insurers and that applying to property-liability insurers.
   a.   contracts and forms
   b.   rates
   c.   reserves
   d.   assets and surplus values
   e.   investments
   f.   agents' licensing and trade practices
   g.   claims practices

5-6.   Maria Rodriguez, your client, is reluctant to buy whole life insurance, because she has heard of some insurers becoming insolvent. She is concerned that her insurance company might not be able to perform its obligations by the time she dies and her heirs need the insurance proceeds. How does insurance regulation seek to protect insurance buyers like Maria when an insurance company becomes insolvent?

5-7.   List the arguments for and against regulation of insurance by the states.

5-8.   What criteria can a financial planner use to help clients select insurers for their insurance programs?

5-9.   What criteria can a financial planner use to help clients choose reliable and competent agents or brokers for their insurance programs?

Self-Test Questions

T   F   5-1.   The general purpose of insurance regulation is to protect the public against insolvency or unfair treatment by insurers.

T   F   5-2.   At the state level, insurance is regulated by legislative, administrative, and court action.

T   F   5-3.   The insurance commissioner has the power to, among other things, enforce the laws passed by the legislature and interpreted by the courts, license insurers and agents, and investigate to determine whether insurers and agents are meeting the requirements of the statutes.

T   F   5-4.   Insurance regulators will reject any insurance rates that are discriminatory.

T   F   5-5.   Life insurance is subject to direct rate regulation under prior approval laws that require that rates be approved before they can be used.

T   F   5-6.   Insurers must comply with state laws that govern the types of securities they may purchase for investment.

T   F   5-7.   Although unfair trade practices are illegal in all states, most states now permit rebating and twisting.

T   F   5-8.   Most premium taxes insurers pay to the states are used to pay for the cost of insurance regulation.

T   F   5-9.   The key to assessing the financial strength of an insurer is the size of the insurer.

T   F   5-10.   In addition to financial strength, other important criteria for selecting an insurer are its willingness to pay claims, the service it provides, and the cost of its products.

T   F   5-11.   The dominant factor in the selection of an agent is friendship.

NOTES

1. *Self Regulation and Antitrust*, prepared remarks of Robert Pitofsky Chairman, Federal Trade Commission DC Bar Association Symposium, February 18, 1998, Washington, DC. http://www.ftc.gov/speeches/pitofsky/self4.htm accessed 3/18/04.
2. See *Clamp-All Corp. v. Cast Iron Soil Pipe Institute*, 851 F.2d 478, 487 (1st Cir. 1988), *cert. denied*, 488 U.S. 1007 (1989).
3. *Allied Tube & Conduit Corp. v. Indian Head, Inc.*, 486 U.S. 492, 500–01 (1988).
4. The insurance code for an individual state can exceed several hundred pages.
5. Today it is difficult to rationalize such a decision, but in 1868 the now famous decision stated, "Issuing a policy of insurance is not a transaction of commerce. They are not commodities to be shipped or forwarded from one state to another and then put up for sale. . . . Such contracts are not interstate transactions, though the parties may be domiciled in different states. They are, then, local transactions and are governed by local law." (*Paul v. Virginia*, 231 U.S. 495)
6. 64 United States 1162.
7. C 20, 79th Cong., 1st sess.
8. Most of the states use this title of "commissioner of insurance," eight use "director of insurance," and three use "superintendent of insurance."
9. Reciprocal exchanges, Lloyd's associations, fraternals, and some health insurance associations do not legally become incorporated by this process. They do, however, file similar statements of their present status and proposed activities as stated in their charters and bylaws.
10. Rebating is allowed in two states, but only under very limited circumstances.

6

Basic Legal Principles and Contract Analysis

Learning Objectives

An understanding of the material in this chapter should enable the student to

---

6-1. Describe the unique aspects of an insurance contract that differentiate it from other goods and services.

6-2. Explain the general legal requirements of an insurance contract.

6-3. Describe the special legal characteristics of an insurance contract.

6-4. Explain how to analyze the various parts of an insurance contract.

Chapter Outline

This chapter begins by describing some fundamental attributes of insurance. Financial planners must understand these basics to make effective use of insurance as a financial planning tool. Some of these attributes are, in a sense, so obvious that they almost go without saying. But it is necessary to state them in order to understand the nature and importance of insurance.

Private insurance is usually provided through a written contract, known as an insurance policy. (Sometimes, insurance begins with a binding oral agreement between the insurer, or its agent, and the insurance applicant; the oral binder is later replaced by a written contract.) The most tangible product resulting from the insurance transaction is the insurance policy—a legally enforceable written contract. The effectiveness of insurance depends to a high degree on contract law, which governs the making and enforcement of contracts. Most financial planners are not attorneys, and they should not therefore deal in depth with legal issues. However, financial planners need to understand the basic principles described in this chapter that relate to contracts.

INSURANCE: AN INTANGIBLE CONTRACT

The insurance policy consists of tangible pieces of paper. However, insurance is more than mere pieces of paper; those pieces of paper contain the insurer's promise to pay money. Unlike tangible assets that have intrinsic value, insurance is an intangible asset that represents value. Other intangible assets include stock certificates and savings bonds.

Unlike most physical goods, which are purchased for immediate use, consumers usually view insurance as a product that provides future benefits when loss payments are made. A hurricane, an auto accident, a premature death, or a retirement are all *future* possibilities for the insurance purchaser. A policyowner who focuses on the future benefits, however, is likely to overlook the significant immediate benefit of insurance: freedom from worry about financial losses.

Many people who buy insurance are convinced they will never have a loss. They buy insurance "just in case," but at the same time they think, "It will never happen to me." It's true that most families carry insurance for many years without having a serious accident and/or without experiencing serious damage to their home. Only the unfortunate minority who suffer losses come to realize the substantial benefits of insurance. Insurance is activated by contingencies that might or might not occur, contingencies that normally do not happen very often.

Insurance transfers the financial risk of losses to the insurer, an organization that is in the business of bearing risks. Insurance is affordable because it involves an exchange of unequal values. The insurance buyer pays a relatively small premium, or a series of premiums, in exchange for the insurer's promise to pay for a potentially large loss.

GENERAL LEGAL REQUIREMENTS

The rights and obligations of the parties to an insurance agreement are determined largely by the general laws that govern contracts. The agreement by which insurance is effected is a contract in which the insurer, in consideration of the policyowner's payment of a specified sum, agrees to make good the losses suffered through the occurrence of a designated unfavorable contingency.

A contract has been defined as "an agreement enforceable by law." A more complete definition would include the following essentials required by law:

- offer and acceptance
- legal purpose
- competent parties
- consideration

Absence of any of the essential elements prevents enforcement of any contract. To be valid and enforceable, insurance contracts must meet these four general legal requirements.

Offer and Acceptance

The first requirement of a legally enforceable contract involves offer and acceptance. A contract requires both an offer by one party to the contract and acceptance of that offer by another party. In insurance, the offer is usually made in a request for coverage by the prospect, or applicant. The simplest method, used for many types of property and liability insurance, is an oral request to an agent either in person or by telephone. In life insurance and in many forms of health insurance, the offer must be made in a written application.

Before a contract is effective, acceptance of the offer is necessary. As noted earlier, with property and liability insurance, the agent often has authority to bind, or accept, the offer even without receiving any payment from the applicant. The protection may commence immediately, if desired, based entirely on the oral request of the applicant and the oral acceptance by the agent.

In life insurance, the method and timing of legal acceptance are different. The applicant usually submits the written application and the first premium payment as the offer to the insurer through the agent, who issues a conditional receipt. Acceptance is held by most courts to occur if the applicant meets the normal underwriting standards of the insurer, including a medical examination if required. Then coverage becomes effective as of the time of the application and premium payment. If the applicant does not meet the underwriting standards of the insurer, the insurer may make a counteroffer with a different contract, which the prospect may accept or reject upon delivery by the agent. If the premium is not paid with the application, the offer to insure is made by the insurer after reviewing the application. The insurance is accepted and becomes effective when the contract is delivered to the applicant while the applicant is in good health and the premium is paid.

Example 1:	Shelley completed an application for $25,000 of non-medical (no examination required) life insurance on her own life and gave it to the insurer's agent with a check for the first premium. Shelley died in an auto accident 2 days later. Three weeks later, the insurer reviewed the application and found that Shelley, at the time of the application, met the insurer's normal underwriting standards. The insurer is obligated to pay $25,000 to Shelley's beneficiary.
Example 2:	Same facts as above, except that Shelley did not pay the premium. In this case, the insurer is not obligated to pay anything.

Legal Purpose

To be legally binding, any contract must meet the second requirement—a legal purpose or object. The courts will not enforce an insurance contact if it has an illegal purpose or is contrary to public policy. For example, a thief might purchase a property insurance policy, listing stolen property. The courts will not require the insurer to pay a claim brought by the thief if that property is then lost or destroyed. Likewise, the courts will not enforce a life insurance contract if it is proven that the applicant who purchased the insurance did so intending to murder the insured and collect the insurance proceeds.

Punitive damages claims provide a good example of the public policy issue. Courts award punitive damages, in some cases, to punish the defendant in a liability claim who has committed some particularly egregious act. Some states do not permit insurance to pay punitive damages claims on behalf of an insured on the basis that the insured is not really punished unless the insured pays punitive damages with his or her own funds. Some liability insurance policies exclude coverage for punitive damages, but even a policy without an exclusion cannot be enforced in states where insurers are not permitted to pay punitive damages.

Competent Parties

Valid contracts require that the party making the offer and the one accepting the offer be legally competent to make the agreement. In insurance, the most common problem arises in connection with applicants who are under the age of legal majority, which differs by state. Minority age applicants may have the option of repudiating contracts up to the time they reach legal adulthood, unless the contracts are for necessities such as food, shelter, or clothing. Some insurance contracts are thus voidable by applicants who are minors, and these applicants will receive a full return of the premiums paid if they later decide to make them void. Some states have made exceptions for life, health, and auto insurance contracts by establishing special age limits of 14 or 16; beyond this age, minors are considered to have the legal capacity to insure themselves, and a contract is binding on them.

A similar problem may occur in insurance purchased by legally insane or intoxicated persons. They cannot make legal contracts, because they fail to understand the agreement.

Insurers, too, must be competent to enter into a legal contract by meeting state charter and license requirements. In cases where legal capacity is lacking, many courts have nevertheless held the contracts binding on the insurer, or on its corporate officers personally, rather than penalizing a good-faith purchaser of the coverage.

Consideration

The final requirement for a valid contract is some "consideration" exchanged by both parties to the agreement—a right or something of value given up or an obligation assumed. In insurance, the applicant typically makes a premium payment, or the contract may become effective on the basis of the applicant's promise to pay and to meet other conditions of the contract. The insurer's consideration is its promise to pay for specified losses or to provide other services to the policyowner.

SPECIAL LEGAL CHARACTERISTICS

The next section of this chapter concerns special legal characteristics of the insurance contract. These are not necessarily unique to insurance contracts, but they help describe the fundamental ideas on which insurance contracts are based. A good understanding of these characteristics should help the financial planner, insurance advisor, and consumer to read insurance contracts and comprehend the underlying legal concepts that are essential to most insurance contracts. Figure 6-1 summarizes the characteristics.

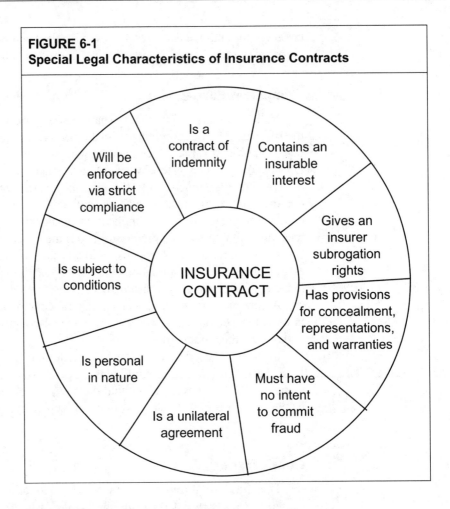

FIGURE 6-1
Special Legal Characteristics of Insurance Contracts

(Insurance Contract characteristics)
- Is a contract of indemnity
- Contains an insurable interest
- Gives an insurer subrogation rights
- Has provisions for concealment, representations, and warranties
- Must have no intent to commit fraud
- Is a unilateral agreement
- Is personal in nature
- Is subject to conditions
- Will be enforced via strict compliance

Unilateral Nature

unilateral contract   The insurance contract is a *unilateral contract* because only one party, the insurer, makes a legally enforceable promise. If the insurer fails to fulfill the promises it makes, such as to pay the specified benefits at the death of the insured, it may be held legally liable for breach of contract. After the premium is paid and the insurance is in force, the policyowner has no further promises to keep, although, of course, failure to live up to policy conditions may release the insurer from the contract.

Unlike an insurance contract, most contracts are bilateral. If Able agrees to sell a car to Baker for $7,000 and Baker agrees to buy it for that amount, they have formed a bilateral contract. If Able later decides not to sell the car, Baker can sue him to enforce the contract or, if the contract is breached, to pay damages. Likewise, if Baker changes his mind and decides not to buy the car, Able can insist that Baker honor his contract.

Personal Nature

The insurance contract is personal and covers the person rather than the property concerned. We may speak of insuring property, but this is not technically accurate. An insurer cannot guarantee that possessions will not be lost, or even guarantee replacement with items of like quality and kind. The insurer can, however, indemnify the person who has incurred the loss. Consider an individual who pays for a property insurance contract and subsequently sells the property without canceling the insurance. In the event of loss, the insurer will make no payment, because the insured has suffered no loss. Insurance payment is contingent on loss to an insured party, not merely on loss of the property described in the policy.

One result of the personal nature of insurance is that many insurance contracts are not freely assignable, or transferable, by the policyowner to other parties. Most insurance contracts, with the exception of life insurance, represent a personal agreement between the insurer and the policyowner. To permit a property or liability insurance contract to be assignable without the insurer's approval would be unfair to the insurer. Only by knowing and investigating each policyowner can the insurance company accurately calculate the potential losses it is insuring.

A life insurance policy can be assigned to another party, such as a charity. Assigning ownership of a life insurance policy does not generally change the insured's life expectancy.

Conditional Nature

conditional contract

Insurance is a *conditional contract*, because the insurer is obligated to pay claims, defend the insured against liability claims, or perform other services, depending on whether the insured (or the life insurance beneficiary) has complied with policy conditions. Insurance policy conditions place some limitations on the insurer's obligations to perform by paying claims. Any failure by the insured to comply with policy conditions may relieve the insurer of its obligation.

An insurance contract condition is usually regarded as either precedent (before) or subsequent (after) the time at which a promise becomes binding on the promisor. An illustration of a common condition precedent, which must take place before a promise becomes binding, is the requirement in many insurance contracts that an insurer must have proper notice and proof of loss before the claim is payable. Note that the policyowner who has a loss has no contractual obligation to file an insurance claim, but the insurer is not obligated to pay unless the policyowner makes a claim in the proper manner. An example of a condition subsequent is an insured's obligation to cooperate with the insurer in defending a liability claim. If the insured does not cooperate, that failure subsequently relieves the insurer of its earlier obligation to pay.

Some Characteristics of an Insurance Contract

- *Unilateral*. Only one party, the insurer, can be held liable for breach of contract.
- *Personal*. It covers a *person,* even if the policy is property insurance.
- *Conditional*. The obligation of one party, usually the insurer, depends on the fulfillment of certain conditions by the other party, usually the policyowner.

Contract of Adhesion

contract of adhesion

The insurance contract is characterized as a *contract of adhesion* because the insurer ordinarily prepares all its details, and the policyowner has no part in drafting its clauses or determining its wording. When applying for insurance, the applicant either accepts the policy as prepared by the insurer (adheres to it), or does not purchase the insurance. Insurers sometimes modify some types of contracts to meet the individual needs of large clients, but even when so modified, the contract with its amendments is prepared by the insurance company. In contrast, a *bargaining contract* is one in which both parties contribute to the terms and conditions.

The insurer does not always create the wording for the contract. Sometimes legislation requires that specific wording be used. Other times the policyowner may be a large corporation that asks for and obtains special contract provisions. In these cases, the intent of the entire contract, and of both the insurer and the policyowner, will probably be considered in court interpretations of any contract ambiguities.

Benefit of Doubt to Policyowner

Because the insurer has the advantage in drawing up the agreement and is expected to represent clearly the intent of the parties when the terms of the policy are ambiguous, obscure, or susceptible to more than one interpretation, the construction most favorable to the policyowner generally prevails.[1] This rule is based on the assumption that the insurer is under a duty to make its meaning clear. When the insurer has failed to be clear, the benefit of the doubt goes to the policyowner. This benefit applies only when the court decides that the contract is unclear, not every time the policyowner misinterprets or does not understand a provision. Sometimes this principle may help policyowners, offsetting their lack of participation in drawing up the insurance contract.

Need for Policyowners to Read Contract

Where there is no ambiguity, an insurance contract is to be enforced in accordance with its terms. If the contract is clear and understandable, few interpretations are necessary. Consideration must be given to the generally understood meaning of the terms used and to the entire context to determine the nature and extent of coverage.

The law holds persons to be bound by the terms of a written contract that they sign or accept, regardless of whether they have acquainted themselves with all of its terms and conditions.[2] Many insurance contracts are complicated and difficult to understand.

Most people do not read their policies. Policyowners assume that a policy meets their needs and let it go at that. However, when a loss occurs, claiming ignorance of the policy's terms because of failure to read the agreement is no defense. The policyowner's failure to read the contract does not change or extend the rights of the policyowner as stated in the written policy. A financial planner's advice to insurance buyers should be: "To avoid problems (and uncertainties), know what is in your insurance policy by reading it, having it explained, or both."

Oral Evidence

parol evidence rule

In connection with the insurance contract, the rule of law applying to oral evidence, referred to in legal terminology as the *parol evidence rule,* has been expressed in a leading case. "It is a fundamental rule, in courts both of law and equity, that parol contemporaneous evidence is inadmissible to contradict or vary the terms of a valid written instrument."[3] Thus, for example, a policyowner may not usually contradict the written contract by saying that the agent promised that the policy covered a specific type of loss.

Although the written contract is not ordinarily subject to modification by oral evidence, the language of the policy is nevertheless not binding in clear cases of mutual mistake of fact or when there is a mistake on one side and fraud inducing it on the other. In these cases, the injured party has a right in equity to ask that the contract be reformed to the true agreement. An example might be a contract that misspells the name of the insured.

Oral evidence also can be helpful to the policyowner. Usually, when information is given to the agent at the time of an application or loss, this knowledge is also assumed to be knowledge of the insurer.

Contract of Indemnity

contract of indemnity

Most property, liability, and health insurance contracts are *contracts of indemnity*. This common-law principle, modified by state statute, means that a policyowner is entitled to payment only to the extent of financial loss or legal liability. In other words, the policyowner should not be allowed to profit from the loss. The policyowner might not be made completely whole because of policy limits and other policy provisions and limitations such as deductibles.

Example: Assume an insured has an individual major medical policy with a $1 million lifetime limit. Also assume that the policy limits hospital room and board benefits to the cost of semiprivate accommodations. Further, assume that the insured is hospitalized and incurs $25,000 in hospital bills, $1,200 of which is for the extra cost of a private room occupied at the insured's request. The policy will reimburse the insured for $23,800 of the hospital expenses, less policy deductibles and percentage participation. Therefore, the insured has been reimbursed to the extent of his or her financial loss, subject to policy limits and provisions.

indemnity

Contracts of indemnity support the principle of *indemnity*. Indemnity refers to financial compensation that makes people whole following a loss. In accord with the principle of indemnity, the purpose of insurance is to indemnify people entitled to its benefits in an attempt to make them financially whole. Insurance does not necessarily make people completely whole, as insurance benefits are subject to policy limits, deductibles, and other limitations.

valued contract

Although most insurance contracts are contracts of indemnity, some are *valued contracts*. The amount of recovery under a valued contract does not depend on the financial amount of the loss but rather on the amount specified in the policy. Life insurance is the most common example. The insurer must pay the stated death benefit if the insured dies. The insurer cannot, for example, deny full payment under a $1 million life insurance policy by arguing that the insured's life was worth only $650,000.

Insurable Interest

insurable interest

Most insurance contracts contain an element of *insurable interest*. An insurable interest is a right or relationship with regard to the subject matter of the insurance contract such that the policyowner would suffer financial loss from its damage, loss, or destruction.

The purposes of requiring an insurable interest in insurance contracts are to prevent gambling and to decrease moral hazard. Without an insurable interest, an insurance contract might be a wager or gambling contract. The contract also could provide an undesirable incentive to cause losses or injuries purposely. When an insurable interest exists, no profit results from an insurance claim settlement, because policyowners merely receive repayment for the loss they have suffered.

A property owner has an insurable interest in that property, because the owner could suffer a financial loss if the property is destroyed by fire, windstorm, or some other peril. Mortgagees, bailees, and creditors may have insurable interests, and often several persons have an insurable interest in the same property. A homeowner may insure his or her interest in property, for example, while at the same time the policy insures the mortgagee's interest up to the value of the mortgage loan.

The continuance of life and good health serves as the basis for many other examples of insurable interest. Death, injury, or sickness may result in financial losses to the persons insured or to their families, creditors, business partners, or employers. The right of persons to insure their own lives, as well as the right of close family members to insure blood relatives, is based on a presumed insurable interest. Other insurable interests for life or health insurance are based on actual potential losses, either increased expenses or reduced income potential, resulting from the relationship to the insured. For example, a creditor may insure the life of a debtor, normally up to the amount of the loan, or a business person may insure a partner's life for the potential loss that his or her death would cause for the partnership.

When must an insurable interest exist? The situation is different with life insurance than with property insurance. Life insurance requires an insurable interest only when the insurance contract is purchased. The insurer is obligated to pay a life insurance claim even if the current policyowner does not have an insurable interest in the insured's life at the time of the insured's death.

With property insurance, an insurable interest must exist at the time of the loss. It is not enough for an insurance policy to be in force that lists the property that was damaged. The policy must also provide coverage for a party who has an insurable interest in that property. Without an insurable interest, that party would have no loss. In practice, people do not usually buy property insurance unless they have an insurable interest, and insurers do not usually sell property insurance to people with no insurable interest in the property.

Insurable interest never becomes an issue in liability insurance. Unless a claim is made, there is no need to raise the issue. If a claim is made, the claim itself proves that the insured could have a liability claim that would result in financial loss.

Subrogation Rights

subrogation

The common-law doctrine of *subrogation* provides that an insurer who has paid a claim takes over any rights of recovery that the insured might have against another party responsible for the loss. In common law, a person who causes a loss to another is responsible for that loss.

> ***Example:***   Jonathan's negligent burning of trash sets fire to his neighbor Laura's house. Therefore, Jonathan will be held responsible for paying for the damage to Laura's house. Laura will probably submit a claim to the

insurance company that provided her homeowners policy. The insurer will pay Laura's claim, subject to any deductible, and then take over Laura's rights to recover from Jonathan. (Jonathan might be protected by liability insurance that ultimately pays the claim on Jonathan's behalf, but that's not the issue here.)

The right of the insurer against other negligent persons usually does not rest on any contractual relationship. As a general rule, an insurer has the right of subrogation even when there is no subrogation clause in the indemnity contract. For the most part, an insurance policy's subrogation clause merely makes the policyowner aware of this common-law doctrine. In some cases, however, the clause might also modify the insurer's subrogation rights.

The right of subrogation by the insurer is limited in amount to the loss payment made to the insured. The insurer may not make a profit by subrogating against the person who caused the loss and recovering a larger amount than the insurer has paid. In fact, subrogation rights are often of little value to the insurance company. There may be no doubt that someone else was responsible for the loss, but to recoup its loss payments (1) the insurer must prove the liability of the wrongdoer and (2) the negligent party must have the financial ability to pay for the loss he or she caused. In many cases, the expense or difficulty of legal proof may prevent the insurer from exercising its subrogation rights. If it might cost $1,000 to collect a $600 claim, the subrogation right may be worthless.

The importance of subrogation differs greatly for various types of insurance. In life insurance, subrogation is not used at all. Subrogation is commonly used in property and liability insurance and, to a lesser extent, in health insurance.

A more common illustration of subrogation is found in auto insurance. If the insurer first pays under collision coverage for damage to the insured's car caused by the negligent driver of another car, then the insurer takes over the rights of the policyowner by subrogation and files a claim against the other driver involved in the accident to receive reimbursement. If the insured does not receive full payment from the insurer because of a deductible in the policy, the insured retains the right to file a claim against the other driver for that deductible. Often the insurer files a joint suit for the loss on its own behalf and on behalf of the insured, but the insurer is not obligated to do so.

Three final points should be made about subrogation. First, insurers often agree in their contracts that they will not pursue a subrogation claim against anyone who is an insured under the policy.

Example: Suppose Theresa lends her car to Jared, who causes an accident while driving it. Assuming Theresa has collision coverage on her auto policy, the insurer will pay Theresa, the car owner with the insurable interest in the car. The insurer will not subrogate against Jared, because he is also an insured.

Second, some insurance contracts permit an insured to waive rights of recovery before any loss occurs.

> ***Example:***   An insured signed a lease agreement that the landlord is not responsible for any damage to the tenant's property. If the landlord's negligence causes a fire that damages the tenant's property, the tenant then has no right to recover from the landlord. The tenant's fire insurance will pay for the tenant's loss. Because the tenant has no rights of recovery to transfer to the insurer, the tenant's insurer cannot take over those (nonexistent) rights and recover from the landlord.

Third, the policy or court interpretations of subrogation may specify the insured's right to retain any subrogation proceeds if the insured has not been fully indemnified for a loss because of deductibles, copayments, exclusions, or inadequate limits. In some cases, the insurer and the insured will share the proceeds on a pro rata basis. In other cases, the insured must be fully indemnified before the insurer is entitled to any recovery.

Effect of Concealment, Misrepresentations, and Fraud

concealment

Concealment and misrepresentation are easily confused. *Concealment* is failure to affirmatively disclose relevant information. Concealment occurs, for example, if an applicant for property insurance knows that the building is in imminent danger of collapsing but does not disclose this fact to the insurer. This building's condition is obviously a material fact that would affect the insurer's underwriting decision.

misrepresentation

Misrepresentation, on the other hand, involves an insurance applicant's knowingly making a false statement of a material fact. The applicant who owns the about-to-collapse building would be guilty of misrepresentation if he or she stated that the building was in sound structural condition. To clarify the distinction between concealment and representation, concealment is concealing material information and misrepresentation is knowingly providing false information. An applicant conceals by maintaining silence when there is an obligation to speak; he or she misrepresents by making an untrue statement.

voidable contract

Either concealment or misrepresentation may make an insurance contract voidable. A *voidable contract* may be affirmed or rejected at the option of one of the parties, although it is binding on the other. If an insurance applicant has concealed or misrepresented material information, the insurer may have a right not to honor contract. But the insurer may also choose to honor the contract. A policyowner rarely has the right to treat an insurance policy as voidable. Perhaps such a situation could arise if the insurer or its agent has grossly misrepresented the contract benefits.

void contract

Sometimes people confuse the terms *void* and *voidable*. A *void contract* has no legal effect, and neither party may enforce it. For example, an illegal gambling contract cannot be enforced through the courts; strong-arm enforcement systems are sometimes used, but that's not the point here. Concealment and misrepresentation make insurance contracts voidable, not void.

fraud

Concealment and misrepresentation often involve *fraud,* as figure 6-2 explains.

If an applicant commits fraud in procuring an insurance policy, the policy may be voidable by the insurer. A policyowner's fraud in connection with a loss or at any other time may also make an insurance contract voidable by the insurer.

FIGURE 6-2
Elements of Fraud

Courts consider six elements when evaluating allegations of fraud. The first five elements must be present to rescind a contract on the basis of fraud. The sixth element must also be necessary for a plaintiff to obtain damages.
The six elements of fraud are as follows:

- *False representation*
  A party must misrepresent a past or existing fact.
- *Knowingly made*
  A party must know a fact to be false or must have made the representation in reckless indifference toward the truth or falsity of the statement made.
- *Intent to influence or deceive*
  One party must have intended to influence or deceive another party.
- *Material fact*
  The misrepresented fact must have influenced or induced the other party to enter the contract or affected the terms under which the other party would have been willing to contract.
- *Reasonable reliance*
  The innocent party must show justification in relying on the statement.
- *Detriment*
  In a suit for damages, the plaintiff must show injury or loss.

Source: Wiening, Eric A., *Foundations of Risk Management and Insurance,* Malvern, PA: American Institute for CPCU, 1st ed., 2002, p. 9.10.

Warranties

warranty

When the application for the insurance contract is made a part of the policy, the answers to specific questions on the application may be considered *warranties*. If false, they make the policy voidable by the insurer regardless of their materiality. Some warranties may also be specifically added in the policy such as the promise of the policyowner in a burglary policy that an alarm system or security guard will be maintained.

The difference between a warranty and a representation is that a warranty is a part of the contract itself and must therefore be strictly complied with, whereas a representation is usually an incidental statement preceding the contract, although it may be an inducement to it. The difference, in effect, is that to make the contract voidable, a warranty need only be false, whereas a representation must be both false and material.

To constitute a warranty, a statement must not only be intended, but must also be definitely indicated as a warranty, either by its incorporation into the policy or by specific reference. Where there is any doubt as to whether a warranty was intended, the statement is to be regarded as a representation and must be shown to be material in order to defeat the policy.

Many states have modified by legislative act the strict application of the doctrine of warranties for most kinds of insurance except ocean marine insurance. When the doctrine has been thus modified, the insurance is sometimes voidable only if a loss occurs during a breach of warranty or is caused thereby, or if the breach materially increases the risk. In effect, this causes most warranties in insurance contracts today to be considered representations. In some lines of insurance, the application itself specifies that statements contained in it are representations, not warranties. Warranties incorporated into insurance policies should be complied with to the letter, for some courts still tend to enforce the original strict rule of declaring the policy voidable when a warranty is breached, regardless of how trivial or immaterial the loss.

ANALYZING AN INSURANCE CONTRACT

The typical insurance contract appears to be a long, complex, formidable legal document. However, an insurance policy is much less formidable to a financial planner who has learned a system or framework for analyzing insurance contracts. The remainder of this chapter provides such a framework. The following discussion includes some examples that involve insurance policy extracts that are taken out of context. Later chapters, which consider types of insurance that deal more specifically with various coverages, will examine these provisions in context.

The provisions of the typical insurance contract can be grouped into the following categories, depending on the purposes they serve: declarations, definitions, insuring agreements, exclusions, conditions, and miscellaneous provisions. The contract also may be modified by adding endorsements or riders.

Declarations

declarations

Every insurance contract has a set of declarations, although they are not always labeled. *Declarations* are factual statements that identify the specific person, property, or activity being insured and the parties to the insurance transaction; they also provide descriptive information about the insurance being provided. They are usually grouped together in the initial section of the policy and are computer-printed for the individual contract, rather than preprinted for all contracts of the same type.

The declarations section of a life insurance policy typically shows the names of the insurer and the agent, the name and age of the insured, the name of the policyowner if different from the insured, the type of policy, the amount of insurance, the policy number, the effective date, the premium, and a listing of attachments to the policy showing items such as supplementary benefits and the beneficiary designation. In property and liability insurance contracts, the declarations section of the policy shows similar types of information as well as the address of the property or activity covered, a listing of endorsements attached to the policy, the names of additional persons or organizations whose interests are insured (such as a mortgagee), the period of coverage, and any applicable deductibles.

Definitions

definitions

Because an insurance policy is a contract of adhesion, the insurer must define carefully what it covers or does not cover. As mentioned earlier, ambiguities in the contract are likely to be construed against the insurer. The *definitions* in the policy explain the key policy terms and are a major help in precisely defining the insured's intentions.

Often words or phrases that are included among the definitions appear in boldface type or quotation marks elsewhere in the policy. The definitions are usually grouped together in an early section of the policy or appear near the end of the policy, serving as a kind of glossary. Examples of a few terms that may appear in the definitions section of the following types of insurance contracts are

- life insurance—you, we, designated office (of the insurer), beneficiary, and new policy
- disability income insurance—monthly earnings, qualifying period, and total disability
- auto insurance—bodily injury, family member, occupying (an auto), your covered auto, and trailer

- homeowners insurance—business, insured location, occurrence, and residence employee

One of the more important definitions in many policies stipulates who is an insured. This definition is discussed in more detail in later chapters as it applies to specific lines of insurance. In homeowners policies, "an insured" refers to the person named in the declarations, his or her spouse and relatives if residents of the household, and persons under age 21 residing in the household and in the care of the named insured, spouse, or resident relatives. Full-time students are also included as insureds, provided they were residents of the household before moving out to attend school, are relatives under the age of 24, or are under the age of 21 and in the care of the named insured or another relative. In the liability section of the personal auto policy, the definition of who is insured includes the named insured and his or her spouse if a resident of the household and for up to 90 days after ceasing to be a member of the household. The definition also includes family members, also defined in the policy, who are residents of the household, anyone using a covered auto, and any person or organization that might be held vicariously liable for use of the auto. Thus, Tom's personal auto policy protects even Tom's employer, as an insured, against liability claims involving Tom's car. If Tom strikes a pedestrian while using his car on business, and the pedestrian sues Tom's employer, Tom's employer is covered as an insured.

Words and phrases not specifically defined in the contract are interpreted according to the following general principles:

- Everyday language is given its ordinary or normal meaning.
- Technical terms are assigned their technical definitions.
- Terms that have an established legal meaning are given that meaning.
- Where appropriate, meanings of words take into account local, cultural, and trade usage considerations.

Insuring Agreements

insuring agreement

The *insuring agreement* is the core of any insurance policy. This agreement (or agreements, as many contracts contain several insuring agreements) spells out the basic promise of the insurance company. Examples of these promises are to pay the face amount of the policy in the event of the insured's death, to defend the insured in any suit alleging liability associated with an auto accident, to pay the actual cash value of personal property damaged by a covered peril, and to pay up to $250 per day for loss of earnings because of the insured's attendance at a court hearing at the insurer's request.

The main insuring agreements in insurance policies are usually either the open-perils type or the named-perils type. An open-perils agreement, also known as an all-risks agreement, covers all losses except those that the policy specifically excludes. All policies have at least a few exclusions, and some have many. For example, a whole life insurance policy is an open-perils policy because it covers death from any cause except a few specified ones, such as death by suicide during the policy's first one or 2 years and, in some policies, death by war or specifically excluded activities such as skydiving or crop dusting.

The named-perils or specified-perils approach to the insuring agreement is used in the personal property coverage of most homeowners policies. This agreement covers only losses that arise from one of the listed perils. If the peril is not listed, the loss is not covered. For example, one form of homeowners policy states that it covers direct physical loss caused by fire; lightning; windstorm; hail; explosion; riot; civil commotion; aircraft; vehicles; smoke; vandalism; malicious mischief; theft; falling objects; weight of ice, snow, or sleet; accidental discharge or overflow of water or steam from certain household systems; and a few other perils. Flood is not contained in the list, so loss to personal property due to flood is not covered.

Exclusions

exclusions
    As noted earlier, every insurance policy has *exclusions* identifying types of claims that the insurer does not cover. The exclusions usually apply either to certain perils, types of losses, types of property, or types of activities. For example, in major medical expense insurance, loss due to the peril of occupational injury or illness is usually excluded because the loss is covered under workers' compensation insurance. In long-term care insurance, costs of care for which the insured is reimbursed under a government program are excluded. In homeowners insurance, the property of unrelated boarders is excluded. And in auto insurance, losses arising from use of the vehicle in a prearranged or organized racing contest in a facility designed for racing are excluded.

The following are the principal reasons for the presence of exclusions in insurance policies:

- Some perils are uninsurable by private insurers.[4] Examples of such perils are wear-and-tear losses to auto and losses due to war.
- Some conditions pose a major increase in risk not contemplated in the basic premium for the coverage. Examples of these conditions are, in auto insurance, the use of an auto to carry persons for a fee other than in a simple carpooling arrangement and, in medical expense insurance, the cost of long-term custodial care.
- Some losses are best covered by other types of policies. For example, collision damage to an auto is not covered by a homeowners policy, and losses due to occupational injury may be excluded by a disability income insurance policy.
- Coverage of some losses would pose too great a potential moral hazard. For example, loss of more than $200 in cash is excluded by homeowners policies.

- Some coverages are not needed by most policyowners, so they should not have to pay for them. For example, most individual medical expense insurance policies exclude or limit maternity coverage.

A practical reason for exclusions is to hold down the premium cost of coverage for policyowners.

Conditions

The insuring agreement is not an absolute promise by the company with "no strings attached." Instead, the promise is a qualified one, enforceable only if the policyowner fulfills the conditions spelled out in the policy. Those conditions may be grouped together in a section of the policy labeled "Conditions," or they may be scattered throughout the policy and its endorsements or riders.

The policyowner must fulfill most of the conditions in an insurance policy before the insurer may be held liable for a loss. An example of these conditions, called conditions precedent (introduced earlier in this chapter), is timely payment of premiums.

Many conditions relate to claims. Most policies, with the exception of life insurance, contain provisions pertaining to the time period within which the insurer must be notified of a loss and the time period within which the insured must file a formal proof of loss. The information that must be included with the formal proof of loss may also be specified.

The insured must fulfill other conditions, called conditions subsequent (also introduced earlier), after the insurer has become liable in order to avoid releasing the insurer from liability. All policies specify that the insured must cooperate with the insurer. Disability income insurance policies include the condition that the insurer can require the insured to submit to examinations by an insurer-selected physician at reasonable intervals during the continuation of a claim. Property and liability insurance policies include the condition that the insured must do nothing to jeopardize the insurer's right to recover from responsible third parties and the condition that the insured must cooperate with the insurer in legal proceedings against the insurer by a third-party claimant.

Miscellaneous Provisions

Some provisions in insurance contracts do not fall into any of the preceding categories of declarations, definitions, insuring agreements, exclusions, or conditions. These provisions may deal with policy continuation, valuation of losses, or other administrative aspects of the policy.

Policy Continuation

Some of the more important miscellaneous provisions in an insurance policy relate to the policyowner's right to continue the coverage in force. Although policies can be issued for a specific term and terminate at the end of that term, many policies allow the policyowner to renew the policy and/or allow the insurer to refuse renewal. These policy renewal provisions fall into four categories: noncancelable, guaranteed renewable, nonrenewable for stated reasons only, and optionally renewable. In addition, some policies are cancelable.

noncancelable

Noncancelable. Some types of insurance policies are *noncancelable,* giving the policyowner the right to renew the coverage at each policy anniversary date, although possibly only until some stated age such as age 65. A noncancelable policy may not be terminated by the insurer during the period of coverage. Moreover, in a truly noncancelable policy, the future rates for the coverage are guaranteed in the contract itself. Examples of noncancelable policies are life insurance policies[5] and some disability income insurance contracts. The term noncancelable may not be as broad as it first seems because the National Association of Insurance Commissioners (NAIC) allows the term to be used in a health insurance policy as long as the policy continues to at least age 50 or at least 5 years if issued to a person aged 44 or older.

Guaranteed Renewable. A guaranteed renewable policy provides a bit less certainty for the policyowner regarding the right to continue coverage. Guaranteed renewable policies are most often found in the health insurance area. Like a

guaranteed renewable

noncancelable policy, a *guaranteed renewable* policy gives the policyowner the right to renew the coverage at each policy anniversary date, but usually only until a stated age such as age 65. The coverage may not be canceled by the insurer during the period of coverage. However, in a guaranteed renewable policy, the insurer does not guarantee future rates for the coverage. Instead, the insurer retains the right to raise the rates for broad classes of insureds, but not just for individual insureds with poor claims experience. Again, the NAIC allows the term to be used for policies that are guaranteed renewable only until age 50 or for at least 5 years if issued to persons aged 44 or older.

Example: Several years ago, Eric Burton bought long-term care insurance for himself and his wife, Claire. They didn't want all their life savings to be depleted by the cost of nursing home or custodial care if they later needed it. They also wanted to leave their assets to their children and not burden them with providing health care for their parents.

The Burtons were extremely satisfied with their guaranteed renewable policies until a couple months ago when their premiums soared from $3,250 per month to almost $5,000. They were shocked, especially because they had believed that the premiums would never increase.

Although the guaranteed renewable provision in their contracts stated that their premiums would never rise based on Eric's and Claire's age or claims history, the insurer had reserved the right to increase premiums based on broad classes of insureds. Experience with long-term care insurance revealed that the insurer had initially underestimated the cost of providing the coverage, so a rate increase became necessary. Unlike in a noncancelable contract, future premium rates are not guaranteed.

Nonrenewable for Stated Reasons Only. Some policies that are otherwise guaranteed renewable allow the insurer to refuse to renew the policy for reasons specifically listed in the policy. These might include the attainment of a certain age. However, if this is the only condition, the policy still often qualifies as guaranteed renewable. Other conditions for nonrenewal include termination of the policyowner's employment in some disability income insurance policies and the nonrenewal of all policies bearing the same form number as the policyowner's.

Optionally Renewable. This optionally renewable provision, found in most property and liability insurance policies, gives the insurer the unilateral right to refuse to renew a policy at the end of any period for which premiums have been paid. Even if the insurer agrees to renew the policy, it has the right to alter the policy's provisions. Some states have enacted legislation that allows an insurer to nonrenew only on annual anniversary dates. In addition, regulations may require the insurer to give specified periods of advance notice to policyowners whose coverage will not be renewed.

Cancelable. A few property and liability policies are cancelable during the period for which premiums have been paid. However, midterm cancellations by the insurers is not allowed for auto and homeowners policies in many states. When a policy can be canceled, the policy and/or state law determines the period of advance notice that must be given to the policyowner. If the policy is cancelled by the insurer, a pro rata share of the premium must be returned.

Valuation of Losses

Another type of miscellaneous provision in several types of insurance policies requires insureds to share in the amount of the loss. For example, deductibles are common in homeowners insurance, auto physical damage insurance, and medical expense insurance. The most common form of deductible is an initial deductible, under which the insurer will pay claims to the extent that they exceed a specified amount. The amount, such as $500, may apply to each claim, as is common in property insurance policies, or to a period of time, such as a calendar year, as in medical expense policies. A similar provision in the form of a waiting or elimination period, during which no benefits are payable at the start of a disability, is found in equipment breakdown insurance, disability income insurance, and long-term care insurance.

Other loss-sharing provisions are the coinsurance clause and copayment requirement in major medical and other types of medical expense coverage. Under these types of provisions, the insured is required to assume a portion of certain covered expenses. For example, the insurer may pay 80 percent of certain medical expenses under a coinsurance clause, while the insured assumes 20 percent. Or the insured may pay a $10 or $20 copayment for each doctor's visit.

Several types of insurance contain a miscellaneous provision that explains how the insurer will respond if other insurance covers the same loss. For example, the property insurance portion of homeowners policies provides that the insurer will pay only that proportion of the loss that the limit of liability applicable in the homeowners policy bears to the total amount of insurance in all policies covering the loss. The liability section specifies that the homeowners coverage is excess over other valid and collectible insurance, except insurance written specifically to provide excess coverage over that of the homeowners policy. An umbrella policy, described in chapter 18, is the most common example of a liability insurance policy specifically written to provide excess liability coverage. Group health insurance often contains a coordination-of-benefits provision to prevent duplication of benefits when an insured is covered by more than one group health insurance plan. For example, if a wife has coverage as an employee under her own plan and is a dependent under her husband's plan, her coverage as an employee is primary and her coverage as a dependent is excess.

Other Provisions

The following illustrate a few other miscellaneous policy provisions:

- Life insurance policies include a description of the optional modes of settlement under which the beneficiary may receive the death proceeds and a clause explaining the policyowner's right to assign the policy to another. There is also an incontestable clause stating that the insurer does not have the right to contest a death claim if the policy has been in force for at least 2 years during the insured's lifetime. In addition, policies contain an explanation of how the death proceeds will be calculated if the insured's age or sex has been misstated. If the policy is issued by a mutual insurer, the policyowner's right to vote for the company's board of directors is also described.
- In annuity contracts, a provision allows the annuitant to delay or accelerate the date when the annuity benefits are to begin; a description of how to change the beneficiary of any death proceeds is also included.

- Personal umbrella liability contracts contain a clause describing how the policy may be canceled by the policyowner or the insurer and a specification that the umbrella policy is excess over all other valid and collectible insurance.
- Disability income insurance policies may include a clause specifying to whom the policy benefits will be paid and another clause stating that the policy and the application attached to it constitute the entire agreement between the parties.
- In major medical expense policies, a lengthy provision explains how coordination of benefits is achieved when more than one policy applies to a loss; other provisions explain the application of the deductible, coinsurance, and stop-loss aspects of the coverage and the procedures for appealing the denial of benefits.
- In homeowners policies, several loss-settlement provisions describe losses that are covered on the basis of the cost to replace with new materials, called replacement cost, and losses where coverage includes a deduction for depreciation, referred to as actual cash value, as well as how a dispute between the insurer and insured over the amount of a loss may be resolved through an appraisal process.
- Personal auto insurance policies contain a provision stating that bankruptcy or insolvency of the insured will not relieve the insurer of any of its obligations under the policy, a description of how coverage applies in a state other than the one where the auto is principally garaged, and an explanation of how disputes between the insured and the insurer on matters of coverage may be resolved through arbitration.
- Several types of policies, including life, health, and annuity contracts, provide a grace period of 30 or 31 days. If a premium is paid after its due date but within the grace period, the coverage is still in effect. Note that property and liability insurance policies do not provide a grace period.
- Some types of policies allow for reinstatement of the coverage under certain conditions after the policy has lapsed. In life insurance, the right to reinstate usually is available only for 3 years following the lapse and only if the policy has not been surrendered for cash or the period of extended term insurance has not expired. Reinstatement requires submission of satisfactory evidence of insurability, the payment of all overdue premiums with interest, and the repayment or reinstatement of all policy indebtedness. In health insurance, payment of the overdue premiums reinstates the policy unless the insurer requires an application. If so, the policy is reinstated only if the application is approved. The reinstated policy is subject to a 10-day waiting period for sickness, but there is no waiting period for accident. No provision is made for reinstatement in the most common property and liability insurance policies.

Endorsements or Riders

endorsement (rider)

An *endorsement*, or in life insurance a *rider*, is a provision added to the policy, sometimes for an extra premium charge or a premium reduction, by which the scope of its coverage is clarified, enlarged, or restricted. An endorsement may alter the declarations such as identifying an additional named insured in an auto policy. Endorsements also may add new definitions to the policy, such as the underinsured motorists endorsement to an auto policy, or modify exclusions in the policy such as removing earthquake from the list of excluded perils in a homeowners policy. Endorsements may even modify a policy condition, such as amending a 30-day notice of nonrenewal to conform with the statute of a particular state that requires a 60-day notice, or a miscellaneous provision such as limiting the insurer's right to cancel the policy to only specified reasons. Similarly, a rider may modify the insuring agreement—for example, adding a waiver-of-premium benefit to a life insurance policy.

As a general legal principle, whenever the wording in an endorsement or rider conflicts with the terms of the policy to which it is attached, the endorsement or rider takes precedence. This principle is based on the assumption that an alteration of the basic agreement between the policyowner and insurer more accurately reflects the true intent of the parties than does the basic agreement itself.

Contents of an Insurance Contract

- Declarations—statements of fact that identify the parties to the insurance transaction, the amount of insurance, the property or activity being covered, the effective date of the coverage, etc.
- Definitions—precise meanings of terms used in the contract, like "family member," "disability," "covered auto," etc.
- Insuring agreements—the promises made by the insurer such as to pay, to defend, to reimburse, etc.
- Exclusions—the perils, properties, types of losses, circumstances, etc. that the insurance does not cover
- Conditions—the duties that (usually) the insured must fulfill before the other party is held to the terms of the contract
- Miscellaneous provisions—other clauses that don't fall into the above categories such as those concerning policy continuation, loss valuation, optional modes of settlement, etc.
- Endorsements or riders—provisions added to the policy to modify or clarify the coverage, sometimes for an extra premium or a reduced premium

MINI-CASE: AMY AND JOHN SCHULTZ

Because their cars were getting old, Amy and John Schultz decided to trade in Amy's Saturn and buy a new car before going on a 2-week cross-country vacation. As soon as they got home from the dealership, they called their insurance agent, provided the necessary information on the new car, and discussed their coverage options. The agent said they would receive a bill for the additional premium involved in insuring their new car and assured them coverage on the new car was now bound, and they were protected immediately.

Amy and John also asked their insurance agent if they could obtain some life insurance coverage before they left on their trip next week. The agent informed them that they should come down to her office, complete an application, and pay the premium, but that she could not assure them that the policy would be in force in time for their vacation trip. On the way to the agent's office, John told Amy not to tell the agent that Amy had recently been treated for depression.

a. If Amy and John complete life insurance applications today, pay the premiums, and their applications are approved, when will their policies become effective?

b. In completing a life insurance application, Amy provides an incorrect answer to the question about whether she had ever been treated for depression. How, if at all, will this affect Amy's life insurance coverage?

(See answer section for answers to mini-case.)

SOURCES FOR FURTHER IN-DEPTH STUDY

- For a detailed discussion of the legal aspects of life insurance policies:
  - Graves, Edward E., and Christensen, Burke A., editors, *McGill's Legal Aspects of Life Insurance*, 4th ed., Bryn Mawr, PA: The American College Press, 2004. Phone 888-263-7265. Web site address www.theamericancollege.edu
- For a detailed discussion of insurance contract analysis, with emphasis on property-liability insurance:
  - Wiening, Eric A. and Malecki, Donald S., *Insurance Contract Analysis*, 1st ed., Malvern, PA: American Institute for Chartered Property Casualty Underwriters, 1992. Chapter 2, "Reading an Insurance Policy," provides a detailed framework for policy analysis.
  - Wiening, Eric A., *Foundations of Risk Management and Insurance*, 1st ed., Malvern, PA: American Institute for Chartered Property Casualty Underwriters, 2002. Chapter 11 contains a less complete

version of the material in the preceding listing. Phone 800-644-
2101. Web site address www.aicpcu.org.

- Wollner, Kenneth S., *How to Draft and Interpret Insurance Policies,*
  1st ed., West Bloomfield, MI: Casualty Risk Publishing, LLC, 1999.
  Phone 800-862-9792. Can be ordered at www.irmi.com.

CHAPTER REVIEW

Answers to mini-case, review questions, and self-test questions start on page 793.

Key Terms

unilateral contract	voidable contract
conditional contract	void contract
contract of adhesion	fraud
parol evidence rule	warranty
contract of indemnity	declarations
indemnity	definitions
valued contract	insuring agreement
insurable interest	exclusions
subrogation	noncancelable
concealment	guaranteed renewable
misrepresentation	endorsement (rider)

Review Questions

6-1. Your client, Maria, complains that buying insurance is just like buying a new
      car in that you shop around, trying to get the best deal, but you don't get to
      enjoy the new car until you actually close the deal and drive it home. What
      unique aspects of an insurance contract differentiate it from other goods and
      services?

6-2. Define the following legal requirements of an enforceable contract:
      a. offer and acceptance
      b. legal purpose
      c. competent parties
      d. consideration

6-3. Define the following legal characteristics of an insurance contract:
      a. unilateral nature
      b. personal nature
      c. conditional nature

6-4. Your client, Sue Litigator, would like to know her legal rights concerning the
      following situations:

    a. Sue claims that one of the provisions in the insurance contract is unclear.

    b. Sue wants to ignore a portion of the contract she did not read.

    c. Sue claims that the insurance agent told her something that contradicts the language of the contract.

6-5. Teddy, your client's son, says he has heard that if he has an accident with his old car, the insurance company will buy him a new car. Explain to Teddy how auto insurance works as a contract of indemnity.

6-6. After her accident-prone cousin's second car accident within 2 months, your client, Julie, asks you if she could buy insurance on the cousin's new car. Julie thinks this might be a good investment, because the cousin is such a bad driver that she will probably have another accident, and the insurance company will then have to pay Julie if Julie has insured the car. You tell Julie that she cannot insure somebody else's car. Briefly give three reasons for requiring an insurable interest in insurance contracts.

6-7. Explain whether your client has an insurable interest in the following situations:

    a. Your client loaned a large amount of money to a friend who is starting a business.

    b. Your client owns and drives a fancy red sports car.

    c. Your client owned a precious stone that was destroyed soon after he gave it to his girlfriend.

6-8. Cheryl Eng, a client of yours, was responsible for an auto accident that damaged the other driver's car. Cheryl was pleased to hear that the other driver had insurance that paid for the damage to his car. Cheryl has just learned that the other driver's auto insurance company has asked Cheryl's insurer for reimbursement. "Can they do that?" she asks you. Briefly describe how the doctrine of subrogation applies to insurance contracts.

6-9. Explain the difference between concealment and misrepresentation by an applicant for insurance.

6-10. Explain the purpose of each of these components of a typical insurance contract:

    a. declarations

    b. definitions

    c. insuring agreements

    d. exclusions

    e. conditions

6-11. Explain the major distinction between a noncancelable policy and a guaranteed renewable policy.

6-12. The wording in an endorsement to your client's insurance policy conflicts with the terms of the policy itself. What is the significance of this conflict for your client?

Self-Test Questions

T F 6-1. An insurance contract is of little value to the policyowner unless a claim for coverage is presented.

T F 6-2. Insurance transfers the financial risk of uncertain perils to the insurer.

T F 6-3. The offer to buy life insurance can be transmitted orally.

T F 6-4. A 16-year-old client can always void his auto insurance policy because he is still a minor.

T F 6-5. An insurance contract is a bilateral contract.

T F 6-6. Property and liability insurance policies are freely assignable by policyowners without the insurer's approval.

T F 6-7. An example of a condition precedent in an insurance contract is that the insured is required to cooperate with the insurer in defending a liability claim.

T F 6-8. Most insurance contracts are contracts of adhesion.

T F 6-9. If there is an ambiguous clause in an insurance contract, the courts will typically interpret the clause in favor of the policyowner.

T F 6-10. Under a contract of indemnity, the insurer pays an amount that reflects the amount of the loss up to the policy limit, subject to other policy provisions.

T F 6-11. Life insurance policies are considered contracts of indemnity.

T F 6-12. Under the principle of subrogation, if the insurer indemnifies the insured for a loss, the insurer obtains whatever rights the insured had against responsible third parties.

T F 6-13. The misrepresentation or concealment of a material fact by an applicant for insurance will void a contract that the insurer has issued to the applicant.

T F 6-14. An innocent misrepresentation by an applicant for insurance constitutes fraud.

T F 6-15. Some exclusions are found in insurance policies because the risks are typically covered by other insurance.

T F 6-16. The requirement that the insured must cooperate with the insurer in legal proceedings against the insurer by a third-party claimant is an example of a condition subsequent.

T F 6-17. Under an initial deductible, the insurer will pay for all losses up to a specified deductible amount.

T F 6-18. As a general legal principle, whenever the wording in an endorsement or rider conflicts with the terms of the policy to which it is attached, the endorsement or rider takes precedence.

NOTES

1. *Knouse v. Equitable Life Insurance Company of Ohio*, 181 Pac. (2d) 310.
2. This is the general rule. See *Grace v. Adams*, 100 Mass. 505. However, some cases seem to say that the policyowner does not have to read his or her policy. Special situations sometimes occur, such as those in which the policyowner has reasonably relied upon advice of a professional agent, but it is unwise for policyowners to assume that courts will be lenient in excusing policyowners from a contract's written terms.
3. *Northern Assurance Co. v. Grand View Building Assn.*, 182 U.S. 380 (1902).
4. See the discussion of the requirements of insurable risks in chapter 1.
5. Term life insurance policies usually may be renewed only to a specified age, such as age 65 or 75, whereas whole life policies may be renewed for the insured's entire lifetime.

7

Social Security, Medicare, and Other Government Programs

Learning Objectives

An understanding of the material in this chapter should enable the student to

7-1.   Describe the extent of coverage under the Social Security and Medicare programs, and explain how the programs are financed.

7-2.   Explain the requirements for eligibility under Social Security, and identify the types and amounts of benefits available.

7-3.   Explain the requirements for eligibility under Medicare, and describe the benefits available under Parts A and B.

7-4.   Describe the Medicare Advantage program.

7-5.   Describe the prescription drug coverage available under Medicare.

7-6.   Discuss the adequacy of Social Security and Medicare financing, and identify the ways in which long-term financial stability might be maintained.

7-7.   Describe the federal income tax treatment of Social Security and Medicare contributions and benefits.

7-8.   Describe the nature of unemployment insurance, temporary disability income insurance, and workers' compensation insurance.

Chapter Outline

Financial planners and insurance agents should understand social insurance because it lays a foundation of basic coverages on which private employer-provided and individual insurance plans are built.

Social insurance programs in the United States fall into several categories. The five described in this chapter are

- Social Security
- Medicare
- unemployment insurance
- temporary disability insurance
- workers' compensation insurance

Two other programs, which are not covered, are established by the Railroad Retirement Act and the Railroad Unemployment Insurance Act. These acts provide benefits to railroad workers that are similar to the benefits provided to other persons by Social Security and state unemployment insurance programs.

The reasons for social insurance programs and their general characteristics are covered in chapter 1. This chapter is devoted to a discussion of specific programs. The major emphasis is on Social Security and Medicare, which are totally federal programs. The other three social insurance programs that are covered vary from state to state and are touched upon in a more general manner.

SOCIAL SECURITY AND MEDICARE

In a broad sense, the term *social security* can be used to refer to any of several programs resulting from the Social Security Act of 1935 and its frequent amendments over the years. The act established four programs aimed at providing economic security for the American society: (1) old-age insurance, (2) unemployment insurance, (3) federal grants for assistance to certain needy groups (the aged, the blind, and children), and (4) federal grants for maternal and child welfare, public health work, and vocational rehabilitation.

OASDHI

The main focus in this chapter is on the old-age insurance program and the benefits that have been added to that program over the years. These additional benefits include survivors insurance (1939), disability insurance (1956), hospital insurance (1965), and supplementary medical insurance (1965). Taken together, these programs constitute the old-age, survivors, disability, and health insurance (*OASDHI*) program of the federal government. This program is often separated into two broad parts. The first part is the old-age, survivors, and disability insurance (OASDI) program.

Over the years OASDI has become commonly referred to as Social Security, and this is the terminology that will be used in this book. The remainder of the OASDHI program is called Medicare.

The following discussion of Social Security and Medicare begins with a description of the extent of coverage under the programs and the way the programs are financed. It then focuses on the eligibility requirements and benefits under the various parts of the programs. Because of the many differences between Social Security and Medicare, the discussion largely treats each program separately. This is followed by a discussion of the adequacy of the funding of these programs. Finally, there is a description of the tax implications of Social Security and Medicare benefits and contributions.

More detailed information about Social Security and Medicare than what is in this chapter can be found on their Web sites: www.socialsecurity.gov and www.medicare.gov. Throughout the chapter, there are many dollar amounts that are indicated as being for 2005. These amounts are subject to annual indexing, and the amounts are posted on these respective Web sites in October or November for the next year.

Extent of Coverage

Over 95 percent of the workers in the United States are in covered employment under the Social Security program and over 98 percent under the Medicare program. This means that these workers have wages (if they are employees) or self-employment income (if they are self-employed) on which Social Security and Medicare taxes must be paid. The following are the major categories of workers who are not covered under the programs or who are covered only if they have met specific conditions:

- civilian employees of the federal government who were employed by the government prior to 1984 and who are covered under the Civil Service Retirement System or certain other federal retirement programs. This exclusion applies only to Social Security benefits. *All* federal employees have been covered for purposes of Medicare since 1983.
- railroad workers. Under the Railroad Retirement Act, employees of railroads have their own benefit system that is similar to Social Security. However, they are covered under Social Security for purposes of Medicare.
- some state and local government employees. Historically, employees covered under state and local government retirement plans have been covered under Social Security only if a state entered into a voluntary agreement with the Social Security Administration. Under such an agreement, the state may either require that employees of local governments be covered or allow the local governments to decide

whether to include their employees. In addition, the state may elect to include all or only certain groups of employees. It is estimated that more than 80 percent of state and local government employees have Social Security and Medicare coverage as a result of such agreements. In addition, coverage under Medicare is compulsory for state and local employees hired after March 1986, and coverage under Social Security is compulsory for employees hired after July 1, 1991, if they do not participate in a public retirement system.

- American citizens working abroad for foreign affiliates of U.S. employers, unless the employer owns at least a 10 percent interest in the foreign affiliate and has made arrangements with the Secretary of the Treasury for the payment of Social Security and Medicare taxes. However, Americans working abroad are covered under Social Security and Medicare if they are working directly for U.S. employers rather than for their foreign subsidiaries.

- ministers who elect out of coverage because of conscience or religious principles

- workers in certain jobs such as student nurses, newspaper carriers under age 18, and students working for the school at which they are regularly enrolled or doing domestic work for a local college club, fraternity, or sorority

- certain family employment. This includes the employment of a child under age 18 by a parent. This exclusion, however, does not apply if the employment is for a corporation owned by a family member.

- certain workers who must satisfy special earnings requirements. For example, self-employed persons are not covered unless they have net annual earnings of $400 or more.

Tax Rates and Wage Bases

Part B of Medicare is financed by a combination of monthly premiums paid by persons eligible for benefits and contributions from the federal government. Part A of Medicare and all the benefits of the Social Security program are financed through a system of payroll and self-employment taxes paid by all persons covered under the programs. In addition, employers of covered persons are also taxed. These taxes are often referred to as FICA taxes because they are imposed under the Federal Insurance Contributions Act.

In 2005, an employee and his or her employer pay a tax of 7.65 percent each on the first $90,000 of the employee's wages. Of this tax rate, 6.2 percent is for Social Security, and 1.45 percent is for the hospital insurance portion of Medicare. The Medicare tax rate of 1.45 percent is also levied on all wages in excess of $90,000. The tax rates are currently scheduled to remain the same after 2005, but the $90,000 wage base is adjusted annually for changes in the

Paying for Social Security and Medicare

- Social Security—Employees pay 6.2 percent of the first $90,000 (2005) of earnings. Employers pay the same. Self-employed persons pay 12.4 percent of first $90,000 (2005) of self-employment income.
- Medicare Part A—Employees pay 1.45 percent of all earnings. Employers pay the same. Self-employed persons pay 2.9 percent of all self-employment income.
- Medicare Part B—Covered persons pay a $78.20 (2005) monthly premium. General revenues of the federal government cover the remainder (about 75 percent) of the program's cost.

national level of wages. Therefore, if wage levels increase by 4 percent in a particular year, the wage base for the following year will also increase by 4 percent. The tax rate for the self-employed is 15.3 percent on the first $90,000 of self-employment income and 2.9 percent on the balance of any self-employment income. This is equal to the combined employee and employer rates.

Over the years, both the tax rates and wage bases have risen dramatically to finance increased benefit levels under Social Security and Medicare as well as new benefits that have been added to the program. In 1950, a tax rate of 1.5 percent was levied on the first $3,000 of wages. These figures increased to 4.8 percent and $7,800 in 1970, and 7.65 percent and $51,300 in 1990. Starting in 1991, a two-tier program was introduced with a tax of 7.65 percent (6.2 percent for Social Security and 1.45 percent for Medicare) on the first $53,400 of wages and the Medicare tax of 1.45 percent on the next $71,500. By 1994, all wages were subject to the Medicare tax.

The adequacy of the current funding structure to pay for Social Security and Medicare benefits continues to be a source of public concern and political debate. This issue is addressed in more detail after the programs are described.

SOCIAL SECURITY: ELIGIBILITY

To be eligible for benefits under Social Security, an individual must have credit for a minimum amount of work under the program. For 2005, a worker receives one credit (also referred to as a quarter of coverage) for each $920 in annual earnings on which Social Security taxes were paid. However, no more than four credits may be earned in any one calendar year. Consequently, a worker who pays Social Security taxes on as little as $3,680 ($920 x 4) at any time during the year will receive the maximum four credits. As in the case of the wage base, the amount of earnings necessary for a credit is adjusted annually for changes in the national level of wages.

Credits are the basis for establishing an insured status under Social Security. The three types of insured status are fully insured, currently insured, and disability insured.

Fully Insured

fully insured

A person is fully insured under Social Security if either of two tests is met. The first test requires 40 credits of coverage. Once a person acquires this credit, he or she is *fully insured* for life even if covered employment under Social Security ceases.

Under the second test, a person who has a minimum of six credits is fully insured if he or she has at least as many credits as there are years elapsing after 1950 (or after the year in which he or she reaches age 21, if later) and before the year in which he or she dies, becomes disabled, or reaches age 62, whichever occurs first. Therefore, a worker who reached age 21 in 1993 and died in 2005 would need 11 credits for his or her family to be eligible for survivors benefits.

Currently Insured

currently insured

If a worker is not fully insured, certain survivors benefits are still available if a *currently insured* status exists. To be currently insured, it is only necessary that a worker have earned at least six credits during the 13 calendar quarters ending with the quarter in which his or her death occurs.

Disability Insured

disability insured

To receive disability benefits under Social Security, it is necessary to be *disability insured*. At a minimum, a disability-insured status requires that a worker (1) be fully insured and (2) have a minimum amount of work under Social Security within a recent time period. In connection with the latter requirement, workers aged 31 or older must have earned at least 20 credits during the 40 calendar quarters ending with the quarter in which disability occurs; workers aged 24 through 30 must have earned credits equal to at least one-half the number of calendar quarters from the time they turned 21 and the quarter in which disability begins; and workers under age 24 must have earned six credits during the 12 calendar quarters, ending with the quarter in which disability begins.

A special rule for blind persons states that they are exempt from the recent-work rules and are considered disability insured as long as they are fully insured.

SOCIAL SECURITY: TYPES OF BENEFITS

The Social Security program provides three principal types of benefits: retirement (old-age) benefits, survivors benefits, and disability benefits.

Retirement Benefits

A worker who is fully insured under Social Security is eligible to receive monthly retirement benefits as early as age 62. However, the election to receive benefits prior to the full Social Security retirement age results in a permanently reduced benefit.

full retirement age

Full retirement age (sometimes referred to as *normal retirement age*), or the age at which nonreduced retirement benefits are paid, is 65 for workers born in 1937 or before. As shown in table 7-1, a gradually increasing full retirement age applies to workers born in 1938 and later.

TABLE 7-1 Retirement Age for Nonreduced Benefits	
Year of Birth	**Full Retirement Age**
1937 and before	65 years
1938	65 years, 2 months
1939	65 years, 4 months
1940	65 years, 6 months
1941	65 years, 8 months
1942	65 years, 10 months
1943–54	66 years
1955	66 years, 2 months
1956	66 years, 4 months
1957	66 years, 6 months
1958	66 years, 8 months
1959	66 years, 10 months
1960 and later	67 years

In addition to the retired worker, the following dependents of persons receiving retirement benefits are also eligible for monthly benefits:

- a spouse aged 62 or older. Benefits are permanently reduced, however, if this benefit is elected prior to the spouse's reaching full retirement age. This benefit is also available to a divorced spouse under certain circumstances if the marriage lasted at least 10 years.
- a spouse of any age if the spouse is caring for at least one child of the retired worker who is (1) under age 16 or (2) disabled and entitled to a child's benefit as described below. This benefit is commonly referred to as a *mother's* or *father's benefit.*
- dependent, unmarried children under age 18. This child's benefit will continue until age 19 as long as a child is a full-time student in elementary or secondary school. In addition, disabled children of any age are eligible for benefits as long as they were disabled before reaching age 22.

It is important to note that retirement benefits, as well as all other benefits under Social Security and Medicare, are not automatically paid upon eligibility but must be applied for.

Survivors Benefits

All categories of survivors benefits are payable if a worker is fully insured at the time of death. However, three types of benefits are also payable if a worker is only currently insured. The first is a lump-sum death benefit of $255, payable if there is a surviving spouse or children.

Two categories of persons are eligible for income benefits as survivors if the deceased worker was either fully or currently insured at the time of death:

- dependent, unmarried children under the same conditions as previously described for retirement benefits
- a spouse (including a divorced spouse) caring for a child or children under the same conditions as described for retirement benefits

The following categories of persons are also eligible for benefits, but only if the deceased worker was fully insured:

- a widow or widower aged 60 or older. However, benefits are reduced if taken prior to full retirement age. This benefit is also payable to a divorced spouse if the marriage lasted at least 10 years. In addition, the widow's or widower's benefit is payable to a disabled spouse at age 50 as long as the disability commenced no more than 7 years after the (1) worker's death or (2) end of the year in which entitlement to a mother's or father's benefit ceased.
- a parent aged 62 or over who was a dependent of the deceased worker at the time of death

Social Security Blackout Period

No benefits are payable for the surviving spouse of a deceased covered worker from the time the youngest child reaches age 16 (or is no longer disabled in certain cases) until the surviving spouse is 60.

Disability Benefits

A disabled worker under full retirement age is eligible to receive benefits under Social Security as long as he or she is disability insured and meets the definition of disability under the law. The definition of disability is very rigid and requires a mental or physical impairment that prevents the worker from engaging in any substantial gainful employment. The disability must also have lasted (or be expected to last) at least 12 months or be expected to result in death. A more liberal definition of disability applies to blind workers who are aged 55 or older. They are considered disabled if they are unable to perform work that requires skills or abilities comparable to those required by the work they regularly performed before reaching age 55 or becoming blind, if later.

Disability benefits are subject to a waiting period and are payable beginning with the 6th full calendar month of disability. In addition to the benefit paid to a disabled worker, the other categories of benefits available are the same as those described under retirement benefits.

As previously mentioned, certain family members not otherwise eligible for Social Security benefits may be eligible if they are disabled. Disabled children are subject to the same definition of disability as workers. However, disabled widows or widowers must be unable to engage in any gainful (rather than substantial gainful) employment.

Eligibility for Dual Benefits

In many cases, a person is eligible for more than one type of Social Security benefit. Probably the most common situation occurs when a person is eligible for both a spouse's benefit and a worker's retirement or disability benefit based on his or her own Social Security record. In this and any other case when a person is eligible for dual benefits, only an amount equal to the higher benefit is paid.

Termination of Benefits

Monthly benefits to any Social Security recipient cease upon his or her death. When a retired or disabled worker dies, the family members' benefits that are based on the worker's retirement or disability benefits also cease, but the family members are then eligible for survivors benefits.

Disability benefits for a worker technically terminate at full retirement age but are then replaced by comparable retirement benefits. Any benefits payable because of disability may cease at an earlier date if medical or other evidence shows that the definition of disability is no longer satisfied. However, the disability benefits continue during a readjustment period that consists of the month of recovery and 2 additional months. As an encouragement for them to return to work, disabled beneficiaries for whom there is no evidence that their disability has otherwise terminated are allowed a 9-month trial work period during which benefits are not affected regardless of how much the beneficiary earns. At the end of that period, a beneficiary's earnings are evaluated to determine if the earnings are substantial ($830 per month in 2005). If earnings then exceed this amount for 3 months, benefits are suspended but can be reinstated during the next 36 months without starting a new application process should the earnings fall below this level.

As long as children are not disabled, benefits usually terminate at age 18 but may continue until age 19 if the child is a full-time student in elementary or secondary school.

A surviving spouse's benefit terminates upon remarriage unless remarriage takes place at age 60 or later.

SOCIAL SECURITY: BENEFIT AMOUNTS

Calculating Benefits

primary insurance amount (PIA)

With the exception of the $255 lump-sum death benefit, the amount of all Social Security benefits is based on a worker's primary insurance amount. The *primary insurance amount (PIA)* is the monthly amount a worker receives if he or she retires at full retirement age or becomes disabled, and it is the amount on which benefits for family members are based. The actual PIA calculation is complex and performed by the Social Security Administration when a beneficiary is eligible for benefits. It involves indexing past wages on which taxes were paid to current wage levels, eliminating some years with the lowest or no earnings, and averaging the indexed wages for the remaining years. The result is then put into a formula that is weighted in favor of lower-income workers.

In 2005, the average PIA for a worker who retires is about $1,000. A worker who has continually earned the maximum income subject to Social Security taxes can expect to have a PIA for retirement purposes of about $1,925 if he or she retires in 2005. The maximum PIA in 2005 for purposes of disability and survivors benefits ranges from approximately $1,925 to $2,100. The higher PIA results for workers who are disabled or who die at younger ages. Table 7-2 shows the Social Security Administration's estimated average monthly benefit that various categories of beneficiaries receive in 2005.

TABLE 7-2
Estimated Average Monthly Social Security Benefits, 2005

Category of Beneficiary	Amount
All retired workers	$ 955
Aged couple, both receiving benefits	1,574
Widowed mother and two children	1,979
Aged widow(er) alone	920
Disabled worker, spouse, and one or more children	1,497
All disabled workers	895

If a worker is retired or disabled, these benefits are paid to family members, as shown in table 7-3. If the worker dies, survivors benefits are as shown in table 7-4.

However, the full benefits described above may not be payable because of a limitation imposed on the total benefits that may be paid to a family. This family maximum is again determined by a formula and is usually reached if three or more family members (including a retired or disabled worker) are eligible for benefits.

TABLE 7-3
Benefits for Family Members of a Disabled or Retired Worker

Family member	Percentage of Worker's PIA
Spouse at full retirement age	50%
Spouse caring for disabled child or child under 16	50%
Child under 18 or disabled	50% each

TABLE 7-4
Benefits for Survivors of a Deceased Worker

Family Member	Percentage of Worker's PIA
Spouse at full retirement age	100%
Spouse caring for disabled child or child under 16	75%
Child under 18 or disabled	75% each
Dependent parent	82.5% for one, 75% each for two

If the total amount of benefits payable to family members exceeds the family maximum, the worker's benefit (in the case of retirement and disability) is not affected, but the benefits of other family members are reduced proportionately.

Example: Sam Chen died, leaving a spouse aged 42 and three children. All four family members are eligible for 75 percent of Sam's PIA of $1,200. Ignoring the family maximum, the benefits total $3,600 ($900 for each family member). However, the family maximum, using the prescribed formula for 2005 is $2,226. Therefore, each family member has his or her benefit reduced to $556 (rounded to the next lower dollar). When the first child loses benefits at age 18, the other family members' benefits increase to $742 (ignoring any automatic benefit increases, including the family maximum).

When a second family member loses eligibility, the remaining two family members each receive the full benefit of $900 because the total benefits the family receives are now less than the $2,226 calculated by the formula.

Other Factors Affecting Benefits

Benefits Taken Early

If a worker elects to receive retirement benefits prior to full retirement age, benefits are permanently reduced by 5/9 of one percent for each of the first 36 months that the early retirement precedes full retirement age and 5/12 of one percent for each month in excess of 36. For example, for a worker who retires 3 years before full retirement age, the monthly benefit is only 80 percent of that worker's PIA. A spouse who elects retirement benefits prior to full retirement age has benefits reduced by 25/36 of one percent per month for each of the first 36 months and 5/12 of one percent for each month in excess of 36. A widow or widower has benefits reduced proportionately from 100 percent at full retirement age to 71.5 percent at age 60. If the widow or widower elects benefits prior to age 60 because of disability, there is no further reduction.

Many Americans retire before the age at which they are eligible for nonreduced Social Security benefits. In some cases, an individual may need the Social Security benefits to meet regular living expenses. In other cases, however, an individual may have income or investments to bridge the gap until full retirement age. Then the decision becomes: Do I elect early benefits at a reduced amount for a longer period of time or larger benefits that will start later? There is no precise answer. As a general rule, if a person expects to live to 78 years or older, the better decision is to select the reduced benefits. However, the "breakeven" age will vary by such factors as when early benefits start, gender, the category of Social Security benefits, and the interest rate at which funds can be invested.

Delayed Retirement

Workers who delay applying for benefits until after full retirement age are eligible for an increased monthly benefit. Benefits are increased for each month of late retirement until age 70. For persons born from 1917 until 1924, the increase is 1/4 of one percent per month, which is equal to 3 percent for delaying application for benefits for one full year. To encourage later retirement, the monthly percentage gradually increases. Table 7-5 shows the percentage for each month of deferral as well as the maximum percentage increase that is available if the worker postpones retirement until age 70.

It should be pointed out that these increases apply to a worker's PIA as determined at the time he or she applies for retirement benefits. If a person continues to work during the period of delayed retirement and covered wages are sufficiently high, it is possible for a worker's PIA to be a higher dollar amount than it would have been at full retirement age. Therefore, the increased monthly retirement benefit from working past full retirement age may be greater than the percentages in the table.

TABLE 7-5
Increase for Delayed Retirement

Year of Birth	Monthly Percentage Increase	Maximum Percentage Increase
1917–24	1/4	115
1925–26	7/24	117 ½
1927–28	1/3	120
1929–30	9/24	122 ½
1931–32	5/12	125
1933–34	11/24	127 1/2
1935–36	1/2	130
1937	13/24	132 1/2
1938	13/24	131 5/12
1939	7/12	132 2/3
1940	7/12	131 1/2
1941	15/24	132 1/2
1942	15/24	131 1/4
1943–54	2/3	132
1955	2/3	130 2/3
1956	2/3	129 1/3
1957	2/3	128
1958	2/3	126 2/3
1959	2/3	125 1/3
1960 and later	2/3	124

Earnings Test

earnings test

Through the 1999 tax year, benefits were reduced for Social Security beneficiaries under age 70 if they had wages that exceeded a specified level. For tax years beginning after 1999, Congress repealed this *earnings test* in and after the month in which a beneficiary attains the full retirement age. However, the earnings test still applies to beneficiaries under full retirement age. They are allowed annual earnings of up to $12,000 in 2005, and this figure is subject to annual indexing for later years. If a beneficiary earns more than this amount, his or her Social Security benefit is reduced by $1 for each $2 of excess earnings. There is one exception to the test: The reduction is $1 for every $3 of earnings in excess of $31,800 (in 2005) in the calendar year a worker attains the full retirement age for earnings in months prior to such age attainment. Once the beneficiary reaches full retirement age, he or she can earn any amount without a Social Security reduction.

Social Security Earnings Test

- Beneficiaries who have reached full retirement age—no loss of benefits regardless of annual wages
- Beneficiaries who are under full retirement age—$1 of benefits lost for every $2 of annual wages in excess of $12,000 (2005). A more liberal test applies in the calendar year a worker attains the full retirement age.

The reduction in a retired worker's benefits that results from excess earnings is charged against the entire benefits that are paid to a family and based on the worker's Social Security record. If large enough, this reduction may totally eliminate all benefits otherwise payable to the worker and family members. In contrast, excess earnings of family members are charged against their individual benefits only. For example, a widowed mother who holds a job outside the home may lose her mother's benefit, but any benefits her children receive are unaffected.

Cost-of-Living Adjustments

Social Security benefits increase automatically each January as long as there has been an increase in the Consumer Price Index (CPI) for the one-year period ending in the third quarter of the prior year. The increase is the same as the increase in the CPI since the last cost-of-living adjustment, rounded to the nearest 0.1 percent. Benefits do not automatically decrease if the CPI declines.

Offset for Other Benefits

Disabled workers under full retirement age who also receive workers' compensation benefits or disability benefits from certain other federal, state, or local disability programs will have their Social Security benefits reduced to the extent that the total benefits received (including family benefits) exceed 80 percent of their average current earnings at the time of disability. In addition, the monthly benefit of a spouse or surviving spouse is reduced by two-thirds of any federal, state, or local government pension that is based on earnings not covered under Social Security on the last day of employment.

SOCIAL SECURITY: REQUESTING BENEFIT INFORMATION

Social Security Statement

The Social Security Administration annually sends a *Social Security Statement* to all persons aged 25 or older who have covered employment under Social Security and are not currently receiving monthly benefits. The statement enables an employee to verify his or her contributions to the Social Security and Medicare programs. It also contains an estimate of benefits that are available upon retirement, disability, or death.

The statement helps employees to understand their total benefit package as well as facilitate the correction of any errors in earnings records while information is readily available. As a general rule, requests for corrections must be made within 3 years, 3 months, and 15 days following the year in which wages were paid or self-employment income was earned. However, clerical or fraudulent errors can be corrected after that time.

MEDICARE: ELIGIBILITY

Part A, the hospital portion of Medicare, is available at no monthly cost to any person aged 65 or older as long as the person is entitled to monthly retirement benefits under Social Security or the railroad retirement program. Civilian employees of the federal government aged 65 or older are also eligible. It is not necessary for these workers actually to be receiving retirement benefits, but they must be fully insured for purposes of retirement benefits. The following persons are also eligible for Part A of Medicare at no monthly cost:

- persons aged 65 or older who are dependents of fully insured workers aged 62 or older
- survivors aged 65 or older who are eligible for Social Security survivors benefits
- disabled persons at any age who have been eligible to receive Social Security benefits for 2 years because of their disability. This includes

workers under age 65, disabled widows and widowers aged 50 or over, and children 18 or older who were disabled prior to age 22.

- workers who are either fully or currently insured and their spouses and dependent children with end-stage renal (kidney) disease who require renal dialysis or kidney transplants. Coverage begins either the first day of the 3d month after dialysis begins or earlier for admission to a hospital for kidney-transplant surgery.

Most persons aged 65 or over who do not meet the previously discussed eligibility requirements may voluntarily enroll in Medicare. However, they must pay a monthly Part A premium and also enroll in Part B. The monthly Part A premium in 2005 is $375 for individuals with fewer than 30 credits of coverage under Social Security and $206 for individuals with 30 to 39 credits. The premium is adjusted annually, and the $375 amount reflects the full average cost of providing benefits to a Part A beneficiary.

Any person eligible for Part A of Medicare is also eligible for Part B. A monthly premium must be paid for Part B. This premium ($78.20 in 2005) is adjusted annually and represents only about 25 percent of the cost of the benefits provided. The general revenues of the federal government finance the remaining cost of the program. As a result of the Medicare Prescription Drug, Improvement, and Modernization Act, the Part B premium will continue to equal 25 percent of Part B benefit costs, but only for beneficiaries with modified adjusted gross income under $80,000 for a single person and $160,000 for a couple. Beginning in 2006, higher-income persons will pay a larger premium that increases with income. These increases will be phased in over 5 years, until persons with income above $200,000 ($400,000 for a couple) will have a Part B premium equal to 80 percent of the cost of the benefits provided. Starting in 2007, these income figures will also be indexed.

Persons who receive Social Security or railroad retirement benefits are automatically enrolled in Medicare if they are eligible. If they do not want Part B, they must reject it in writing. Other persons eligible for Medicare must apply for benefits. As a general rule, anyone who rejects Part B or who does not enroll when initially eligible may later apply for benefits during a general enrollment period that occurs between January 1 and March 31 of each year. The monthly premium is increased by 10 percent for each 12-month period during which the person was eligible but failed to enroll.

Medicare secondary rules make employer-provided medical expense coverage primary to Medicare for certain classes of individuals who are over 65, who are disabled, or who are suffering end-stage renal disease. These persons (and any other Medicare-eligible persons still covered as active employees under their employer's plans) may not wish to elect Medicare because it largely constitutes duplicate coverage. When their employer-provided coverage ends, these persons have a 7-month special enrollment period to elect Part B coverage, and the late enrollment penalty is waived.

Medicare is also secondary to benefits received by persons (1) entitled to veterans' or black lung benefits, (2) covered by workers' compensation laws, or (3) whose medical expenses are paid under no-fault insurance or liability insurance. Medicare secondary rules are covered in more detail in chapter 12.

MEDICARE PART A: HOSPITAL BENEFITS

Medicare Part A

Medicare Part A provides benefits for expenses incurred in hospitals, skilled-nursing facilities, and hospices. Some home health care benefits are also covered. In order for benefits to be paid, the facility or agency providing benefits must participate in the Medicare program. Virtually all hospitals are participants, as are most other facilities or agencies that meet the requirements of Medicare.

Part A of Medicare, along with Part B, provides a high level of benefits for medical expenses. As described in the next few pages, however, deductibles and copayments may be higher than in prior group or individual coverage. In addition, certain benefits that were previously provided may be excluded or limited. For this reason, persons without supplemental retiree coverage from prior employment may wish to consider purchasing a Medicare supplement (medigap) policy in the individual marketplace.

Hospital Benefits

Part A pays for inpatient hospital services for up to 90 days in each benefit period (also referred to as a spell of illness). A benefit period begins the first time a Medicare recipient is hospitalized and ends only after the recipient has been out of a hospital or skilled-nursing facility for 60 consecutive days. A subsequent hospitalization then begins a new benefit period.

In each benefit period, Medicare pays covered hospital expenses in full for 60 days, subject to an initial deductible ($912 in 2005). This deductible is adjusted annually to reflect increasing hospital costs. Benefits for an additional 30 days of hospitalization are also provided in each benefit period, but the patient must pay a daily copayment ($228 in 2005) equal to 25 percent of the initial deductible amount. All recipients also have a lifetime reserve of 60 additional days that they may use if they exhaust the regular 90 days of benefits. However, once a reserve day is used, it cannot be restored for use in future benefit periods. When using reserve days, patients must pay a daily copayment ($456 in 2005) equal to 50 percent of the initial deductible amount.

There is no limit on the number of benefit periods a person may have during his or her lifetime. However, there is a lifetime limit of 190 days of benefits for treatment in psychiatric hospitals.

Covered inpatient expenses include the following:

- room and board in semiprivate accommodations. Private rooms are covered only if required for medical reasons.
- nursing services (except private-duty nurses)
- use of regular hospital equipment such as oxygen tents or wheelchairs
- drugs and biologicals ordinarily furnished by the hospital
- diagnostic or therapeutic items or services
- operating room costs
- blood transfusions after the first three pints of blood. Patients must pay for the first three pints of blood unless they get donors to replace the blood.

There is no coverage under Part A for the services of physicians or surgeons.

Skilled-Nursing Facility Benefits

In many cases, a patient may no longer require continuous hospital care but may not be well enough to go home. Consequently, Part A provides benefits for care in a skilled-nursing facility if a physician certifies that the patient needs skilled-nursing care or rehabilitative services for a condition that was treated in a hospital within the last 30 days. In addition, the prior hospitalization must have lasted at least 3 days. Benefits are paid in full for 20 days in each benefit period and for an additional 80 days with a daily copayment ($114 in 2005) equal to 12.5 percent of the initial hospital deductible. Covered expenses are the same as those described for hospital benefits.

A skilled-nursing facility may be a separate facility for providing such care or a separate section of a hospital or nursing home. The facility must have at least one full-time registered nurse, and it must provide nursing services at all times. Every patient must be under the supervision of a physician, and a physician must always be available for emergency care.

One very important point should be made about skilled-nursing facility benefits. Custodial care is not provided under any part of the Medicare program unless skilled-nursing or rehabilitative services are also needed and covered. Older individuals often need custodial care to help them with such personal needs as walking, bathing, dressing, or taking medication. This care may be short-term in nature, but often it is long-term and a major health care expense. Long-term care insurance and other sources for obtaining long-term care are discussed in chapter 15.

Home Health Care Benefits

If a patient can be treated at home for a medical condition, Medicare pays the full cost for an unlimited number of home visits provided by a home health agency. To receive these benefits, a person must be confined at home and treated under a home health plan set up by a physician. The care needed must include skilled-nursing services, physical therapy, or speech therapy. In addition to these services, Medicare pays for the cost of part-time home health aides, medical social services, occupational therapy, and medical supplies and equipment provided by the home health agency. There is no charge for these benefits other than a required 20 percent copayment for the cost of such durable medical equipment as oxygen tanks and hospital beds. Medicare does not cover home services that are furnished primarily to assist people in activities of daily living (ADLs) such as housecleaning, preparing meals, shopping, dressing, or bathing.

If a person has only Part A of Medicare, Part A covers all home health care benefits. If a person has both Parts A and B, Part A covers the first 100 visits that commence within 14 days of a hospital stay of at least 3 days. Part B covers all other home health visits.

Hospice Benefits

Hospice benefits are available under Part A of Medicare for beneficiaries who are certified as being terminally ill with a life expectancy of 6 months or less. Although a hospice is thought of as a facility for treating the terminally ill, Medicare benefits provided by a Medicare-approved hospice are available primarily to patients in their own homes. However, inpatient care can be provided if the patient needs it. In addition to including the types of benefits described for home health care, hospice benefits include drugs, bereavement counseling, and inpatient respite care when family members need a break from caring for the ill person.

To qualify for hospice benefits, a Medicare recipient must elect such coverage in lieu of other Medicare benefits, except for the services of the attending physician or services and benefits that do not pertain to the terminal condition. There are modest copayments for some services. A beneficiary may cancel the hospice coverage at any time (for example, to pursue chemotherapy treatments) and return to regular Medicare coverage. The beneficiary can elect hospice benefits again but must be recertified as terminally ill.

Exclusions

There are some circumstances under which Part A of Medicare does not pay benefits. In addition, there are times when Medicare acts as the secondary payer of benefits. Exclusions under Part A include the following:

- services outside the United States and its territories or possessions. However, there are a few exceptions to this rule for qualified Mexican and Canadian hospitals. Medicare pays benefits if an emergency occurs in the United States and the closest hospital is in one of these countries. However, persons living closer to a hospital in one of these countries than to a hospital in the United States may use the foreign hospital even if an emergency does not exist. Finally, there is coverage for Canadian hospitals if a person needs hospitalization while traveling the most direct route between Alaska and another state in the United States. This latter provision does not apply to persons vacationing in Canada.

- elective luxury services such as private rooms or televisions
- hospitalization for services that are not necessary for the treatment of an illness or injury such as custodial care or elective cosmetic surgery

Under these circumstances, Medicare is the secondary payer of benefits:

- when there is primary coverage under an employer-provided medical expense plan for (1) an employee or spouse aged 65 or older or (2) a disabled beneficiary
- when medical care can be paid under any liability policy or policies that provide no-fault benefits for vehicle accidents
- in the first 30 months for end-stage renal disease when an employer-provided medical expense plan provides coverage. By law, employer plans cannot specifically exclude this coverage during this period.

Medicare pays only if complete coverage is not available from these sources and then only to the extent that benefits are less than would otherwise be payable under Medicare. Medicare secondary rules are discussed in more detail in chapter 12.

MEDICARE PART B: MEDICAL INSURANCE

Benefits

Medicare Part B

Medicare Part B provides benefits for most medical expenses not covered under Part A. These include

- physicians' and surgeons' fees. Under certain circumstances, Medicare also provides benefits for the services of chiropractors, podiatrists, and optometrists.
- diagnostic tests
- X rays
- physical therapy
- blood transfusions
- drugs and biologicals that cannot be self-administered
- radiation therapy

- medical supplies such as surgical dressings, splints, and casts
- rental of medical equipment such as oxygen tents, hospital beds, and wheelchairs
- prosthetic devices such as artificial heart valves or lenses after a cataract operation
- ambulance service if a patient's condition does not permit the use of other methods of transportation
- mammograms and Pap smears
- diabetes glucose monitoring and education
- diabetic screening for persons at risk of diabetes (beginning in 2005 as a result of the Medicare Prescription Drug, Improvement, and Modernization Act)
- screening blood test for early detection of heart disease (also beginning in 2005)
- colorectal cancer screening
- bone mass measurement
- prostate cancer screening
- pneumococcal vaccination and flu shots
- dilated eye examinations for beneficiaries at high risk for glaucoma
- home health care services as described for Part A when a person does not have Part A coverage or when Part A benefits are not applicable

Exclusions

Although the preceding list may appear to be comprehensive, there are numerous medical products and services Part B does not cover, some of which represent significant expenses for the elderly. These exclusions include

- most drugs and biologicals that can be self-administered except drugs that are used for osteoporosis, oral cancer treatment, and immunosuppressive therapy under specified circumstances
- routine physical, eye, and hearing examinations except those previously mentioned. However, as part of the Medicare Prescription Drug, Improvement, and Modernization Act, all Medicare beneficiaries are now eligible for a one-time physical examination within 6 months of enrolling in Part B.
- routine foot care
- immunizations except pneumococcal vaccinations or immunization required because of an injury or immediate risk of infection
- cosmetic surgery unless it is needed because of an accidental injury or to improve the function of a malformed part of the body

- dental care unless it involves jaw or facial bone surgery or setting fractures
- custodial care
- eyeglasses, hearing aids, or orthopedic shoes

In addition, benefits are not provided to persons eligible for workers' compensation or to those treated in government hospitals. Benefits are provided only for services received in the United States, except for physicians' services and ambulance services rendered for a hospitalization that is covered in Mexico or Canada under Part A. Part B is also a secondary payer of benefits under the same circumstances described for Part A.

Amount of Benefits

The benefits available under Part B are subject to a number of different payment rules. A few charges are paid in full without any cost sharing. These include (1) home health services, (2) pneumococcal vaccinations and flu shots, (3) certain surgical procedures that are performed on an outpatient basis in lieu of hospitalization, (4) diagnostic preadmission tests performed on an outpatient basis within 7 days prior to hospitalization, (5) mammograms, and (6) Pap smears.

For other charges, there is a $110 calendar-year deductible in 2005. (As a result of the Medicare Prescription Drug, Improvement, and Modernization Act, the deductible will be indexed for medical care inflation beginning in 2006.) When the deductible is satisfied, Part B pays 80 percent of approved charges for most covered medical expenses other than professional charges for mental health care and outpatient services of hospitals and mental health centers. Medicare pays only 50 percent of approved charges for the mental health services of physicians and other mental health professionals. There is a separate payment system under which Medicare determines a set payment for each type of service for outpatient services of hospitals and mental health centers. This amount varies across the country to reflect factors such as the level of hospital wages. For some services, Medicare patients are required to pay an amount equal to 20 percent of the set payment amount, and Part B pays 80 percent. For other services, there is a fixed copayment that may be more or less than 20 percent of the set payment amount. In no case can the amount a Medicare patient pays for a single service exceed a dollar figure equal to the Part A hospital deductible ($912 in 2005).

The approved charge for doctors' services covered by Medicare is based on a fee schedule issued by the Centers for Medicare & Medicaid Services, the federal agency that administers Medicare. A patient will be reimbursed for only 80 percent of the approved charges above the deductible—regardless of the doctor's actual charge. Most doctors and other suppliers of medical services accept an assignment of Medicare benefits and therefore are prohibited from charging a patient in excess of the fee schedule. They can, however, bill the patient for any portion of the approved charges that Medicare did not pay because of the annual deductible and/or coinsurance. They can also bill for any services that Medicare does not cover.

Doctors who do not accept assignment of Medicare benefits cannot charge a Medicare patient more than 115 percent of the approved fee for nonparticipating doctors. Because the approved fee for nonparticipating doctors is set at 95 percent of the fee paid for participating doctors, a doctor who does not accept an assignment of Medicare benefits can charge a fee that is only 9.25 percent greater than if an assignment had been accepted (115 percent x 95 percent = 109.25 percent). As a result, some doctors either do not see Medicare participants or limit the number of such patients they treat.

The previous limitation on charges does not apply to providers of medical services other than doctors. Although a provider that does not accept assignent can charge any fee, Medicare pays only what it would have paid if the provider accepted assignment. For example, if the approved charge for medical equipment is $100 and the actual charge is $190, Medicare reimburses $80 (.80 x $100), and the Medicare recipient must pay the balance.

MEDICARE PART C: MEDICARE ADVANTAGE (MEDICARE+CHOICE)

original Medicare

In 1985, Congress amended the Medicare program to allow a beneficiary to elect coverage under a health maintenance organization (HMO) as an alternative to traditional Medicare Parts A and B, usually referred to as *original Medicare*. At first, the number of persons who elected this option was relatively small. Many of the elderly had not had HMO coverage during their working years and viewed it with some skepticism. In addition, many HMOs continued to focus on expanding their traditional market of younger, healthier individuals rather than entering a new and demographically different market. Furthermore, there were complex federal rules that had to be satisfied to enter the Medicare market.

The situation slowly changed as more HMOs got into the Medicare market and the public became more familiar with HMO coverage. Moreover, as medical costs continued to rise, the election of an HMO option made more sense from a cost standpoint. As a result, HMO coverage for Medicare beneficiaries grew rapidly in the mid- to late 1990s, and approximately one out of six beneficiaries obtained such coverage.

Under the 1985 rules, an HMO was basically given 95 percent of what Medicare would expect to pay to provide benefits if a beneficiary who elected HMO coverage had stayed in the traditional Medicare program. In turn, the HMO was expected to provide at least the same benefits that were available under Medicare. Although an HMO could provide additional benefits and charge an extra premium, some HMOs have provided additional benefits, such as prescription drugs, without charging an additional premium. These zero-premium plans have been very popular among Medicare beneficiaries. Although they must continue to pay the Part B Medicare premium, these bene-iciaries can receive coverage that is broader than original Medicare and have no reason to purchase a Medicare supplement policy.

In 1999, Part C of Medicare (called Medicare+Choice) went into effect. It expands the choices available to most Medicare beneficiaries by allowing them to elect health care benefits through one of several alternatives to original Medicare, as long as the providers of these alternatives enter into contracts with the Centers for Medicare & Medicaid Services.

The Medicare+Choice plans include

- HMOs. Most of the HMOs previously in the Medicare market became part of the Medicare+Choice program.
- preferred-provider organizations (PPOs). Beginning in 2005, PPOs can begin to offer Medicare Advantage plans on a regional basis that is broader than the typical service areas used for non-Medicare Advantage participants. The Secretary of Health and Human Services will determine these regions. This will give PPOs a broader base from which to solicit members and should also increase competition. These regional plans must use a single deductible and out-of-pocket limit for Part A and Part B benefits.
- provider-sponsor organizations (PSOs). These are similar to HMOs but established by doctors and hospitals that have formed their own health plans.
- private fee-for-service plans
- private contracts with physicians

These plans must provide all benefits available under original Medicare. They may include additional benefits as part of the basic plan or for an additional fee.

Through 2004, beneficiaries were able to enroll in a Medicare+Choice plan or switch options (including reenrollment in original Medicare) at any time. Beginning in 2005, there will be a limited period each year during which beneficiaries can change their plans.

The initial reaction to Medicare+Choice was less than overwhelming. Few new providers of alternative coverage entered the marketplace, and the enrollment in alternatives to the original Medicare program had decreased after several years of growth. One reason is that the Medicare+Choice rules were extremely complex, and it is questionable if many of the potential providers could have entered the market in a viable way. As a result, there was a decrease in the number of HMOs that offered coverage. Although some HMOs continued to enter the Medicare market or expand their service areas for Medicare beneficiaries, a larger number of HMOs either ceased to provide Medicare coverage or reduced their service areas. Although many of those who lost Medicare coverage had other HMOs available, a change to another HMO often required the use of different physicians and hospitals. Other HMO participants had no choice but to return to the original Medicare program. Finally, some HMOs no longer offered zero-premium plans, they increased premiums, and/or they reduced benefits. These changes stem from two factors. First, HMO costs have increased significantly in recent years, partially because of large increases in the cost of prescription drugs, which are a major source of medical expenses for the elderly. Second, the rate of growth of Medicare payments to HMOs has been reduced so that many HMOs are receiving increases that fail to match their increases in expenses.

Medicare Advantage

The situation, however, may change as a result of provisions in the Medicare Prescription Drug, Improvement, and Modernization Act. The act changes the name of Medicare+Choice to *Medicare Advantage*, and all materials for such plans must use this terminology by January 1, 2006. The act makes numerous administrative changes to the program aimed at increasing participation. The method for calculating reimbursement to participating plans has been changed, and many plans are receiving larger reimbursements. This has already resulted in some plans increasing benefits and/or lowering premiums.

In 2005, beneficiaries are able to enroll in a Medicare Advantage plan or switch plans (including reenrollment in original Medicare) once during the first 6 months of the year. Beginning in 2006, an annual change will be allowed only during the first 3 months of the year.

In 2006, Medicare Advantage plans will be required to submit proposals to participate in the program. Such proposals are subject to negotiation, and the Secretary of Health and Human Services will determine whether a plan can participate in the program based on statutory criteria. This procedure is similar to that used to select the medical expense plans available to employees of the federal government under the Federal Employees Health Benefits Program.

Is a Medicare Advantage Plan an Appropriate Option?

It is clear from the earlier part of this chapter that the original Medicare program provides less than complete protection for medical expenses. As a result, many retirees have some type of medical expense coverage to provide additional benefits. Some retirees have this coverage under employer-provided postretirement medical expense plans; other retirees purchase a Medicare supplement (medigap) policy. These alternatives are described in detail in chapter 13, the second of two chapters devoted to private medical expense insurance.

The selection of a Medicare Advantage plan is also a viable option that may provide broad coverage at a relatively modest cost. However, Medicare Advantage plans are not available in all parts of the country, and the number of plans in a given area may be very limited. In addition, most of the plans that are currently in existence are structured as HMOs. For a retiree who was covered by an HMO plan while working, the nature of the coverage will be familiar, and the HMO plan may even be with the same insurer that provided coverage previously. For other retirees, the inherent nature of such plans may be less than desirable. For example, HMOs control the selection of physicians that a member can use. The selection of a Medicare Advantage plan may require a retiree to stop seeing a long-time trusted physician and select a physician who participates in the HMO network. On the other hand, the retiree's physician may already be in the HMO network and no change will be necessary. HMOs also have limited coverage when a member receives medical care outside the plan's relatively small geographic service area. Retirees who plan to spend winter or summer months at another location may have limited coverage except in emergency situations unless they return home for treatment.

The decisions regarding HMO coverage are essentially the same for retirees as they are for actively working persons. HMOs, their nature, and their advantages and drawbacks are discussed in chapter 12.

MEDICARE PART D: PRESCRIPTION DRUG COVERAGE

Medicare Part D

Along with numerous other changes to Medicare and the establishment of health saving accounts, the Medicare Prescription Drug, Improvement, and Modernization Act adds a prescription drug program to Medicare— *Medicare Part D*. Until Part D becomes effective in 2006, the act provides for Medicare-approved drug discount cards. The act also gives employers a financial incentive to provide or continue to provide drug coverage to retirees as an alternative to enrollment in Part D.

Drug Discount Cards

Since spring 2004, most Medicare beneficiaries have been able to purchase a drug discount card. Insurance companies, retail pharmacies, Medicare Advantage plans, and other entities can sponsor these cards. The cards are not available to beneficiaries who have prescription drug coverage through Medicaid (public assistance for low-income individuals), TRICARE for Life (for retired military personnel), the Federal Employees Health Benefits Program, or a plan of their current or former employer. In addition, members of Medicare Advantage plans that already provide discount cards to members cannot purchase another card. Estimates were that a beneficiary's drug costs would decrease by 10 to 25 percent, but savings for most persons have not been this high.

An individual can purchase only one card and the cost cannot exceed $30. Sponsors are required to pass any discounts they negotiate on the purchase of drugs to cardholders and to publish a price list of the drugs they cover.

Certain low-income seniors will also be eligible for annual subsidies of up to $600 to help them pay the cost of prescription drugs. With the subsidies, this group of older Americans often enjoys significant savings.

Information on the cost and benefits of available cards as well as pharmacy locations and drug costs can be found on the Medicare Web site—www.medicare.gov—or the AARP Web site—www.aarp.org.

Prescription Drug Coverage

In 2006, Medicare Part D will replace Medicare-approved drug discount cards. Part D is a subject of considerable controversy. More liberal members of Congress argue that it does not go far enough to meet seniors' needs. More conservative members of Congress contend that its cost will saddle the government with another major entitlement. Some also view Part D as a boon to the pharmaceutical industry. Moreover, the rules for this program are very complex. Therefore, Part D may change before it ever becomes effective. Even if no changes are made, many regulations still need to be issued to fully implement the program. Therefore, the following discussion is general, and readers should be aware of ongoing developments. One source of this information is the Medicare Web site: www.medicare.gov.

Eligibility and Cost

Part D is a voluntary prescription drug benefit that is available to all Medicare beneficiaries entitled to Part A and enrolled in Part B. This includes persons who participate in any of the various Medicare Advantage plans. The act provides that most eligible persons will have access to at least two privately operated prescription drug plans in the region in which they live. The plans must meet certain standards and be approved by the Secretary of Health and Human Services. There are provisions in the act for the Secretary to arrange prescription drug coverage on an alternative basis if fewer than two drug plans are approved. Beneficiaries who participate in Medicare Advantage plans would obtain their prescription drug coverage through that plan as long as it was an approved provider.

It is estimated that the premium will average about $35 per month per person. This represents about 26 percent of the actual cost of coverage, with the balance paid to the drug plan by the federal government. The premium is partially or totally waived for persons with very low incomes.

Covered Drugs

formulary

It is expected that each Medicare prescription drug plan will develop a *formulary,* which is a list of approved drugs that the plan will cover. Although these formularies do not have to cover every prescription drug, they must cover at least two prescription drugs in each therapeutic category and class. Formularies can be changed at any time during the year, but participants may change drug plans only once per year. As a result, some participants may find that there will no longer be coverage for a drug that they have been taking.

Benefits

The act provides for a standard prescription drug program but also allows for alternative plans to be approved if the plans meet certain requirements and are at least actuarially equivalent to the standard plans. The standard prescription drug program will have an annual deductible of $250 in 2006. This amount and other dollar figures mentioned below will increase in later years if the expenditures for prescription drugs by Medicare beneficiaries increase.

After the deductible has been satisfied, the plan will pay 75 percent of the next $2,000 of prescription drug costs the plan covers. Benefits then cease until a beneficiary's total drug costs (including the deductible) reach $5,100. At this point, the beneficiary will have had out-of-pocket costs of $3,600 in addition to the $420 annual premium. The plan will then pay 95 percent of covered drug costs in excess of $5,100.

The following example shows that beneficiaries with $810 or less in annual prescription drug expenditures will receive no net benefit from Part D. Approximately half of Medicare beneficiaries fall into this category and will need to decide whether or not they should purchase coverage. The negative side of not signing up when initially eligible is that there will be a financial penalty for enrollment at a later date when a beneficiary might have significantly higher drug costs. This penalty is in the form of a premium that will be higher by at least one percent for every month of later enrollment. The percentage increase may actually be greater if the Secretary of Health and Human Services determines that a larger penalty is actuarially justified.

Example: Roger incurs $810 in covered drug costs during the year.

Payment by drug plan: .75 x ($810 – $250) $420
Less premium ($35 per month)   −420
                                                                      0

Percentage of drug cost Roger pays   100%

The next example shows that Medicare beneficiaries with $5,100 or less in annual prescription drug expenditures will also pay a significant percentage of their drug costs.

Example: Wendy and her husband, Keith, have annual prescription drug costs of $2,318 and $5,100 respectively. (Wendy's costs are equal to the average prescription drug costs for Medicare recipients.)

Wendy and Keith will each receive $1,500 under their Part D drug plans. This amount is equal to 75 percent of the first $2,000 in drug costs in excess of the $250 deductible. In Wendy's case, she will have out-of-pocket costs equal to $1,238 or 53 percent of her expenditures. This $1,238 figure is calculated as follows:

Premium	$ 420
Deductible	250
25% of first $2,000 above deductible	500
100% of expenses in excess of $2,250	68
	$1,238

In Keith's case, expenses in excess of $2,250 are $2,850, and his total out-of-pocket costs and premium are $4,020 or about 79 percent of his drug expenditures.

The percentage of drug costs will drop as costs exceed $5,100 because Part D plans pay 95 percent of this excess amount.

Example: Todd takes several expensive drugs for an assortment of ailments. This year, he expects drug costs to be $20,000. As in the previous example for Keith, Todd will have out-of-pocket costs of $4,020 for the first $5,100 of drug expenditures. Of the remaining $14,900 in expenditures, he will be responsible for only 5 percent, or $745. Thus his total out-of-pocket costs are $4,765 or about 24 percent of his expenditures.

Qualifications for Drug Plans

The act establishes several criteria for Part D prescription drug plans that are designed to protect beneficiaries. Some of these include the following:

- Plans must give beneficiaries information on access to covered drugs, how the plan formulary works, copayment and deductible requirements, and any medication therapy management program.
- Plans must have a mechanism to respond to beneficiary questions, including toll-free telephone access.
- Plans must provide meaningful procedures for hearing and resolving grievances.
- Plans must allow any willing pharmacy to participate as long as it complies with the terms and conditions of the plan.
- Each pharmacy that dispenses drugs must inform the beneficiary of any differential between the price of a drug and the price of the lowest-priced generic drug that is therapeutically equivalent.
- Plans must include in their provider network a sufficient number of pharmacies that dispense drugs other than by mail order to ensure convenient access.
- Plans must make information on formulary changes available through the Internet and must give beneficiaries adequate notice of changes.
- Plans must provide quality-assurance measures and systems to reduce medication errors and adverse drug interaction.
- Plans must offer medication management programs to beneficiaries with multiple chronic diseases.

Employer Incentives

One concern of Congress was that employers or unions that provided prescription drug coverage to retirees would drop this coverage and, possibly, other retiree medical expense coverage after the act was passed. To prevent this from occurring, the act offers a subsidy to employers or unions that continue drug coverage as long as it is at least actuarially equivalent to the coverage under a standard prescription drug program.

The annual subsidy, which becomes effective in 2004, is equal to 28 percent of the cost of providing a retiree with up to $5,000 in prescription drug benefits, subject to a $250 deductible. After 2006, these dollar amounts will be indexed.

ADEQUACY OF FINANCING

partial advance funding

Social Security and Medicare are based on a system of funding that the Social Security Administration refers to as *partial advance funding*. Under this system, taxes are more than sufficient to pay current benefits and thus provide some accumulation of assets for the payment of future benefits. Partial advance funding falls somewhere between pay-as-you-go financing, which was once the way Social Security and Medicare were financed, and full advance funding as used by private insurance and retirement plans. Under pay-as-you-go financing, taxes are set at a level to produce just enough income to pay current benefits; under full advance funding, taxes are set at a level to fund all promised benefits from current service for those making current contributions.

All payroll taxes and other sources of funds for Social Security and Medicare are deposited into four trust funds: an old-age and survivors fund, a disability fund, and two Medicare funds. Benefits and administrative expenses are paid out of the appropriate trust fund from contributions to that fund and any interest earnings on accumulated assets. The trust funds have limited reserves to serve as emergency funds in periods when benefits exceed contributions such as in times of high unemployment. However, current reserves are relatively small and could pay benefits for only a limited time if contributions to a fund ceased. In addition, the reserves consist primarily of IOUs from the Treasury because the contributions have been "borrowed" to finance the government's deficit.

In the early 1980s, considerable concern arose over the potential inability of payroll taxes to pay promised benefits in the future. Through a series of changes, the most significant being the 1983 amendments to the Social Security Act, these problems appeared to have been solved for the Social Security program—at least in the short run. The changes approached the problem from two directions. On one hand, payroll tax rates were increased; on the other hand, some benefits were eliminated and future increases in other benefits were scaled back. However, the solutions of 1983 have not worked. Without further adjustments, the trust funds will have inadequate resources to pay claims in the foreseeable future. Although the old-age and survivors fund will continue to increase—it will be quite large by the time the current baby boomers retire—and benefits will then exceed income, the fund will begin to decrease as the percentage of retirees grows rapidly. Current projections indicate that the assets of the combined old-age and survivors trust fund and the disability trust fund will run out about 2040.

Because of an increasing number of persons aged 65 or older and medical costs that continue to grow at an alarming rate, there is also concern about the Medicare portion of the program. Estimates are that its trust funds will be depleted by about 2020.

It is obvious that changes must be made—either now or later—in the Social Security and Medicare programs. Probably the most important step in finding a solution is to convince the public that changes in this very popular entitlement program are necessary. Changes, of course, have significant political implications. Although most members of Congress realize the need for reform, neither political party has been willing to compromise and take the necessary initiative for fear of losing public support.

In the broadest sense, the solution lies in doing one or both of the following: increasing revenue into the trust funds or decreasing benefit costs. Changes that would increase revenue include the following:

- increasing the Social Security and/or Medicare tax rate
- increasing the wage base on which Social Security taxes are paid
- using more general tax revenue to fund the programs
- subjecting a greater portion of income benefits to taxation and depositing the increased tax revenue into the trust funds
- investing all or a portion of trust fund assets in higher-yielding investments than Treasury securities

Suggested changes that have been made for decreasing benefit costs include the following:

- increasing full retirement age beyond the planned increase to age 67
- raising the early retirement age beyond 62
- lowering the benefit formula so that future retirees will receive somewhat reduced benefits
- reducing cost-of-living increases
- imposing a means test for benefits
- shifting more of the inflation risk to workers through the use of separate accounts for all or part of each worker's contributions. This would give the worker some control over his or her account.
- increasing the Medicare eligibility age beyond 65
- raising Medicare deductibles and copayments
- increasing the Medicare Part B premium for everyone, or possibly only for higher-income retirees
- lowering or slowing the growth of payments to Medicare providers
- encouraging or requiring Medicare beneficiaries to enroll in managed care plans

In May 2001, President Bush announced the establishment of a bipartisan commission to study the Social Security program and report specific recommendations to preserve Social Security for seniors while building wealth for younger Americans. The commission was asked to make its recommendations using the following six guiding principles for modernizing the program:

- Modernization must not change Social Security benefits for retirees or near-retirees.

- The entire Social Security surplus must be dedicated to Social Security only.
- Social Security payroll taxes must not increase.
- Government must not invest Social Security funds in the stock market.
- Modernization must preserve Social Security's disability and survivors components.
- Modernization must include individually controlled, voluntary personal accounts, which will augment the Social Security safety net. This concept is often referred to as privatization.

In late 2001, the commission issued a report. Rather than recommending one specific plan to reform Social Security, it put forth three alternative proposals that contained the President's guiding principles. Two of the three proposals would also significantly increase benefits for low-income workers over what the current program pays. Although the various proposals received some degree of support, there are critics who argue for different changes. The net effect is that no reform has yet taken place. However, President Bush is making Social Security reform a major goal of his second term in office.

Any single change to the Social Security program will probably offend one important group of voters or another. As a result, the ultimate solution (which may or may not follow the commission's recommendations) will probably involve a combination of several of the previously mentioned suggestions for change so that everyone will bear a little of the pain.

TAX TREATMENT OF SOCIAL SECURITY AND MEDICARE

Deductibility of Premiums

Employer contributions to the Social Security and Medicare program are tax deductible for federal income tax purposes. Any employee contributions are paid with after-tax dollars. Self-employed persons, however, are able to deduct one-half of their Social Security and Medicare taxes as business expenses. In addition, Part B premiums are treated the same as other medical expense premiums for individual insurance and may be deductible as described in chapter 13.

Taxation of Benefits

Benefits received in the form of monthly income under Social Security are partially subject to income taxation for some Social Security recipients. To determine the amount of Social Security benefits subject to taxation, it is necessary to calculate modified adjusted gross income, which is the sum of following:

- the taxpayer's adjusted gross income (disregarding any foreign income and savings bond exclusions)
- the taxpayer's tax-exempt interest received or accrued during the year
- one-half of the Social Security benefits for the year

If the modified adjusted gross income is $25,000 or less for a single tax-payer ($32,000 or less for married taxpayers filing jointly), Social Security benefits are not taxable. If the modified adjusted gross income is between $25,001 and $34,000 ($44,000 for married taxpayers filing jointly), up to 50 per-cent of the Social Security benefit is includible in taxable income. If the modi-fied adjusted gross income exceeds $34,000 ($44,000 for married taxpayers filing jointly), up to 85 percent of the Social Security benefit is includible in taxable income. The exact amount of the taxable Social Security benefit is determined by complex formulas that are beyond the scope of this discussion.

Medicare benefits and any lump-sum Social Security benefits are received tax free.

OTHER SOCIAL INSURANCE PROGRAMS

The remainder of this chapter is devoted to social insurance programs other than Social Security and Medicare. Unemployment insurance is a joint federal and state program, and workers' compensation insurance and tempor-ary disability laws are solely under state control. Because the programs of each state are unique, the discussion in this chapter is general in nature. Readers should familiarize themselves with the programs in their own state and not assume that these programs will always conform to the general-izations that follow. Detailed information on a specific state's program can be obtained from the state agency that administers the program.

Unemployment Insurance

unemployment insurance

Prior to the passage of the Social Security Act in 1935, relatively few employees had any type of protection for income lost during periods of unemployment. The act stipulated that a payroll tax was to be levied on covered employers for the purpose of financing *unemployment insurance* programs that were to be established by the states under guidelines issued by the federal government. Essentially, the federal law levied a federal tax on certain employers in all states. If a state established an acceptable program of unemployment insurance, the taxes used to finance its program could be offset against up to 90 percent of the federal tax. If a state failed to establish a program, the federal tax would still be levied, but no monies collected from the employers in that state would be returned for purposes of providing benefits to the unemployed there. Needless to say, all states quickly established unemployment insurance programs. These programs (along with a federal program for railroad workers) now cover over 95 percent of all working persons, but major gaps in coverage exist for domestic workers, agricultural workers, and the self-employed.

There are several objectives to the current unemployment insurance program. The primary objective is to provide periodic cash income to workers during periods of involuntary unemployment. Benefits are generally paid as a matter of right, with no demonstration of need required. Although federal legislation has extended benefits during times of high unemployment, the unemployment insurance program is basically designed for workers whose periods of unemployment are short-term; the long-term and hard-core unemployed must rely on other measures, such as public assistance and job-retraining programs, when unemployment insurance benefits are exhausted.

A second major objective of unemployment insurance is to help the unemployed find jobs. Workers must register at local unemployment offices, and they receive unemployment benefits through these offices. Another important objective is to encourage employers to stabilize employment. As described below, this is accomplished through the use of experience rating to determine an employer's tax rate. Finally, unemployment insurance contributes to a stable labor supply by providing benefits so that skilled and experienced workers are not forced to seek other jobs during short-term layoffs, thereby remaining available to return to work when called back.

Financing Benefits

Unemployment insurance programs are financed primarily by unemployment taxes levied by both the federal and state governments. The federal tax is equal to 6.2 percent of the first $7,000 of wages for each worker, but this tax is reduced by up to 5.4 percentage points for taxes paid to state programs. The practical effect of this offset is that the federal tax is actually equal to 0.8 percent of covered payroll. A few states levy an unemployment payroll tax equal to only the maximum offset (5.4 percent on the first $7,000 of wages), but most states have a higher tax rate and/or levy their tax on a higher amount of earnings.

No state levies the same tax on all employers. Rather, states use a method of experience rating whereby all employers, except those that have been in business for a short time or those with a small number of employees, pay a tax rate that reflects their actual experience, within limits. Thus, an employer who has laid off a large percentage of employees will have a higher tax rate than an employer whose employment record has been stable.

An employer who has good experience often has to pay a state tax of less than one percent of payroll and possibly even as little as 0.1 percent. On the other hand, some employers pay a state tax as high as 9 or 10 percent. Regardless of the amount of actual state tax paid, the employer still pays the 0.8 percent federal tax.

The major argument for experience rating is that it provides a financial incentive for employers to stabilize employment. Those who oppose its use, however, contend that many employers have little control over economic trends that affect employment. In addition, they argue that tax rates tend to escalate in bad economic times and thus may actually be an obstacle to economic recovery.

Individual states collect the entire unemployment insurance tax and deposit it in the Federal Unemployment Insurance Trust Fund, which is administered by the Secretary of the Treasury. Each state has a separate account that is credited with its taxes and its share of investment earnings on assets in the fund. Unemployment benefits in the state are paid from this account. The federal share of the taxes the fund receives is deposited into separate accounts and used for administering the federal portion of the program and for giving grants to the states to administer their individual programs. In addition, the federal funds are available for loans to states whose accounts have been depleted during times of high unemployment.

Eligibility for Benefits

The right to benefits depends on the worker's attachment to the labor force within a prior base period. In most states, this base period is the 52 weeks or four quarters prior to the time of unemployment. During this base period, the worker must have earned a minimum amount of wages or worked a minimum period of time, or both.

The right to benefits is also contingent on an unemployed worker's being both physically and mentally capable of working. The worker must also be available for work. Benefits may be denied if he or she refuses suitable work or places substantial restrictions on the type of work he or she will accept. In addition to registering with a local unemployment office, most states require a worker to make a reasonable effort to seek work.

Most unemployment programs have a one-week waiting period before benefits commence. Benefits are not paid retroactively for that time of unemployment.

All states have provisions in their laws under which a worker may be disqualified from receiving benefits. This disqualification may take the form of (1) a total cancellation of benefit rights, (2) the postponement of benefits, or (3) a reduction in benefits. Common reasons for disqualification include the following: voluntarily leaving a job without good cause, discharge for misconduct, refusal to accept suitable work, involvement in a labor dispute, and receipt of disqualifying income such as dismissal wages, workers' compensation benefits, benefits from an employer's pension plan, or primary insurance benefits under Social Security.

Benefits

The majority of states pay "regular" unemployment insurance benefits for a maximum of 26 weeks; the remaining states pay benefits for slightly longer periods. In most states, the amount of the weekly benefit is equal to a specified fraction of a worker's average wages during the highest calendar quarter of the base period. The typical fraction is 1/26, which yields a benefit equal to 50 percent of average weekly earnings for that quarter. Other states determine benefits as a percentage of average weekly wages or annual wages during the base period. Some states also modify their benefit formulas to provide relatively higher benefits (as a percentage of past earnings) to lower-paid workers. Benefits in all states are subject to minimum and maximum amounts. Minimum weekly benefits typically fall within the range of $20 to $100, maximum benefits in the range of $210 to $450, and average benefits in the range of $200 to $275. In addition, a few states currently provide additional benefits if there are dependents who receive regular support from the worker.

States also provide reduced benefits for partial unemployment. Such a condition occurs if a worker is employed less than full-time and has a weekly income less than his or her weekly benefit amount for total unemployment.

There is also a permanent federal-state program of "extended" unemployment benefits for workers who exhaust regular benefits during periods of high unemployment. When a state's unemployment rate exceeds a specified level, it automatically triggers the availability of these benefits. The federal government and the states involved finance the benefits equally, and they can be paid for up to 13 weeks, as long as the total of regular and extended benefits does not exceed 39 weeks.

In 1988, Congress created a program of unemployment assistance to individuals whose unemployment is the direct result of a major disaster as declared by the President and who are not otherwise eligible for regular unemployment insurance benefits. To be eligible for benefits under this program, an individual must have worked or been scheduled to work in an area that was declared a federal disaster area, as were parts of New York after the terrorist attacks on September 11, 2001. In addition, benefits are paid only if the individual cannot work because of the disaster and the work he or she cannot perform is his or her primary source of income and livelihood. The state where a disaster occurred administers the benefits, and the benefit amounts are the same as regular unemployment insurance benefits. The benefits are paid for up to 26 weeks but cease once the disaster assistance period (which is usually also 26 weeks) is over. The federal government, through the Federal Emergency Management Agency, provides the funds for these "disaster" benefits.

In periods of severe economic conditions on a national basis, the federal government often enacts legislation to provide additional benefits that are financed with federal revenue. The most recent program, which ran through 2003 for new claims, provided up to 13 weeks of benefits to persons who had exhausted regular benefits.

Temporary Disability Laws

temporary disability law

At their inception, state unemployment insurance programs were usually designed to cover only unemployed persons who were both willing and able to work. Programs denied benefits to anyone who was unable to work for any reason, including disability. Some states amended their unemployment insurance laws to provide coverage to the unemployed who subsequently became disabled. However, five states—California, Hawaii, New Jersey, New York, and Rhode Island—and Puerto Rico went one step further by enacting *temporary disability laws* under which employees can collect disability income benefits, regardless of whether their disability begins while they are employed or unemployed. Although variations exist among the states, these laws (often referred to as nonoccupational disability laws because benefits are not provided for disabilities covered under workers' compensation laws) are generally patterned after the state unemployment insurance law and provide similar benefits.

Eligibility

Every jurisdiction requires that an employee must have worked for a specified time and/or have received a minimum amount of wages within some specific period prior to disability to qualify for disability income benefits. The usual waiting period for benefits is 7 days. In some jurisdictions, the waiting period is waived if the employee is hospitalized.

Benefits

Benefits are a percentage, ranging from 50 percent to 66 2/3 percent, of the employee's average weekly wage for some period prior to disability, subject to maximum and minimum amounts. Benefits are generally paid up to 26 weeks if the employee remains disabled that long.

Workers' Compensation Laws

Prior to the passage of workers' compensation laws, it was difficult for employees to receive compensation for their work-related injuries or diseases. Group benefits were meager and the Social Security program had not yet been enacted. The only recourse for employees was to sue their employer for damages. In addition to the time and expense of such actions (as well as the possibility of the employee's being fired), the probability of a worker's winning such a suit was small because of the three common-law defenses available to employers. Under the contributory negligence doctrine, a worker could not collect if his or her negligence had contributed in any way to the injury sustained. Under the fellow-servant doctrine, the worker could not collect if his or her injury had resulted from the negligence of a fellow worker. And finally, under the assumption-of-risk doctrine, a worker could not collect if he or she had knowingly assumed the risks inherent in the job.

workers' compensation law

To help solve the problem of uncompensated injuries, *workers' compensation laws*—a form of both social insurance and employers' liability insurance—were enacted to require employers to provide benefits to employees for losses resulting from work-related accidents or diseases. These laws are based on the principle of liability without fault. Essentially, an employer is absolutely liable for providing the benefits prescribed by the workers' compensation laws, regardless of whether the employer would be considered legally liable in the absence of these laws. Benefits, with the possible exception of medical expense benefits, are subject to statutory maximums.

All states have workers' compensation laws. In addition, the federal government has enacted several similar laws. The Federal Employees Compensation Act provides benefits for the employees of the federal government and the District of Columbia. Other federal acts require benefits for various groups of persons who might be exempt from state workers' compensation laws.

Type of Law

Most workers' compensation laws are compulsory for all employers covered under the law. A few states have elective laws, but the majority of employers do elect coverage. If they do not, their employees are not entitled to workers' compensation benefits and must sue for damages resulting from occupational accidents or diseases. However, the employer loses the right to the three common-law defenses previously described.

Financing Benefits

Most states allow employers to comply with the workers' compensation law by purchasing coverage from insurance companies. Several of these states also have competitive state funds from which employees may obtain coverage, but these funds usually provide benefits for fewer employers than insurance companies do. Five states have monopolistic state funds that are the only source for obtaining coverage under the law. Workers' compensation insurance is discussed further in chapter 19.

Ways to Comply with Workers' Compensation Laws

Depending on the state, the ways to comply with workers' compensation laws include the following:

- Purchase insurance from a private insurance company
- Purchase insurance from a competitive state fund
- Purchase insurance from a monopolistic state fund
- Qualify as a self-insurer

Almost all states, including some with monopolistic state funds, allow employers to self-insure their workers' compensation exposure. These employers must generally post a bond or other security and receive the approval of the agency that administers the law. Although the number of firms using self-insurance for workers' compensation is small, these firms account for approximately one-half of the employees covered under such laws.

In virtually all cases, the employer bears the full cost of providing workers' compensation benefits. Insurance premiums are set at a level that covers both the costs of expected claims and the insurer's sales and administrative expenses and other services. Obviously, if an employer self-insures benefits, the ultimate cost will include the claims paid plus any administrative expenses.

Employers who purchase coverage pay a premium that is calculated as a rate per $100 of payroll, based on the occupations of their workers. For example, rates for office workers may be as low as $.10, and rates for workers in a few hazardous occupations may exceed $50. Most states also require that employers with total workers' compensation premiums above a specified amount be subject to experience rating. That is, the employer's premium is a function of benefits paid for past injuries to the employer's workers. To the extent that savings in workers' compensation premiums offset or eliminate safety costs, experience-rating laws encourage employers to take an active role in correcting conditions that may cause injuries.

Covered Occupations

Although it is estimated that about 90 percent of the workers in the United States are protected by workers' compensation laws, the percentage varies among the states from less than 70 percent to more than 95 percent. Many laws exclude certain agricultural, domestic, and casual employees. Some laws also exclude employers with a small number of employees. Furthermore, coverage for employees of state and local governments is not universal.

Eligibility

Before an employee can be eligible for benefits under a workers' compensation law, he or she must work in an occupation covered by that law and be disabled or killed by a covered injury or illness. The typical workers' compensation law provides coverage for accidental occupational injuries (including death) arising out of and in the course of employment. In all states, this includes injuries arising out of accidents, which are generally defined as sudden and unexpected events that are definite in time and place. Every state has some coverage for illnesses resulting from occupational diseases. Although the trend is toward full coverage for occupational diseases, some states cover only those diseases that are specifically listed in the law.

Benefits

Workers' compensation laws typically provide four types of benefits: medical care, disability income, death benefits, and rehabilitation benefits.

Medical Care. Benefits for medical expenses are usually provided without any limitations on time or amount. They are not subject to a waiting period.

Disability Income. Disability income benefits are payable for both total and partial disabilities. It does not matter whether a disability is temporary or permanent.

Most workers' compensation laws have a waiting period for disability income benefits that varies from 2 to 7 days. Benefits in many states are paid retroactively to the date of the injury if an employee is disabled for a specified period of time or is confined to a hospital.

Disability income benefits under workers' compensation laws are a function of an employee's average weekly wage over some time period, commonly the 13 weeks immediately preceding the disability. For total disabilities, benefits are a percentage (usually 66 2/3 percent) of the employee's average weekly wage, subject to maximum and minimum amounts that vary substantially by state. Benefits for temporary total disabilities continue until an employee returns to work; benefits for permanent total disabilities usually continue for life but have a limited duration (such as 10 years) in a few states.

Benefits for partial disabilities are calculated as a percentage of the difference between the employee's wages before and after the disability. In most states, the duration of these benefits is subject to a statutory maximum. Several states also provide lump-sum payments to employees whose permanent partial disabilities involve the loss (or loss of use) of an eye, an arm, or other body part. These benefits, determined by a schedule in the law, may be in lieu of or in addition to periodic disability income benefits.

Death Benefits. Most workers' compensation laws provide two types of death benefits: burial allowances and cash income payments to survivors.

Burial allowances are a flat amount in each state and vary from $300 to $5,000; benefits of $1,000 and $1,500 are common.

Cash income payments to survivors, like disability income benefits, are a function of the worker's average wage prior to the injury resulting in death. Benefits are usually paid only to a surviving spouse and children under 18. Some states require employees to pay benefits until the spouse dies or remarries and all children reach 18. Other states require benefits for a maximum time, such as 10 years, or until a maximum dollar amount has been paid, such as $50,000.

Rehabilitation Benefits. All states have provisions in their workers' compensation laws for rehabilitative services for disabled workers. Benefits are included for medical rehabilitation as well as for vocational rehabilitation, including training, counseling, and job placement.

Federal Taxation of Other Social Insurance Benefits

Unemployment insurance benefits are included in a recipient's gross income. Workers' compensation benefits are received free of income taxation.

Benefits received under temporary disability laws must be included in gross income. However, disabled persons with gross incomes below a specified level may be eligible for a federal tax credit. In jurisdictions where unemployed persons can also receive disability income benefits, any benefits paid to them are considered unemployment insurance benefits and taxed accordingly.

SOURCES FOR FURTHER IN-DEPTH STUDY

- *Social Security Manual*, Erlanger, KY: The National Underwriter Company (updated annually). Phone 800-543-0874. Web site address www.nuco.com
- Rejda, George E., *Social Insurance and Economic Security,* 6th ed., Englewood Cliffs, NJ: Prentice-Hall, Inc., 1999. Phone 800-282-0693. Web site address www.prenhall.com
- Social Security Administration. Web site address www.ssa.gov
- Centers for Medicare & Medicaid Services. Web site address www.cms.gov
- Department of Labor for information on unemployment insurance. Web site address www.dol.gov

CHAPTER REVIEW

Answers to review questions and self-test questions start on page 793.

Key Terms

OASDHI	Medicare Part B
fully insured	original Medicare
currently insured	Medicare Advantage
disability insured	Medicare Part D
full retirement age	formulary
primary insurance amount (PIA)	partial advance funding
earnings test	unemployment insurance
Social Security Statement	temporary disability law
Medicare Part A	workers' compensation law

Review Questions

7-1. How are the Social Security and Medicare programs financed?

7-2. As of this year, Evelyn Grey, aged 37, had 28 credits under Social Security. She earned 24 of these credits prior to the birth of her first child 11 years ago. She has earned four credits since she reentered the labor force one year ago.
   a. Is Grey fully insured? Explain.
   b. Is Grey currently insured? Explain.
   c. Is Grey disability insured? Explain.

7-3. Describe the retirement benefits available under Social Security.

7-4. What categories of persons are eligible for Social Security survivors benefits?

7-5. a. What is the definition of disability under Social Security?
   b. What categories of persons may be eligible for disability benefits?

7-6. a. Explain the relationship between a worker's PIA and the benefits available for dependents and survivors.
   b. What happens if the total benefits for a family exceed the maximum family benefit?

7-7. Explain how a worker's retirement benefits under Social Security are affected if that person elects early or delayed retirement.

7-8. Describe the earnings test applicable to the Social Security program.

7-9. Describe the automatic cost-of-living adjustment provision under Social Security as it relates to benefit amounts.

7-10.   With respect to Part A of Medicare:
  a.   Describe the types of benefits that are available.
  b.   Explain the extent to which deductibles and copayments are required.
  c.   Identify the major exclusions.

7-11.   With respect to Part B of Medicare:
  a.   Describe the types of benefits that are available.
  b.   Explain the extent to which copayments are required.
  c.   Identify the major exclusions.

7-12.   How does Medicare Advantage increase the options available to Medicare beneficiaries for obtaining medical expense coverage?

7-13.   Describe the prescription drug coverage that will be available under Part D of Medicare with respect to each of the following:
  a.   eligibility and cost
  b.   covered drugs
  c.   benefits
  d.   employer incentives

7-14.   a.   What is the nature of the Social Security and Medicare trust funds?
  b.   Identify possible actions that can better ensure the adequacy of these trust funds.

7-15.   Explain the extent to which Social Security benefits are taxed to recipients.

7-16.   a.   What are the objectives of unemployment insurance?
  b.   How is the program financed?
  c.   How is benefit eligibility determined?

7-17.   What is the nature of temporary disability laws?

7-18.   a.   What is the purpose of workers' compensation insurance?
  b.   What types and amounts of benefits are available?

7-19.   Explain the extent, if any, to which benefits from unemployment insurance, temporary disability insurance programs, and workers' compensation insurance are included in a recipient's gross income for federal income tax purposes.

Self-Test Questions

T   F   7-1.   A person is fully insured under Social Security if he or she has 40 credits.

T   F   7-2.   A person born in 1962 will be eligible to receive full Social Security retirement benefits when he or she reaches age 65.

T   F   7-3.   The definition of disability under Social Security is very rigid.

T   F   7-4.   The primary insurance amount is the amount of the Social Security benefit a worker will receive if he or she retires at full retirement age or becomes disabled.

T   F   7-5.   A family will usually reach the maximum benefit under Social Security if three or more family members are eligible for benefits.

T   F   7-6.   If a person continues to work during the period of delayed retirement, it is possible for a worker's primary insurance amount to be higher than it would have been at full retirement age.

T   F   7-7.   There is a reduction in Social Security benefits under the earnings test for a 72-year-old person who goes back to work and earns $40,000 annually.

T   F   7-8.   Part A, the hospital portion of Medicare, is available to any person aged 65 or older who is entitled to monthly retirement benefits under Social Security.

T   F   7-9.   Part A of Medicare pays for inpatient hospital services for up to 365 days for an uninterrupted stay in a hospital.

T   F   7-10.   A Medicare beneficiary who was released last week from the hospital but is going back after 7 days will start a new benefit period for Part A purposes.

T   F   7-11.   Part A of Medicare provides benefits for home health care.

T   F   7-12.   Part B of Medicare pays for prostate cancer screening and certain other preventive care.

T   F   7-13.   Subject to dollar maximums, Part B of Medicare provides benefits for eyeglasses, hearing aids, and orthopedic shoes.

T   F   7-14.   By electing a Medicare Advantage plan, a Medicare beneficiary may have more comprehensive benefits than those provided by original Medicare.

T   F   7-15.   Medicare Part D (prescription drug coverage) is a mandatory benefit financed by additional FICA taxes.

T   F   7-16.   Medicare Part D will pay 90 percent of prescription drug costs after a beneficiary satisfies a $500 deductible.

T   F   7-17.   Social Security and Medicare are based on a system of funding that the Social Security Administration refers to as partial advance funding.

T   F   7-18.   Unemployment insurance is intended to provide short-term benefits (typically 26 weeks) to workers who lose their jobs.

T   F   7-19.   Workers' compensation laws are based on the principle of liability without fault.

T   F   7-20.   In virtually all cases, employees must bear the full cost of providing workers' compensation benefits.

T   F   7-21.   Workers' compensation benefits are included in a recipient's gross income for income tax purposes.

8

Introduction to Life Insurance

Learning Objectives

An understanding of the material in this chapter should enable the student to

8-1. Identify the family and business purposes of life insurance.

8-2. Explain the methods of providing life insurance protection.

8-3. Describe the three traditional types of life insurance.

8-4. Describe variations on the traditional types of life insurance.

8-5. Describe the life insurance provided by employers and other types of groups.

Chapter Outline

A human life possesses many values, most of them irreplaceable and not conducive to measurement. These values are founded on religious, relational, and societal bases. From a religious standpoint, for example, human life is regarded as immortal and endowed with a value beyond the comprehension of mortal man. In a person's relationship with other human beings, a set of emotional and sentimental attachments is created that cannot be measured in monetary terms or supplanted by material things. A human may be capable of artistic achievements that contribute in a unique way to the culture of a society.

Although not oblivious to these values—in fact, life insurance has strong moral and social overtones—these values are not the foundation of life insurance. Chapter 6 explained that life insurance is a valued contract and not a contract of indemnity. When an insured dies, life insurance does not pay whatever that person was worth. Still, life insurance is directly concerned with the economic value of a human life. A person's *human life value* is derived from earning capacity and the financial dependence of other lives on that earning capacity. More precisely, a person's human life value can be measured in terms of the present value of that portion of estimated future earnings, which, if he or she lives long enough to achieve all of the earnings, will be used to support dependents. Financial planners must be able to apply the concept of human life value in order to identify appropriate ways to meet their clients' insurance needs.

human life value

Example: Vance is a 30-year-old male whose estimated average earnings will be $50,000 per year until he retires at age 65. If we assume that one-half his income will be used to support dependents, his economic value to dependents is $25,000 per year for 35 years or $875,000 ($25,000 x 35 = $875,000). However, at age 30 his human life value is not this $875,000 total, but the present value of a stream of income in the amount of $25,000 for 30 years. Using a rate of 6 percent compound interest, the present value of this cash flow is calculated at $362,456.

Stated differently, if Vance's dependents had $362,456 today and invested it at 6 percent compound interest, they could withdraw $25,000 per year for the next 30 years before running out of money. Based on these assumptions, Vance's current human life value is $362,456.

Although this simple example illustrates the human life value concept that equates the value of a person's life with the income stream that person generates, the human life value concept has many obvious flaws that limit its usefulness as a financial planning tool. Perhaps most obvious is the assumption that income will be level over a number of years. Later discussions in chapter 10 show how this basic concept can be refined.

Because the human life value may arise out of either a family or a business relationship, we will begin the discussion of life insurance by looking at its purposes for families and businesses. The chapter continues with an analysis of the basic methods of providing life insurance protection. The focus of the chapter then turns to the types of individual life insurance policies. First, the three traditional types of life insurance (term insurance, whole life insurance, and endowment policies) are discussed. Then the chapter looks at some of the newer variations of life insurance policies: current assumption whole life insurance, variable life insurance, universal life insurance, variable universal life insurance, and joint-life insurance. The final section of the chapter is devoted to group insurance, a marketing variation of some types of life insurance previously mentioned.

PURPOSES OF LIFE INSURANCE

In terms of earning capacity, a human life may be worth millions of dollars. Yet earning power alone does not create an economic value that can logically serve as the basis of life insurance. A human life has an economic value only if some other person or organization can expect to derive pecuniary advantage through its existence. If an individual is without dependents and no other person or organization stands to profit through his or her living either now or in the future, then that life, for all practical purposes, has no monetary value that needs to be perpetuated. Such an individual is rare. Most income producers either have dependents or can expect to acquire them in the normal course of events. Even income earners with no family dependents often provide financial support to charitable organizations. In either case, a basis exists for insurance.

Preservation of Family's Economic Security

In many cases, an income producer's family is completely dependent on his or her personal earnings for subsistence and the amenities of life. In other words, the "potential" estate is far more substantial than the existing estate—the savings that the family has accumulated. If he or she lives and stays in good health, the income earner will eventually realize his or her total income potential, to the benefit of the family and others who derive financial gain from such efforts. When an income earner dies, the unrealized portion of his or her total earnings potential is lost, and in the absence of other measures, the family might soon find itself destitute or reduced to a lower standard of living.

Life insurance contracts can create a fund at death to partially or fully offset the lost income of the insured. Life insurance enables the income earner to leave the family in the same economic position that they would have enjoyed had the decedent lived.

Obligation to Provide Protection

Most people assume major responsibility for the support and maintenance of their dependents during their lifetimes. In fact, they consider providing for their families to be one of the rewarding experiences of life. Additionally, the law attaches a legal obligation to the support of a spouse and children. Thus, if there is a divorce or legal separation, the court will normally decree support payments for dependent children and possibly alimony for the dependent spouse. In some cases, these payments, including alimony, continue beyond the provider's death if the children are still dependent or if the former spouse has not remarried.[1] Nevertheless, it takes a high order of responsibility for a parent to voluntarily provide for continuation of income to dependents after his or her own death. It virtually always involves a reduction in the individual's current standard of living. Yet most would agree that any person with a dependent spouse, children, or parents has a moral obligation to provide them with the protection afforded by life insurance, to the extent that his or her financial means permit.

Business Purposes of Life Insurance

Life insurance also serves a wide variety of purposes in the business world. The primary purposes of life insurance in business are key person indemnification, business continuation, and protection for employees and executives. Business applications are discussed in chapter 10. Group life insurance coverage for employees is discussed later in this chapter.

METHODS TO PROVIDE LIFE INSURANCE PROTECTION

There are two basic approaches to life insurance:

- term insurance, which is temporary
- cash value insurance, which is permanent protection that builds up a reserve or savings component.

A financial planner who invests the effort required to understand these two fundamental approaches will also recognize the answers to the questions likely to perplex clients, such as:

- Why is term insurance only temporary?
- How can an insurer provide permanent life insurance protection?
- What is the source of life insurance policy reserves?

In addition to the distinction between term insurance and permanent insurance, life insurance can also be categorized on the basis of whether premium levels are guaranteed throughout the premium-paying period or whether either the policyowner or the insurer has some flexibility as to the amount of premium to be paid. Several of the newer, nontraditional types of policies described later in this chapter have a degree of flexibility in their premiums.

Term Insurance Approach

yearly renewable term insurance

Term insurance is the simplest form of insurance that life insurance companies offer. *Yearly renewable term insurance* provides protection for a period of one year only but permits the policyowner to renew the policy for successive periods of one year without furnishing a medical examination or other evidence of insurability. Term insurance can also be written for longer periods such as 5 or 10 years. In all cases, however, the right to renew is usually limited to a specified period or to a specified age. If the insured dies while the term policy is in force, the face amount is paid to the designated beneficiary. If the insured does not die during the period of protection, no benefits are payable at the expiration of the policy or on the insured's subsequent death.

To clarify the term insurance approach, the following discussion deals only with the net premium and does not include the insurer's operating expenses. The net premium for term insurance is determined by the death rate for the attained age of the individual involved. Subject to minor exceptions, the death rate increases with age, so the term insurance policy's net premium needed to pay death claims increases at the start of each new term. Moreover, because death rates rise at an increasing rate as ages increase, the net premium also rises at an increasing rate, much like a flight of steps with successively higher risers.

If the surviving members of the insured group continue to renew their term insurance, the steadily rising premiums necessary to cover death claims become increasingly unaffordable. As premiums increase, healthy individuals will tend to give up their protection, while those in poor health may sacrifice to renew their policies, regardless of cost. This is a type of adverse selection, a concept discussed in earlier chapters. The withdrawal of the healthy members accelerates the increase in the death rate among the continuing members, and it can produce death claims in excess of premiums unless the insurance company's net premium rates provide ample margins. An insurer cannot adjust its rates if they prove to be inadequate, because the rates at which the policy can be renewed are usually guaranteed for the entire period of renewability. For these reasons, companies that offer term insurance on an individual basis limit the time during which the insurance can be renewed, such as up to age 65.

At older ages, the premium rates for term insurance are extremely high. However, many individuals need coverage that extends throughout their lifetime. This need led to the development of cash value or permanent life insurance.

Cash Value Approach

cash value life insurance

Cash value life insurance is just what the name implies—an approach to insurance under which premiums are sufficient not only to pay the insurer's mortality costs (death claims) and expenses but also to build a savings fund (or cash value) within the policy. That savings fund's growth depends in part on the premiums paid, and it is designed to result in the fund's equaling the face amount of the policy by the last age shown in the mortality table, such as age 100.

In many cash value policies, the annual premium does not increase from year to year but remains level throughout the premium-paying period. This does not mean that the policyowner must pay premiums as long as insurance protection is in force, but only that all required premiums will be the same amount.

As previously mentioned, net premiums tend to rise as a result of increasing death rates. If those premiums are leveled out, those paid in the early years of the contract must be more than sufficient to meet current death claims, while those paid in the later years generally will be less than adequate to meet incurred claims. This is a simple but significant concept in the practice of life insurance.

reserve

In cash value life insurance, the net premiums beyond those needed for death claims in the early years of the contract create an accumulation that is held in trust[2] by the insurance company for the benefit of, and to the credit of, the policyowners. This accumulation, called a *reserve*, is an amount that the insurance company must accumulate and maintain to meet definite future obligations. The manner in which the fund is to be accumulated and invested is strictly regulated by law, and the fund is usually referred to as the *legal reserve*. Technically, the reserve is a liability account on the insurer's balance sheet. The reserve is not allocated to individual policies, but it may be viewed as an aggregate of individual savings accounts established for the benefit of the policyowners.[3]

Figure 8-1 compares the net level premium for a type of cash value policy known as whole life with the net premium that would be required for a yearly renewable term policy. The age of issue in both cases is 25.

Assume that an annual net level premium of $6.09 per $1,000 of insurance is paid for the whole life policy as long as the insured lives. This premium is the actuarial equivalent of a series of increasing net premiums on the yearly renewable term basis, ranging from $1.16 per $1,000 of insurance at age 25 to $956.94 at age 99.

The mortality table used in this example assumes that everyone who survives to age 99 will die during the following year, producing a net premium

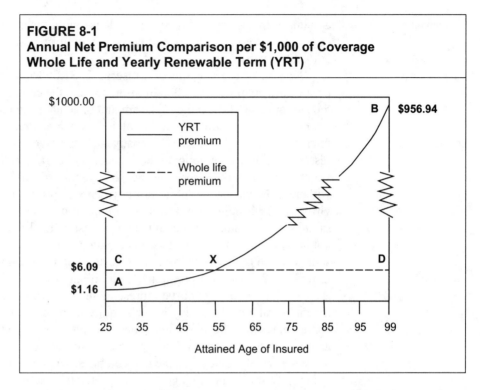

FIGURE 8-1
Annual Net Premium Comparison per $1,000 of Coverage
Whole Life and Yearly Renewable Term (YRT)

at age 99 on the yearly renewable term basis equal to the $1,000 face of the policy, less the interest earned on the premium during the year.

In figure 8-1, line CD, the net level premium for the whole life policy, bisects the curve AB, the rising net premiums for the term policy, between the ages of 53 and 54. The disparity between the areas bounded by AXC and BXD shows that excess net premiums (AXC) in the early years of a whole life contract (or, for that matter, any type of insurance contract except term) will offset the deficiency in the net premiums of the later years when the term insurance net premium is in the hundreds of dollars. In addition, with the aid of compound interest, the excess premium will accumulate a reserve equal to the face of the policy by the time the insured reaches the terminal age in the mortality table. In contrast, the yearly renewable term contract will have no reserve at the expiration of the contract. The risk (possibility of death) under a contract that provides protection for the whole of life is one "converging into a certainty," while the risk under a yearly renewable term policy (except for the final year in the mortality table) is a mere contingency—one that may or may not occur. A permanent or cash value life insurance contract must provide for a death claim that is certain to occur, the only uncertainty being the time of its occurrence.

Under a cash value contract, the accumulated reserve becomes part of the face amount payable at the insured's death. From the standpoint of the insurance company, the effective amount of insurance is the difference between the face

net amount at risk

amount of the policy and the reserve. This amount is called the *net amount at risk*. As the reserve increases, the net amount at risk decreases if the face amount remains constant.

Because of the accumulated reserve, a $1,000 permanent life insurance policy does not provide $1,000 of insurance and the company is not "at risk" for the face amount of the policy. The amount of actual insurance is always the face amount, less the policyowner's total excess net premium payments, plus interest. From the insurance company's perspective, the accumulation is the reserve, and from the policyowner's perspective, it is the cash value, which is slightly less than the reserve in the early years. Because the policyowner can withdraw the excess net premium payments in the form of the cash value at virtually any time, these excess net premium payments can be regarded as a savings or accumulation account. Thus, a cash value life insurance policy does not provide pure insurance but a combination of protection and cash values, the sum of which is always equal to the face amount of the policy. This is illustrated in figure 8-2 for a level-premium whole life policy of $1,000 issued at age 25.

The area below the curve represents the reserve under the contract or, as mentioned above, the policyowner's equity in the contract. The area above the curve represents the company's net amount at risk and the policyowner's amount of protection. As the reserve increases, the amount of protection decreases. At any given age, the two combined will equal the face amount of the policy. By the insured's age 95, the protection element of the contract has

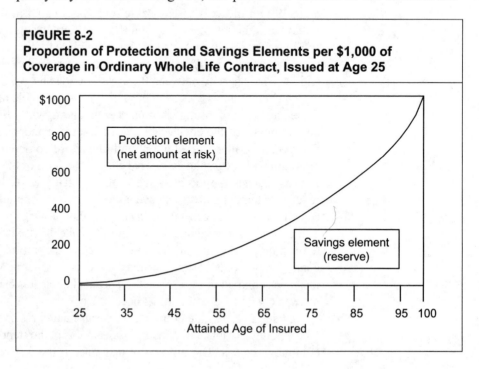

FIGURE 8-2
Proportion of Protection and Savings Elements per $1,000 of Coverage in Ordinary Whole Life Contract, Issued at Age 25

become relatively minor, and by age 100—frequently, the end of the contract—it has completely disappeared. At age 100, the policyowner will receive $1,000, composed entirely of the policy's cash value element.

This combination of protection and accumulated cash values is characteristic of all permanent life insurance. Fundamentally, one contract differs from another only by the proportions in which they combine the two elements.

Yearly renewable term insurance is all protection with no cash value, while single premium life insurance is at the other end of the spectrum, with the highest cash values and the lowest net amount at risk. Accumulated cash values should be thought of as a degree of prefunding. Single premium policies are fully prefunded, and lower premium policies that develop cash values are only partially prefunded. The shorter the premium-paying period, the higher the relative proportion of cash value to death benefit.

Nearly all operations of a life insurance company feel the effect of the cash value or permanent life insurance plan. The reserve accounts for a major portion of the aggregate assets of life insurance companies. The need to invest funds presents the life insurance institution with a challenge, but also enables it to materially contribute to economic expansion. The cash value makes the life insurance contract one of the most flexible and valuable contracts in existence, and one of the most acceptable forms of collateral for credit purposes. The cash value or permanent life insurance plan is most significant because it is the only practical arrangement to provide insurance protection for an individual's entire life span, without the possibility that the cost will become prohibitive.

Effect of the Cash Value

- Serves as a major source of an insurer's investable funds
- Adds to the flexibility of the life insurance policy
- Is useful as collateral for credit purposes
- Makes permanent death protection possible

Guaranteed Premiums

In most types of life insurance policies, the periodic premiums to be paid throughout the premium-paying period of coverage are known in advance and guaranteed by the insurance company. However, these premiums are not necessarily level over time. For example, in a yearly renewable term policy, the annual premium increases are usually guaranteed by the insurer at the issue of the contract. A similar guarantee is provided with respect to the renewal premiums for 5-year, 10-year, and other renewable term policies. Even in cash value policies, the annual premiums can be both nonlevel and guaranteed. For

modified whole life insurance

example, *modified whole life insurance* guarantees a level premium for the first few policy years, with a higher guaranteed level premium thereafter.

Flexible Premiums

In several types of life insurance policies, some of which are described later in this chapter, the premium is flexible, at the option of either the policyowner or the insurance company. For example:

reentry term insurance

- In *reentry term insurance,* the insurer uses one schedule of renewal premiums if the insured can prove his or her continuing insurability and a higher schedule of renewal premiums if the insured's health has declined so that he or she no longer qualifies for the lower rate.
- In universal life insurance—a cash value, permanent type of policy discussed in more detail later in this chapter—the policyowner can elect to pay, within limits, more or less than the target premium established at the issue of the contract.
- In current assumption whole life insurance, discussed in detail later, the insurer periodically redetermines the premium, based on experience and assumptions for mortality, expenses, and interest.

Flexible premiums naturally affect the cash value of permanent insurance. The modified premium of the universal life policy, or the redetermined premium of the current assumption whole life policy, influence the growth of the policy's savings element.

TRADITIONAL TYPES OF LIFE INSURANCE

There are three traditional types of life insurance:

- term insurance
- whole life insurance
- endowments

Term Insurance

As described earlier, term insurance provides life insurance protection for a limited period only. The face amount of the policy is payable if the insured dies during the specified period, and the insurer pays nothing if the insured survives.

Like most property and liability insurance contracts, term insurance provides temporary insurance. A person who buys a one-year property insurance policy pays for one year of insurance coverage. The insurer pays for any covered claims that occur during that year. At the conclusion of that one-year period, the insurer has no further obligation unless the policy is renewed for another year. Likewise, if a person insures his or her life under a 5-year term contract, no obligation is incurred by the insurance company unless the death of the insured occurs within the term. The company considers all premiums paid for the term protection to be fully earned by the end of the term, whether or not a loss has occurred, and the policy has no further value.

The premium for term insurance is initially relatively low, even though it includes a relatively high expense loading and an allowance for adverse selection. Premiums can be low because most term contracts do not cover the period of old age when death is most probable and the pure cost of insurance is high.

Renewability

Many term insurance contracts contain an option to renew for a limited number of additional periods of term insurance, usually of the same length. The simplest policy of this type is the yearly renewable term policy, which is a one-year term contract renewable for successive periods of one year each. Longer term contracts, such as 10-year term, may also be renewable.

renewability
Renewability refers to the right to renew the contract without a medical examination or other evidence of insurability. When the term policy contains no renewal privilege, or when it can be renewed only upon evidence of insurability satisfactory to the company, the insured may find that he or she cannot continue coverage as long as needed. Because of poor health, a hazardous occupation, or some other reason, the insured might be unable to secure a renewal of the contract or to obtain any other form of life insurance. The renewal feature protects the insurability of the insured.

Under a term insurance policy, the premium increases with each renewal and is based on the insured's attained age at the time of the renewal. Within each contract period, however, the premium is level. The schedule of renewal rates is included in the original contract, and the company cannot change these rates while the contract remains in force. As a safeguard against adverse selection, companies historically did not permit renewals beyond a specified age such as 65. Renewals that continue the coverage to later ages are now commonly available.

Convertibility

convertibility
A term policy might be convertible, permitting the policyowner to convert, or exchange, the term contract for permanent insurance within a specified time frame, without evidence of insurability. This *convertibility* feature serves the needs of those who want permanent insurance but are temporarily unable to afford the higher premiums that whole life and other types of cash value life insurance require. Convertibility is also useful when the policyowner desires to postpone the final decision as to the type of permanent insurance until a later date when, for some reason, it may be possible to make a more informed choice.

Attained Age versus Retroactive Conversion

- Attained age method: New premium is based on insured's age at time of conversion; policy form is one that the insurer issues at that time.
- Retroactive (original age) method: New premium is based on the insured's age when the term insurance was first taken out; policyowner must make a lump-sum payment equal to the difference in the reserves or premiums plus interest on the old and new policies; policy form is one that the insurer issued when the term insurance was first taken out.

Thus, convertible term insurance provides a way to obtain temporary insurance with the option to purchase permanent insurance.

The conversion from term to permanent insurance may be effective as of the date of the conversion or as of the original date of the term policy. If the term policy is converted as of the current date, conversion is usually referred to as the *attained age method* because the current age determines the premium rate. A conversion using the original date of the term policy is referred to as the *original age method* or a *retroactive conversion*. When the conversion is effective as of the original date, the premium rate for the permanent contract is that which would have been paid had the new contract been taken out originally, and the policy form is that which would have been issued originally. The advantage of the lower premium is obvious, but in many cases, the contract issued at the original date contains actuarial assumptions or other features that are more favorable than those incorporated in current policies.

Offsetting the advantages of the original age method, however, is the financial adjustment—a payment by the policyowner to the company—which may be quite substantial if the term policy has been in force for several years. The financial adjustment can be computed on a variety of bases, but many companies specify that the payment will be the larger of (1) the difference in the reserves under the policies being exchanged or (2) the difference in the premiums paid on the term policy and those that would have been paid on the permanent plan, with interest on the difference at a stipulated rate. The purpose of the financial adjustment, regardless of how it is computed, is to place the insurance company in the same financial position in which it would have been had the permanent contract been originally issued.

Nonlevel Term Insurance

The preceding discussion has presumed that the amount of insurance is level or uniform throughout the term of the policy. The amount of insurance, however, may increase or decrease throughout the period of protection. As a matter of fact,

decreasing term insurance

a substantial—if not predominant—portion of term insurance provides systematic decreases in the amount of insurance from year to year. This type of term insurance, appropriately called *decreasing term insurance*, may be written as a separate contract, as a rider to a new or existing contract, or as an integral part of a combination contract. Decreasing term insurance is often used to provide the funds necessary to pay off a mortgage loan if the insured dies.

Example:	Jonathan, aged 34, and his wife Laura, aged 30, buy a house with the aid of a 20-year $200,000 mortgage. Jonathan is the primary breadwinner, and they qualified for the mortgage based on his salary. They plan to begin a family, and it would be unmanageable for Laura to be burdened with the mortgage payments if Jonathan dies. To address this specific need, Jonathan purchases a 20-year decreasing term insurance policy.

Increasing term insurance can be provided on a year-to-year basis through the operation of a common provision in cash value life insurance policies, referred to as the *fifth dividend option*, discussed further in chapter 9. Increasing term insurance can help meet families' needs for the death benefit to increase with inflation or salary increases, and it also has business applications. These concepts are discussed in chapter 10.

Term Insurance

- Protection during the term of the policy (for example, one year, 5 years)
- Premium that covers current mortality and expenses (no cash value)
- Renewability
  - "Renewable term," which may be renewed for subsequent terms, without evidence of insurability, at a higher premium
    - Premium based on attained age
    - Becomes expensive at higher ages
    - Common to have age limit—for example, 65, on renewals
  - Level premium for each term
- Convertibility (option to convert to permanent insurance)
  - Attained age—premium based on age at conversion
  - Retroactive (original) age—lump-sum catch-up premium
- Nonlevel term
  - Decreasing term (for example, to pay off mortgage)
  - Increasing term

Areas of Usefulness

Term insurance is suitable when either (1) the need for protection is purely temporary, or (2) the need for protection is permanent, but the policyowner temporarily cannot afford the premiums for permanent insurance. In the first case, term insurance is the complete answer, but it should be renewable in the event that the temporary need extends over a longer period than originally anticipated. The second case requires that the policy be convertible. The conversion privilege spans the gap between the need for permanent insurance and the financial ability to meet the need. Thus, the renewable and convertible features serve quite different functions and, ideally, should be incorporated in all term policies.

Whole Life Insurance

whole life insurance

In contrast with term insurance, which pays benefits only if the insured dies during a specified period of years, *whole life insurance* provides for the payment of the policy's face amount at the death of the insured, regardless of when death occurs. This characteristic—protection for the whole of life—gives the insurance its name. The expression has no reference to the manner in which the premiums are paid, only to the duration of the protection:

- *Ordinary life* premiums are paid throughout the insured's lifetime.
- *Limited-payment life* premiums are paid only during a specified period.

Characteristics of Whole Life Insurance

Whole life insurance has the following characteristics:

- It offers permanent protection.
- It accumulates a cash value.
- A policy can be either participating or nonparticipating.

As explained later in this section, a participating policy may pay a dividend. It is called a participating policy, because the policy enables the policyowner to *participate* in the insurance company's favorable experience.

Permanent Protection. The protection the whole life contract affords is permanent—the term never expires, and the policy never has to be renewed or converted. If policyowners continue to pay premiums or pay up their policies, they have protection for as long as they live, regardless of their health; eventually, the face amount of the policy will be paid. This is a valuable right because virtually all people need some insurance as long as they live, if only to pay for last-illness and funeral expenses.

In one sense, whole life can be regarded as an endowment. As discussed later in this chapter, an endowment insurance contract pays the face amount of the policy, whether the insured dies prior to the endowment maturity date or survives to the end of the period. If age 100 is considered to be the end of the endowment period—as well as the terminal age in the mortality table—then a whole life policy is equivalent to an endowment contract that pays the face amount as a death claim if the insured dies before age 100 or as a matured endowment if he or she survives to age 100.

Cash Value or Accumulation Element. As level premium permanent insurance, whole life insurance accumulates a reserve that gradually reaches a substantial level and eventually equals the face amount of the policy. The contract emphasizes protection, but it also accumulates a cash value that can be used to accomplish a variety of purposes.

Cash values are not generally available during the first year or two of the insurance contract because of the insurer's cost of putting the business on the books. Common exceptions are single-premium policies and some durations of limited-payment whole life policies where initial premiums exceed all first-year expenses incurred to create the policy and maintain policy reserves. The cash values that accumulate under whole life insurance can be utilized as cash surrender values, paid-up insurance, or extended term insurance. These nonforfeiture options are discussed in chapter 9 along with options available for borrowing cash values.

nonparticipating policy

participating policy

Participating versus Nonparticipating. Whole life policies can be issued as *nonparticipating* or *non-dividend-paying policies*. Historically, nonparticipating policies were associated with stock life insurance companies. The insurance company retains all gains from favorable experience for its shareholders.

Whole life policies issued as *participating policies* anticipate charging a small extra margin in the fixed premium with the intention of returning part of the premium later in the form of policyowner dividends. This approach allows the insurance company to maintain a stronger contingency margin and still adjust the cost to policyowners downward after periods of coverage have been evaluated. Policyowner dividends are based on favorable experience such as higher-than-expected investment returns or lower-than-expected mortality and/or expenses for operations.

Although participating policies were originally offered by mutual life insurers, the appeal of policyowner dividends prompted stock life insurance companies to offer participating policies. Many stock life insurance companies offer a choice of both participating and nonparticipating policies. Almost all policies mutual companies sell are participating policies.

Policyowner dividends are generally declared annually, based on the insurance company's experience. Investment results usually account for the largest portion of dividends. The amount of dividends cannot be guaranteed, and it is illegal for an agent to present projections of future dividends as if they were guaranteed or certain. If insurance company experience turns unfavorable, policyowner dividends may decline, or they may cease altogether. The policy-owner chooses among the dividend options for the use of his or her dividends, as discussed in the next chapter.

Types of Whole Life Insurance

There are two types of whole life insurance: ordinary life insurance and limited-payment life insurance.

ordinary life insurance

Ordinary Life Insurance. As mentioned earlier, *ordinary life insurance* (also called continuous premium whole life) is a type of whole life insurance with premiums that are assumed to be paid until the insured's death. It is desirable to define ordinary life insurance in this way because, in an increasing number of cases, policyowners purchase life insurance without intending to pay premiums for the life of the insured. In many cases, they purchase the insurance with the intention of using dividends to pay up the insurance prior to the life expectancy of the insured. In other cases, the plan may be to eventually surrender the insurance for an annuity or for a reduced amount of paid-up insurance. Ordinary life should not be envisioned as insurance on which the policyowner must pay premiums for a lifetime, or even into the insured's extreme old age. Rather, it should be viewed as a contract that provides permanent protection for the lowest total premium outlay and some flexibility to meet changing needs and circumstances for both long-lived persons and those with average-duration lifetimes. Ordinary life is the most basic lifelong coverage any life insurance company offers.

Calculating the premium rate for an ordinary life contract assuming that premiums will be payable throughout the insured's life produces the lowest premium rate for any type of whole life policy. Naturally, the longer the period over which the premium payment is spread, the lower each periodic premium will be. However, lower premiums also result in lower cash values than other types of whole life policies. Nevertheless, many financial advisors believe that the ordinary life contract offers the optimal combination of protection and savings.

Limited-payment insurance contracts provide benefits that justify the higher premium rates. If, however, the policyowner's objective is to secure the maximum amount of permanent insurance protection per dollar of premium outlay, then an ordinary life contract will best serve his or her purposes. Its moderate cost can bring the policy within reach of most purchasers except those in the older age brackets.

limited-payment life insurance

Limited-Payment Life Insurance. *Limited-payment life insurance* is a type of whole life insurance for which premiums are limited by contract to a specified number of years. The extreme end of the limited-payment policies spectrum is the single-premium whole life policy. However, few people can afford the premium or are willing to pay that much in advance.

The limitation in limited-payment policies can be expressed in terms of the number of annual premiums or the age beyond which premiums will not be required. Policies with premiums limited by number usually stipulate one, 5, 7, 10,

15, 20, 25, or 30 annual payments. These policies are usually referred to as, for example, 20-pay life. The greater the number of premiums payable, naturally, the more closely the contract approaches the ordinary life design. For those who prefer to limit their premium payments to a period measured by a terminal age, companies make policies available that are paid up at a specified age—typically, 60, 65, or 70. These policies are often referred to, for example, as life paid up at 65 or more simply, life at 65. The objective of these age-related premium horizons is to confine premium payments to the insured's working years.

Because the value of a limited-payment whole life contract at the date of issue is precisely the same as that of a contract purchased on the ordinary life basis, and it is presumed that there will be fewer premium payments under the limited-payment policy, it follows that each premium must be larger than the comparable premium under an ordinary life contract. Moreover, the fewer the premiums specified or the shorter the premium-paying period, the higher each premium will be. The higher premiums, however, are offset by greater cash and other surrender values. Thus, the limited-payment policy will provide a larger fund for use in an emergency and will accumulate a larger fund for retirement purposes than will an ordinary life contract issued at the same age. On the other hand, if death takes place within the first several years after issuance of the contract, the total premiums paid under the limited-payment policy will exceed those payable under an ordinary life policy. The comparatively long-lived policyowner, however, will pay considerably less in premiums under the limited-payment plan than on the ordinary life basis.

The limited-payment policy contains the same surrender options, dividend options, settlement options, and other features of ordinary life policies.

It is important to differentiate between a limited-payment policy, which guarantees paid-up status at the end of the premium-paying period, and a vanishing premium approach, which uses policyowner dividends to pay all of the premiums as soon as the dividends are adequate to do so. Vanishing premium approaches were popular during the early 1980s when the high interest rates insurers could earn made possible a rapid build-up in cash values. However, dividends are not guaranteed. By the early 1990s, customers who had purchased policies expecting the premiums to vanish found that they had to make continuing premium payments to keep these policies in force. It is important to remember that dividends are not guaranteed and may decline in the future, and if dividends are inadequate to pay the premiums under the vanishing premium approach, the policyowner will have to resume actual premium payments out of pocket or let the policy lapse. There is no guarantee that so-called vanishing premiums will actually vanish or, if they do vanish, that they will never reappear.

Endowment Policies

endowment life insurance

Endowment life insurance policies are a variation of cash value life insurance. They not only provide level death benefits and cash values that increase with duration so that a policy's cash value equals its death benefit at maturity, but they also allow the purchaser to specify the policy's maturity date. Among the wide variety of endowments available are 10-, 15-, 20-, 25-, 30-, 35-, and 40-year endowments (or longer), or the maturity date can be a specific age of the insured such as 55, 65, 70, or older. As mentioned earlier, whole life insurance is identical in design to an endowment at age 100, when the cash value equals the death benefit.

The endowment contract was designed to provide a death benefit during an accumulation period that is equal to the target accumulation amount. Purchasing an endowment policy with a face amount equal to the desired accumulation amount ensures that the funds will be available whether or not the insured survives to the target date. In the past, the policy was popular for policyowners who were beyond the chronological midpoint of their careers and sought accumulation for retirement or other objectives. During the late 1970s and early 1980s, when inflation was in double digits, consumer demand shifted away from long-term fixed-dollar contracts, including nearly all forms of life insurance, particularly endowment policies.

Although endowment contracts were readily available, sales were declining in the United States even before the 1984 federal income tax law change eliminated the tax-advantaged buildup of most endowment policies' cash values. Congress was concerned that life insurance policies (especially endowments) with high cash values relative to their death benefit amounts were being used as tax-advantaged accumulation vehicles by the wealthy.

Since 1984, sales of new endowment contracts have been very limited. Although contracts are still available from a few insurers, most new sales are for

---

Whole Life Insurance

- Permanent protection—never expires if premium is paid
- Level premium—does not increase with age
- Premium in early years that exceeds current mortality and expenses
- Accumulation of cash value
- Participating versus nonparticipating
    - Participating—extra premium returned as dividend
    - Nonparticipating—no dividends
- Ordinary life insurance (continuous premium whole life)—premiums paid until insured's death
    - Lowest premium for permanent insurance
    - Lower cash values than other types
- Limited payment life insurance
    - Premiums paid for a specified number of years or to a specified age
    - Goal—premiums confined to working years

policies used in tax-qualified retirement plans where other factors control the tax treatment.

Outside of the United States, especially in countries with high savings rates, the endowment policy is still quite successful and widely purchased to accumulate funds for a variety of purposes, including to fund retirement or children's higher education.

VARIATIONS OF TRADITIONAL POLICIES

Numerous variations of traditional life insurance policies have been developed in recent years. Some of these are

- current assumption whole life insurance
- variable life insurance
- universal life insurance
- variable universal life insurance
- joint-life insurance

Current Assumption Whole Life Insurance

current assumption whole life insurance

A *current assumption whole life insurance* (CAWL) policy is a whole life policy with a premium charge that varies with changes in the insurer's actual or anticipated mortality, expense, and interest earnings experience. The insurer makes *assumptions* regarding the policy's mortality, investment returns, and expenses. If the insurer's assumptions are accurate, the policy performs as expected. If the insurer's results exceed the assumptions, either the premiums drop, or the cash value or the death benefit increases. The opposite occurs if the insurer's results are worse than it assumed. Whatever the premium charge is at a given time, that premium is a fixed obligation for the policyowner. If the premium is not paid, the policy will lapse after the grace period. CAWL policies are usually issued on a nonparticipating basis.

As each premium is paid, it is added to the policyowner's accumulation account. An expense charge and a mortality charge to cover the policy's share of current death claims are deducted. Also, an interest credit is added to the account. These charges and the credit are based on current mortality, expense, and interest assumptions, subject to a guaranteed maximum charge for mortality and expenses and a guaranteed minimum interest rate credit. The cash surrender value of the policy at any point is equal to the value of the accumulation account minus a surrender charge that gradually reduces to zero after a specified time such as after the first 15 or 20 years of the policy's life.

CAWL policies have been marketed in low-premium and high-premium designs. Both reflect the general features described above.

Low-Premium Design

With the low-premium design, sometimes called interest-sensitive or indeterminate premium whole life, the policyowner initially pays a low-level premium in comparison to that paid for a traditional nonparticipating whole life policy. This premium is guaranteed for the first few (generally 3 or 5) policy years. At the end of the guarantee period, the insurer redetermines the premium required to keep the CAWL policy in force under then-current assumptions, given the amount already available in the accumulation account. Redetermination of the required premium will again occur on specified policy anniversary dates or at specified intervals such as every 5 years.

If, on a particular redetermination date, the premium charge increases because anticipated experience assumptions have worsened, the policyowner has the option of paying the new, higher premium and keeping the policy's death benefit unchanged. Alternatively, he or she may continue to pay the old, lower premium and accept a reduction in the death benefit. If the premium charge is reduced because assumptions have improved, the policyowner may pay the new, lower premium with no change to the death benefit. Alternatively, he or she may elect to continue to pay the old, higher premium with the same death benefit as formerly but with a more rapid buildup of the accumulation account. The policyowner may even have the option, if he or she can provide satisfactory evidence of insurability, to continue to pay the old, higher premium and increase the policy's death benefit. Therefore, with a low-premium CAWL policy, changes in current mortality, expense, and, especially, interest assumptions can affect the policy's premium, cash value, and death benefit.

High-Premium Design

With the high-premium design of CAWL insurance, sometimes called vanishing premium whole life insurance, the policyowner pays a relatively high level premium compared to that of traditional whole life insurance. The high

---

Distinctive Features of Current Assumption Whole Life Insurance

- Usually nonparticipating, but favorable experience may reduce or eliminate premium charges
- Guaranteed maximum premium based on maximum mortality and expense charges and minimum interest rate credit
- Premiums that must be paid when due, or policy lapses
- Low-premium design—premiums redetermined periodically as current conditions warrant
- High-premium design—policy may reach paid-up status for a time, perhaps even permanently

premium charge causes a much more rapid buildup of the accumulation account than would occur in the low-premium design. If the insurer's mortality, expense, and interest results are favorable enough, the accumulation account will grow to an amount that eventually equals or exceeds the net single premium needed to pay up the policy under then-current assumptions. At that time, the policyowner can elect to stop paying premiums. However, unlike a traditional paid-up whole life policy, which guarantees that premiums will never have to be paid again, the CAWL does not guarantee that premiums will not have to be resumed if experience and assumptions worsen sufficiently. Indeed, the CAWL policy does not guarantee that premiums will ever completely vanish.

Variable Life Insurance

variable life insurance

Variable life insurance was the first life insurance policy designed to shift the uncertainty of investment gains or losses to policyowners. This product had a long and expensive gestation period. It not only had to run the gauntlet of state insurance department approvals but it also needed, and finally acquired after many years of negotiations, approval by the Securities and Exchange Commission (SEC).

The premium in a variable life policy is fixed and guaranteed not to increase. A variable life insurance policy provides no guarantee of either interest rate or minimum cash value. Theoretically, the cash value can go down to zero, and if it does, the policy will terminate. As the SEC pointed out, in order for policyowners to gain the additional benefit of better-than-expected investment returns, they also must assume all the risk of investment losses. Consequently, the SEC required that variable life policies be registered and that all sales be subject to the requirements imposed on other registered securities. In other words, policy sales may be made only after the prospective purchaser has read the policy prospectus. The SEC also required that the insurance company be registered as an investment company and that all sales agents be registered with the SEC for the specific purpose of variable life insurance policy sales. Agents who sell variable life insurance policies must be licensed as both life insurance agents and securities agents.

Investment Choices

Variable life insurance policies give the policyowner several investment options into which the cash value can be directed. The policyowner is free to put all of the funds into one of these choices or to distribute the funds among the options in whatever proportions he or she desires. Some insurance companies have more than a dozen funds from which to choose. There are usually a variety of stock funds, including growth stock funds, income stock funds, balanced stock funds, and international stock funds. Bond fund offerings include different durations and different types of issuers (large corporations, small corporations, state governments, and the federal government) as well as Government National Mortgage Association (GNMA) funds and collateralized mortgage obligations (CMOs).

In addition, many insurance companies offer a managed fund as one of the portfolio choices. The policyowner can put all of the policy funds into a managed portfolio fund and have a professional money manager working for the insurance company make the investment allocation decision. This option appeals to policyowners who do not want to spend a lot of time learning about the market and making investment decisions.

Some insurance companies have allied with large mutual fund groups that make their entire range of mutual funds available. These agreements enable smaller life insurance companies to gain access to the administrative services already in place in these large mutual fund family groups.

Because the policyowner is allowed to direct the policy cash value, the policyowner becomes the portfolio director, within limits. Obviously, the policyowner has no control over the selection of assets and the timing of trades. The insurance company's portfolio management team makes those investment decisions. With variable life insurance, the policyowner participates in portfolio investment and, consequently, benefits directly from better-than-expected results and bears the risk of poor investment performance. The results of the investment performance are credited directly to the policy's cash values.

Ability to Tolerate Investment Fluctuations. Individuals who are already experienced in equity investments are quite comfortable with the variable life insurance policy. However, this policy is subject to daily portfolio fluctuations and can provoke great anxiety in individuals who are not accustomed to or risk tolerant enough to be comfortable with market value fluctuations.

Market volatility is part of the challenge of marketing variable life policies. Many life insurance agents are reluctant to sell a policy that depends on the policyowner's investment decisions for its success. Agents are afraid that some purchasers will expect the life insurance agent to offer investment advice.

A variable life policy is a market-driven product, and its popularity, to some extent, is influenced by general investment market conditions. This type of policy becomes more acceptable to consumers after a long period of market increases and falls out of favor when the market experiences a general price decline.

Insurance Charges

If favorable investment choices are made, variable life insurance enables the policyowner's money to work harder. But variable life insurance contracts are not exclusively investments. They are, in fact, life insurance contracts, and they include mortality charges for the death benefits. Consequently, the return on the invested funds within a variable life insurance contract will never equal the return on a separate investment fund that invests in assets of a similar type and quality but does not provide a death benefit.

Variable life insurance is not a short-term investment vehicle. The combination of sales load, mortality charges, and surrender charges will significantly reduce any potential gains in the policy's early years.

Linkage of Death Benefits with Investment Performance

Because the primary objective of life insurance is to provide death benefits, it makes sense to link superior investment performance with increases in the death benefit level. Theoretically, this is a way to keep up with inflation. In fact, studies indicate that such a linkage would more than keep pace with inflation. However, there is an important caveat. Although investment performance in equities tends to equal or exceed inflation in the economy over the long term, there is little or no correlation in the short term. In other words, it is possible for inflation to exceed increases in the investment performance for short durations of time such as 2 or 3 years. This is another reason to regard life insurance as a long-term financial security purchase and not as a short-term investment.

There are two ways to link the policy's death benefit to the associated portfolio's investment performance—the level additions method and the constant ratio method, discussed later. Regardless of the linkage design, all of the contracts provide a minimum guaranteed death benefit. Also, all have the purchaser select a target level of investment performance as a benchmark against which actual investment performance will be measured. Performance in excess of the target level will fund incremental increases in the death benefit; performance below the target amount requires downward adjustments in the death benefits to make up for the deficit.

Usually, variable life policies have positive excess investment earnings in the early years of the contract, and they provide incremental increases in the death benefit before the investment earnings drop below the target rate. Most variable life insurance policies issued since 1976 have experienced investment earnings over the target rate more frequently and for longer durations than they have experienced investment earnings below the target rate. There is no guarantee

---

Distinctive Features of Variable Life Insurance

- The policyowner selects the types of investments into which the savings element will be directed.
- Premiums are fixed.
- There is no minimum guaranteed crediting rate or minimum cash value.
- Policies can be sold only with a prospectus.
- The minimum death benefit is guaranteed to equal the policy's original face amount.
- Above that minimum, the death benefit depends on the investment performance of the policyowner-selected separate account(s).
- Policy loans are allowed, but to a smaller percentage of the cash value than in traditional contracts.
- Contracts contain the usual range of nonforfeiture options.

that this will always be true, but the expectation is that overall investment earnings will exceed the target amount over the bulk of the policy duration.

Level Additions Model. The level additions model uses investment returns in excess of the target rate to purchase additional insurance. The face amount or death benefit will rise as long as investment performance equals or exceeds the target rate. This model does not cause as rapid an increase or decrease as the constant ratio method of linking the policy's death benefit to investment performance. The strength of the level addition design is that it does not require an ever-increasing investment return to support incremental increases in death benefits. Additional coverage is added more slowly, but it is more easily supported once it is added. Similarly, downward adjustments in death benefits are less rapid, and they are less likely to accelerate downward in future years. Furthermore, policies that use the level additions design provide a minimum face value guarantee equal to the amount of coverage when the policy was first purchased.

Constant Ratio Method. The constant ratio method also uses the excess investment earnings as a net single premium to purchase an additional amount of coverage. Under this method, the additional coverage is not a level amount, but rather a decreasing benefit amount. The policy is designed to maintain a ratio between the death benefit and the policy reserve that prevents the investment element of the contract from becoming excessive relative to the protection element. Under this policy design, more volatile increments are added to or subtracted from the contract as investment performance differs from the target amount. Like the level additions model, this design has a minimum death benefit guarantee equal to the initial face amount of the policy.

Policy Cash Values

Policy premiums paid under variable life insurance contracts are often subject to an administrative charge. The balance of the premium payment goes into the cash value account, from which mortality charges are deducted. The actual value of the cash component is determined by the net asset value of the separate account funds that make up the policy portfolio. The cash value of a variable life policy fluctuates daily. Each day's net asset value is based on the closing price for the investments in the portfolio on that trading day.

As with traditional life insurance contracts, the policyowner has access to the cash value via policy loans. Variable life insurance policies usually limit maximum policy loans to a slightly smaller percentage of the total cash value than is traditionally available in whole life policies. Policy loans may be repaid at any time in part or in full, but there is no requirement that policy loans be repaid in cash at any time during the existence of the life insurance contract. Interest accrues on any unpaid loan balance. As in any other form of whole life policy, policy loans under a variable life insurance policy reduce the death benefit payable. The policy loan is always fully secured by the remaining cash value in the policy. Whenever the outstanding loans plus accrued interest equal the remaining cash value, the net cash value becomes zero and the policy terminates.

The net cash value in the contract is also closely related to the nonforfeiture options available under the policy. Variable life insurance contracts provide the same range of nonforfeiture options as do traditional whole life policies. The net cash surrender value may be obtained by surrendering the contract to the insurance company, or the net cash value may be applied as a single premium to purchase either a reduced amount of paid-up insurance or the same amount of extended term insurance. The duration of the extended term insurance will be the longest period of coverage for the same death benefit amount that can be obtained from the insurance company for the policy's net cash value.

Prospectus

Variable life insurance policies must be sold with an accompanying prospectus. The prospectus the SEC mandates is similar in many respects to the prospectus required for new stock issues. This prospectus is a full and accurate disclosure of all the contract provisions, including expenses, surrender charges, and investment options. Although the prospectus is a lengthy and detailed document that most purchasers are reluctant to read, it is an important source of information not available elsewhere.

Expense Information. The prospectus has very detailed information about all of the expense charges the insurance company levies against variable life insurance contracts. These charges include commissions paid to soliciting agents, state premium taxes, administrative charges, collection charges, and any fees for specific future transactions.

In addition, the prospectus sets forth the manner in which charges are made against the asset account to cover the cost of insurance under the contract. This is usually referred to in the prospectus as the cost-of-insurance charge. The prospectus specifies exactly what rate will be used to determine cost-of-insurance charges and explicitly specifies if there is any maximum rate above the intended rate. The prospectus also explains the manner in which charges are levied against the separate account itself—essentially the fees associated with managing the various investment accounts from which the policyowner may choose. Part of that charge is always some specified percentage (usually less than one percent) of the assets in the separate accounts themselves. There also may be specific charges to establish and maintain the trusts necessary for managing those assets.

Surrender Charges. The prospectus clearly spells out the charge applicable to policy surrenders. In most cases, this information is set forth in a schedule, listing each policy year with its applicable percentage surrender charge. Surrender charges are applicable only if the policy is surrendered for its cash value, allowed to lapse, or (under some contracts) adjusted to provide a lower death benefit. Surrender charges are commonly levied during the first 10 to 15 years of the contract.

Investment Portfolio Information. The prospectus sets forth the objectives of each of the available investment funds and a record of their historical performance. There is detailed information on the current holdings of each of the available portfolios, usually supplemented by information about trades of equities or debt instruments over the previous 12 months. It gives further information about earnings during that same period of time and usually for longer intervals of prior performance if those portfolio funds have been in existence long enough to give investment results for trades over 5 or 10 years. The prospectus fully discloses any investment restrictions applicable to these portfolios as indicated in the trust instruments themselves.

The prospectus also includes projections of future performance under the contract if portfolio funds generate an assumed level of investment earnings over the projected interval. Under SEC regulations, the permissible rates of return that can be projected are the gross annual rates after tax charges but before any other deductions at 0, 4, 6, 8, 10, or 12 percent. The insurer decides which of those permissible rates to project.

Universal Life Insurance

universal life insurance

Universal life insurance was the first variation of whole life insurance to offer truly flexible premiums. These policies shift some of the possibility of investment fluctuations to the policyowner because the cash value can be increased by interest credited in excess of the guaranteed interest rate, but the policies do not allow the policyowner to direct the investment portfolio. Two other features of universal life insurance policies are (1) the policyowner's ability to withdraw part of the cash value without having the withdrawal treated as a policy loan and (2) the choice of either a level death benefit design or an increasing death benefit design.

Flexible Premiums

Universal life insurance has the unusual feature of completely flexible premiums after the first year—the only time a minimum level of premium payments for a universal life policy is rigidly required. As usual, the first year's premium can be arranged on a monthly, quarterly, semiannual, or annual basis. The insurance company requires only that it equals or exceeds a minimum specified level of first-year premium payments. After the first policy year, the policyowner can determine how much premium to pay and even whether or not to pay premiums—with one constraint.

The one constraint regarding premium payments is that the aggregate premiums paid, regardless of their timing, must be adequate to cover the costs of maintaining the policy. Consider the analogy of an auto's gas tank, where premium payments are like filling the tank. Premium payments (tank refills) can be made frequently to keep the tank nearly full at all times. With that approach, the auto is never likely to run out of gas. The same auto, however, can operate on a just-in-time philosophy, where premium payments (or additional fuel) of minimal amounts are made only as frequently as necessary to keep the policy (the car) from running out of gas.

Under a universal life insurance policy, if the policy's cash value is allowed to drop too low (the cash value is inadequate to cover the next 60 days of expense and mortality charges), the policy will lapse. If an additional premium payment is made soon enough, the policy may be restarted without a formal reinstatement process. However, if an injection of additional funds comes after the end of the grace period, the insurance company may force the policyowner to request a formal reinstatement before accepting any further premium payments.

Prefunding

The higher the amount or proportion of prefunding through premium payments, the more investment earnings will be credited to the policy and utilized to cover mortality and administrative costs. All premium suggestions are based on some assumed level of investment earnings, and the policyowner must accept the possibility that actual investment earnings might be less than necessary to support the suggested premium. Even though investment earnings cannot go below the guaranteed rate, a long-term shortfall may necessitate either an increase in premiums or a reduction in coverage at some future point.

Under traditional contracts with cash values, the only mechanism for returning policy overfunding in the early years is policyowner dividends. With universal life policies, however, the accumulations from prefunding are credited to the policy's cash value and are quite visible to the policyowner. The earnings rates applied to those accumulations are also clearly visible as they fluctuate with current economic conditions. This open disclosure for universal life policies eliminates some of the doubts about fair treatment often directed at whole life insurance.

Withdrawal Feature

As previously noted, another feature of universal life policies is the policyowner's ability to make partial withdrawals from the policy's cash value without incurring any indebtedness. In other words, money can be taken out of the policy's cash value just like a withdrawal from a savings account. There is no obligation to repay those funds, nor is interest incurred on the amount withdrawn. Withdrawals do affect the policy's future earnings because the fund still intact to earn interest for future crediting periods is reduced by the amount of the withdrawal. The extent to which the withdrawal reduces the death benefit depends on the type of death benefit in force.

Target Premium Amount

Nearly every universal life policy is issued with a target premium amount. The target amount is the suggested premium to be paid on a level basis throughout the contract's duration or for a shorter period of time if a limited-payment approach was originally intended to fund the policy. The target premium amount is merely a suggestion and carries no liability if it is inadequate to maintain the contract to any duration, much less to the end of life.

In some insurance companies, the target premium is actually sufficient to keep the policy in force (under relatively conservative investment return assumptions) through age 95 or 100 and to pay the cash value equivalent to the death benefit amount if the insured survives either to age 95 or 100. On the other hand, some companies with a more aggressive marketing stance have chosen lower target premiums, which may not be adequate to carry the policy in force to advanced ages even under more generous (if questionable) assumptions of higher investment returns over future policy years. If, in fact, the investment return credited to the policy's cash value falls short of the amount assumed to derive the target premium, the policy may essentially run out of gas before age 95 or 100. In these cases, the policyowner will be faced with two options: (1) to increase the premium level or (2) to reduce the death benefit amount. Neither one of these options is necessarily desirable, but they are the only acceptable ways under the contract's provisions to correct for unfulfilled optimistic assumptions about investment returns in the contract's early years.

Some insurance companies have introduced a secondary guarantee associated with their target premium. These companies have pledged contractually to keep the policy in force for, say, 15 to 20 years and to pay the full death benefit as long as the premium has been paid in an amount equal to or greater than the target premium amount at each suggested premium-payment interval. Even these guarantees do not extend to age 95 or 100, but they ensure that the premium suggested as a target will be adequate to provide the coverage for at least as long as the guarantee period.

The flexible features of universal life premiums allow policyowners to make additional premium payments above any target premium amount at any time and without prior negotiation or agreement with the insurance company. The only limitation on paying excess premiums is associated with the income tax definition of life insurance, which is discussed in chapter 10. However, the insurance company reserves the right to refuse additional premium payments under a universal life policy if the policy's cash value is large enough to encroach on the legal upper limit allowed for cash values relative to the level of death benefit granted in the policy.

The premium flexibility also allows the policyowner to skip premium payments, again without any prior negotiation or notification, or to pay premium amounts lower than the target premium suggested at the time of purchase. The lower limitations on premium payments have two constraints. The first is that nearly every company specifies a minimum acceptable amount for any single payment. The second is that there must be enough cash value in the contract to meet the mortality and administrative charges for the next 60 days. In other words, if the tank is running on empty, more premium is required.

Death Benefit Type

Universal life insurance gives policyowners a choice between level death benefits and increasing death benefits. The level death benefit design is much like the traditional whole life design. When the death benefit stays constant and the cash value increases over the duration of the contract, the net amount at risk, or the protection element, decreases. The one new aspect of a level death benefit design under universal life policies is not really a function of universal life itself but a function of the tax law definition of life insurance requiring that a specified proportion of the death benefit is derived from the net amount at risk. Whenever the cash value in the contract gets high enough that this proportion is no longer satisfied, the universal life policy starts increasing the death benefit, even though the contract is called a level death benefit contract. This phenomenon does not occur until ages beyond normal retirement, and it is not a significant aspect of this design.

The increasing death benefit design is a modification that was introduced with universal life policies. Under this approach, there is always a constant net amount at risk that is superimposed over the policy's cash value, whatever it may be. As the cash value increases, so does the total death benefit payable under the contract. A reduction in the cash value will reduce the death benefit. This design pays the policy's stated face amount plus its cash value at the insured's death. Policies with an increasing death benefit design overcome the criticism of whole life policies that the death benefit consists partially of the contract's cash value. By selecting the increasing death benefit option under a universal life policy, the policyowner

---

Distinctive Features of Universal Life Insurance

- Premium flexibility
- Market rates of interest credited
- Unbundling of cost elements
- Partial withdrawals allowed
- Differential interest crediting rates if policy loans are outstanding
- "Back-end" expense loads in case of surrender
- Choice of death benefit designs (level or increasing)

is ensuring that the death benefit will be composed of the cash value and an at-risk portion equal to the original face value of the contract.

Effect of Policy Loans

Another aspect of policy design in universal life policies is the differential crediting rate on the cash value, depending on whether there are policy loans outstanding. Most insurance companies credit current interest rates on the cash value as long as there are no policy loans outstanding. Once the policyowner borrows funds from the cash value, the insurance company usually credits a lower interest rate or earnings rate to the portion of the cash value associated with the policy loan.

Internal Funds Flow

Although universal life insurance policies are still relatively young in the overall realm of life insurance products, some companies' policies are already in their fifth or sixth series. As with all products, the individual policy designs constantly evolve in response to the economy, competitive pressures, and market demand.

Most of the first generation of universal life policies were heavily front-end loaded products. They took a significant proportion of each premium dollar as administrative expenses, and the remaining portion was then credited to the policy's cash value account. In most insurance companies, the mortality rate then charged against the cash value for the amount at risk was often about 50 percent of the guaranteed maximum mortality rate set forth in the policy contract for the insured's attained age.

The difference between the mortality rate actually charged and the maximum permitted mortality rate published in the policy represents the safety margin the life insurance company holds in reserve. If the future mortality costs for the block of policies turn out to be more than initially assumed, the insurance company can increase the mortality charge, as long as it does not exceed the guaranteed maximum rates specified in the contract.

As noted, from each premium dollar paid for universal life insurance, deductions are made for expenses and mortality. In addition, the universal life cash value account is increased at the current crediting rate to reflect investment earnings on that cash value. These dollars help to reduce the policyowner's current and future out-of-pocket premium expenses. The actual rate credited is a discretionary decision on the part of the insurance company, and it tends to fluctuate freely, reflecting current market conditions.

Interest crediting rates have been the focal point of most of the competition among companies that sell universal life policies. There has been very little emphasis on the mortality rates charged or the expense charges levied against incoming premiums. In reality, all three factors constitute the total cost of

---

Cash Value Account for a Universal Life Policy

	Ending account balance, previous period
plus	Flexible premium paid
minus	Current expense charge (guaranteed maximum)
minus	Current mortality charge (guaranteed maximum)
plus	Interest credit at current rate (guaranteed minimum)
minus	Partial withdrawal (if any)
equals	Ending account balance, current period

---

insurance. Interest rates can be (and have been) intentionally elevated to a level above what the investment portfolio actually supports, but they are still viable because of compensating higher levels of mortality charges and expense deductions. When consumers choose to focus on only one of the three elements, it is not surprising that marketing efforts zero in on that element. Assessment of overall policy efficiency requires that all factors be considered in concert.

Many universal life insurance policies are now based on a back-end loading design. In other words, they lower or eliminate up-front charges levied against incoming premium amounts and, instead, impose new or increased surrender charges applicable to the cash value of a policy surrendered during the contract's first 7 to 15 years. Surrender charges are usually highest during the first policy year and decrease on a straight-line basis over the remaining years until the year in which the insurance company expects to have amortized all excess first-year expenses. At that point, the surrender charge is reduced to zero and is not applicable at later policy durations.

Competitive pressures have caused many insurance companies to minimize front-end loading in order to emphasize that nearly all premium dollars go directly into the cash value account. The actual expenses are still being exacted internally, but it is not easy for the consumer to discern the manner in which they are handled. For example, expenses can be embedded in the spread between actual mortality costs and actual mortality charges or in the spread between investment earnings and the interest rate credited to the cash value account.

Variable Universal Life Insurance

variable universal life insurance

Variable universal life insurance is one of the more recently developed variations of whole life. This policy incorporates all of the premium flexibility features of the universal life policy with the policyowner-directed investment aspects of variable life insurance.

One of the most interesting aspects of variable universal life insurance is that it eliminates the direct connection between investment performance above or below some stated target level and the corresponding formula-directed adjustment in death benefits. Instead, variable universal life insurance adopts the death benefit designs applicable to universal life policies—either a level death benefit or an increasing death benefit design where the policy pays a constant fixed amount of protection in addition to the cash accumulation account. Under the first option, the death benefit usually does not change, regardless of how positive or negative the investment performance under the contract. If the policyowner wants to vary the death benefit with the performance of the investments under the contract, he or she must choose the increasing death benefit design. Any increase or decrease is a direct result of the accumulation balance.

Variable universal life policies offer the policyowner a choice among a specified group of separate investment accounts that the insurance company itself usually creates and maintains. Some insurance companies have made arrangements with other investment companies to utilize separate account portfolios that those investment management firms create and maintain.

Like variable life insurance, variable universal life insurance policies are classified as securities and subject to regulation by the SEC. The SEC requires registration of the agents who market the product, the separate accounts that support the contracts, and the contracts themselves. In addition, policies must conform with the SEC requirements that the investment funds be in separate accounts that are segregated from the insurance company's general investment portfolio and are therefore not subject to creditors' claims on the insurer's general portfolio should the company face financial difficulty. As with all insurance, variable universal life contracts are also subject to regulation by state insurance commissioners.

Because variable universal life is a registered investment product, policies must be accompanied by a prospectus, which is governed by the same rules that are applicable to prospectuses for variable life insurance policies. The prospectus provides the necessary information for a meaningful evaluation and comparison of policies.

Variable universal life insurance is similar to universal life insurance, but with the added feature that the policyowner chooses the investments, as under fixed-premium variable life insurance contracts. Variable universal life offers the policyowner both flexibility and the potential for investment gain or loss. There are no interest rate or cash value guarantees and very limited guarantees on the applicable maximum mortality rates. Policyowners have wide-open premium flexibility under this contract and can choose to fund it at whatever level they desire, as long as it is at least high enough to create coverage similar to yearly renewable term insurance and not in excess of the amount that would

Distinctive Features of Variable Universal Life Insurance

- Premium flexibility of universal life
- Death benefit design flexibility of universal life
- Investment flexibility of variable life

drive the cash accumulation account above the maximum threshold set forth in the Internal Revenue Code. Policyowners do not need to negotiate with or inform the insurer in advance of any premium modification or cessation.

These variable universal life contracts permit partial withdrawals that work like those under universal life policies. Early partial withdrawals may be subject to surrender charges, which apply to surrenders during the policy's early years, when the insurance company is still recovering excess first-year acquisition costs. The surrender charges vanish at a specified policy duration.

Policyowners can aggressively prefund variable universal life insurance so that later the policy can completely support itself from its cash value. If large premiums are contributed to the contract, this self-support can be accomplished in a relatively short period. As with universal life insurance, variable universal life policies have no guarantee that once the cash value is large enough to carry the policy, it will always be able to do so. The policyowner assumes the uncertainty of investment return and, to a limited extent, some of the uncertainty of mortality rate charges. Consequently, the policyowner may either pay more premiums or reduce the death benefit at some future time if, in fact, the cash value subsequently dips below the level needed to totally prefund the remaining contract years.

Choosing the increasing death benefit option under the variable universal life contract, affords policyowners an automatic hedge against inflation. This inflation protection is general in nature and subject to a timing mismatch in that investment experience may not keep pace with short-term bursts of inflation. Over the long haul, however, the investment-induced increases in coverage should equal, if not exceed, general increases in price levels.

As with variable life, the policyowner is able to switch investment funds from one of the available choices to any other single fund or combination whenever desired. Some insurance companies limit the number of fund changes permitted before charging the policyowner for additional changes. Policyowners can switch investment funds without incurring any internal or external taxation of inherent gains in the funds. The internal buildup of the cash value is tax deferred at least as long as the policy stays in force and will be tax exempt if the policy matures as a death claim.

Joint-Life Insurance

The typical life insurance contract is written on the life of one person and is technically known as *single-life insurance*. A contract written on more than one life is known as a *joint-life policy*, also called a *first-to-die policy*. Strictly speaking, a joint-life contract is one written on the lives of two or more persons and payable upon the death of the first person to die. Joint-life policies are fairly common for funding business buy-sell agreements.

joint-life (first-to-die) policy

survivorship (second-to-die) policy

The policy is called either a *survivorship policy* or a *second-to-die policy* if the face amount is payable upon the death of the last of two or more lives insured under a single contract. Survivorship policies have become quite popular as a means of funding federal estate taxes of wealthy couples whose wills make maximum use of tax deferral at the first death.

Joint-life policies are usually some form of cash value insurance. A term insurance rider may be used to increase the overall amount of protection in the cash value policy. Some first-to-die policies consist solely of term insurance.

GROUP LIFE INSURANCE

The discussion of life insurance up to this point has focused on individual insurance. However, for many people, group insurance is their principal, or perhaps only, source of life insurance protection. One indication of the important role of group life insurance is that, of the total life insurance in force in the United States, about 42 percent is group coverage.[4] Group purchases also represent the fastest growing portion of life insurance sales.

By far the most common type of coverage issued under group life plans is term insurance, accounting for about 95 percent of the total. The remainder consists mainly of universal life insurance or variable universal life insurance.

State law establishes the groups that are eligible for group life insurance. In general, the minimum size required is 10 lives. Five types of groups are usually eligible: individual employer groups, negotiated trusteeships (also known as Taft-Hartley trusts), trade associations, creditor-debtor groups, and labor union groups. Of these, the most common eligible group is the employees of a common employer.

In a typical group term life insurance plan covering employees, a benefit schedule is included to define the classes of employees that are eligible for coverage and to specify the amount of life insurance that will be provided to the members of each class. The employee also is given a conversion privilege; certain supplemental benefits may be provided as well.

Eligibility

To be eligible, an employee must be in a covered classification of workers, work on a full-time basis, and be actively at work. He or she may be required to fulfill a probationary period and, in some cases, to show insurability and meet premium contribution requirements.

The employer defines the classes of workers that will be eligible for the group life insurance; eligibility is usually restricted to full-time workers such as those who work at least 30 hours per week. Many group life insurance master contracts also contain an actively-at-work requirement, meaning that the employee is not eligible for coverage if absent from work due to sickness, injury, or other reasons on the otherwise effective date of coverage. Coverage commences when the employee returns to work.

probationary period   The master contract may also specify a *probationary period* of employment with the employer, such as 6 months, that an employee must satisfy before he or she is eligible for coverage. After the employee fulfills the required probationary period, he or she then becomes eligible for coverage.

Most group life coverage is provided without individual evidence of insurability. However, this evidence is required in some cases such as when an employee decides after the eligibility period has expired that he or she wants the coverage.

If the group plan is contributory, meaning that covered employees pay a portion of the premium, the coverage will not take effect until the employee properly authorizes payroll deduction. Usually, a 31-day eligibility period is provided during which the employee may make the decision on this matter without having to show evidence of insurability.

Benefit Amounts

The amount of group life insurance on each covered worker is normally set according to a schedule, rather than a choice for the employee. The most common schedules are based on earnings or position. In an earnings schedule, the amount of insurance is often equal to some multiple of earnings, such as two times the employee's annual earnings, rounded up to the next $1,000 and subject to a maximum benefit of, for example, $100,000. In a position schedule, different benefit amounts are provided based on each employee's position within the firm. For example, the president and vice presidents might have $100,000 of coverage, managers $60,000, salespersons $40,000, and other employees $20,000.

Convertibility

Any employee whose group life insurance ceases has the right according to the master contract to convert to an individual insurance policy. For example, an individual who terminates his or her employment or ceases to be a member of an eligible classification of employees has the right to convert. Conversion does not require proof of insurability and must occur within the first 31 days of eligibility to convert. The individual policy may be any type the insurer offers *except term insurance*, and the face amount may not exceed the amount of group life insurance being terminated. The premium for the individual policy is based on the employee's attained age at the time of conversion.

Supplemental Benefits

A group life insurance plan may provide certain supplemental benefits. For example, the plan may make additional amounts of insurance available to some or all classes of employees. Proof of insurability is usually required to obtain the additional amount, except when the amount of coverage is small and the employer does not usually pay any part of the premium for it. Employees who need additional protection can pay premiums for supplemental coverage by payroll deduction. However, the premium is not necessarily any less expensive than coverage that an employee might be able to purchase in the individual marketplace.

Dependent life insurance may also be available as a supplemental benefit. Coverage is generally optional, with the employee paying the entire cost. The amount of insurance is usually modest such as $5,000 on the employee's spouse and $1,000 on each dependent child over 14 days of age and under age 21. The employee typically is not allowed to select which of his or her eligible dependents will be covered but must decide on an all-or-none basis.

COMPARISON OF LIFE INSURANCE TYPES

This chapter has discussed the similarities and differences among the various types of individual life insurance. Variations within each type of plan exist, but some generalizations, which are summarized in table 8-1, can be made. The table is arranged in a sequence that roughly reflects the increasing complexity of various types of life insurance, ranging from term insurance to variable universal life insurance.

TABLE 8-1
Types of Life Insurance

Type	Protection Period	Premium	Death Benefit	Cash Value
Term	Temporary, often renewable	Increases with each renewal as scheduled and guaranteed	Level, increasing, or decreasing	None
Reentry term	Temporary	Fixed for one or more years, then increases based on one of two schedules, depending on insured's health	Usually level	None
Whole life	Permanent	Fixed and level	Fixed and level	Guaranteed and scheduled
Single premium whole life		One up-front premium payment		
Modified whole life		Level for first few years, then higher guaranteed premium		
Ordinary whole life		Premiums payable for life		
Limited-pay whole life		Premiums payable for specified period		

TABLE 8-1
Types of Life Insurance (Continued)

Type	Protection Period	Premium	Death Benefit	Cash Value
Endowment life insurance	Specified maturity date	Payable until maturity date	Fixed and level	Guaranteed and scheduled; equals death benefit at maturity
Current assumption whole life	Permanent	Can vary, depending on insured's mortality, expense, interest experience; guaranteed maximum	Fixed and level	Guaranteed and scheduled plus accumulation fund
Low-premium design		Premiums redetermined periodically	Insured may decrease death benefit to avoid premium increase	
High-premium design		Relatively high premium, which may cease	Fixed and level	High premiums speed cash buildup, possibly to a point where no premium is required
Variable life	Permanent	Fixed and level	Depends on cash value; guaranteed minimum	Not guaranteed; depends on investment performance; policyowner chooses investment account(s)
Universal life	Permanent	Flexible after first year	Level or increasing	Guaranteed minimum interest rate plus excess interest; insurer chooses investments; partial withdrawals permitted
Variable universal life	Permanent	Flexible after first year	Depends on cash value	Depends on investment performance; policyowner chooses investment account(s); no guarantees; partial withdrawals permitted

MINI-CASE: AMY AND JOHN SCHULTZ

As you recall, Amy Schultz, who is 28, and her husband John, who is 33, are both engineers employed by SKH, Inc. John has an annual salary of $95,000. Amy currently earns $55,000 a year. They Schultzes have $60,000 in a money market account. They have just purchased their first house, which is 80 years old and across the street from an elementary school, for $240,000 with 20 percent down and a 15-year mortgage at an interest rate of 5 percent.

SKH provides group benefits that include life insurance of two times their salaries. Amy and John currently own no individual life insurance policies, but they have now decided to buy life insurance for three reasons: First, as first-time homeowners, they are concerned about Amy's ability to make mortgage payments, based only on her income, if John should die. Second, they plan to have children soon and ultimately to put the children through college. Finally, if possible, they would like to provide an inheritance for their children. They are concerned, however, about the potential effects of future inflation.

a. Do Amy and John have temporary life insurance needs or permanent life insurance needs? Explain.

b. What type of life insurance does Amy and John's employer probably provide?

c. What type of life insurance would enable Amy to pay off the mortgage if John should die?

d. What type(s) of life insurance would enable Amy and John to ensure that funds are available for their children's education even if one or both parents dies?

(See answer section for answers to mini-case.)

SOURCES FOR FURTHER IN-DEPTH STUDY

- Graves, Edward E., editor, *McGill's Life Insurance*, 4th ed., Bryn Mawr, PA: The American College Press, 2004. Phone 888-263-7265. Web site address www.theamericancollege.edu
- Black, Kenneth, Jr., and Skipper, Harold D., Jr., *Life and Health Insurance*, 13th ed., Englewood Cliffs, NJ: Prentice-Hall, Inc., 2000. Phone 800-282-0693. Web site address www.prenhall.com

CHAPTER REVIEW

Answers to mini-case, review questions, and self-test questions start on page 793.

Key Terms

human life value	cash value life insurance
yearly renewable term insurance	reserve

net amount at risk
modified whole life insurance
reentry term insurance
renewability
convertibility
decreasing term insurance
whole life insurance
nonparticipating policy
participating policy
ordinary life insurance
limited-payment life
    insurance

endowment life insurance
current assumption whole life
    insurance
variable life insurance
universal life insurance
variable universal life
    insurance
joint-life (first-to-die) policy
survivorship (second-to-die)
    policy
probationary period

Review Questions

8-1.   Your client, Marty Gibson, is an auto mechanic in his 30s with two children in elementary school. His wife, Cindy, works part-time as a cosmetologist. The Gibsons struggle to meet daily expenses and to pay off the substantial medical bills resulting from Cindy's serious case of Lyme disease. Why, Marty asks, should he incur an additional expense by buying life insurance? Explain to Marty the purposes of life insurance, and identify the type of life insurance that would provide the most protection at the lowest cost.

8-2.   Explain the differences between yearly renewable term insurance and level premium cash value insurance. (Ignore the loading to cover expenses, profit, and contingencies.)

8-3.   Your financial planning client requires some life insurance to meet various needs. You begin to discuss some products available to meet those needs. How would you answer the following questions?
    a.   What is the difference between term and whole life insurance regarding
        (1) the permanence of death protection provided
        (2) the benefit promises if the client lives until the end of the policy
        (3) the use of premiums to save money as well as provide death protection
    b.   If your client buys a 10-year term policy, can the client extend it at the end of 10 years to satisfy new needs?
    c.   If the client buys a 10-year term policy and then needs a more permanent form of insurance, can the client switch the policy to whole life insurance?
    d.   Is there a policy that would pay the balance of the client's mortgage when the client dies to relieve the family of that burden?
    e.   What is the difference between ordinary life and limited-payment whole life in terms of the
        (1) permanence of protection
        (2) amount of premium outlay per year
        (3) relative size of their cash values

8-4. Your financial planning client says she's heard that some life insurance policies pay dividends and others don't. She asks you to explain.

8-5. Your financial planning client tells you that his grandmother bought a $50,000 20-year endowment policy 30 years ago that paid her even though she didn't die. The client asks you
   a. how that type of policy works
   b. whether it would make sense for him to buy one today

8-6. Describe each of the following as it relates to variable life insurance:
   a. guarantees with respect to interest rate or minimum cash value
   b. SEC requirements
   c. investment choices
   d. insurance charges
   e. linkage of death benefits with investment performance
   f. policy cash values
   g. contents of the prospectus

8-7. Describe each of the following as it relates to universal life insurance:
   a. flexible premiums
   b. prefunding
   c. withdrawal
   d. target premium amount
   e. death benefit type
      (1) level death benefit design
      (2) increasing death benefit design
   f. effect of policy loans
   g. internal funds flow

8-8. Explain to your client how a universal life policy with a level death benefit design can take on an array of different forms (depending on how much premium is paid to the insurance company), ranging from being comparable to yearly renewable term insurance to being comparable to limited-payment whole life insurance.

8-9. Explain why a universal life policy with
   a. the level death benefit design may not always provide a level death benefit
   b. the increasing death benefit design may not always provide an increasing death benefit

8-10. Explain how variable universal life insurance is similar to
   a. variable life insurance
   b. universal life insurance

8-11. Martha and Steve Miller have a handicapped daughter who is dependent on them for daily care. If either Martha or Steve dies, they would need to hire somebody to help with their daughter's care. This creates a specific need for funding. If both of them die, the daughter would be institutionalized and would need a much larger amount of funding to pay for her care. Briefly describe how each of the following life insurance policies might meet the Millers' needs:

a.   joint-life or first-to-die

b.   survivorship or second-to-die

8-12.   Your client, Jane, took your advice and purchased individual life insurance when she was a self-employed management consultant. She has just taken a full-time position with a large corporation that provides a benefits package including group life insurance. Jane asks you to explain how group life insurance works so she can decide whether to make any changes in her individual life insurance program. Explain the following features of a typical group life insurance plan covering employees:

a.   employee eligibility requirements

b.   evidence of insurability requirements

c.   benefit amounts

d.   convertibility

e.   supplemental benefits

Self-Test Questions

T   F   8-1.   Individuals may be legally obligated to provide for family support after their death.

T   F   8-2.   Yearly renewable term insurance pays the policy face value if the insured is alive at the end of the protection period.

T   F   8-3.   Yearly renewable term insurance premiums increase each year because of increases in the death rate.

T   F   8-4.   With a level premium policy, level premiums in excess of the policy's share of death claims in the early years of the contract are accumulated at interest in a reserve.

T   F   8-5.   To safeguard against adverse selection, insurers that offer term insurance on an individual basis typically allow it to be renewed, regardless of the insured's age at the time of renewal.

T   F   8-6.   With a whole life policy, the policyowner receives a combination of increasing cash values and decreasing (pure insurance) protection.

T   F   8-7.   With renewable term insurance, the policyowner/insured would be permitted to renew the policy if he or she had contracted a terminal disease prior to a renewal date.

T   F   8-8.   Decreasing term insurance has little use for financial planning purposes.

T   F   8-9.   Term insurance tends to be suitable when the need for protection is either purely temporary or permanent but the insured temporarily cannot afford the premiums for permanent insurance.

T   F   8-10.   Ordinary life insurance provides protection for a longer period of time than does limited-payment whole life insurance.

T   F   8-11.   Life insurance policies that provide for the payment of policyowner dividends are participating policies.

T   F   8-12.   Because of federal income tax reform in 1984, endowment policies play a major role in financial planning in the United States today.

T   F   8-13.   In exchange for investment flexibility, variable life insurance shifts the investment risk to the policyowner and provides no guarantee of either interest rate or minimum cash value.

T   F   8-14.   With variable life insurance, cash values reflect investment performance, but death benefit amounts do not.

T   F   8-15.   Variable life insurance policies may be sold without an accompanying prospectus.

T   F   8-16.   With universal life insurance, the policyowner can skip premium payments (after the first one) and the policy will stay in force as long as there is enough money in the policy's cash value account to cover current mortality and expense charges.

T   F   8-17.   With universal life insurance, death benefits are always level unless the cash value gets too close to the death benefit to comply with federal income tax law.

T   F   8-18.   Variable universal life insurance incorporates the premium flexibility features of the universal life policy with the policyowner-directed investment aspects of variable life products.

T   F   8-19.   A joint-life policy is payable upon the death of the last of two or more lives insured under the single contract.

T   F   8-20.   Most group life coverage is provided without individual evidence of insurability.

NOTES

1. In such an event, the parent and ex-spouse are required to provide life insurance or to set funds aside in trust.
2. This is not a trust fund in the legal sense, which would require the insurance company to establish separate investment accounts for each policyowner and render periodic accountings.
3. In practice, each policy is credited with a cash value or surrender value, which is not the same as the reserve but also has its basis in the redundant premiums of the early years.
4. Data concerning the amount, growth, and types of group life insurance in force are taken from *Life Insurance Fact Book 2003*, published by the American Council of Life Insurance.

Life Insurance Policy Provisions

Learning Objectives

An understanding of the material in this chapter should enable the student to

9-1.   Describe the policy declarations page.

9-2.   Explain the effect of standard policy provisions laws.

9-3.   Describe the provisions that are required in life insurance policies.

9-4.   Indicate the provisions that are prohibited in life insurance policies.

9-5.   Identify the optional provisions that may be found in life insurance policies.

9-6.   Describe three types of riders that policyowners often add to their life insurance policies.

9-7.   Describe the effect of state requirements for policy filing and approval.

Chapter Outline

The previous chapter introduced the types of life insurance. This chapter looks more closely at the life insurance contract. We will review provisions and riders associated with life insurance so that financial planners can understand them and therefore help their clients make use of the contract privileges available to them.

Chapter 1 mentioned two of the parties involved in a life insurance policy, the insured and the policyowner. This chapter mentions another party—the beneficiary. Often three different parties are involved, but one of these parties can also serve two roles.

beneficiary

- The *insured* is the person whose life is insured. Life insurance benefits are paid if that person dies.
- The *policyowner* is the party that owns the insurance contract and that generally has the right to change, renew, or cancel a policy. In individual insurance, this also includes the right to name the beneficiary. Often, the policyowner of an individual policy is also the insured. However, a parent may be the policyowner of a life insurance policy that covers a child, and one spouse may own a policy that insures another spouse. In group insurance, the policyowner is an entity, such as an employer, and each insured typically can name his or her own beneficiary.
- The *beneficiary* or *beneficiaries* are the person or persons who are entitled to receive death benefits. In individual life insurance, the policyowner may also be the beneficiary. Of course, the insured who dies cannot also be the beneficiary. However, the insured's estate may be the beneficiary.

We will discuss beneficiaries in greater detail later in this chapter.

Chapter 6 noted that most insurance contracts, including life insurance contracts, are contracts of adhesion, which means that the policyowner and the insurer do not negotiate the contract's terms.

As explained in more detail in chapter 6, by completing an application, the applicant is making an offer, thereby taking the first step to create an enforceable contract. The applicant specifies what type and amount of insurance he or she would like to purchase. Based on this information, the insurer will decide whether it wishes to accept the offer and issue an insurance contract.

The applicant cannot negotiate the wording of the insurance policy. Because the prospective policyowner can only accept or reject the contract the insurer issues, the contract of adhesion rule provides that all ambiguities in the contract of insurance will be resolved in favor of the policyowner and against the insurer. This rule of law is not entirely fair to insurance companies, because there are substantial limitations on the insurer's freedom to draft the insurance contract as it wishes. Insurers are required by law to include many types of provisions and in some cases are required to use or not use certain words.

Many states require that the contracts avoid complex sentences and arcane legal terminology in order to make the contracts easier for the consumer to read and understand. Although laudable, this requirement for simplicity can conflict with the lawyers' need to be certain that a contract will be interpreted exactly as the drafter intended. Over many years, courts have given certain legal terms specific meanings on which lawyers have come to rely in drafting contracts. This legalese may be difficult for the uninitiated to understand, but it offers a certainty that lawyers prefer. The practice in the United States is to favor less technical language over the certainty of interpretation. Lawyers will have to rely on current and future cases to develop that certainty as the courts interpret the simplified language of modern contracts.

State law controls a variety of required, prohibited, and optional life insurance policy provisions. Before an insurer can sell a policy in a particular jurisdiction, it must file the policy provisions with that state's insurance department for approval.

POLICY DECLARATIONS PAGE

Although the placement of the provisions may vary from company to company, the declarations pages of most life insurance contracts are quite similar and have the following information:

- the name of the insurance company
- specific details for the policy. These include the name of the insured and the name of the policyowner, the identity of the beneficiary or beneficiaries, the face amount of the policy, the policy number, and the policy date or issue date (some declarations pages include both dates).

- a general description of the type of insurance the policy contract provides. For example, the declarations page of a traditional participating whole life policy might read as follows:

  > Whole Life—Level Face Amount Plan. Insurance payable upon death. Premiums payable for life. Policy participates in dividends. Dividends, dividend credits, and policy loans may be used to help pay premiums.

- a statement about the policy's free-look provision. This is a provision that gives the policyowner a period of time, usually 10 days, to return the policy after acceptance. The following is an example of such a provision:

  > You may return this contract no later than 10 days after you receive it. All you have to do is take it or mail it to one of our offices or to the agent who sold it to you. The contract will be canceled from the start, and a full premium refund will be made promptly.

- the insurer's promise to pay. This is the core of the insurance contract. A typical statement reads as follows:

  > We will pay the beneficiary the sum insured under this contract promptly if we receive due proof that the insured died while this policy was in force. We make this promise subject to all of the provisions of this contract.

The remainder of the required and optional provisions are not usually included on the declarations page.

REQUIRED PROVISIONS

standard policy provisions laws

The *standard policy provisions laws* of the various states require that life and health insurance policies include certain provisions but allow the insurance companies to select the actual wording as long as it is at least as favorable to the policyowner as the statutory language. However, companies must submit the wording to the state insurance department and have it approved. Some of the standard provisions do not apply to certain types of insurance contracts, such as term, single premium, and nonparticipating policies. Insurers are not required to include standard policy provisions in policies to which they would not apply. For example, because term policies do not build a cash value, these policies are not required to include nonforfeiture provisions that would preclude loss of the cash value when a policy terminates.

Grace Period

grace period

The *grace period* provision grants the policyowner an additional period of time to pay any premium after it has become due. Although the provision is now required by law, acceptance of a slightly overdue premium was a common practice among insurers before laws compelled insurers to include the provision in the contract. Because of the provision, a policy that would have lapsed for nonpayment of premiums continues in force during the grace period. The premium remains due, however, and if the insured dies during the grace period, the insurer may deduct the overdue premium from the death benefit.

Although insurers could charge interest on the unpaid premium for the late period, they do not typically do so. If the insured survives the grace period but the premium remains unpaid, the policy lapses. However, cash value life insurance policies are required to include a nonforfeiture provision, discussed in a later section, that may enable the policyowner to continue coverage.

As with all renewal premiums, the policyowner has no obligation to pay the premium for the insurance coverage provided under the grace period clause. Thus, it might be said that the policyowner has received "free" insurance during that time, but only when the insured does not die within the grace period.

The standard length of the grace period is 30 or 31 days in fixed-premium policies. In flexible-premium policies, such as universal life insurance, a grace period of 60 or 61 days is common. If the last day of the grace period falls on a nonbusiness day, the period is usually extended to the next business day.

Late Remittance Offers

It is important to distinguish between the grace period rules and a late remittance offer that the insurer makes after the grace period expires. They are not the same, and there is usually no provision in the contract concerning a late remittance offer. Such an offer is made solely at the insurer's option. It is not a right of the policyowner or an obligation of the insurer included in the insurance contract under the requirements of the law.

Some insurers will make a late remittance offer to a policyowner whose coverage has lapsed after the grace period has expired. This is not an extension of the grace period, and coverage is not continued as a result of the offer. A late remittance offer is intended to encourage the policyowner to reinstate the policy; it does not extend coverage. The inducement from the insurer is that coverage may be reinstated without providing evidence of insurability. The policyowner accepts a late remittance offer by paying the premiums due and meeting any other conditions the insurer imposes. The most common condition is that the insured must be alive when the late premium payment is made.

Example: Hope misplaced her life insurance bill, and as a result she failed to pay her term life insurance premium when it was due. Because Hope's life insurance policy has 30-day grace period, as required by law, she can continue her life insurance coverage without interruption as long as she pays the premium before the 30-day period has run out. If she dies during that period and has not paid the premium before she dies, the insurance company will deduct the overdue premium from the death benefit.

Suppose Hope is also strapped for cash and does not pay her term life insurance premium within the grace period. Hope's coverage would normally lapse at this point, and the insurer would have no further obligation to Hope. However, in an effort to retain Hope as a customer, the insurer may voluntarily make a late remittance offer to accept her payment belatedly without requiring evidence of insurability. Of course, Hope must be alive when the premium is paid.

Policy Loans

policy loan

The law requires that a life insurance contract permit policy loans if the policy generates a cash value. *Policy loans* give the policyowner access to the cash value that accumulates inside the policy without having to terminate the policy. The policyowner merely requests a loan, and the life insurer lends the funds confidentially. The loan provisions in the policy specify what portion of the cash value is available for loans and how interest will be determined. In most policies, over 90 percent of the cash value is available for loans—some policies may restrict the amount of loanable funds to 90 percent of the cash value—and the policyowner may borrow any portion of the available cash value. Policyowners indicate in their request the amount desired. A policyowner can take more than one policy loan as long as the aggregate amount of all outstanding loans plus accrued interest does not exceed the policy's cash value available for loan.

Policy loans accrue interest on the borrowed funds. When purchasing a policy, the policyowner usually selects one of two different approaches to setting the policy loan interest. The policy will contain either (1) a fixed rate as specified in the policy or (2) a variable interest tied by formula to some specified index. One variable approach is to use Moody's composite yield on seasoned corporate bonds or some other index that is regularly published in the financial press such as *The Wall Street Journal* or *The Journal of Commerce*. Another index may be the interest rate being credited to the cash value plus a specified spread.

Policy Loan Provision

- No credit questions asked
- Policyowner may borrow up to 90 percent to 100 percent of cash value
- Technically, insurer can delay lending for up to 6 months
- Fixed or variable interest rates charged
- Unpaid interest added to the loan balance
- No repayment schedule or requirement
- Indebtedness repaid when policy is surrendered or matures as a claim
- May include automatic premium loan feature

The policyowner has the option of paying loan interest in cash or adding the unpaid interest charge to the balance of the outstanding loan. The policyowner can choose to pay any part of the loan and interest he or she desires; there is no repayment schedule or requirement. If the policyowner makes any repayments, they are totally at his or her discretion as to both timing and amount. If the policyowner does not pay the policy loan and accrued interest in cash, the life insurer recovers the outstanding balance of the loan and accrued interest either from (1) the death benefits if the insured dies or (2) the cash surrender value if the policy terminates. In fact, the policy automatically terminates if the policy loan balance plus unpaid interest ever exceeds the policy's cash value.

automatic premium loan option

Some whole life policies give policyowners an *automatic premium loan option*. When the policyowner selects this option, any delinquent premium is automatically paid by a new policy loan. This keeps the policy in force as long as there is adequate cash value to cover each delinquent premium. The policy, however, will terminate if the cash value is exhausted.

A policy loan has negative consequences on benefits and can reduce the amount credited to the cash value and/or the level of policyowner dividends. The death benefit payable to the beneficiary is reduced by the full amount of policy loans outstanding and accrued interest under most types of policies. Policy loans also reduce nonforfeiture benefits.

Policy loans result in the life insurer's release of funds that would otherwise have been invested. If investment return on the insurer's portfolio exceeds the rate paid on the policy loan, the insurer experiences a reduction in earnings. Therefore, the insurance company usually takes steps to offset such loan-induced losses to preserve an approximate equity between policyowners who leave their cash values invested and those who preclude the insurer from reaping the higher yield. In traditional participating whole life policies, policyowner dividends were not affected by policy loans, but most participating whole life policies sold today use direct recognition to reduce dividends on policies with outstanding loans. This not only adjusts for the differential in earnings but also discourages policy loans.

State statutes allow life insurers to delay lending funds for up to 6 months after they are requested. Although insurers almost never exercise this right, it serves as a form of emergency protection in case policyowners' demands for loans accelerate to the point that the insurer must liquidate other assets at significant losses to satisfy the loan demands.

Example:	Helen and Gary desperately need a new car. They do not qualify for an auto loan because they already have substantial medical bills due to their children's illnesses, as well as credit card debt. Helen remembers the cash value in her whole life insurance policy and wonders whether that might provide a way to finance the car.
	The law requires that Helen's policy include a loan provision that Helen can access with no credit-check requirements. The insurer will charge interest on the loan, but Helen will not be required to make payments on a fixed schedule. Although these features seem attractive, Helen must also realize that the loan reduces not only the current and future cash value of the policy but also the benefits payable upon her death. If she does not repay the loan and the amount she has borrowed plus unpaid interest exceeds the policy's cash value, her life insurance policy will terminate. In short, Helen should probably think twice about taking steps that could impair the important protection her life insurance policy provides. Insurance on Helen's life might be especially important if her children have medical problems and the family is financially strapped.

Incontestable Clause

incontestable clause

Brief mention was made in chapter 6 of a life insurance policy provision called the *incontestable clause*. This clause is a provision that prohibits the insurer from disputing or "contesting" the validity of the policy after it has been in force for a certain time period. State laws differ as to the form of the clause prescribed, but no state permits a clause that would make the policy contestable for more than 2 years.

The following is a sample incontestable clause:

Except for nonpayment of premium, we will not contest this contract after it has been in force during the lifetime of the insured for 2 years from the date of issue.

After a policy has been in effect for the period of time the incontestable clause prescribes (normally 2 years), the insurance company cannot have the policy declared invalid. The courts have generally recognized three exceptions to this rule, deeming that the incontestable clause does not apply because the contract was void from its inception. These three exceptions are as follows:

- The applicant had no insurable interest at the inception of the policy.
- The policy was purchased with the intent to murder the insured.
- There was a fraudulent impersonation of the insured by another person (for example, for purposes of taking the medical exam).

The incontestable clause exists due to a belief that a life insurance policy's beneficiaries should not suffer for mistakes made in the application. The beneficiary is protected by the incontestable clause even if the error in the application is based on a fraudulent or material misrepresentation by the applicant or by a failure to meet a condition precedent to the existence of the contract.

After the insured's death, it would be extremely difficult, if not impossible, for the beneficiary to disprove the allegations of the insurance company that there were irregularities in procuring the policy. If there were no time limit on the insurance company's right to question the accuracy of the information in the application, there would be no certainty during the life of the policy that the benefits promised would be payable at maturity. Honest policyowners need assurance that at the insured's death, the beneficiary will receive a check. The incontestable clause gives policyowners that assurance. The clause is based on the theory that, after the insurance company has had a reasonable opportunity to investigate the circumstances surrounding issuance of a life insurance policy, it should thereafter relinquish the right to question the validity of the contract.

The typical incontestable clause makes the policy incontestable after it has been in force during the lifetime of the insured for a specified period. This means that if the insured dies during that period, the policy never becomes incontestable. As a result, if the insured dies a few days before the contestable period expires, the policy remains contestable by the insurer even if it is not notified of the death claim until after that period expires.

Example:	Donald took out a life insurance policy on February 16, 2003, naming his wife as the beneficiary. The policy contained the typical 2-year incontestable clause. Donald dies on February 9, 2005. Knowing that Donald had lied

about his health on the insurance application, Donald's wife waits until February 17, 2005, before filing the claim. Will she collect the proceeds? Probably not. Because the life insurance policy was not in force for 2 years *during Donald's lifetime*, it never became incontestable.

Other points are worth noting. First, refusal to pay a claim because of nonpayment of the premium is not governed by the incontestable clause. Second, some insurers specify in their incontestable clause that it does not apply to disability benefits or accidental death benefits that may be provided as part of the life insurance policy. Third, the policy provision relating to misstatement of the insured's age or gender, described later in this chapter, takes precedence over the incontestable clause.

Divisible Surplus

divisible surplus

An insurer's *divisible surplus* is that portion of an insurer's surplus declared as a dividend to be distributed to the owners of participating policies. The divisible surplus provision appears only in participating policies, because it would not be relevant in a nonparticipating policy. The provision requires the insurer to determine and apportion any divisible surplus among the insurer's participating policies at frequent intervals.

A typical divisible surplus provision reads as follows:

> While this policy is in force, except as extended term insurance, it is entitled to the share, if any, of the divisible surplus that we shall annually determine and apportion to it. This share is payable as a dividend on the policy anniversary.

In addition, some contracts provide that payment of a dividend is conditional on payment of all premiums then due. The provision in most contracts notes that a dividend is not likely to be paid before the second anniversary of the policy.

Dividend Options

dividend options

The application for a participating life insurance policy asks the policyowner to select among several of the following *dividend options*, thus indicating how any available dividends are to be used:

- *cash option.* The policyowner receives dividends in cash.
- *reduction of premiums.* The policyowner simply subtracts the amount of the dividend from the premium currently due and remits the difference to the insurer.

- *accumulation at interest.* The dividends are maintained in the equivalent of an interest-bearing savings account for the policyowner. A minimum rate of interest is guaranteed, but a higher rate of interest may be credited if conditions warrant. The accumulated dividends may be withdrawn at any time. If not withdrawn, they are added to the death proceeds or to the nonforfeiture value if the policy is surrendered.
- *purchase of paid-up additions.* Each dividend is used to purchase, on an attained-age basis, a small amount of additional, fully paid-up whole life insurance. The purchase is made at rates that do not contain a loading for expenses, and no evidence of insurability is required.
- *purchase of term insurance.* Some insurers that offer this *fifth dividend option* use a portion of the dividend to buy one-year term insurance equal to the policy's then cash value, with the remainder used to buy paid-up additions or to accumulate at interest. Other insurers use the entire dividend to buy one-year term insurance. In either case, the term insurance is purchased on the basis of the insured's attained age.

fifth dividend option

Other dividend options that may be available enable the policyowner to shorten the premium-paying period or to cause the policy to mature as an endowment. In the former case, the policy becomes paid up when its reserve, together with the reserve value of the dividends, equals the net single premium for a paid-up policy that the company could issue to the insured on the basis of his or her attained age. In the latter case, the insurer pays the face amount of the policy when the reserve, together with the reserve value of the dividends, equals the policy's face amount.

Entire Contract

Ordinarily, we would expect that a contract of any type includes all the provisions that are binding on the parties. However, this is not always the case. Sometimes one contract includes the terms of another document without actually including that second document in the contract. This is done by referring to the other document and incorporating it into the contract by that reference, a practice known as incorporation by reference. Entire contract statutes grew out of an attempt to prohibit insurers' use of incorporation by reference and to make life insurance contracts more understandable for consumers. One goal was to ensure that the policyowner was given a copy of all documents that constitute the conract. Another was to preclude any changes in the contract after it had been issued.

entire contract provision

The various states impose different requirements concerning the entire contract. Some states require an *entire contract provision* disclosing that the policy and the application constitute the entire contract; other states simply provide that the policy and the application are the contract, regardless of what the policy may say.

A sample provision is as follows:

This policy and any attached copy of an application form the entire contract. We assume that all statements in an application are made to the best of the knowledge and belief of the person who makes them; in the absence of fraud, they are deemed to be representations and not warranties. We rely on those statements when we issue the contract. We will not use any statement, unless made in an application, to try to void the contract, to contest a change, or to deny a claim.

Reinstatement

**reinstatement
provision**

Reinstatement provisions allow a policyowner to reacquire coverage under a policy that has lapsed. This right is valuable to both the policyowner and the insurer. The various state laws and the insurance contracts impose certain requirements that the policyowner must meet to reinstate the policy.

A typical reinstatement clause provides the following:

This policy may be reinstated within 3 years after the due date of the first unpaid premium, unless the policy has been surrendered for its cash value. The conditions for reinstatement are that (1) the insured must provide evidence of insurability satisfactory to us, (2) the policyowner must pay all overdue premiums plus interest at 6 percent per year, and (3) the policyowner must repay or reinstate any policy loan outstanding when the policy lapsed, plus interest.

Generally, insurers do not permit reinstatement of a policy that has been surrendered for its cash value, and this prohibition is often included in the contractual definition of the requirements for reinstatement.

Example: When Rick completed a life insurance application, he mentioned his high blood pressure, controlled with medication, but disclosed no other health problems. Soon after the policy was issued, a PSA blood test, given as part of a routine physical, led Rick to discover that he had prostate cancer, which had apparently been developing over the past few years. Rick was surprised at this discovery.

A *representation* is a statement in an insurance application that is substantially true to the best of the applicant's knowledge and belief. A false representation of a material fact is a *misrepresentation*. It now seems

misrepresentation

clear that Rick already had prostate cancer when he completed the insurance application. He did not know it, however, and he represented his condition to the best of his knowledge; Rick did not warrant that he had no health problems. The *entire policy provision* makes it clear that the insurer cannot use Rick's statement to void Rick's policy unless the insurer can prove that Rick was aware of his condition and intentionally misrepresented it.

Rick also had another life insurance policy that lapsed 2 years earlier when he failed to pay a renewal premium. Given his serious health problem, Rick decides to reinstate the policy since he is still within the 3-year reinstatement period. The *reinstatement provision* in Rick's policy requires that he provide satisfactory evidence of insurability. Because he is no longer able to do so, Rick will not be able to reinstate this policy.

Misstatement of Age or Gender

The insured's age and gender are fundamentally important factors in the evaluation of the risk the life insurance company assumes. Rather than voiding the contract based on any misrepresentation of any insured's age or gender, the practice is to adjust the policy's premium or benefits to reflect the truth. The incontestable clause does not preclude adjustments in the policy's premiums based on misstatements of age or gender; the incontestable clause only

misstatement of age or gender clause

precludes disputes over the policy's validity. Also, because a *misstatement of age or gender clause* (often called a misstatement of age or sex clause) appears in the contract, an adjustment based on that clause would be an attempt to enforce the terms of the contract, not to invalidate it.

A sample provision in an individual life insurance policy might read as follows:

> If the age or gender of the insured has been misstated, we will adjust all benefits payable under this policy to that which the premium paid would have purchased at the correct age or gender.

Example: Jim took out a life insurance policy for an annual premium of $1,300. He stated that his age was 41, when in fact he was 46. When he died, the company discovered the misstatement of age. The insurer will pay an amount less than the face of the policy to Jim's beneficiary—specifically, the amount of insurance that an annual premium of $1,300 would have bought for a 46-year-old male.

However, if the insured is still alive when the age or gender misrepresentation is discovered, the parties typically will agree to adjust the premium to the correct amount, rather than to adjust the benefits. An adjustment of premium is also the method used in group life insurance, whether the insured is living or not. A majority of states require a provision that adjusts for misstatements of age, but fewer than half require a provision that applies to misstatement of gender.

Nonforfeiture Provisions

When insurers developed the concept of insurance policies with level premiums over the insured's lifetime, the goal was to make life insurance more affordable to older policyowners. As explained in chapter 8, in the early years of the policy, the level premium was higher than necessary to cover the mortality costs. The excess portion of the premium in the policy's early years, and the interest it earned, built up a cash reserve that was used to help pay the mortality costs at older ages, which then exceeded the attained age level premium. A question soon arose over who was entitled to those reserves when a policy lapsed in the early years. Initially, the policyowner forfeited these reserves, but this was clearly inequitable, and the practice was soon modified. Today, that question has been answered by nonforfeiture laws.

The states require that insurers assure policyowners who voluntarily terminate their contracts a fair return of the value, if any, built up inside their policies. These laws are known as *nonforfeiture laws*. As late as the middle of the 19th century, insurance policies in the United States made no provision for refunds of excess premiums paid on cash value policies upon the policyowner's termination of the policy before maturity. However, in 1861, Massachusetts recognized that the policyowner had a right to at least a portion of those funds, and the first nonforfeiture law was enacted in that state. By 1948, that idea had evolved into the Standard Nonforfeiture Law, and subsequent versions of the law have become effective in all jurisdictions. Policies issued since that date have provided at least the minimum surrender values prescribed by the version of the law in effect when the policy was issued.

The NAIC Standard Nonforfeiture Law for Life Insurance, which has been widely adopted by the states, does not require specific surrender values. The only requirement is that surrender values are at least as large as those that would be produced by the method the law prescribes. In addition, each policy must contain a statement of the method used to determine the surrender values and benefits provided under the policy at durations not specifically shown.

After a traditional cash value policy has been in effect for a minimum number of years—usually 3—the insurer must use part of the reserved excess premium to create a guaranteed minimum cash value. Nonforfeiture laws require that a life insurance policy must make certain options available regarding how a policyowner can use the policy's cash value. The insurer must make that value available to the policyowner in cash as a surrender value and must give the policyowner a choice of two other *nonforfeiture options*: (1) paid-up insurance at a reduced death benefit amount or (2) extended term insurance for the net face amount of the policy. These options are illustrated in figure 9-1. If the policyowner has not elected a nonforfeiture option, the policy must provide that one of these two options will be effective automatically if the policy lapses. Under most plans and issue ages, nonforfeiture values are made available by the end of the second policy year.

nonforfeiture options

Cash Surrender Option

The policyowner may surrender the policy at any time for its cash value, less any policy indebtedness, plus accumulated dividends. In that event, the protection terminates and the company has no further obligation under the policy. As with policy loans, a 6-month delay clause applies to cash surrenders, although it is extremely rare for an insurer to exercise this right to delay payment.

Reduced Paid-up Insurance Option

The next option permits the policyowner to take a reduced amount of paid-up whole life insurance, payable upon the same conditions as the original policy. The amount of the paid-up insurance is the amount that can be purchased at the insured's attained age with the net cash value (cash value, less any policy indebtedness, plus any dividend accumulations) applied as a net single premium. Note that the paid-up insurance is purchased at net rates, meaning they contain no expense loading, which may constitute a sizable savings to the policyowner.

Extended Term Insurance Option

The extended term option provides term insurance in an amount equal to the original face amount of the policy, increased by any dividend additions or deposits, and decreased by any policy indebtedness. The length of the term is that which can be purchased at the insured's attained age with the net cash value applied as a single premium. If the policyowner fails to elect an option within a specified period after default of premiums, this option usually automatically goes into effect.

Annuity Alternative

Surrender values may also be used to purchase an annuity for retirement income. If the life insurance policy does not specifically give the policyowner

FIGURE 9-1
Face Value with Various Nonforfeiture Options

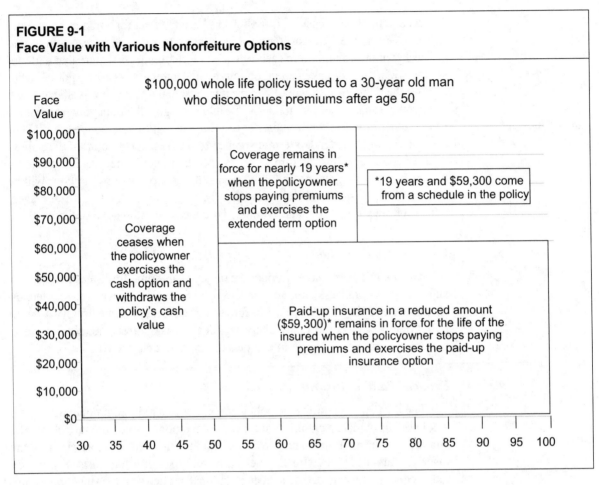

$100,000 whole life policy issued to a 30-year old man who discontinues premiums after age 50

Face Value

Coverage ceases when the policyowner exercises the cash option and withdraws the policy's cash value

Coverage remains in force for nearly 19 years* when the policyowner stops paying premiums and exercises the extended term option

*19 years and $59,300 come from a schedule in the policy

Paid-up insurance in a reduced amount ($59,300)* remains in force for the life of the insured when the policyowner stops paying premiums and exercises the paid-up insurance option

the right to take the cash value in the form of a life income, purchased at net rates, the insurer will usually grant the privilege on request. Some policyowners purchase ordinary life insurance to protect their families during the child-raising period with the objective of eventually using the cash values for their own retirements. The cash value, supplemented by Social Security benefits, private retirement plan benefits, and income from other savings, could provide a policyowner with an adequate retirement income.

Nonforfeiture Options

- Surrender the policy for cash.
- Buy a reduced amount of paid-up permanent insurance.
- Buy the same amount of extended term insurance.
- If the insurer allows, purchase an annuity.

Nonforfeiture options in universal and variable life insurance policies have special characteristics that differentiate them from traditional whole life policies. First, variable life policies provide no guarantees as to the minimum nonforfeiture values available under any of the three options. Second, universal and variable life policies in force under the reduced paid-up option or the extended term option may require further adjustments of the coverage if investment earnings or interest crediting rates fall significantly.

Example:	Following the death of her invalid husband, Rob, who was the beneficiary on her life insurance policy, Becky no longer wishes to pay premiums on the whole life insurance policy she has carried for the past 20 years. She contacts her financial advisor, who reminds her that her policy has accumulated a substantial cash value and that she will not need to forfeit this value because she has several options. Becky must select one of them:

- She can surrender the policy and take the money in cash.
- Rather than taking cash, Becky can probably arrange to surrender the policy and take the money as an annuity (periodic payments for the remainder of her life).
- She can stop paying premiums but keep permanent insurance in force with a reduced face limit.
- She can stop paying premiums and keep the full face limit of the insurance in force as term insurance that will expire at the end of a specified term.

If Becky chooses to keep life insurance in force, she will need to change the beneficiary to, perhaps, her children, her grandchildren, and/or a charity.

Settlement Options

settlement options

The standard policy provisions of the various states require that a life insurance policy include certain settlement option tables for the policy's death proceeds if the *settlement options* include installment payments or annuities. These tables must show the minimum amounts of the applicable installment or annuity payments.

The types of settlement options, other than the lump-sum or cash option, most commonly found in life insurance policies are the interest option, the fixed-period option, the fixed-amount option, and one or more life income options.

Interest Option

Under the interest option, the insurer temporarily retains the death proceeds and pays only the interest to the beneficiary periodically such as monthly or annually. The policy guarantees a minimum rate of interest, although insurers frequently pay a higher rate if investment earnings warrant it. The company pays the death proceeds at a specified later date at the request of the beneficiary, or on the occurrence of a specified event such as the beneficiary's death.

Fixed-Period Option

Under the fixed-period option, the insurer makes installment payments consisting of both the death proceeds and interest to the beneficiary over a specified period of time such as 10 years following the insured's death. Again, there is a guaranteed minimum interest rate. If the insurer pays a higher rate than the guaranteed rate, the amount of the installment payment increases accordingly.

Fixed-Amount Option

The insurance company makes level periodic installments of a specified amount to the beneficiary under the fixed-amount option. The payments consist of a portion of the death proceeds and interest earnings, and they continue for as long as the funds that the insurer holds last. Unlike the fixed-period option, excess interest earnings under the fixed-amount option do not increase the size of the periodic payments. Rather, they extend the length of time during which the payments will continue.

Life Income Options

Under a life income option, the policy's death proceeds are used as a single premium to purchase an annuity for the beneficiary. Various forms of annuities may be available, but the most common ones are a straight life income, a life income with a period certain, a life income with some type of refund feature, and a joint-and-survivor life income. Details concerning these life income options are contained in chapter 11.

Example:	As the beneficiary on his late wife Edna's $250,000 life insurance policy, Bob is entitled to receive benefits. He consults his financial advisor to decide how

best to handle these policy proceeds, and the advisor informs Bob that he can take the money in cash but that the policy also provides these other options:

- interest option. Bob can let the insurer keep the $250,000 for now, in effect lending it to the insurer, and have the insurer pay him interest at a rate no lower than the rate specified in the policy. Bob can receive the death proceeds later or arrange for them to be payable at his death.
- fixed-period option. Rather than taking the money as a lump sum, Bob can take it in payments over a fixed period of, say, 10 years, with the insurer paying at last a guaranteed minimum rate of interest.
- fixed-amount option. Instead of taking the money over a fixed period of time, Bob can choose to receive periodic payments in a fixed amount for as long as the money lasts, with the insurer paying at least a minimum guaranteed rate of interest. (The money will last longer if interest rates are higher.)
- life income option. Bob can use the $250,000 death proceeds to provide him with an income for as long as he lives.

Bob's choice among these options will depend on a variety of factors such as his age, his health, other income sources, and his interest in leaving an estate for his heirs or other beneficiaries.

PROHIBITED PROVISIONS

Although the state laws are not uniform, most states prohibit insurers from including certain provisions in their policies. For various reasons, courts or state legislatures have determined that these prohibited contract provisions violate public policy. There are five generally prohibited provisions:

- The insurance producer, who is the agent of the insurance company, may not be made the agent of the policyowner for purposes of filling out the application for insurance. If the producer were acting as an agent of the applicant, then any concealment or misrepresentation in the application would be binding on the policyowner even if the producer was aware of the true facts.

- Nonpayment of a loan cannot cause a forfeiture. The state laws generally provide that as long as the cash value of the insurance policy exceeds the total indebtedness on the policy, the policyowner's failure to repay the loan or to pay interest on the loan may not cause a forfeiture of the policy.

- An insurer cannot promise something on the declarations of the policy and take it away in the "fine print." This is spelled out in laws called *less value statutes* because the insurer is prohibited from providing a settlement option that is of less value than the death benefit of the policy.

- The insurance laws of several states prohibit use of a policy provision that gives the policyowner too short a time in which to bring suit against the insurer. Statutes of limitations place an upper limit on the time during which legal action can be brought for alleged wrongs of various types, but sometimes parties to a contract can agree on a shorter period. Some states allow insurers to include a shorter time period in their policies; the permissible periods vary from one to 6 years. Other states do not allow insurers to reduce the time specified in the statute of limitations. These laws protect the interests of the insurers and the public. Insurers are protected because the laws allow them to impose shorter limitation periods than otherwise permitted in the state. This benefits insurers because it requires plaintiffs to sue while information relevant to the insurance policy is still easy to obtain. The public is protected because the statutes do not allow insurers to shorten the limitation period so much that the public does not have sufficient time to determine whether a lawsuit is worthwhile.

backdating

- Although not directly related to a policy provision, state laws typically include a limitation concerning the effective date of the policy as specified on its declarations page. The limitation involves the practice of *backdating*, which means to issue the policy as if it had been purchased when the insured was younger. The consumer advantage is that the policyowner pays lower periodic premiums for the policy because the premium is based on the younger age. The consumer disadvantage is that the policyowner must pay the premium for the backdated period, during which no coverage existed. Statutes generally limit backdating to no more than 6 months.

OPTIONAL PROVISIONS

Numerous other provisions are neither required nor prohibited. Some of these relate to the beneficiary designation.

Beneficiary Provisions

Several provisions in a life insurance policy relate to designation of the beneficiary who receives policy proceeds upon the death of the insured. The first reference to the beneficiary appears on the policy's declarations page. There, the policyowner names the primary, and perhaps a contingent, beneficiary.

primary beneficiary

The *primary beneficiary* is the person or organization that is to receive the proceeds if he, she, or it survives the insured. The policyowner may name more than one person or organization, with a percentage of the proceeds allocated to each. The policyowner may even name the insured's estate as the primary beneficiary, although naming the estate is usually unwise because it subjects the proceeds to transfer taxes and costs that can be avoided. Naming the estate as primary beneficiary may be acceptable, however, if the proceeds are small and/or designed to pay only last-illness costs, funeral expenses, estate debts, and taxes. Among the parties often named as primary beneficiaries are the policyowner (if different from the insured), the heirs of the insured, other donee beneficiaries (such as charitable organizations), and creditors of the insured.

contingent beneficiary

A *contingent beneficiary* is a person or organization that is to receive the proceeds only if the primary beneficiary predeceases the insured or loses entitlement to any of the proceeds for some other reason (for example, if a charity named as primary beneficiary goes out of existence or if the primary beneficiary murders the insured). If the primary beneficiary is eligible to receive the policy proceeds, that extinguishes the rights of the contingent beneficiary.

When life insurance proceeds are payable under a settlement option (other than the lump-sum cash option), a contingent payee, as contrasted with a contingent beneficiary, may have a claim on the proceeds. For example, assume that the primary beneficiary begins receiving the policy's death proceeds under the life income with a 10-year period certain. If he or she dies after, say, 7 years, the remaining 3 years of income would go to the named contingent payee, who may or may not be the same person or organization as the contingent beneficiary.

Whether primary or contingent, beneficiaries may be named specifically (for example, my wife, Anne J. Kirby) or as a class (for example, the children born to my wife, Anne J. Kirby, and me). In either case, the policyowner should make every effort to be clear in spelling out who is to receive the proceeds. For example, simply designating "my husband" is unclear, as the policyowner may have more than one husband during her lifetime. Or simply designating "my grandchildren" is unclear because the policyowner's children may have adopted children, children from different marriages, or children from outside the state of marriage. Class designations present many possible problems in identifying who is a member of the class; therefore, insurers often limit the use of such designations.

Example: Dolores named her husband to receive the death proceeds of her life insurance policy. She also specified that if her husband predeceased her, the proceeds would be paid to her brother. The settlement option Dolores selected was the 10-year fixed period option. Dolores dies in 2005, her husband in 2004, and her brother in 2008.

Who gets what?

- The husband is the *primary beneficiary* but he gets nothing because Dolores outlived him.
- The brother is the *contingent beneficiary* but became the primary beneficiary when the husband died. The brother gets 3 years of death benefit payments.
- The brother's heirs or his estate are the *contingent payees* and get 7 years of death benefit payments.

The declarations page of the life insurance policy, in addition to identifying the beneficiaries, may also state whether they are named revocably or irrevocably. If the policyowner names a beneficiary revocably, the policyowner can change the designation at any time prior to the insured's death without the beneficiary's consent. If the policyowner names the beneficiary irrevocably, however, the policyowner must obtain the beneficiary's consent before making a beneficiary change. Usually, an irrevocable designation also requires that the beneficiary consent to the policyowner's exercise of other ownership rights in the policy such as surrendering it for cash or borrowing against the cash value.

Provisions in the body of the life insurance policy concerning the beneficiaries are not standardized. Policies often contain provisions that specify the conditions under which a policyowner can change the beneficiary designation. Also, the policy may describe the right of the beneficiary to name or change the contingent payee, who will receive the remaining proceeds if the beneficiary dies before all the death proceeds have been distributed. The policy can also specify that, if the beneficiary predeceases the insured and if no contingent beneficiary has been named or is alive when the insured dies, the proceeds will be paid to the policyowner or to his or her estate.

Other Optional Provisions

Life insurance policies usually contain optional provisions concerning suicide, ownership, assignment, and changes of plan. Increasingly, they also include a provision concerning accelerated benefits. Common optional provisions are as follows:

suicide provision
- *suicide provision.* An insurer can elect to cover suicide from the day it issues the policy. However, this is unusual, and most insurance contracts do not provide coverage for a death by suicide within the first one or 2 years after the policy issue date. If the policy does not contain a suicide exclusion provision, then the policy covers a death by suicide, and the death benefit is payable to the beneficiary regardless of when the suicide occurs.

  The following is a typical insurance contract suicide provision:

  > Suicide of the insured, while sane or insane, within 2 years of the issue date, is not covered by this policy. In that event, we will pay only the premiums paid to us, less any unpaid policy loans.

ownership provision
- *ownership provision.* Ordinarily, the insured is the applicant and owner of the policy. The ownership provision in the life insurance contract describes the rights of the owner. The typical ownership provision stipulates that the owner of the policy is the insured unless the application states otherwise. The provision usually states that the policyowner may change the beneficiary, assign the policy to another party, and exercise other ownership rights. If the provision describes these powers, it will also define how such powers are to be exercised in order to be recognized by the insurance company.

assignment provision
- *assignment provision.* In contract law, assignment is the act of transferring a property right. As with most contracts and most interests in property, the policyowner has, as a matter of law, the right to assign some or all of his or her rights to another person or an entity. The right to assign an ownership interest in a life insurance policy exists even without an assignment provision in the contract. However, most contracts include an assignment clause that clearly specifies the conditions under which the policyowner may make an assignment. The purpose of these conditions in a life insurance contract is to make the insurer aware of the assignment to eliminate future disputes. A sample assignment clause might provide the following:

  > You may assign this policy if we agree. We will not be bound by an assignment unless it has been received by us in writing at our home office. Your rights and the rights of any other person referred to in this policy will be subject to the assignment. We assume no responsibility for the validity of an assignment. An absolute assignment will be the same as a change of ownership to the assignee.

plan change provision
- *plan change provision.* This provision acknowledges that the parties may agree to change the terms of the contract. A sample plan change provision might read as follows:

Subject to our rules at the time of a change, you may change this policy to another plan of insurance, you may add riders to this policy, or you may make other changes if we agree.

accelerated benefits provision

- *accelerated benefits provision.* Some insurers have added a provision that permits the policyowner to withdraw a portion of death benefits under certain circumstances. These accelerated benefits or living benefits provisions state that if the insured becomes terminally ill, then the policyowner may withdraw a portion of the policy's death benefit. According to the NAIC Accelerated Benefits Model Regulation, the condition that permits the payment of the accelerated benefits must be a medical condition that drastically limits the insured's life span expectation (for example, to 2 years or less). The regulation also lists several examples of a qualifying medical condition: acute coronary artery disease, a permanent neurological deficit resulting from a cerebral vascular accident, end-stage renal failure, AIDS, or other such medical condition as the commissioner may approve. To qualify as accelerated benefits, the lifetime payments must reduce the death benefit otherwise payable under the contract. About half of the states have adopted regulations or statutes similar to the NAIC model.

RIDERS TO LIFE INSURANCE POLICIES

Common riders that policyowners can add to their life insurance policies include those concerning accidental death benefits, the guaranteed purchase option (also known as the guaranteed insurability option), and waiver of premium in the event of the insured's disability.

Accidental Death Benefits

accidental death benefits

Insurers add *accidental death benefits* to some contracts in the form of a rider, or amendment, to the policy. The rider is also known as the *double indemnity provision* because it usually doubles the standard death benefit if the insured dies accidentally.

In the absence of a specific definition of accidental death, *accident* means an unintentional event that is sudden and unexpected. An accidental death is one that is caused by an accident. This statement seems quite clear, but it is not always easy to apply. An insured may have been mortally injured in an accident, then died from a disease. The accidental death benefit is payable only if the accident was the cause of death. If the insured is in an auto accident but dies from a heart attack, the accidental death benefit is payable only if the accident is proven to have triggered the heart attack.

The standard practice of including a time limit in the accidental death benefit provision somewhat mitigates the problems caused by cases in which there may be more than one cause of death. In the most common type of provision, the death must occur within 90 days of the accident said to have caused the injury.

These basic definitions preclude coverage for any death that is the natural and probable result of a voluntary act. An unchallenged principle of law is that people are presumed to expect and intend the probable or foreseeable consequences of their actions. This concept is sometimes described by the term *assumption of risk*. If an individual plays Russian roulette, jumps off buildings, or runs with the bulls in Pamplona, Spain, his or her death as a result of those activities cannot be described as accidental.

A sample accidental death benefit provision is as follows:

> We will pay this benefit to the beneficiary when we have proof that the Insured's death was the result, directly and apart from any other cause, of accidental bodily injury, and that death occurred within one year after that injury and while this rider was in effect.

Some life insurance agents routinely include an accidental death benefit rider in virtually every life insurance contract they sell. The cost of the rider is small because a small percentage of all deaths occur as a result of accident. On the other hand, there is little reason for an individual to carry more insurance for an accidental death than for any other type of death, except perhaps as an appeal to the policyowner's gambling instinct.

Guaranteed Purchase Option

guaranteed purchase (insurability) option

Another popular policy provision is the *guaranteed purchase option*, also called the *guaranteed insurability option*. This provision helps policyowners protect themselves against the possibility that the insured might become uninsurable. Under the typical provision, the policyowner may purchase the right to acquire additional insurance in specified amounts at specified times or ages. Typically, this provision allows additional purchases every 3 years, upon marriage, and after the birth of a child, provided the events occur before the insured reaches a specified maximum age, often age 45. This right to purchase additional insurance can be valuable because the insured need not provide evidence of insurability to exercise the option. Another benefit of the guaranteed purchase option is that the new coverage is usually not subject to a new suicide provision or a new incontestable clause.

There is a ceiling on the maximum amount of insurance available under the guaranteed purchase option and a maximum age at which the option may be exercised. Once the insured passes an age or event that triggers the right to purchase additional insurance and does not exercise the option, that option lapses, but future options are not affected.

Guaranteed Purchase Option

- Allows purchase of specified additional amounts of insurance at specified times and ages
- No need to show evidence of insurability
- No new suicide exclusion or incontestable period
- Options not cumulative

Waiver of Premium

waiver-of-premium rider

A *waiver-of-premium rider* in the event of the insured's disability is another commonly available rider. According to a typical waiver-of-premium rider, if the insured becomes totally disabled as defined in the rider or policy, the insurance company will waive payment of premiums on the policy during the continuance of the insured's disability.

The disability waiver of premium has some limitations. For example, the insurer will not grant the waiver if the insured's disability begins after a specified age. In addition, the provision usually will not waive premiums if the disability is self-inflicted or the result of an act of war.

In any contract, it is important to pay close attention to the wording of the waiver-of-premium rider. For example, these riders usually require that the disability last for at least 6 months before premiums will be waived. Some riders specify that only premiums due thereafter will be waived, while others provide that the insurer will refund premiums that were paid during the 6 months, as well as waive premiums due thereafter.

Care should be taken to examine the definition of total disability used in the rider. A common definition of total disability is the inability to perform the essential duties of the insured's own job or of any job for which he or she is suited by reason of training or experience. However, some riders contain definitions that are less liberal to the insured.

POLICY FILING AND APPROVAL

If a policy is sold in a state but does not include a required provision or has not been filed with the state for approval, the courts will treat the policy as if it did include all of the required provisions under the law of that jurisdiction. The policyowner or beneficiary will be permitted to enforce the policy against the insurer as if it complied in all respects with the applicable state law. The state insurance commissioner is responsible for the compliance of insurance companies doing business in that state with that state's laws regarding the permitted and prohibited policy provisions. A policy may not be issued or delivered in a state until it has been approved by the state insurance department.

In some states, the insurer can assume that the policy has been approved if it has not been advised otherwise within a fixed period of time, such as 30 days, after submission to the state insurance department. In other states, the insurer may not issue the policy until it has received notice of approval from the department.

If an insurer issues a policy that the insurance department has not approved, the policyowner can seek a refund of premiums (because the contract is voidable) or seek enforcement of the policy. If there is a suit, the courts will enforce the unapproved contract against the insurer on behalf of the beneficiary. If the unapproved policy does not include a provision that would have been required for approval, the courts will treat the policy as if it did contain such a provision. Furthermore, if a required provision is more favorable to the policyowner than one actually included in the contract, the courts will treat the contract as if it included the more favorable provision. The insurer that violates the laws requiring filing of the policy and approval of its provisions by the state is also subject to fines or other penalties such as revocation of the insurer's right to do business in that state.

MINI-CASE: AMY AND JOHN SCHULTZ

Amy and John have recently decided to buy life insurance because (1) as first-time homeowners, they are concerned about Amy's ability to make mortgage payments, based only on her income, if John dies, (2) they plan to have children soon and ultimately to put them through college, and (3) they would like to provide an inheritance for their children. They are also concerned about the potential effects of future inflation.

After considering their options, Amy and John decide to buy participating life insurance policies that cover both their lives. The insurance application requires them to select a dividend option and gives them the opportunity to select three optional riders.

   a. Describe the factors Amy and John should consider when selecting a dividend option.

   b. Describe the factors Amy and John should consider when evaluating each of the following optional riders:

     (1) accidental death benefits

     (2) guaranteed purchase option

     (3) waiver-of-premium rider

(See answer section for answers to mini-case.)

SOURCE FOR FURTHER IN-DEPTH STUDY

- Graves, Edward E., and Christensen, Burke A., *McGill's Legal Aspects of Life Insurance*, 4th ed., Bryn Mawr, PA: The American College Press, 2004. Phone 888-263-7265. Web site address www.theamericancollege.edu

CHAPTER REVIEW

Answers to mini-case, review questions, and self-test questions start on page 793.

Key Terms

beneficiary
standard policy provisions laws
grace period
policy loan
automatic premium loan option
incontestable clause
divisible surplus
dividend options
fifth divided option
entire contract provision
reinstatement provision
representation
misstatement of age or gender
    clause

nonforfeiture options
settlement options
backdating
primary beneficiary
contingent beneficiary
suicide provision
ownership provision
assignment provision
plan change provision
accelerated benefits provision
accidental death benefits
guaranteed purchase (insurability)
    option
waiver-of-premium rider

Review Questions

9-1. What information usually appears on the declarations page of most life insurance policies?

9-2. Frank purchased a participating whole life policy many years ago, and over time, several questions have arisen regarding his coverage. Which policy provision should be reviewed to clarify each of the following questions, and what would that provision typically suggest?
  a. Frank just discovered that his premium was due 2 weeks ago. Is the coverage still in force?
  b. Frank is facing a liquidity crunch. He needs some cash but does not want to exercise a nonforfeiture option. Can his life insurance policy help?
  c. When Frank purchased the policy, he lied about his health history. Will this prevent his beneficiary from collecting the face amount of the coverage?
  d. Frank has been using his dividends to help pay premiums. Are other options available to him?
  e. When he applied for his policy, Frank understated his age to get a lower premium. What effect, if any, will this have on the benefits payable to his beneficiary when Frank dies?

9-3. Describe the two options, in addition to cash surrender values, that life insurance companies are required to provide under the Standard Nonforfeiture Law.

9-4. Describe the settlement options that life insurance policies most commonly provide.

9-5. What is the difference between
   a. a primary beneficiary and a contingent beneficiary
   b. the rights of the policyowner when the beneficiary is named revocably versus irrevocably

9-6. Bill purchased a $500,000 whole life policy 10 years ago. When his marriage and business recently failed, he became distraught and committed suicide. Would Bill's beneficiary receive the $500,000 policy death benefit?

9-7. Harold has the AIDS virus. His prognosis is not good, and he has exhausted all of his financial resources on treatment. His life insurance contract includes an accelerated benefits (living benefits) provision. How can this provision benefit Harold?

9-8. When Rita purchased a whole life policy, she added a double indemnity rider and was surprised to learn that adding the rider did not double her premium. Rita believes that she "slipped one past" the insurance company. Is Rita overlooking something?

9-9. How does a guaranteed purchase option protect an insured policyowner who may need additional life insurance protection in the future?

9-10. Susan, a 61-year old widow, has decided to stop paying the premiums on the $250,000 whole life policy that named her late husband as primary beneficiary and her three grandchildren as contingent beneficiaries. It's not that she needs the money she would receive by cashing in the policy because Susan was the beneficiary of a substantial life insurance policy on her late husband, but that she no longer sees a need for life insurance. Susan had thought of taking the life insurance policy's cash surrender value and using it to set up a trust to fund her grandchildren's college expenses, but she has just learned that the policy also provides other nonforfeiture options. What factors should Susan consider in evaluating her other options?

Self-Test Questions

T   F   9-1. Standard policy provision laws require that life insurance policies include certain provisions that are worded precisely as contained in the statute.

T   F   9-2. If the insured dies 2 weeks after the premium was due but not paid, the life insurance company must pay the beneficiary only an amount equal to the premiums paid in the past plus interest.

T   F   9-3. If the insured dies or surrenders the policy while a loan is outstanding, the insurer deducts the loan and accrued interest from the amount otherwise payable.

T   F   9-4.   After John's policy has been in force for 2 years during John's lifetime, the insurer can no longer contest the policy based on a false answer in the application about John's health.

T   F   9-5.   The use of dividends to purchase paid-up additions may be advantageous because the purchase is made at rates that do not contain a loading for expenses.

T   F   9-6.   If Bill dies 20 years after purchasing his whole life policy and the insurer discovers that he had understated his age in the application, the company will have to pay the face amount to the beneficiary because the 2-year contestability period is over.

T   F   9-7.   If the premium for a whole life insurance policy is overdue at the end of the grace period, the policy will lapse and automatically pay the cash surrender value to the policyowner.

T   F   9-8.   If Sarah named her husband as primary beneficiary and her children as contingent beneficiaries of her life insurance policy, and her husband predeceases her, the death proceeds from Sarah's policy will be paid to her husband's estate unless she has changed the beneficiary designation.

T   F   9-9.   If Teresa commits suicide 5 years after purchasing her whole life policy, the insurer will pay the face amount to the beneficiary.

T   F   9-10.   The person who has the power to exercise the rights in a life insurance policy is called the insured.

T   F   9-11.   Although accidental death benefit riders typically exclude death by suicide, they do pay for most deaths caused by disease.

T   F   9-12.   If a person purchases a life insurance policy that the state insurance department has not approved, the policyowner can seek a refund of premiums paid or seek to enforce the policy.

Life Insurance Planning and Purchasing Decisions

Learning Objectives

An understanding of the material in this chapter should enable the student to

10-1.   Explain the key approaches to determining the amount and type of life insurance appropriate for a client.

10-2.   Explain the key methods for measuring the cost of life insurance.

10-3.   Describe the issues involved in the replacement of a life insurance policy.

10-4.   Explain the reason for and methods used to treat substandard risks.

10-5.   Explain the regulation, ethics, taxation, and planning considerations of policy viatication.

10-6.   List and explain business uses of life insurance.

10-7.   Describe the taxation of life insurance benefits and premiums.

10-8.   Describe the uses of life insurance in estate planning.

Chapter Outline

As the preceding chapters have shown, many types of life insurance coverage are available, and each type has many different features. Therefore, clients who are considering the purchase of life insurance must make a variety of decisions with which the financial planner should be able to provide assistance. The present chapter provides guidance for financial planners regarding making life insurance recommendations, along with the implications of those recommendations.

LIFE INSURANCE PLANNING

Life insurance planning includes determining both how much and what type of insurance is needed. The first of these tasks is usually completed based on an analysis of the client's needs. The second task begins with a decision between temporary versus permanent coverage and proceeds to the selection of a particular type of policy.

This chapter assumes that clients are serious about their financial futures and that the financial services professional has established enough trust for the information-gathering and analysis process to proceed. Problem solving in this arena requires complete and accurate information about the client's finances. In addition, the planner must understand the client's priorities and goals or objectives. The planner must gather this information before making any recommendations.

The chapter begins with a discussion on determining the appropriate amount and type of life insurance to provide future income for persons who depend on the insured for support. It also discusses other uses of life insurance, following an overview of estate and gift taxation. An understanding of these tax rules is necessary to appreciate the role life insurance can play in estate planning.

Appropriate Amount of Life Insurance

Many different approaches are used to determine the amount of life insurance appropriate for any given client. Some of these approaches include the following:

- *multiple of income approach*—a simplistic approach that determines life insurance needs based on the client's current annual income
- *financial needs analysis approach*—an approach that determines how much life insurance is needed to provide a principal sum that will be liquidated to meet survivors' lump-sum and ongoing income needs
- *capital needs analysis approach*—an approach that determines how much life insurance is needed to provide a principal sum adequate to fund survivors' needs while preserving the principal

Multiple of Income Approach

How much life insurance should a client purchase? Some financial journalists recommend that people have life insurance and liquid assets in amounts ranging from 5 to 7 times their annual income. This simplistic approach is easy to explain, and it requires few computations. However, this approach ignores specific information about assets the client has already accumulated and any external sources of funds such as trusts and inheritances. This approach can err in either direction—that is, it can either overinsure or underinsure the client.

More sophisticated approaches to determine needs are described below. These approaches translate the client's needs into estimated costs, then evaluate assets and existing coverage to determine how much of the funding is already in place. Any deficit between the intended goals and objectives and current financial sources is usually a candidate for additional coverage.

Financial Needs Analysis Approach

financial needs analysis

The *financial needs analysis* approach is commonly used to determine how much life insurance a person should carry. This approach identifies survivors' immediate cash needs and ongoing income needs and assumes life insurance policy proceeds will be liquidated to meet them. The financial needs approach begins with estimates of the family's financial needs if the client were to die today. The two main categories of financial needs approaches are lump-sum needs at death and ongoing income needs.

Lump-Sum Needs at Death. This lump-sum need category deals with needs at the client's death that require immediate cash. These needs include

- final illness costs insurance does not cover
- repayment of outstanding debt, perhaps including the home mortgage loan that becomes due and payable upon death
- estate taxes, if applicable
- probate and attorney's expenses
- funeral, burial, or cremation expenses, as applicable
- operational expenses to cover survivors' ongoing, short-term household expenses such as mortgage or rental payments, utility bills, property insurance premiums, property taxes, food, clothing, transportation costs, and the costs of childcare or education
- an emergency fund

Although it does not address specific identifiable expenses, an emergency fund provides an important safety net or shock absorber that will help survivors cope with unexpected costs that could otherwise devastate a family in a strained financial situation. An emergency fund enables the family to meet emergencies without sacrificing funds it needs for ongoing expenses. Determining emergency fund needs should take into consideration any liquid or near-liquid assets that survivors could use to cover emergencies. Money market accounts and listed securities that can readily be liquidated can reduce the extent to which life insurance proceeds are needed to address emergencies.

Children's educational needs might be considered either a lump-sum need or an ongoing income need, depending on the specific situation. Both the amount of the need and the timing of the need depend on the number of children and their ages, the costs associated with the educational institutions they will attend, the number of years for which educational support is to be provided, and the portion of educational expenses the parents intend to fund. Some families' educational goals include a public school education, while others intend to pay for private preparatory schools and an Ivy League college education that includes a graduate degree.

Ongoing Income Needs. In addition to a lump-sum cash need to manage specific, immediate expenses, most clients' surviving dependent family members have ongoing financial needs that require a flow of income that continues until the dependents can support themselves. Some families can reasonably expect all members to become self-sufficient soon after the head of the household dies. In other families, such an expectation is so unrealistic that a client who does not provide for the survivors' support is guilty of neglect. Some surviving spouses never become self-sufficient, and there often is no intent that the surviving spouse support himself or herself.

Many families wish to prefund survivors' income needs at least until the youngest child becomes self-sufficient, typically when the child completes his or her formal education. Some families have special-needs children who never will become self-sufficient; these children can have ongoing income needs that extend for many years beyond the death of both parents.

Survivors' ongoing income needs are commonly analyzed in four categories:

- readjustment income for the period immediately after death
- adjusted income starting after the initial transition period, continuing until the youngest child becomes self-sufficient
- income for the surviving spouse, if any, after the children have become self-sufficient and before the spouse is again eligible for Social Security benefits (the blackout period)
- surviving spouse's income after renewed eligibility for Social Security benefits and initial eligibility for private pension benefits

Because the purpose of life insurance is to fund the unfunded portion of these objectives, all existing funds that can provide part or all of these needs should be considered. For simplicity and efficiency, most planners suggest using a percentage of the insured's current income as the target income level, rather than calculating a composite of each separate anticipated need. That the survivors will need about 70 percent of the predeath income to carry on after the insured's death is often assumed, but a higher or lower percentage may be more accurate depending on a particular family's circumstances.

Social Security benefits are the most commonly available source of income for survivors. These benefits are discussed in chapter 7. Other potential sources of income include employer-provided plan benefits such as deferred compensation, group life insurance, any qualified plan participation funds that are not forfeited or terminated upon the employee's death, and perhaps the surviving spouse's earnings.

At this point in the process, a financial planner has helped the client determine the income necessary to provide a readjustment income and meet each of the other income objectives. The planner has also identified existing benefits or sources of income and estimated their anticipated levels. The gap between needs and income for each period is a deficit that must be addressed. The next step in the planning process is to determine the present value of all future additional income needs. The total income need is simply the sum of the present values of income deficiencies for each separate period. This entire process is illustrated in the following example.

Case Example of Financial Needs Analysis

A simplified case situation will illustrate the use of the financial needs analysis method to determine the amount of life insurance needed.

Ted and Maggie Stringer are a young married couple with a 4-year-old daughter, Laura. Ted is aged 31 and is a bank executive earning $48,000 per year. Maggie, aged 27, is an elementary school teacher earning $28,000 per year.

Following a series of conversations with Ted and Maggie, their financial planner has summarized their objectives or needs in today's dollars, if Ted were to die today, as follows:

- Lump-sum needs at Ted's death
    - Funeral expenses $5,000
    - Estate clearance (attorney's fees,
      debts, taxes, etc.)   5,000
    - Mortgage retirement   140,000
    - Emergency fund   15,000
    - Education fund for Laura   100,000
          Total $265,000
- Income needs after Ted's death
    - Readjustment period income for one year $ 65,000
    - Dependency period income per year for
      17 years $ 50,000
    - Life income per year for Maggie after Laura
      finishes college $ 40,000

The financial planner next gathers information about the sources of funds Ted and Maggie already have for meeting the above needs. Their principal resources are as follows:

- Group term life insurance on Ted provided by
  the bank (face amount) $96,000
- Individual universal life insurance on Ted
  (face amount) $50,000
- Investments (mutual funds and 401(k) plan,
  market value) $20,000
- Checking account (average balance) $ 2,045
- Social Security lump-sum death benefit $ 255
- Social Security survivorship benefits (Laura
  until she finishes high school at age 18) $ 6,000/yr.
- Maggie's income $28,000/yr.
- Maggie's combined Social Security retirement
  benefits and miscellaneous income at
  age 65 for life $15,000/yr.

Notice that no specific amount of Social Security survivorship benefits is identified for Maggie. Instead, Maggie's earned income is assumed to cause her to forfeit these benefits as long as she is working. A further assumption for purposes of simplicity is that Maggie's income is shown as an annual average, rather than an estimated amount year by year. Also, notice that a combined income of $15,000 per year is assumed for Maggie beginning at her projected retirement age of 65 from her pension, Social Security benefits, and miscellaneous sources. Note that Maggie will not be eligible for full Social Security retirement benefits until age 67.

As noted earlier, the family needs a total of $265,000 as a lump sum at Ted's death. The present sources of funds with which to meet this need total only $166,000, consisting of group insurance of $96,000, individual insurance of $50,000, and investments of $20,000. The checking account and Social Security lump-sum death benefit are ignored. Thus, a first need is for an additional $99,000 to meet the lump-sum needs (the difference between $265,000 and $166,000).

A time line, as shown in figure 10-1, is useful for planning the income needs of the family. The uppermost set of lines shows the desired income level of $65,000 for the readjustment period of one year, followed by $50,000 per year for the dependency period of 17 years until Laura's age 22, followed by $40,000 per year as the income Maggie needs, beginning at her age 45 and continuing for the rest of her life. Below the lines are the various sources of income available to provide the desired income, consisting of a Social Security benefit for Laura until her age 18, an unspecified mix of Maggie's Social Security benefits and earned income until age 65, and Maggie's pension, Social Security benefits, and miscellaneous income beginning at age 65 and continuing for life.

The period of time in this graph, spanning 40 years or more, can be broken into five component segments. For each segment, figure 10-1 shows the income gap, or the difference between the desired or needed income during each period and the available income at that time. This gap amounts to

$65,000 minus $34,000, or $31,000, for one year; followed by
$50,000 minus $34,000, or $16,000, for 13 years; followed by
$50,000 minus $28,000, or $22,000, for 4 years; followed by
$40,000 minus $28,000, or $12,000, for 20 years; followed by
$40,000 minus $15,000, or $25,000, for the rest of Maggie's life

The amount of life insurance proceeds needed today to fill the income gap is the present value of each of the separate gaps. If discounted at an assumed after-tax rate of return of 6 percent per year, the total present value can be found with a calculator's net present value (NPV) function or by using an Excel® spreadsheet as shown in figure 10-2. As indicated, assuming Maggie lives to age 85, the net present value is approximately $294,000.

FIGURE 10-1
The Stringers' Income Needs and Available Resources

On this basis, the total additional life insurance that should be written on Ted's life is $99,000 for the lump-sum needs and $294,000 for the survivors' income needs, or approximately $393,000. (Note that a similar approach can be used to determined the amount of life insurance Maggie should have.)

There are two difficulties with this amount of insurance:

- Maggie could outlive this income because an assumption was made that she would live for no more than 20 years, or to age 85, after she retired. The insurance needs would increase by approximately $8,000 if a life expectancy of age 100 were used. Note how little additional insurance is required to guarantee income for a longer time if that time is far in the future.
- No inflationary increase in the annual income is provided to the survivors.

	A	B	C	D	E
1	**FIGURE 10-2** **Maggie's Needs Analysis Calculations upon Ted's Death**				
2					
3	**Maggie's Age**	**Year**	**Need**	**Income**	**Gap**
4	27	1	$65,000	$34,000	$31,000
5	28	2	$50,000	$34,000	$16,000
6	29	3	$50,000	$34,000	$16,000
7	30	4	$50,000	$34.000	$16,000
8	31	5	$50,000	$34,000	$16,000
9	32	6	$50,000	$34,000	$16,000
10	33	7	$50,000	$34,000	$16,000
11	34	8	$50,000	$34,000	$16,000
12	35	9	$50,000	$34,000	$16,000
13	36	10	$50,000	$34,000	$16,000
14	37	11	$50,000	$34,000	$16,000
15	38	12	$50,000	$34,000	$16,000
16	39	13	$50,000	$34,000	$16,000
17	40	14	$50,000	$34,000	$16,000
18	41	15	$50,000	$28,000	$22,000
19	42	16	$50,000	$28,000	$22,000
20	43	17	$50,000	$28,000	$22,000
21	44	18	$50,000	$28,000	$22,000
22	45	19	$40,000	$28,000	$12,000
23	46	20	$40,000	$28,000	$12,000
24	47	21	$40,000	$28,000	$12,000
25	48	22	$40,000	$28,000	$12,000
26	49	23	$40,000	$28,000	$12,000
27	50	24	$40,000	$28,000	$12,000
28	51	25	$40,000	$28,000	$12,000
29	52	26	$40,000	$28,000	$12,000
30	52	27	$40,000	$28,000	$12,000
31	54	28	$40,000	$28,000	$12,000
32	55	29	$40,000	$28,000	$12,000
33	56	30	$40,000	$28,000	$12,000
34	57	31	$40,000	$28,000	$12,000
35	58	32	$40,000	$28,000	$12,000
36	59	33	$40,000	$28,000	$12,000
37	60	34	$40,000	$28,000	$12,000
38	61	35	$40,000	$28,000	$12,000
39	62	36	$40,000	$28,000	$12,000
40	63	37	$40,000	$28,000	$12,000
41	64	38	$40,000	$28,000	$12,000
42	65	39	$40,000	$15,000	$25,000
43	66	40	$40,000	$15,000	$25,000
44	67	41	$40,000	$15,000	$25,000
45	68	42	$40,000	$15,000	$25,000
46	59	43	$40,000	$15,000	$25,000

	A	B	C	D	E
	FIGURE 10-2 (Continued) **Maggie's Needs Analysis Calculations upon Ted's Death**				
	Maggie's Age	**Year**	**Need**	**Income**	**Gap**
47	70	44	$40,000	$15,000	$25,000
48	71	45	$40,000	$15,000	$25,000
49	72	46	$40,000	$15,000	$25,000
50	73	47	$40,000	$15,000	$25,000
51	74	48	$40,000	$15,000	$25,000
52	75	49	$40,000	$15,000	$25,000
53	76	50	$40,000	$15,000	$25,000
54	77	51	$40,000	$15,000	$25,000
55	78	52	$40,000	$15,000	$25,000
56	79	53	$40,000	$15,000	$25,000
57	80	54	$40,000	$15,000	$25,000
58	81	55	$40,000	$15,000	$25,000
59	82	56	$40,000	$15,000	$25,000
60	83	57	$40,000	$15,000	$25,000
61	84	58	$40,000	$15,000	$25,000
62	85	59	$40,000	$15,000	$25,000
63	86	60	$40,000	$15,000	$25,000
64	87	61	$40,000	$15,000	$25,000
65	88	62	$40,000	$15,000	$25,000
66	89	63	$40,000	$15,000	$25,000
67	90	64	$40,000	$15,000	$25,000
68	91	65	$40,000	$15,000	$25,000
69	92	66	$40,000	$15,000	$25,000
70	93	67	$40,000	$15,000	$25,000
71	94	68	$40,000	$15,000	$25,000
72	95	69	$40,000	$15,000	$25,000
73	96	70	$40,000	$15,000	$25,000
74	97	71	$40,000	$15,000	$25,000
75	98	72	$40,000	$15,000	$25,000
76	99	73	$40,000	$15,000	$25,000
77	100	74	$40,000	$15,000	$25,000

Basis of NPV calculation:
PV to age 85: $293,552.86 = E4+NPV(0.06,(E5:E62))
PV to age 100: $301,823.13 = E4+NPV(0.06,(E5.E77))

As to the first point, additional life insurance on Ted at a later date, if he does not die soon, or electing a life income settlement option for a portion of the life insurance death proceeds could provide a partial solution. Alternatively, at some point, Maggie could use the then unliquidated capital sum from the life insurance proceeds to purchase an annuity. Annuities, which are discussed in chapter 11, can provide an income for Maggie's lifetime. Then, too, if all else fails, perhaps Laura will be able and willing to help support her mother in Maggie's later years.

As for the latter point regarding inflation, several approaches can alleviate the problem. For example, Social Security benefits for survivors and retirees are automatically adjusted annually for inflation. Also, a rate of interest lower than 6 percent could be used to calculate the present value of the income. The lower discount rate would create a larger amount of additional life insurance needed but would allow for modest periodic increases in the income it provides. Alternatively, Ted's life insurance could be increased later by including a guaranteed insurability option in the policy and/or by using policy dividends to buy additional insurance. Another possible approach is for Ted to buy a variable or variable universal type of life insurance policy. The premium cost, however, may be prohibitive at this point in light of the Stringers' present income and the large amount of life insurance needed.

The financial needs analysis approach requires estimating the beneficiary's likely age at death and planning for the capital sum to be fully liquidated at that date or later. The problem is that the person might live longer than the plan has projected. Any liquidation planning predicated on the beneficiary's death at an early age runs a high probability of using all the proceeds while the beneficiary still needs them.

Capital Needs Analysis Approach

capital needs analysis

The *capital needs analysis* approach resembles the financial needs analysis approach, just described. However, the capital needs analysis approach relies on meeting income needs with the earnings on a principal sum, without liquidating that sum. Capital is therefore retained rather than being consumed.

The capital needs analysis approach is most appropriate for a client who wishes not only to meet the financial needs of surviving family members but also to leave an estate that will pass to other heirs or be used for charitable purposes. It should be pointed out that preserving capital requires a substantially larger capital sum than consuming it during the survivor's remaining lifetime. When used to assess a client's life insurance needs, the capital needs approach is therefore likely to require a much higher insurance recommendation than the financial needs analysis approach, as shown in the following example.

Example: Based on a 5 percent interest assumption, a $1 million capital sum will provide a monthly income of approximately $10,500 for 120 months under the financial needs approach. At the end of that period, the capital sum will have been liquidated.

Under the capital needs analysis approach, a $1 million capital sum will provide a monthly income of about $4,200, but the income will continue indefinitely. To provide a monthly income of $10,500 would require a capital sum of about $2.5 million.

If capital is to be retained, determination of the amount of life insurance to own based on needs proceeds as in the capital liquidation approach. Then a personal balance sheet of the client is prepared. All the liabilities, immediate cash needs, and all assets that do not produce income, such as the residence, are subtracted from the total assets. The remainder is the client's present income-producing capital. The last step is to compute the amount of additional capital needed to achieve the desired income objective net of all other income sources.

The amount of additional capital needed to meet the desired objective is found by dividing the amount of additional income needed by the applicable interest rate that represents the after-tax rate of investment return anticipated on the capital sum. For example, if $100,000 per year of additional income is desired, and the capital sum generating those income payments can realistically be expected to generate a 5 percent return after taxes, a $2 million fund is sufficient ($100,000 ÷ .05 = $2,000,000).

Obviously, the lower the after-tax investment return rate, the higher the capital fund needed to produce the same amount of income. Similarly, higher marginal tax rates will lower the after-tax return rate and increase the size of the fund needed to generate the income.

The choice between capital liquidation and capital retention is not necessarily an all-or-nothing decision. A planner may use a combination of the two approaches, liquidating some of the client's capital and retaining some of it, as a compromise approach to filling the gap between the income needs of the survivors and the other available sources of income.

Life Insurance and Retirement Needs

The income needs described to this point do not include the client's own retirement. The client who survives long enough to retire does not need to fund most of the needs previously described in this chapter, but he or she then has a need for retirement income. Financial planners need to consider this contingency in determining not only the amount but also the type of insurance a family head should carry. Term insurance can provide the necessary capital sum upon the death of the insured, but permanent insurance cannot only meet the family's capital needs upon the client's death but also build a cash value that helps address the postretirement needs of the insured and his or her spouse.

Appropriate Type of Life Insurance

After the needed amount of life insurance has been determined, there is a question about the most appropriate types of life insurance for the client. Too often, this question resolves itself into the highly debatable and often emotional matter of term life insurance versus permanent life insurance. In fact, each of these types has a legitimate role in life insurance planning for a client.

Chapter 8 describes the characteristics of term insurance, including

- the temporary nature of the coverage. Even the right to renew or to convert expires at some point.
- the low initial premium cost per $1,000 of coverage because of the absence of a savings element
- the rising premium, at an increasing rate, at the expiration of each period of coverage
- the inclusion in the rate of a margin to offset the adverse selection among term insurance purchasers
- the availability of a death benefit that can be level over time, decreasing, or, in some cases, increasing

Needs that term insurance can and should meet are encountered daily. One of the most obvious is to hedge a loan. A term policy in the amount of the loan payable to the lender protects the lender against possible loss, and it relieves the insured's estate of the burden of repaying the loan if the insured dies. An entrepreneur who has invested heavily in a speculative business venture should protect his or her family and estate by obtaining term insurance in the amount of the investment. A parent with young children is likely to need more insurance while the children are dependent than he or she will need when they are grown and self-sufficient. Additional insurance during the child-raising period can be provided through term insurance, frequently through decreasing term insurance superimposed on a permanent policy.

On the other hand, some needs for life insurance are permanent, or at least extend over a very long period. For example, a client's need for funds with which to provide a life income for his or her spouse may not arise in the next few years, or even by age 65. A wealthy client's need for a substantial sum with which to meet estate clearance costs at his or her death or that of his or her spouse is likely to extend for several decades. Permanent life insurance is an efficient, cost-effective way to partially fill these needs.

Nonetheless, some financial planners find virtually no legitimate role for permanent insurance in life insurance planning for their clients. They argue that clients are best served by providing for their death protection needs initially through low-premium term coverage and by meeting their other needs through investing the premium dollars saved in a separate fund. Buying term and investing the difference, or separating the savings and protection elements of the life insurance contract, is based on the assumption that an individual can invest his or her surplus funds more wisely and with a greater return than the life insurance company can. This argument should be analyzed in terms of the objectives of any investment program: safety of principal, yield, and liquidity.

Regarding safety of principal, the life insurance industry has compiled a solvency record over the years that is unmatched by any other type of business organization. Losses to policyowners have been relatively rare despite periods of war, depression, and inflation. Even the few insurance companies seized by regulators in recent years have been able to honor most of their policyowners' contracts.

Life insurance companies unquestionably obtain the highest possible yield commensurate with the standard of safety they have set for themselves and the regulatory constraints within which they operate. Precise measurement of their yield is complicated by several aspects of life insurance accounting. Comparisons of the returns earned by life insurers depend on which invested assets are being considered, and whether they are total invested assets or various separate blocks of assets supporting variable insurance and annuity products.

At certain times, many individuals may be able to secure a higher yield than that provided by a life insurance company by investing in common stocks or other equity investments, and some exceptional investors will be able to do it under virtually any circumstances. The typical life insurance policyowner is unlikely, over a long period, to earn a consistently higher yield than a life insurance company without taking on a greater degree of speculative investment risk. As described later, annual increases in cash values are not subject to federal income taxes as they accrue, while the earnings from a separate investment program are often taxed as ordinary income.

With respect to the third objective of an investment program, the liquidity of a life insurance contract is unsurpassed. The policyowner's cash value can be taken out at any time with no loss of principal. This can be accomplished through surrender for cash, policy loans, or in many newer life insurance products, partial withdrawals. Unlike equity investments, the policyowner virtually never faces the possibility of liquidating his or her assets in an unfavorable market. Unlike other loans, policy loans cannot be called because of inadequate collateral.

More important perhaps than any of the preceding factors is the question of whether savings under a separate investment program will actually take place. Fixed-premium life insurance that develops cash values is a form of "forced" saving. Periodic premiums provide a simple and systematic mechanism for saving, and when the savings feature is combined with the protection feature, there is also far more incentive for the policyowner to save consistently than otherwise might be present. An individual who voluntarily buys a bond a month, who purchases a flexible-premium form of life insurance, or who sets a certain amount per month in another type of savings program might skip a month or two if some other use of money is more appealing. If, however, failure to set

---

Buy Term and Invest the Difference?
Factors to Consider

- Safety of principal and income
- Rate of return
- Liquidity
- Assurance that saving will be done

aside the predetermined contribution to a savings program would result in loss of highly prized insurance protection that might be irreplaceable, he or she will be far more likely to make the savings effort.

The foregoing is not to disparage other forms of investment. All have their place in an individual's financial program. Permanent life insurance, however, can be the foundation for funding lifelong financial needs, particularly if there is a long-term need for life insurance.

If permanent life insurance is to play a role in financial planning for a client, each of the types of such insurance should be considered. The characteristics of several types of permanent life insurance are described in chapter 8. Among the distinguishing characteristics that may make one type preferable over another for a particular client are the following:

- *length of the planned premium-paying period.* The shorter this period, the higher the periodic premium. The client should consider limited-payment whole life to confine premium payments to his or her years of earned income. Alternatively, the client could purchase ordinary life but use dividends or a nonforfeiture option to avoid the need for lifelong premium payments.
- *emphasis on saving versus protection.* Again, limited-payment life builds up the savings component more rapidly than ordinary life. If very heavy emphasis is to be placed on the savings element, the client should consider a very short premium-paying period, perhaps even single-premium whole life, or an endowment, although some of the advantage of the tax-deferred buildup of the savings element can be lost.
- *time when death benefits are needed.* If the principal need for funds is at the death of the main income earner, a single-life policy is appropriate. However, if the principal need for funds is to provide estate liquidity when the surviving spouse dies, the client should consider a joint-life or survivorship (second-to-die) policy.
- *desire for inflation protection.* Variable life, universal life, or variable universal life insurance can provide increasing amounts of death benefit protection. In these and other types of insurance, the use of dividends to buy additional insurance or the use of a guaranteed insurability option is also helpful.
- *importance of yield versus safety in the savings component.* If the client's risk-tolerance permits, variable, universal, or variable universal life may be appropriate as a way to achieve a higher yield.
- *unbundling of cost components.* If the client wants to know where his or her premium dollars go, he or she should consider variable, universal, or variable universal life insurance.
- *premium-payment flexibility.* Universal life or variable universal life can be appropriate if premium flexibility is important to the client.

MEASURING THE COST OF LIFE INSURANCE

Of course, one of the important factors in a rational life insurance purchasing decision is the cost. If all other factors are equal, low-cost insurance obviously is preferable. If the other factors are unequal, the prospective purchaser needs to weigh price differentials against the differences in other factors that are important to him or her. Therefore, meaningful cost information is an essential element in intelligent decision-making.

At one time, it was common for insurers and their agents to show the net cost of a policy as equal to the sum of the premiums to be paid during the first, for example, 20 years of the policy, minus the sum of the dividends anticipated during that period, and minus the cash value available at the end of that period. The rather ludicrous result of this traditional net cost method was often a net cost of less than zero. Purchasers were asked to believe not only that their insurance for the 20 years would be free but also that the insurer would pay them for the privilege of giving them the coverage!

The weakness of the traditional net cost method was the disregard for the time value of money. Specifically, the method ignored that premiums must be paid out by purchasers every year, whereas most of the dividends and cash values are not available until much later. Also, dividend growth patterns, and perhaps those of cash values, can differ significantly for different insurance companies.

Example: Under the traditional 20-year net cost method, if the annual premium for a $100,000 policy is $1,600, the 20th-year cash value is $28,000, and the projected dividends total $7,200, the annual net cost per $1,000 of coverage would be shown as

Premiums ($1,600 x 20)	$32,000
Minus dividends	7,200
Minus cash value	28,000
Net cost	–$ 3,200
Net cost per $1,000 (–$3,200 ÷ 100)	–$ 32.00

The National Association of Insurance Commissioners (NAIC) has developed a model regulation to improve the quality of the cost information prospective life insurance buyers receive. The regulation requires insurers to give the prospective purchaser a buyer's guide that contains a clear explanation of products and how to shop for them, and a policy summary that contains essential information pertaining to the particular policy under consideration. The policy summary is required to disclose two interest-adjusted cost indexes that reflect the time value of money by recognizing that money is paid and received at different times and that costs can be better compared by using a spec[...] interest assumption. These two indexes are referred to as a surrender cost ind[...] and a net payment cost index.

Surrender Cost Index

surrender cost index

The *surrender cost index* is useful when the client's main concern is the level of cash values. This index indicates the cost of surrendering the policy for the cash value at some future point in time such as 20 years. The index shows the average amount of each annual premium that is not returned if the policy is surrendered for its cash value.

To compute the surrender cost index, the usual steps are:

(1)   Assume that each annual premium, paid at the beginning of the year, is placed in an account to accumulate at 5 percent interest until the end of a 20-year period.

(2)   Assume that each annual dividend, paid at the end of the year, is placed in an account to accumulate at 5 percent interest until the end of the 20-year period.

(3)   Subtract the 20th-year cash value and the result of step (2) from the result of step (1).

(4)   Divide the result of step (3) by 34.719. This interest factor converts it into an equivalent level annual amount that, if paid at the beginning of each year over a 20 year period, would accrue to the value in step (3). With this computation, the cost is discounted over 20 years at 5 percent to a beginning-of-year annuity.

(5)   Divide the result of step (4) by the number of thousands of dollars in the policy's death benefit. The result is the estimated level annual cost per $1,000 of coverage.

Net Payment Cost Index

net payment cost index

The other interest-adjusted cost index is the *net payment cost index,* useful when the client's main concern is the death benefit to be paid at the end of the 20th year, rather than the cash value. The procedure for calculating this index is identical to that for the surrender cost index, except that in step (3) there is no subtraction of the 20th-year cash value.

Although the use of these cost indexes is subject to caveats, including that the indexes do not reflect actual net costs to the individual policyowner, the prospective cost estimates can be valuable in giving the applicant a relative sense of which similar policies are high or low in cost. Note, however, the actual cost of a life insurance policy to an individual depends on his or her own circumstances and the actual cash flows experienced under the policy. This actual cost cannot be ascertained until the contract expires by death, maturity, or surrender.

Example: Assume that a policy has a $100,000 death benefit. Assume also that the level annual premiums, if accumulated at 5 percent compound interest from the time of payment until the end of the 20th policy year, would amount to $75,931. Further assume that the 20th year cash value is $35,900. Last, assume that the anticipated dividends, if accumulated at 5 percent compound interest from the time of receipt until the end of the 20th policy year, would amount to $14,119. The 20-year surrender cost index would be

Accumulated premiums	$75,931.00
Minus accumulated dividends	14,119.00
Minus cash value	35,900.00
Cost	$25,912.00
Discounted over 20 years at 5 percent,	
to a beginning-of-year annuity	= $746.33
Divided by 100 units of coverage	= $7.46

The net payment cost index would not entail subtraction of the cash value. It would therefore be

Accumulated premiums	$75,931.00
Minus accumulated dividends	14,119.00
Cost	$61,812.00
Discounted over 20 years at 5 percent,	
to a beginning-of-year annuity	= $1,780.34
Divided by 100 units of coverage	= $17.80

LIFE INSURANCE POLICY REPLACEMENT

replacement

Life insurance purchasing decisions may involve the *replacement* of an old policy with a new one. An existing insurance policy may be replaced by another policy from the same insurer or by a policy issued by a different insurer. Twisting, an illegal practice discussed in chapter 5, takes place when a policyowner is induced to discontinue and replace a policy through agent or insurer distortion or misrepresentation of the facts. However, replacement can occur in the absence of any distortion or misrepresentation.

The replacing agent's motives may or may not be laudable. If an agent accurately discloses the facts and the replacement works to the policyowner's benefit, replacement does not present a social problem. However, because of high first-year commissions on new policies, agents have financial incentives not only to take business away from another insurer but also to replace a policy in their own company to generate another first-year commission. Furthermore, insurers who seek new business may not be averse to taking it away from a competitor, even when doing so may not benefit the policyowner.

Traditionally, most replacements were considered detrimental to the policyowner because he or she had already incurred the high first-year expenses, because the premiums under the new policy might be higher due to the insured's increased age, and because the suicide and incontestable provisions might expire sooner, if they have not already done so, under the existing policy. However, with sometimes higher interest rates and improved mortality experience, policyowners may be able to improve their situations by replacing an existing policy with either the same or a different company. However, proposed replacements need to be carefully evaluated.

To protect policyowners' interests, the NAIC developed the Unfair Trade Practices Act, which contains prohibitions against misrepresentation, including misrepresentations to induce the lapse, forfeiture, exchange, conversion, or surrender of any life insurance policy. The NAIC has also adopted what is now called the Life Insurance and Annuities Replacement Model Regulation, which focuses on giving the buyer full disclosure of information in a fair and accurate manner and providing ample time to review the information before making a final decision.

When an agent submits an application for life insurance or an annuity to the insurer, he or she must include a statement about whether the policy is a replacement. If a replacement is involved, the agent must give the applicant a prescribed notice that alerts the applicant to the need to compare the existing and the proposed benefits carefully and to seek information from the agent or insurer from whom he or she purchased the original policy. The replacing insurer must advise the other insurer of the proposed replacement and provide information on the new policy. The replacing insurer must also give the applicant at least a 20-day free look at the new policy, during which time he or she has an unconditional right to a full refund of all premiums paid if he or she decides not to retain the policy. The existing insurer or agent has 20 days to furnish the policyowner with information on the existing policy, including the premium, cash values, death benefits, and dividends. Both insurers and agents are responsible for the accuracy of the information submitted to the person whose policy is being considered for replacement.

Some Issues in Policy Replacement

- Pay high first-year expenses again?
- Higher premium?
- New suicide clause?
- New incontestable clause?
- More or less favorable policy terms?

SUBSTANDARD COVERAGE

In life insurance, an individual who belongs to a class with a higher-than-standard mortality rate is referred to as a substandard risk. The individual may still be considered insurable by an insurer's underwriter, but only on a substandard basis. This situation occurs in about 6 percent to 7 percent of all new policies issued, and it introduces some additional complexities into the life insurance purchasing decision.

A group or classification that an insurer rates as substandard, such as male applicants who have elevated blood pressure readings, is expected to produce a higher mortality rate than a group of normal lives. The group concept must be emphasized because, as with insuring standard applicants, there is no certainty about any individual's longevity expectations. All assumptions therefore are based on the anticipated average experience of a large number of individuals.

The law of large numbers should be reiterated in any consideration of substandard insurance, involving, as it does, extra cost or restricted benefits for the policyowner or beneficiary. Some believe that if an individual is placed in a substandard classification and subsequently lives to a ripe old age, the company erred in its treatment of the case. However, if 1,000 persons, each of whom is suffering from a particular physical impairment, are granted insurance, the death rate among them will be greater than the death rate among a group of people the same age who are free of any discernible impairments. To allow for the higher death rates or extra mortality that will certainly occur within the substandard group, the company must collect an extra premium from or impose special terms on all who are subject to the extra mortality. The insurer does not expect that every member of the group will survive for a shorter period than the normal life expectancy, just that a larger proportion of the people in a standard group will attain normal life expectancy.

Incidence of Extra Mortality

If a group of substandard applicants is to be fairly treated, the degree of extra mortality the group represents and the approximate period in life when the extra mortality is likely to occur must both be known within reasonable limits. The timing of claims makes a great deal of difference financially to the insurer, whether the extra claims are expected to occur primarily in early life, middle age, old age, or at a level rate throughout the individuals' lifetimes. If the extra mortality occurs during the early years of the policies, when the net amount at risk is relatively large, the burden on the insurance company will be greater than if it occurs later, when the net amount at risk is relatively small. Therefore, between two substandard groups representing the same aggregate amount of extra mortality, the group whose extra mortality is concentrated later in life should pay a smaller extra premium than the group whose extra mortality occurs earlier.

The majority of companies assume that each substandard applicant falls into one of three broad groups. In the first group, the additional hazard increases with age; in the second group, the hazard remains approximately constant at all ages; in the third, the hazard decreases with age. Examples of each type of hazard are easy to find. High blood pressure presents an increasing hazard. Occupational hazards represent a fairly constant hazard, as do certain types of physical defects. Impairments attributable to past illnesses and surgical operations are usually hazards that decrease with time.

Treatment of Substandard Applicants

Several methods have been devised to provide insurance protection to people with impaired health. In general, companies make an effort to adapt the method to the type of hazard the substandard applicant represents.

Increase in Age

rate-up age method

One method of treatment is to *rate up* the age of the applicant. Under this *rate-up age method*, the applicant is assumed to be a number of years older than his or her real age, and the policy is written accordingly. For example, if a male applicant, aged 25, is placed in a classification that is expected to produce an extra mortality equivalent to the rate for a male aged 33, the applicant would be rated up 8 years and thereafter treated in all respects as if he were 33 years of age. His policy would contain the same surrender and loan values and would be entitled to the same dividends, if any, as any other similar contract issued at age 33. This method of dealing with substandard applicants is often used when the extra mortality is decidedly increasing and will continue to increase indefinitely.

The chief appeal of this method for the insurance company is its simplicity. Policies can be dealt with for all purposes as standard policies issued at the assumed age. No separate set of records is required; no special calculations of premium rates, cash and other surrender values, reserves, and dividends are involved. For the applicant, the method is attractive because the higher premium is accompanied by correspondingly higher surrender values and dividends, if the policy is participating.

Extra Percentage Tables

extra percentage tables

Extra percentage tables provide the most common method of dealing with substandard applicants who present an increasing hazard. These tables classify applicants into groups based on the expected percentage of standard mortality and charge premiums that reflect the appropriate increase in mortality. The number of substandard classifications can vary from three to 12, depending to some extent on the degree of extra mortality the company is willing to underwrite. For example, a company might establish three acceptable substandard classifications with expected average mortalities of 150, 175, and 200 percent of standard, respectively. In effect, a special mortality table that reflects the appropriate degree of extra mortality is prepared for each substandard classification, and a complete set of gross premium rates is computed for each classification. Depending on company practice and state law, surrender values may be based on the special mortality table or may be the same as surrender values under policies issued to standard applicants.

Flat Extra Premium

flat extra premium

A third method of underwriting substandard applicants is to assess a *flat extra premium*. Under this method, the standard premium for the policy in question is increased by a specified number of dollars per $1,000 of insurance. Assessed as a measure of the extra mortality involved, the flat extra premium does not vary with the age of the applicant. The extra premium may be paid throughout the premium-paying period of the policy, or it may be terminated after a period of years when the extra hazard has presumably disappeared.

The flat extra premium method is generally used when the hazard is thought to be constant, for example, deafness or partial blindness, or decreasing, as with a family history of tuberculosis or the aftermath of a serious illness or surgical operation, in which case the flat extra premium is usually temporary. The flat extra premium is widely used to cover the extra mortality associated with certain occupations and avocations.

The flat extra premium is not reflected in policy values and dividends. It is assumed that the entire amount of the extra premium is needed each year to pay additional claims and expenses. The dividends and guaranteed values are identical to those of a comparable policy without the flat extra premium.

Liens

lien

When the extra mortality to be expected from an impairment is of a distinctly decreasing and temporary nature, such as that associated with convalescence from a serious illness, an insurer may create a *lien* against the policy for a number of years, with the amount and term of the lien depending on the extent of the impairment. If this method is utilized, the policy is issued at standard rates and is standard in all respects except that, should death occur before the end of the period specified, the amount of the lien is deducted from the proceeds otherwise payable. Consequently, the death benefit is reduced during the first few years of coverage.

The lien method has a psychological appeal in that few persons who are refused insurance at standard rates believe themselves to be substandard applicants and tend to resent the company's action in classifying them that way. If the only penalty involved is a temporary reduction in the amount of protection, most applicants are willing to go along with the company's decision, confident that they will survive the period of the lien and thus prove the company wrong.

A practical and serious disadvantage of the method is that the reduction in coverage occurs in the early years of the policy, when the need for protection is presumably the greatest. Frequently, the beneficiary has no knowledge of the lien, and the company's failure to pay the face amount of the policy can be the source of great disappointment and resentment, to the detriment of the company's reputation in the community. There is also a possibility that the lien is in conflict with laws in certain states that prohibit any provision that permits the company to settle a death claim with a payment smaller than the policy's face amount.

Other Methods

When the degree of extra mortality is small or when its nature is not well known, the insurer may make no extra charge but, if the policy is participating, place all of the members of the group in a special class for dividend purposes, adjusting the dividends in accordance with the actual experience. Alternatively, the insurer may simply limit the plan of insurance to one with a high savings component.

Ways to Deal with Substandard Applicants

- Hazard increases with age
  - Age rate-up
  - Extra percentage table
- Hazard remains constant
  - Flat extra premium
- Hazard decreases with time or is temporary
  - Flat extra premium
  - Lien
  - Special dividend class
  - Limit policy type to one with high savings component

Removal of Substandard Rating

Frequently, a person who is classified as substandard and insured on that basis by one company subsequently applies for insurance with another company, or even the same company, and is found to be standard in all respects. Under these circumstances, the person's natural reaction is to request the removal of the substandard rating. The insurer must determine whether to remove the rating.

Theoretically, the rating should not be removed unless the impairment on which it was based was known to be temporary or was due to occupation or residence. At the time the policy was originally issued, the insured was placed in a special classification whose members were presumably impaired to approximately the same degree. The company knew that some of the members of the group would die within a short period, while others would survive far beyond their normal expectancy. If the company reduces the premiums for those whose health has improved, the insurer should also be permitted to increase the premiums of those whose health has deteriorated. Because the premiums of those in the latter category cannot be adjusted upward, the premiums of those in the former category should not logically be reduced.

As a practical matter, however, the company is virtually forced to remove the substandard rating of a person who can demonstrate current insurability at standard rates. If the insurer does not do so, the policyowner will almost surely surrender the substandard insurance and replace it with insurance at standard rates with another company. Thus, the common practice is to remove the extra premium upon proof that the insured is no longer substandard.

Value of Substandard Insurance

Substandard insurance is of great social importance because it makes insurance protection available to millions of American families that would otherwise be without it. It is perhaps fair to conclude that life insurance is now available to all except those subject to such excessive rates of mortality as to entail premiums beyond their ability or willingness to pay.

VIATICAL AGREEMENTS

Financial planners realize that part of insurance planning pertains to alternative uses of the life insurance policy. At certain times, the benefits payable at the insured's death may become less important than the cash that may be available from the policy during the insured's last months. The policyowner may need access to funds during the insured's final months for funding experimental treatments or other treatments insurance does not cover, for keeping the insured comfortable at home rather than in an institution, or simply for financing enjoyable final experiences.

Numerous alternatives may be available if the policyowner needs funds prior to the dying insured's death. First, the policyowner can access the cash value in the form of a loan. Alternatively, the policyowner may use the cash value as collateral for a loan from a bank or from a family member, possibly from the beneficiary against the future death benefit. In both of these cases, the policy will remain in force and premiums will continue to be due, which may be prohibitive for the policyowner. Another alternative to accessing additional funds is to utilize the policy's accelerated benefits provision. This provision is discussed in chapter 9. The policyowner should check with the insurance company to see whether this alternative is available, as some insurers will allow payment of an accelerated death benefit even when the provision is not included in the policy.

viatical settlement

Finally, the policyowner may enter into a *viatical settlement*. The agreement is a contract for the policyowner, or viator, to sell the life insurance policy to a third party, the viatical settlement provider, who purchases the policy. The settlement provider becomes the new policyowner, is responsible for future premium payments, and is entitled to receive the death benefit at the insured's death.

In the viatical settlement purchase agreement, in exchange for the rights to the insurance policy, the viator receives a lump-sum cash settlement from the settlement provider. This lump sum is a percentage of the death benefit, based on various factors, such as the insured's life expectancy, the premiums that will be required to keep the policy in force, the insurer's financial strength, and the settlement provider's required rate of return. Settlements generally are paid in the range of 40–80 percent of the death benefit.

The policyowner may engage a viatical settlement broker to comparison shop for the best offer and negotiate the agreement between the viator and the viatical settlement provider. The broker will usually charge a fee of 5–7 percent of the policy's face amount. Alternatively, policyowners can comparison shop on their own to find the best offer. Most life insurance policies can be viaticated, including (under some circumstances) term insurance and group policies. Any policy must have been in force for at least 2 years so that the contestability period is past.

Regulation and Ethics

Viaticals for Viators

Viatical settlements became available in the mid-1980s in response to a new demand created by the AIDS epidemic. AIDS patients, as well as patients with other terminal illnesses such as cancer, rely on viatical settlements to help with expenses during the insured's final months. Regulation of these transactions did not follow until years after their introduction and, as discussed in this section, remains inadequate to protect the public.

Viatical settlements are not considered securities and are not subject to SEC regulation. Regulation of viaticals is left to the states. The NAIC developed the 1993 Viatical Settlement Model Regulation Act, which provides guidelines to help state insurance commissioners protect viators. The act mandated full disclosure to consumers and established fair payment guidelines based on the estimated life expectancy of the insured. The act requires that the viatical settlement provider grant a 15-day cooling off period during which the viator can rescind the viatical agreement. Nearly half of the states have adopted the act. Additionally, some, but not all, states require licensing of viatical settlement brokers and viatical settlement providers.

Due to the lack of disclosure requirements, the provider's financial strength may not be known. Because there is little financial protection to the viator, consumer groups recommend that the viator insist that an independent escrow agent hold the funds to ensure that they will be available to pay the viator.

Viaticals for Investors

After the settlement is complete, viatical settlement providers may retain the insurance as an asset in their investment portfolios. Alternatively, the settlement provider may offer the insurance contract to a third-party investor, who will pay the settlement provider cash in exchange for the ownership rights to the policy. Depending on the conditions of sale, the investor or, more commonly, the settlement provider may pay any remaining premiums.

Investment in insurance policies as the result of viatication is not well regulated, and fraudulent practices have tainted the industry. Viatical salespeople have promised investors high returns with no risk, and they have often misrepresented the life expectancy of the insured. Further, dishonest practices such as the sale of nonexistent policies to investors have made front page news in the past few years. Additionally, the fraudulent practice of clean sheeting, or inducing terminally ill individuals to apply for life insurance and then selling those policies to investors, has been identified.

The current inadequacy of regulation has created a climate with potential for abuse of both the viator and the investor. The viator is not assured of a fair and adequate payment at a time of physical, emotional, and financial vulnerability. The morality of investing in a viatication contract may be difficult for some investors because, the earlier the insured dies, the higher the return to the investor.

When a life insurance policy is viaticated, the new policyowner has no insurable interest in the life of the insured. Insurance laws require that insurable interest exists only at the time of application, not throughout the life of the policy. However, the ownership of the policy by a complete stranger could create an incentive for the investor to encourage the death of the insured. Although there has been no evidence in the United States of homicide of an insured by an investor, some experts caution that the contract could encourage murder for profit.

Tax Treatment

The Health Insurance Portability and Accountability Act of 1996 (HIPAA) defined situations under which viatical and accelerated death benefits are tax exempt on the federal level. The insured must be terminally ill, having been certified by a physician as having a life expectancy of 24 months or less or chronically ill, defined as permanently and severely disabled. Also, if the viator's state requires licensing, the viatical settlement provider must be licensed with the state. If the state does not require licensing, the settlement provider must meet selected requirements of the NAIC Model Act. Most, but not all, states also exempt these settlements from taxation if they meet these conditions. Even in states where viatical settlements are tax exempt, capital gains taxes may be imposed on the difference between the settlement received and the total premiums paid.

Planning Considerations

A major weakness in using viatical settlement is that at the death of the insured, the policy will not provide death benefits to the surviving family but rather to the investor. Thus, income and burial protection will not be provided to the survivors. However, needs may have changed since the policy was purchased, and the death benefit may no longer be necessary for the surviving family.

Other weaknesses of the viatical approach are less obvious. First, the proceeds may make the viator ineligible for assistance for which he or she otherwise would be eligible. This assistance may include Medicaid, Supplemental Social Security Income, Aid for Families with Dependent Children, food stamps, and state prescription programs. The proceeds may also be subject to creditors' claims.

Another weakness of the viatical settlement is that personal and medical information may be passed along to the investor. This information may include the insured's identifying information, life expectancy, and other medical information. With no privacy regulation, the policyowner has no control over who may have access to this information. A contractual agreement regarding privacy should be a consideration to a potential viator who is comparison shopping for a settlement provider.

Viatication can provide much needed financial relief to a dying client. The financial planner should help the client explore all other options available, and consider both the benefits and the shortcomings of viatication. The client should compare provider offers as to the amount of cash offered, as well as other factors such as reputation, financial strength, state licensure, and privacy provisions. A thorough review of the client's tax situation should also be undertaken to ensure that the settlement will be tax exempt. The financial planner should help the client reach the solution that will best serve the client's needs and provide for the client's wishes as to the financial security of the surviving family.

BUSINESS USES OF LIFE INSURANCE

The discussion of life insurance in this and the preceding chapters has explicitly or implicitly assumed its use for family purposes. Life insurance also serves a number of functions in the business world, and for these purposes, additional factors bear on the purchase decision. In this text, only a few of the many ways in which life insurance can be used in a small business situation are described—namely, indemnifying a small business for death of a key employee; funding a business buy-sell agreement; serving as a group employee benefit plan; and furnishing an executive compensation benefit under a split-dollar plan.

Other uses and the sometimes intricate tax aspects of business life insurance are described in more advanced texts.

Key Person Indemnification

The success of a closely held business often depends on the personal services of a key employee. The loss of a key employee's services due to death or disability will probably result in a loss of income, at least temporarily, to the closely held business. In addition, the business could incur increased expenses if a replacement employee has to be recruited at a higher salary and requires extensive training.

What makes someone a key employee? He or she might have a specialized skill critical to the success of the particular closely held business. Potential replacements may possess this same skill, but replacement employees might have to be recruited at higher salary levels. Or perhaps the employee has a significant customer or client base and is responsible for attracting significant amounts of business. As another example, the employee might be a source of capital if his or her loss would damage the closely held business's credit rating.

Valuing the Key Employee

Determining the key employee's value to the closely held business is very speculative. The actual valuation method depends on the characteristic of the employee that creates the key employee status. Determining the value of the key employee who attracts substantial business might be relatively easy. The net income resulting from the business he or she produces in excess of the amount of net income that could be expected from a similarly situated but less effective employee could be capitalized in some manner. In other cases, the firm may have to consider various subjective factors to arrive at a proxy for the key employee's value. For example, the firm should consider replacement salaries and the training required for a replacement employee to become effective.

Key Employee Life Insurance

key employee life insurance

A business can purchase *key employee life insurance* on the key employee to cover the possibility of an income loss and/or increase in expenses resulting from the key employee's death. Insurance covering loss as a result of the key employee disability is discussed in chapter 14. Term insurance can be purchased if the primary concern is the key employee's dollar value to the business. Decreasing term might be appropriate because the key employee loss exposure decreases as the insured approaches retirement. Key employee life insurance, however, is usually coupled with some other purpose such as providing a retirement benefit for the key employee. Permanent life insurance is typically purchased to meet this objective. The business receives the life insurance death benefit as indemnification for the income loss and/or increase in expenses resulting from the key employee's death. If the insured survives to retirement, the corporation can use the cash surrender value to fund a retirement benefit. Another approach is for the business to transfer the policy to the employee at retirement.

Example:	Chuck Keller is a key employee of Pontco. What makes him a key employee? Because of Chuck's ebullient personality and his vast technical knowledge, he sells more industrial cranes than Pontco's five other salesmen combined. If Chuck were to die or become disabled before his normal retirement age, Pontco's sales revenues would suddenly plummet, at least in the short run. Pontco can purchase key employee life insurance to protect against this possibility. The death benefit Pontco receives in the event of Chuck's demise will stabilize Pontco by helping to offset this drop in revenue. Two approaches are possible:

- Yearly renewable term insurance, with a term long enough to last until Chuck's normal retirement age, can be used to protect Pontco.
- A permanent life insurance policy could both protect Pontco and reward Chuck by funding some additional retirement benefits if he survives to retirement.

The business should be the owner and beneficiary of key employee life insurance. The premiums for key employee life insurance are nondeductible, and death benefits are received tax free.

Funding Buy-Sell Agreements

The death or disability of an owner of a closely held business typically disrupts the business and often leads to its failure. Life insurance can be used to provide the funds necessary to finance a buy-sell agreement that preserves the value of the business. When a business owner dies, the executor of his or her estate must collect, preserve, and distribute the decedent's assets. Of course, these assets include both the business and personal assets owned by the decedent at the time of his or her death. The closely held business presents many difficulties for the executor unless the decedent has appropriately planned for business continuation.

buy-sell agreement   A properly designed buy-sell agreement ensures that the estate can sell its interest in the closely held business for a reasonable price. A *buy-sell agreement* is a contract that binds the owner of a business interest to sell at his or her death, and a designated buyer to buy at that time, the business interest for a specified or determinable price. The purchasers of the business interest, perhaps the surviving co-owners of the business, will obtain the business interest and avoid the difficulties associated with passing it through probate. Without an appropriate continuation plan, the executor may be compelled to sell the business interest to pay the estate's settlement costs and federal estate taxes and/or state inheritance taxes. The settlement costs must be paid in cash promptly after the business owner's death. Under these circumstances, the executor has a tenuous bargaining position, and a forced sale of the business interest may yield far less than its full fair market value. The surviving co-owners also face a great deal of uncertainty. The survivors may be pressured to provide distributions of business income to the decedent's heirs. They may also face the prospect that the executor or the heirs will choose to sell the business interest to outsiders.

Benefits of the Buy-Sell Agreement

Proper estate planning with a buy-sell agreement offers several advantages, which include:

- a guarantee that there will be a market for the closely held business interest
- liquidity for the payment of death taxes and other estate settlement costs
- establishment of the estate tax value of the decedent's business interest, making the estate planning process more reliable for the owner
- continuation of the business in the hands of the surviving owners and/or employees
- improved credit risk because the probability of continuation of the business is enhanced

Basic Structure of a Buy-Sell Agreement

A properly designed buy-sell agreement has several provisions that are generally included. Among these are the following:

- *purpose of the agreement.* A buy-sell agreement should contain a statement indicating its purpose. One advantage of including a statement of purpose is to document the intent of the agreement should a dispute arise later.
- *commitment of the parties.* The agreement should clearly state the obligation of all parties. For example, it should be clear that the estate of the deceased business owner will sell the business interest to the parties who become purchasers under the terms of the agreement.

- *lifetime transfer restrictions.* Most buy-sell agreements contain a first-offer provision that prevents the parties to the agreement from disposing of the business interest to outsiders while all the parties are living.
- *purchase price.* The buy-sell agreement should specify a purchase price or, in the alternative, a method for determining the purchase price at which the business interest will be bought and sold.
- *funding provisions.* The terms of the agreement should specify how the purchase price will be funded. For example, if the agreement is funded with life insurance, the agreement should indicate how such life insurance will be structured and paid for.

Continuation Agreements for Partnerships and Corporations

entity agreement

In the case of a partnership or closely held corporation, the agreement may be structured under either an entity agreement or a cross-purchase approach. Under an *entity agreement*, the firm itself enters into an agreement with each owner specifying that, on the death of an owner, the firm will buy and the deceased's estate will sell the business interest of the deceased. Technically, the firm liquidates the interest of the deceased partner or redeems the stock of the deceased stockholder. The firm carries life insurance on each owner, with the firm as beneficiary, to provide the money to fund the agreement.

cross-purchase agreement

Under a *cross-purchase agreement*, each partner or stockholder is both a seller and a purchaser. The agreement provides that, on the death of one owner, his or her estate will sell, and the other owners will buy, the deceased's interest. To fund this type of agreement, each owner should carry and be the beneficiary of insurance on the lives of the other owners. For example, if there are three equal partners, the two surviving partners will each purchase one-half, or another agreed-upon share, of a deceased partner's interest.

Continuation Agreements for Sole Proprietorship

The sole proprietorship is by far the most common form of business organization. By definition, there is only one owner of the firm, so on his or her death, there are no surviving co-owners to serve as purchasers of the deceased's business interest. Nevertheless, the advantages of having a binding buy-sell agreement are as important for a sole proprietorship as they are for a closely held corporation or a partnership. The new issue in a proprietorship is to find the appropriate purchaser.

Often, the sole proprietor has no family successors who are capable and/or willing to step in at the sole proprietor's death. However, there may be a key employee or group of employees who would like to be purchasers of the business. Such individuals, if available, are logical choices for two reasons. First, the key employee or employees of the sole proprietorship are familiar with the business. This is particularly important if the business requires unique skills to perform its function. Second, the key employees may be willing to enter into a buy-sell agreement to protect their own future employment. Without a buy-sell agreement, the sole proprietorship is often liquidated or sold to outsiders at the death of the proprietor. This could leave the key employees unemployed and without a future in the proprietorship. If there are no key employees or natural successors to the sole proprietor, the sole proprietor could seek a buyer from competitors who might want to take over the proprietor's business at some point in the future.

The life insurance arrangements for a sole proprietorship buy-sell agreement are relatively simple. The purchasing party is obligated to provide sale proceeds to the deceased proprietor's estate. Accordingly, the owner and beneficiary of the life insurance should be the purchasing party. The purchaser should obtain sufficient coverage on the life of the sole proprietor to make the required payments to the estate.

Life Insurance as an Employee Benefit

Group term life insurance is a benefit plan provided by an employer to a group of participating employees. Such plans are also known as *Sec. 79 plans,* referring to the section of the Internal Revenue Code that applies to them. These plans allow the employer a tax deduction for premium payments on behalf of a participant unless the premium amounts exceed the tax code's reasonable compensation test, which is unlikely.

If the coverage provided by the plan is nondiscriminatory, the first $50,000 of coverage is provided tax free to all plan participants. The taxable amounts of coverage—that is, amounts above $50,000—are taxed according to a premium rate schedule, referred to as Table I, provided by IRS regulations. These rates are as shown in table 10-1.

If a plan is contributory, an employee's taxable income is reduced by any employee contributions for the entire amount of coverage.

Example:	Jill, aged 55, has a salary of $60,000 and receives $120,000 in group term life insurance as an employer-paid fringe benefit. The first $50,000 of this insurance is tax free. The remaining $70,000 is treated as taxable income. The amount her employer actually pays the insurance company is irrelevant. For tax purposes, the amount of taxable income Jill receives is determined based on the Sec. 79 cost per month, which, as shown in table 10-1, is .$43 per thousand per month for a person aged 55. As far as the Internal Revenue Service is concerned, Jill receives a taxable income of 70 x $.43 x 12, or $361.20, in addition to her taxable salary. Her employer reports this additional income to the IRS on her W-2 form.

If Jill paid $20 per month for her coverage, her annual taxable income for this benefit would be reduced by $240 to $121.20.

TABLE 10-1
Uniform Premium Table I

Age	Cost per Month per $1,000 of Coverage
24 and under	$ .05
25–29	.06
30–34	.08
35–39	.09
40–44	.10
45–49	.15
50–54	.23
55–59	.43
60–64	.66
65–69	1.27
70 and over	2.06

If the plan discriminates in favor of key employees with respect to coverage or benefits, the actual premiums paid on behalf of these key employees for their entire amount of coverage are taxable as ordinary income to them, but other employees still receive the previously mentioned favorable tax treatment. A key employee generally includes the shareholder-employees and officers of a closely held corporation. The actual nondiscrimination rules are complex and beyond the scope of this book. However, a plan is generally nondiscriminatory if (1) it covers at least 70 percent of a firm's employees, (2) key employees make up fewer than 15 percent of plan participants, and (3) benefits are either a flat amount or a uniform percentage of salary.

Split-Dollar Life Insurance Plans

split-dollar life insurance

Split-dollar life insurance is a form of permanent life insurance frequently used prior to 2003 as an executive compensation benefit. In a traditional split-dollar plan, a corporation and an employee split a life insurance policy covering the life of the employee. The corporation contributes an amount equal to the annual increase in the cash surrender value, while the executive pays the remainder of the annual premium. In the past, the executive was taxed only for the PS 58 cost of one-year term insurance funded by the employer. PS 58 rates are one-year term insurance rates the federal government uses to measure the taxable economic benefit employees receive from the pure insurance protection split-dollar plans and qualified retirement plans provide.

Under split-dollar, the death benefit is split between the participating executive and the corporation as follows:

- The corporation receives a return of its contributions, which equals the cash surrender value.
- The beneficiary named by the insured receives a death benefit equal to the net amount at risk.

The Sarbanes-Oxley Act, enacted in 2002 to bar insider loan transactions, struck a major blow to split-dollar life insurance. Sarbanes-Oxley prohibits a publicly traded company from using corporate funds to personally finance its directors or officers. A second blow took place when the IRS and the Treasury Department issued final regulations in December 2003. The new regulations clearly make split-dollar plans less attractive.

Under current regulations, split-dollar arrangements are treated in one of two ways for tax purposes. If the employee owns the policy and the employer pays part of the premium, the employer's contribution is treated as a loan, and the employee is taxed on the difference between the market interest rate and any interest being charged by the employer. If the employer owns the policy and pays the premium, the employee is taxed based on the economic benefit he or she receives; the value of the current life insurance protection and the employee's interest in the policy's cash value increase are treated as taxable income to the employee.

TAX TREATMENT OF LIFE INSURANCE

Quite often, especially for affluent clients, financial planners recognize that a life insurance purchase can legitimately serve to reduce the client's federal tax burden. The subject of federal income, estate, and gift taxes is sufficiently broad and deep to fill an entire textbook, and many authors have done so. In this chapter, only a thumbnail sketch of some of the most common tax aspects of individual life insurance is included. The major aspects of the tax treatment of annuities are explained in chapter 11.

Income Taxation of Death Proceeds

In general, and subject to some exceptions, proceeds paid under a life insurance contract by reason of the insured's death are excludible from gross income for federal income tax purposes. The basic requirement for the income tax exclusion for life insurance proceeds is that they be paid because of the death of the insured. Current law also extends the exclusion to certain viatical settlements and accelerated death benefits made on behalf of an insured who is terminally ill and expected to die within 24 months.

Transfer-for-Value Rule

transfer-for-value rule

The most important exception to the general rule of exclusion of life insurance death proceeds from federal income taxation is the *transfer-for-value rule*. This rule provides that if a policy is transferred from one owner to another for valuable consideration, the income tax exclusion is lost. When the insured dies in these cases, the policy beneficiary will recover income tax free only the amount the transferee-owner paid for the policy, plus any premiums subsequently paid. The transfer-for-value rule is not limited to an outright sale of a policy. This rule can also apply when a noncash consideration for a policy transfer can be inferred.

Thus, the transfer-for-value rule is an exception to the general rule of exclusion for policy proceeds. There are also exceptions to the exception (a common phenomenon in tax law). Policy transfers that are not jeopardized by the transfer-for-value rule are as follows:

- transfers in which the transferee-owner is the insured
- transfers to a partner of the insured
- transfers to a partnership in which the insured is a partner
- transfers to a corporation of which the insured is a shareholder or officer
- transfers in which the transferee's tax basis of the policy is determined by reference to its basis to the transferor

A policyowner's basis is initially determined by adding the total premiums paid into the policy and subtracting the dividends, if any, that the insurer has paid. If nontaxable withdrawals have previously been made from the policy, such amounts also reduce the policyowner's basis. Policy loans generally have no effect on basis unless the policy is a modified endowment contract, as discussed later.

Income Tax Definition of Life Insurance

The full exclusion for life insurance death proceeds depends in part on whether the policy itself meets the definition of life insurance under the Internal Revenue Code. There are two alternative tests under this definition. A policy qualifies as life insurance for income tax purposes if it satisfies either of these two tests. The determination whether a policy qualifies is not performed by the consumer or agent, but rather by the insurance company that makes this information available.

cash value accumulation test

The first test, the *cash value accumulation test,* generally applies to more traditional cash value policies such as whole life policies. Under this test, the cash value is generally limited to the net single premium that would be needed to fund the policy's death benefit. The insurance company calculates the net single premium using an assumed interest rate and certain mortality charges.

**guideline premium
and corridor test**

The second two-pronged test is the *guideline premium and corridor test.* Policies that are designed to pass the second test must meet both of the requirements. The guideline premium requirement limits the total premium that may be paid into the policy at any given time. This limit varies with each life insurance company based on its own expenses and its own mortality experience. The limit also varies with the insurer's own interest assumptions, subject to specified IRS limits. The policy meets the corridor or death benefit requirement, the second prong of the test, if the contract's death benefit exceeds a specified multiple of its cash value at all times. This multiple varies according to the insured's attained age. Generally, universal life and other similar types of policies are tested under this second, two-pronged test.

Settlement Options

Death proceeds distributed as a series of payments under a settlement option generally include an element of interest earned after the death of the insured, which is taxable. However, the portion of a settlement option payment that represents principal (the policy's face amount) still qualifies for the income tax exclusion.

The portion that represents the death benefit is calculated by prorating the face amount over the option's payment period. This is the excludible portion. Any excess amount of each payment represents interest. If the interest-only option is used, all interest paid or accrued is taxable. If the fixed-amount option is used, the payment period is calculated by determining the number of fixed payments needed to exhaust the policy's face amount at its guaranteed interest rate. If a life-income option is used, the present value of any refund or period-certain feature is subtracted from the excludible amount to be prorated.

Income Taxation of Living Proceeds

Amounts paid under a life insurance contract while the insured is still living can take several forms. The most common of these are policy dividends, withdrawals from the policy's cash value or investment fund, policy loans, and proceeds from the cash surrender of a policy.

To determine the income tax effect of most of these transactions, the policyowner's tax basis in the policy must first be known. However, it is important to remember that if a policy is surrendered, the principal amount of any loan outstanding against the policy is includible in the surrender value of the policy for tax purposes.

Policy dividends are treated as a nontaxable return of premium and reduce the policyowner's basis. If total dividends paid exceed total premiums, dividends are taxable to that extent. If dividends are used to reduce premiums or otherwise paid back into the policy (for example, to buy paid-up additions), the basis reduction caused by the payment of the dividend is offset by a corresponding basis increase when the dividend is reinvested in the policy because it is then treated as an additional premium payment.

If a policy is surrendered for cash, the taxable amount is the total surrender value minus the policyowner's current basis in the policy. Dividends left with the insurer to accumulate at interest are not included in the surrender value for tax purposes because they have already reduced the policyowner's basis in the contract.

Example:	Aaron Sloan, aged 40, owns a level premium whole life policy. He has paid $25,000 in premiums and has received $4,000 in dividends from the policy. The face amount of the policy is $100,000. Its total cash value is $29,000. The policy is also subject to an outstanding loan of $15,000. Aaron decides to surrender his policy for cash. The tax effects of Aaron's surrender of his policy are as follows:

Surrender Value

Policy loan	$15,000
Plus net cash value ($29,000 total value less $15,000 policy loan)	14,000
Total surrender value	$29,000

Basis

Premium paid	$25,000
Less dividends	4,000
Total basis	$21,000

Taxable Gain

Surrender value	$29,000
Less basis	21,000
Taxable gain	$ 8,000

inside buildup

The *inside buildup,* or increase in the cash value or investment fund of a permanent life insurance policy, is not subject to taxation as long as it is left inside the policy. Loans from a policy are not taxable unless the policy is a modified endowment contract. If a policyowner withdraws funds from a policy's cash value, the general rule is that the withdrawal is first treated as a nontaxable return of basis. The excess, if any, of the amount of the withdrawal over the policyowner's current basis is taxable in the year of withdrawal. However, there are important exceptions to this general rule. These exceptions include certain withdrawals from universal life policies and withdrawals from policies classified as modified endowment contracts.

If a withdrawal is made from a policy that results in a reduction in the policy's death benefit during the first 15 years of the policy, the withdrawal may first be taxed as income to the extent of income earned within the contract. A death benefit reduction resulting from a cash value withdrawal typically occurs in a universal life contract. This income first, or LIFO (last in, first out), method of taxation is the reverse of the general rule of basis first, or FIFO (first in, first out), taxation that life insurance typically enjoys.

modified endowment contract (MEC)

A policy is treated as a *modified endowment contract (MEC)* if it fails a test called the *7-pay test*. This test is applied at the inception of the policy and again if the policy experiences a material change. A material change generally includes most increases and certain decreases in future benefits. A common example of a material change is an increase in death benefits under the policy, resulting from a flexible premium payment.

The 7-pay test is designed to impose MEC status on policies that take in too much premium during the first 7 policy years, or in the 7 years after a material change. For each policy, a net level premium is calculated. If the total premium actually paid into the policy at any time during the 7-year testing period is more than the sum of the net level premiums that would be needed to result in a paid-up policy after 7 years, the policy is a MEC. Simply stated, the 7-pay test is designed to discourage a premium schedule that would result in a paid-up policy before the end of a 7-year period.

Any life insurance policy that falls under the definition of a MEC is also subject to an income, first or LIFO, tax treatment with respect to loans and most distributions from the policy. A 10 percent penalty tax also generally applies to the taxable portion of any loan or withdrawal from a MEC unless the taxpayer has reached age 59 1/2. With respect to loans (not withdrawals) from a MEC, the policyowner does receive an increase in basis in the policy equal to the amount of the loan that is taxable. However, as shown in the example, the nontaxable portion of a loan from a MEC will not affect the policyowner's basis. A nontaxable portion of a withdrawal, on the other hand, will reduce the basis.

Example: Assume that Aaron Sloan's policy in the previous example is a MEC and that he takes the $15,000 loan from the policy this year. Prior to the loan, Aaron has a total of $8,000 in untaxed gain in the policy. However, the withdrawal of any untaxed gain from the policy triggers a taxable event. Therefore, the loan will first be treated as a taxable event to the extent of $8,000. The remaining $7,000 of the loan is not taxable to Aaron. The $8,000 taxable portion of the loan will also be subject to the 10 percent penalty tax because Aaron is under age 59 1/2. Aaron's basis in the policy will be increased by $8,000 (the taxable portion of the loan). Therefore, Aaron's basis is now $29,000 ($21,000 + $8,000).

Deductibility of Premium Payments

As a general rule, premium payments for individual life insurance policies are not deductible for federal income tax purposes. This rule applies, regardless of who owns the policy and whether it is used for personal or business purposes. In certain situations, however, life insurance premiums can be deductible because they also fit the definition of some other type of deductible expense, not because they are premium payments. For example, a premium payment for a policy on behalf of a charitable organization is deductible by the payor if the charity owns the policy outright. The premium is deductible because it is treated as a charitable contribution, not because it is a life insurance premium. Similarly, in cases where a corporation pays the premium on a policy that covers an employee and the death benefit is payable to the employee's beneficiary, the employer can deduct the premium as compensation paid to the employee. Another situation in which premium payments can fit the definition of a particular deductible expense is when premium payments constitute alimony, made on behalf of an ex-spouse.

Transfer Taxation of Life Insurance

In addition to income taxation, the federal transfer tax system can apply to life insurance. The following pages provide a brief overview of the transfer tax system and the general transfer tax treatment of life insurance products.

Federal Transfer Tax System

The federal tax system consists of three components—gift taxes, estate taxes, and generation-skipping taxes. The federal estate and gift taxes are separate tax systems imposed on different types of transfers. The generation-skipping transfer taxes are separate taxes applied under different rules in addition to any applicable estate or gift taxes. This component of the transfer tax system is not addressed in this book.

Federal Gift Tax

gift tax

gift

The federal *gift tax* is a tax imposed on transfers of property by gift during the donor's lifetime. This tax applies only if both of the following two elements of a *gift* are present:

- a completed transfer and acceptance of property
- a transfer for less than full and adequate consideration

The essential elements of a taxable gift reveal some noteworthy facts. First, only property transfers are subject to gift taxation. Thus, the transfer of services by an individual is not a taxable gift. Second, the taxation of a transfer does not require an element of donative intent; simply, the transfer must be made for less than full consideration.

The lifetime amount that a person can gift on a tax-exempt basis is $1 million. This amount remains constant through 2010, then increase with inflation thereafter.

annual exclusion

Annual Exclusion. Much of the planning and complexity associated with gift tax planning involves the *annual exclusion*. In 2005, qualifying gifts of $11,000 or less could be made annually by a donor to any number of donees without gift tax. The exempt amount can be increased to $22,000 if the donor is married and the donor's spouse elects to split gifts on a timely filed gift tax return. With gift splitting, each spouse gives half the gift. The annual exclusion amount is indexed to inflation, and it increases in $1,000 increments. The annual exclusion is in addition to the tax-exempt amount described in the previous paragraph.

To qualify for an annual exclusion, the gift must provide the donee with a present interest. Outright interests or current income interests in a trust provide the beneficiary with a present interest. Trust provisions that provide the beneficiaries with current withdrawal powers can be used to qualify gifts to a trust for an annual exclusion even if the trust provides for deferred benefits. Use of the annual exclusion in the transfer of life insurance products is discussed later in the chapter.

Deductions from the Gift Tax Base. Two types of gifts are fully deductible from the transfer tax base. First, the marital deduction provides that unlimited qualifying transfers a donor makes to his or her spouse are fully deductible from the gift tax base. The marital deduction proves quite useful if it is necessary to rearrange ownership of marital assets in the implementation of an estate plan. This deduction is similar to the marital deduction against federal estate taxes discussed later. Second, qualified gifts to a qualified charity are deductible.

Federal Estate Tax

estate tax

The federal *estate tax* is a tax imposed on the transfer of property at death. The most difficult task in calculating the estate tax is often the determination of the assets included in the decedent's estate tax base. Some of the included assets are obvious, such as individually owned property, but the estate tax rules often cause the inclusion of property in surprising circumstances. For example, property previously transferred by a decedent can be brought back to the estate tax base by provisions in the statute.

gross estate

Gross Estate. The starting point in the federal estate tax calculation is determining the property included in the decedent's *gross estate*. The gross estate includes the property in the probate estate, which is all property that passes under the deceased's will or, in the absence of a valid will, under the state intestacy law, but it also includes property transferable by the decedent at death by other means. The decedent's gross estate includes, among other things, the following:

- property individually owned by the decedent at the time of death
- (some portion of) property held jointly by the decedent at the time of death
- insurance on the decedent's life if either (1) the decedent held an incident of ownership or transferred it by gift within 3 years of death or (2) the proceeds are deemed payable to the estate
- property transferred by the decedent during his or her lifetime if the decedent retained (1) a life interest in the property, (2) a reversionary interest valued at greater than 5 percent of the property at the time of death, or (3) a right to revoke or amend the transfer at the time of death

Items Deductible from the Gross Estate. Certain items are deductible from the gross estate for estate tax calculation purposes: legitimate debts of the decedent, reasonable funeral and other death costs of the decedent, and the reasonable cost of estate settlement such as the executor's commission and attorney fees. As with the gift tax, qualifying transfers to a surviving spouse are deductible under the marital deduction rules. Because the marital deduction is unlimited, the usual dispositive scheme (100 percent to the surviving spouse) for married individuals results in no federal death taxes for a married couple until the death of the survivor of the two spouses. As a client's wealth increases, sophisticated planning is needed to make optimal use of the marital deduction. (Planning for the marital deduction for life insurance proceeds is discussed later in this chapter.) Moreover, the federal estate tax charitable deduction provides that transfers at death to qualifying charities are fully deductible from the estate tax base.

Credit against the Estate Tax. Prior to 2005, there was a state death tax credit that provided a reduction against the federal estate tax for state death taxes paid by the estate. This credit is no longer available.

The Taxable Estate. The 2001 Economic Growth and Tax Relief Reconciliation Act significantly revised federal estate taxation. The act increased the exclusion amount, which can pass by death on a tax-exempt basis, to the levels indicated in table 10-2. The act also reduced the marginal tax rates, which are based on the amount in excess of the exclusion amount. Further, the exclusion amount increases and the marginal tax rate decreases for larger estates periodically through 2009, and in 2010 the exclusion amount will be unlimited. At the time this book is being written, the estate portion of the act will sunset at the end of 2010. Estate taxation will then revert to the law that was in effect in 2001, which had a smaller exclusion amount. However, the Bush administration is committed to repealing the estate tax, and the sunset provision may be repealed.

Federal Gift Taxation of Life Insurance

Gifts of life insurance are treated in the same manner as gifts of any other assets as far as the annual exclusion ($11,000 for 2005) is concerned. That is,

TABLE 10-2
Exclusion Amounts for Estate Taxation

Year of Death	Exclusion Amount
2003	$1,000,000
2004–2005	1,500,000
2006–2008	2,000,000
2009	3,500,000
2010	Unlimited
2011	1,000,000

the outright gift of a policy is a transfer of property that provides a present interest. The system used for determining the value of the gifted policy is beyond the scope of this introductory discussion.

Sometimes there is an inadvertent gift of life insurance policy proceeds. This can happen when a policy one individual owns on another's life matures by reason of the insured's death and a person other than the policyowner has been named as beneficiary. For example, if a wife purchases a policy on her husband's life and names her children as beneficiaries, the proceeds that otherwise would have been payable to her are payable instead to her children at her husband's death. The transaction is treated as if the policyowner—the wife—had received the proceeds and made a gift in that amount to her children. Moreover, gift splitting will not be allowed because there is no longer a spouse with whom to split the gift.

Federal Estate Taxation of Life Insurance

As explained earlier, estate taxes are payable on property included in a decedent's gross estate if the decedent's estate exceeds the available deductions and credits. Frequently, life insurance is the single largest asset or group of assets in the gross estate. Including life insurance can often mean the difference between a federal estate tax liability and no tax liability. For this reason, it is important to look at the factors that determine when life insurance is included in the decedent-insured's gross estate for federal estate tax purposes:

- Life insurance proceeds payable to the executor, that is, to or for the benefit of the insured's estate, are includible in the estate, regardless of who owned the contract or who paid the premium.
- Life insurance proceeds are included in the estate of an insured if he or she possessed an incident of ownership in the policy at the time of his or her death.
- Life insurance proceeds are included in the gross estate of an insured who transferred incidents of ownership in the policy by gift within 3 years of his or her death.

Life Insurance Payable to the Executor. In general, life insurance should not be made payable to a decedent's estate. There are many reasons in addition to avoiding federal estate taxation why estate planners seldom recommend such a beneficiary designation. These reasons include the following:

- Insurance payable to a decedent's estate subjects the proceeds to the claims of the estate's creditors.
- Insurance payable to a decedent's estate subjects the proceeds to costs of probate administration, such as executor's fees, but provides no corresponding advantages.

incident of ownership

Possession of Incidents of Ownership. When insurance proceeds are paid to a named beneficiary other than the insured's estate, *incidents of ownership* in the policy at the time of death are the key criteria for determining inclusion. If the insured held an incident of ownership at the time of his or her death, the policy is included in his or her gross estate. An incident of ownership is broadly defined as an element of ownership or degree of control over a policy. Incidents of ownership include, but are not limited to, the power to

- change the beneficiary
- assign the policy
- borrow on the policy
- surrender the policy
- exercise any of the other essential contract rights or privileges

Merely being the beneficiary of a policy's death benefit is not an incident of ownership.

Like any other property, the insurance policy is an asset that a policyowner can freely assign in a gift or sale. Thus, the policyowner may transfer limited interests to others while retaining some of the privileges and rights in the policy. However, to remove the proceeds from the scope of the federal estate tax, the insured must divest himself or herself of all significant rights and privileges under the contract.

Transfers of Policies within 3 Years of Death. Policies are often transferred to others so that policy proceeds will not be in the insured's gross estate when he or she dies. Inclusion will still result, however, if the insured dies within 3 years of a gratuitous transfer. Under this 3-year rule, life insurance transferred to a third party for less than full consideration within 3 years of the insured's death is automatically includible in the insured's gross estate. Transfers made more than 3 years before the insured's death are not normally includible in the insured's estate if the insured has retained no incidents of ownership. In addition, a sale to a third party for the full fair market value of the policy will not be included even if the sale occurs within 3 years of the insured's death.

Life Insurance and the Federal Estate Tax Marital Deduction. Life insurance proceeds payable at the insured's death to his or her surviving spouse can qualify for the federal estate tax marital deduction. Because the marital deduction is unlimited, the full value of life insurance proceeds payable in a qualifying manner to the surviving spouse is deductible from the insured's gross estate.

USES OF LIFE INSURANCE IN ESTATE PLANNING

The goal of life insurance in the estate plan depends on many factors specific to the client. The goals for life insurance in general, however, can be divided into two categories: Life insurance can serve either as an estate enhancement or as an estate liquidity/wealth replacement device. The goals of a specific client for his or her life insurance planning depend on age, family circumstances, and financial status.

Estate Enhancement Purposes

In many cases, a client's estate at death will not be sufficient to provide for the basic needs of his or her heirs. This is particularly true for (1) young clients, (2) clients with family members dependent on their income, and/or (3) clients with small- to moderate-sized estates. These clients generally have estate enhancement as the primary goal for their life insurance coverage. They may still have their peak earning years in front of them. The basic support needs of their family, such as educational, medical, and retirement savings programs, depend on this income. It is essential for these clients to investigate their life insurance coverage needs and secure sufficient insurance to enhance their estates to a size that is, at the very least, adequate to handle their dependent family members' basic needs. Life insurance is the perfect estate enhancement device to replace the financial loss created by premature death. The methods to determine the amount of life insurance a client needs for this purpose are discussed earlier in this chapter.

Estate Liquidity/Wealth Replacement Purposes

For older clients or clients with large estates, estate liquidity/wealth replacement is the primary goal of life insurance coverage. Their children's support and educational expense needs are usually things of the past. In addition, these older clients are nearing the end of their income-producing years and should, presumably, have less future income to replace. Their needs for estate enhancement from life insurance should have diminished in importance relative to their estate liquidity/wealth replacement needs.

A prospective insured may need coverage for estate liquidity/wealth replacement for the following purposes:

- *probate expenses.* Estate settlement costs usually increase with the size of the estate. The cost for professionals such as executors, attorneys, accountants, and appraisers to settle an estate is often based on a percentage of the total size of the probate estate. Generally, the larger the estate, the greater the complexity and need for costly professional help. One advantage of life insurance is that it avoids probate if paid to a named beneficiary.
- *death taxes.* As discussed above, federal estate taxes, as well as other taxes, also increase with the size of the estate. Federal estate taxes, and state death taxes in many states, are based on a progressive rate schedule. Thus, wealthy individuals often desire life insurance to replace the wealth lost to death taxes.
- *liquidity needs.* Wealthy clients often face an additional problem. Frequently, their accumulated wealth contains assets that are not liquid. For example, wealthy individuals often own closely held businesses that may be unmarketable to outsiders. Death taxes and other estate settlement costs are based on the full value of such assets the estate owns and must be paid in cash. The liquidity problems an estate faces often result in the forced sale of estate assets on undesirable terms.

Estate Planning Techniques with Life Insurance

There are many practical uses for life insurance in the estate planning context. Three are described briefly here:

- gifts of policies to family members
- providing estate liquidity
- the second-to-die policy

Gifts of Policies to Family Members

Although the 3-year rule causes estate tax inclusion if the insured transfers incidents of ownership within 3 years of his or her death, transferring or assigning the policy to family members might still be an appropriate planning step. The insured simply has to live more than 3 years following the transfer to avoid inclusion of the proceeds in his or her estate. And even if the insured dies within 3 years, he or she will be no worse off from an estate tax standpoint because the policy would have been included in any event had the transfer or assignment not occurred.

There are many reasons why estate planners recommend a life insurance policy gifting program. Some of the reasons are as follows:

- The donee feels no richer after the gift of the life insurance policy and will seldom dispose of it foolishly.

- The donor-insured's financial position is not markedly affected by making a gift of life insurance.
- The gift tax cost to transfer a policy is usually nominal compared to the potential estate tax savings if a person is in a situation when the gift tax applies. Through efficient use of the donor-insured's annual exclusion, the gift of the policy and subsequent premiums can actually avoid gift taxes entirely.
- The gift of a life insurance policy is particularly advantageous for older donors whose estate planning concerns have risen in priority in relation to their other financial planning goals. Usually, older insureds can select appropriate beneficiaries with more certainty, and they are less concerned about a policy's cash surrender value. If a life insurance policy is gifted more than 3 years before the donor's death, the transfer tax savings is substantial.

Providing Estate Liquidity

Unless the executor of an estate wishes to go through a series of complex and burdensome requests for an extension, the estate tax due must be paid within 9 months of the date of death. If the gross estate is composed of liquid assets, the executor or administrator faces no problem in meeting the 9-month deadline successfully. For example, if the estate is composed of sufficient cash, marketable securities, or life insurance proceeds, there will be ample liquidity to ensure that the tax can be paid within the required time. Conversely, if the federal estate tax liability exceeds the amount of liquid assets available, there will be an estate liquidity deficit. To meet the 9-month deadline, a forced liquidation of assets, possibly at a loss, will be necessary.

Life insurance is the most effective way to supply needed dollars to meet federal estate tax obligations for these reasons. First, the dollars, in the form of death proceeds, are free of federal income taxation. Second, if someone or some entity other than the insured owns the life insurance, the policy's face amount will not be included as part of the decedent's gross estate. Finally, a sizable death benefit may be purchased for pennies on the dollar in the form of premium payments.

Second-to-Die Policy

The federal estate tax marital deduction is now unlimited in nature and scope. Consequently, there is a propensity by estate owners to leave their entire estates to their surviving spouses, which ensures no estate tax liability at the first death. There is, unfortunately, a serious flaw in this approach.

The concept of the federal estate tax marital deduction is based on deferral, rather than complete avoidance, of estate tax liability. Although the deduction is unlimited, to use the deduction to its fullest extent creates a stacking of estate taxes at the second death. The estate tax liability from the first to die is added to that of the second to die. The result is a higher estate tax liability overall.

The unlimited marital deduction has created a need for greater planning for the death of the second spouse. That is why the second-to-die policy, described in chapter 8, was instituted. At the death of the first spouse, no death benefit is paid; at the death of the second spouse, the policy proceeds are paid to the named beneficiary.

Second-to-die coverage is often a perfect fit in a married couple's estate plan. The most common use of second-to-die coverage is in an estate plan in which taking the unlimited marital deduction after the death of the first spouse will result in more substantial death taxes at the death of the second spouse. With second-to-die coverage, policy benefits will be paid when the insured married couple incurs these more substantial taxes—at the second death of the two spouses.

Survivorship Life Insurance (Second-to-Die Coverage)

- Pays the death benefit only at the death of the surviving spouse
- The federal estate tax system allows an unlimited marital deduction
- Problem: the estate tax bill at the death of the surviving spouse
- Solution: death benefit payable at the second death on a far less costly basis than two separate policies

CHECKLIST FOR EVALUATING AND COMPARING LIFE INSURANCE POLICIES

☐ What are the provisions concerning premium payments?

___ Are they level or rising at each renewal date?
___ Are they flexible at the policyowner's option at each renewal date?
___ Are they payable for life or for a specified number of years?

☐ What is the initial policy premium?

___ What is the 20-year surrender cost index?
___ What is the 20-year net payment cost index?

☐ Is the duration of death benefit protection for a limited number of years? If yes,

___ Is the policy renewable for additional periods? If yes, until when?
___ Is the policy convertible to permanent coverage? If yes, until when?

☐   What is the initial amount of death benefit protection?

☐   How does the amount of death protection change thereafter?

☐   Does the policy contain a savings element? If yes,

    ___ Is there a minimum guaranteed amount?
    ___ Is there a minimum guaranteed interest rate?
    ___ In what year is it first available?
    ___ Will it grow with inflation?
    ___ What nonforfeiture options are available?
    ___ Are withdrawals permitted?
    ___ Are policy loans allowed?
    ___ What is the interest rate for policy loans?
    ___ Is an automatic premium loan option available?
    ___ Is the inside buildup tax deferred?
    ___ Are policyowner-directed types of investments available?

☐   Is the policy participating? If yes,

    ___ When are dividends likely to be available for the first time?
    ___ Are dividends useable to buy additional term or permanent insurance?
    ___ Are dividends affected by policy loans?
    ___ What is the interest rate if dividends are left to accumulate?
    ___ What is the insurer's track record of meeting dividend projections?

☐   What settlement options does the policy contain?

☐   How soon can the policy be made to mature as an endowment?

☐   What is length of the contestable period?

☐   What is length of the suicide exclusion?

☐   What is length of time available to reinstate?

☐   Are accelerated benefits available?

☐   Is an accidental death benefit rider available?

☐   Is a guaranteed purchase (insurability) rider available?
    ___ What is the amount that may be bought?
    ___ What is the frequency of purchase dates?

☐   Is a waiver-of-premium rider available?

___ What is the definition of disability?
___ What is the length of the waiting period?
___ Are premiums waived retroactively to the start of disability?
___ Is there an age before which disability must occur?

MINI-CASE: JEAN AND STEVE GREEN

This case involves Amy Schultz's parents, Jean and Steve. Amy Schultz's father, Steve, aged 52, and her mother, Jean, aged 53, are a married couple with an independent adult daughter, Amy, aged 28, and a son, Tim, aged 20, who has completed 2 years of college. Steve is a social worker for a religious organization with a $40,000 salary and few benefits. Because the organization faces budget pressures, his salary is not likely to increase. Jean is the president of a small private college and earns a $150,000 salary.

Although Steve's salary is relatively small, both he and Jean believe his work is important, and he expects to continue this work until he takes a full retirement at age 66. If Jean should die, Steve plans to live in their house and maintain his current lifestyle until he becomes eligible for a pension and full Social Security benefits and moves to an inexpensive apartment in the sunbelt where he will live on the income from his pension and Social Security.

For planning purposes, Steve believes it is reasonable to assume a 6 percent rate of return on his investments.

a. Based on the following information and Steve's assumptions (whether or not you agree with them), use a needs analysis approach to determine whether Jean has adequate life insurance and, if not, how much additional insurance you would recommend.

Lump-sum Needs at Jean's Death	
Estate clearance fund	$ 12,000
Mortgage retirement fund	180,000
Emergency fund	10,000
Education fund for Tim	80,000
Income Needs after Jean's Death	
Readjustment period (1 year)	$120,000
Dependency period income (14 years)	100,000
Resources Available	
Jean's group term life insurance	$300,000
Jean's defined-contribution retirement plan	520,000

b. What are the shortcomings of this approach in determining Steve and Jean's life insurance needs?

(See answer section for answers to mini-case.)

SOURCES FOR FURTHER IN-DEPTH STUDY

- For more on life insurance planning and company operations:
  - Graves, Edward E., editor, *McGill's Life Insurance*, 4th ed., Bryn Mawr, PA: The American College Press, 2004. Phone 888-263-7265. Web site address www.theamericancollege.edu
  - Black, Kenneth, Jr., and Skipper, Harold D., Jr., *Life and Health Insurance*, 13th ed., Englewood Cliffs, NJ: Prentice-Hall, Inc., 1999. Phone 800-282-0693. Web site address www.prenhall.com
  - *Life Insurance Fact Book* (published annually), Washington, DC: American Council of Life Insurance. Available online at www.acli.org. Phone 202-624-2000.
- For highly detailed information on the determination of the cost of life insurance, various issues of Belth, Joseph M., editor, *The Insurance Forum* (a monthly publication), Elletsville, IN: Insurance Forum, Inc. Phone 812-876-6502.
- For a thorough treatment of the complex subject of many of the business uses of life insurance, Kurlowicz, Ted; Ivers, James F. III; and McFadden, John J., *Planning for Business Owners and Professionals*, 10th ed., Bryn Mawr, PA: The American College Press, 2005. Phone 888-263-7265. Web site address www.theamericancollege.edu
- For the answer to virtually any question on the federal taxation of life insurance, *Tax Facts 1* (published annually), Erlanger, KY: The National Underwriter Company, Phone 800-543-0874. Web site address www.nuco.com

CHAPTER REVIEW

Answers to mini-case, review questions, and self-test questions start on page 793.

Key Terms

financial needs analysis	buy-sell agreement
capital needs analysis	entity agreement
surrender cost index	cross-purchase agreement
net payment cost index	split-dollar life insurance
replacement	transfer-for-value rule
rate-up age method	cash value accumulation test
extra percentage tables	guideline premium and corridor
flat extra premium	test
lien	inside buildup
viatical settlement	modified endowment contract
key employee life insurance	(MEC)

gift tax
gift
annual exclusion

estate tax
gross estate
incident of ownership

Review Questions

10-1. Life insurance plays a key role in most clients' financial plans. What two basic tasks are involved in life insurance planning?

10-2. Before gathering the information required for determining the amount of additional life insurance your client needs, explain to your client the key steps involved and types of information required in the financial needs analysis approach.

10-3. Sophie Jones, a single mother and corporate manager on the "fast track," needs help to determine the amount of additional life insurance she needs to provide support for her children if she should die before they finish college. After gathering information regarding the family's needs in the event of Sophie's death, you find that support for the children, including college educations would require $300,000 to meet lump-sum needs. Also, taking into account reasonable assumptions regarding inflation, after-tax investment returns, and Social Security benefits for the children, you calculate that a present value of $200,000 would be required to meet the children's income support needs if Sophie were to die today. Fact-finding indicates that Sophie already has $200,000 of group term life insurance and $50,000 in savings. How much additional life insurance would Janet need if the principal will be liquidated to help meet the family's needs?

10-4. Describe the steps in the capital needs analysis approach for determining the amount of additional life insurance your client needs. Explain how that approach differs from the financial needs analysis approach.

10-5. Many clients have heard the argument that they should "buy term and invest the difference" argument against the use of permanent life insurance. This argument is based on the assumption that an individual can invest his or her surplus funds more wisely and with greater returns than a life insurance company can. Analyze this argument in terms of the following objectives of an investment program: safety of principal, yield, and liquidity.

10-6. Discuss the distinguishing characteristics that may make one type of permanent life insurance preferable over another type for a particular client.

10-7. A financial planning client of yours received a buyer's guide and policy summary from an agent trying to sell him some additional life insurance. Your client asked the agent several questions, but the agent said, "Don't worry about that detail. We're just required by law to give it to you. Our policy is a good buy." Answer the following questions your client asked:

a. The summary says the policy has a surrender cost index of $7.35 per $1,000 of coverage. What does that number indicate, and generally how was it calculated?

b. How does the net payment cost index shown in the summary differ from the surrender cost index?

c. Why is there so much concern with taking interest into account in these calculations? Why can't you just calculate the cost of a life insurance policy by adding the premiums for 20 years and subtracting the sum of the illustrated dividends for 20 years and the 20th year cash value?

10-8. You suggested to a financial planning client that she might want to consider replacing a life insurance policy she already owns with a new one. She quickly replied, "An agent told me at a cocktail party last week that you should never replace a life insurance policy. In fact, it's against the law." Advise her by answering the following questions:

a. Why might replacement of an existing policy be advantageous to a client?

b. If replacement itself is not illegal, what type of replacement is illegal?

c. What requirements are typically imposed on the replacing agent, the replacing insurer, and the existing insurer or agent by state law?

10-9. A client of yours applies for life insurance, and he is placed in a substandard classification. He says, "So my job is hazardous. I'm in great health as the underwriting showed. Besides, no one has ever died on a job site where I've worked except from bad health. What's the deal?" Explain to your client the rationale for substandard insurance.

10-10. Briefly describe several methods life insurers use to handle substandard risks. Be sure to indicate the type(s) of substandard risk for which each is most commonly used.

10-11. Describe the benefits and pitfalls of a policyowner's viaticating an insurance policy.

10-12. Suzie Pomeranz, a financial planning client, owns her own rapidly growing business with two minority stockholders. As CEO, she asks for advice in dealing with the following:

a. The firm has a number of salespersons, but one, Betty, is the superstar in terms of generating and closing deals. Suzie is concerned with the loss of income, the extra expenses, and the potential effect on the corporate credit rating if Betty were to die. What can you suggest as a solution, and how might it be funded?

b. The two minority stockholders who own a total of 40 percent of the voting stock are also corporate vice presidents. They have expressed concern to Suzie about their futures because, if she were to die, her majority shares would currently pass to her playboy son Lance, who has already indicated he would change operations significantly to focus on current return to the owners rather than on long-term growth. What could you suggest as a means to financially protect the interests of both Suzie's estate and the two minority stockholders in the event of Suzie's death? How might your recommended solution be funded?

c. Suzie feels that because the business is growing rapidly due to the very productive contributions of her employees, as an employee benefit, they should all be provided with life insurance protection equal to two times their salary. What would you suggest as a cost-effective way to accomplish this objective?

10-13. Describe the general rules and key exceptions with regard to the federal income tax treatment of the following aspects of life insurance:
a. death proceeds distributed in a lump sum
b. death proceeds distributed under a settlement option
c. policy dividends
d. inside buildup of a policy's cash value
e. withdrawal of funds from a policy's cash value
f. policy loans
g. loans and most other distributions from a policy that falls under the definition of a MEC
h. premium payments

10-14. Describe the following aspects of the federal gift tax system:
a. the essential elements of a taxable gift
b. the annual exclusion
c. deductions from the gift tax base

10-15. List and explain briefly the key factors taken into account in calculating the federal estate tax.

10-16. In each of the following situations, indicate whether the proceeds of the life insurance policy would be included in your client John's estate for federal estate tax purposes upon his death and, if so, why:
a. John's wife purchased a policy on John's life. She was the policyowner and paid all the premiums. She named John's estate as primary beneficiary so there would be sufficient liquidity to pay estate taxes and she would not be required to sell the family home upon his death.
b. John purchased a policy on his own life and named his children as beneficiaries. Although he was initially the policyowner, he transferred all the rights in the policy to his wife 5 years ago except the right to change the beneficiary.
c. John purchased a policy on his own life and named his children as beneficiaries. Although he was initially the policyowner, he gave all the rights in the policy to his wife 2 years before his death.

10-17. Discuss some key uses of life insurance in estate planning.

Self-Test Questions

T F 10-1. Using a simple multiple of earnings method to determine the amount of life insurance needed ignores key information about how much a client has already accumulated.

T F 10-2. The financial needs analysis approach considers both lump-sum needs at death and ongoing income needs.

T F 10-3. With the financial needs analysis approach, the amount of additional life insurance needed is determined by subtracting the resources already available from the resources needed by the surviving dependents if the client should die today, assuming all future income payments are composed solely of investment earnings on a capital sum.

T F 10-4. A major advantage of the financial needs analysis approach is that it does not take into account factors that may be difficult to forecast such as Social Security benefits and future earnings by a spouse.

T F 10-5. Although term insurance is available in the marketplace, virtually all client life insurance needs are best met with whole life insurance.

T F 10-6. The basic fallacy of the traditional net cost method for measuring the cost of life insurance is that it ignores the time value of money.

T F 10-7. The surrender cost index indicates the cost of surrendering the policy for the cash value at some future point in time.

T F 10-8. All life insurance policy replacements involve twisting and thus are detrimental to the policyowner.

T F 10-9. If a group of substandard risks is to be treated fairly, the degree of extra mortality the group represents and the approximate period in life when the extra mortality is likely to occur must both be known within reasonable limits.

T F 10-10. The most common method of dealing with risks that present an increasing hazard is to assess a flat extra premium.

T F 10-11. It is common practice to remove the extra premium upon proof that the insured is no longer substandard.

T F 10-12. Viatication, or the selling of a life insurance policy to a viatical settlement provider, is a securities transaction subject to SEC regulation.

T F 10-13. Federal privacy laws regarding viaticals protect insureds from being identified and their medical information from being provided to third-party investors.

T F 10-14. One of the common uses of life insurance in business is to serve as an alternative to a properly designed buy-sell agreement.

T   F   10-15.   In a traditional split-dollar plan, the executive contributed an amount equal to the annual increase in the policy's cash surrender value, while the corporation paid the remainder of the annual premium.

T   F   10-16.   In nearly all cases, the beneficiary of a life insurance policy must include the proceeds paid by reason of the insured's death in the beneficiary's gross income for federal income tax purposes.

T   F   10-17.   The inside buildup in a permanent life insurance policy is subject to taxation if it is left inside the policy.

T   F   10-18.   Federal gift taxes apply if there is a completed transfer and acceptance of property for less than full and adequate consideration.

T   F   10-19.   The federal gift tax applies to lifetime transfers of property as well as to transfers occurring at death.

T   F   10-20.   If Sally transfers all incidents of ownership in a life insurance policy on her life to her grown son through a gift and she dies a year later, the life insurance is automatically included in her estate.

T   F   10-21.   The primary goal of life insurance coverage for young clients is estate liquidity, whereas for older clients it tends to be estate enhancement.

11

Annuities

Learning Objectives

An understanding of the material in this chapter should enable the student to

11-1.   Explain the nature of annuities, and compare and contrast them with life insurance.

11-2.   Contrast the various types of annuities.

11-3.   Explain the key features of single-life annuities.

11-4.   Explain the key features of joint annuities.

11-5.   Explain the key features of variable annuities.

11-6.   Explain the key features of equity-indexed annuities.

11-7.   Describe actuarial considerations regarding annuities.

11-8.   Describe the taxation of annuities during the accumulation and liquidation periods.

11-9.   Explain uses of annuities, including structured settlements.

Chapter Outline

annuity

annuitant

Financial planners need to understand annuities in order to help their clients make decisions about liquidating a principal sum. Annuities are useful not only in retirement planning but also for other purposes. This chapter discusses the annuity products life insurance companies sell. An *annuity* is a periodic payment that will begin at a specified or contingent date and continue throughout a fixed period or for the duration of a designated life or lives. The person on whose life the duration of the payments is based is called the *annuitant.* The annuitant is usually but not always the person who receives the periodic payments. Payments under the annuity contract may be on an annual, semiannual, quarterly, or monthly basis, depending on the conditions of the agreement. Usually, payments are made monthly.

annuity certain

life annuity

temporary life annuity

If annuity payments are to be made for a definite period of time without being linked to the duration of a specified human life, the agreement is known as an *annuity certain*. If the payments are to be made for the duration of a designated life, the agreement is called a *life annuity* or, more accurately, a single-life annuity. This annuity is also referred to as a whole life annuity to distinguish it from a *temporary life annuity*, under which payments are made during a specified period of time, but only for as long as a designated person is alive. In other words, a temporary life annuity terminates with the death of the designated individual or at the expiration of the specified period of time, whichever occurs earlier. The word *life* in the title of an annuity indicates that the payments are based on life contingencies or continue only as long as a designated person is alive. This chapter is concerned primarily with life annuities created by insurance companies.

Annuity Definitions

- annuitant—the person on whose life the duration of payments may be based; usually also the person receiving the payments
- annuity certain—payments made for a definite period of time; no relationship to how long the annuitant lives
- life (whole life) annuity—payments made until the annuitant dies; the word "life" in the title indicates that payments are based on life contingencies
- temporary life annuity—payments made until the annuitant dies or for a specified period of time, whichever time period is shorter

---

In order to introduce the annuity concept, this chapter focuses on the various types of annuities and the ways in which annuities can be structured to accumulate and disperse assets. The tax treatment of annuities occupies a page of discussion late in the chapter. We do not want to leave the mistaken approach that annuities are used primarily to provide a stream of retirement income that, incidentally, provides some tax advantages. In reality, tax deferral during the accumulation phase is the most significant reason for many annuity purchases.

NATURE OF ANNUITIES

Comparison with Life Insurance

The primary function of life insurance is to *create* an estate or principal sum; the primary function of an annuity is to *liquidate* a principal sum, regardless of how it was created. Despite this basic dissimilarity in function, both life insurance and annuities are based on the same fundamental pooling, mortality, and investment principles.

Both life insurance and annuities can protect against loss of income. Life insurance furnishes protection against loss of income arising out of premature death; an annuity provides protection against loss of income arising out of excessive longevity. While life insurance can provide a financial hedge against dying too soon, an annuity can provide a hedge against living too long. From a financial standpoint, both contingencies are undesirable.

A second common feature that life insurance and annuities share is the pooling technique. Insurance is a pooling arrangement where all members contribute so that the dependents of those who die prematurely are partially compensated for loss of income. An annuity is a pooling arrangement where those who die prematurely contribute so that those who live beyond their life expectancy will not outlive their income.

A third common feature that life insurance and annuities share is that contributions are based on probabilities of death and survival derived from a mortality table. For reasons that will be apparent later, the same mortality table is not used for both sets of calculations. Finally, for both life insurance and annuities, premiums (often referred to as deposits) are discounted for the compound interest that the insurance company will earn on them.

Life Insurance Compared with Annuities

Life Insurance	Annuities
• Protects against loss of income resulting from premature death	• Protect against loss of income arising out of excessive longevity
• Pooling arrangement in which those who live beyond their life expectancy compensate dependents of those who die prematurely	• Pooling arrangement in which those who die prematurely contribute to the income of those who live beyond their life expectancy
• Premiums based on a mortality table	• Premiums based on a different mortality table
• Premiums discounted to reflect interest earned by the insurer	• Premiums (deposits) discounted to reflect interest earned by the insurer

---

Annuity Principle

Like life insurance, the annuity concept is founded on the unpredictability of any given human life. A person may have accumulated a principal sum to be liquidated for old-age support over the person's remaining years. However, the individual must accurately predict the number of years remaining. With average health and vitality for his or her age, the individual could expect to live exactly the calculated life expectancy, based on a mortality table. But because survival beyond this predicted life expectancy is possible, to be conservative, the accumulated principal would have to be adequate to fund a longer period than the annuitant is likely to live. Even then, there is some danger of finding the assets and income totally consumed prior to death.

On the other hand, the annuitant might die after only a few years, leaving funds to the estate that could have been used to provide more comforts during the decedent's lifetime. If the annuitant is willing to pool savings with those of other people in the same situation, the administering agency, relying on the laws of probability and large numbers, can provide all the participants with an income of a specified amount as long as they live—regardless of longevity. In this way none of the participants could outlive their income. This arrangement relies on participants' willingness to have all or a portion of their unliquidated principal at the time of death used to supplement the principal of those who live beyond their life expectancy. Therefore, each payment to the annuitant is composed partly of the annuitant's principal, the unliquidated principal of other annuitants who die early, and investment income on these funds.

Classifications of Annuities

As figure 11-1 shows, annuities can be classified in many different ways, depending on the point of emphasis.

The distribution of benefits may extend only for the life of the annuitant or may include some minimum guaranteed total payout. The annuity may cover only one life, or it may depend on the longevity of two (or more) persons. The benefit payments may begin immediately or at some future date. The annuity may be purchased through a single premium or through installment premiums. Last, the amount of each annuity payment may be fixed or variable. The discussion that follows provides details on the types and characteristics of annuities.

Number of Lives Covered

The annuity may cover a single life or more than one life. The conventional form is the single-life annuity. A contract that covers two or more lives may be a joint annuity or a joint-and-last-survivor annuity. The seldom-issued *joint* or

joint (joint-life) annuity

joint-and-last-survivor annuity

joint-life annuity provides that the income ceases at the first death among the lives covered. A *joint-and-last-survivor annuity*, on the other hand, provides that the income ceases only at the last death among the lives covered. In other words, payments under a joint-and-last-survivor annuity continue for as long as either of two or more specified persons lives. This annuity contract is very useful, and widely marketed, especially for husband and wife couples. Annuity contracts that involve more than two lives are uncommon.

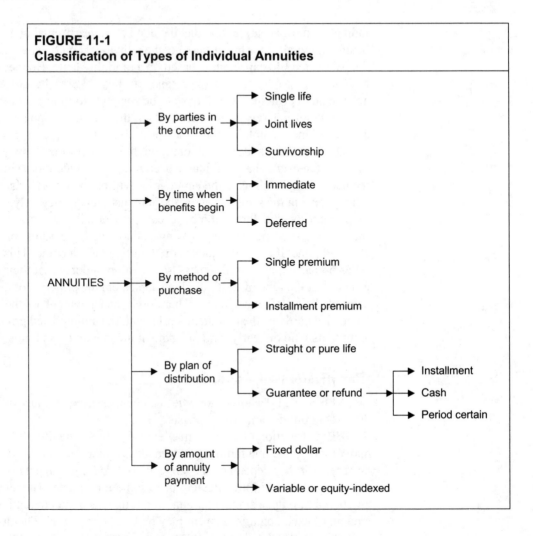

FIGURE 11-1
Classification of Types of Individual Annuities

Time When Benefit Payments Commence

immediate annuity

Annuities can also be classified as immediate or deferred. An *immediate annuity* makes the first benefit payment one payment interval after the date of purchase. If the contract provides for monthly payments, the first benefit payment is due one month after the date of purchase; if annual payments are called for, the first payment is due one year after the date of purchase. An immediate annuity is always purchased with a single premium; the annuitant exchanges a principal sum for a lifetime income or some other payment promise.

deferred annuity

Under a *deferred annuity*, a period longer than one payment interval must elapse after purchase before the first benefit payment is due. As a matter of fact, normally at least several years elapse between the date of purchase and the time when payments commence. A deferred annuity is suitable for many people, including those of ordinary means who want to accumulate a sum for their old age.

Method of Premium Payment

Deferred annuities can be purchased with either single premiums or periodic premiums. Originally, an annuity was developed as a contract purchased with a lump sum, perhaps accumulated from a successful business venture or an inheritance. The lump sum was paid in exchange for an immediate income of a stipulated amount. Immediate annuities are still purchased with a lump sum, but most annuities today are purchased on an installment basis. Periodic payments may be scheduled level deposits or may be flexible deposits with the amount and timing at the purchaser's discretion. The deferred annuity provides an attractive and convenient method of accumulating over time the necessary funds for an adequate old-age income.

Nature of the Insurer's Obligation

pure (straight life) annuity

When discussing deferred annuities, it is important to distinguish between the accumulation period, during which premiums (deposits) are paid *to* the insurer and the liquidation period, during which benefits are paid *by* the insurer. During the liquidation period, a *pure annuity,* also known as a *straight life annuity,* provides periodic—usually monthly—income payments that continue as long as the annuitant lives and terminate at that person's death. Most deferred annuities sold to individuals provide that all premiums paid will be refunded, with or without interest, if the insured dies during the accumulation period. In any case, a pure annuity is considered to be fully liquidated upon the death of the annuitant, regardless of how soon after the beginning of the liquidation period death may occur. There is no guarantee that the insurer will pay any particular number of monthly payments during the liquidation period. This nonrefund feature applies to the liquidation period of not only deferred annuities but also immediate annuities.

refund annuity

A pure annuity will make no additional payments after the death of an annuitant, even if the annuitant dies very early in the liquidation period. In contrast, a *refund annuity* includes a promise to return all, or at least part, of the purchase price of the annuity in some manner. As might be expected, refund annuities are far more popular than pure annuities. Refund annuity contracts take several forms, as discussed in the following sections.

Example: Betsy, aged 60, is retiring and wants to take the $100,000 in vested funds from her employer's retirement plan in a lump sum. She plans to use this money to purchase an annuity to fund her retirement.

She learns that the insurer offers a life annuity that will pay her $558 per month until she dies, whether she lives for one month or 50 years. Betsy is not thrilled with the idea that her $100,000 retirement fund could pay as little as $558 in benefits (or even nothing at all if she dies within the first month).

She also learns that the insurer offers a refund annuity that will pay her a little less money, $551 per month for life, *and* guarantee payments for at least 10 years, even if she does not live that long. Betsy chooses the 10-year certain annuity.

Fixed or Variable Benefit Amounts

Annuities may provide a fixed number of dollars for each benefit payment or a varying payment based on the investment performance of the assets underlying **fixed annuity** the annuity. The conventional *fixed annuity* provides payments of a fixed amount over a specified period or throughout the lifetime of one or more persons. Significant inflation during some recent periods, however, focused attention on the **variable annuity** need to protect the purchasing power of benefits. In response to this need, *variable annuity* contracts were developed to provide benefits that vary with changes in investment performance, a proxy for changes in purchasing power.

SINGLE-LIFE ANNUITIES

Liquidation Period

liquidation period

This section discusses various arrangements for the payment of benefits during the *liquidation period* of an annuity. The liquidation period is the period during which the capital sum is paid out. The capital sum here is either (1) the single premium that funds an immediate annuity or (2) the periodic premiums during the accumulation period, plus interest accrued on those payments, that fund a deferred annuity. In other words, we will describe the various arrangements under which a principal sum can be liquidated on the basis of life contingencies. Although this discussion refers specifically to annuities, the same principles apply to the liquidation of a principal sum under the life-income option of a life insurance policy. These principles also apply when an annuity is used in lieu of a lump-sum payment to settle a liability claim; this is referred to as a structured settlement and will be explained in greater detail later in the chapter.

Pure Annuities

As stated previously, a pure annuity provides periodic benefit payments for the lifetime of the annuitant. The consideration paid for the annuity is fully earned by the insurance company when the benefit payments begin. The payments can be made monthly, quarterly, semiannually, or annually. The more frequent the periodic payments, the more costly the annuity for the owner. The insurer must charge more due to the greater expense of writing frequent checks, the loss of interest earnings by the insurance company, and the greater probability that the annuitant will live to receive at least some of the payments. For example, if the annuitant dies 6 months and one day after purchasing the annuity, he or she would have received six monthly payments if the benefit payment is monthly but no benefit payments if the benefit is payable annually.

Occasionally, annuities are made apportionable—that is, they provide for a pro rata payment covering the period from the date of the last regular payment to the date of death. This feature necessitates an increase in the purchase price as compared with premiums for the usual type of annuity calculated on the assumption that there will be no such pro rata payment.

The pure annuity provides the maximum income per dollar of outlay, and for that reason, it is perhaps most suitable for people with only a limited amount of capital. According to typical actuarial assumptions, $1,000 of capital will provide monthly income between $7 and $10 for males aged 65 and between $6 and $9 for females aged 65 under a straight life annuity. If payments are guaranteed for 10 years, whether the annuitant lives or dies, the monthly income will be reduced approximately $.50 for each $1,000 increment. On an investment of $100,000, the difference in monthly income will be $50, which might be the difference between dependency and self-sufficiency for an elderly person. For a person aged 70, the difference in monthly income from $100,000 will be $100, and at 75, the difference will be $175—too large to ignore.

At younger ages, because of the high probability of survival, the difference in income between an annuity without a refund feature and one with a refund feature is extremely small. A person aged 35 can obtain an annuity with a 5-year guarantee for the same cost as a pure annuity and an annuity with a 10-year guarantee at the sacrifice of only a few cents of monthly income per $1,000 of outlay. Even someone aged 55 can obtain a 10-year guarantee at a reduction in monthly income of less than $.50. In general, the chances for males under 60 and females under 65 to survive the typical periods of guaranteed payments are so high that little in monthly income is gained by giving up the refund feature. Even so, if a particular younger-aged annuitant does die early during the liquidation period and he or she has not opted for a refund feature, the financial loss to the heirs can be substantial.

Refund Annuities

Most people have strong objections to placing a substantial sum of money into a contract that promises little or no refund to their heirs if the annuitant dies at an early age. Therefore, to make annuities marketable, insurance companies have found it necessary to add a refund feature. The refund feature can take two general forms: a promise to provide at least a certain number of annuity payments whether the annuitant lives or dies, or a promise to refund all or a portion of the purchase price in the event of the annuitant's early death.

Table 11-1 summarizes these refund features.

TABLE 11-1 Refund Features During Liquidation		
	Annuitant Dies:	**Then**
Pure annuity	During liquidation	No further payments
Life annuity with period certain	During period certain	Payments to contingent payee for remainder of period certain
	After period certain	No further payments
Installment refund	When total payments < purchase price	Payments to contingent payee until purchase price is recovered
	When total payments ≥ purchase price	No further payments
Cash refund annuity	When total payments < purchase price	Lump sum paid to contingent payee equal to purchase price minus total payments
	When total payments ≥ purchase price	No further payments
50% refund annuity	When total payments < 50% x purchase price	Payments on lump sum paid to contingent payee equal to (50% x purchase price) minus total payments
	When total payments ≥ 50% x purchase price	No further payments
Modified cash refund annuity	When payments < accumulated contributions	Lump sum paid to contingent payee equal to accumulated contribution minus total payments
	When payments ≥ accumulated contributions	No further payments

life annuity certain

Life Annuity Certain. One type of contract goes under various names, including *life annuity certain*, life annuity certain and continuous, life annuity with installments certain, life annuity with a period certain guarantee, and life annuity with minimum guaranteed return. This annuity pays a *guaranteed minimum number of monthly payments,* regardless whether the annuitant lives or dies, and payments continue for the whole of the annuitant's life if he or she lives beyond the guaranteed period. Contracts can be written with payments guaranteed for 5, 10, 15, 20, or even 25 years, although not all insurers offer such a wide range of choices.

As figure 11-2 illustrates, the life annuity certain can be viewed as a combination of two components: an annuity certain and a pure deferred life annuity. The annuity certain covers the period of guaranteed payments and provides the payments regardless of whether the annuitant is living. The pure deferred life annuity becomes effective if the annuitant is still alive at the end

---

FIGURE 11-2
Two Components of a Life Annuity Certain

Annuity Liquidation Period (Years)	
Annuity Certain	**Pure Deferred Life Annuity**
Payments will be made whether annuitant is dead or alive.	If annuitant is still alive, payments will be made until annuitant dies.
1 2 3 4 5	6 7 8 9 10, etc.
As the annuity certain period is reduced, the refund annuity provides a higher benefit for a given purchase price (or lower price for a given benefit).	As the annuity certain period is increased, the refund annuity provides a lower benefit for a given purchase price (or higher price for a given benefit).
The cost for this period varies directly with the length of the term for which payments are guaranteed.	The cost for this period decreases as the age at which the commencement of the deferred life annuity increases.

---

of the period of guaranteed payments, and it provides continuing lifetime benefits. If the annuitant does not survive the period of guaranteed payments, no payments are made under the deferred life annuity, and no refund is forthcoming.

All other things being equal, an annuity with a period certain is always more expensive per dollar of income than a straight life annuity because it is not based solely on life contingencies. Some of the payments are a certainty; the only cost-reducing factor is the compound interest earned on the unliquidated portion of the purchase price. Therefore, the longer the term of the period certain—or to put it more specifically, the longer the period of guaranteed payments—the more costly this type of refund annuity is or the lower the yield on the purchase price. Because the annuity certain is not based solely on life contingencies, the cost of an annuity certain does not depend on the age of the annuitant; it varies directly with the length of the term. At any particular age, however, the longer the period of guaranteed payments, the less expensive the deferred life annuity will be because the higher the age at which the deferred life annuity commences, the smaller the probability that the annuitant will survive to that age. This means that the larger the number of guaranteed payments, the smaller the portion of the purchase price going into the deferred life annuity.

installment refund annuity

Installment Refund Annuity. Under an *installment refund annuity,* if the annuitant dies before receiving monthly payments equal to the purchase price of the annuity, the payments will continue to a designated beneficiary or beneficiaries until the full cost is recovered. Of course, payments to the annuitant continue as long as he or she lives, even though the purchase price may long since have been recovered in full.

Example: Assume that Stan, aged 65, purchases an immediate annuity for $100,000. This annuity will provide a monthly life income of about $750 on an installment refund basis. If Stan dies after receiving 100 payments ($75,000), the payments will continue to a designated beneficiary until an additional $25,000 is paid out, for a total of $100,000. If Stan dies after 13 years, there will be no further payments because the entire purchase price already will have been recovered.

---

cash refund annuity

Cash Refund Annuity. The *cash refund annuity* promises, at the death of the annuitant, to pay to the annuitant's estate or to a designated beneficiary a lump sum amounting to the difference, if any, between the purchase price of the annuity and the sum of the monthly payments. The only difference between the cash refund and installment refund annuities is that in the former, the unrecovered portion of the purchase price is refunded in a lump sum at the time of the annuitant's death; in the latter, the monthly installments are continued until the purchase price has been fully recovered. The cash refund annuity is naturally somewhat more expensive because the insurance company loses the interest it would have earned while liquidating the remaining portion of the purchase price on an installment basis. Under the cash refund annuity, the insurer uses the interest earnings on the unliquidated portion of the premiums of all annuitants receiving benefits to fund benefit payments in excess of any particular annuitant's purchase price.

50 percent refund annuity

50 Percent Refund Annuity. A *50 percent refund annuity* contract guarantees a minimum return of one-half of the purchase price, a compromise between the straight life annuity and the 100 percent refund annuity. Under this contract, if the annuitant dies before receiving benefits equal to half of the cost of the annuity, monthly installments continue until the combined payments to both the annuitant and a designated beneficiary equal half of the cost of the annuity. Usually, if the beneficiary so elects, he or she can receive the present value of the remaining payments in a lump sum. Because the guarantee under this contract is smaller than that under the 100 percent refund annuity, the income per dollar of purchase price is larger.

Another form of annuity sometimes provides that, regardless of the number of payments received prior to the annuitant's death, 50 percent of the cost of the contract will be returned in the form of a death benefit. This contract is not a refund annuity in the strict sense. Instead, the company uses one-half of the premium to provide a straight life annuity and holds the other half on deposit. It uses earnings from the half it holds on deposit to supplement the annuity benefits the other half of the premium provides. At the annuitant's death, the insurer returns the premium deposit to the annuitant's estate or to a designated beneficiary in the form of a death benefit.

modified cash refund annuity

Modified Cash Refund Annuity. Finally, the *modified cash refund annuity* is found in contributory pension plans. This contract promises that if the employee dies before receiving retirement benefits equal to the accumulated value of his or her contributions, with or without interest, the difference between the employee's benefits and contributions will be refunded in a lump sum to the employee's estate or to a designated beneficiary. In other words, the refund feature is based on the employee's contributions and not on the portion of the total cost of the annuity paid by the employer.

Comparisons. Monthly income amounts one insurer provides under various forms of annuities per $1,000 of premium accumulations are shown in table 11-2. This table illustrates the small cost of a refund feature at age 60 or 65 and the high cost at more advanced ages. Note that at the highest age shown, the refund form is less expensive—or, conversely, purchases more monthly benefit than a life annuity with a 10-year guarantee. Remember, however, that the benefits under each of the forms are the actuarial equivalent of those under all the other forms, and the annuitant must choose the form that is most appropriate to his or her financial and family circumstances.

Insurance companies can design annuity contracts with any period certain or with a refund guarantee for any specified percent from 0 to 100 percent of the purchase price. In practice, however, each insurer is likely to offer only a few options, primarily due to the costs of getting regulatory approval for each type of contract.

TABLE 11-2
Monthly Annuity Benefits Available per $1,000 of
Purchase Price (Immediate Annuities)

Type	Male Age				
	60	65	70	75	80
Life	$5.85	$6.54	$7.47	$8.89	$10.90
10-year certain + life	5.73	6.32	6.98	7.79	8.65
Refund	5.62	6.18	6.49	7.74	8.90

Type	Female Age				
	60	65	70	75	80
Life	$5.81	$6.16	$6.91	$8.07	$9.71
10-year certain + life	5.51	6.03	6.62	7.40	8.33
Refund	5.45	5.93	6.49	7.28	8.36

The figures shown in table 11-2 remain fixed over their payment period. However, an annuitant may want benefit payments to increase with rises in the cost of living. One alternative is to purchase a variable annuity which is discussed later in this chapter. There is no guarantee, however, as to the level of future payments. Another alternative is to select a fixed income payment that is adjusted for inflation. Only a few insurers offer such payment options, and they are not widely selected by annuitants when they are available. For example, one insurer allows the annuitant to select an inflation factor of 1, 2, 3, 4, or 5 percent. For an annuitant aged 65, the initial payment is reduced by 25 percent if he or she selects a 3 percent inflation factor and 43 percent for a 5 percent inflation factor. Each year, however, the payment amount increases by the selected inflation factor, regardless of the actual inflation rate. This insurer also allows the annuitant to select an income that will be adjusted by changes in the consumer price index, subject to a maximum 10 percent annual increase.

Accumulation Period

accumulation period

The preceding discussion of annuities related entirely to their liquidation phase, with no discussion concerning how the funds for payout had been accumulated. With deferred annuities, during an *accumulation period*, funds are invested at the insurance company to grow to the amount necessary to fund benefits promised at a specified future date.

Annuity contracts that allow flexible premium payments during the accumulation phase cannot specify in advance the level of benefit payments that will be paid during the liquidation phase. Instead, these annuities specify the amount of benefit for each $1,000 of fund balance when the annuity switches over to the liquidation phase.

Almost without exception, deferred annuities sold to individuals promise to return all premiums, with or without interest, if the annuitant dies during the accumulation period. The usual contract provides for a return of either gross premiums without interest or the cash value, whichever is larger. This contract is a type of refund annuity with respect to the period of accumulation.

Under private pension plans, employer contributions are almost invariably used to purchase pure deferred annuities with respect to the accumulation period. If the purchaser dies prior to the date the income is scheduled to commence, there is no refund of premiums. If the employee terminates employment before retirement, the employer recovers the employer's contributions, plus interest, but if the employee dies, employer contributions on his or her behalf remain with the insurance company to provide benefits to employees who remain with the employer until retirement. This annuity can be purchased at a much lower premium than one that promises to return contributions, with the result that the employer can either finance the pension plan at the lowest possible outlay or can provide larger retirement benefits than it could otherwise afford.

Structuring the Annuity Contract

The premiums for an annuity contract bought with periodic premiums can be quoted in units of $100 of annual premium or in terms of the annual premium needed to provide a monthly life income of $10 at a designated age.

In every deferred annuity except a variable annuity, which is described later, a minimum rate of interest on the cash value is guaranteed throughout the accumulation period. Many annuities, however, also provide a secondary guaranteed rate that is higher than the minimum floor rate. The secondary guaranteed rate usually applies only for the first several years of the accumulation period, with a higher rate for short periods than for long periods. At the conclusion of the initial guarantee period, a lower or unspecified secondary guaranteed rate, perhaps zero, will apply.

The effect of cash withdrawals should also be considered when evaluating a secondary guaranteed rate during the accumulation period. Some insurers reduce this secondary rate, sometimes even retroactively, if funds are withdrawn from the cash value rather than left to eventually be taken in annuity benefits.

After the secondary guaranteed rate expires, some contracts contain a bail-out provision that allows the contract to be terminated without a surrender charge. The bail-out may be allowed if the interest rate falls below a stipulated rate, often 2 percentage points below the secondary guaranteed rate. The bail-out provision may seem much more attractive than it really is for two reasons: (1) Competitors are unlikely to be able to pay higher rates if and when the release is triggered, and (2) interest on a cash-out will be subject to income taxes and possibly a 10 percent penalty tax. In the event of the annuitant's death before age 65 or other scheduled start of the liquidation period, the company will return the accumulated gross premiums without interest or the cash value, whichever is larger. The cash value is equal to the gross premiums plus interest at a guaranteed rate, after deducting an expense charge. After about 10 years, the cash value exceeds the accumulated value of premiums paid without interest, and it becomes the effective death benefit. Note that, although this is an annuity contract, there is an insurance element during the accumulation period in that the death benefit exceeds the cash value.

Evaluating a Secondary Guaranteed Interest Rate

- At what rate will funds accumulate?
- For how long does the rate apply?
- After the rate expires, is a subsequent rate guaranteed?
- What will the effect of withdrawals be on the rate?
- After the rate expires, can the contract be terminated without a surrender charge?

The annuitant can withdraw the full cash value at any time during the deferral period, whereupon the contract terminates and the company has no further obligation. Under some contracts, the annuitant can borrow against the cash value, and the loan will not bring about a termination of the contract.

Liquidation Options

At the maturity date, the annuitant can elect to have the accumulation applied under any of the annuity forms the company offers. Depending on the option the owner elects at maturity, the actual monthly income might be more or less than the amount originally anticipated, based on the owner's payout option selection at the time of issue. Moreover, the annuitant usually has a *cash option* of taking a lump sum in lieu of an annuity. The cash option exposes the company to serious adverse selection. Persons in poor health tend to withdraw their accumulations in cash, while those in excellent health usually choose an annuity. To offset this selection, if the annuitant selects the cash option, some companies provide a retroactive reduction in the investment earnings rate applied to accumulations under a deferred annuity. The resulting penalty can be a substantial dollar amount.

cash option

Under most contracts, the annuitant can choose to have the benefit payments commence at an earlier or a later date than the one originally specified in the contract, with a subsequent adjustment in the amount of monthly benefits. Beginning the income at an earlier age than the age specified in the contract amounts to converting the cash value to an immediate annuity. There is usually no age limit below which the benefit payments must not begin, although the option is subject to the general requirement that the periodic income payments equal or exceed a stipulated minimum amount.

There is usually an upper age limit, sometimes as high as age 80 or as low as age 70, beyond which commencement of the income benefits cannot be postponed. The option to postpone the commencement of benefit payments can be particularly attractive if the annuitant is still in good health at the original maturity date and plans to work for a few more years. The life income payable at any particular age, whether the maturity date is moved ahead or set back, is the same amount that would have been provided had the substituted maturity date been the one originally selected and funded with the actual amount accumulated.

JOINT ANNUITIES

Joint annuities share most characteristics of single life annuities, discussed in the preceding section, except that joint annuities involve more than one annuitant. The two basic types of joint annuities were briefly mentioned earlier in this chapter. The joint-life annuity, provides income benefits only until the death of the first of two or more annuitants. The joint-and-last-survivor annuity, continues benefit payments until the last of the named annuitants dies.

Joint-Life Annuity

A joint-life annuity provides an income as long as the two or more persons named in the contract live. Because the income ceases at the first death among the covered lives, the coverage is relatively inexpensive. This contract is always sold as a single premium immediate annuity.

This contract has a very limited market. It might be appropriate for two persons—elderly sisters, for example, who have an income from a stable source large enough to support one but not both of the sisters. If they can purchase a joint-life annuity in an amount adequate to support one sister without disturbing the other income, the combined income will be adequate for their needs while both sisters are alive. Upon the death of one of the sisters, the income from the original source will meet the survivor's needs.

Joint-and-Last-Survivor Annuity

A joint-and-last-survivor annuity is a far more marketable contract than the joint-life annuity because the income under this form of annuity continues as long as any of two or more persons live. This arrangement is ideal for a husband and wife or for families in which there is a permanently disabled dependent child.

For most combinations of ages, the joint-and-last-survivor annuity is the most expensive of all annuity forms. According to one insurer, an accumulation of $18,469 is required to provide an income of $100 per month on the joint-and-last-survivor basis to a man and woman both aged 65. If the man is 65 and the woman 60, a sum of $19,068 is needed to provide $100 per month on the joint-and-last-survivor basis. Compare those figures to the approximate amount of $15,290 that is required, according to the $6.54 rate shown in table 11-2, to provide a life income of $100 per month with no refund feature only to a man aged 65.

The joint-and-last-survivor annuity can be purchased as a single-premium immediate annuity at a cost somewhat higher than the accumulation figures quoted above, as an optional form under an annual-premium deferred annuity, or in conjunction with the settlement of life insurance or endowment proceeds.

Although a typical joint-and-last-survivor contract does not contain a refund feature, most insurance companies offer a contract that guarantees 120 monthly installments, and a few offer 240 guaranteed installments. Under these contracts, if the last survivor dies before the minimum number of payments has been made, the remaining installments continue to a designated beneficiary. As with single-life annuities, the designated beneficiary may be permitted to take the present value of the remaining installments as a lump sum. When both husband and wife are 65, a life income of $100 per month with 120 guaranteed installments requires an accumulation of $18,589—only $120 more than a similar annuity without a refund feature.

The conventional joint-and-last-survivor annuity continues the same income to the survivor as was paid while both annuitants were alive. A common modification, which reduces the cost, decreases the income to the survivor to two-thirds of the original amount. This contract, the *joint-and-two-thirds annuity,* is based on the assumption that the survivor does not require as much income as the two annuitants. This contract written in an original amount of $100 per month on the lives of a husband and wife, both aged 65, requires an accumulation of slightly more than $15,960.

In a *joint-and-one-half annuity*, the income to the survivor is reduced to one-half of the original amount. This form has not had the popular appeal of the joint-and-two-thirds annuity. Many insurers have introduced other options besides the two-thirds and one-half options for continuation at the death of the first annuitant.

The joint-and-last-survivor form is widely used by private pension plans to pay retirement benefits to married plan participants. When the employee elects the joint-and-two-thirds annuity, many plans reduce the income only if the employee dies first. If the employee's spouse dies first, the employee continues to receive the full income. Federal law requires written consent of the nonemployee spouse in order to drop the survivorship benefit.

VARIABLE ANNUITIES

For a contract to offer benefits with stable purchasing power, the contract should provide more dollars if prices rise and fewer dollars if prices decline. Theoretically, benefits could be adjusted as the appropriate price index, such as the consumer price index, changes. From the standpoint of insurance companies, however, there is no mechanism by which the value of the assets backing the annuity can be adjusted automatically to reflect changes in the dollar value of the annuity promises. As a practical solution, variable annuity contracts have been developed that provide benefits adjusted to changes in the market value of the assets—typically common stocks—in which the annuity reserves are invested. The tie to common stock is based on the theory that over a long period of time, the market value of a representative group of common stocks tends to conform rather faithfully to changes in the consumer price level. Moreover, inasmuch as the insurance company's liabilities to its annuitants are expressed in terms of the market value of the assets offsetting the liabilities, funds for the payment of annuity benefits are available in the appropriate proportions at all times.

Proponents of the variable annuity believe that annuitants need protection against inflation and that a common stock investment program administered by a life insurance company is the best approach yet developed. Critics of the variable annuity approach question whether continuing inflation is inevitable, and even if it is, whether common stock investments provide an effective hedge against rising prices in the short run. These critics also cite the absence of any guaranteed minimum interest rate credit as an important disadvantage of the variable annuity.

Accumulation Units

accumulation unit

At present, variable annuities are most often issued on a deferred basis. During the accumulation period, premium payments—or deposits, as they are frequently called—are applied to the purchase of accumulation units. The *accumulation unit* is assigned an arbitrary value, such as $10, at the inception of the plan, and the initial premiums purchase accumulation units at that price. Thereafter, the units are revalued each month to reflect changes in the market value of the common stock that makes up the company's variable annuity portfolio. On any valuation date, the value of each accumulation unit is determined by dividing the market value of the common stock underlying the accumulation units by the aggregate number of units. Dividends are usually allocated periodically to the participants and applied to the purchase of additional accumulation units, although they may simply be reinvested without allocation and permitted to increase the value of each existing accumulation unit. Capital appreciation or depreciation is always reflected in the value of the accumulation units, rather than in the number of units. (In other words, both realized and unrealized gains and losses are reflected for individual participants through an increase or decrease in the value of their accumulation units.) A portion of each premium payment is deducted for expenses, and the remainder is invested in accumulation units at their current market value.

A hypothetical accumulation is shown in table 11-3. In this example, the initial purchase is made at age 35 with a premium high enough to cover a $200 purchase of units each month after paying insurer expenses. The assumptions behind the table 11-3 numbers are that the accumulation units change value once each year and that a full $200 is available each month to acquire more units. The units in this example grow at approximately 7.5 percent in most years but fluctuate more or less than that in some years as stock prices are prone to do over short intervals. In this case, there is an accumulation of $258,459.62 at the end of the 30th year (end of age 64 or beginning of age 65) consisting of 31,751.80 accumulation units.

Annuity Units

annuity unit

At the beginning of the liquidation period, the accumulation units are exchanged for *annuity units*. The number of annuity units the annuitant acquires depends on the company's assumptions as to mortality, dividend rates, and expenses, and on the market value of the assets underlying the annuity units. In essence, the number of annuity units is determined by dividing the dollar value of the accumulation units ($258,459.62 in the table 11-3 example) by an actuarial factor (assumed to be $35 in this case) designed to provide a benefit of $1 per year for the annuitant's remaining lifetime. While the owner's number of accumulation units increases with each premium payment and each allocation of dividends during the accumulation period, the number of annuity units

TABLE 11-3
Variable Annuity Accumulation Units
Deferred Annuity Purchased at Age 35 at $200 per Month

Year	Age	Unit Value	New Units	Total Units	Total Value
1	35	$1.00	2,400.00	2,400.00	$ 2,400.00
2	36	1.08	2,232.56	4,632.56	4,980.00
3	37	1.16	2,076.80	6,709.36	7,753.50
4	38	1.24	1,931.91	8,641.26	10,735.01
5	39	1.34	1,797.12	10,438.38	13,940.14
6	40	1.07	2,242.99	12,681.37	13,569.07
7	41	1.15	2,086.50	14,767.88	16,986.75
8	42	1.24	1,940.93	16,708.81	20,660.76
9	43	1.88	1,276.60	17,985.41	33,812.56
10	44	2.12	1,132.08	19,117.48	40,529.06
11	45	2.28	1,053.09	20,170.57	45,968.74
12	46	2.45	979.62	21,150.20	51,816.39
13	47	2.63	911.28	22,061.47	58,102.62
14	48	2.83	847.70	22,909.17	64,860.32
15	49	3.04	788.56	23,697.73	72,124.84
16	50	3.27	733.54	24,431.27	79,934.21
17	51	3.52	682.36	25,113.63	88,329.27
18	52	3.78	634.76	25,748.39	97,353.97
19	53	3.50	685.71	26,434.10	92,519.37
20	54	3.25	738.46	27,172.57	88,310.84
21	55	3.00	800.00	27,972.56	83,917.70
22	56	3.60	666.67	28,639.23	103,101.24
23	57	4.01	598.50	29,237.74	117,243.32
24	58	4.97	482.90	29,720.63	147,711.55
25	59	5.76	416.67	30,137.70	173,590.85
26	60	6.25	384.00	30,521.30	190,758.13
27	61	7.16	335.20	30,856.50	220,932.51
28	62	7.90	303.80	31,160.29	246,166.32
29	63	8.09	296.66	31,456.96	254,486.78
30	64	8.14	294.84	31,751.80	258,459.62

remains constant throughout the liquidation period (7,384.6 annuity units in this case). However, the units are revalued each year, to reflect the current market price of the common stock and the mortality, investment, and expense experience for the preceding year.[1] The dollar income payable to the annuitant each month is determined by multiplying the number of units the annuitant owns by the current value of one unit. During the liquidation period, the higher the market price of the stock and the greater the dividends, the greater the dollar income of the annuitant.

Some of the more recent variable annuity contracts differ from the above by using only one unit throughout the contract period, by discounting for mortality before as well as after retirement, and by limiting variations in the unit value to investment experience only.

> **Accumulation Units versus Annuity Units in a Variable Annuity**
>
> - Accumulation units: The number of units bought and the value of each unit vary depending on when the purchases are made.
> - Annuity units: The number of annuity units distributed periodically is constant, but the value varies depending on when the distributions are made.

Surrender Provisions

When a variable annuity is sold as an individual contract, surrender privileges are made available but on a much more restricted basis than in connection with ordinary annuities. When a variable annuity is used as part of a pension plan, surrender values are not generally made available. Under all plans, the current value of the accumulation units is payable to a designated beneficiary, if any, or to the estate, usually as a continuing income. However, a lump-sum settlement is possible at the death of the participant during the accumulation period.

Regulation

In a landmark decision,[2] the United States Supreme Court held that an individual variable annuity contract is a security within the meaning of the Securities Act of 1933 and that any organization that offers such a contract is an investment company subject to the Investment Company Act of 1940. Any company that offers individual variable annuity contracts is subject to dual supervision by the Securities and Exchange Commission (SEC) and the various state insurance departments. Persons selling variable annuities must pass the Series 6 licensing exam of the National Association of Securities Dealers (NASD).

EQUITY-INDEXED ANNUITIES

equity-indexed annuity

Equity-indexed annuities are a variation of fixed-interest, traditional deferred-annuity products. These annuities were introduced in the mid-1990s. Fixed-interest annuities were very attractive during the high-interest-rate era of the 1980s and early 1990s. Their appeal waned, however, as interest rates dropped and stock market yields significantly surpassed the yields in traditional fixed-interest annuities.

An equity-indexed annuity offers guaranteed minimum interest rates and, at the same time, pays a higher return if a specified stock index increases enough to provide a higher yield. They are designed to appeal to persons who want to participate in high-equity investment yields without bearing the full downside investment risk they assume through the purchase of a variable annuity.

The equity-indexed annuity provides only a portion of the capital gain of the stocks that make up the applicable index, commonly the Standard & Poor's Composite Index of 500 Stocks. Variable annuities are still the only annuity products that provide most of the full yield of the equity investments to the owner/annuitant.

Participation Rate Formula

Prospective purchasers of equity-indexed annuities should understand that their potential return based on increases in the value of the index is determined by the formula approach set forth in the contract. Generally, this formula includes a participation rate as well as the increase in the index from the beginning of the term to the verified anniversary-date value of the index. The participation rate is a percentage (always less than 100 percent) of the defined increase that will be used to calculate the crediting amount. The insurer sets this participation rate, which is subject to change. Some companies do not even specify the current participation rate in their promotional materials. Often, the participation rate is guaranteed for a specified term such as the first 5 or 7 years. The insurance company reserves the right to change the participation rate at the expiration of each term, but the company usually guarantees the then-current rate for the subsequent term.

Most contracts anticipate a series of terms of uniform length, much like renewals of 5-year term life insurance. However, some contracts reserve the insurer's right to modify the term period available for continuation at the expiration of any existing term. In most designs, a higher increase from the index calculation is available only at the end of the applicable term unless the owner dies or the contract is converted to benefit-payout status (annuitized) before the end of the term. The higher value based on the index will not apply if the contract is terminated before the end of the term.

The participation rate restricts the amount of the index gain, if any, that can be applied to produce more than the guaranteed yield. The participation rate and the guaranteed interest rate are linked. Higher participation rates may be available from some insurers if the purchaser accepts a lower guaranteed interest rate. One company guarantees that the participation rate will never be lower than 25 percent. Illustrations are often based on 80 percent or 90 percent participation rates. The participation rate cannot be changed more than once per year under most contracts.

Another aspect of the indexed benefit is that some contracts include a cap on the crediting rate that is applied to the accumulated value of the contract. This cap prevents full formula participation in times of very rapid index increases.

As downside protection, most contracts specify a floor of zero percent as the minimum extra interest crediting rate applicable to the accumulated value. This prevents the application of a negative percentage in the formula to reflect plunges in the index value. The intent is that the fixed-interest-rate guarantee is the worst possible outcome, and if the equity index does better, the accumulation can be even better than the guaranteed accumulation.

No Securities and Exchange Commission Regulation

Equity-indexed annuities are classified as fixed annuities and may be sold by agents who are not licensed to sell variable products. Thus, the agent has a product that offers a minimum accumulation guarantee but is partly influenced by equity performance. The agent is allowed to sell the product without having to acquire the training and licensing necessary to enter the variable-annuity market.

The SEC, which is currently examining insurance products, could decide that equity-indexed annuities really are a variable product rather than a fixed product. Many experts argue that the current definitions of terms to which the SEC adheres are broad enough for such an interpretation without changing any existing authorizations or guidelines. Others believe equity-indexed annuities cannot be classified as variable products without some action to change the SEC definitions.

Guarantees

The minimum guarantees under equity-indexed annuities are lower than those for traditional fixed-interest annuities. In fact, the rates actually guaranteed apply to less than the full amount paid as a premium. The guaranteed rate is usually applied to 90 percent of the amount paid to purchase the annuity. The percentage (10 percent in this example) not included in the guarantees can be used to cover insurer expenses. With this approach, usually 3 or 4 years elapse before the guaranteed amount equals or exceeds the original purchase amount. The contract indicates the specified interest rate applied each year to the contract value. This rate remains fixed unless both the contract owner and the insurance company later agree to a negotiated change. Many of the existing equity-indexed annuities have guaranteed rates in the range of 2 percent to 3.5 percent.

Value of Contract at End of Term

At the end of each term or participation period, the value of the annuity is the greatest of the following three amounts:

- the contract value based on the minimum interest rate guarantees
- the accumulated value derived by applying the participation rate to the increase in the index on the applicable anniversary. This amount is subject to any cap on the maximum crediting rate and to any floor on the minimum crediting rate.
- the premiums paid through the end of the term, minus any withdrawals

In many contracts, the same procedures are used to calculate the death benefit payable if the owner dies during the deferral phase of the contract.

Terminating an equity-indexed annuity before the end of a specified term usually results in loss of the index-crediting option. The termination is usually the greater of the following two amounts:

- the guaranteed-interest contract value
- the aggregate purchase amount minus adjustments for any partial withdrawals previously taken

Indexes

Although the most commonly used index is the Standard & Poor's Composite Index of 500 Stocks, some insurers use another index specified in the contract. These are generally established indexes that regularly appear in financial publications such as the *Wall Street Journal*. However, some insurers use international indexes or a composite of two or more established indexes. The definition of the index is under the insurance company's control. Theoretically, the company could change the definition of the index after the contract is created, leaving open the possibility of intentional manipulation of the index in the future.

Asset Match

All financial products involve risks to the issuer, and the equity-indexed annuity is no exception. The issuer needs to invest in assets that will provide an adequate return to honor the contractual promises.

Because the index participation promises some results that are above those of bond returns when the stock index outperforms the bond market, how can a company invest assets to produce the higher return? The closest match is achieved by investing the funds in the same stocks that make up the index. However, some insurers have chosen to invest in derivatives and other financial assets that they believe will track well with the index, even though these choices are not a composite of the items that make up the index. Over the long run, there could be a significant difference between investment results and contractual obligations. If the investment results exceed the contractual obligations, there will be no problem honoring the annuity contract terms. Conversely, underperformance of asset returns relative to obligations could threaten the insurer's financial viability. Purchasers should feel more comfortable with issuing companies whose investments closely resemble the index to which the benefits are related.

ACTUARIAL CONSIDERATIONS FOR ANNUITIES

The insurance company's cost of providing annuity benefits is based on the probability of survival, rather than the probability of death. In itself, this fact would seem to have no greater significance than that the insurance company actuaries, in computing premiums for annuities, have to refer to the actuarial probabilities of survival rather than probabilities of death. As a matter of fact, however, writing annuities poses a unique set of actuarial problems.

First, insurance companies have found that the mortality, or probability of death, among annuity purchasers tends to be lower, age for age, than that of persons who purchase life insurance, due mainly to adverse selection against the company. Individuals who know that they have serious health impairments rarely, if ever, purchase annuities. In fact, many persons contemplating the purchase of immediate annuities subject themselves to a thorough medical examination to make sure that they have no serious impairments before committing their capital to annuities. On the other hand, people who know or suspect that they have an impairment usually seek life insurance. Whatever its origin, the mortality difference between life insurance insureds and annuitants is so substantial that special annuity mortality tables must be used to calculate annuity premiums.

Second, the trend toward lower mortality, resulting in longer lifespans, has been a favorable development for insurers with respect to life insurance but an unfavorable development with respect to annuities. Many annuity contracts, including the accumulation period, run for 60 to 75 years, and rates that were adequate at the time of issue can, with the continued increase in longevity, prove inadequate over the years. All mortality tables, of course, contain a safety margin—which, for life insurance mortality tables, means higher death rates than those likely to be experienced, and for annuity mortality tables, lower rates of mortality than anticipated. Although long-run decline in mortality rates increases the safety margin in life insurance mortality tables, this decline shrinks the margin in annuity mortality tables, sometimes to the point of extinction. Therefore, an annuity mortality table that accurately reflects the mortality among annuitants at the time it was compiled gradually becomes obsolete and eventually overstates the expected mortality.

Finally, a high percentage of annuitants are women, who as a group enjoy greater longevity than men. This gender difference in longevity forced companies to use a rate differential between male and female annuitants long before a rate differential based on gender was applied to the sale of life insurance

---

Annuitants Never Die—Well, Hardly Ever

- Purchasers of annuities have generally lower mortality rates than others (adverse selection).
- Mortality rates for most people, including annuitants, have been declining.
- A high percentage of annuitants are women, who have greater average longevity than men.

policies. However, court decisions have required insurers to base some group annuity contracts on unisex mortality rates.

Revised Mortality Tables

Life insurance companies cope with these mortality differences in various ways. First, the insurers can compute annuity premiums on the basis of mortality tables that reflect annuitants' lower mortality.

For many years, companies used age setbacks for rates. The setbacks were used to recognize mortality differences between annuity and life insurance purchases. For example, the rate for an age-65 applicant may have been based on a 2-year age setback, thereby increasing the premium for a given amount of income to that based on the mortality of an age 63 individual. Ages for females were usually set back 4 or 5 years in addition to the setback for males, in recognition of the gender differential in mortality.

The 2000 Annuity Mortality Table[3] enables insurers, by means of projection factors, to make long-range adjustments for future reductions in mortality rates. Modern annuity tables all contain a set of projection factors that can be used to adjust the mortality assumptions for all ages from year to year or, instead, to project the basic rates of mortality to some future date. The projections make allowances for anticipated future improvements in mortality.

Interest Assumptions

Historically, insurance companies attempted to hedge future improvement in annuitant mortality by using an unrealistically low interest assumption in the premium formula. The rates were substantially lower than those used to calculate life insurance premiums. This technique can be quite effective because an interest margin of 25 basis points can absorb a general reduction in mortality of 6 or 7 percent. Intensified competition among insurance companies and between insurance companies and investment media, however, has now caused companies to adopt interest assumptions much closer to the level of their actual investment earnings.

Use of Participating Basis

A third approach to adjusting annuity prices for anticipated future increases in life expectancy is to compute the premiums and/or benefits on a participating basis, which permits conservative assumptions with respect to all factors in the premium calculations. Annual-premium annuities issued by mutual companies are almost invariably participating during the liquidation period. Some stock companies also issue annuities that are participating during the accumulation period. Single-premium immediate annuities, whether written by mutual or stock companies, are usually not participating.

FEDERAL INCOME TAX TREATMENT

Annuities enjoy a significant federal income tax advantage of accumulating on a tax-deferred basis, with the investment income that is credited to the contract not taxable until the annuitant or beneficiary receives it.

Amounts Received during Accumulation Period

Amounts received as loans and withdrawals during an annuity's accumulation period are taxable to the extent of income earned on the contract. This represents a kind of LIFO (last in, first out) tax treatment.[4] Also, a 10 percent penalty tax generally applies to the taxable portion of these amounts unless they are made after the taxpayer's age 59 1/2 or by reason of the taxpayer's death or disability.

Amounts Received during Liquidation Period

The portion of benefit payments taxable during the liquidation period depends on the applicable exclusion ratio. This ratio is calculated by dividing the amount invested in the annuity by the total amount expected to be received. The exclusion ratio is then multiplied by the amount of each payment to the annuitant to determine the excluded amount, which is presumed to be a return of the investment in the contract. The balance of each payment is taxable.

The amount invested in the contract is generally the premiums paid, minus any previous nontaxable distributions and minus the actuarial value of any period certain or other guarantee feature. The amount the annuitant can expect to receive depends on the type of payout option he or she selected. If the annuity provides payments for a fixed period of time, the total payments to be received constitute the expected amount to be received. If the annuity provides a life income, the expected amount to be received is based on life expectancy tables from the U.S. Treasury Department.[5]

After the annuitant has received excludible amounts equal to the investment in the contract, he or she has fully recovered the basis in the annuity. Thereafter, under current tax law, any remaining benefit payments are fully taxable to the annuitant. If he or she dies before the basis is fully recovered, a deduction is applicable for the unrecovered amount in the taxpayer's final return.

USES OF AN ANNUITY

The market for annuities comprises two broad categories of individuals:

- those who have already accumulated an estate, either through inheritance or by their own personal efforts
- those who are seeking to accumulate an estate

Wealthy individuals purchase annuities as a hedge against adverse financial developments. Business reverses, unwise investments, and reckless spending can destroy large estates. Insurance company records abound with cases of individuals who at one time were wealthy but whose fortunes melted away, leaving payments from annuities they purchased in their more affluent days as their sole source of income. There are also numerous cases of individuals who are dependent on relatives for whom they had purchased annuities during a more solvent period. Wealthy people, then, purchase annuities in a search for security, with yield a secondary consideration.

Yield is a primary consideration for those individuals, often middle-aged or elderly, who have accumulated a modest estate and envision this estate as the source of financial security during the remaining years of their lives. The life annuity, or the joint-and-last-survivor form for couples, promises a continuation of the benefit payments and some deferral of income taxes as long as the annuitant or annuitants live. Although some people are reluctant to invest their capital in an annuity because they want to leave an estate to their children or other close relatives, others feel that a greater responsibility is to provide for their own old-age maintenance, relieving the children of that burden.

A retired couple might not need to invest their entire capital accumulation in an annuity to provide for their old-age support. In such a case, the couple might purchase an appropriate annuity with the remainder of the estate to be distributed to their children, or to a charitable cause, either during the couple's lifetime or after their deaths. Annuities can also be used to provide a living bequest to a charitable, educational, or religious organization.

Finally, the annuity is also an attractive savings medium for the person who has not yet accumulated an estate but wants to achieve financial independence in old age. He or she can make premium deposits on a flexible schedule, and the accumulation grows on a tax-deferred basis.

CHARITABLE GIFT ANNUITIES

The goals of many financial planning clients include contributing to a religious organization, an educational organization, or another charity while also providing an adequate life income for themselves or others and, of course, minimizing taxes. Charitable gift annuities can simultaneously address all three goals.

A client who enters into a gift annuity agreement donates cash or other assets to a sponsoring charity. In exchange for the gift, the charity enters into a contract to provide the donor or other beneficiaries with fixed payments for the life of the annuitant(s).

Because a client's donation is an irrevocable gift, the client is entitled to an immediate income tax deduction based in part on the value of the donated asset. The client's tax deduction is not the value of the donated asset, but rather the difference between the date-of-gift value of the asset and present value of the annuity contract as determined by IRS tables that take into account both the age of the donor and the applicable federal interest rate. Clients who own property that has appreciated in value receive an added tax benefit if they donate the property itself rather than selling it and donating the cash proceeds. Subject to limitations beyond the scope of this discussion, the client, in effect, is allowed to spread payment of capital gains taxes on the appreciation in asset value over an extended period of time. A further benefit results from the fact that assets used to fund the gift annuity are generally removed from the client's taxable estate.

Besides receiving immediate tax benefits, the client receives a periodic annuity payment. The payment may be annual, monthly, or at some other interval. Only part of these payments is taxable income, because a portion of the payments is deemed to be a tax-free return of the donor's gift during the donor's expected lifetime under federal tax regulations. In the case of gifts of appreciated capital assets, the taxable component of each annuity payment consists of ordinary income and a statutorily defined share of the unrealized capital gains inherent in the gift asset, taxed at applicable capital gains tax rates.

Virtually any kind of annuity arrangement—immediate, deferred, single-life, joint-life, and so forth—may be used. Gift annuity rates are a bit lower than the rates available from an insurance company. The charity benefits from this differential. From the client's standpoint, part of this financial disadvantage is offset by the tax advantages of a charitable gift annuity. Remember also that clients purchase a charitable gift annuity in large part because they want the charity to receive a benefit. Most charities use gift annuity rates established by the American Council on Gift Annuities. Current rates are published at its Web site (www.acga-web.org). These rates are based on actuarial studies of annuitants' death rates. However, the rates are often negotiable in individual situations. For example, a charity might negotiate a lower rate for a donation of appreciated property that will be difficult or costly to sell. Or a client might be willing to accept a lower rate in exchange for a larger charitable deduction. Alternatively, the charity might be willing to negotiate a higher rate for a large donation from a favored donor. In some states, regulations require a charity that uses higher-than-suggested rates to prove that its assumptions are within the state's regulatory laws. Many states require charities to maintain sufficient reserves to meet annuity obligations and satisfy regulatory requirements. If the rate of return is too high above established rate tables, the IRS may disallow the contribution as a gift.

Benefits to the charity include any difference between its earnings and its costs of providing periodic payments. The charity also benefits from the residual value of the donated property, if any, after the death of the annuitant(s). Sometimes, of course, a client will outlive his or her normal life expectancy. In such cases, the charity may not realize net gift proceeds from that particular annuity transaction.

Benefits to the client include the following:

- The client receives an immediate income tax deduction when making the initial donation.
- The client or the client's designee receives an income stream for the duration of his or her life with a rate of return higher than the rate available through interest or dividends alone.
- Only a portion of the income stream is taxable, and, in some cases, that portion may be taxed at preferential long-term capital gains rates.
- The client's charity receives a benefit.
- No commission is involved in the sales transaction.

Although they provide many benefits, charitable gift annuities are not without their disadvantages, nor do they completely solve the problem of providing an adequate cash stream for retired clients. Gift annuities provide a fixed income stream that is not adjusted for inflation. Clients should also invest in securities or maintain an additional source of funds that enables them to cope with increasing future expenses.

Even more significant, in many cases, is the fact that charitable annuities may provide fewer financial safeguards than the annuities from insurance companies. It is very important to evaluate the charity's long-term solvency. If a charity goes bankrupt or faces financial difficulty, the annuitant is merely a general creditor, and the client may have neither income nor recourse.

Clients who would like to donate property outright but cannot do so because they also need to provide for their own needs during retirement often use charitable gift annuities. Property can be willed to a charity, but this produces no immediate income tax benefit. Some clients also find that a charitable gift annuity is a useful means of disposing of appreciated property or other assets that a surviving spouse would be unwilling or unable to manage.

Example:	Polly, aged 75, decides to donate $100,000 to her university under a gift annuity agreement. The payment rate at her age is 7.1 percent, so she will receive a payment of $7,100 each year for the remainder of her life. More than two-thirds of each annual payment will be free of federal income tax. Polly will also receive a substantial income tax deduction in the year of her gift.
	If Polly wished, she could also name her brother or another loved one to continue to receive annual payments, for his or her life, after Polly dies. The payment rates and tax benefits in this case would be reduced because payments are likely to be made for a longer period. There may also be transfer tax obligations flowing from the creation of an income gift in favor of nonspousal income beneficiaries.

STRUCTURED SETTLEMENTS

structured settlement

The courts have been involved in thousands of cases involving bodily injury or wrongful death in which the negligent party was required to pay at least $1 million in damages. It is usually acceptable to the court for large awards of this type to be paid as *structured settlements*, which are periodic payments instead of, or in addition to, a single lump-sum payment. Insurance companies issue immediate annuity contracts that guarantee the payments over the required lifetime or over the mandated support period. These contracts are specifically tailored to the needs of the claimants, who are the injured or wronged parties.

Although making periodic payments over time for claimant damages can be traced to the 1950s, independent full-time structured settlement specialists were not common until the 1970s. Since then, the number of cases using structured settlement contracts to satisfy plaintiffs' claims has grown substantially. The most frequent cases in which a structured settlement can be appropriate involve general liability, medical malpractice, defective products, auto accidents, or workers' compensation injuries.

Liability claims adjusters and/or defense attorneys work together with a structured settlement specialist to arrange appropriate settlements. Suitable structured settlements provide an adequate amount of immediate cash for liquidity needs, as well as reimbursement for past expenses, legal fees, and other cash needs. If the recipient is unable to work, an income stream can be designed to fund his or her normal living expenses, custodial and medical services, rehabilitation costs, and where appropriate, tuition for educational programs.

Annuities Utilized in Structured Settlements

The customary structured settlement uses an annuity to provide periodic payments that meet the recipient's financial needs as much as possible. The claimant receives periodic payments of income that are tax free during his or her life, and thereafter, the claimant's beneficiaries receive payments for the balance of any guarantee period. Two of the requirements for the claimant's income-tax-free treatment are the absence of any evidence of ownership by the annuitant of the annuity that funds the structured settlement and the absence of constructive receipt or economic benefit in the annuity itself. Therefore, the defendant, who is the legal owner of the annuity, and the insurer predetermine all timing decisions, as well as the exact amount of money.

step-rate annuity

If the claimant has no reduction in life expectancy from the injuries that caused the claim, standard rates are applied for life annuities. Likewise, standard rates are used for fixed-period annuities because there is no life contingency. An example of a fixed-period annuity is payment of $1,000 per month for 5 years and $2,000 per month during years 6 through 10. This is also referred to as a *step-rate annuity*. Annuity benefit payments can generally be increased on a compound annual rate, ranging from 3 percent to 6 percent. In addition to life income guarantees, period-certain and joint-life guarantees can be used, depending on the circumstances. The insurer may issue a rated age or substandard life annuity if the claimant's life expectancy has been reduced.

In a catastrophic injury case, the structured settlement broker submits the medical data to different insurance companies for evaluation. Each company makes its own judgment as to the claimant's life expectancy and bases its annuity quotes on that opinion. Life expectancy estimates vary among companies, just as substandard life insurance varies among insurers. The lower the life expectancy, the lower the annuity cost. Then the broker presents the bids to the defendant and his or her legal counsel to make an informed selection.

Generally, only defendants in bodily injury and wrongful death cases or their insurers can purchase this kind of annuity, and the number of insurance companies that issue such contracts is rather small.

Advantages of Structured Settlements

Figure 11-3 describes the structured settlement approach from the perspective of a liability claims adjuster. The advantages for each of the other involved parties are described below.

The advantages of a structured settlement for each of the individual entities involved—the injured party, the plaintiff's attorney, the judge, and the public—are explained below.

For the Injured Party

Financial Security. The major advantage of a structured settlement for the injured party is financial security. A lifetime income is especially practical and desirable when a minor or someone acknowledged to be incompetent is involved or whenever there is reason to be concerned about protecting the injured party's, or the surviving family's, future finances.

Benefits That Match Needs. An injured party needs regular income to meet living expenses and medical care costs. On occasion, when future medical costs are estimated to be substantial but the timing of these costs is unknown, a medical trust, similar to an emergency fund, can be created with the defendant as grantor under the trust agreement.

Management of Benefits. Claimants and their families or guardians are usually not trained to manage large sums of money. The use of periodic payments in a structured settlement significantly reduces the risk of dissipation of funds through mismanagement, imprudent investment, unwise expenditures, misuse, or even neglect.

FIGURE 11-3
Structured Settlements—A Liability Claims Adjuster's Perspective

A **structured settlement** is a method of resolving a claim that gives the claimant some payment immediately but defers much of the payment into the future. The future payment is usually disbursed over a period of time rather than in one lump sum. A liability insurer normally arranges a structured settlement by purchasing an annuity from a life insurance company and naming the claimant as "beneficiary" so that the claimant will receive periodic payments for a set number of years. The advantage to the claimant is that the interest earned on these annuities is tax-free, whereas if the claimant invests the lump-some payment, interest on those investments is taxable. The advantage to the insurer is that the additional tax-free income may make the settlement more attractive to the claimant. This tax-free feature may be enough to help parties overcome an impasse, because the claimant receives more money in total than with a lump-sum payment.

Structured settlements are useful for addressing the following claimant needs:

- ongoing regular medical treatments
- adequate income to replace wages that can no longer be earned
- ongoing household help
- occupational therapy and rehabilitation
- educational needs for children
- lump-sum needs on an occasional basis for medical equipment replacement
- payment of legal fees on a lump-sum or an extended basis
- trusts, endowments, or annuities to take care of dependents or contingencies that may arise

Factors to consider in determining the amount and terms of a structured settlement are

- the life expectancy of the claimant
- the likely cost of future medical expenses, including rehabilitation, physical therapy, future surgeries, nursing home costs, home services, prosthetic devices, wheelchairs, and other equipment
- cost of reasonable monthly living expenses, including mortgages, taxes, maintenance, food, clothing, and similar items
- cost of dependents' needs
- legal fees
- lump sums for special contingencies

Source: Jones, James R., *Liability Claim Practices*, 1st ed., Malvern, PA: Insurance Institute of America, 2001. Phone 800-644-2101. Web site address www.aicpcu.org

---

Guaranteed Payment. Because the income payments are guaranteed for life or for a fixed period, the settlement can never be prematurely exhausted.

Income-Tax-Free Payments. Whether payments are in a lump sum or periodic, they represent bodily injury damages, which are excluded from income tax.[6]

For the Plaintiff's Attorney

Attorneys are assured that their client's settlement is guaranteed and will not be subject to the potential dissipation of a lump-sum settlement. Some attorneys even believe that recommending a structured settlement insulates them from exposure to legal malpractice because they are not taking a sizable portion of the total value of the entire benefit payable as a lump sum right in the beginning.

For the Judge

Under the structured settlement, guaranteed periodic payments for life ensure the plaintiff's ongoing financial security for a lifetime. The judge or jury simply identifies the amount of monthly need rather than the actuarially equivalent lump-sum present value of payments over an uncertain number of years.

For the Public

The public benefits from the structured settlement because the injured party does not become a ward of the state and is assured a guaranteed income and proper care. In addition, a structured settlement avoids the delay of prolonged litigation, reducing court costs and placing fewer burdens on the already overloaded judicial system.

Disadvantages of Structured Settlements

If the life insurance company becomes insolvent, the annuitant may have a delay of benefit payments. Also, the annuitant will absorb all of the losses in excess of any state guaranty fund limitations. Further, the benefit payments may be reduced with the new insurer. Therefore, structured settlement specialists should select only the most secure and well-managed insurance companies.

The periodic payment schedule cannot be changed, so problems can occur if more immediate cash is needed than the stream of payments provides. This may be due to an unprecedented financial reversal, a medical necessity, an educational need, or greater than expected inflation. The original design of the structured settlement should therefore anticipate increasing payments annually (or at least periodically), build in periodic deferred lump sums, or include a medical trust for future medical and custodial needs.

IMPAIRED RISK ANNUITIES

As mentioned earlier, annuities are generally purchased by people who anticipate a long life span. However, some structured settlements that use annuities involve victims whose life expectancy has been reduced as a result of their injuries. Annuities can also be used to provide for specific long-term care needs, often when an individual is unable to qualify for long-term care insurance. Individuals who need long-term care have life expectancies, on the average, that are of shorter duration.

impaired risk annuity

An *impaired risk annuity* takes into account the annuitant's reduced life expectancy. The applicant's health is considered in the underwriting process, and the annuity payments are increased (or the premium lowered) in relation to the shorter life expectancy.

Some annuities contain a long-term care rider. With such a rider, the periodic payment increases when the annuitant is determined to need long-term care. For the most part, this involves satisfying the same criteria that trigger benefits under a long-term care insurance policy, discussed in chapter 15.

Example:	Grace recently retired at age 63 and is interested in turning some of her assets into a lifetime income stream to supplement her retirement income. She was just diagnosed with the very early stages of Parkinson's disease. Her physician has told her that her health will slowly decline, but it should be several years before she needs any type of long-term care. Although Grace cannot qualify for long-term care insurance, she is able to purchase a single-premium annuity that will guarantee her $2,000 of monthly income. The annuity has a rider that increases this amount to $4,000 per month if Grace satisfies the criteria for needing long-term care. Grace feels that the annuity payments and her other resources will be sufficient to meet her future needs, whether or not they involve long-term care.

CHECKLIST FOR EVALUATING AND COMPARING ANNUITIES

Accumulation Period

☐ Is the annuity funded with a single premium? If yes, how much?

☐ Is the annuity funded with periodic premiums? If yes,

    ___ Are premiums fixed or flexible?
    ___ What is the annual premium?
    ___ What is the premium frequency?
    ___ For how many years are premiums payable?

☐ Is there a minimum interest rate guaranteed for the length of the accumulation period?

☐ Is a secondary interest rate guaranteed? If yes,

    ___ What is the rate?
    ___ How long is it guaranteed?
    ___ What happens after it expires?
    ___ Is a bail-out option provided?

☐ What is the benefit amount for death or surrender of the contract?

    ___ If there is a return of premiums, is it with interest?
    ___ When will the cash value exceed premiums paid?
    ___ Are there surrender charges? If yes, describe.

Liquidation Period

☐ When does the liquidation period begin?

    ___ Is there an option to accelerate the starting date?
    ___ Is there an option to delay the starting date? If yes, how long?
    ___ Is a cash option available at the start of the liquidation period?

☐ How much is the periodic benefit payment?

☐ Is the periodic benefit amount guaranteed or variable?

☐ Is the benefit payment based on the insurer's investment results?

☐ Is the benefit payment based on a stock market index? If yes,

    ___ What is the participation rate?
    ___ What is the index?
    ___ Is there a cap on participation?
    ___ Is there a guaranteed minimum?

☐ How frequently is the periodic benefit paid?

☐ Do the benefit amounts continue for only a specified number of years? If yes, how many?

☐ Do the benefit payments continue for only one lifetime? If yes,

    ___ Is there any period certain? If yes, how long?
    ___ Are there any installment or cash refund features? If yes, how much?

☐ Do the benefit payments continue for two lifetimes? If yes,

___ Are the benefit payments reduced after the first death? If yes, by how much?

___ Is there any guaranteed minimum amount of the total benefit payments? If yes, what is the amount?

MINI-CASE: CLARA HARRIS

Clara Harris is the grandmother of Amy Schultz whom we have met in several earlier cases. Clara is 75 and recently lost her husband after a long struggle with Alzheimer's disease.

Clara and her husband lived well after his retirement. Just prior to his death, they had annual Social Security benefits of $18,000, pension income of $38,000, and savings and investment income of $4,000. Upon his death, these benefits decreased to a total of $33,000 per year. Unfortunately, many of Clara's expenses are fixed costs, such as the costs of maintaining her home and auto insurance, and these will not decrease. Clara would also like to take cruises with friends as she and her husband did before his illness.

Clara estimates that she will need close to $45,000 per year for living costs if she does not dip into her savings, and she would like to have closer to $50,000. She is also concerned about the effect of inflation on her income. Clara is in excellent health, and there is a family history of longevity.

Clara's largest asset is a home that she and her husband built 50 years ago on a four-acre site along a scenic river. Although the house is modest, the property is now worth $500,000 to developers who would build two or three luxury homes on it. Clara loves her home and wants to stay in it as long as she possibly can, even if she has to rely on some degree of custodial care. Clara also has about $100,000 in savings and investments. This amount was about $150,000 larger until Clara spent that amount on caregivers and nursing home care for her husband during his illness. Clara has no financial liabilities.

Clara's husband was a firm believer in life insurance and maintained a whole life insurance policy with a death benefit of $200,000 and named Clara as beneficiary.

Clara's four children are all financially well off. They want her to live well and have told her that they do not need any inheritance. However, she would like to maintain a significant portion of her net worth so that she can leave something to each of her 11 grandchildren. She does not want the expenses of long-term care to substantially eat into her estate if she can avoid it. She also does not want to become a burden on her children if she needs long-term care. (We will come back to this issue in the mini-case for chapter 15.)

a. Explain how Clara might use an annuity to generate her desired income.
b. How could Clara plan for the effect of inflation on her income?

(See answer section for answers to mini-case.)

SOURCES FOR FURTHER IN-DEPTH STUDY

- Chandler, Darlene K., *The Annuity Handbook: A Guide to Nonqualified Annuities*, 3d ed., Erlanger, KY: The National Underwriter Company, 2002. Phone 800-543-0874. Web site address www.nuco.com
- For further information about structured settlements, see the National Structured Settlement Trade Association. Web site address www.nssta.com

CHAPTER REVIEW

Answers to mini-case, review questions, and self-test questions start on page 793.

Key Terms

annuity	life annuity certain
annuitant	installment refund annuity
annuity certain	cash refund annuity
life annuity	50 percent refund annuity
temporary life annuity	modified cash refund annuity
joint (joint-life) annuity	accumulation period
joint-and-last-survivor annuity	cash option
immediate annuity	accumulation unit
deferred annuity	annuity unit
pure (straight life) annuity	equity-indexed annuity
refund annuity	structured settlement
fixed annuity	step-rate annuity
variable annuity	impaired risk annuity
liquidation period	

Review Questions

11-1. A client seems surprised when you mention that annuities have a lot in common with life insurance, because she thought annuities were more like mutual funds. Explain how annuities and life insurance are
a. dissimilar in function
b. based on the same principles

11-2. Ben Thayer is retiring and plans to live off a combination of Social Security and investments made during his working years, but he worries that he might outlive his investments. Explain how an annuity can guarantee a lifetime income to an individual.

11-3. Indicate how annuities can be classified by
a. plan of distribution
b. parties in the contract

    c.   time when benefits begin

    d.   method of purchase

    e.   amount of annuity payment

11-4.   Penny Youngman's employer provides no 401(k) plan or other retirement program, but Penny is investing roughly one-third of her current income in savings bonds and other investments. When she retires, she plans to use most of her life savings to buy an annuity that will pay her living expenses. A friend has suggested that Penny consider a deferred annuity, rather than purchasing an immediate annuity when she retires. Explain how immediate and deferred annuities differ with regard to

    a.   the method of premium payment possible

    b.   the existence of accumulation and/or liquidation periods

11-5.   Your client, Jim Smith, wishes to supplement, over time, the funds he is accumulating in his corporate pension so that he will be able to more adequately meet the anticipated needs for him and his wife after he retires in 20 years. Jim has indicated in his discussions with you that he is willing to take sufficient investment risk in an attempt to protect his retirement savings and benefits from inflation. What features would you have Jim consider in purchasing an annuity to accomplish his goal?

11-6.   Ann Peterson purchased an immediate annuity for $300,000 at retirement, received two monthly payments, and died. What would happen after Ann died if her annuity was

    a.   a pure annuity

    b.   a life annuity with 20-years certain

    c.   an installment refund annuity

11-7.   Describe the operation of a variable annuity issued on a deferred basis in terms of the role of accumulation units and annuity units.

11-8.   Describe the key features of equity-indexed annuities.

11-9.   Explain the three approaches that life insurance companies use to adjust annuity prices for anticipated future increases in life expectancy.

11-10. Lynn Straw's financial goals, as a recent retiree with substantial assets and no dependents, include providing a retirement income and making a major donation to her favorite educational institution. Explain how a charitable gift annuity might simultaneously accomplish both of Lynn's goals while also providing tax advantages.

11-11. Explain how an annuity is used in a typical structured settlement.

11-12. Discuss the advantages and disadvantages of structured settlements.

11-13. What type of annuity would be most advantageous for a client whose life expectancy has been reduced by various health problems?

Self-Test Questions

T   F   11-1.   The person whose life governs the duration of payments in an annuity is called the annuitant.

T   F   11-2.   Annuities serve essentially the same function as life insurance.

T   F   11-3.   If Jack would like to accumulate money for his planned retirement in 20 years, he should purchase an immediate annuity with periodic premiums.

T   F   11-4.   If Rachel purchased a life annuity with 20-years certain to liquidate her retirement savings and was still alive at the end of 20 years, her annuity benefit payments would cease.

T   F   11-5.   An installment refund annuity promises to keep paying installment benefits to the annuitant and/or beneficiary until the total equals the purchase price of the annuity plus interest at a guaranteed rate.

T   F   11-6.   A joint-and-last-survivor annuity continues to pay benefits as long as any of the annuitants are alive.

T   F   11-7.   During the liquidation period, a variable annuity promises to pay a variable number of annuity units of fixed value in each payment period.

T   F   11-8.   Equity-indexed annuities offer a minimum guaranteed interest rate.

T   F   11-9.   Annuity considerations are generally calculated using the same mortality rates as are used in calculating life insurance premiums.

T   F   11-10.   A charitable gift annuity has the same financial safeguards as an annuity an insurance company provides.

T   F   11-11.   If properly designed, a structured settlement can provide periodic payments of income that the claimant receives tax free during his or her life and that the claimant's beneficiaries receive thereafter for the balance of any guaranteed period.

T   F   11-12.   For a client in poor health, the underwriter might offer an impaired risk annuity that requires a higher premium for the same benefits.

NOTES

1. More precisely, the value of an annuity unit at the end of each fiscal year is obtained by dividing the current market value of the funds supporting the annuity units by the total number of annuity units expected to be paid over the future lifetimes of all participants then receiving annuity payments, in accordance with the assumptions as to mortality, investment earnings, and expense rates for the future.
2. *Securities and Exchange Commission v. Valic,* 359 U.S. 65 (1959).
3. http://www.soa.org/research/rp00_mortalitytables.pdf.
4. Different treatment is applicable for amounts invested in the annuity before August 14, 1982.
5. Special rules apply to the calculation of the exclusion ratio for equity-based annuity contracts.
6. IRC Sec. 104(a)(2). Also see Rev. Ruls. 79-220, 79-313, and 77-230.

Medical Expense Insurance As an Employee Benefit

Learning Objectives

An understanding of the material in this chapter should enable the student to

---

12-1.   Describe the development of medical expense coverage.

12-2.   Describe traditional major medical expense coverage, and explain how this approach has incorporated managed care provisions.

12-3.   Identify the reasons for the use of managed care, and describe the recent developments that pertain to the quality of care.

12-4.   Describe the various types of managed care plans.

12-5.   Describe the nature and purpose of consumer-directed medical expense plans.

12-6.   Explain why benefit carve-outs are used with medical expense plans, and describe the carve-outs used for prescription drugs, vision benefits, and behavioral health.

12-7.   Describe the provisions found in medical expense plans that pertain to eligibility, coordination of benefits, Medicare, and claims.

12-8.   Describe the nature of dental insurance plans.

12-9.   Explain the rationale for supplemental medical expense plans for executives, and describe the nature of such plans.

12-10. Explain the tax implications of employer-provided medical expense premiums and benefits for employers and employees.

Chapter Outline

health insurance

The next four chapters of this book are devoted to various aspects of health insurance. Although the term *health insurance* is often used in a narrow sense to mean protection against financial loss resulting from medical bills, the term actually has a much broader meaning. In this book, health insurance refers to

medical expense insurance

protection against the financial consequences of poor health. These financial consequences can result from incurring medical bills as the result of an accident or illness (including dental expenses) for which *medical expense insurance* provides protection. Poor health can also result in lost income and additional expenses. Protection against lost income is provided by disability income insurance, and long-term care insurance covers one significant expense that can be a result of poor health. This and chapter 13 focus on medical expense insurance; chapters 14 and 15 cover disability income insurance and long-term care insurance, respectively. Chapter 7 describes health insurance provided by the Social Security and Medicare programs.

Medical expense insurance is arguably the most important type of insurance protection to most Americans and the type of protection that causes the most anxiety if it is lost or unaffordable. It is also the type of personal insurance for which the greatest dollar outlay is made. However, approximately 90 percent of the persons who have medical expense insurance obtain it as an employee benefit, and their employers pay a major portion of the cost of coverage for most working persons. Employer-provided coverage is the focus of this chapter. It is important for the financial planner to understand a client's coverage to determine whether it is adequate. If it is not, sometimes the client can obtain supplemental coverage. It is equally important to know when supplemental coverages, such as dread disease policies, may be inappropriate because they only duplicate employer-provided coverage or provide poor or inadequate protection for the client's actual needs.

It is also important for financial planners to know what alternatives are available when a client's employment or insurance coverage terminates. The next chapter covers various forms of individual coverage. These coverages can also be used for clients who are self-employed or work for employers that do not have a group insurance plan.

Medical expense insurance is the most significant type of employee benefit in terms of both the number of persons covered and the dollar outlay. With the exception of employers with a small number of employees, virtually all employers offer some type of medical expense plan. In almost all cases, coverage identical to that offered for employees is also available for eligible dependents. In the absence of employee contributions, the cost of providing medical coverage for employees will be several times greater for most employers than the combined cost of providing life insurance and disability income insurance.

Group medical expense coverage is not as standardized as other types of employer-provided coverage such as group life insurance and group disability income insurance. Coverage may be provided through Blue Cross and Blue Shield plans (often called the Blues), health maintenance organizations (HMOs), and preferred-provider organizations (PPOs), as well as insurance companies. In addition, a large and increasing percentage of the benefits is provided under plans that are partially or totally self-funded (self-insured) by the employer. An overall medical expense plan may be limited to specific types of medical expenses, or it may be broad enough to cover almost all medical expenses. Even when broad coverage is available, it may provide benefits either under a single contract or under a combination of contracts. Furthermore, in contrast to other types of group insurance, benefits may be in the form of services rather than cash payments.

Finally, the skyrocketing cost of providing medical expense benefits over a long period of time has led to changes in coverage and plan design aimed at controlling these costs. Many of these changes have resulted in more similarities among providers of medical expense coverage than existed in the past.

Over the last decade, two major issues—affordability and accessibility of medical care—have led to profound changes in the health care industry. Not only has there been a continued shift to managed care plans (discussed in detail later) but the entire character of the health care industry has also changed. Where once there was a distinction among the providers of care (such as doctors and hospitals) and the organizations that financed the care (such as insurers, the Blues, and HMOs), this distinction is now blurred. For example, physicians and hospitals have established HMOs and PPOs, and physicians may be employees of managed care plans. There are those who feel that in the not-too-distant future most Americans will receive their medical expense coverage from one of a small number of large organizations that both provide medical care and finance the cost of that care.

The issues surrounding medical care have also become a concern of government. Many states have enacted programs to make coverage available to the uninsured, including those who work for employers with a small number of employees. At the federal level, lively debate over health care has occurred and is likely to continue.

HISTORY OF MEDICAL EXPENSE INSURANCE

Development of Medical Expense Coverage

Until the 1930s, medical expenses were borne primarily by ill or injured persons and their families. Blue Cross and Blue Shield Plans, as well as HMOs, were developed during the Great Depression, and the Blues were the predominant providers of medical expense coverage through the 1940s. HMOs remained only a small player in the marketplace for medical expense coverage until the last two decades.

Insurance companies were only modestly successful in competing with the Blues until a new product was introduced in 1949—major medical insurance. By the mid-1950s, insurance companies surpassed the Blues in premium volume and number of persons covered.

The number of persons with medical expense insurance plans grew rapidly during the 1950s and 1960s. For the first time, the federal government became a major player in providing medical expense coverage by creating national health insurance programs for the elderly and the poor. The first program—Medicare—provides benefits for persons aged 65 and older. The second program—Medicaid—provides medical benefits for certain classes of low-income individuals and families.

By 1970, expenditures for health care equaled 7.3 percent of GDP (gross domestic product), and the country saw the first large-scale debate over national health insurance. The result was legislation to encourage HMOs. The Employee Retirement Income Security Act (ERISA) also freed self-funded plans from state regulation and hastened the growth of this financing technique.

Attempts to rein in the cost of medical care since the 1970s seemed to have little effect, and health care expenditures now account for about 15 percent of GDP. Still, over 40 million Americans, including many employed persons and their families, remain uninsured.

The many efforts by employers to contain these rising health care costs include the following:

- increased use of employer self-funding
- cost-shifting to employees. It has become increasingly common for employers to raise deductibles and require employees to pay a larger portion of their medical expense coverage.
- increased use of managed care plans that are alternatives to HMOs such as PPOs and point-of-service (POS) plans
- requiring or encouraging managed care plans. Many employers have dropped traditional medical expense plans, and they offer managed care alternatives only. However, another prevalent approach is for employers to offer employees a financial incentive to join managed care plans.
- introduction of consumer-directed medical expense plans

Data collected by the Kaiser Family Foundation[1] show that enrollment in medical expense plans that can be characterized as traditional indemnity plans has dropped from over 70 percent to 5 percent since the early 1990s. During the same period, the number of enrollees in plans that use PPOs has increased significantly to 55 percent. Point-of-service plans and HMOs have grown more slowly and now account for about 15 percent and 25 percent, respectively, of the number of enrollees.

One important change is hidden in these statistics—the increasing trend toward self-funding of medical expenses by employers. It is estimated that over 50 percent of all workers are covered under plans that are totally or substantially self-funded. Note that the way benefits are provided under a self-funded plan can vary—the employer may design the plan to provide benefits on an indemnity basis or as an HMO or a PPO.

A Look at the Future

As in past decades, the health care system will continue to evolve in the first decade of this millennium. What the changes will be is only speculation, but a few observations can be made about the current environment:

- Premium rates for employer-provided medical expense plans are increasing at the highest percentage since the early 1990s; these high percentage increases are predicted to continue in the foreseeable future. As a result, employers will continue to look for ways to control their costs, including cost-shifting to employees.
- Surveys indicate that a large majority of Americans, including those with HMO coverage and other forms of managed care, are satisfied with their own health care plan. The relatively low degree of dissatisfaction, however, is higher among plans with the greatest degree of managed care.
- Surveys also indicate that despite satisfaction with their own coverage, Americans are becoming less satisfied with and less confident about the health care system.
- There is a growing backlash against managed care, particularly HMOs. Two observations can be made about this trend. First, many persons appear to have based their opinions on media reports and stories from friends, not on their own experiences. Second, this backlash has attracted the attention of Congress and the states. Some legislation has resulted at the state level. However, managed care plans are also becoming increasingly flexible and consumer friendly, possibly to prevent further legislation aimed at managed care reform. (Managed care reform is discussed later in this chapter.)
- Federal legislation continues to change the character of medical expense insurance plans. For example, the Medicare Prescription Drug, Improvement, and Modernization Act was passed in 2003. In addition to making significant changes in Medicare (see chapter 7), the act also encouraged the growth of consumer-directed medical expense plans with the creation of health savings accounts.

TRADITIONAL PLANS

Prior to the mid-1970s, most employees were covered by what are commonly referred to as traditional, or indemnity, plans. However, these plans have evolved. Although they are still far from what might be called managed care plans, these plans increasingly contain provisions designed to control costs and influence the behavior of persons who need medical care.

Historically, medical expense coverage consisted of separate basic benefits for hospital expenses, surgical expenses, and physicians' visits. Coverage was limited, and many types of medical expenses were not covered. However, the available coverage was "first dollar," in that covered expenses were paid in full without deductibles and coinsurance. Over time, employers began to offer more extensive benefits to employees. Although this broader coverage is usually provided through a single major medical contract, some employees are still covered under medical expense plans that consist of selected basic coverages typically provided by Blue Cross and/or Blue Shield. In most cases, these basic coverages are supplemented by a major medical contract so that the effect is essentially the same as if a single major medical contract was used.

Before proceeding further, two comments need to be made about the importance of this section of the chapter. First, interest in various types of plans will undoubtedly vary by the state in which a reader resides. It was pointed out earlier that only about 5 percent of employees and their families are covered under traditional plans. However, this percentage varies significantly by state. For example, HMO enrollments are small (10 percent or less) in about 20 percent of the states—mostly states with small and heavily rural populations. In these states, most employees and their families are covered by traditional plans or PPOs, which can be viewed as traditional major medical plans that have adopted a wide range of managed care characteristics. In another 20 percent of the states—typically populous and urban states—40 to 55 percent of employees and their families are covered by HMOs and almost all of the remaining employees and families are covered by other forms of managed care.

Second, the discussion of traditional medical expense plans largely follows their historical development. Much of the terminology and coverage of legislation introduced here also applies to the managed care approaches to medical care that are discussed later.

Major Medical Coverage

**major medical
insurance**

Major medical insurance protects against catastrophic medical expenses, with few exclusions or limitations. The distinguishing features of major medical expense plans include a broad range of covered expenses, deductibles, coinsurance, and high overall maximum benefits.

Covered Expenses

Major medical plans give broad coverage for necessary expenses incurred for medical services and supplies that a physician has ordered or prescribed. These services and supplies, which are specified in the contract, generally include the following:

**Basic Characteristics of Major Medical
Expense Insurance**

- Wide range of covered expenses
- Use of deductibles
- Use of coinsurance
- High maximum benefits

- hospital room and board. Traditionally, coverage has not been provided either for confinements in extended care facilities or for home health care. However, major medical plans now often include such coverage. Some plans also provide benefits for room and board in alternative facilities such as birthing centers.
- other hospital charges
- charges of outpatient surgical centers
- anesthetics and their administration
- services of doctors of medicine or osteopathy. Coverage for the services of other medical practitioners (such as chiropractors or podiatrists) may also be included.
- professional services of registered nurses. The services of other nurses (such as nurse midwives) may also be covered.
- prescription drugs
- physical and speech therapy
- diagnostic X ray and laboratory services
- radiation therapy
- blood and blood plasma
- artificial limbs and organs
- pacemakers
- casts, splints, trusses, braces, and crutches
- rental of wheelchairs and hospital beds
- ambulance services

Even though coverage is broad, major medical contracts contain certain exclusions and limitations.

Exclusions. The list varies, but exclusions in most major medical contracts preclude coverage for charges arising from the following:

- occupational injuries or diseases to the extent that benefits are provided by workers' compensation laws or similar legislation
- care provided by family members or when no charge would be made for the care received in the absence of the insurance contract

- cosmetic surgery, except as required by the Women's Health and Cancer Rights Act, unless such surgery is to correct a condition resulting from either an accidental injury or a birth defect (if the parent has dependent coverage when the child is born)
- most physical examinations, unless such examinations are necessary for the treatment of an injury or illness. However, plans are increasingly providing preventive medicine that might involve specific types of physical examinations.
- convalescent, custodial, or rest care
- dental care except for (1) treatment required because of injury to natural teeth and (2) hospital and surgical charges associated with hospital confinement for dental surgery
- eye refraction, or the purchase or fitting of eyeglasses or hearing aids
- expenses either paid or eligible for payment under Medicare or other federal, state, or local medical expense programs
- experimental services

preexisting-conditions provision

Most major medical plans also contain an exclusion for preexisting conditions. However, such a *preexisting-conditions provision* applies only for a limited time, after which the condition is no longer considered preexisting and covered in full, subject to any other contract limitations or exclusions.

A *preexisting condition* is typically defined as any illness or injury for which a covered person received medical care during the 3-month period prior to the person's effective date of coverage. Usually, the condition is no longer considered preexisting after the earlier of (1) a period of 3 consecutive months during which no medical care is received for the condition or (2) 12 months of coverage under the contract by the individual.

It is also not unusual, particularly with large employers, for the preexisting-conditions clause to be waived for persons who are eligible for coverage on the date a master contract becomes effective. However, future employees will be subject to the provision, but its effect may be shortened or eliminated by the portability provision of the Health Insurance Portability and Accountability Act (HIPAA) as discussed later. HIPAA also limits the use of preexisting-conditions provisions with respect to newborn or adopted children. Preexisting-conditions provisions also cannot apply to pregnancy.

The exclusion for cosmetic surgery is subject to the Women's Health and Cancer Rights Act, which amended ERISA and applies to all types of group health plans as well as individual medical expense insurance. Under the provisions of the federal act, any benefit plan or policy that provides medical and surgical benefits for mastectomy must also provide coverage for the following: (1) reconstruction of the breast on which the mastectomy has been performed, (2) surgery and reconstruction of the other breast to produce a symmetrical appearance, (3) prostheses, and (4) physical complications of the mastectomy, including lymphedemas.

The federal Pregnancy Discrimination Act requires that benefit plans of employers with 15 or more employees treat pregnancy, childbirth, and related conditions the same as any other medical condition. In the absence of a state law to the contrary, pregnancy may be and is sometimes excluded under group insurance contracts written for employers with fewer than 15 employees.

Limitations. Major medical plans also contain "internal limits" for certain types of medical expenses. Although the expenses are covered, the amounts paid under the contract are limited. For example, benefits are rarely paid for charges that exceed what is reasonable and customary, room-and-board benefits are generally limited to the charge for semiprivate accommodations unless other accommodations are medically necessary, and benefits for infertility treatments might be subject to 50 percent coinsurance or a maximum dollar limitation.

Treatment of Mental Illness, Alcoholism, and Drug Addiction. It is common for major medical plans to provide limited benefits for treatment for mental and nervous disorders, alcoholism, and drug addiction. Unless state laws require that these conditions be treated like any other medical condition, inpatient coverage is often limited to a specific number of days each year (commonly 30 or 60). Outpatient benefits, which are even more limited, are often subject to 50 percent coinsurance and to a specific dollar limit per visit.

It has been common for major medical plans to impose an annual maximum (such as $1,000) and/or an overall maximum lifetime limit (such as $25,000) on benefits for mental and nervous disorders, alcoholism, and drug addiction. However, the provisions of the Mental Health Parity Act, which apply only to employers with more than 50 employees, prohibit a group health plan, insurance company, or HMO from setting annual or lifetime *dollar* limits on mental health benefits that are less than the limits that apply to other medical and surgical benefits. Besides imposing no dollar limitations on benefits for alcoholism or drug addiction, the act is noteworthy for other things it does not do. It does not require employers to make any benefits available for mental illness, and it does not impose any other restrictions on mental health benefits. Employers can still impose limitations such as an annual maximum on number of visits or days of coverage and different cost-sharing provisions for mental health benefits than those that apply to other medical and surgical benefits.

Also note that some states require more comprehensive coverage than the federal act and/or mandate benefits for employers with a smaller number of employees.

Deductibles

deductible

A *deductible* is the initial amount of covered medical expenses an individual must pay before he or she receives benefits under a major medical plan. For example, if a plan has an annual deductible of $200, the covered person is responsible for the first $200 of medical expenses incurred each year. The major medical plan then pays covered expenses in excess of $200, subject to any limitations or coinsurance.

The simplest and most common form of deductible is the *initial deductible*. Essentially, a covered person must satisfy this deductible before the plan will pay any insurance benefits. However, the deductible can vary with respect to (1) the amount of the deductible, (2) the frequency with which it must be satisfied, and (3) the expenses to which it applies.

Deductible Amounts. Deductible amounts for any covered person tend to be relatively small. Most deductibles are fixed-dollar amounts that apply separately to each person and usually fall within the range of $100 to $500. In most major medical expense plans, the deductible must be satisfied only once during any given time period (usually a calendar year), regardless of the number of causes from which medical expenses arise.

Deductibles apply to each covered individual, including an employee's dependents. To minimize the family's burden of satisfying several deductibles, however, most major medical expense plans contain a family deductible. Once the family deductible is satisfied, future covered medical expenses of all family members are paid just as if every member of the family had satisfied his or her individual deductible.

The most common type of family deductible waives any future deductible requirements for other family members once a certain number of family members (generally two or three) have satisfied their individual deductibles.

Example: A family deductible might specify that the first $100 per year for each covered family member is the deductible. However, if three of five covered members of the family have each satisfied the deductible in a given year, the family needs to meet no further deductibles for that year. Thus, after Mom, Dad, and child #1 each incur $100 or more of covered expenses during the year, no further deductible applies to the expenses of child #2 and child #3 incurred after the family deductible is satisfied.

common accident provision

Most major medical expense contracts also contain a *common accident provision*, whereby if two or more members of the same family are injured in the same accident, the covered medical expenses for all family members are at most subject to a single deductible, usually equal to the individual deductible amount.

Deductible Frequency. A deductible usually applies to medical expenses incurred within a specified 12-month period, typically a calendar year (January 1 to December 31). Under such a *calendar-year deductible,* expenses incurred from January 1 apply toward the deductible. Once the deductible has been satisfied, the balance of any covered expenses incurred during the year is then paid by the major medical plan, subject to limitations and coinsurance.

Many plans with a calendar-year deductible also have a carryover provision that allows any expenses (1) applied to the deductible and (2) incurred during the last 3 months of the year to also be applied to the deductible for the following year.

Expenses to Which the Deductible Applies. Most major medical plans have a single deductible that applies to all medical expenses. However, some plans have two (or more) deductibles that apply separately to different categories of medical expenses. In some major medical plans, the deductible does not apply to certain expenses, in effect giving the covered person first-dollar coverage for these charges.

Coinsurance

coinsurance (medical expense insurance)

Major medical expense plans contain a coinsurance provision whereby the plan pays only a specified percentage (in most cases, 80 percent) of the covered expenses that exceed the deductible. For purposes of medical expense insurance, the term *coinsurance* as used in this book refers to the percentage of covered expenses a medical expense plan pays. Thus, a plan with 80 percent coinsurance, sometimes referred to as an 80/20 plan, pays 80 percent of covered expenses while a person who receives benefits under the plan must pay the remaining 20 percent. In some plans, a percentage participation, such as 20 percent, is specified. As commonly used, a *percentage participation* refers to the percentage of covered medical expenses that a medical expense plan does not pay and that a person receiving benefits must pay. Note that percentage participation is sometimes referred to as a *copayment,* but copayment usually implies a fixed-dollar amount that an insured must pay for a covered service. To make the matter even more confusing, some insurers refer to the percentage participation, rather than their portion of the benefit payment, as coinsurance. In addition, as discussed in chapter 16, the term is also used in property insurance in a way that involves a penalty for underinsurance.

Example:	If a comprehensive major medical expense plan has a $200 calendar-year deductible and an 80 percent coinsurance provision that applies to all expenses, an individual who incurs $1,200 of covered medical expenses during the year (assuming no limitations) will receive an $800 reimbursement, calculated as follows:

Covered expenses	$1,200
Less deductible	200
	$1,000
Multiplied by coinsurance percentage	.80
	$ 800

Just as deductibles vary, so do coinsurance provisions. Sometimes different coinsurance percentages apply to different categories of medical expenses. For example, outpatient psychiatric charges may be subject to 50 percent coinsurance, while other covered medical expenses are subject to 80 percent coinsurance. In addition, certain medical expenses may be subject to 100 percent coinsurance (and usually no deductible), which in effect means that the expenses are paid in full, subject to any limitations. Such full coverage is most likely to exist (1) for those expenses over which an individual has little control (such as hospitalization), (2) when there is a desire to provide first-dollar coverage for certain expenses, or (3) when there is a desire to encourage the use of the most cost-effective treatment (such as outpatient surgery, preadmission testing, or birthing centers).

In the case of catastrophic medical expenses, the coinsurance provision could result in an individual's having to assume a large dollar amount of his or her own medical expenses. Consequently, many major medical expense plans **stop-loss limit** place a limit, often called a *stop-loss* (or coinsurance) *limit* or cap, on the amount of out-of-pocket expenses that a covered person must bear during any time period. For example, a plan with an 80 percent coinsurance provision might have an annual stop-loss limit of $2,000. As long as aggregate claims for the year subject to coinsurance are $10,000 or less, the insured will be required to assume 20 percent of his or her own medical expenses. At $10,000 of claims, the insured will have reached the stop-loss limit of $2,000, and additional claims during the year will be paid in full.

Most plans apply the stop-loss limit only to amounts paid by the insured because of the coinsurance provision. However, some plans also include any deductibles that have been paid in determining when a stop-loss limit has been reached.

Stop-loss limits commonly range from $1,000 to $5,000. Like deductibles, the stop-loss limit is often waived for other family members after two or three family members satisfy their individual limits.

Maximum Benefits

Many major medical contracts contain a lifetime maximum benefit that applies to all medical expenses paid (after the application of deductibles and coinsurance) during the entire period an individual is covered under the contract. Most benefit maximums fall in the range of $1 million to $2 million. In some instances, the benefit amount is unlimited.

In addition to the overall lifetime maximum, major medical contracts sometimes have *internal maximums*. For example, a plan may have a $1 million overall lifetime maximum but a $10,000 lifetime maximum for benefits relating to alcoholism and drug addiction.

Managed Care Provisions in Traditional Plans

Historically, medical decisions were between the covered persons and their health care providers, and medical expense plans did little to manage or control patients' treatment. Over time, however, medical expense plans have gradually increased their control. For years, many plans have required preadmission certification of the need for hospital treatment and supported the cost of second opinions for surgical treatment. It is also common to cover treatment provided in facilities other than hospitals. Other managed care provisions and practices that traditional plans may contain include the following:

- preapproval of visits to specialists
- increased benefits for preventive care
- carve-outs of benefits that can be provided cost effectively under arrangements that employ various degrees of managed care. Examples include prescription drugs, treatment of mental illness, and substance abuse treatment. These types of carve-outs are discussed later as part of managed care plans.

Some traditional major medical plans actually make wide use of managed care techniques; the primary factor that prevents them from being called managed care plans is that there are few restrictions on access to providers.

Preadmission Certification

preadmission certification

As a method of controlling costs, medical expense plans have adopted utilization review programs. One aspect of these programs is *preadmission certification*. Such a program requires that a covered person, or his or her physician, obtain prior authorization from the plan for any nonemergency hospitalization. Authorization usually must also be obtained within 24 to 48 hours of admissions for emergencies.

Most plans reduce benefits if the preadmission certification procedure is not followed. If a patient enters the hospital after a preadmission certification has been denied, many plans do not pay for any hospital expenses, whereas other plans provide a reduced level of benefits.

Second Surgical Opinions

second surgical opinion

Most major medical expense policies provide benefits for *second surgical opinions* in an attempt to control medical costs by eliminating unnecessary surgery. A voluntary approach for obtaining second surgical opinions is often used. If a physician or surgeon recommends surgery, a covered person may seek a second opinion and the medical expense plan bears the cost. Some plans also pay for a third opinion if the first two opinions disagree. When there are divergent opinions, the final choice is up to the patient, and the plan's regular benefits are usually paid for any resulting surgery.

Some medical expense plans require mandatory second opinions, which may apply to any elective and nonemergency surgery but frequently apply only to a specified list of procedures. In most cases, a surgeon the insurance company or other provider of benefits selects must give the second opinion. If conflicting opinions arise, a third opinion may be obtained. The costs of the second and third opinions are paid in full. In contrast to voluntary provisions, mandatory provisions generally specify that benefits are paid at a reduced level if surgery is performed either without a second opinion or contrary to the final opinion.

Alternative Facilities for Treatment

Many traditional medical expense plans provide coverage for treatment in facilities that are alternatives to hospitals. Initially, this coverage was provided primarily to the extent that it reduced hospital benefits that were otherwise covered. Although this is still the primary effect of this coverage, it is often an integral part of medical expense plans, and benefits are provided even if they might not have been covered under a plan limited solely to treatment received in hospitals.

extended care facility

Extended Care Facility Benefits. Many hospital patients recover to a point where they no longer need the full level of care a hospital provides but still require a medically supervised period of convalescence. *Extended care facilities* (often called convalescent nursing homes or skilled-nursing facilities) have been established in many areas to provide this type of care. Treatment in these facilities, which are sometimes adjacent to hospitals, can reduce daily room-and-board charges—often substantially. As a result, a small but increasing number of contracts include benefits for situations where extended care facilities are used in lieu of hospitalization to contain medical care costs.

Extended care facility coverage provides benefits to inpatients in an extended care facility, which is typically defined as an institution that furnishes room and board and 24-hour-a-day skilled-nursing care under the supervision of a physician or a registered professional nurse. It does not include facilities that are designed as a place for rest or domiciliary care for the aged. Facilities for the treatment of drug abuse and alcoholism are often excluded from the definition.

The maximum length of time for which extended care benefits will be paid is usually limited to a specific number of days; 60 days is fairly common.

home health care

Home Health Care Benefits. *Home health care* coverage is similar to extended care facility benefits but designed for when the necessary part-time nursing care ordered by a physician following hospitalization can be provided in the patient's home. Coverage is for (1) nursing care (usually limited to a maximum of 2 hours per day) under the supervision of a registered nurse, (2) physical, occupational, and speech therapy, and (3) medical supplies and equipment such as wheelchairs and hospital beds.

In most cases, the benefits payable are equal to a percentage, frequently 80 percent, of reasonable-and-customary charges. Benefit payments are limited to either a maximum number of visits (such as 60 per calendar year) or to a period of time (such as 90 days after benefits commence).

hospice care

Hospice Benefits. Hospices for the treatment of terminally ill persons are a recent development in the area of medical care. *Hospice care* does not attempt to cure medical conditions but is devoted to easing the physical and psychological pain associated with dying. In addition to providing services for the patient, a hospice may offer counseling to family members. Although a hospice may be a separate facility, this type of care is frequently provided on an outpatient basis in the dying person's home.

Hospice benefits may be subject to a maximum such as $5,000.

birthing center

Birthing Centers. Another recent development in medical care is *birthing centers*, which are designed to provide a homelike facility for the delivery of babies. Nurse-midwives perform deliveries in a facility separate from a hospital, and mothers and babies are released shortly after birth.

Preapproval of Visits to Specialists

Many persons elect to bypass their primary care physicians, such as family physicians and pediatricians, and use specialists as their main access to medical care. This practice results in additional costs but, in the opinion of much of the medical community, does not improve medical outcomes. To counter this practice, some medical expense plans require that a visit to a specialist be preceded by a visit to a primary care physician. It is not necessary for the primary care physician to actually certify that a trip to a specialist is needed, only that he or she has been told that the patient plans to make such a visit. The rationale for this procedure is that the primary care physician may convince the patient that the primary care physician is able to treat the condition and that a specialist is unnecessary, at least at that time. If a specialist is needed, the primary care physician is also in a better position to recommend the right type of specialist and to coordinate health care for persons seeing multiple specialists.

The patient's failure to use the primary care physician as a quasi-gatekeeper will result in a reduction in benefits. Usually, benefits will still be paid but at a lower level.

Benefits for Preventive Care

Most traditional medical expense plans provide at least a few benefits for preventive care. Probably the most frequent benefits, because of state mandates for group insurance contracts, are well-baby care, childhood immunizations, and mammograms. Plans may also go as far as to provide routine physicals for children at specified ages and, perhaps, for all covered persons, typically subject to an annual maximum benefit such as $150 or $200. Coverage for routine adult physicals, however, is much more likely under managed care plans.

MANAGED CARE PLANS

The preceding discussion dealt with various methods traditional plans have used to control patient care. Managed care plans, discussed in this section, take a much more direct approach. Over the last few years, the number of persons having medical expense coverage from managed care plans has grown rapidly. Slightly over 50 percent of managed care participants are enrolled in PPOs, and the remaining participants are split between traditional HMOs and point-of-service (POS) plans. Each of these types of managed care plans is discussed later in the chapter.

managed care

Although managed care plans have evolved over the last few years, it is generally felt that a true *managed care* plan should have five basic characteristics:

- *controlled access to providers.* It is difficult to control costs if participants have unrestricted access to physicians and hospitals. Managed care plans attempt to encourage or force participants to use predetermined providers. By limiting the number of providers, managed care plans are better able to control costs by negotiating provider fees. Because a major portion of medical expenses results from referrals to specialists, managed care plans tend to use primary care physicians as gatekeepers to determine the necessity and appropriateness of specialty care.

- *comprehensive case management.* Successful plans perform utilization review at all levels. This involves reviewing a case to determine the type of treatment necessary, monitoring ongoing care, and assessing the appropriateness and success of treatment after it has been given.
- *preventive care.* Managed care plans encourage preventive care and the attainment of healthier lifestyles.
- *risk sharing.* Managed care plans are most successful if providers share in the financial consequences of medical decisions. Newer managed care plans have contractual guarantees to encourage cost-effective care. For example, a physician who minimizes diagnostic tests may receive a bonus. Ideally, such an arrangement will eliminate unnecessary tests, not discourage tests that should be performed.
- *high-quality care.* A managed care plan will not be well received and selected by participants if there is a perception of inferior or inconvenient medical care. In the past, too little attention was paid to this aspect of cost containment. Newer managed care plans not only select providers more carefully but also monitor the quality of care on a continuing basis.

Basic Characteristics of Managed Care Plans

- Controlled access to specialists and hospitals
- Emphasis on case management, including utilization review
- Encouragement of preventive care and healthy lifestyles
- Sharing by medical care providers in the financial consequences of medical decisions
- Careful selection and monitoring of medical providers

This section on managed care first looks at the issue of quality of care and discusses some recent developments. It then describes the types of managed care plans.

Quality of Care

A difficult question to answer is whether persons covered by managed care plans receive the same quality of care as persons covered under traditional medical expense plans. If the sole objective of a managed care plan is to offer coverage at the lowest possible cost, there may be a decline in the quality of care. However, some type of quality assurance program is one aspect of any managed care plan.

The results of numerous surveys and studies on the quality of medical care plans have been mixed. Some studies show that persons in managed care plans are less likely than persons in traditional medical expense plans to receive treatment for a serious medical condition from specialists, and they are also likely to have fewer diagnostic tests. There are those who argue that family physicians can treat a wide variety of illnesses and avoid unnecessary diagnostic tests and referrals to specialists. An opposing argument contends that the decline in the use of diagnostic tests indicates a corresponding decline in the level of medical care. Other studies show that persons in managed care plans are much more likely than the rest of the population to receive preventive care and early diagnosis and treatment of potentially serious conditions such as high blood pressure and diabetes. In addition, managed care plans are viewed as having been successful in coordinating care when it is necessary for a person to see several different types of specialists. There is no doubt that there are some small provider networks with a limited choice of specialists, but most networks are relatively large or allow persons to select treatment outside the network. There are also many managed care plans that do refer patients to highly regarded physicians and hospitals or include these providers in their network.

As managed care matures and becomes more widespread, there is an increasing focus by some employers on quality. This has led many employers, particularly large employers, to require that managed care organizations for their employees meet some type of accreditation standards. Several not-for-profit organizations set these standards and provide the accreditation.

Recent Developments

As previously mentioned, the majority of employers and employees are reasonably satisfied with managed care plans but have increasing concerns. However, physicians and other providers are much less satisfied, primarily because of decreased control over medical decisions for their patients and a loss of income. As a result, there has been what the media describe as a "backlash against managed care." In some ways, this terminology is inaccurate. First, some of the public's concerns, such as lack of complete mental health parity and inadequate coverage for certain preventive medical screenings, apply to the entire health care system, not just to managed care. Second, although some dissatisfactions are aimed at all types of managed care plans, many are targeted solely at practices of HMOs.

This backlash has had several results:

- States continue to enact legislation to address many of the concerns.
- Managed care organizations voluntarily modify their practices in light of legislative activity and competitive forces.
- The federal government continues to grapple with consumer legislation.

State Reform

State legislatures in recent years have passed several types of laws aimed at managed care reform. Some of these changes bring managed care plans closer to traditional indemnity plans in both coverage and cost. Some of these laws, passed by anywhere from a dozen to almost all states, include

- rules that prohibit managed care organizations from including anti-gag clauses in their contracts. Such clauses prevent doctors from discussing with patients treatment options that may not be covered under their health plans or from referring patients who are very ill for specialized care by providers outside the plan.
- grievance, review, and appeal procedures
- mandatory point-of-service options that require managed care organizations to permit enrollees to seek treatment from nonnetwork providers by paying a portion, but not all, of the expenses incurred with these providers. In effect, such legislation transforms a traditional HMO into a point-of-service plan.
- emergency room coverage that requires a plan to pay emergency room charges whenever a prudent layperson considers a situation to be an emergency
- mental health parity laws that require either complete parity for benefits arising from physical illnesses and mental illnesses or complete parity for physical illnesses and certain severe mental illnesses such as schizophrenia, depression, or bipolar disorder
- minimum stays for certain procedures such as maternity or breast cancer surgery
- plastic surgery mandates that require all health insurance contracts or health plans to provide coverage for certain types of reconstructive surgery. This legislation may apply to the repair of birth defects only, or it may apply to a broader list of situations in which reconstruction might be needed as a result of mastectomies, trauma, infections, tumors, or disease.
- legislation that allows women covered under managed care plans to have direct access to obstetricians/gynecologists without obtaining approval or a referral from their health plan. A few states require direct access to other types of providers such as dermatologists.

Voluntary Reform by Managed Care Organizations

Many managed care organizations have voluntarily initiated reforms. Some reforms are probably a result of the natural evolution of a new form of financing and providing health care; other changes have occurred because of competition among managed care organizations for market share. Most reforms are reactions to legislation that is proposed or passed by the states. After a few states enact a certain type of managed care legislation, managed care organizations nationwide often revise their plans to address the concerns that resulted in the legislation.

Just as it is for other types of businesses, the threat of legislation, at either the state or federal level, is also a major impetus for voluntary changes by managed care plans. Such voluntary reform may forestall more restrictive government regulation.

Federal Reform

Congress has addressed some health care concerns with the passage of such legislation as the following acts, which are mentioned in this chapter: the Health Insurance Portability and Accountability Act, the Mental Health Parity Act, and the Women's Health and Cancer Rights Act.

At the time this book is being revised, there are bills in Congress that would add more federal legislation to the health care environment. These include expanded consumer rights for patients and limitations on malpractice suits. However, there are differences of opinion as to what should be done, and these often vary by political party. Readers should monitor legislative developments and their potential effect on health care plans.

Health Maintenance Organizations

health maintenance organization (HMO)

Health maintenance organizations (HMOs) are generally regarded as organized systems of health care that provide a comprehensive array of medical services on a prepaid basis to voluntarily enrolled persons (usually referred to as members) living within a specified geographic region. HMOs act like insurance companies and the Blues in that they finance health care. Unlike insurance companies and the Blues, however, they also deliver medical services. HMOs can be either profit or not-for-profit organizations. They may be sponsored or owned by insurance companies, the Blues, consumer groups, physicians, hospitals, labor unions, or private investors.

Even though the term health maintenance organization is a relatively modern term, the concept of the HMO is not. For many years, prepaid group practice plans (as they were called) have operated successfully in many parts of the country. However, growth was relatively slow until the passage of the Health Maintenance Organization Act of 1973. This act resulted from a belief on the federal government's part that HMOs were a viable alternative method of financing and delivering health care and thus should be encouraged with grants for feasibility studies and development and loans (or loan guarantees) to assist them in covering initial operating deficits. Many HMOs were formed as the result of these grants and loans.

The act introduced the concept of the federal-qualified HMO. To become federally qualified, an HMO must meet certain requirements (set forth in the act) to the satisfaction of the Secretary of Health and Human Services. In return for a periodic prepaid fee from members and/or employers, an HMO must provide a broad array of benefits to its members at no cost or with nominal copayments.

In addition, the HMO must meet the following other requirements regarding its operations:

- a fiscally sound operation, including provisions against the possibility of insolvency
- annual open enrollment periods
- an ongoing quality assurance program

The need now for a federal HMO law is debatable. Most states already have similar legislation. Although newer HMOs may forgo federal qualification, the majority of older HMOs still retain that status, and the majority of HMO members are covered under federally qualified plans. It is felt that this grants them a "seal of approval" from the federal government. In addition, many employers will deal only with federally qualified HMOs.

Characteristics of HMOs

HMOs have several characteristics that distinguish them from traditional medical expense contracts that are offered by insurance companies and the Blues.

Comprehensive Care. HMOs offer their members a comprehensive package of health care services, generally including benefits for outpatient services as well as for hospitalization. Members usually get these services at no cost except the periodically required premium. However, in some cases, a copayment, such as $5 or $10 per physician's visit, may be imposed for certain services. HMOs emphasize preventive care and provide such services as routine physicals and immunizations.

Delivery of Medical Services. HMOs provide for the delivery of medical services that in some cases, are performed by salaried physicians and other personnel the HMO employs. Although this approach is in contrast to the usual fee-for-service delivery system of medical care, some HMOs do contract with providers on a fee-for-service basis.

In addition, members are required to obtain their care from providers of medical services who are affiliated with the HMO. Because HMOs may operate in a geographic region no larger than a single metropolitan area, this requirement may result in limited coverage for members if treatment is received elsewhere. Most HMOs do have out-of-area coverage but only in the case of medical emergencies.

HMOs also emphasize treatment by primary care physicians to the greatest extent possible. These practitioners fulfill a gatekeeper function and historically have controlled access to specialists. The traditional HMO covers benefits provided by a specialist only if the primary care physician recommends the specialist, who may be a fellow employee in a group-practice plan or a physician who has a contract with the HMO. The member has little or no say regarding the specialist selected, which has been one of the more controversial aspects of HMOs and one that has discouraged larger enrollment. In response to consumer concerns, many HMOs now make the process of seeing a specialist easier. Referrals can often be made by nurses in physicians' offices or by HMO staff members whom members can contact by telephone. Some HMOs, referred to as direct-access or self-referral HMOs, allow members to see network specialists without going through a gatekeeper. However, the specialist may have to contact the HMO for authorization before proceeding with tests or treatment. A variation of an HMO, called a point-of-service plan, allows even more choice.

Cost Control. HMOs emphasize control of medical expenses. By providing and encouraging preventive care, HMOs attempt to detect and treat medical conditions at an early stage, thereby avoiding expensive medical treatment in the future.

The use of salaried employees by many HMOs may also result in lower costs because the physician or other care provider has no financial incentive to prescribe additional, and possibly unnecessary, treatment. In fact, the physicians and other medical professionals in some HMOs may receive bonuses if the HMO operates efficiently and generates a surplus.

Types of HMOs

There are several types of HMOs: closed-panel, individual practice associations, and mixed model.

Closed-Panel. The earliest HMOs can best be described as closed-panel plans under which members must use physicians employed by the plan or by an organization with which it contracts. Because most closed-panel plans have several general practitioners, members can usually select their physician from among those accepting new patients and make medical appointments just as if the physician was in private practice. However, there is frequently little choice among specialists because a plan may have a contract with only one physician or a limited number of physicians in a given specialty.

The number of closed-panel plans is relatively small, but they account for almost 20 percent of all HMO members. These HMOs may operate in a variety of ways with respect to providing physicians' services. They may own their own facilities and hire their own physicians, who are paid a salary and possibly an incentive bonus. They are more likely, however, to enter into contracts with one or more groups of physicians to provide services. In many cases, these groups are paid on a capitation basis, which means that they receive a predetermined fee per year for each member and must provide any and all covered services for this fee.

Closed-panel plans may own their own hospitals, laboratories, or pharmacies or contract with other entities to provide their services.

Individual Practice Associations. Many newer HMOs have been formed as individual practice associations (IPAs). This type of plan has more flexibility with respect to members' ability to choose physicians and physicians' ability to participate in the plan. About 45 percent of HMO members are in individual practice associations.

In IPAs, participating physicians practice individually or in small groups at their own offices. In most cases, these physicians accept both nonmanaged care patients (on a traditional fee-for-service basis) and HMO members. IPAs are often referred to as open-panel plans, because members choose from a list of participating physicians. The number of physicians participating in this type of HMO is frequently larger than the number participating in group practice plans and may include several physicians within a given specialty. Because most of the newer HMOs are IPAs, the percentage of HMO members served by these plans continues to grow.

Several methods may be used to compensate physicians who participate in an IPA. The most common is a fee schedule based on the services provided to members. To encourage physicians to be cost effective, it is common for plans to have a provision for reducing payments to physicians if the experience of the plan is worse than expected. On the other hand, the physicians may receive a bonus if the experience of the plan is better than expected. Particularly with respect to general practitioners, some individual practice association plans pay each physician a flat annual capitation for each member who has elected to use him or her. For this annual payment, the physician must see these members as often as necessary during the year.

It is unusual for IPAs to own their own hospitals or other medical facilities. Rather, they enter into contracts with local hospitals or other organizations to provide the necessary services for their members.

Mixed-Model HMOs. About 35 percent of HMO members are covered by mixed-model plans. This means that the organization of the plan is a combination of the approaches previously described. Such a combination generally occurs as a plan continues to grow. For example, a plan might have been established as a closed HMO but at a later time decided to expand its capacity or geographic region by adding physicians under an IPA arrangement. Some mixed models have also resulted from the merger of two plans that each used a different organizational form.

Types of HMOs

- Closed-panel
- Individual practice association
- Mixed-model

Preferred-Provider Organizations

A concept that continues to receive considerable attention from employers and insurance companies is the preferred-provider organization (PPO). A few PPOs have existed on a small scale for many years, but since the early 1980s, PPOs have grown steadily in number and in membership. Today, PPOs provide coverage for medical expenses to more Americans than do HMOs, primarily because of covered persons' flexibility to choose their own medical providers.

Insurance companies own the majority of PPOs. Some are owned by HMOs to diversify their health plan portfolios. Still others have a variety of ownership forms, including third-party administrators, private investors, and groups of physicians and/or hospitals.

PPOs are regulated by the states but somewhat less strictly than HMOs. Note that most PPO contracts also meet the regulatory definition of insurance and are subject to the same regulation by state insurance departments as traditional insurance contracts with respect to contract provisions and benefit mandates.

What Is a PPO?

preferred-provider organization (PPO)

The term *preferred-provider organization (PPO)* tends to be used in two ways. One way is to apply it to health care providers that contract with employers, insurance companies, union trust funds, third-party administrators, or others to provide medical care services at a reduced fee. Using this definition, a PPO may be organized by the providers themselves or by other organizations such as insurance companies, the Blues, HMOs, or employers. Like HMOs, they may take the form of group practices or separate individual practices. They may provide a broad array of medical services, including physicians' services, hospital care, laboratory costs, and home health care, or they may be limited only to hospitalization or physicians' services. Some of these types of organizations are very specialized and provide specific services such as dental care, mental health benefits, substance abuse services, maternity care, or prescription drugs. In this book, these providers are referred to not as *PPOs* but as *preferred providers* or *network providers.*

The second use of the term *PPO,* and the one generally assumed when the term is used throughout this book, is to apply it to benefit plans that contract with preferred providers to obtain lower-cost care for plan members. PPOs typically differ from HMOs in several respects. First, the preferred providers are generally paid on a fee-for-service basis as their services are used. However, fees are usually subject to a schedule that is the same for all similar providers within the PPO contracts, and providers may have an incentive to control utilization through bonus arrangements. Second, employees and their dependents are not required to use the practitioners or facilities that contract with the PPO; rather, they can make a choice each time they need medical care, and benefits are also paid for care from nonnetwork providers. Employees are offered incentives to use network providers; they include lower or reduced deductibles and copayments as well as increased benefits such as preventive health care. Third, most PPOs do not use a primary care physician as a gatekeeper; employees do not need referrals to see specialists.

Characteristics of a Typical PPO

- A network of medical care providers contracts to offer medical services to plan participants at reduced rate.
- Medical care providers are usually paid on a fee-for-service basis.
- Members have a choice of using network or nonnetwork providers.
- Members who opt to use a network provider pay lower deductibles or copayments or receive broader types of covered care.

Variations. Over time, PPOs have continued to evolve. Some PPOs compensate providers on a capitation basis, while others perform a gatekeeper function. If a member's primary care physician does not recommend a specialist, benefits may be reduced. With these changes, it is sometimes difficult to determine the exact form of a managed care organization. However, those that operate as traditional HMOs generally provide medical expense coverage at a slightly lower cost than those that operate as traditional PPOs, but there are wide variations among HMOs as well as among PPOs. Therefore, a careful analysis of quality of care, cost, and financial stability is necessary before selecting a particular HMO or PPO.

Another variation of the PPO is the *exclusive-provider organization (EPO)*. The primary difference is that an EPO does not provide coverage outside the preferred-provider network, except in those infrequent cases when the network does not contain an appropriate specialist. This aspect of an EPO makes it very similar to an HMO. The number of EPOs is small.

exclusive-provider organization (EPO)

Benefit Structure

The basic benefit structure of a PPO is similar to that of the traditional major medical contract, which is discussed earlier in this chapter. The most significant difference is that PPOs include a higher level of benefits for care received from network providers than for care received from nonnetwork providers. Many PPOs have extensive networks of preferred providers, particularly in the geographic areas in which they operate; hence, there is little reason to seek care outside the network. However, other PPOs have more limited networks, so their members' need for treatment from nonnetwork providers is greater.

The level of benefits under PPOs may vary because of differences in deductibles, coinsurance, maximum lifetime benefits, and precertification rules. There may also be a few additional benefits that are available only if care is received from a network provider. Finally, procedures for filing claims also differ. The major purpose of these differences is to encourage an employee or dependent to receive care from preferred providers who have agreed to charge the plan a discounted fee.

Deductibles. A PPO may have annual deductibles that apply separately to network and nonnetwork charges—for example, $100 and $250, respectively. However, many PPOs have no deductible for network charges or waive this deductible for certain medical services such as emergency or preventive care.

Coinsurance. Most PPOs use coinsurance percentages that are 20 percent (and occasionally 30 percent) lower when care is received from nonnetwork providers. The most frequently found provision applies 90 percent coinsurance to network charges and 70 percent coinsurance to nonnetwork charges. Coinsurance provisions of 100/80, 90/80, and 100/70 are also frequently used. As with deductibles, the percentage participation may be waived for certain medical services. In addition, different stop-loss limits or coinsurance caps, such as $1,000 and $3,000, may apply to network and nonnetwork charges.

Although PPOs typically have higher coinsurance percentages for network charges than do traditional major medical plans, a covered person may be responsible for modest copayments in some circumstances. For example, there might be a copayment of $5 to $20 for each visit to a primary care physician.

Maximum Benefits. Although there are variations, most PPOs have a lifetime maximum of $1 million for nonnetwork benefits. The lifetime maximum for network benefits is seldom less that $2 million and may even be unlimited.

Precertification Rules. PPOs often have precertification requirements for many types of hospitalizations, outpatient procedures, and medical supplies. For network benefits, the person responsible for obtaining the needed precertification is the network provider, and the covered person is not penalized if the network provider fails to obtain the proper precertification. However, this responsibility shifts to the employee or family member for nonnetwork services. If precertification is not obtained when required, there usually is a reduction in benefits.

Additional Network Benefits. For the most part, PPOs pay benefits for the same medical procedures, whether they are performed by a network or nonnetwork provider. A few procedures, however, may be covered only if they are received from network providers. For example, routine physical exams may be covered only in the network. In addition, there might be coverage for more outpatient psychiatric visits if a network provider is used.

Claims. There are no claim forms required for network services. The covered person merely pays any required copayment, and the provider of medical services does the paperwork needed to receive the additional amounts payable by the plan.

Point-of-Service (POS) Plans

point-of-service (POS) plan

A newer type of managed care arrangement is the *point-of-service (POS) plan*. A *POS plan* is a hybrid arrangement that combines aspects of a traditional HMO and a PPO. With a POS plan, participants in the plan elect, at the time medical treatment is needed, whether to receive treatment within the plan's tightly managed network, usually an HMO, or outside the network. Expenses received outside the network are reimbursed in the same manner as described earlier for nonnetwork services under PPO plans.

There are two basic types of POS plans: the open-ended HMO and the gatekeeper PPO. An open-ended HMO is by far the most common form and is the HMO industry's response to the demand for more consumer flexibility in the choice of providers, even though it increases costs somewhat. It essentially consists of traditional HMO coverage with an endorsement for nonnetwork coverage. It can take the basic form of any of the HMOs previously described. However, at any time, a member can elect to go outside the HMO network of medical care providers.

It can be argued that any PPO is actually a POS plan. However, the normal usage of the term POS implies a higher degree of managed care than is found in most PPOs. A gatekeeper PPO requires the PPO participant to elect a primary care physician in the manner of an HMO participant. This physician acts as a gatekeeper to control utilization and refer members to specialists within the PPO network. At any time care is needed, however, a covered person can elect to go outside the network.

Under some POS plans, a covered person can go outside the plan's network without informing the plan. In other POS plans, the person must notify the gatekeeper that he or she is seeking such treatment.

COMPARISON OF TYPICAL MEDICAL EXPENSE PLANS

This chapter has discussed the various types of medical expense plans and how they differ. Although variations within each type of plan exist, some generalizations, which are summarized in table 12-1, can be made. The degree of managed care increases as one moves from left to right in the table. However, the cost of the plans, on the average, decreases as the degree of managed care increases. In addition, a higher degree of managed care is generally associated with lower annual premium increases by a plan.

CONSUMER-DIRECTED MEDICAL EXPENSE PLANS

consumer-directed medical expense plan

The first half of the new decade has seen considerable interest in the concept of the *consumer-directed medical expense plan*. Such plans, also referred to by such names as consumer-driven health care and consumer-choice plans, give the employee increased choices and responsibilities with the selection of his or her own medical expense coverage. Some consumer-directed models also have a greater accountability for health plans and providers.

There are two general approaches to consumer-directed medical expense plans—defined-contribution medical expense plans and the use of savings accounts.

Defined-Contribution Medical Expense Plans

defined-contribution medical expense plan

Even though some consumer-directed approaches for medical expense plans are in their infancy or still in the proposal stage, they have existed in the form of the *defined-contribution medical expense plan* for some time. For

TABLE 12-1
Comparison of Health Insurance Plans

	Traditional Major Medical Contracts	PPOs	POS Plans	HMOs
Provider choice	Unlimited	Unlimited, but benefits are greater if network provider is used	Unlimited, but benefits are greater if network provider is used	Network of providers must be used; care from nonnetwork providers covered only in emergencies
Use of gatekeeper	None	None	Used for access to network specialists	Used for access to specialists
Out-of-pocket costs	Deductibles and percentage participation	Deductibles and percentage participation, which are lower if network providers are used; may have small copayment for network services	Small copayments for network services; deductibles and percentage participation for nonnetwork services	Small copayments for some services
Utilization review	Traditionally little, but a few techniques are likely to be used now	More than traditional plans, but less than HMOs; network provider may be subject to some controls	Like HMOs for network services; like PPOs for nonnetwork services	Highest degree of review, including financial incentives and disincentives for providers
Preventive care	Little covered other than that required by law	Usually more coverage than traditional major medical plan but less coverage than HMOs and POS plans	Covered	Covered
Responsibility for claims filings	Covered person	Plan providers for network services; covered person for nonnetwork services	Plan providers for network services; covered person for nonnetwork services	Plan providers

example, many employers make two or more medical expense plans available to their employees, such as an HMO, a PPO, and an indemnity plan. The employer contribution to the cost of coverage for each plan may be a defined dollar amount that is pegged to a fixed percentage of the cost of the least expensive plan, usually an HMO. Therefore, employees who elect a more expensive PPO or indemnity plan must make a greater out-of-pocket contribution for coverage than if they had selected the HMO.

Example: The Weir Corporation makes three medical expense plans available to its employees—an HMO, a point-of-service plan, and a PPO. For a single employee, the corporation pays an amount equal to 90 percent of the cost of the least expensive plan, which is the HMO. For the three plans, the employee contribution is as follows:

	Total Monthly Premium	Employer Contribution	Employee Contribution
HMO	$275.70	$248.13	$27.57
POS plan	330.67	248.13	82.54
PPO	419.09	248.13	170.96

A similar approach is used to determine the cost of dependent coverage for which the corporation contributes an amount equal to 50 percent of the cost of HMO coverage.

There is no question that defined-contribution plans have driven large numbers of employees to medical expense plans with higher degrees of managed care. However, managed care plans historically have provided a broad scope of coverage, including prescription drugs, yet limited the member's payment for these services to a modest copayment such as $10. In doing so, these plans greatly diminish the motivation of their members to contain costs when they seek services. From a member's viewpoint, the broad array of services is available for only the cost of the copayment. Even as many managed care plans have become less restrictive, copayment levels have usually changed little. Such marginal copayments applicable to the wide array of more easily available services may explain, at least in part, the decline in the overall personal out-of-pocket payments from nearly 25 percent of health care spending in 1980 to less than 15 percent today.[2]

Use of Savings Accounts

Newer types of defined-contribution medical expense plans have features other than just fixed employer contributions. At a minimum, these approaches force employees to make financial decisions that involve their health care. Typically, an employer might provide employees with a medical expense plan that has a very high deductible, perhaps as much as $5,000 per year. This type of plan is often referred to as a *high-deductible health plan.* The employer also contributes a lower or equal amount, such as $2,500 per year, to some type of savings account from which the employee can make tax-free withdrawals to pay medical expenses that are not covered because of the deductible. The employee can carry forward any unused amount in the account and add it to the next year's employer contribution. Such a plan gives the employee an immediate incentive to purchase medical care wisely because, if medical expenses exceed the amount in the account, the employee will have to pay the full cost of medical expenses out of his or her own pocket until the deductible is satisfied. The plan often incorporates a preferred-provider network of health care professionals. As long as an employee receives medical treatment within the network, any charges that the employee must pay because of the deductible are limited to the amount negotiated with the preferred provider.

high-deductible health plan

Employers might use this approach for all employees, but most employers make it available as an option to a more traditional medical expense plan. In addition, because of the newness of the approach to providing medical expense coverage, employers often limit these plans to a select group of employees on a trial basis.

The rationale for using a high-deductible medical expense plan along with a savings account is that significant cost savings can occur for two primary reasons. First, the expensive cost of administering and paying small claims is largely eliminated, as demonstrated by the fact that a major medical policy with a $2,500 deductible can often be purchased for about one-half the cost of a policy with a $250 deductible. Second, employees now have a direct financial incentive to avoid unnecessary care and to seek out the most cost-effective form of treatment.

A very small number of employers have used this approach for some time with positive results. Costs have been lowered or have risen less rapidly than would otherwise be expected. Employees' reactions have generally been favorable. But, as with almost any approach to cost containment, this type of medical expense plan has its critics. It is argued that employees will minimize treatment for minor medical expenses and preventive care that would have been covered under a plan without a high deductible. Critics contend that this avoidance of medical care may lead to major expenses that could have been averted or minimized with earlier treatment. However, some types of consumer-directed medical expense plans waive the deductible for preventive care. Another criticism is that a high-deductible plan tends to favor healthy individuals and those in high income tax brackets. A final criticism is that this type of medical expense plan does not focus on the problem of the uninsured. In rebuttal to this criticism, proponents argue that any technique that lowers costs for employers will ultimately benefit everyone and encourage small employers to provide coverage that would have previously been unaffordable.

Some consumer-directed medical expense plans that use the savings-account approach have been designed so that employer decisions about specific benefit plans are eliminated, or at least minimized. Some employers view this as a way of minimizing their legal exposure for health care decisions because a certain level of responsibility is transferred back to employees and health care providers. Under such a plan, an employee can use an employer contribution (along with any additionally needed employee contribution) to shop at some type of "health care supermarket," where many different types of medical expense plans are available. These plans are often required to provide detailed information about their operations so that consumers can make more informed decisions in selecting a medical expense plan. An insurer or some type of Internet provider may offer these plans, and the employer may or may not be involved in the selection of the supermarket that an employee uses. Most consumer-directed medical expense plans that use the savings-account approach, however, make only a single medical expense plan available to employees.

health reimbursement arrangement

There are three basic types of savings accounts. One of these—called a *health reimbursement arrangement* (or HRA) is an unfunded arrangement. There are no restrictions on the type of underlying policy, and the employer makes an annual credit to an employee's account. If an employee does not use the funds in an account during the year, the balance rolls over to the following year. At termination of employment, the account usually terminates and any remaining funds belong to the employer.

Two other types of savings accounts are Archer medical savings accounts and health savings accounts (HSAs). Persons other than employees can also establish these accounts. Both accounts are described in chapter 13.

BENEFIT CARVE-OUTS

The use of benefit carve-outs by medical expense plans has grown in recent years, often as a method of cost containment via managed care techniques. In addition, many medical expense plans have come to realize that they cannot always provide as high a quality of care as a well-managed specialty provider. Carve-outs for prescription drugs, vision care, dental care, and behavioral health have been common for a number of years. Increasingly, carve-outs are being used to better manage a wide variety of medical conditions such as pregnancy, asthma, and diabetes.

A benefit *carve-out* can best be defined as coverage under a medical expense plan for a health care service that has been singled out for individual management by a party other than the employer or the employer's primary health plan provider. Some types of carve-outs predate managed care as it is now known. For example, many employees have long been covered under separate prescription drug plans. The early emphasis under these plans, however, was on discounts with preferred providers of prescription drugs. Today, prescription drug plans and other types of carve-outs use a wider variety of managed care techniques.

An employer can purchase a medical expense plan to provide benefits to its employees for most types of medical care and then enter into a separate contract with another provider for the carved-out benefit. However, in many cases, it is the insurance company, Blue Cross–Blue Shield plan, HMO, or PPO that enters into the carve-out arrangement with a "subcontractor" that manages the benefits. From the standpoint of employers and employees, the benefit is part of the employer's plan.

It should be pointed out that the vendors who provide carve-outs often act as managed care plans for a single medical expense benefit and take on characteristics of HMOs or PPOs. They also have learned over time that their type of specialty care should sometimes be accompanied by a unique benefit structure. This is one reason why mental health and prescription drug benefits are often subject to different deductibles, copayments, or benefit limitations than those used for most types of medical expenses.

There are numerous types of benefit carve-outs. The three discussed in this chapter are prescription drugs, vision benefits, and behavioral health.

Prescription Drugs

Although separate prescription drug plans have existed for many years, the initial focus was on obtaining lower costs through discounts with participating pharmacies and mail-order suppliers of drugs. The situation changed significantly in the early 1980s when pharmacy benefit managers (PBMs) appeared in the marketplace. It is estimated that over 75 percent of prescription drugs are provided through PBMs, and that fewer than 10 large PBMs cover over 80 percent of the health plan participants who receive drugs in this manner. PBMs may be affiliated with pharmaceutical companies or health care providers such as insurance companies. They may also be independently owned.

PBMs administer prescription drug plans on behalf of self-funded employers, HMOs, PPOs, insurance companies, Blue Cross–Blue Shield plans, and third-party administrators. PBMs' on-line capabilities enable them to offer considerable flexibility in designing a prescription drug program for a specific employer or benefit plan provider. PBMs have been leaders in the integration of formularies into prescription drug plans. A *formulary* is a list, developed by a committee of pharmacists and physicians, of preferred medications for a specific medical condition.

The typical prescription drug plan covers the cost of drugs (except those dispensed in a hospital or in an extended care facility) that are required by law to be dispensed by prescription. Drugs for which prescriptions are not required by law are usually not covered even if a physician orders them on a prescription form. One frequent exception to this general rule is injectable insulin, which is generally covered despite the fact that in many states it is a nonprescription drug. No coverage is provided for charges to administer drugs or the cost of therapeutic devices or appliances such as bandages or hypodermic needles. It is also common to exclude benefits for a quantity of drugs in excess of a specified amount each time a prescription is filled.

Contraceptive drugs are usually covered but may be excluded. Some prescription drug plans take a middle approach by covering these drugs only when they are prescribed for treating some medical condition rather than for preventing conception. (Note that recent court decisions and the position of the Equal Employment Opportunity Commission seem to indicate that an employer will have a more difficult time defending a legal challenge by female employees over the failure to provide less-than-complete coverage for prescription contraceptives.) Drugs for treatment of infertility or sexual dysfunction, such as Viagra, may or may not be covered.

Drug plans are increasingly requiring precertification for the use of certain expensive drugs.

Most prescription drug plans have a copayment that a covered person pays for any prescriptions filled; in some cases, it is a flat amount that usually varies from $5 to $15 per prescription. Other plans have one copayment amount for generic drugs and a higher one for brand-name drugs. A three-tier structure, such as a $10 copayment for brand-name generic drugs, $20 for brand-name formulary drugs, and $30 for nonformulary drugs, is becoming increasingly common as well. Some plans provide financial incentives for prescriptions filled by mail-order pharmacies or on the Internet. A few plans have quarterly, semiannual, or annual spending caps. For example, benefits might be limited to $500 per person per quarter or $3,000 per year per family.

Two basic methods are used to provide prescription drug coverage: a reimbursement approach and a service approach. Under plans using a reimbursement approach, a covered individual personally pays the cost of prescription drugs and files a claim for reimbursement.

The majority of prescription drug plans use a service approach. Under this approach, participating pharmacies provide drugs to covered persons upon receipt of prescriptions, proper identification (usually a card issued by the plan), and any required copayments. The pharmacy then bills the provider of coverage (usually electronically) for the remaining cost of any prescription filled. Prescriptions filled at nonparticipating pharmacies are often covered but on a reimbursement basis.

Vision Benefits

Carve-out vision benefits may be provided by insurance companies, Blue Cross-Blue Shield plans, plans of state optometric associations patterned after Blue Shield, closed-panel HMO-type plans established by local providers of vision services, vision care PPOs, or third-party administrators.

Over half of the persons covered under employer-provided medical expense plans have some type of vision coverage, and the majority of this coverage is provided under a carve-out arrangement. Normally, a benefit schedule is used that specifies the types and amounts of certain benefits and the frequency with which they will be provided. Table 12-2 is an example of one such schedule. If a provider of vision services writes the plan, it is common for a discount, such as 20 percent, to be available for costs incurred with the provider that the schedule of benefits does not cover. Under some plans, most benefits are provided on a service basis rather than being subject to a maximum benefit. These plans usually cover only the cost of basic frames, which the covered persons can upgrade at an additional expense.

TABLE 12-2
Example of Benefit Schedule

Type of Benefit	Maximum Amount
Any 12-month period	
Eye examination	$ 45
Lenses, pair	
single vision	45
bifocal	75
trifocal	125
lenticular	200
contact (when medically necessary)	300
contact (when not medically necessary)	125
Any 24-month period	
Frames	60

Exclusions commonly exist for any extra charge for plastic lenses or the cost of safety lenses or prescription sunglasses. Benefits are generally provided for eye examinations by either an optometrist or an ophthalmologist, and larger benefits are sometimes provided if the latter is used. Vision care plans do not pay benefits for necessary eye surgery or treatment of eye diseases because these services are covered under a medical expense plan's regular coverage. However, many vision plans make benefits available for elective procedures to improve vision such as LASIK surgery. This benefit is usually in the form of a discounted fee from a provider who has a relationship with the plan.

Behavioral Health

Behavioral health benefits have always presented a challenge for medical expense plans. There is less uniformity in treatment standards for mental health, alcoholism, and drug addiction than for most other medical conditions. This, and the difficulty of monitoring treatment, has often led to unnecessary, expensive, and dangerous treatment by less-than-scrupulous providers of behavioral health care. Historically, benefit plans addressed these problems by having very limited benefit levels. But even these benefit levels had a tendency to encourage more expensive inpatient care over outpatient treatment, which, in most cases, appears to be as clinically effective. Moreover, there was little follow-up care after treatment. With rapidly increasing costs for behavioral health, employers and providers of benefit plans are increasingly carving out this benefit by contracting with vendors that use managed care techniques. Even with the use of carve-outs, plans continue to limit behavioral health benefits to a level significantly below that for other medical conditions.

Characteristics of a successful behavioral health program, whether or not it is a carve-out arrangement, include the following:

- the use of case management to design and coordinate treatment plans and to monitor the need for follow-up care
- a mechanism for referring a patient to the program. In many cases, this is through a primary care physician gatekeeper.
- the development of a provider network that specializes in behavioral health. In addition to physicians, the network will include psychologists and therapists. It will also include alternatives to hospital treatment such as residential centers, halfway houses, and structured outpatient programs. Benefits may or may not be provided if patients seek nonnetwork treatment. If it is covered, there is usually a lower benefit level than for network treatment.
- 24-hour patient access to care. Persons who have behavioral health problems often need immediate crisis intervention. Of course, the availability of such care needs to be well communicated to patients.

PLAN PROVISIONS

Medical expense plans have numerous provisions that concern financial planners. This section discusses provisions that pertain to eligibility, coordination of benefits, the relationship with Medicare, and claims. The next chapter covers other provisions that pertain to persons whose active employment has ceased.

Eligibility

The eligibility requirements for medical expense coverage are essentially the same as those for other types of group insurance—an employee must usually be in a covered classification, must satisfy any probationary period, and must be employed full-time.

Eligibility requirements may be different somewhat if an employer changes insurance companies. However, eligible employees who were covered under the old plan are automatically covered under the new plan and are exempt from any probationary periods.

Dependent Eligibility

Typically, the same medical expense benefits that are provided for an eligible employee are also available for that employee's dependents. If the employee does not elect dependent coverage under a contributory plan within 31 days after dependents are eligible, future coverage is available only during an open enrollment period or when satisfactory evidence of insurability is provided. However, if an employee was previously without dependents (and therefore had no dependent coverage), any newly acquired dependents (by birth, marriage, or adoption) are eligible for coverage as of the date that they gain dependent status.

The term *dependents* most commonly refers to an employee's spouse who is not legally separated from the employee and any unmarried dependent children (including stepchildren, adopted children, and children born out of wedlock) under the age of 19. However, coverage is usually provided for such children to age 23 or 26 if they are full-time students. In addition, coverage may also continue (and is required to continue in some states) for children who are incapable of earning their own living because of a physical or mental infirmity. Such children are considered dependents as long as this condition exists, but periodic proof of the condition may be required. If an employee has dependent coverage, all of the employee's newly acquired dependents (by birth, marriage, or adoption) are automatically covered.

Portability

The Health Insurance Portability and Accountability Act also affects eligibility for medical expense coverage. HIPAA's provisions, which apply to both insured and self-funded plans, do not allow an employee to take specific insurance from one job to another. Rather, they put limitations on preexisting-conditions exclusions and allow an employee to use evidence of prior insurance coverage to reduce or eliminate the length of any preexisting-conditions exclusion when the employee moves to another employer-provided medical expense plan. The act's provisions on portability generally override state laws unless state laws provide more liberal portability.

Restrictions for preexisting conditions are limited to a maximum of 12 months (18 months for late enrollees). In addition, the period for preexisting conditions must be reduced by the length of coverage under a prior medical expense plan as long as there has not been a break in coverage of 63 days or more. The prior coverage can have been under an individual policy, an employer-provided group plan (either insured or self-funded), an HMO, Medicare, or Medicaid.

The act requires an employer to give persons who lose group coverage a certificate that specifies the period of coverage under the plan they are leaving, including any period of COBRA coverage. COBRA is discussed in detail in chapter 13.

Benefits for Domestic Partners

In the mid-1980s, a few employers' plans began to define the term *dependent* broadly enough to include unmarried domestic partners. For example, one plan covers unmarried couples as long as they live together, show financial interdependence and joint responsibility for each other's common welfare, and consider themselves life partners. This type of requirement is fairly typical, as is the additional requirement that the employee's relationship must have lasted some specified minimum period of time such as 6 or 12 months. The employee must usually give the employer an affidavit that these requirements have been satisfied.

An estimated 25 percent of employers now provide medical expense benefits to domestic partners. (A smaller percentage of employers offer other types of group benefits.) Most plans provide benefits to domestic partners engaged in either heterosexual or homosexual relationships. Some plans provide benefits only to persons of the opposite sex of the employee, while a small number of plans limit benefits only to persons of the same sex. The rationale for the latter is that persons of opposite sexes can obtain benefits by marrying, whereas this option is not generally available to persons of the same sex.

Coordination of Benefits

In recent years, the percentage of individuals who have duplicate group medical expense coverage has increased substantially and is estimated to be about 10 percent. Probably the most common situation is one in which a husband and wife both work and have coverage under their respective employer's noncontributory plan. If the employer of either spouse also provides dependent coverage on a noncontributory basis, the other spouse (and other dependents if both employers provide such coverage) is covered under both plans. If dependent coverage is contributory, it is necessary for a couple with children to elect such coverage under one of their plans. Because a spouse is considered a dependent, he or she also has duplicate coverage when the election is made. Duplicate coverage may also arise when an employee has two jobs, or children are covered under both a parent's and a stepparent's plans.

In the absence of any provisions to the contrary, each group medical expense plan is obligated to provide benefits in cases of duplicate coverage as if no other coverage exists. To prevent individuals from receiving benefits that exceed their actual expenses, most group medical expense plans contain a **coordination-of-** *coordination-of-benefits (COB) provision,* which establishes priorities for the **benefits (COB)** payment of benefits by each plan covering an individual.
provision

Most COB provisions are based on the NAIC Group Coordination of Benefits Model Regulation. This regulation is periodically revised, and almost all states have adopted all or portions of one of the versions. As with all NAIC model legislation and regulations, some states have adopted the COB provisions with variations.

Although some flexibility is allowed, virtually all COB provisions apply when other coverage exists through another employer's group insurance plans or group benefit arrangements (such as the Blues, HMOs, or self-funded plans). They may also apply to no-fault automobile insurance benefits and to student coverage that educational institutions either sponsor or provide. However, these provisions virtually never apply (and cannot in most states) to any other coverages provided under contracts purchased on an individual basis outside of the employment relationship.

As a general rule, coverage under multiple policies will allow a person to receive benefits equal to 100 percent of his or her medical expenses. The coverage determined to be primary will pay as if no other coverage exists. If some expenses are not reimbursed (because, for example, of deductibles, copayments, or policy limitations), the secondary coverage will pick up the balance as long as it is less than what that coverage would have paid if it were the only coverage in existence.

Determination of Primary Coverage

The usual COB provision stipulates that any other plan without the COB provision is primary and that any plan with it is secondary. If more than one plan has a COB provision, the following priorities are established:

- Coverage as an employee is usually primary to coverage as a dependent. The exception occurs if a retired person is covered (1) by Medicare, (2) under a retiree plan of a former employer, and (3) as a dependent of a spouse who is an active employee. In this case, coverage as a dependent is primary, Medicare is secondary, and the retiree plan pays last.
- Coverage as an active employee (or as that person's dependent) is primary to coverage as a retired or laid-off employee (or as that person's dependent).
- Coverage as an active employee (or that person's dependent) is primary to a plan that provides COBRA continuation benefits.
- If the specific rules of a court decree state that one parent must assume responsibility for his or her child's health care expenses, and the plan of that parent has actual knowledge of the terms of the court decree, then that plan is primary.
- If the parents of dependent children are married or are not separated (regardless of whether they have ever been married) or if a court awards joint custody without specifying that one parent has the responsibility to provide health care coverage, the plan of the parent whose birthday falls earlier in the calendar year is primary and the plan of the parent with the later birthday is secondary.
- If the parents of dependent children are not married, are separated (regardless of whether they have ever been married), or are divorced and if there is no court decree allocating responsibility for the child's health care expenses, the following priorities apply:
  - The plan of the parent with custody is primary.
  - The plan of the stepparent who is the spouse of the parent with custody is secondary.
  - The plan of the parent without custody is tertiary.
  - The plan of the stepparent who is the spouse of the parent without custody pays last.
- If none of the previous rules establishes a priority, the plan covering the person for the longest period of time is primary. However, if this rule also fails to determine the primary plan, then benefit payments are shared equally among the plans.

Relationship with Medicare

Because most employees and their dependents are eligible for Medicare upon reaching age 65 (and possibly under other circumstances), a provision that eliminates any possible duplication of coverage is necessary. The simplest solution is to exclude any person eligible for Medicare from eligibility under the group contract. In most cases, however, this approach conflicts with the Age Discrimination in Employment Act, which prohibits discrimination in benefit plans for active employees.

Medicare Secondary Rules

Employers with 20 or more employees must make coverage available under their medical expense plans to active employees aged 65 or older and to active employees' spouses who are eligible for Medicare. Unless an employee elects otherwise, the employer's plan is primary and Medicare is secondary. Except in plans that require large employee contributions, it is doubtful that employees will elect Medicare to be primary because employers are prohibited from offering active employees or their spouses a Medicare carve-out, a Medicare supplement, or some other incentive not to enroll in the employer's plan.

Medicare is the secondary payer of benefits in two other situations. The first situation involves persons who are eligible for Medicare benefits to treat end-stage renal disease with dialysis or kidney transplants. Medicare provides these benefits to any insured workers (either active or retired) and to their spouses and dependent children, but the employer's plan is primary during the first 30 months of treatment only; after that time Medicare is primary and the employer's plan is secondary.

Medicare is also the secondary payer of benefits to disabled employees (or disabled dependents of employees) under age 65 who are eligible for Medicare and covered under the medical expense plan of large employers (defined as plans with 100 or more employees). Medicare, however, does not pay anything until a person has been eligible for Social Security disability income benefits for 2 years. The rule applies only if an employer continues medical expense coverage for disabled persons; there is no requirement for such a continuation.

Medicare Carve-Outs and Supplements

An employer's plan may cover certain persons aged 65 or older who are not covered by the provisions of the Age Discrimination in Employment Act—specifically, retirees and active employees of firms with fewer than 20 employees. Although there is nothing to prevent an employer from terminating coverage for these persons, many employers provide them with either a Medicare carve-out or Medicare supplement.

Medicare carve-out

Medicare supplement

With a *Medicare carve-out*, plan benefits are reduced to the extent that benefits are payable under Medicare for the same expenses. As an alternative, some employers use a *Medicare supplement* that provides benefits for certain specific expenses not covered under Medicare. These include (1) the portion of expenses Medicare does not pay because of deductibles, coinsurance, or copayments and (2) certain expenses that Medicare excludes. Such a supplement may or may not provide benefits similar to those available under a carve-out plan.

Claims

Medical expense contracts that provide benefits on a service basis (such as HMOs and the Blues) or that use preferred providers generally do not require covered persons to file claim forms. Rather, the providers of services perform any necessary paperwork and are then reimbursed directly.

Medical expense contracts that provide benefits on an indemnity basis typically require that the insurance company (or other provider) be given a written proof of loss (that is, a claim form) concerning the occurrence, character, and extent of each claim. This form usually contains portions that must be completed and signed by the employee, a representative of the employer, and the provider of medical services.

The period during which an employee must file a claim depends on the provider of coverage and any applicable state requirements. An employee generally has at least 90 days (or as soon as is reasonably possible) after medical expenses are incurred to file. Some insurance companies require that they be notified within a shorter time (such as 20 days) about any illness or injury on which a claim may be based, even though they give a longer time period for the actual filing of the form itself.

Individuals have the right under medical expense plans to assign their benefits to the providers of medical services. Such an assignment, which authorizes the insurance company to make the benefit payment directly to the provider, may generally be made by completing the appropriate portion of the claim form. In addition, the insurance company has the right to examine any person for whom a claim is filed at its own expense and with the physician of its own choice.

DENTAL INSURANCE

Over the last 25 years, dental insurance has increased significantly as an employee benefit. Dental benefits may be offered by insurance companies, dental service plans (often called Delta Dental plans), the Blues, and managed care plans such as dental HMOs (called DHMOs). Like medical expense coverage, a significant portion of dental coverage is also self-funded by employers. Some employees also have dental benefits under discount plans, which are described later.

Although group dental insurance contracts have been patterned after group medical expense contracts, some of their provisions are different, while others are unique to dental coverage. These provisions pertain to benefits, exclusions, and benefit limitations. In contrast to medical expense plans, for which an employer usually pays a substantial share of the premium cost, a large percentage of dental plans are provided as voluntary benefits. This requires an employee to pay 100 percent of the premium cost.

Benefits

Most dental insurance plans pay for almost all types of dental expenses, but a particular plan may provide more limited coverage. One characteristic of dental insurance that is seldom found in medical expense plans is the inclusion of benefits for both routine diagnostic procedures (including oral examinations and X rays) and preventive dental treatment (including teeth cleaning and fluoride treatment). In fact, a few dental plans actually require periodic oral examinations as a condition for continuing eligibility. There is clear evidence that the cost of providing these benefits will be more than offset by the prevention of the expensive dental procedures required when a condition is not discovered early or when a preventive treatment has not been given.

In addition to benefits for diagnostic and preventive treatment, benefits for dental expenses may be provided for the following categories of dental treatment:

- restoration (including fillings, crowns, and other procedures used to restore the functional use of natural teeth)
- oral surgery (including the extraction of teeth, as well as other surgical treatment of diseases, injuries, and defects of the jaw)
- endodontics (treatment for diseases of the dental pulp within teeth such as root canals)
- periodontics (treatment of diseases of the surrounding and supporting tissues of the teeth)
- prosthodontics (replacement of missing teeth and structures by artificial devices such as bridgework and dentures)
- orthodontics (prevention and correction of dental and oral anomalies through the use of corrective devices such as braces and retainers)

For benefit plan design purposes, these treatments are usually divided into the following categories of dental services:

- service level I—preventive and diagnostic services
- service level II—basic services, including minor restorative procedures (fillings), and endodontic, periodontic, and oral surgery services

- service level III—major services, including major restorations (crowns, inlays, onlays, veneers), and prosthodontic procedures (dentures, bridges)
- service level IV—orthodontic services

Most dental plans provide benefits for the first three service levels; some plans provide benefits for service level IV. These service levels are key to designing plans in which members have focused financial incentives to seek routine services for prevention of future expenses and have a greater stake in more costly major services decisions. Thus, for example, a typical dental plan will aim to provide its most complete payment for level I services and somewhat less complete payment for level II services, while providing the least complete benefit for level III and level IV services (if covered).

Benefit Payment Methods

Dental plans have several types of benefit payment methods. Plans that pay benefits on an indemnity basis usually make payments on the basis of reasonable-and-customary charges. Most plans have annual deductibles in the neighborhood of $50 to $100. However, the deductible typically does not apply to level I services. Coinsurance is also common. It is typically 80 percent or higher for level I services, with 100 percent being the most common. Level II services are usually subject to coinsurance in the range of 70 to 85 percent. Level III and level IV services typically have coinsurance of between 50 and 60 percent.

A very few indemnity plans have scheduled maximum benefits. These benefits are provided on a first-dollar basis with no deductibles or specified coinsurance percentage. Benefit maximums, however, are usually lower than reasonable-and-customary charges, thereby forcing employees to bear a portion of the costs of their dental services.

Dental plans that are structured as PPOs usually have deductibles and co-insurance similar to indemnity plans except that higher coinsurance percentages are used when services are received from network providers. In-network benefits are also paid on the basis of negotiated charges with providers.

Deductibles and coinsurance are usually not used for most service levels in DHMO plans as long as network providers are used. However, the member may be responsible for varying copayments for level II and level III services. Level IV services are usually subject to coinsurance, often 50 or 60 percent.

Exclusions

All dental plans contain exclusions, but the number and type vary. Some of the more common exclusions are charges for the following:

- services that are purely cosmetic, unless necessitated by an accidental bodily injury while a person is covered under the plan. (Orthodontics, although they are often used for cosmetic reasons, can usually also be justified as necessary to correct abnormal dental conditions.)
- replacement of lost, missing, or stolen dentures, or other prosthetic devices
- duplicate dentures or other prosthetic devices
- services that do not have uniform professional endorsement

Limitations

Dental insurance plans also contain numerous limitations that are designed to control claim costs and to eliminate unnecessary dental care. In addition to deductibles and coinsurance, virtually all dental plans have overall benefit maximums. Except for DHMOs, which usually do not have a calendar-year limit, most plans contain a calendar-year maximum (varying from $500 to $2,500) but no lifetime maximum. However, some plans have only a lifetime maximum (such as $5,000), and a few plans contain both a calendar-year maximum and a lifetime maximum. These maximums may apply to all dental expenses, or they may be limited to all expenses except those that arise from orthodontics (and occasionally periodontics). In the latter case, benefits for orthodontics will be subject to a separate, lower lifetime maximum, which is typically between $500 and $2,000.

Most dental plans limit the frequency with which some benefits will be paid. Routine oral examinations and teeth cleaning are usually limited to once every 6 months, and full-mouth X rays to once every 24 or 36 months. The replacement of dentures may also be limited to one time in some specified period (such as 5 years).

The typical dental plan also limits benefits to the least expensive type of accepted dental treatment for a given dental condition. For example, if either a gold or silver filling can be used, benefit payments will be limited to the cost of a silver filling, even if a gold filling is inserted.

Discount Plans

Although they cannot be classified as an insurance plan, dental discount plans play a role in providing dental services to many Americans. A discount plan, often referred to as a referral or access plan, provides members with a discount on the purchase of professional services. Dental discount plans usually have a modest monthly fee—such as $5 or $7 per person—that may be paid by an employer. In return, the employee receives a discount on specified dental services as long as the services are received from providers affiliated with the discount plan's network. The employee pays the discounted fee. There is no other reimbursement to either the dental provider or employee.

Discounts are often in the range of 20 to 30 percent, but they may be higher or lower. The discounts may also vary by type of dental procedure. Dental professionals are willing to grant these discounts in anticipation of an increased volume of business.

ADDITIONAL BENEFITS FOR EXECUTIVES

Some employers have plans that provide additional medical and dental benefits for executives. Although this group of employees is most likely to be able to pay for the expenses such plans cover, these supplemental benefits are frequently viewed as a way to attract and retain key employees.

From a purely administrative standpoint, it would be relatively easy to self-fund these benefits, but the benefits, as explained later under the section on federal taxation, would most likely represent taxable income to employees. As a result, these additional executive benefits are usually insured as either separate coverage or as a rider to the plan that covers other employees.

This type of plan usually covers the executives and their dependents. Benefits almost always include coverage to provide reimbursement for deductibles and coinsurance under the employer's plan that apply to all covered employees. It is also common to find coverage for annual physicals and the extra cost of private hospital rooms. In addition, there frequently is extra coverage, although possibly limited to an annual maximum, such as $10,000, for expenses such as mental or emotional treatment, hearing care, vision care, and dental work.

FEDERAL TAX TREATMENT

In many respects, the federal tax treatment of employer-provided medical and dental expense premiums and benefits parallels that of other group coverage if they are provided through an insurance company, a Blue Cross–Blue Shield plan, an HMO, or a PPO. Contributions by the employer for an employee's coverage or coverage of the employee's dependents are tax deductible to the employer as long as the employee's overall compensation is reasonable. Employer contributions do not create any income tax liability for an employee. Moreover, benefits are not taxable to an employee except when they exceed any medical expenses incurred. The value of any employer-provided coverage for an employee's domestic partner, minus any employee contributions, represents taxable income to the employee unless the partner qualifies under IRS rules as the employee's dependent.

One major difference between group medical expense coverage and other forms of group insurance is that a portion of an employee's contribution for coverage may be tax deductible as a medical expense if that individual itemizes his or her income tax deductions. Under the Internal Revenue Code, individuals are allowed to deduct certain medical care expenses (including dental expenses) for which no reimbursement was received. This deduction is limited to expenses (including amounts paid for insurance) that exceed 7.5 percent of the person's adjusted gross income.

However, employees may receive even more favorable tax benefits if they elect salary reductions through a cafeteria plan for medical (and dental) premiums and expenses that would otherwise be unreimbursable by insurance. If an employer's cafeteria plan has a premium-conversion plan, an employee may elect a salary reduction to pay his or her premium contribution. If the cafeteria plan includes a flexible spending account (FSA), an employee can elect an additional salary reduction to fund medical expenses that are not covered by the employer's plan because of deductibles, coinsurance, exclusions, and limitations. The employee must elect the reduction prior to the beginning of the plan year and forfeit amounts not used for benefits during the year.

Salary reductions also reduce income for purposes of Social Security and Medicare taxes and therefore may reduce future Social Security benefits. In most states, they lower income for purposes of state income taxes. As the following example shows, the use of salary reductions can have a significant effect on an employee's spendable income by lowering taxes paid.

Example: Charlie is a single employee with an annual income of $75,000. He pays $1,000 per year toward the cost of his employer-provided medical expense coverage. He expects to have $2,000 in unreimbursed medical and dental expenses for the year. Charlie's marginal federal income tax bracket is 25 percent. This percentage is increased to 28 because of state income taxes. Charlie's standard deduction and exemptions for income tax purposes are $15,000.

Without a cafeteria plan, Charlie's federal and state taxes are calculated as follows:

Annual Income	$75,000
Minus standard deduction and exemptions	−15,000
Taxable income	$60,000
Income taxes (.28 x $60,000)	$16,800
Social Security and Medicare taxes (.0765 x $75,000)	5,738
Total taxes	$22,538

If Charlie participates in his employer's premium-conversion plan and FSA, Charlie's taxes are calculated as follows:

Annual income	$75,000
Minus contribution for premium-conversion plan	−1,000
Minus FSA contribution	−2,000
Minus standard deduction and exemptions	− 15,000
Taxable income	$57,000
Income taxes (.28 x $57,000)	$15,960
Social Security and Medicare taxes [.0765 x ($75,000 − $3,000)]	5,508
Total taxes	$21,468

Self-employed persons (for example, sole proprietors), partners, and persons who own more than 2 percent of the stock of an S corporation are not considered employees. If a sole proprietorship, partnership, or S corporation pays the cost of medical expense coverage for those persons or their family members, this amount constitutes taxable income to the proprietor, partner, or 2 percent owner. However, the proprietor, partner, or S corporation may be entitled to an income tax deduction for this amount. The deduction cannot exceed the individual's earned income from the proprietorship, partnership, or S corporation that provides the medical expense plan. In addition, the deduction is available only if the person is not eligible to participate in any subsidized medical expense plan of another employer for whom the person or his or her spouse works. The remainder of the cost of the medical expense coverage can be deducted as an itemized expense to the extent that it and other medical expenses exceed the 7.5 percent threshold that was previously described.

The tax situation may be different if an employer provides medical expense benefits through a self-funded plan (referred to in the Internal Revenue Code as a self-insured medical reimbursement plan), under which employers either (1) pay the providers of medical care directly or (2) reimburse employees for their medical expenses. If a self-funded plan meets certain nondiscrimination requirements for highly compensated employees, the employer can deduct benefit payments as they are made, and the employee will have no taxable income. If a plan is discriminatory, the employer will still receive an income tax deduction. However, all or a portion of the benefits received by highly compensated employees, but not by other employees, will be treated as taxable income.

MINI CASE: AMY AND JOHN SCHULTZ

Amy and John have had excellent medical expense coverage under their employer's traditional indemnity medical expense plan. Each is covered separately and pays a monthly premium of $45. However, the cost of the plan to their employer has skyrocketed and the current plan is being eliminated. They will now have a choice of three alternative plans with the following monthly costs:

- an HMO with a monthly employee cost of $30
- a POS plan with a monthly employee cost of $75
- a PPO plan with a monthly employee cost of $130

Amy and John see the same primary care physician and are in excellent health. Although John is willing to change physicians if necessary, Amy would prefer not to. She also would be very reluctant to change her gynecologist. Both are aware of the need to visit specialists because Amy's mother recently had breast cancer and John's mother has diabetes. Amy and John value their ability to visit a specialist of their choice.

What factors should Amy and John evaluate in selecting a new medical expense plan?

(See answer section for answers to mini-case.)

SOURCES FOR FURTHER IN-DEPTH STUDY

- Beam, Burton T., Jr., *Group Benefits: Basic Concepts and Alternatives,* 10th ed., Bryn Mawr, PA: The American College Press, 2004. Phone 888-263-7265. Web site address www.theamericancollege.edu
- Rosenbloom, Jerry S., editor, *The Handbook of Employee Benefits*, 5th ed., New York: McGraw-Hill, 2001. Phone 800-262-4729. Web site address www.books.mcgraw-hill.com
- *Kongstvedt, Peter R., Managed Care: What It is and How It Works,* 2d ed., Gaithersburg, MD: Aspen Publishers, Inc., 2002. Phone 800-638-8437. Web site address www.aspenpublishers.com

CHAPTER REVIEW

Answers to mini-case, review questions, and self-test questions start on page 793.

Key Terms

health insurance
medical expense insurance

major medical insurance
preexisting-conditions provision

deductible
common accident provision
coinsurance (medical expense
    insurance)
stop-loss limit
preadmission certification
second surgical opinion
extended care facility
home health care
hospice care
birthing center
managed care
health maintenance organization
    (HMO)
preferred-provider organization
    (PPO)

exclusive-provider organization
    (EPO)
point-of-service (POS) plan
consumer-directed medical expense
    plan
defined-contribution medical
    expense plan
high-deductible health plan
health reimbursement arrangement
carve-out (medical expense
    insurance)
coordination-of-benefits (COB)
    provision
Medicare carve-out
Medicare supplement

Review Questions

12-1.   What observations can be made about the future of the health care system?

12-2.   Your client, Sue, is covered by an employer-provided major medical policy. Which of the following medical expenditures that Sue incurred are covered under the policy?
   a.   She required hospitalization in a semiprivate room for a period of 20 days following an operation on her heart.
   b.   She had cosmetic surgery on her nose to improve her looks.
   c.   She required care as an inpatient at an extended care facility after release from a 4-day stay in the hospital following a serious operation.
   d.   She received custodial or rest care for 5 days at her home after release from an overnight stay in the hospital following minor surgery.
   e.   She required a prescription drug for her arthritis that costs $500 per month.

12-3.   Most major medical plans contain an exclusion for preexisting conditions. How does this exclusion differ from the other exclusions found in major medical plans?

12-4.   Your client is concerned about the types of deductibles that apply to her medical expense plan. Explain to her how the following deductibles operate:
   a.   initial deductible
   b.   family deductible

12-5.   Peggy is covered under a comprehensive major medical plan that has a $250 calendar-year deductible and an 80 percent coinsurance provision. If Peggy incurs $1,500 of covered medical expenses during the year (assuming no limitations), how much of this will she have to pay out of pocket?

12-6.   What are the basic characteristics of a managed care plan?

12-7.   What are the characteristics of HMOs that distinguish them from insurance companies and/or the Blues?

12-8.   How do preferred-provider organizations (PPOs) differ from traditional major medical contracts?

12-9.   Briefly describe how a point-of-service (POS) plan is a modification of a traditional HMO arrangement.

12-10. What is the value of benefit carve-outs to medical expense plans?

12-11. Describe the two general approaches to consumer-directed medical expense plans.

12-12. Briefly describe the following types of benefit carve-outs:
   a.   prescription drugs
   b.   vision benefits
   c.   behavioral health

12-13. What persons may be eligible for coverage under an employee's medical expense plan?

12-14. How does the Health Insurance Portability and Accountability Act (HIPAA) affect eligibility under medical expense plans?

12-15. A child in the custody of her mother is covered as a dependent under the major medical coverage of both her father and her stepfather. Which coverage is primary if both coverages are subject to the usual coordination-of-benefits provision?

12-16. Explain when Medicare is the primary and when it is the secondary payer of benefits for individuals who are also covered under an employer medical expense plan.

12-17. Explain whether a group dental plan typically covers each of the following dental expenses:
   a.   X rays
   b.   root canal
   c.   replacement of lost dentures
   d.   teeth whitening
   e.   braces

12-18. What types of additional medical expense benefits may be available to executives?

12-19. To what extent are employee contributions for medical expense coverage deductible for federal income tax purposes?

12-20. Explain how premium-conversion plans and flexible spending accounts (FSAs) result in tax savings for employees.

Self-Test Questions

T   F   12-1. Medical expense insurance is the most significant type of employee benefit in terms of both the number of persons covered and the dollar outlay.

T   F   12-2. Maternity-related expenses are usually excluded from major medical plans.

T   F   12-3. Major medical plans contain internal limits for certain types of medical expenses.

T   F   12-4. Many major medical plans with a calendar-year deductible also have a carryover provision that allows any expenses applied to the deductible and incurred during the last 3 months of the year also to be applied to the deductible for the following year.

T   F   12-5. Many major medical expense plans place a limit on the amount of out-of-pocket expenses that a covered person must bear during any time period.

T   F   12-6. Extended care facility benefits cover rest or domiciliary care for the aged.

T   F   12-7. Basic hospice care benefits cover treatments that attempt to cure seriously ill patients.

T   F   12-8. Managed care plans typically encourage preventive care and the attainment of healthier lifestyles.

T   F   12-9. HMOs typically provide out-of-area coverage for all medical services because their scope is national.

T   F   12-10. Cost controls of HMOs tend to discourage preventive care.

T   F.   12-11. A PPO often has different deductibles and coinsurance that apply to network and nonnetwork charges.

T   F   12-12. PPOs typically provide benefits for a much wider array of medical procedures if nonnetwork providers are used.

T   F   12-13. An exclusive-provider organization (EPO) is so named because it allows members to pay an additional premium for the right to see the most prominent specialist in a medical field.

T   F   12-14. A point-of-service plan allows members to be reimbursed for treatment received outside the HMO network.

T F 12-15. Consumer-directed medical expense plans give employees increased choices and responsibilities with the selection of medical expense coverage.

T f 12-16. High-deductible medical expense plans give employees an incentive to avoid unnecessary medical care.

T F 12-17. Benefit carve-outs are often used as a method of cost containment through the use of managed care techniques.

T F 12-18. Most prescription drug plans cover nonprescription drugs as long as a physician orders them on a prescription form.

T F 12-19. A successful behavioral health program should permit patient access on a 24-hour basis.

T F 12-20. For purposes of group medical expense benefits, a 27-year-old woman is fully covered as a dependent child under her father's coverage if she is living at home and is a full-time student.

T F 12-21. Most group medical expense plans contain a coordination-of-benefits (COB) provision under which coverage as an employee is primary to coverage as a dependent.

T F 12-22. If an employee who is eligible for Medicare works full-time for a large employer, Medicare is the primary medical expense coverage, and the employer's plan is secondary.

T F 12-23. The typical dental plan limits benefits to the least expensive type of accepted dental treatment for a given dental condition.

T F 12-24. Premium contributions by an employer to group medical and dental coverage for an employee are considered taxable income to the employee.

T F 12-25. Flexible spending accounts (FSAs) typically reduce employees' spendable income.

NOTES

1. The Henry J. Kaiser Family Foundation and Health Research and Educational Trust, *Employer Health Benefits, 2004.*
2. Centers for Medicare & Medicaid Services, Office of the Actuary, National Health Statistics Group.

13

Individual Medical Expense Insurance

Learning Objectives

An understanding of the material in this chapter should enable the student to

13-1.   Explain COBRA and the various other alternatives for continuing employer-provided medical expense coverage.

13-2.   Describe the various types of medical expense coverage available in the individual marketplace.

13-3.   Explain how the market has evolved to make it easier for unhealthy individuals to obtain medical expense insurance.

13-4.   Describe Archer MSAs and health saving accounts.

13-5.   Describe the premium and renewability provisions found in medical expense contracts.

13-6.   Explain the federal income tax rules that apply to individual medical expense insurance.

Chapter Outline

The previous chapter was devoted to a discussion of employer-provided medical expense insurance to active employees and their dependents. This coverage is the source of medical expense protection for almost two-thirds of all Americans under age 65. The majority of this chapter is devoted to the private insurance protection available to persons in this age group who do not qualify for this employer-provided coverage. Although the chapter title uses the word *individual,* some of the insurance available is a continuation of prior employer-provided coverage. In addition, Archer MSAs and health savings accounts may be used within an employment relationship.

Numerous circumstances account for the need for individual medical expense insurance. These include

- the lack of employer-provided coverage for some employees, usually those who work for small employers
- the termination of employment for reasons such as voluntarily quitting, being fired or laid off, becoming disabled, or retiring
- the termination of dependent coverage, even when employee coverage continues. This can occur because of divorce, separation, or a child becoming too old.
- not being in the labor market. Some people have the resources to forego employment. Others, for many reasons, are unable to find or hold jobs.
- self-employment

It is important to point out that less than 10 percent of the population under age 65 obtains private individual medical insurance for themselves and their families. An estimated 15 percent of the population has no medical expense insurance, and almost as many are covered by Medicaid. One reason for this lack of individual coverage is its significant cost. Although legislation has made coverage potentially available for more persons in recent years, there is still a severe affordability problem. For example, the premium for a person in his or her late 50s can be several thousand dollars per year.

Another segment of the population that often obtains individual coverage consists of those persons eligible for Medicare. As mentioned in chapter 7, Medicare has some limitations, including no out-of-country coverage, extremely limited coverage for prescription drugs, and higher copayments than many major medical policies. More than 60 percent of individuals over the age of 65 have some type of coverage to supplement Medicare.

Several topics are covered in this chapter. These include the ways in which employer-provided coverage can be continued, types of individual coverage for those under age 65, Medicare supplements, policy provisions, and the tax treatment of premiums and benefits. Finally, there is a checklist for evaluating and comparing policies. Financial planners can use this information to help their clients assess and choose needed coverage.

CONTINUATION OF EMPLOYER-PROVIDED COVERAGE

In the absence of any provisions for continuation or conversion, employer-provided coverage on an employee generally ceases on the earliest of the following:

- the date on which employment terminates. In some plans, coverage ceases on the last day of the month in which employment terminates.
- the date on which the employee ceases to be eligible
- the date on which the master contract for the employer-provided coverage terminates
- the date on which the overall maximum benefit of major medical coverage is received
- the end of the last period for which the employee has made any required contribution

Coverage on any dependent usually ceases on the earliest of the following:

- the date on which he or she ceases to meet the definition of dependent
- the date on which the coverage of the employee ceases for any reason except the employee's receipt of the overall maximum benefit
- the date on which the dependent receives the overall maximum benefit of major medical coverage

- the end of the last period for which the employee has made any required contribution for dependent coverage

However, insurance coverage often is available past these dates because of federal legislation or employer practices. In some cases, the former coverage can be continued, at least for a period of time; in other cases, the prior employment results in the availability of individual coverage without evidence of insurability.

Continuation of Coverage under COBRA

COBRA

The Consolidated Omnibus Budget Reconciliation Act of 1985 (*COBRA*) requires that group health plans allow employees and certain beneficiaries to elect to have their current health insurance coverage extended at group rates for up to 36 months following a "qualifying event" that results in the loss of coverage for a "qualified beneficiary." The term *group health plan* as used in the act is broad enough to include medical expense plans, dental plans, vision care plans, and prescription drug plans, regardless of whether benefits are self-funded by the employer or provided through other entities such as insurance companies or managed care organizations. Long-term care coverage is not subject to COBRA rules. COBRA applies to group health plans even if employees pay the full cost of coverage as long as the plan would not be available at the same cost to an employee if he or she were not employed. However, there is one exception to this rule: Voluntary benefit plans under which the employer's only involvement is to process payroll deductions are not subject to COBRA.

The act applies only to employers who had the equivalent of 20 or more full-time employees on a typical business day during the preceding calendar year; certain church-related plans and plans of the federal government, however, are exempt from the act. Failure to comply with the act will result in an excise tax of up to $100 per day for each person denied coverage. The tax can be levied on the employer as well as on the entity (such as an insurer or HMO) that provides or administers the benefits.

qualified beneficiary

A *qualified beneficiary* is defined as any employee, or the spouse or dependent child of the employee, who on the day before a qualifying event was covered under the employee's group health plan. In addition, the definition includes any child who is born to or placed for adoption with the employee during the period of COBRA coverage. This change gives automatic eligibility for COBRA coverage to the child as well as the right to have his or her own election rights if a second *qualifying event* occurs.

qualifying event

Under the act, each of the following is a qualifying event if it results in the loss of coverage by a qualified beneficiary:

- the death of the covered employee
- the termination of the employee for any reason except gross misconduct. This includes quitting, retiring, or being fired for something other than gross misconduct.
- a reduction of the employee's hours so that the employee or dependent is ineligible for coverage
- the divorce or legal separation of the covered employee and his or her spouse
- for spouses and children, the employee's eligibility for Medicare
- a child's ceasing to be an eligible dependent under the plan

The act specifies that a qualified beneficiary is entitled to elect continued coverage without providing evidence of insurability. The beneficiary must be allowed to continue coverage identical to that available to employees and dependents to whom a qualifying event has not occurred. Coverage for persons who elect COBRA continuation can be changed when changes are made to the plan that covers active employees and their dependents.

Each qualified beneficiary must be allowed to continue coverage from the qualifying event until the earliest of the following:

- 18 months for employees and dependents when the employee's employment has terminated or coverage has been terminated because of a reduction in hours. This period is extended to 29 months for a qualified beneficiary if the Social Security Administration determines that the beneficiary was or became totally disabled at any time during the first 60 days of COBRA coverage.
- 36 months for other qualifying events
- the date the plan terminates for all employees
- the date the coverage ceases because of a failure to make a timely payment of premium for the qualified beneficiary's coverage
- the date the qualified beneficiary subsequently becomes entitled to Medicare or becomes covered (as either an employee or dependent) under another group health plan, provided the group health plan does not contain an exclusion or limitation with respect to any preexisting condition. If the new plan does not cover a preexisting condition, the COBRA coverage can be continued until the earlier of (1) the remainder of the 18- or 36-month period or (2) the time when the preexisting-conditions provision no longer applies.

If a second qualifying event (such as the death or divorce of a terminated employee) occurs during the period of continued coverage, the maximum period of continuation is 36 months.

Example: When Peter Gonzalez terminated employment, he and his family were eligible for 18 months of COBRA coverage. When he died 15 months after electing the coverage, a second qualifying event occurred for his spouse and dependent children. The normal period of COBRA continuation resulting from an employee's death is 36 months. Because the spouse and children had already had COBRA coverage for 15 months, the second qualifying event extended the potential period of coverage for an additional 21 months.

At the termination of continued coverage, a qualified beneficiary must be offered the right to convert to an individual insurance policy if a conversion privilege is generally available to employees under the employer's plan.

When a qualifying event occurs, the employer must notify the benefit plan administrator, who then must notify all qualified beneficiaries within 14 days. In general, the employer has 30 days to notify the plan administrator. However, an employer may not know of a qualifying event if it involves divorce, legal separation, or a child's ceasing to be eligible for coverage. In these circumstances, the employee or family member must notify the employer within 60 days of the event, or the right to elect COBRA coverage will be lost. The time period for the employer to notify the plan administrator begins when the employer is informed of the qualifying event, as long as this occurs within the 60-day period.

The continuation of coverage is not automatic; a qualified beneficiary must elect it. The election period starts on the date of the qualifying event and may end not earlier than 60 days after actual notice of the event to the qualified beneficiary by the plan administrator. Once coverage is elected, the beneficiary has 45 days to pay the premium for the period of coverage prior to the election.

Under COBRA, the cost of the continued coverage may be passed on to the qualified beneficiary, but the cost cannot exceed 102 percent of the cost to the plan for the period of coverage for a similarly situated active employee to whom a qualifying event has not occurred. The extra 2 percent is supposed to cover the employer's extra administrative costs. The one exception to this rule occurs for months 19 through 29 if an employee is disabled, in which case the premium can be as high as 150 percent. Qualified beneficiaries must have the option of paying the premium in monthly installments. In addition, there must be a grace period of at least 30 days for each installment.

Because of cost economies associated with employer-provided coverage, COBRA is more often than not the most cost-effective way to obtain medical expense coverage. With significant cost variations in both the group and individual insurance markets, however, it is wise to shop around. For example, a young, healthy person might find the purchase of individual coverage to be significantly less expensive.

Continuation of Coverage in Addition to COBRA

Even before the passage of COBRA, it was becoming increasingly common for employers (particularly large employers) to continue group insurance coverage for certain employees—and sometimes their dependents—beyond the usual termination dates. Obviously, when coverage is continued now, at a minimum an employer must comply with COBRA. However, an employer can be more liberal than COBRA by paying all or a portion of the cost, providing continued coverage for additional categories of persons, or continuing coverage for a longer period of time. Some states have continuation laws for insured medical expense plans that might require coverage to be made available in situations that COBRA does not cover. One example is coverage for employees of firms with fewer than 20 employees; another is coverage for periods longer than those COBRA requires.

Retired Employees

Many employers continue coverage on retired employees. Although coverage can also be continued for retirees' dependents, it is often limited only to spouses. Retired employees under age 65 usually have the same coverage as the active employees have. However, coverage for employees aged 65 or older (if included under the same plan) may be provided under a Medicare carve-out or a Medicare supplement. The lifetime maximum benefit for persons eligible for Medicare is often much lower (such as $5,000 or $10,000) than for active employees.

Because of changes in accounting rules for retiree medical expense coverage and increasing benefit costs, many employers have lowered or eliminated retiree benefits or are considering such a change. There are legal uncertainties, however, as to whether benefits that have been promised to retirees can be eliminated or reduced. Many employers also feel that there is a moral obligation to continue these benefits. As a result, most employers are not altering plans for current retirees or active employees who are eligible to retire. Rather, the changes apply to future retirees only. These changes, which seem to be running the gamut, include the following:

- the elimination of benefits for future retirees
- the shifting of more of the cost burden to future retirees by reducing benefits. Such a reduction may be accomplished by providing lower benefit maximums, covering fewer types of expenses, or increasing copayments.
- adding or increasing retiree sharing of premium costs after retirement

- shifting to a defined-contribution approach to funding retiree benefits. For example, an employer might agree to pay $5 per month toward the cost of coverage after retirement for each year of an employee's service. Many plans of this nature have been designed so that the employer's contribution increases with changes in the consumer price index, subject to maximum increases such as 5 percent per year.
- encouraging retirees to elect benefits from managed care plans. With this approach, retirees are required to pay a significant portion of the cost if coverage is continued through a traditional indemnity plan.

Surviving Dependents

Coverage may also continue for the survivors of deceased active employees and/or deceased retired employees. Coverage for the survivors of active employees does not commonly continue beyond the period COBRA requires, and coverage for the survivors of retired employees may be limited to surviving spouses. In both instances, the continued coverage is usually identical to what was provided prior to the employee's death. It is also common for the employer to continue the same premium contribution level.

Laid-off Employees

Medical expense coverage can be continued for laid-off workers, and large employers frequently provide such coverage for a limited period. Few employers provide coverage beyond the period COBRA requires, but some employers continue to make the same premium contribution, at least for a limited period of time.

Disabled Employees

Medical expense coverage can be continued for an employee (and dependents) when he or she has a temporary interruption of employment, including one arising from illness or injury. Many employers also cover employees who have long-term disabilities or have retired because of a disability. In most cases, this continuation of coverage is contingent on satisfaction of some definition of total (and possibly permanent) disability. When coverage is continued for disabled employees, an employer must determine the extent of employer contributions. For example, the employer may continue the same premium contribution as for active employees. There is nothing, however, to prevent a different contribution rate—either lower or higher.

Extension of Benefits

extension of benefits

When coverage is terminated rather than continued, most employer-purchased medical expense contracts have an *extension of benefits* for any covered employee or dependent who is totally disabled at the time of termination. The disability must have resulted from an illness or injury that occurred while the person was covered under the contract. Generally, the same level of benefits is available as before termination. Although some contracts cover only expenses associated with the same cause of disability, other contracts cover any expenses that would have been paid under the terminated coverage, regardless of cause. The extension of benefits generally ceases after 12 months or when the individual is no longer totally or continuously disabled, whichever comes first.

Conversion

Except when termination results from the failure to pay any required premiums, medical expense contracts usually contain (and are often required to contain) a conversion provision, whereby most covered persons whose group coverage terminates are allowed to purchase individual medical expense coverage without evidence of insurability and without any limitation of benefits for preexisting conditions. Conversion provisions are rare in dental insurance contracts.

Covered persons commonly have 31 days from the date of the group coverage's termination to exercise this conversion privilege, and coverage is then effective retroactively to the date of termination. This conversion privilege is typically given to any employee who has been insured for at least 3 months, and it permits the employee to convert his or her own coverage as well as any dependent coverage. In addition, a spouse or child whose dependent coverage ceases for any other reason may also be eligible for conversion (for example, a spouse who divorces or separates, and children who reach age 19).

A person who is eligible for both the conversion privilege and the right to continue the group insurance coverage under COBRA has two choices when eligibility for coverage terminates. He or she can either elect to convert under the provisions of the policy or elect to continue the group coverage. If a person makes the latter choice, COBRA rules specify that he or she must again be eligible to convert to an individual policy within the usual conversion period

---

Conversion Privilege

- Requires no evidence of insurability
- Provides full coverage of preexisting conditions
- Allows 31 days for conversion
- Coverage retroactive to start of 31-day period
- Includes right to convert dependents' coverage
- May not be available to anyone covered by Medicare
- May not be available if conversion would result in overinsurance

(31 days) after the maximum continuation-of-coverage period ceases. Policy provisions may also make the conversion privilege available to persons whose coverage terminates prior to the end of the maximum continuation period.

The insurance company or other provider of the medical expense coverage has the right to refuse to issue a conversion policy to anyone (1) who is covered by Medicare or (2) whose benefits under the converted policy, together with similar benefits from other sources, would result in overinsurance according to the insurance company's standards. These similar benefits may be found in other coverages that the individual has (either group or individual coverage) or for which the individual is eligible under any group arrangement.

The use of the word *conversion* is often a misnomer. In actuality, a person whose coverage terminates is given only the right to purchase a contract on an individual basis at individual rates. Most Blue Cross and Blue Shield plans and some HMO plans offer a conversion policy that is similar or identical to the terminated group coverage. Insurance companies may, however, offer a conversion policy (or a choice of policies) that contains a lower level of benefits than existed under the former employer-provided coverage.

Some plans offer a conversion policy that is written by another entity. For example, an HMO might enter into a contractual arrangement with an insurance company. In some cases, the HMO and insurance company are commonly owned or have a parent-subsidiary relationship.

Self-funded plans, which are exempt from state laws that mandate a conversion policy, may still provide such a benefit. Rather than providing coverage directly to the terminated employee, an agreement is made with an insurance company or other provider of medical expense coverage to make a policy available.

Group-to-Individual Portability

The Health Insurance Portability and Accountability Act (HIPAA) makes it easier for individuals who lose employer-provided medical expense coverage to find alternative coverage in the individual marketplace. The purpose of the federal legislation is to encourage states to adopt their own mechanisms to achieve this goal, and most states have complied. The federal rules apply in a state only if the state does not have its own plan. The state alternative must do all the following:

- provide a choice of health insurance coverage to all eligible individuals
- impose no preexisting-conditions restrictions
- include at least one policy form of coverage that is either comparable to comprehensive health coverage offered in the individual marketplace or comparable to, or a standard option of, coverage available under the group or individual laws of the state

If a state fails to adopt an alternative to federal regulation, then insurance companies, HMOs, and other health plan providers in the individual marketplace are required to make coverage available on a guaranteed-issue basis to individuals with 18 or more months of creditable coverage, whose most recent coverage was under a group health plan. However, coverage does not have to be provided to an individual who has other health insurance or who is eligible for COBRA coverage, Medicare, or Medicaid. No preexisting-conditions exclusions can be imposed. Health insurers have three options for providing coverage to eligible individuals:

- They may offer every health insurance policy they offer in the state.
- They may offer their two most popular policies in the state, based on premium volume.
- They may offer a low-level and a high-level coverage, as long as they contain benefits that are similar to other coverage the insurer offers in the state.

Rules similar to those described in chapter 12 for group health insurance coverage require the renewal of individual coverage.

TYPES OF POLICIES AVAILABLE

A variety of medical expense policies is available in the individual marketplace. These can be purchased from insurance companies and, in some cases, from managed care organizations. Some of these policies provide broad coverage; other policies provide more limited coverage. It should also be pointed out that many associations, such as AARP and professional societies, have programs through which their members can obtain coverage.

Individual Major Medical Policies

Many insurance companies offer major medical insurance in the individual marketplace. In some cases, these are traditional indemnity policies; covered persons have complete freedom to choose any medical provider and have the same level of benefits paid. In other cases, the policies are actually individual PPO coverage, with a lower level of benefits if services are received from providers outside the PPO network. With a few exceptions, such as those mentioned below, the coverage available is very similar to what is found under employer-provided medical expense plans.

Unlike employer-provided coverage, for which an employee must accept the plan limits as determined by the employer, the purchaser of individual coverage has some choices to make. The most frequent choice is the selection of the annual deductible. The number and dollar amount of options vary by company, but a set of choices ranging from $150 to $2,500 is quite common. Most policies are sold with deductibles of $250, $500, or $1,000. A few insurers offer major medical contracts with very high deductibles, ranging from a low of $10,000 or $20,000 to a high of $1 million. These policies also have very high lifetime maximums. Some insureds pay the deductible amounts out of their own pockets. However, such "catastrophic" insurance is often used as an umbrella or excess major medical policy to fill gaps after an underlying medical expense plan reaches its maximum limits. Some insureds also use catastrophic insurance as supplementary coverage when their managed care plan excludes or limits nonnetwork benefits.

Some policies have a maximum lifetime benefit of $1 million or $2 million; other policies have several options, which might vary from $250,000 to $5 million or more. With today's health care costs, it is questionable if a limit below $1 million qualifies as adequate coverage.

A similar choice might exist with respect to a policy's coinsurance percentage. Some companies' policies have the same coinsurance percentage for all contracts; other companies allow a choice. For example, one company lets the purchaser of a policy select whether the policy will pay 50, 80, 90, or 100 percent of covered expenses. The latter option is available only if the purchaser also selects a high deductible.

Some major medical policies cover prescription drugs like any other medical expenses; other policies impose limitations such as separate copayments, maximum annual benefits, or different coinsurance percentages. Still other policies make prescription drug coverage an optional benefit that must be added by the purchase of a policy rider.

Maternity coverage frequently requires the purchase of a separate rider for coverage. Benefits are often subject to a waiting period of 10 or 12 months. Benefits may also be paid at something less than their full level during the first year or two of coverage.

Individual policies are likely to have slightly less generous benefits than employer-provided coverage. For example, there may be more limited coverage for mental and nervous disorders. Because of state-mandated benefits, however, individual policies might provide broader coverage than major medical coverage that would exist under a self-funded, employer-provided plan. Examples in some states are coverage for acupuncture treatment or mammograms. It is such state mandates that encourage many employers to self-fund benefits because ERISA exempts noninsured plans from state insurance mandates.

HMO Coverage

Many HMOs sell individual coverage, which usually is identical to coverage offered to employers for their benefit plans. However, the emphasis on first-dollar coverage and preventive medicine often makes the HMO coverage more expensive than the coverage available under major medical policies. Some HMOs offer coverage only to persons who have lost employer-provided coverage from the same HMO. Other HMOs market their coverage to everyone; the premium is sometimes lower for persons who converted from employer-provided coverage. Although the situation is changing somewhat, HMOs have historically emphasized the marketing of coverage through employer plans and have marketed individual coverage less aggressively than insurance companies.

Medicare Supplement (Medigap) Policies

Chapter 7 is partially devoted to a discussion of the benefits available under Medicare. Although it is a program that provides significant benefits to many Americans, Medicare has several limitations that can lead to large out-of-pocket costs for some beneficiaries. The reasons for these costs include the following:

- a significant Part A deductible for each spell of illness
- no stop-loss limit for Part B expenses
- very limited coverage for treatment outside the United States
- very limited coverage for prescription drugs outside a hospital or skilled-nursing facility until Part D goes into effect

Estimates indicate that about two-thirds of Medicare recipients have some type of coverage to supplement Medicare; this group is split about equally between those with coverage provided by a former employer and those who purchase coverage in the individual marketplace. As mentioned in the previous chapter, employer-provided coverage for retirees may take the form of either a Medicare carve-out or a Medicare supplement.

medigap insurance

Medicare supplement insurance in the individual marketplace is frequently referred to as *medigap insurance*. As the name implies, the objective is to fill some of the gaps left after Medicare benefits have been exhausted. When originally developed, medigap plans were as diverse as the companies that sold them. This led to confusion in the marketplace and to questionable sales practices and duplications of coverage. As a result, the federal government began to take a greater interest in what was going on, and it eventually enacted legislation to deal with the structure and marketing of medigap plans.

In 1990, the medigap market became directly subject to federal regulation when Congress directed the National Association of Insurance Commissioners (NAIC) to develop a group of standardized medigap policies. Congress mandated several other features, including a 6-month open enrollment period, limited preexisting-conditions exclusions, prohibition of the sale of duplicate coverage, increased individual loss ratios, and guaranteed renewability.

Basic Benefits

The NAIC adopted 10 standard medigap plans; all 10 require including a core of specified basic benefits. States may approve, and insurers may offer, fewer than the 10 standard plans, but all states must permit the core benefits to be sold. Most states now permit the sale of all 10 plans, but a few limit the types sold, and a few states are not affected by the mandate because alternative standardized programs were already in place prior to the federal legislation.

The basic benefits that all plans must include consist of the following:

- hospitalization—the copayment or cost sharing of Part A benefits for the 61st through the 90th day of hospitalization and the 60-day lifetime reserve. In addition, coverage is extended for 365 additional days after Medicare benefits end.
- medical expenses—the Part B percentage participation for Medicare-approved charges for physicians' and medical services after a beneficiary has satisfied the Part B deductible
- blood—the payment for the first 3 pints of blood each year

Other Types of Benefits

Medigap plans that can be sold include, in addition to the basic benefits, an array of benefits that provide additional coverage for benefits included in Medicare or that add coverage for benefits not included in Medicare. These benefits include paying

- the Part A copayment for the 21st through the 100th day of skilled-nursing facility care
- the hospital inpatient Part A deductible for each benefit period
- the Part B deductible
- charges for physicians' and medical services that exceed the Medicare-approved amount (either 80 or 100 percent of these charges)
- 80 percent of the charges for emergency care in a foreign country (with several limitations)
- an at-home provider to give assistance with activities of daily living (ADLs) while a beneficiary qualifies for Medicare home health care benefits (with certain limitations)
- limited annual amounts for preventive care (flu shots, physicals, screening tests, and so forth)
- 50 percent of outpatient prescription drug charges after a $250 deductible with either a $1,250 or $3,000 calendar-year benefit limit. As explained later, this benefit will not be available after 2005.

The 10 medigap plans are illustrated in table 13-1. The policies available in the individual marketplace must be identified by the letters A through J. The most widely available Medicare supplement plans are A, C, D, and F. Plan A generally represents less than 5 percent of Medicare supplement sales, however. Plan F represents more than half, while plans C and D make up approximately a third of total sales. Medicare SELECT policies (described below), which are generally less available, represent no more than 10 percent of total Medicare supplement sales.

With two exceptions, insurance companies cannot offer policies that provide benefits that differ from these available options. The first exception is that the companies can offer two high-deductible medigap policies. These policies are otherwise identical to plans F and J. The deductible amount—$1,730 in 2005—is subject to annual changes based on the consumer price index.

Medicare SELECT policy

The second exception is for policies issued under the Medicare SELECT program, which has been in existence since 1994. A *Medicare SELECT policy* is one of the 10 standard medigap policies, but it can exclude or limit

TABLE 13-1
Medicare Supplement (Medigap) Policies

Benefits	A	B	C	D	E	F	G	H	I	J
Basic	X	X	X	X	X	X	X	X	X	X
Skilled-nursing facility (days 21–100)			X	X	X	X	X	X	X	X
Part A deductible		X	X	X	X	X	X	X	X	X
Part B deductible			X			X				X
Part B excess charges						100%	80%		100%	100%
Foreign travel emergency			X	X	X	X	X	X	X	X
At-home recovery				X			X		X	X
Preventive medical care					X					X
Prescription drugs (until 2006)								$1,250	$1,250	$3,000

benefits (except in emergencies) for medical services if they are not received from network providers. Medicare SELECT policies are issued by insurance companies as PPO products and by some HMOs. As a general rule, the cost of a Medicare SELECT policy is 15 to 25 percent less than the cost of a comparable medigap policy that does not use such preferred-provider networks. An insured who has a Medicare SELECT policy has the right to switch to a regular medigap policy the same company sells, as long as the new policy has equal or less coverage than the Medicare SELECT policy.

It should be pointed out that the rules for standardized policies apply to the individual marketplace. Group Medicare supplements that employers offer to their retirees are not considered medigap policies and may differ. In addition, three states—Massachusetts, Minnesota, and Wisconsin—had medigap programs prior to the NAIC standards. These programs were allowed to continue, and the policies issued are somewhat different from those previously described. However, they are required to contain the basic medigap benefits available in all other states.

Eligibility

Persons aged 65 or older may buy any available Medicare supplement policy, regardless of health status, at any time during the 6-month period after initial enrollment for Medicare Part B benefits. Insurance companies are allowed to exclude benefits for no more than 6 months because of preexisting conditions. Some policies, however, immediately provide benefits for preexisting conditions or have an exclusion period shorter than 6 months. If a person initially elects a managed care option in lieu of regular Medicare benefits, the person will be eligible to purchase a Medicare supplement policy, without evidence of insurability, if he or she leaves the managed care option during the first 12 months of coverage and returns to regular Medicare benefits. Similarly, a person who drops Medicare supplement coverage and elects a managed care option can regain Medicare supplement coverage if he or she decides to drop the managed care option during the first 12 months of coverage.

In addition, a person can obtain a medigap policy without evidence of insurability because of the termination of an employer-provided plan that supplements Medicare, or because a Medicare Advantage plan no longer provides coverage or the person loses eligibility by moving out of the plan's service area.

Changes in 2006

As chapter 7 explains, the Medicare Prescription Drug, Improvement, and Modernization Act adds a new prescription drug benefit program to Medicare that becomes effective January 1, 2006. Implementation of this program will affect the array of standard Medicare supplement plans just discussed. In addition, the act authorizes two new Medicare supplement plans with consumer-directed health plan features.

Beginning in 2006, insurance companies may no longer issue new Medicare supplement policies with drug benefits (plans H, I, and J). Persons already insured under these policies have several options. They may continue to renew them with drug benefits included as long as they do not enroll in the new Medicare prescription drug program. If they enroll in the program, they may keep their existing Medicare supplement policies in force, but the drug benefit will be eliminated and the premium adjusted accordingly. Alternatively, they can purchase another available Medicare supplement policy that has no drug benefit.

The two new Medicare supplement plans (also with no drug benefit), designated as plans K and L, provide the basic Medicare supplement benefits plus the Part A hospital deductible and skilled-nursing facility care for days 21 through 100. Compared to current Medicare supplement plans, plans K and L require cost sharing by the insured for certain covered services, subject to an out-of-pocket limit.

Plan K requires the insured to pay 50 percent of the following:

- Part A deductible
- daily copayment for days 21 through 100 of skilled-nursing facility care
- first three pints of blood
- percentage participation for Part B services

When the insured's out-of-pocket payments for these services plus the Part B deductible equal $4,000, Plan K will pay 100 percent of the self-responsible amounts for Medicare services for the rest of the calendar year. However, provider charges that exceed Medicare-approved amounts do not count toward the annual out-of-pocket limit.

Plan L is similar to Plan K except that the insured must pay 25 percent rather than 50 percent. In addition, the out-of-pocket limit is $2,000.

Other Individual Health Insurance Coverages

Several other forms of health insurance coverage are relevant to the discussion of individual medical expense insurance. This section focuses on dental, temporary medical, international travel medical, hospital-surgical, hospital indemnity, and specified disease policies available in the individual insurance market.

Dental Insurance

Most dental coverages are offered through group contracts under employer-provided plans. Individual policies are available, but they are not widely purchased because of their relatively high cost in relation to the maximum benefits available. Individual dental coverages are similar in most aspects to the employer-provided benefits described in the previous chapter. However, they are more likely to provide the following:

- lower maximum benefits per calendar year for all services with lower internal benefit limits for specified services, such as orthodontia, if offered
- higher patient copayments
- longer waiting periods for specified basic and major dental services

Coverage is sometimes made available for an additional premium under individual major medical policies.

Temporary Medical Insurance

temporary medical insurance

Temporary medical insurance (sometimes called short-term medical insurance) generally provides coverage for periods between 30 days and one year to under-age-65 individuals and their dependents who are between permanent medical plans. This market includes people who are

- between jobs
- graduating from college
- waiting for group coverage to become effective
- dependents who are no longer eligible under a parent's plan
- temporary or seasonal employees

These plans are quite similar to individual major medical policies; applicants usually have a choice of deductibles and coinsurance percentages. These plans are nonrenewable, but an individual may purchase an additional policy beyond the original policy period if he or she is insurable, and any condition that occurred during prior coverage will be considered a preexisting condition under subsequent coverage periods. Some companies do not limit the number of additional periods for which coverage is available; other companies impose a maximum period of total coverage such as one year.

International Travel Medical Insurance

international travel medical insurance

International travel medical insurance is available for international travelers. U.S. citizens traveling abroad, foreign nationals traveling anywhere internationally (such as Canadians who winter in the United States), and recent immigrants to the United States may purchase some form of this coverage. In addition to vacation travelers, this market includes employees of domestic, international, and multinational corporations that require their employees to travel abroad, missionary groups, and intercultural and student exchange programs.

The period of coverage can range from a minimum of 15 days to a maximum of one year; optional renewal of some policies is up to 5 years. Benefits cover the expenses of inpatient and outpatient hospitalizations as well as medical and related services. Deductibles may be selected from a range of $100 to $2,500. Coinsurance levels are frequently available at 80 percent up to a specific dollar amount—$5,000, for example—with a benefit payment of 100 percent thereafter to the policy maximum. Such maximums may range from $50,000 to as high as $1 million. The expense of repatriating mortal remains in the event of death and medical evacuation to a person's home country for more suitable treatment or after an extended hospitalization are usually covered. Coverage typically ceases when a person returns to his or her home country.

Generally, the health-related benefits are folded into a broader policy covering many non-health-related travel contingencies, and they may also provide assistance in making arrangements to obtain covered services.

Hospital-Surgical Policies

hospital-surgical policy

Hospital-surgical policies provide coverage for a limited number of days of hospitalization, and the daily benefit can be less than the cost of semiprivate accommodations. Surgical benefits are usually paid on a fee-schedule basis. Depending on the policy, benefits may be available for expenses associated with physician's visits, maternity, and extended care facilities.

Such policies are typically inadequate for prolonged sicknesses, serious accidents, or the significant medical expenses that can arise outside a hospital setting. Although this type of medical policy is obviously better than no medical expense coverage, it is no substitute for a major medical policy. Purchasers of hospital-surgical policies are generally lower-income individuals and families who are unlikely to be financial planning clients.

Hospital Indemnity, Specific Disease, and Critical Illness Insurance

Three types of medical expense insurance are designed to supplement the benefits available under principal policies of medical expense insurance. These policies—hospital indemnity insurance, specified disease insurance, and critical illness insurance—share certain characteristics. They help the insured to face the significant additional financial consequences of a serious episode of illness or injury by providing direct cash payments, usually made without regard to other coverages. These payments may be used for

- out-of-pocket expenses of medical treatment left uncovered by even a comprehensive medical plan
- associated nonmedical expenses such as travel, lodging, meals, child care, and loss of income

Hospital indemnity insurance, specified disease insurance, and critical illness insurance are no substitute for adequate medical expense and disability income insurance. And if medical expense and disability income coverages are adequate, there are many financial planners who question whether such supplemental policies are necessary, particularly if a person has appropriate financial reserves for emergencies.

**hospital indemnity
insurance**

Hospital Indemnity Insurance. *Hospital indemnity insurance* gives the insured a fixed daily cash benefit during a covered hospitalization. A spouse or dependent child is usually eligible for coverage, although benefits may be reduced.

The policy provides daily benefits in the event of hospital confinement in a specified dollar amount (such as $150 per day) for a defined period (such as 90 days). These additional benefits are available as a standard feature or as a rider:

- a lump-sum payment on the first day of hospital confinement
- an intensive care benefit, such as $100, for a specified number of days in addition to the standard daily payment
- payment for emergency room and related physician services due to an illness or accident, with limitations on duration or expense per event or per year
- daily payment for recovery after a qualified hospital stay
- an accidental death benefit

**specified disease
insurance**

Specified Disease Insurance. *Specified disease insurance* (also referred to as dread disease insurance) provides benefits to insured individuals and covered family members upon the diagnosis of, or medical events related to the treatment of, a disease named in the policy. It does not cover accidents or injuries. Specified disease insurance for cancer only was once the most prevalent form of this insurance. Today, however, most policies cover cancer in addition to other diseases, which might include many or all of the following:

- Addison's disease
- amyotrophic lateral sclerosis
- botulism
- Budd-Chiari syndrome
- cystic fibrosis
- diphtheria
- encephalitis
- poliomyelitis
- Q fever
- rabies
- Reye's syndrome
- rheumatic fever
- Rocky Mountain spotted fever
- sickle-cell anemia

- histoplasmosis
- Legionnaires' disease
- lupus erythematosus
- malaria
- meningitis
- multiple sclerosis
- muscular dystrophy
- myasthenia gravis
- osteomyelitis

- Tay-Sachs disease
- tetanus
- toxic shock syndrome
- trichinosis
- tuberculosis
- tularemia
- typhoid fever
- undulant fever
- whooping cough

Specified disease policy benefits vary widely. Benefit provisions may utilize a combination of three payment structures: per-day or per-service, expense-incurred, or a lump-sum payment. Benefits are contingent on a diagnosis of the specified disease, but payments will cover the first day of care or confinement even though the diagnosis is made at some later date. This retroactive application of benefits usually applies to relevant services received within 90 days prior to the diagnosis. Table 13-2 presents a summary of illustrative benefits.

TABLE 13-2
Specified Disease Insurance: Summary of Selected Benefits

Service	Benefit
Hospital confinement	$300 daily for up to 90 days; $600 daily in coronary or intensive care unit up to 30 days
Surgery	Up to $7,500 per fee schedule
Anesthesia	Up to 25 percent of the surgical benefit
Physician's attendance	Actual charges up to $35 per day for in-hospital visits
Chemotherapy, radiation, immunotherapy, or radio-active isotopes therapy	50 percent of the first $50,000 of charges and 100 percent of the next $100,000, limited to $125,000 per calendar year
Experimental treatment	Up to $25,000 for experimental bone marrow transplant and $2,500 for donor-related expenses plus transportation
Transportation and lodging	Up to $50 per day for lodging, mileage, or coach airfare for travel for insured and companion (each)
Ambulance	Actual charges for an ambulance to the hospital and up to $5,000 for air ambulance
Artificial limbs and prostheses	Actual charges with lifetime maximum of $2,000 per insured person
Equipment	Up to $1,000 per calendar year for rental or purchase

Specified disease policies frequently offer a first-occurrence benefit that pays a one-time amount for each covered person who receives a diagnosis of internal cancer. The amount may range from $1,000 to as high as $50,000 or more.

critical illness insurance

Critical Illness Insurance. *Critical illness insurance* (sometimes referred to as serious illness insurance) is a relatively new form of supplemental medical insurance that provides a substantial one-time lump-sum cash benefit for a listed critical illness. Some of these conditions result from injury as well as disease and include specified major surgeries.

The applicant selects a maximum benefit amount, which can range from $10,000 to several hundred thousand dollars. The maximum benefit is payable only once—upon the first diagnosis of a condition or specified surgical treatment that it is covered. Each covered condition and surgical treatment is explicitly defined in the policy. Typically, the maximum benefit is payable for the following medical conditions or major surgery:

- Alzheimer's disease
- blindness
- life-threatening cancer
- deafness
- heart attack
- major organ transplant
- multiple sclerosis
- paralysis
- renal failure
- stroke

The policy may also provide a lesser benefit, such as 25 percent of the maximum benefit, for each of the following:

- initial coronary angioplasty (surgical treatment)
- initial coronary artery bypass (surgical treatment)
- initial diagnosis of cancer in its original site (other than skin cancer)

The percentage payment of the maximum benefits for the above conditions is payable only once; the maximum benefit is reduced by the amount paid, and the premium is also reduced accordingly. The policyowner is notified of the new maximum amount and the new premium. The policy terminates on the date the maximum benefit amount is paid under the terms of the policy.

INSURING THE UNHEALTHY

Historically, persons with a preexisting medical condition had a difficult time obtaining individual medical expense coverage. If the medical condition was severe, insurers would often decline coverage. If the medical condition was less severe, insurers might write coverage on a nonstandard basis by doing one or more of the following: charging an additional premium, excluding the condition, or imposing a waiting period before benefits would be payable for the condition.

Over time, the ability of the unhealthy to obtain coverage has improved significantly. If there is prior employer-provided coverage, federal legislation like COBRA and HIPAA eliminates the availability, but not necessarily the affordability, problem for many persons. States have also increasingly addressed the issue of access to individual medical expense coverage. Some of these state actions, such as the mandate of a conversion provision in group medical expense contracts, date back many years. In addition, some Blue Cross and Blue Shield plans, in return for preferential regulatory and tax status, offer periodic enrollment periods when normal medical underwriting requirements are reduced or waived.

In more recent years, more than half of the states have established some type of high-risk pool, whereby anyone turned down for medical expense coverage in the normal marketplace can obtain coverage through the pool. Although these pools vary among the states, basic major medical coverage is usually available, but benefits for preexisting conditions are often subject to waiting periods. Premiums tend to be higher than regular medical expense insurance, but state subsidies keep premiums below the level needed to fully cover expenses and claims costs.

The best way to find out about the options for insuring an unhealthy person is to contact the insurance department of the state where that person resides.

CONSUMER-DIRECTED MEDICAL EXPENSE PLANS

As mentioned in chapter 12, one approach to consumer-directed medical expense plans is the use of savings accounts. Two techniques that take this approach are Archer medical savings accounts (Archer MSAs) and health savings accounts (HSAs). The ability to establish new Archer MSAs will be phased out, and HSAs have been designed as their replacements. Individuals can establish Archer MSAs and HSAs. Employers can also establish them for the benefit of the individual employees. If an employee changes employers or leaves the workforce, the savings account (but not necessarily the underlying insurance plan) remains with the individual.

Archer Medical Savings Accounts

HIPAA provides favorable tax treatment for medical savings accounts (MSAs) under a pilot project that began on January 1, 1997, and continues through 2005. In 2001, these MSAs were given the name Archer MSAs. During this period, the act allows for the establishment of up to 750,000 Archer MSAs. However, fewer than 100,000 have actually been established despite great initial enthusiasm about their potential success. No more Archer MSAs can be established after 2005, but those that are in existence at the end of 2005 can remain in effect.

During the first 6 years of this pilot project, Archer MSAs were evaluated and debated. With the basic concept receiving strong support from the insurance industry and the more conservative members of Congress, health savings accounts (HSAs) became successors to Archer MSAs as part of the Medicare Prescription Drug, Improvement, and Modernization Act of 2003. HSAs and how they differ from Archer MSAs are discussed later.

General Nature

Archer MSA

An *Archer MSA* is a personal savings account from which unreimbursed medical expenses, including deductibles, percentage participation, and co-payments, can be paid. Coverage can be self-only or include family members. The Archer MSA must be in the form of a tax-exempt trust or custodial account established in conjunction with a high-deductible health plan (HDHP). (HDHPs are discussed later in this chapter.) An Archer MSA is established with a qualified trustee or custodian in much the same way that an IRA is established. Some insurers that sell HDHPs for use with Archer MSAs also market the Archer MSA accounts; other insurers leave it to the purchasers of HDHPs to establish their Archer MSAs with other institutions.

Eligibility

Two types of individuals are eligible to establish and maintain Archer MSAs:

- an employee (or spouse of an employee) of a small employer (generally one with fewer than 50 employees) who obtains self-only or family coverage through a high-deductible health plan sponsored by that employer
- a self-employed person (or spouse of a self-employed person) maintaining an individual or family high-deductible health plan covering that individual. These persons need to seek out a custodian or trustee for their Archer MSAs.

An HDHP, for purposes of Archer MSA participation, is a plan that has the following deductibles and annual out-of-pocket limitations. These amounts are for 2005 and subject to inflation adjustments:

- In the case of individual coverage, the deductible must be at least $1,750 and cannot exceed $2,650. The maximum annual out-of-pocket expenses cannot exceed $3,500.
- In the case of family coverage, the deductible must be at least $3,500 and cannot exceed $5,250. The maximum annual out-of-pocket expenses cannot exceed $6,450.

The deductible must apply to all medical expenses the plan covers, including preventive care.

An insurance company or a managed care organization, such as an HMO, can write a high-deductible plan. Currently, insurance companies write high-deductible plans, sometimes in the form of traditional major medical products but usually as PPO products. No HMOs have yet established high-deductible plans.

A high-deductible plan can be part of a cafeteria plan, but the Archer MSA must be established outside the cafeteria plan.

With some exceptions, a person who is covered under an HDHP is denied eligibility for an Archer MSA if he or she is covered under another health plan that does not meet the definition of a high-deductible plan but provides any benefits that the HDHP covers. The exceptions include coverage for accident, disability, dental care, vision care, and long-term care as well as liability insurance, insurance for a specified disease or illness, and insurance that pays a fixed amount per period of hospitalization.

Contributions

Either the account holder of an Archer MSA or the account holder's employer, but not both, may make a contribution to an Archer MSA. If the employer makes a contribution, even one below the allowable limit, the account holder may not make a contribution. Contributions must be in the form of cash.

Contributions by an employer are tax deductible to the employer and are not included in an employee's gross income or subject to Social Security and other employment taxes. Employee contributions are deductible in computing adjusted gross income. As with IRAs, individuals' contributions must generally be made by April 15 of the year following the year for which the contributions are made.

The amount of the annual tax-deductible contribution to an employee's account is limited to 65 percent of the policy deductible for the health coverage if the Archer MSA is for an individual. The figure is 75 percent if an Archer MSA covers a family. If each spouse has an Archer MSA and one or both of the Archer MSAs provide family coverage, the aggregate contribution is equal to 75 percent of the deductible for the family coverage with the lower deductible. The contribution is split equally between the two persons unless they agree to a different division.

The actual Archer MSA contribution that can be deducted in a tax year is limited to 1/12 of the annual amount, as described in the previous paragraph, times the number of months that an individual is eligible for Archer MSA participation. For example, assume that the deductible under an individual's health plan is $1,800, The maximum annual contribution to the Archer MSA is then 65 percent of this amount, which is $1,170, and the monthly amount is $97.50. If the individual is covered under a high-deductible plan only for the first 8 months of the year, then the annual deductible contribution is eight times $97.50, or $780. Note, however, that there are no requirements that contributions be made on a monthly basis or at any particular time. In this example, the full $1,170 could have been made early in the year. The amount over $780 would then be an excess contribution.

An excess contribution occurs to the extent that contributions to an Archer MSA exceed the deductible limits or are made for an ineligible person. Any excess contribution made by the employer is included in the employee's gross income. In addition, account holders are subject to a 6 percent excise tax on excess contributions for each year these contributions are in an account. This excise tax can be avoided if the excess amount and any net income attributable to the excess amount are removed from the Archer MSA prior to the last day prescribed by law, including extensions, for filing the account holder's income tax return. The net income attributable to the excess contributions is included in the account holder's gross income for the tax year in which the distribution is made.

An employer that makes contributions to Archer MSAs is subject to a nondiscrimination rule that requires the employer to make comparable contributions for all employees who have Archer MSAs. However, full-time employees and part-time employees (those working fewer than 30 hours per week) are treated separately. The comparability rule requires that the employer contribute either the same dollar amount for each employee or the same percentage of each employee's deductible under the health plan. Failure to comply with this rule subjects the employer to an excise tax equal to 35 percent of the aggregate amount contributed to Archer MSAs during the period when the comparability rule was not satisfied.

Employer contributions belong to the employee and are nonforfeitable.

Account Growth

Unused Archer MSA balances carry over from year to year, and there is no prescribed period in which they must be withdrawn. Earnings on amounts in an Archer MSA are not subject to taxation as they accrue.

Distributions

An individual can take distributions from an Archer MSA at any time. The amount of the distribution can be any part or all of the account balance. Subject to some exceptions, distributions of both contributions and earnings are excludible from an account holder's gross income if used to pay medical expenses of the account holder and the account holder's family, as long as other sources of insurance do not pay these expenses. For the most part, the eligible medical expenses are the same ones that would be deductible, ignoring the 7.5 percent of adjusted gross income limitation, if the account holder itemized his or her tax deductions. Tax-free withdrawals are permitted for the purchase of long-term care insurance, COBRA continuation coverage, or health coverage while an individual receives unemployment compensation. However, tax-free withdrawals are not otherwise permitted for the purchase of health insurance. In addition, in any year a contribution is made to an Archer MSA, tax-free withdrawals can be made to pay the medical expenses of only those persons who were eligible for coverage under an Archer MSA at the time the expenses were incurred. For example, Archer MSA contributions cannot be withdrawn tax free to pay the unreimbursed medical expenses of an account holder's spouse who is covered under a health plan of his or her employer that is not a high-deductible plan.

Distributions for reasons other than paying eligible medical expenses are included in an account holder's gross income and subject to a 15 percent penalty tax unless certain circumstances exist. The penalty tax is not levied if the distribution is made after the account holder turns 65 or because of the account holder's death or disability. In addition, the penalty tax does not apply to funds rolled over to a new Archer MSA as long as the rollover is done within 60 days. Transfers of Archer MSA accounts as a result of divorce are also tax free.

Effect of Retirement

Individuals who retire retain ownership of balances in their Archer MSAs. Distributions can be taken under the tax rules as previously described, but no additional contributions can be made.

Retirees under age 65 may still wish to participate in a consumer-directed health plan. They are eligible to establish health savings accounts, which are discussed later in this chapter. They can also roll over Archer MSA balances to such a newly established account.

Estate Tax Treatment

Upon death, the remaining balance in an Archer MSA is includible in the account holder's gross estate for estate tax purposes. If the beneficiary of the account is a surviving spouse, the Archer MSA belongs to the spouse and he or she can deduct the account balance in determining the account holder's gross estate. The surviving spouse can then use the Archer MSA for his or her medical expenses. If the beneficiary is anyone else, or if no beneficiary is named, the Archer MSA ceases to exist.

Health Savings Accounts

health savings account (HSA)

In addition to providing prescription drug coverage for older Americans, the Medicare Prescription Drug, Improvement, and Modernization Act established the *health savings account (HSA)*. Like Archer MSAs, HSAs are savings accounts for use with high-deductible medical expense plans and from which certain unreimbursed medical expenses can be paid. They are designed to be successors to Archer MSAs, and the two have many features in common. They also have some notable differences that make them more attractive than Archer MSAs and available to a much larger pool of consumers. While there is considerable interest in these products among health insurers, their development is proceeding cautiously. Employers, who are expected to take the lead in establishing these new arrangements, are evaluating how HSAs fit into their health benefit programs. HSAs could have been established as early as 2004, but because employer plans are often on a calendar-year basis, 2005 is the earliest that many employers can establish medical expense plans that incorporate HSAs. It is also the first year that many insurers will make HSA products available directly to individuals.

Although they are similar to the Archer MSAs, HSAs raise a number of specific issues about their development and use. The Treasury Department continues to issue clarifications, known as "guidance," to address these issues. The following discussion focuses on how HSAs are similar to Archer MSAs and how they differ. It also incorporates many key points of the Treasury Department's guidance. Updated and detailed information from the Treasury Department is available from the government's Web site at www.treas.gov/offices/ public-affairs/hsa.

General Nature

Like an Archer MSA, an HSA is a personal savings account fully owned by the account holder. Its use can be limited to an individual or include dependents, and the account can be used to pay unreimbursed medical expenses. HSAs must be funded, and the funds are held by a qualified trustee or custodian under the same rules that apply to Archer MSAs.

Some of the many insurers that intend to sell HDHPs for use with HSAs also plan to market the HSAs. Other insurers will market only the HDHPs.

Eligibility

The eligibility rules for HSAs are much broader than those for Archer MSAs. HSAs can be established by employees, the self-employed, and anyone else who meets the following rules for qualification:

- The individual must be covered by a high-deductible health plan. That plan may be insured or self-insured if offered by an employer as long as it meets the criteria for a qualifying high-deductible plan.
- The individual is not eligible to be claimed as a dependent on another person's federal income tax return.
- With certain exceptions, the individual must not be covered by other health insurance. These exceptions are the same as those for Archer MSAs and include policies that provide coverage for specified disease or illness, a fixed payment for a period of hospitalization, accidents, disability, dental care, vision care, or long-term care.

Generally, an individual covered by Medicare (by attaining age 65 or disability) or receiving Veterans Administration benefits is considered as having another health plan and, therefore, may not contribute to an HSA. Nevertheless, an individual who is (1) eligible for Medicare but not enrolled or (2) eligible to receive medical benefits through the Veterans Administration but not receiving them may contribute to an HSA. Individuals covered by TRICARE (the insurance program for members of the uniformed services) are not eligible.

An employer can establish HSAs for its employees, or an individual (whether employed or not) may establish his or her own HSA.

High-Deductible Health Plan (HDHP)

For purposes of HSA participation, a high-deductible health plan is defined as having the following deductibles and annual out-of-pocket limitations for 2005:

- In the case of individual coverage, the deductible must be at least $1,000, and annual out-of-pocket expenses cannot exceed $5,100.
- In the case of family coverage, the deductible must be at least $2,000, and annual out-of-pocket expenses cannot exceed $10,200.

As with HDHPs for use with Archer MSAs, the above figures are subject to annual indexing for inflation. If these high-deductible plans use preferred-provider networks, they can have higher out-of-pocket limits for services provided outside the network, and any deductibles for nonnetwork services are not taken into account when determining the out-of-pocket limits specified above.

One point should be emphasized about the deductible for family coverage. It is not a family deductible as was described in the discussion on major medical insurance. In that situation, there is an individual deductible that applies to each family member as well as a separate deductible for the family. This is sometimes referred to as a stacked deductible, and policy benefits are paid for any family member once his or her deductible is satisfied, even if the family deductible has not been met.

In the case of a high-deductible policy used with an HSA, there will usually not be an individual deductible if a policy is written for a family. Rather, there will be a single deductible—referred to as a common deductible—that must be satisfied before any benefits are payable, even if all claims are for one family member. It is permissible, however, to use a stacked deductible, but only if the individual deductible is equal to at least the required HSA family deductible of $2,000. For example, a policy with an individual deductible of $2,500 and a family deductible of $5,000 is acceptable.

The following incurred expenses do not count toward the plan's required deductible and out-of-pocket limitations:

- out-of-pocket amounts, including deductibles, for services received from nonnetwork health care providers, if the plan uses a preferred-provider network
- amounts above a plan's reasonable specific service or lifetime maximums
- amounts in excess of reasonable and customary fees
- penalties for failure to obtain a plan-required certification

Nevertheless, copayments count toward the out-of-pocket limit, even if the plan does not consider copayments as contributing toward the satisfaction of the deductible.

Preventive Care

Generally, an HDHP cannot provide benefits before the deductible is satisfied, but there is an exception for benefits for preventive care. An HDHP may provide benefits for the following preventive care services before the insured satisfies the plan's required high deductible:

- annual physicals, immunizations, and screening services
- routine prenatal and well-child care
- tobacco cessation programs and obesity weight-loss programs
- employee assistance, disease management, or wellness programs
- treatment of a related condition that is incidental or ancillary to a preventive care service or screening, such as removal of polyps during a diagnostic colonoscopy

- drugs or medications taken by a person who has developed risk factors for a disease before the disease manifests itself or to prevent the reoccurrence of a disease from which the person has recovered

An example of the last item above is the drug treatment of high cholesterol to prevent heart disease, or the treatment of recovered heart attack or stroke victims with medications to prevent a recurrence. Preventive care generally does not include treatment of existing conditions.

Contributions

Contributions to an HSA for a self-employed or unemployed individual are made directly by that person. For an employed person, contributions can be made by the employer, the employee, or a combination of the two. Family members may also make contributions to an HSA on behalf of other family members. Unlike Archer MSAs, contributions to the HSA can also be made under a cafeteria plan.

Contributions by an individual are deductible for federal income tax purposes even if the individual does not itemize deductions. Employer contributions are deductible by the employer and do not represent taxable income to an employee. Generally, if an employer contributes, the same nondiscrimination rule for comparable contributions that was described for Archer MSAs applies. However, the comparability rules do not apply to contributions made through cafeteria plans. An employer may contribute to the HSA of each eligible employee in an amount equal to the amount of the employee's HSA contribution or a percentage of that amount.

The maximum annual contribution to an HSA in 2005 is $2,650 for an individual and $5,250 for families. These amounts are subject to annual indexing for inflation and are not a function of the deductible amount for the high-deductible policy. The amounts, however, are aggregate amounts that apply to all HSAs and Archer MSAs that an individual or family might have.

Individuals aged 55 or older are also permitted an additional annual contribution of up to $600 in 2005. This amount will increase by $100 per year until it reaches $1,000 in 2009. If both a husband and wife are aged 55 or older, the additional contribution is available to each of them.

Account balances from Archer MSAs can be rolled over to HSAs on a tax-free basis.

As with Archer MSAs, the tax-deductible contribution is limited to 1/12 of these amounts for each month of participation in an HSA. However, the full contribution for a year can be made at any time. Excess contributions are treated in the same manner as for Archer MSAs.

Account Growth

Unused amounts in an HSA accumulate on a tax-free basis and carry over to subsequent years without limit. The size of an HSA balance carried over from prior years has no effect on the amount of a current year's contribution.

Distributions

Distributions from HSAs are tax free as long as they are used to pay for qualified medical expenses. These medical expenses are the same as those described for Archer MSAs. Therefore, tax-free distributions can also be used to pay premiums for long-term care insurance, COBRA continuation coverage, and health insurance while an individual receives unemployment insurance. Distributions are deferrable to a taxable year other than the year in which the qualified expenses are incurred; there is no time limit on when a distribution must occur.

Even though contributions cannot be made after an individual reaches age 65 and becomes a Medicare beneficiary, tax-free distributions can still be used for qualified medical expenses, which include Medicare premiums and premiums for medical expense coverage under employer-sponsored plans. However, tax-free distributions cannot be used to pay premiums for Medicare supplement policies.

Distributions are permitted for other reasons, but they are subject to income taxation and possibly to a 10 percent penalty tax. The penalty tax does not apply in the case of distributions after an individual's death, disability, or the attainment of age 65.

Effect of Retirement

Retirees can continue HSAs that were established prior to retirement, and the rules for contributions and distributions are as previously described.

Retirees who did not have an HSA prior to retirement can establish one at that time as long as all the proper rules are satisfied. This HSA may present an opportunity for a retiree to reduce income taxes. The requirement of having a high-deductible plan, however, will probably negate this advantage if an individual has substantial medical expenses.

There are fees involved in establishing an HSA. These fees may affect any potential tax advantages if an HSA is established near the time of Medicare enrollment.

Example: Kathleen retired at age 60 from her job as an attorney. Her medical expense coverage had been under an Archer MSA and a high-deductible health plan. Her current account balance is $9,360. She enjoys excellent health and is in a high income tax bracket. She likes the concept of consumer-directed health plans and has decided to establish an HSA and to roll over her Archer MSA balance into this account. To be eligible for the HSA, she purchased a major medical policy with an annual deductible of $2,500. She plans to make the maximum allowable contribution to the HSA. For 2005, this is $2,650.

Estate Tax Treatment

Upon the account holder's death, the remaining balance in an HSA is treated in the same manner as the balance in an Archer MSA if a spouse is the beneficiary. If the beneficiary is anyone else, the beneficiary must include the fair market value of the account in his or her gross income for tax purposes.

POLICY PROVISIONS

Premiums

Premiums for individual health insurance policies can be paid annually, semiannually, quarterly, or possibly monthly. The total premiums for a year will be higher than the annual premium if paid in installments. Several factors may affect the level of premiums. These include age, sex, occupation, and whether the insured has certain avocations or is a smoker.

Most policies have a 30-day grace period. If the premium is paid during this period, the policy will continue in force with no lapse in coverage. If a premium is not paid within the grace period, the policy will lapse as of the beginning of the grace period.

Most policies contain a provision whereby a lapsed policy can be reinstated for some period of time after it lapses. Some insurers will automatically reinstate a policy if a premium is received within a short period of time following the grace period. Otherwise, the insurer may wish to reunderwrite the policy. No benefits are paid for losses that occur between the date of lapse and a policy's reinstatement. Accidental injuries sustained after the date of reinstatement are covered from the date of reinstatement. However, there is usually a 10-day waiting period before losses from sickness are covered.

Renewability

It is important to look at the provision in a medical expense policy regarding renewability. Because of the uncertain nature and cost of future medical claims, it is rare to find noncancelable policies, unless they provide very limited benefits. Many policies are guaranteed renewable to at least age 65 when a person qualifies for Medicare. Many policies, however, limit their obligation to continue coverage if the insurer decides to stop writing that particular type of insurance contract. Insurers that issue optionally renewable policies are required to give the policyowner advance notice of any intention not to renew, usually at least 30 days.

FEDERAL TAX TREATMENT

The tax situation for self-employed individuals is discussed in the previous chapter. Other individuals who itemize deductions are allowed to deduct most unreimbursed medical care expenses (including dental expenses) to the extent the total of these expenses exceeds 7.5 percent of adjusted gross income. Premiums paid for medical expense and dental insurance are included as an expense for purposes of this deduction. However, premiums for policies that pay a stated periodic payment to a person while hospitalized, regardless of benefits from other sources, are considered premiums for disability income insurance and are not deductible.

As a result of trade legislation passed in 2002, a tax credit is available to certain taxpayers. These include (1) individuals who are certified as having lost their jobs because of trade-related reasons, such as competition from foreign imports, and (2) individuals who are at least age 55 and receiving benefits from the Pension Benefit Guaranty Corporation. The credit is equal to 65 percent of the cost of the premium for continuing coverage under COBRA (and possibly for the purchase of certain other medical expense coverage) for an individual and his or her eligible family members. The credit, however, is not available to a taxpayer who has medical expense coverage under Medicare, Medicaid, or an employer-sponsored plan for which the employer pays at least 50 percent of the cost of the coverage.

As a general rule, benefits received from individually paid medical expense and dental insurance are not subject to income tax, even if they exceed expenses actually incurred. One exception includes benefits received for expenses that were deducted in prior years.

CHECKLIST FOR EVALUATING AND COMPARING MEDICAL EXPENSE INSURANCE

☐ What is the type of coverage?

___ Major medical
___ HMO
___ PPO

___ Point-of-service
___ Archer MSA or HSA
___ Other

☐ What is the annual policy premium?

☐ Are there any discounts for good health or healthy behaviors such as not smoking?

☐ Are there any preexisting conditions that are not covered? If so, for how long?

☐ To what extent is each of the following services covered? Identify any exclusions or limitations that apply to each service that will affect the client or family.

___ Inpatient hospital services
___ Outpatient surgery
___ Physician visits (in the hospital)
___ Office visits
___ Skilled-nursing care
___ Medical tests and X rays
___ Prescription drugs
___ Mental health care
___ Drug and alcohol abuse treatment
___ Home health care visits
___ Rehabilitation facility care
___ Physical therapy
___ Speech therapy
___ Hospice care
___ Maternity care
___ Chiropractic visits
___ Preventive care and checkups
___ Well-baby care
___ Dental care
___ Vision care

☐ Are there any lifetime maximum limits? If so, what are they?

☐ What is the annual deductible?

___ Per person
___ Per family

☐ What coinsurance or copayments apply?

    ___ After meeting deductible
    ___ Per office visit
    ___ For inpatient hospital care

☐ What is the stop-loss limit?

☐ What preauthorization or certification procedures must be met?

☐ If coverage is individually purchased, what are the provisions for renewal?

MINI-CASE: MARY AND SAM SCHULTZ

Mary and Sam Schultz are the parents of John Schultz, who has been the subject of earlier mini-cases. Sam is 64 and would like to retire from a job that he no longer enjoys. His employer provides no medical expense coverage for retirees. Mary, aged 62, has never worked outside the home and has been in frail health since suffering a stroke two years ago. She also has diabetes. Sam's health is excellent, and he rarely sees a doctor.

The Schultzes currently have medical expense protection under a PPO Sam's employer provides, and they have been very satisfied with the benefits that have been available for Mary's care.

Mary and Sam realize that adequate medical expense coverage after his retirement is a necessity. Although they are financially secure, their retirement income is not unlimited. Therefore, they would like to obtain adequate coverage in the most cost-effective manner.

Discuss the options available to Mary and Sam at each of the following times:

    a. before Sam is eligible for Medicare
    b. after Sam is eligible for Medicare but before Mary is eligible
    c. after Mary is eligible for Medicare

(See answer section for answers to mini-case.)

SOURCES FOR FURTHER IN-DEPTH STUDY

- For a discussion of continuing coverage after termination of employment, Beam, Burton T., Jr., *Group Benefits: Basic Concepts and Alternatives*, 10th ed., chapter 12, Bryn Mawr, PA: The American College Press, 2004. Phone 888-263-7265. Web site address www.theamericancollege.edu

- For a discussion of individual medical expense coverages:
  - Thomas P. O'Hare, *Individual Medical Expense Insurance*, 3d ed., Bryn Mawr, PA: The American College Press, 2004. Phone 888-263-7265. Web site address www.theamericancollege.edu
  - *Supplemental Health Insurance*, Washington, DC: Health Insurance Association of America, 1998. Phone 202-824-1600. Web site address www.hiaa.org

CHAPTER REVIEW

Answers to mini-case, review questions, and self-test questions start on page 793.

Key Terms

COBRA
qualified beneficiary
qualifying event
extension of benefits
medigap insurance
Medicare SELECT policy
temporary medical insurance

international travel medical
  insurance
hospital-surgical policy
hospital indemnity insurance
specified disease insurance
critical illness insurance
Archer MSA
health savings account (HSA)

Review Questions

13-1. COBRA requires that group health plans allow employees and certain beneficiaries to elect to have their current health coverage extended following a "qualifying event." Briefly describe the
  a. types of plans COBRA covers
  b. various qualifying events
  c. categories of qualified beneficiaries

13-2. Explain how the Health Insurance Portability and Accountability Act makes it easier for individuals who lose employer-provided medical expense coverage to find alternative coverage in the individual marketplace.

13-3. What are the basic benefits all Medicare supplement policies must include?

13-4. What are the eligibility criteria for Medicare supplement insurance?

13-5. Describe the following types of individual health insurance coverages:
  a. temporary medical insurance
  b. international travel medical insurance
  c. hospital-surgical policies
  d. hospital indemnity insurance

    e.   specified disease insurance

    f.   critical illness insurance

13-6. Who is eligible to establish an Archer MSA?

13-7. Explain the rules that apply to Archer MSAs with respect to
    a.   contributions
    b.   distributions

13-8. Who is eligible to establish an HSA?

13-9. How do HSAs differ from Archer MSAs?

13-10. Explain why insurers rarely issue medical expense policies on a noncancelable basis.

Self-Test Questions

T   F   13-1. The term *group health plan* as used for COBRA purposes is broad enough to include long-term care plans.

T   F   13-2. A qualified beneficiary can obtain COBRA coverage after a qualifying event without having to provide evidence of insurability.

T   F   13-3. COBRA coverage is automatic for qualified beneficiaries who lose their group health coverage because of a qualifying event.

T   F   13-4. The insurance company has the right to refuse conversion of group medical expense coverage for anyone who is covered under Medicare.

T   F   13-5. The HIPAA group-to-individual portability rules apply in a state only if the state does not have its own plan.

T   F   13-6. AARP and many professional societies have programs through which their members can obtain medical expense coverage.

T   F   13-7. The purchaser of an individual major medical policy has to select the annual deductible and lifetime maximum limit he or she wants in the policy.

T   F   13-8. ERISA requires that self-funded, employer-provided medical expense plans include state-mandated benefits.

T   F   13-9. HMO coverage for individuals is typically less expensive than an individual major medical policy.

T   F   13-10. Only 10 percent of Medicare recipients have some type of coverage to supplement Medicare.

T   F   13-11. Group Medicare supplements employers offer to their retirees may differ from individual Medicare supplement policies.

T   F   13-12. Insurance companies are allowed to permanently exclude benefits for preexisting conditions from their Medicare supplement policies.

T   F   13-13. Most specified disease insurance policies in the marketplace today cover only cancer.

T   F   13-14. More than half of the states have established some type of high-risk pool, whereby anyone turned down for medical expense coverage in the normal marketplace can obtain coverage through the pool.

T   F   13-15. Coverage under an Archer MSA can be limited to an individual or include dependents.

T   F   13-16. Both the account holder of an Archer MSA and the account holder's employer may make a contribution to the account.

T   F   13-17. A high-deductible health plan used with an HSA must apply the policy deductible to any preventive care the policy covers.

T   F   13-18. A surviving spouse who is the beneficiary of an HSA can use the account balance for his or her own medical expenses.

T   F   13-19. Individuals who itemize deductions for income tax purposes are allowed to deduct all unreimbursed medical expenses, regardless of their amount.

14

Disability Income Insurance

Learning Objectives

An understanding of the material in this chapter should enable the student to

14-1. Explain the need for and sources of disability income protection.

14-2. Briefly describe how sick-leave plans work.

14-3. Describe in detail the characteristics of group disability income plans.

14-4. Explain the income tax treatment of employer-provided disability income benefits.

14-5. Describe in detail the characteristics of individual disability income policies.

14-6. Describe the business uses of disability income insurance.

Chapter Outline

In terms of its financial effect on the family, long-term disability is more severe than death. In both cases, income ceases. In the case of long-term disability, however, family expenses—instead of decreasing because the family has one less member—may actually increase due to the cost of providing care for the disabled person. Financial planners need to understand the disability risk and the methods for managing this risk.

The purpose of disability income insurance is to partially (and sometimes totally) replace the income of persons who are unable to work because of sickness or accident. Any employee may miss a few days of work from time to time; however, there is a tendency to underestimate both the probability and potential severity of disabilities that last for longer periods. At all working ages, the probability of being disabled for at least 90 consecutive days is much greater than the chance of dying. About half of all employees will have a disability that lasts at least 90 days sometime during their working years, and one out of every 10 persons can expect to be permanently disabled before reaching age 65.

SOURCES OF COVERAGE

Disability income protection can come from several sources: social insurance programs, employer-provided benefits, and individually purchased policies. These sources are discussed in this chapter. Not discussed is an additional source of recovery often available to individuals who become temporarily or permanently disabled as the result of an off-the-job auto accident or some other nonoccupational occurrence caused by the negligence of another party. The disabled person may recover damages from the negligent party or his or her insurance company as the result of a settlement or court judgment. As discussed in chapter 11, this recovery may involve a lump-sum payment, a structured settlement, or both.

Social Insurance Programs

Several types of disability coverage under social insurance programs are discussed in chapter 7. For example, persons suffering injury or illness in the workplace will be covered under workers' compensation programs. Although benefits may be payable for life for total disabilities and may be as high as two-thirds of predisability income, benefits are subject to maximum dollar amounts that make them inadequate for all but lower-paid workers. Benefits of limited duration are also available in a few states under temporary disability laws.

Most employed persons are potentially eligible for disability benefits under the Social Security program if they are disabled longer than 5 months. However, the Social Security definition of disability is more restrictive than that in most individual or group insurance policies. In addition, benefits are likely to

---

Possible Sources of Disability Income Coverage

- Workers' compensation programs
- State temporary disability laws
- Social Security
- Employer-provided sick-leave plans
- Employer-provided short-term disability income insurance plans
- Employer-provided long-term disability income insurance plans
- Individual disability income insurance policies

be inadequate for many workers, particularly those with annual earnings over $30,000. In spite of these limitations, the Social Security program is the major source of disability income, with approximately 5 million disabled workers and over 1.5 million dependents annually collecting in excess of $60 billion in benefits.

Employer-Provided Benefits

Employer-provided income protection consists of two distinct types of plans:

short-term disability income plan

- *short-term disability income plans*, which provide benefits for a limited period of time, usually 6 months or less. Benefits may be provided under sick-leave plans, which are often uninsured, or under insured plans.

long-term disability income insurance

- *long-term disability income insurance*, which provides extended benefits (possibly for life) after an employee has been disabled for a period of time, frequently 6 months

Employers are less likely to provide employees with disability income benefits than with either life insurance or medical expense benefits. Still, it is estimated that at least three-quarters of all employees have some form of employer-provided short-term protection, either in the form of self-funded plans or insured short-term disability income insurance plans. However, only about one-third of employees have any type of employer-provided long-term protection other than Social Security.

The specific types of employer-provided coverage are discussed in a later section of this chapter.

Individual Disability Income Insurance

Many individuals have a need for disability income insurance that social insurance and employer-provided coverage do not meet. However, insurance companies that offer disability income policies are very concerned about overinsurance and the accompanying moral hazard, and, consequently, limit the amount of benefits relative to the individual's income. As a result, many individuals with coverage through their employers or other sources are ineligible for additional disability income protection.

Anyone who earns more than about $25,000 per year from gainful employment and is not already covered by private individual disability income insurance has a significant need for disability income protection. (Individual coverage is often not available to persons with an income below this amount.) Obviously, this includes the self-employed, business owners and partners, individual workers, and anyone who would have an inadequate income if he or she were to become disabled and unable to continue working for compensation.

Unfortunately, disability income insurance is not available for every occupation from every insurance company. Therefore, it is important for persons in many occupations and their financial planners to be aware of variations in the marketplace. For example, some companies do not insure persons in certain hazardous or unstable occupations for disability income; other insurers offer a special disability policy for these occupations; still other insurers offer their regular policy at higher-than-standard premium rates.

Furthermore, many corporate events can alter employer-provided disability income protection and therefore increase the need for individual protection. First, corporate mergers or acquisitions may result in a change in management and management philosophy, which may result in the termination of previously provided benefits. Second, bankruptcy or severe financial problems may prompt management to cut back on such employee benefits as disability income insurance. Third, the insurance company that provides disability income protection through the employer could terminate the policy; if the employer is unable to find another insurance company willing to write the coverage, disability protection ceases. Even if coverage could be obtained from another insurer, management may decide not to seek replacement coverage.

Because most employers do not provide long-term disability income insurance, it is quite possible that an employee who leaves a job in which he or she had disability income protection may not be provided with that protection by a new employer. Such job changes create a definite need for individual disability income protection. One advantage of relying on individual protection rather than on employer-provided group protection is that the individual is not subject to termination of coverage at the whim of corporate decision makers. Also, individual coverage is portable and can go with the insured to new geographic locations and down new career paths.

Disability income coverages are also important for partnerships and closely held corporations. Such coverages can provide the financial means for healthy partners or stockholders to purchase the ownership interest of the disabled partner or stockholder. Business enterprises can also use disability income to pay business overhead and to replace lost income or revenue that results from a key person's disability.

Individual disability income policies are discussed following the sections on employer-provided coverage.

SICK-LEAVE PLANS

Employers provide short-term disability benefits to employees through two approaches: sick-leave plans and short-term disability income insurance

sick-leave plan

plans. *Sick-leave plans* (often called salary continuation plans) are usually uninsured and generally fully replace lost income for a limited period of time, starting on the first day of disability. In contrast, short-term disability income insurance plans (which are covered in the next section of this chapter) usually provide benefits that replace only a portion of an employee's lost income and often contain a waiting period before benefits start, particularly for sickness.

Eligibility

Almost all sick-leave plans are limited to permanent full-time employees. Most plans also require an employee to satisfy a short probationary period (commonly one to 3 months) before being eligible for benefits. Sick-leave plans may also be limited to certain classes of employees such as top management or nonunion employees.

Benefits

Most sick-leave plans are designed to provide benefits equal to 100 percent of an employee's regular pay. Most plans, however, provide a reduced level of benefits after an initial period of full pay.

Several approaches are used to determine the duration of benefits. The most traditional approach credits eligible employees with a certain amount of sick leave such as 10 days each year. Most plans with this approach allow employees to accumulate unused sick leave up to a maximum amount, which rarely exceeds 6 months (sometimes specified as 180 days or 26 weeks).

Another approach bases the duration of benefits on an employee's length of service. For example, an employee with less than 3 months of service may get no sick days. After this limited period, the employee may get 5 days during the next year, with the number of days increasing to 30 with 10 years of service.

An alternative to this approach provides benefits for a uniform length of time (such as 26 weeks) to all employees, except possibly those with short periods of service. However, benefits are reduced to less than full pay after some period of time that is related to an employee's length of service. For example, an employee with 2 years of service might get 4 weeks of sick leave at full pay and 22 additional weeks at half pay. After each additional year of service, the number of weeks at full pay increases by 4, until all 26 weeks would be available at full pay after 6 years of service.

Most sick-leave plans are coordinated with social insurance programs. For example, if an employee is entitled to 100 percent of pay and receives 60 percent of pay as a workers' compensation benefit, the sick-leave plan pays the remaining 40 percent.

INSURED GROUP DISABILITY INCOME PLANS

As previously mentioned, insured group disability income plans consist of two distinct products: short-term coverage and long-term coverage. In many respects, the contractual provisions of both short-term and long-term disability income contracts are the same or very similar. In other respects—notably, the eligibility requirements, the definition of disability, and the amount and duration of benefits—they differ significantly.

Eligibility

Many of the eligibility requirements in group disability income insurance plans are similar to those in other types of group insurance contracts. In addition to being in a covered classification, an employee must usually work full-time and be actively at work before coverage commences. Any requirements concerning probationary periods, insurability, and premium contributions must also be satisfied.

Disability income insurance plans frequently differ in both the classes of employees who are eligible for coverage and the length of the probationary period. Employers are more likely to provide short-term benefits to a wider range of employees, and it is not unusual for short-term plans to cover all full-time employees.

Long-term disability plans often limit benefits to salaried employees, because claims experience has traditionally been less favorable for hourly paid employees. Some long-term plans also exclude employees below a certain salary level, because this category of employees, like hourly paid employees, is considered to have a reasonable level of benefits under Social Security.

Long-term disability income plans tend to have longer probationary periods than short-term disability income plans. While the majority of short-term disability plans either have no probationary period or have a probationary period of 3 months or less, it is common for long-term disability plans to have

Common Eligibility Requirements for Group Disability Income Insurance

- Be a member of a covered class of employees.
- Work full-time.
- Be actively at work.
- Satisfy any probationary period.
- Show any required evidence of insurability.
- Authorize withholding of any required employee contributions.

probationary periods ranging from 3 months to one year. Whereas short-term plans require only that an employee be actively at work on the date he or she is otherwise eligible for coverage, long-term plans sometimes require that the employee be on the job for an extended period (such as 30 days) without illness or injury before coverage becomes effective.

Definition of Disability

Benefits are paid under disability income insurance contracts only if the employee meets the definition of disability as specified in the contract. Virtually all short-term disability income insurance contracts define disability as *the total inability of the employee to perform each and every duty of his or her regular occupation.* A small minority of contracts use a more restrictive definition, requiring that an employee be unable to engage in any occupation for compensation. Partial disabilities are usually not covered, but a few newer plans do provide benefits. In addition, the majority of short-term contracts limit coverage to nonoccupational disabilities because employees have workers' compensation benefits for occupational disabilities.

A few long-term disability income contracts use the same liberal definition of disability that is commonly used in short-term contracts, but the term *material duties* often replaces the term *each and every duty.* These are referred to as *own-occupation* definitions of disability. The majority of long-term disability contracts use a dual definition under which benefits are paid for some period of time (usually 24 or 36 months) as long as an employee is unable to perform his or her regular occupation. After that time, benefits are paid only if the employee is unable to engage in any occupation for which he or she is qualified by reason of training, education, or experience. The purpose of this combined definition is to require and encourage a disabled employee who becomes able after a period of time to adjust his or her lifestyle and earn a livelihood in another occupation.

own-occupation

A more recent definition of disability in some long-term contracts contains both an occupation test and an earnings test. Under the occupation test, a person is totally disabled if he or she meets the definition of disability as described in the previous paragraph. However, if a person does not satisfy the occupation test, he or she is still considered disabled as long as the person satisfies an earnings test—that is, his or her income has dropped by a stated percentage, such as 20 percent, because of injury or sickness. This newer definition makes a group insurance contract similar to an individual disability income policy that provides residual benefits.

The definition of disability in long-term contracts may differ from that in short-term contracts in several other respects. Long-term contracts are somewhat more likely to provide benefits for partial disabilities. However, the amount and duration of such benefits may be limited when compared with those for total disabilities, and the receipt of benefits is usually contingent on a previous period of total disability. In addition, most long-term contracts provide coverage for both occupational and nonoccupational disabilities. Finally, short-term contracts usually have the same definition of disability for all classes of employees. Some long-term contracts use different definitions for different classes of employees—one definition for most employees and a more liberal definition for executives or salaried employees.

Exclusions

Under certain circumstances, disability income benefits are not paid even if an employee satisfies the definition of disability. Common exclusions under both short-term and long-term disability income contracts specify that no benefits will be paid

- for any period during which the employee is not under the care of a physician
- for any disability caused by an intentionally self-inflicted injury
- unless the period of disability commenced while the employee was covered under the contract
- if (or to the extent that) benefits are payable under workers' compensation or similar laws

It was once common for disabilities resulting from pregnancy to be excluded. Such an exclusion is now illegal under federal law if an employer has 15 or more employees. Employers with fewer than 15 employees may still exclude pregnancy disabilities unless they are subject to state laws to the contrary.

Additional exclusions are often found in long-term contracts. These commonly deny benefits for disabilities resulting from

- war, whether declared or undeclared
- participation in an assault or felony. Some insurers have recently expanded this exclusion to include the commission of any crime.
- mental illness, alcoholism, or drug addiction. However, most contracts provide benefits for an employee who is confined in a hospital or institution that specializes in the care and treatment of such disorders; other contracts provide employees with benefits but limit their duration (such as for 24 months per disability).
- preexisting conditions

The exclusion for preexisting conditions is designed to counter the adverse selection and potentially large claims that could occur if an employer established a group disability income plan or if an employee elected to participate in a plan because of some known condition that is likely to result in disability.

Although variations exist, a common provision for preexisting conditions excludes coverage for any disability that commences during the first 12 months an employee is covered under the contract if the employee received treatment or medical advice for the disabling condition both (1) prior to the date the employee became eligible for coverage and (2) within 90 consecutive days prior to the commencement of the disability.

When coverage is transferred from one insurance company to another, it is not unusual, particularly in the case of large employers, for the new insurance company to waive the limitation for preexisting conditions for employees who were insured under the previous contract.

Benefits

Group disability income contracts contain benefit schedules that classify employees and specify the amount of disability income to be provided. They also include provisions pertaining to the length of time that benefits are paid and the coordination of benefits with other available sources of disability income.

Benefit Schedules

There are a variety of benefit schedules in group disability income contracts. Benefits may be available to all employees or limited to specific groups of employees. In addition, benefits may be expressed as either flat-dollar amounts, varying dollar amounts by classification, or a percentage of earnings.

Giving a disabled employee a level of income that is comparable to his or her regular earnings encourages absenteeism and diminishes the incentive to return to work. In general, disability income plans are designed to provide a level of benefits that replaces between 50 and 70 percent of an employee's gross income. Although this may appear to represent a substantial reduction of regular earnings, remember that a disabled employee does not have the usual expenses associated with working such as transportation costs. In addition, disability income benefits financed with after-tax employee contributions are not subject to Social Security and Medicare taxes, and employer-financed benefits are subject to Social Security and Medicare taxes only during the last calendar month in which an employee worked and during the 6 months that follow.

Many short-term disability income plans and the majority of long-term plans base benefits on a single percentage of regular earnings (excluding bonuses and overtime). This percentage varies widely for short-term plans, and benefits as low as 50 percent or as high as 100 percent are not unusual. Many insurers are reluctant to underwrite plans that provide benefits higher than 70 percent of earnings. In some instances, short-term plans may use different percentages such as 100 percent of earnings for 4 weeks and 70 percent of earnings for the remaining benefit period. The length of time

---

Reasons for Limited Benefits

- Return to work is encouraged.
- Work-related expenses are reduced.
- Benefits may not be subject to Social Security taxation.

---

for which the higher level of benefits is provided may also be a function of the length of an employee's service.

Long-term plans typically provide benefits that range from 50 to 70 percent of earnings; 60 and 66 2/3 are the most prevalent percentages. Some plans also use a sliding scale such as 66 2/3 percent of the first $4,000 of monthly earnings and 40 percent of earnings in excess of $4,000.

Plans that determine benefits as a percentage of earnings also commonly place a maximum dollar amount on the benefit that will be provided, regardless of earnings. For example, a long-term plan might be subject to a monthly maximum that varies from $1,000 for some small groups to $4,000 or $5,000 (and sometimes higher) for large groups. The purpose of the maximum is to prevent the absolute benefit from being so high that an employee, by adjusting his or her lifestyle, could live comfortably on the disability income benefit and thus have no financial incentive to return to work.

Period of Benefits

To determine the period for which benefits are paid, it is necessary to determine when benefits begin and how long they are paid. In both respects, there are differences between short-term and long-term plans.

waiting (elimination) period

Short-term Plans. Short-term disability income contracts commonly contain a *waiting period* (often referred to in such contracts as an elimination period). The waiting period is the length of time for which an employee covered under the contract must be disabled before benefits begin. The typical short-term contract has no waiting period for disabilities resulting from accidents, but a waiting period of one to 7 days is used for disabilities resulting from sicknesses. Some plans have a single waiting period that applies to disabilities from either accidents or sicknesses; a few plans have no waiting periods for either. Waiting periods longer than 7 days are occasionally used, particularly when there is a sick-leave plan to provide benefits during the initial portion of a disability. In a few cases, benefits are paid retroactively to the date of disability if the disability lasts for a predetermined period of time, but it is generally felt that retroactive benefits cause employees to prolong their return to work in order to receive benefits for the full period of their disability.

Once an employee begins to receive benefit payments under a short-term disability contract, the benefits continue until the end of the benefit period the

---

Typical Benefit Periods

- Short-term plans—13 weeks or 26 weeks subject to a one- to 7-day waiting period for sickness
- Long-term plans—2 years to life, subject to a 3-month or 6-month waiting period

---

contract specifies, if the employee remains disabled for that long. Although short-term contracts may provide benefits up to 2 years (with long-term contracts providing benefits for periods over 2 years), benefits rarely continue for more than one year. In fact, the majority of short-term contracts stipulate that benefits are paid for either 13 or 26 weeks; the latter period is more prevalent.

In a few cases, the maximum period of benefits applies to a specified duraion of time (such as any consecutive 12 months), regardless of the number of separate disabilities. In most plans, both the maximum benefit period and the elimination period apply to each separate disability. Successive periods of disability caused by the same accident or the same or related sickness are generally considered to be a single disability, unless they are separated by a period of continuous resumption of active employment.

Long-term Plans. Long-term disability income plans have waiting periods of 3 to 6 months; 6 months is more common. The length of the waiting period often corresponds to the length of time benefits are paid under a firm's short-term disability income plan or salary continuation plan. Unlike short-term plans, the waiting periods for sicknesses and accidents are the same.

Long-term disability income benefits may be paid for as short a period as 2 years or as long as the lifetime of the disabled employee. At one time, it was common for long-term disability income benefits to stop at age 65, but this is no longer permissible under the Age Discrimination in Employment Act. Several different approaches are now used for older employees. In a few cases, benefits are paid until age 70 for any disability that occurred before that age. For disabilities occurring at age 70 or later, benefits are paid for a reduced duration. A more common approach is to use a graded benefit period and give benefits to age 65 for employees who are disabled before a specified age. Employees disabled after the specified age receive benefits for a limited duration, as shown in table 14-1.

As in short-term disability income plans, provisions are made in long-term plans for successive disabilities. The majority of contracts stipulate that successive periods of disability that are separated by less than some period (usually varying from 3 to 6 months) of continuous, active full-time employment are considered a single disability unless the subsequent disability (1) arises from an unrelated cause and (2) begins after the employee has returned to work.

TABLE 14-1 Duration of Disability Income Benefits	
Age at Commencement of Disability	**Benefit Duration**
59 and younger	To age 65
60–64	5 years
65–69	To age 70
70–74	1 year
75 and older	6 months

Coordination with Other Benefits

To minimize the possibility of an employee's receiving total benefits higher than his or her predisability earnings, disability income plans commonly stipulate that benefits are coordinated with other sources of disability income. In general, the insurance laws or regulations of most states allow reductions to be made as a result of benefits from social insurance programs and group insurance or retirement plans the employer provides, but not as a result of benefits from individual disability income contracts unless they were purchased by the employer.

Benefits under short-term plans are generally integrated with (1) workers' compensation benefits, if the plan covers occupational disabilities, (2) temporary disability laws, if they are applicable, and (3) Social Security benefits, if the maximum benefit period is longer than 5 months.

Long-term disability income benefits are usually integrated with benefits provided under the following:

- Social Security
- workers' compensation laws
- temporary disability laws
- other insurance plans for which the employer makes a contribution or payroll deduction
- pension plans for which the employer has made a contribution or payroll deduction to the extent that the employee elects to receive retirement benefits because of disability
- sick-leave plans
- earnings from employment, either with the employer or from other sources

It is possible for the integration with other benefits to totally eliminate a long-term disability benefit. To prevent this from happening, many plans provide (and some states require) payment of a minimum benefit such as $50 or

$100 per month. Most plans also contain a provision freezing the amount of any Social Security reduction at the initial level that was established when the claim began.

As a general rule, both the insured and the insurer profit if the insured is able to collect Social Security benefits for a disability; the insured has an increased overall benefit, and the insurer has a substantially lower claim to pay. Consequently, insurers are often willing to provide assistance to claimants by helping them file Social Security claims and appeal decisions to deny claims.

Supplemental Benefits

It is becoming increasingly common to find group long-term disability income plans that provide employees with a base of employer-paid benefits and that allow each covered employee to purchase additional coverage at his or her own expense. For example, a plan may provide basic benefits of 50 percent of earnings and an option for an employee to increase this amount **buy-up plan** to 55, 66 2/3, or 70 percent of earnings. These *buy-up* (or supplemental) *plans* are becoming more popular, because employers feel the need to control the costs of benefits by shifting a greater burden of the cost to employees.

carve-out (benefit plan) Some plans are also designed as *carve-out* plans to provide benefits for certain employees, typically key executives. For example, an employer might design one plan to cover most of its employees, but it might cover top executives with another group plan that provides enhanced benefits in the form of a larger percentage of earnings and a more liberal definition of disability. Another variation of a carve-out plan would provide executives with a lower benefit percentage than other employees would receive, but it could include supplemental benefits in the form of individual disability income policies. In addition to more favorable policy provisions, a carve-out plan might offer better rate guarantees and an overall higher benefit than a group plan could offer. Furthermore, the portability of the individual policy might be attractive to executives but might not necessarily appeal to the employer.

Catastrophic Benefits Rider

A few disability insurers that also sell long-term care insurance have recently started to make available additional benefits if the insured suffers a severe disability that includes cognitive impairment or the inability to perform two or more of six activities of daily living (ADLs). These are the same criteria that trigger benefits in long-term care policies, which are discussed in chapter 15.

The employer can typically purchase benefits that range from an additional 10 to 40 percent of earnings, as long as total-disability benefits do not exceed a specified limit that may be as high as 100 percent of earnings. The employer also selects the length of time the catastrophic benefits are paid, which can vary from one year to the duration of the regular disability benefits the policy provides. (Note that at least one insurer offers a 10 percent benefit for one year as part of its standard disability income policies, with the employer having the option to select larger benefits or a longer benefit duration.) In addition, an employer may have the option to add a flat monthly benefit that is payable if an employee's spouse suffers a cognitive impairment or is unable to perform two or more ADLs.

Other Contract Provisions

Many provisions in group disability income contracts are similar to those in other types of insurance contracts previously discussed and, therefore, are not discussed further in this chapter. These provisions pertain to incontestability, a grace period, the entire contract, and the payment of premiums. The provisions discussed here either are unique to group disability income benefit contracts or differ in certain respects from similar provisions in other types of group insurance contracts.

Claims

The provisions concerning claims under both short-term and long-term disability income contracts are essentially the same. The insurance company must be notified within a relatively short time period—20 or 30 days or as soon as is reasonably possible—after the disability for which benefits are being claimed begins. A formal proof of loss must then be filed with the insurance company, usually within 90 days after the commencement of the disability or after the end of the week, month, or other time period for which benefits are payable. The proof of loss normally consists of a statement by the employee concerning the disability, a statement by the attending physician, and a statement by the employer that indicates the date and reason that active employment ceased. Provisions also require periodic reports from the attending physician or permit the insurance company to request these reports at reasonable intervals. The insurance company also has the right to have the employee examined by a physician of its own choice (and at its own expense) at reasonable time periods during the duration of the claim.

Rehabilitation

As an incentive to encourage disabled employees to return to active employment as soon as possible, but perhaps at a lower-paying job, most insurance companies include a rehabilitation provision in their long-term disability income contracts. This provision permits the employee to enter a trial work period of one or 2 years in rehabilitative employment. During this time, disability benefits continue but are reduced by some percentage (varying from 50 to 80 percent) of the earnings from rehabilitative employment. If the trial work period indicates that the employee is unable to perform the rehabilitative employment, the original long-term benefit is continued and the employee is not required to satisfy a new waiting period.

Although there are seldom other provisions in long-term disability income contracts that require the insurance company to aid in the rehabilitation of disabled employees, it has become increasingly common for insurance companies to provide benefits for rehabilitation when it is felt that the cost of these benefits will be offset by shortening an employee's disability period. These benefits may be in the form of physical therapy, job training, or adaptive aids to enable a disabled person to perform job functions.

In the past, the decision to seek rehabilitation was left to the disabled person. Some insurers now require the person to undertake rehabilitation or have benefits reduced or stopped.

The rehabilitation of disabled persons is continuing to grow in importance among companies. More and more companies are taking a proactive role in managing disability claims by employing more skilled professionals and by intervening earlier in the claims process. Because early intervention is undoubtedly a key factor in getting disabled employees back to work sooner, many benefit consultants think it advantageous for an employer to use the same insurance company for its short-term and long-term disability income plans. This approach enables the insurer's rehabilitation staff to become involved when a claim is filed under the short-term plan rather than waiting until the waiting period for long-term benefits has been met.

Termination

For the most part, the provisions in disability income contracts concerning the termination of either the master contract or an employee's coverage are the same as those in other types of group insurance. There is one notable exception: A conversion privilege is rarely included.

Additional Benefits

Occasionally, there are several types of additional benefits in long-term disability income contracts. The most common are a cost-of-living adjustment (COLA), a pension supplement, and a survivors' benefit.

Some disability income plans have COLAs to prevent inflation from eroding the purchasing power of disability income benefits being received. Under the typical COLA formula, benefits increase annually during the period of disability, along with changes in the consumer price index.

Many firms make provisions in their pension plan for treating disabled employees as if they were still working and accruing pension benefits. Such a provision requires that contributions on behalf of disabled employees be made to the pension plan, usually from the employer's current revenues.

Additional Benefits Sometimes Provided

- Cost-of-living adjustments
- Continued growth of pension benefits
- Income benefit to survivors
- Payments for child care
- Benefits for disability of employee's spouse
- Payment of medical expense insurance premiums

However, some disability income contracts stipulate that the contributions necessary to fund a disabled employee's accruing pension benefits be paid by the disability income contract.

Note also that some pension plans provide disability income benefits by allowing disabled employees to begin receiving retirement benefits when they are totally and permanently disabled. It is common, however, to limit these early retirement benefits to employees who have satisfied some minimum period of service or reached some minimum age. Recently, employee benefit consultants seem to feel that separate retirement and disability income plans are preferable.

Some long-term contracts provide a benefit to survivors in the form of continued payments after the death of a disabled employee. In effect, the disability income payments are continued, possibly at a reduced amount, for periods ranging up to 24 months; 3 to 6 months is more common. Payments are generally made only to eligible survivors, who typically are the spouse and unmarried children under age 21.

Other types of additional benefits are even less common. Examples include child-care payments for disabled employees who can work on a part-time basis, spousal disability benefits payable to the employee, and benefits to pay premiums for medical expense coverage.

FEDERAL INCOME TAXATION OF EMPLOYER-PROVIDED BENEFITS

Deductibility of Contributions

Employer contributions for an employee's disability income insurance are fully deductible to the employer as an ordinary and necessary business expense. Contributions by an individual employee are considered payments for personal disability income insurance and are not tax deductible.

Federal Income Tax Liability of Employees

Employer contributions for disability income insurance result in no taxable income to an employee. Receipt of benefits under an insured plan or sick-leave plan may or may not result in the receipt of taxable income. To make this determination, it is necessary to look at whether the plan is fully contributory, noncontributory, or partially contributory.

Fully Contributory Plan

Under a fully contributory plan, the entire cost of an employee's coverage is paid by after-tax employee contributions, and benefits are received free of income taxation.

Noncontributory Plan

Under a noncontributory plan, the employer pays the entire cost, and benefits are included in an employee's gross income. Some persons who are permanently and totally disabled may be eligible for a tax credit, but this credit is relatively modest. For example, the maximum credit for a married person filing jointly is $1,125, and this figure is reduced if adjusted gross income (including the disability benefit) exceeds $10,000. For purposes of this tax credit, the IRS uses the stringent Social Security definition of disability.

Partially Contributory Plan

Under a partially contributory plan, benefits attributable to employee contributions are received free of income taxation. Benefits attributable to employer contributions are includible in gross income, but employees may be eligible for the tax credit described previously.

The portion of the benefits attributable to employer contributions (and thus subject to income taxation) is based on the ratio of the employer's contributions to the total employer-employee contributions for an employee who has been under the plan for some period of time. For example, if the employer paid 75 percent of the cost of the plan, 75 percent of the benefits would be considered attributable to employer contributions and 25 percent to employee contributions.

Example: Harry is covered under a long-term disability income insurance plan of his employer. Harry and the employer pay 25 percent and 75 percent of the premium cost, respectively. The income tax treatment is as follows:

- The employer's contributions are deductible as a normal business expense and are not taxable as income to Harry.

- Harry's contributions are not tax deductible.
- Twenty-five percent of any disability income benefit payments are tax free to Harry; 75 percent of such payments are taxable as income, but Harry may be eligible for a tax credit if his adjusted gross income is low enough.

INDIVIDUAL DISABILITY INCOME INSURANCE POLICIES

Individual disability income coverages and related disability policies vary widely. Many variations involve such factors as the definition of disability itself, the duration of benefits, the waiting period, whether and how partial-disability benefits are provided, waiver-of-premium protection, how recurring disability is handled, and COLAs.

Definition of Disability

any-occupation

A few private insurance company contracts use a definition of disability that is as restrictive as the Social Security definition, but these should not be considered high-quality products. These definitions are commonly referred to in the insurance industry as *any-occupation* definitions of disability, which means that benefits are payable only if the individual is disabled so severely that he or she cannot engage in any occupation.

Most individual disability income contracts use definitions of disability that are similar to those for group plans discussed earlier in this chapter. Note that most companies, because of adverse claims experience, no longer issue contracts of long benefit duration that have own-occupation definitions of disability for the contract duration. Such policies, many of which are still in force, were once common. The dual definition of disability is the norm; insureds sometimes have a choice regarding how long the own-occupation definition of disability remains in force. When this choice is available, an employee can typically select one of two options that are in the range of 2 to 5 years. A common modification of the own-occupation definition is to continue benefits as long as an insured is not working in some other occupation.

To this point, the definitions discussed deal primarily with total disability. Currently, many individual disability policies also provide benefits for either partial disability or residual disability. Both of these types of benefits are intended to encourage insureds to return to the workforce prior to total recovery. Some experts argue that the absence of these benefits encourages disabled insureds to malinger so that they can collect total-disability benefits. It should be emphasized that partial-disability benefits and, in many policies, residual-disability benefits are payable only following a period for which total-disability benefits have been paid.

Partial-Disability Benefits

partial disability

Partial disability is usually defined as the inability to perform some stated percentage of the duties of the insured's occupation or performance at such a speed that completion of those duties takes a longer-than-normal amount of time; the more severe the limitations, the higher the benefit paid. Theoretically, under such a contract, an individual could return to work on a full-time basis at full salary, and he or she would still be eligible for partial-disability benefits.

Residual-Disability Benefits

residual-disability benefits

Residual-disability benefits provide for a replacement of lost earnings due to less-than-total disability. Here the focus is on how much income reduction has occurred as a result of the disability rather than on the physical dimensions of the disability itself. Residual-disability benefits are particularly well suited for self-employed professionals whose caseloads often determine their income such as accountants, attorneys, and physicians. A disability that reduces their capacity for work would automatically lead to a reduction in income.

Policies providing residual-disability benefits usually specify a fraction (representing the proportion of lost income) that is multiplied by the stated monthly benefit for total disability to derive the residual benefit payable. The numerator of that fraction is usually income prior to disability minus earned income during disability; the denominator of the fraction is income prior to disability. The contract specifies a definition of each form of income. The definitions differ from one insurance company to another, and these differences become extremely important for individuals whose income fluctuates widely. Some contracts may specify predisability income as the average monthly income during the 6 months immediately preceding the onset of disability; others may specify predisability income as the greater of the average monthly income during the 12 months preceding the onset of disability or the highest 12 months of consecutive earnings during the 3 years preceding the onset of disability. There are many variations, but the important concept here is that persons subject to income fluctuation should insist on a definition allowing the *greater* of two different base periods so that they are not unduly penalized as a result of a single base period applied during a slump in income. Most of the definitions either explicitly or implicitly include not only income earned from work activities but also pension or profit-sharing contributions made on behalf of the individual.

The income received during residual disability that is used to calculate the income loss is usually defined to include all money received during the period being evaluated even if the money represents payment for services rendered prior to the disability. However, a few insurance company definitions exclude payments made for services rendered prior to the disability.

Example:	Barbara Graves had a $66,000 annual predisability income and a policy providing $3,500 per month for total disability. She was able to return to work following a total disability and is earning $2,500 per month during the current period of residual disability. Subtracting $2,500 in residual earnings from the predisability income of $5,500 per month results in a lost income of $3,000 per month. The lost-income ratio ($3,000 ÷ $5,500) is then multiplied by the stated monthly benefit for total disability ($3,500) to determine her residual-disability benefit of $1,909 (rounded to the nearest dollar). Most residual-disability benefits cease whenever the income loss drops below 20 percent of the predisability income. If this were the case, residual benefits would cease when Barbara's monthly income exceeds $4,400.

A clause common within residual-disability-benefit provisions specifies that the minimum benefit payable for residual-disability periods is at least 50 percent of that payable for total disability. At least one insurance company provides 100 percent of the total-disability benefit during residual disability if the lost income exceeds 75 percent of the predisability income. Under most policies, residual-disability benefits are payable to the end of the benefit period, but some policies impose an 18- or 24-month limitation on residual benefits for partial disabilities beginning after a specified age such as 54.

Ability to Keep the Coverage in Force

Top-quality contracts are at least guaranteed renewable to some specified age, such as 65, or even for the insured's lifetime; noncancelable contracts are better still. Guaranteed renewable means that the policyowner has the right to continue the coverage in force by paying the premium due. The premium itself may be increased on a class basis for all guaranteed-renewable policies in the classification, but the premium cannot be increased on an individual basis. The important point is that the insurance company does not have the option to refuse renewal of these contracts before the end of the guaranteed-renewal period. Noncancelable disability contracts guarantee that the policyowner can keep the policy in force by paying the premium and that the premium will not increase beyond the scheduled amount specified in the policy.

Cancelable disability income insurance contracts have less generous renewability provisions than guaranteed-renewable or noncancelable ones. These cancelable policies offer very questionable protection for the insured, because the insurance company is allowed to refuse renewal of the contract in some circumstances or to increase the premium.

When Benefits Start

Disability income policies generally have a waiting period before benefit payments begin. Most insurance companies give the purchaser an option to select the duration of this period. Because benefits are paid on a monthly basis at the end of the month, the first benefit payment is made as much a 30 days after the end of the waiting period. Common waiting periods are 30, 60, 90, and 120 days. A few policies are available with a zero-day waiting period but only for disability due to accident; the premium increase to get rid of the waiting period is significant, because benefits are payable for many short-term disabilities.

Many factors should be considered when selecting the waiting period for a disability income policy. The ability of the insured to pay living costs and other expenses during the waiting period is of utmost importance. Another pertinent factor is whether or not the insured has other sources of funds available during short-term disabilities.

Insurance companies differ as to whether they require consecutive days or allow the accumulation of nonconsecutive disability days to satisfy the waiting period. Some policies explicitly spell out that nonconsecutive days will satisfy the waiting period. In other policies, the language is silent on this point, and the company's claims-handling philosophy determines the answer.

Residual-disability benefits that many policies provide have what is commonly known as a qualification period, which specifies the number of days of total disability the insured must sustain before residual-disability benefits are payable. The most generous residual-disability policies have a zero-day qualification period and therefore require no total-disability period prior to eligibility for residual- or partial-disability benefits. Under that type of contract, residual benefits could begin at the end of the waiting period to replace lost income such as the income lost by a surgeon suffering from severe arthritis. A policy that has residual benefits with a qualifying period equal to the waiting period could also start paying residual benefits at the end of the waiting period if the individual had been totally disabled for the entire waiting period and recovered enough to return to work with a reduced income immediately after the end of the waiting period. It is quite common for the qualification period associated with residual benefits actually to exceed the waiting period, but there is not necessarily a connection between the waiting period and the qualification period.

Recurring Disability

Most disability policies have provisions setting forth a specified period of recovery (usually measured by return to work) that automatically separates one disability from another.

Example:	Suppose Jen became disabled as a result of an auto accident and was totally disabled for 6 months. She then returned to work for 8 months before having a relapse and becoming totally disabled again from causes associated with the auto accident. The new disability is treated as a separate disability because Jen's recovery and return to work exceeded 6 months, which is the specified period separating recurring disabilities in most disability income policies. If Jen's return to work lasted fewer than 6 months, her second period of disability would be treated as a continuation of the initial disability, and no new waiting period would apply.

For disability policies with a limited benefit period, it can be advantageous to have each relapse classified as a new disability, which then starts with a new benefit period.

Duration of Benefit Period

Just as disability income policies differ according to definitions of disability and length of waiting period, they also differ according to the duration of benefits that they provide once the individual becomes disabled. Disability contracts often provide choices such as 2 years, 3 years, 5 years, to age 65, or even for the insured's lifetime. Some disability coverages are automatically renewable to age 65 and conditionally renewable to age 70 or 75 if the individual continues to work at his or her occupation. Obviously, the longer the potential benefit period, the higher the premium necessary to support such benefits.

Most companies do not differentiate between disabilities caused by injury and disabilities caused by illness. However, some policies do make such a differentiation. It is not uncommon for these policies to provide lifetime benefits if the disability results from injury but to limit benefits to age 65 if the disability stems from illness. Other companies offer a total range of options or the selection of the maximum benefit period for both injury and illness. For example, an individual could select injury to age 65 and illness to age 65, injury for the insured's lifetime and illness to 65, or the maximum of lifetime for both injury and illness. Companies that differentiate between injury and illness as a source of disability do not usually allow the maximum benefit period for illness to exceed the maximum benefit period for injury.

Policies with short benefit durations do not provide comprehensive protection against disability, but their main appeal is the premium savings associated with the relatively short maximum benefit period. The premium for a 2-year benefit period can be as low as 40 to 50 percent of the premium required to extend benefits to age 65.

In recent years, the predominant maximum benefit period for disability income policies is in the range of age 65 to age 67. This coverage ensures a source of replacement income until the normal retirement age for most individuals. The availability of Medicare, Social Security, pensions, and other benefits makes it less important for people to rely on disability income benefits beyond the mid-60s.

Even those policies purporting to provide lifetime benefits for disability include limitations on disabilities that occur after specified ages such as 50, 55, or 60. Disabilities with their first onset after the specified age are often limited to benefit periods of 2 or 5 years or may terminate at a specified age such as 65, 68, or 70. In other words, lifetime benefit payments are available only for disabilities that initially occur before the specified age limitation and remain continuous and uninterrupted for the remainder of the insured's life.

Policies with long benefit durations are being issued to high-income individuals for significant amounts of coverage such as $10,000 to $20,000 in benefits per month. These policies present a potential liability of millions of dollars to the insurance company. With such potential liabilities, it is under-standable that insurance companies are more restrictive in writing these policies than they are in writing policies of short benefit duration. Fewer occupations qualify for policies with long benefit durations than for policies of short benefit durations. Policies with long benefit durations are rarely available to any occupation that involves physical labor or direct involvement in dangerous processes.

Disability benefits continue for as long as the insured individual is disabled according to the contract provisions. Insurance companies often require repeated verification that the disability still satisfies the qualifications for benefit eligibility. Benefits for total disability cease when the individual has recovered enough that the disability no longer satisfies the criteria of total disability. In policies providing residual benefits, benefit payments may continue at a reduced amount when the individual has recovered enough to return to work but still sustains more than a 20 percent reduction in income.

Level of Benefits Payable

Disability income policies specify the dollar amount of monthly benefits payable during periods of total disability after the insured satisfies the waiting period. At the time of policy issuance, the stated monthly benefit amount should be in line with the insured's income and provide fairly complete protection. Over time, however, the stated benefit amount is likely to become inadequate as the insured's income increases because of both inflation and job promotions. Disability income policies are available with provisions to counteract such erosion in benefit levels. These provisions fall into two different categories. The first category consists of provisions that provide increases in the benefit payments during periods of disability when benefits are being distributed. The second consists of provisions aimed at increasing the benefit level while the coverage is in force but the insured is not disabled.

Cost-of-Living (COLA) Riders

cost-of-living-adjustment (COLA) rider

Provisions dealing with increasing benefits during periods of disability are often referred to as either *cost-of-living-adjustment (COLA) riders* or inflation-protection provisions. They tend to have either a fixed-percentage increase per year or a floating-percentage increase, where the floating amount is determined by some external index such as a consumer price index. These benefits are almost always provided as an optional rider for an additional premium over and above the base policy. Many companies with COLA riders offer purchasers a choice about the percentage increase ceilings on the rider; increases of up to 7 percent are often allowed. However, the higher the percentage, the higher the cost of the rider.

In addition to these annual increase limitations, COLA riders usually contain an aggregate limit on benefit increases such as two times the original monthly benefit amount. For example, an insured may purchase a fixed 5 percent COLA rider to a policy originally providing $2,000 per month in benefits and may subsequently become disabled for a continuous period of 20 years. After the individual has been disabled for one year, the benefit amount increases to $2,100 per month, reflecting the 5 percent increase. After 2 years, the benefit increases to $2,205 if the increases are based on a compound-interest adjustment, or to $2,200 if the increases are based on a simple-interest adjustment. If the COLA rider contains an aggregate limit of twice the original benefit amount, no additional increases are allowed once the benefit amount reaches $4,000.

Increased Predisability Coverage

There are basically three approaches to keeping disability income benefits in step with increased income for insured individuals who are not disabled. The oldest and least attractive method is to purchase new policies to supplement the in-force policies incrementally as income increases. The drawback to this approach is that it requires evidence of insurability every time the individual obtains incremental amounts of coverage. If his or her health deteriorates, additional coverage may not be available at any price.

The second approach to adjusting disability benefit levels is through a rider that guarantees the right to purchase additional coverage at specified future intervals, up to some specified maximum age such as 45, 50, or 55. This approach is similar to the first one in that the individual must purchase additional coverage every time an adjustment is needed, but he or she can acquire the additional amounts at the specified intervals, regardless of the insured's health. However, these incremental purchases are subject to underwriting requirements regarding the individual's current income. In other words, the insurance company will not issue new coverage if the incremental addition increases aggregate disability income benefits above the underwriting guidelines for that individual's current income on the option date.

The third and most attractive way to adjust benefits upward for inflation while the insured is not disabled is to use riders that automatically increase the base benefit amount on a formula basis such as a stated flat-percentage amount at each policy anniversary. Even this approach requires purchasing additional coverage, and the premium will be increased appropriately. As with the second approach, the additional increment of coverage is purchased at premium rates based on the insured's attained age at the time it is added to the policy. The real advantage to this approach is that the changes are automatic unless the policyowner refuses them.

Insurance companies are not required to provide any inflation adjustments, and some insurance companies that sell disability income policies choose not to make such riders available. Insurance companies that offer both options—purchasing additional coverage in the future and automatic percentage increases in benefits—limit future incremental additions and make sure that they are in line with the insured's earnings. These companies often refuse to issue the options if the insured has another policy that already contains such riders or if the base policy was issued on an extra-premium basis due to health problems.

Ways to Keep Up with Inflation Before Becoming Disabled

- Purchase new policies periodically (requires evidence of insurability).
- Purchase a guaranteed insurability (guaranteed purchase) option.
- Purchase a rider that automatically increases the benefit amount periodically.

Premium Payments

Premiums for disability income policies are similar to life insurance policy premiums in that they are based on the policyowner's age at the time of policy issuance and remain level for the duration of the coverage. Consequently, an individual can lock in lower premiums by buying a policy at a younger age and keeping it in force.

Premiums can be paid on an annual, semiannual, quarterly, or monthly basis and can be set up on a payroll-deduction basis or an automatic bank draft plan. Premiums must be paid on a timely basis to keep the coverage in force, but the policies do contain a 31-day grace period for late premium payments. Most insurance companies also allow lapsed policies to be reinstated automatically if the premium is paid within 15 days after the end of the grace period.

Most disability income policies automatically include a waiver-of-premium provision. Some companies waive premiums after 90 days of disability, while other companies waive premiums after 60 days of disability. The shorter the waiting period, the higher the premium for the waiver-of-premium provision if it is charged separately. Disability policies differ as to whether the waiver of premium requires consecutive days or allows aggregate nonconsecutive days from short disability periods to satisfy the waiting period.

Some policies waive only future premiums after the waiver-of-premium waiting period has been satisfied; other policies retroactively waive prior premium payments made after the onset of disability but before the waiver-of-premium eligibility requirements have been met. Once the insured individual recovers and no additional disability benefits are payable, premiums will no longer be waived and premium payments must be resumed. Premium waivers generally do not continue beyond age 65 even in policies providing lifetime benefits.

Return-of-Premium Option

Some insurance companies offer an optional policy provision that returns some portion of premiums at specified intervals such as 5 years or 10 years. For example, one company has an option that returns 60 percent of premiums paid at the end of each 5-year interval if no claims have been made during that period. This particular option can increase premiums by more than 40 percent over the base premium level. Other companies offer variations in the percentage of premium to be returned, such as 70 percent or 80 percent of the premiums paid, and in the duration of the interval over which there must be no claims in order to collect the return of premium.

Rehabilitation Benefits

rehabilitation benefit

Higher-quality disability income policies may include some type of *rehabilitation benefits*, although many insurance policies do not. The policies that do include rehabilitation benefits tend to require the insurance company's prior approval of the rehabilitative program in writing. Some companies limit the amount of rehabilitation benefits to 24 or 36 times the monthly total-disability benefit payable. Receiving rehabilitation benefits generally does not disqualify the individual from collecting total-disability benefits. In other words, the better policies pay the full total-disability benefit and, at the same time, pay additional rehabilitation expenses over and above the monthly benefit payments. Policy provisions often require rehabilitation programs to be furnished by accredited educational institutions, state or local governments, or otherwise licensed and recognized providers of sanctioned rehabilitation training.

Presumptive Disability

Many disability income policies include provisions setting forth specific losses that qualify for permanent total-disability status. They are referred to as *presumptive-disability provisions,* because the individual is presumed to be totally disabled even if he or she is able to return to work or gain employment in a new occupation.

presumptive-disability provision

Presumptive-disability provisions generally include loss of sight, loss of speech, loss of hearing, or the total loss of use of or the severance of both hands, both feet, or one hand and one foot. As with other disability coverages, the presumptive-disability benefits cease if the insured individual recovers to an extent that he or she no longer qualifies for the presumptive disability. For example, an individual may lose the use of both hands because of paralysis from a stroke or other causes. If the individual agradually recovers use of one or both hands, he or she no longer qualifies for presumptive-disability benefits.

Presumptive-disability provisions differ as to whether the benefits are paid as of the first day presumptive-disability requirements have been met or if the regular waiting period still applies.

Incontestability

The laws of all states require that disability income policies contain incontestability provisions. Generally, the incontestable clause specifies that the policy will remain contestable for 2 years after the date of issue during the lifetime of the individual insured. Some insurance companies, however, include a provision that extends the contestable period for any disabilities that occur during the first 2 years of coverage. Under such a policy, if an individual is disabled for 13 months out of the first 2 years of the policy, the policy does not count the 13 months toward satisfying the 24-month period. This type of extension provision is not included in the better disability income policies available in the marketplace.

Treatment of Organ Donations

Disability income policies differ as to how they treat disabilities intentionally induced by the insured for the purpose of donating vital organs or tissue to other human beings. The most generous policies provide the same disability benefits for these operations as for any other covered disability. The normal waiting period is applicable, and then the appropriate level of benefits is provided. Policies containing this coverage usually require that the policy be in force for a minimum of 6 or 12 months before benefits become payable for such purposes.

Social Security Rider

Social Security rider

Many insurance companies offer an optional provision in the form of a *Social Security rider* that requires a separate extra premium to cover additional benefits payable when the individual is disabled under the base policy but does not qualify for Social Security disability benefits. The supplemental benefit is paid over and above the base disability benefit of the underlying policy. When claiming benefits under this option, the insured is generally required to apply for the Social Security or other social insurance benefits, then supply the insurance company with evidence that the benefits have been denied by the Social Security Administration or other governmental agency (which often use a more stringent definition of disability than the insurance company). Some policies also require that the insured must appeal the government's benefit denial before benefits will be paid under this rider. Under most of these riders, the benefit payments are not retroactive, and the first benefit payment is not dispensed until the insurance company has accepted the denial of government benefits. Therefore, in most cases, the first benefit payment will be 13 or more months after the onset of disability.

The reason for this type of rider is that to avoid overinsurance, underwriting guidelines limit the amount of coverage that an individual can purchase. In setting these guidelines, the insurance companies usually take into consideration the level of benefits that might be payable under Social Security for disability purposes. An individual can purchase this rider to supplement the maximum benefit available in the base policy so that total benefits the insured collects from the insurance company are essentially the same as he or she would have collected if the individual qualified for Social Security disability benefits.

Benefits under the Social Security rider terminate for any period that the insured does receive benefits from Social Security or other governmental units specified in the contract. Benefits also terminate at the full Social Security retirement age even if the individual continues to be totally disabled. Election to take early retirement benefits under Social Security also terminates benefits.

Hospitalization Benefits

For an additional premium, some disability income policies provide the option of adding supplemental income benefits for periods of hospitalization. These additional benefits are made available because the insured's need for income can rise during a period of hospitalization due to deductibles, coinsurance provisions, exclusions, and other benefit limitations in medical expense coverage. The benefit payable is for a stated dollar amount, which under some policies begins with the first day of hospitalization and under other policies is subject to a waiting period that may or may not be the same as that for total-disability benefits. These riders generally contain a limitation on the duration of benefits for any single hospitalization.

Some contracts provide no waiting period at all, and hospitalization benefits are payable from the first day of hospitalization, regardless of the length of the waiting period for total-disability benefits. Other contracts have a specified waiting period applicable to the hospitalization rider, which is often the same duration as the waiting period applicable to total-disability benefits, but it may differ.

Dividends

Many insurance companies issuing disability income policies provide participating contracts that pay policyowner dividends. In most cases, little or no dividend payment is made during the first 2 years of coverage; under some policies, no dividends are paid during the first 3 years of coverage. The level of dividends payable is a function of the company's profitability on its disability income policies and thus subject to fluctuation. In general, dividends increase with policy duration. As with dividends in all insurance policies, however, dividends cannot be guaranteed. Any dividend illustration is merely an extrapolation of past experience, adjusted for expectations of future results.

Many disability income policies are issued on a nonparticipating basis and pay no policyowner dividends. Purchasers of these policies know the full cost in advance because there is no future reduction in cost through dividends.

Insurance Company Limitations on Amount of Coverage

Insurance company statistics have shown that the higher the percentage of a person's predisability income that is replaced by disability income benefits, the higher the likelihood that claims experience will exceed claims expected. In other words, high levels of disability benefits tend to stimulate higher aggregate claims. This is especially true if the benefits exceed the cash income available prior to disability. There have been a surprising number of fraudulent claims in disability income insurance where the insured intentionally maimed himself or herself with the express intent of ceasing work and collecting disability income benefits. Some of the more notorious cases have involved medical practitioners who injected painkillers before severing fingers or other extremities of the body. In cases where fraud was detected, the individuals were unable to collect disability income benefits even though they were permanently disabled.

Minimizing Fraudulent Claims

To minimize the motivation for fraudulent claims as well as padding legitimate claims by malingering, insurance companies limit the amount of coverage they will issue to any individual in relation to that individual's income. Generally speaking, disability income coverage is not available for benefit amounts that exceed 60 or 66 2/3 percent of the individual's gross earned income. In fact, as the level of income increases, the percentage of income replacement that insurance companies will issue decreases. High-income professionals are often limited to less than 50 percent of their income level in setting the maximum benefit level for their disability policies.

Some experts advise that the appropriate amount of disability income protection to purchase is the maximum amount available from an insurance company that provides quality coverage. Insurance companies will want to know about existing sources of disability protection such as sick-leave plans and group insurance policies through employers, professional associations, or affinity groups. The financial underwriting aspect of disability income policy issuance is just as important as the medical evaluation.

Business owners who have financial difficulties and face bankruptcy present a high risk of adverse selection. A high stress level increases the likelihood of a stroke, heart attack, or other stress-related disability. Stressed individuals with a history of high blood pressure or heart problems present an even higher risk.

The underwriting process for disability income insurance is much more complex than that for life insurance. Although underwriting for life insurance and for disability income insurance coverages has many similarities, disability coverages entail more refined classifications and, therefore, a more involved evaluation process. The evaluation process is more complicated because disability can be, and often is, a recurrent condition throughout an individual's lifetime. For example, an individual with a bad back may require repeated hospitalization and rehabilitation therapy even though he or she may have a long life. Joint problems associated with knees and elbows often start with injuries at a young age and get progressively worse with wear and the onset of arthritis.

The job of underwriting for disability income insurance is to correctly classify individuals as to how costly their medical maintenance will be over their lifetime. The individual must be classified appropriately on the basis of existing information so that the premium for that individual and similar individuals adequately covers the cost of claims for that group over the duration of their coverage.

Modifying the Standard Issue

Depending on the insurer, 25 percent to 40 percent of issued policies may require some sort of modification or adjustment from the standard issue. As in life insurance, disability premiums can be increased for individuals who present a higher level of risk to the insurance company. Another modification in disability income insurance is to insist on a longer waiting period for some high-risk insureds, which eliminates more of the short-term problems and disabilities. In some cases, a longer waiting period may be applicable to specified causes or conditions, or the insurance company may insist on a relatively long waiting period that applies to all causes of disability. This approach does not preclude coverage for a particular condition, but it limits claim payments to the longer durations. The most limiting modification is an outright exclusion of any benefits associated with disabilities stemming from specified causes or conditions. Although this approach may seem drastic, it at least allows individuals to obtain disability coverage for causes other than the major problem that is preventing them from getting full disability protection.

The disability underwriting process commonly includes one or more requests from the home office for additional information. Although this does delay the issuance of coverage, it does not necessarily indicate that the coverage will not be issued. Disability insurers use many resources in an attempt to insure all applicants who fall within their acceptable risk classifications. Obviously, some risks will not meet the minimum company standards and will be rejected outright. Individual applicants who are rejected by one company may not necessarily be uninsurable; another company may classify risks in a different manner and apply different cutoff standards. Individuals who experience difficulty in obtaining disability income insurance should shop for coverage from other insurers on a sequential basis and should not apply for coverage with many insurers concurrently. Certain brokers who specialize in substandard insurance can be helpful in obtaining disability coverage for individuals with serious health problems.

Policy Exclusions

A few exclusions typically appear in disability income policies. Disabilities resulting from war or any sort of military service are nearly always excluded from coverage by a specific policy exclusion provision. This provision often defines war to include declared wars, undeclared wars, and any acts of war. Exclusions also preclude benefit payments for any sickness or injury sustained during military service, because it is usually covered by military or veterans' benefits. Some policies exclude benefits for disabilities resulting from a normal pregnancy and disabilities resulting from travel in aircraft if the insured has duties relating to the plane's flight or maintenance.

The total exclusion provision in disability policies is usually rather short. Longer exclusion clauses often indicate that the coverage may be less generous than that provided by premier-quality policies.

Conversion to Long-term Care Coverage

A few insurers allow the insured to convert a disability income policy to a long-term care policy when the insured is no longer working or at a point that disability income benefits are no longer available (such as age 65). These provisions are in the early stages of development and may or may not become more common as the sales of separate long-term care policies (discussed in chapter 15) increase.

The conversion does not require evidence of insurability, and the amount of benefits available is often based on what the individual can purchase with the same premium paid for the disability income coverage. As a general rule, benefits are more limited than those in most separate long-term care policies. For example, benefits may be paid only if the insured is confined to a nursing home, whereas many long-term care policies cover other settings for care, including the home.

Federal Income Taxation

Premiums a person pays for individually owned disability income insurance are not deductible for federal income tax purposes; benefits a person receives are tax free.

BUSINESS USES OF DISABILITY INCOME INSURANCE

The disability of business owners or key employees poses a serious risk to a business's financial health. Just as a family suffers from the loss of the income of its breadwinners, a business suffers from the loss of its productive resources. The problems are particularly acute for small enterprises in which the workforce may not be large enough to have a backup for critical tasks that could be interrupted because of disabilities. Good examples of business owners in need of disability income insurance are self-employed attorneys, accountants, physicians, and dentists who operate solo practices and employ a support staff of one or more persons. When these business owners become totally disabled, the primary business activities are often halted. However, it is necessary to maintain the business premises and at least a skeletal support staff so that business can be resumed when the business owner recovers from the disability. For example, accounts receivable must still be collected, and ongoing expenses must still be paid.

Business Overhead Expense Insurance

Business overhead expense policies are available to cover many of the ongoing costs of operating a business while the business owner is totally disabled. These policies tend to be limited to benefit durations of one or 2 years and have relatively short waiting periods. The intent is to keep the necessary staff and premises available for the resumption of business if the business owner recovers from the disability.

Insurance companies are extremely cautious in writing this coverage and in keeping the benefit amount in line with established stable costs for previous periods. Consequently, supporting financial statements to verify the stability of the business and to establish the appropriate level of insurable expenses must accompany the application for this coverage. Insurable expenses include such things as salaries for secretaries, nurses, and other staff necessary to resume business upon the business owner's recovery, as well as the ongoing expenses for rent, utilities, taxes, accounting services, and so forth. Actual expenses are reimbursed at time of disability up to a maximum monthly indemnity selected at the time of policy issue.

Key Person Insurance

Business entities are dependent on their personnel to carry out business activities and generate revenues and profits. Very often, the unique talents and experiences of a few key individuals are crucial to the success of the business entity. The loss of an individual's contributions by reason of disability or death could deal a devastating blow to the financial well-being of the enterprise. In fact, sometimes the dependence is so critical that losing the individual's participation could lead to the bankruptcy or termination of the business. This is particularly true of professionals who operate as sole practitioners.

Many business enterprises have recognized the importance of key individuals who make the most critical contributions and have therefore obtained disability income insurance to cover these key individuals. Benefits from key employee disability policies are payable to the business entity when the insured key employee is disabled. The justification for this coverage is similar to that for key person life insurance policies. Proceeds from key person disability policies can be used to replace lost revenue directly attributable to the key person's disability. It can also be used to fund the search for individuals to replace the insured person, the extra cost of hiring specialized individuals to replace the multiple talents of the insured, and the training costs that may be incurred to prepare replacements to carry out the duties the insured performed. The costs of training, hiring, and compensating are usually rather easy to ascertain, whereas estimating lost revenue is a very difficult and complex task. These policies are not designed to provide continuance of salary for the key employee.

Even though a business entity may determine a desired amount of disability income protection for each key individual, it may not be able to obtain that amount of coverage. The underwriting processes of insurance companies limit the maximum amount of coverage available on any one individual. Companies utilize a wide range of guidelines to set these limitations, and getting an insurer to waive any of these limitations is usually difficult. Sometimes a business entity is able to make a strong enough argument on both financial and economic grounds to justify an exception and obtain the desired amount even though it exceeds underwriting guideline limitations.

Premiums for a business-owned disability income policy are not deductible for federal income tax purposes if benefits are paid to the business; the receipt of these proceeds by the business is free of any federal income tax liability. Payment of those premiums does not create any taxable income for the insured employee.

Salary Continuation for Owners and Key Employees

A business entity can purchase individual disability income policies to fund formal plans to continue salary for disabled owners or key employees. Formal plans can be set up in two different ways. The corporation can own the policy and be the beneficiary under the policy, or the corporation can pay the premiums on a policy owned by the employee to whom benefits will be paid. When the corporation is both the owner and the beneficiary of the policy, premium payments are nondeductible by the corporation and the corporation receives the insurance proceeds free of any federal income tax liability. Premium payments for such coverage are not considered taxable income to the employee.

When the corporation merely pays the premiums on a policy owned by the employee, the premiums are deductible expenses of the corporation as long as they meet reasonable expense criteria. The premium payments are not considered taxable income to the employee; however, benefits paid under the policy are taxable income to the employee.

In some informal plans to continue salary, the corporation pays a large enough bonus to the employee for the employee to buy an individual disability income policy. If the bonus payments are reasonable compensation, they are deductible by the corporation. The bonus is taxable income to the employee. The premium payments made by the employee are not deductible. Any benefit payments the employee receives have no effect on the corporation, and the employee receives them free of any federal income tax liability.

Disability Buy-Sell Funding

A business owner's disability often threatens the viability of that enterprise. Preserving the value of the business often necessitates shifting the business owner's ownership interest to one or more other individuals who can continue to conduct the affairs of the business. In cases that involve multiple ownership of the business, the most likely parties to purchase the ownership interest of a disabled owner are the nondisabled co-owners. Unfortunately, few business owners have adequate amounts of liquid assets to make an outright purchase of the ownership interest from the disabled co-owner.

Just as buy-sell agreements triggered by the death of an owner can be funded with life insurance, buy-sell agreements triggered by the disability of an owner can be funded with disability income insurance. Special disability policies have been designed specifically for the purpose of funding buy-sell agreements. These policies can fund either an installment purchase or a lump-sum buyout.

The types of buy-sell arrangements are similar to those discussed earlier in this book for situations arising from death. However, some extra care is necessary in drafting the agreement. The definition used in the disability policy should be the same definition as that specified in the buy-sell agreement. The waiting period for a buy-sell policy is typically one year or longer in order to avoid triggering the buyout for disabilities that last less than one year. Most buy-sell policies pay the benefit in one lump sum.

Although a discussion is beyond the scope of this book, readers should also be aware that different approaches to buy-sell agreements can have significantly different tax implications.

CHECKLIST FOR EVALUATING AND COMPARING DISABILITY INCOME POLICIES

☐ What is the definition of total disability? If the definition of total disability is a two-step definition, how many years apply to own occupation?

☐ What are the amount and frequency of total-disability benefits?

☐ What waiting (elimination) period applies to total-disability benefits?

☐ What is the duration of total-disability benefits?

☐ Are partial-disability benefits covered? If yes,

___ What is the definition of partial disability?
___ What period of total disability is required before benefits are payable?

☐ Are residual-disability benefits covered? If yes,

___ What is the benefit amount?
___ How long are they payable?
___ Is a prior period of total disability required?

☐ What is the annual policy premium?

☐ Is there a presumptive-disability provision?

☐ Is there coverage for disabilities arising from organ donations?

☐ What cost-of-living increases are available for benefits being paid and coverage in force, and what is the basis on which such increases are made?

☐ Does the policy contain any modifications from standard issue?

☐ What is the renewability provision?

☐ What is the waiver-of-premium provision?

☐ Is there a return-of-premium option?

☐ What are the rehabilitation benefits?

☐ Does the policy contain riders? If yes,

___ What do they cover?
___ Is there an additional premium for their use?

SOURCES FOR FURTHER IN-DEPTH STUDY

- Sadler, Jeff, *Disability Income: The Sale, the Product, the Market,* 2d ed., Erlanger, KY: The National Underwriter Company, 1995. Phone 800-543-0874. Web site address www.nuco.com
- Soule, Charles E., *Disability Income Insurance: The Unique Risk,* 5th ed., Bryn Mawr, PA: The American College Press, 2002. Phone 888-263-7265. Web site address www.theamericancollege.edu

CHAPTER REVIEW

Answers to review questions and self-test questions start on page 793.

Key Terms

short-term disability income plan
long-term disability income
 insurance
sick-leave plan
own-occupation
waiting (elimination) period
buy-up plan
carve-out (benefit plan)

any-occupation
partial disability
residual-disability benefits
cost-of-living-adjustment (COLA)
 rider
rehabilitation benefit
presumptive-disability provision
Social Security rider

Review Questions

14-1. Describe the need for disability income insurance coverage.

14-2. What are the sources of coverage that may protect your client against financial trouble in case of disability?

14-3. What is the nature of sick-leave plans?

14-4. What are the typical eligibility requirements in an insured group disability income plan?

14-5. Explain how the definition of total disability in group long-term contracts may differ from that in group short-term contracts.

14-6. What types of exclusions are in group disability income contracts?

14-7. What types of benefit schedules are in group disability income plans?

14-8. Explain how group disability income benefits are coordinated with other benefits.

14-9. Describe the following additional benefits that are occasionally in group long-term disability income contracts:
 a. cost-of-living (COLA) riders
 b. pension supplements
 c. survivors' benefits

14-10. Describe what the income tax consequences are for each of the following clients who receive disability income benefits from an employer plan:
 a. Kevin receives disability benefits under a fully contributory plan.
 b. Patty receives disability benefits under a noncontributory plan.
 c. Julie receives disability benefits under a partially contributory plan.

14-11. Describe residual-disability benefits, and explain how they are calculated.

14-12. What advice might a planner give a client regarding each of the following aspects of individual disability income insurance policies?
a.   ability to keep the coverage in force
b.   when benefits start
c.   recurring disabilities
d.   duration of benefit period
e.   level of benefits payable
f.   premium payments

14-13. Describe the three approaches an individual who is not disabled can use to keep individual disability income policy benefits in step with the individual's increasing income.

14-14. Describe how the return-of-premium option works.

14-15. Explain why it may be a good idea to add a Social Security rider to an individual disability income policy.

14-16. What are insurance company limits on the amount of coverage that an individual income disability policy can provide?

14-17. Explain how individual disability income policies can be used by a business for
a.   paying business overhead expenses
b.   key person protection
c.   salary continuation for owners and key employees
d.   disability buy-sell funding

Self-Test Questions

T   F   14-1. At all working ages, the probability of being disabled for at least 90 consecutive days is much greater than the chance of dying.

T   F   14-2. The definition of disability under the Social Security program is less restrictive than that in most individual or group disability income contracts.

T   F   14-3. Employer-provided short-term disability income plans typically provide benefits for a limited period of time such as 6 months or less.

T   F   14-4. It is generally possible to provide disability income protection for up to 100 percent or more of a client's income by purchasing a supplemental policy to coordinate with his or her group long-term policy.

T   F   14-5. Most employers provide long-term disability income coverage for their employees.

T   F   14-6. Sick-leave plans generally replace all lost income for a limited period of time, starting on the first day of disability.

T F   14-7.   Most sick-leave plans are open to part-time employees.

T F   14-8.   Most sick-leave plans are coordinated with social insurance programs.

T F   14-9.   Long-term disability plans often limit benefits to salaried employees because claims experience has traditionally been less favorable for hourly paid employees.

T F   14-10. Short-term disability income contracts typically limit coverage to occupational disabilities.

T F   14-11. Group disability income contracts typically specify that no benefits will be paid unless the employee is under the care of a physician.

T F   14-12. Most group disability income contracts exclude disabilities that result from pregnancy.

T F   14-13. Group long-term disability income contracts commonly exclude benefits for disabilities that result from preexisting conditions.

T F   14-14. Group short-term disability income contracts generally have 30-day waiting periods.

T F   14-15. Group long-term disability income contracts typically require disabled employees who return to work to complete a new waiting period before any benefits can be reinstated if they subsequently decide they are unable to keep working.

T F   14-16. The disadvantage of group long-term disability income plans is their inability to provide any cost-of-living adjustments after benefits begin.

T F   14-17. Planners should advise their clients to buy any-occupation individual disability income policies because they are very liberal in defining disability.

T F   14-18. Residual-disability benefits focus on how much income reduction has been sustained as a result of the disability, rather than on the physical dimensions of the disability itself.

T F   14-19. Planners should advise clients to consider individual disability income contracts that are at least guaranteed renewable to some specified age such as 65, or even for the insured's lifetime.

T F   14-20. The premium for an individual disability income policy with a 2-year benefit period can be as low as 40 to 50 percent of the premium required to extend the benefits to age 65.

T F   14-21. Insurance companies often require repeated verification that an individual's disability still satisfies the qualifications for benefit eligibility.

T   F   14-22. The best way to adjust benefits upward for inflation before the insured is disabled is to purchase new policies to supplement the in-force policies incrementally as the insured's income increases.

T   F   14-23. Most individual disability income policies include a waiver-of-premium provision.

T   F   14-24. Individual disability income policies are prohibited from having an incontestability provision because of the potential for fraud.

T   F   14-25. Benefits under a Social Security rider continue even after the insured elects to start receiving Social Security retirement benefits.

T   F   14-26. The underwriting process for individual disability income insurance is much more complex than for individual life insurance.

T   F   14-27. Business overhead expense policies are available to cover many of the ongoing costs of operating a business while the business owner is totally disabled.

T   F   14-28. Benefits from key employee disability policies are payable to the wife or husband of the disabled key employee.

T   F   14-29. Buy-sell agreements triggered by the disability of an owner can be funded with disability policies.

15

Long-Term Care Insurance

Learning Objectives

An understanding of the material in this chapter should enable the student to

15-1. Explain the need for and sources of long-term care.

15-2. Describe the development of long-term care insurance, including the National Association of Insurance Commissioners (NAIC) model legislation.

15-3. Explain the effect of the Health Insurance Portability and Accountability Act (HIPAA) on long-term care insurance.

15-4. Describe the characteristics of individual long-term care policies.

15-5. Describe how group long-term care policies differ from individual policies.

Chapter Outline

Since the early 1980s, long-term care insurance has evolved from being virtually nonexistent to being an important form of insurance product carried by about 6 million persons. The number of insurers with individual long-term care products has gradually increased to about 100, but 10 insurers write over 80 percent of the coverage.[1] The major providers of employee benefits now make group products available. Financial planners need to understand this important product in order to advise their clients.

During its relatively short life, long-term care coverage has been hailed as a major source of financial security and criticized as a coverage that fails to meet consumers' real long-term care needs. State and federal legislation affecting coverage has also been common. In this environment, long-term care products have continued to evolve, with the frequent introduction of newer and more comprehensive products. Long-term care coverage can probably best be described as having grown from infancy to somewhere between the childhood and teenage years. Coverage will change to meet consumer demands and expectations, and the largely untapped market for coverage will continue to grow as the American population ages.

The first portion of this chapter looks at the need for long-term care. This is followed by a brief description of sources of long-term care other than insurance. The chapter continues with a discussion of how and why insurance policies have evolved into the products now being offered. It then contains an analysis of the more common products in the marketplace today—both individual and group. The chapter concludes with a checklist for evaluating and comparing policies.

NEED FOR LONG-TERM CARE

An Aging Population

Long-term care has traditionally been thought of as a problem primarily for the older population. The population aged 65 or over is the fastest-growing age group; today it represents about 11 percent of the population, a figure that is expected to increase to between 20 percent and 25 percent over the next 50 years. The segment of the population aged 85 and over is growing at an even faster rate. While less than 10 percent of the over-65 group is over 85 today, this percentage is expected to double over the next two generations.

An aging society presents changing problems. Those who needed long-term care in the past were most likely to have suffered from strokes or other acute diseases. With longer life spans today and in the future, a larger portion of the elderly are incapacitated by chronic conditions such as Alzheimer's disease, arthritis, diabetes, osteoporosis, and lung and heart disease—conditions that often require continuing assistance with day-to-day needs. The likelihood that a person will need to enter a nursing home increases dramatically with age. One percent of persons between the ages of 65 and 74 reside in nursing homes, and the percentage increases to 6 percent between the ages of 75 and 84. At age 85 and over, the figure rises to approximately 25 percent. Statistics of the Department of Health and Human Services indicate that persons aged 65 or older face a 40 percent chance of entering a nursing home at some time during the remainder of their lives. Nearly half of the persons who enter nursing homes remain longer than one year, and the average nursing home stay is about 2.5 years.

Nursing home statistics tell only part of the story. An even greater percentage of the elderly have age-related conditions that require varying degrees of assistance to enable them to perform normal daily activities. In some cases, this assistance is provided in other types of supportive-living arrangements such as assisted-living facilities and adult foster homes. In many cases, however, the elderly remain in their own homes or the homes of relatives and receive their care from relatives, home health agencies, and community-based programs. The latter programs include meals on wheels and adult day care centers.

The elderly are not the only group of persons who need long-term care. Many younger persons are unable to care for themselves because of handicaps resulting from birth defects, mental conditions, illnesses, or accidents.

Increasing Costs

The Congressional Budget Office estimated the year 2004 national expenditures for care for the elderly in institutional settings at over $92 billion; home health care exceeded $42 billion. These costs, about 11 percent of national health care expenditures, are increasing faster than inflation because of the growing demand for nursing home beds and the shortage of skilled medical personnel. By 2020, these annual amounts are expected to rise to approximately $139 billion for nursing home care and $69 billion for home care.[2]

The out-of-pocket payments for long-term care by individuals who must use personal resources can be astronomical. Currently, average annual nursing home costs are over $60,000 and can be much higher. Although the average nursing home stay is 2.5 years, some stays exceed the average by many years. Two visits a day by a home health aid to help with bathing and dressing and household chores can cost $2,500 a month.[3] By 2030, the annual cost of nursing home care is expected to approximate $200,000 with comparable increases in home care charges.[4]

Inability of Families to Provide Full Care

Traditionally, family members have provided long-term care, often at considerable personal sacrifice and stress. However, it is becoming more difficult for families to provide long-term care for these reasons:

- geographic dispersion of family members
- increased participation in the paid workforce by women and children
- fewer children in the family
- more childless families
- higher divorce rates
- inability of family members to provide care because they, too, are growing old

Inadequacy of Insurance Protection

Private medical expense insurance policies (both group and individual) almost always have an exclusion for convalescent, custodial, or rest care. Some policies do provide coverage for extended-care facilities and for home health care. In both cases, the purpose is to provide care in a manner that is less expensive than care in a hospital. However, coverage is provided only if a person also needs medical care; benefits are not provided if a person is merely "old" and needs someone to care for him or her.

Medicare is also inadequate because it does not cover custodial care unless this care is needed along with the medical or rehabilitative treatment provided in skilled-nursing facilities or under home health care benefits.

SOURCES OF LONG-TERM CARE

There are several sources other than insurance that are available for financing long-term care; however, there are drawbacks associated with each.

One source is to rely on personal financial resources. In addition to income, these resources may include savings, investments, and home equity that is accessed by loans and reverse mortgages. Few individuals have sufficient retirement income to fully meet their potential long-term care expenses. Unless a person has substantial assets on which to draw, this approach may force an individual and his or her dependents into poverty. It may also mean that the person will not meet the financial objective of leaving assets to heirs.

An often overlooked source of providing or financing long-term care is relatives, or even friends. In some cases, family members may act as caregivers themselves; in other cases, they may give financial support to provide care or pay for long-term care insurance premiums. The support of relatives, however, may not last forever. For example, a spouse may no longer be able to provide care because of his or her own physical condition. And aging children may not have the financial resources to continue the same level of support because of their own long-term care needs.

Another source is to rely on welfare. The Medicaid program in most states provides benefits, which usually include nursing home care and home health care (and possibly assisted-living care), to the "medically needy." However, a person is not eligible unless he or she is either poor or has a low income and has exhausted most other assets (including those of a spouse). There is also often a social stigma associated with accepting welfare. In addition, the facilities that accept Medicaid recipients may be located away from family members and/or provide a lower quality of care than a person with adequate resources can purchase.

look-back period

One strategy that is sometimes used is to give a person's assets away at the time nursing home care is needed and ultimately rely on Medicaid. (This will work only if income, including pensions and Social Security, is below specified limits.) However, Medicaid benefits are reduced (or their onset postponed) if assets were disposed of at less than their fair market value within a specific time period (called the *look-back period*) prior to Medicaid eligibility. One solution is to purchase long-term care insurance in an amount sufficient to provide protection for the length of the look-back period. If care is needed, a person can rely on the insurance coverage and transfer assets to heirs. When the insurance coverage runs out and the look-back period is over, the person can apply for Medicaid.

Several states have attempted to encourage better coverage for long-term care by waiving or modifying certain Medicaid requirements if a person carries a state-approved long-term care policy. For example, in Connecticut, a person can apply for and receive Medicaid benefits without having to exhaust current assets if the individual has maintained an approved long-term care policy and its benefits have run out. In essence, these programs increase the assets that a person can retain and still collect Medicaid benefits; the increase in the allowable asset threshold is related to the amount of long-term care coverage carried and exhausted.

continuing care retirement community

Continuing-care retirement communities (CCRCs), also referred to as life care facilities, are growing in popularity as a source to meet long-term care needs. Residents in a CCRC pay an "entrance fee" that allows them to occupy a dwelling unit but usually does not give them actual ownership rights. The entrance fee may or may not be refundable if the resident leaves the facility voluntarily or dies. As a general rule, the higher the refund is, the higher the entrance fee is. Residents pay a monthly fee that includes meals, some housecleaning services, and varying degrees of health care. If a person needs long-term care, he or she must give up the independent living unit and move to the assisted-living or nursing home portion of the CCRC, but the monthly fee usually remains the same.

The disadvantages of this option are that the cost of a CCRC is beyond the reach of many persons, and a resident must be in reasonably good health and able to live independently at the time he or she enters the facility. Therefore, the decision to use a CCRC must be made in advance of the need for long-term care. Once such care is needed or is imminent, this approach is no longer viable.

A few insurers now include long-term care benefits in some cash value life insurance policies. Essentially, an insured can begin to use these accelerated benefits while he or she is still living. For example, if the insured is in a nursing home, he or she might be able to elect a benefit equal to 25 percent or 50 percent of the policy face amount. However, any benefits received reduce the future death benefit payable to heirs. One potential problem with this approach is that the acceleration of benefits may result in the reduction of the death benefit to a level that is inadequate to accomplish the purpose of life insurance—the protection of family members after a wage earner's death. If benefits are accelerated, there is less left for the surviving family. In addition, the availability of an accelerated benefit may give the insured a false sense of security that long-term care needs are being met when, in fact, the potential benefit may be inadequate to cover extended nursing home stays.

long-term care insurance

Finally, there is *long-term care insurance*, which is the subject of the remainder of this chapter. It is a form of health insurance that usually provides coverage for custodial care, intermediate care, and skilled-nursing care. Benefits may also be provided for other types of care such as home health care, adult day care, and assisted living.

Some Ways to Pay for Long-Term Care

- Personal income and assets
- Family support
- Medicaid/welfare programs
- Continuing care retirement communities
- Accelerated benefits in life insurance policies
- Long-term care insurance

DEVELOPMENT OF INSURANCE COVERAGE

It is common for insurance coverages to evolve over time. However, the evolution of long-term care products has been dramatic—both the magnitude of the changes and the speed with which these changes have occurred.

Early Policies

The long-term care policies in existence in the early 1980s were primarily designed to provide care during the recovery period following an acute illness. They seldom met the needs of persons who required long-term care for chronic conditions. The following provisions were characteristic of many of these policies:

- benefit periods of less than one year
- a prerequisite for benefits in a skilled-nursing facility, often a prior hospitalization of 3 to 5 days
- a prerequisite of a higher level of out-of-hospital care before the person could receive benefits for a lower level of care. For example, home health care might be covered, but only if a person had spent 3 to 5 days in a skilled-nursing facility.
- the exclusion of benefits for care needed as a result of Alzheimer's disease or other organic brain diseases
- no inflation protection to meet higher long-term care costs in the future
- lack of guaranteed renewability provisions

In addition, the sale of early long-term care policies was often accompanied by improper sales practices. Consumers were led to believe that policies were much more comprehensive than they actually were. In effect, policyowners felt that they were purchasing "nursing home" insurance that would cover them anytime nursing home care was needed. Only when such care was needed did many of these policyowners realize that their coverage was very limited.

Finally, for many years, there was no favorable tax treatment given to long-term care insurance. Premiums for coverage were not deductible, and benefits and employer-paid premiums under group plans resulted in taxation to employees.

Evolution of Coverage

Criticism of the early long-term care policies created considerable pressure for change. Consumer groups argued for more government regulation. The federal government conducted studies and held hearings, with the results painting a less than flattering picture of long-term care policies. Change itself, however, resulted primarily from the actions of insurance companies themselves and from the state regulators of insurance. But the threat of federal regulation was always present. The negative publicity about early policies had a dampening effect on the public's perception of long-term care insurance. This led many insurance companies to modify their policies and companies entering the business to offer more comprehensive policies. At the same time, the National Association of Insurance Commissioners (NAIC) began to take a very active interest in long-term care insurance. This culminated in the adoption of the Long-term Care Insurance Model Act in 1987. In 1988, model regulations were issued to enable the states to implement the model act. The act and the regulations have been amended many times since. Sometimes these amendments changed previous act provisions; at other times, they addressed new issues. The majority of states have adopted the model act, which is discussed in more detail later. However, the version in force in a given state is not always the latest NAIC version. A few states still have little regulation of long-term care policies, and other states have adopted legislation different from the model act, although it may be similar to that the NAIC recommended.

Considerable changes also took place at the federal level with passage of the Health Insurance Portability and Accountability Act in 1996. This law, referred to as HIPAA, provides favorable tax treatment to long-term care insurance contracts that meet certain standards. These contracts are referred to as *tax-qualified* policies.

The long-term care policies of most insurance companies have gone through many revisions. Although coverage is still not always complete, there is little comparison between the early policies and most of what is marketed today. Not only have policies become more comprehensive over the last few years, but premiums are also lower as a result of intensified competition and the availability of more credible statistics about long-term claims. (However, several insurers have increased premiums recently, particularly for newly written policies.) Existing policyowners are often able to obtain the enhancements in newer policies but frequently at an increased premium. Some companies allow the policyowner to add the enhanced benefits by paying the new premium based on the policyowner's original age of issue. Other companies require evidence of insurability and use attained-age rates.

Most companies that write individual policies now issue only the tax-qualified contracts prescribed by HIPAA. Some companies issue both qualified contracts and *non-tax-qualified* contracts, and a few companies issue only non-tax-qualified contracts. Although purchasers of these contracts do not receive the tax advantages that qualified contracts provide, the nonqualified contracts often include provisions that make it easier to qualify for benefits.

NAIC MODEL LEGISLATION

Because of its widespread adoption by the states, it is appropriate to discuss the NAIC model legislation regarding long-term care. The legislation consists of a model act that is designed to be incorporated into a state's insurance law and model regulations that are designed to be adopted for use in implementing the law. This discussion is based on the latest version of the model legislation, which, as mentioned earlier, seems to be amended almost annually. Even though most states have adopted the NAIC legislation, some states may not have adopted the latest version. However, the importance of the model legislation should not be overlooked. With most insurers writing coverage in more than one state, it is likely that the latest provisions have been adopted by one or more states where an insurer's coverage is sold. Because most insurance companies sell essentially the same long-term care product everywhere they do business, the NAIC guidelines are often, in effect, being adhered to in states that have not adopted the legislation.

Before proceeding with a summary of the major provisions of the NAIC model legislation, it is important to make two points. First, the model legislation establishes guidelines. Insurance companies still have significant latitude in many aspects of product design. Second, many older policies are still in existence that were written prior to the adoption of the model legislation or under one of its earlier versions.

The model legislation focuses on two major areas—policy provisions and marketing. Highlights of the criteria for policy provisions include the following:

- Certain words or terms cannot be used in a policy unless they are specifically defined in accordance with the legislation. Examples include adult day care, home health care services, personal care, and skilled-nursing care.
- No policy can contain renewal provisions other than guaranteed renewable or noncancelable.
- Limitations and exclusions are prohibited except in the following cases:
  - preexisting conditions
  - mental or nervous disorders (but this does not permit the exclusion of Alzheimer's disease)
  - alcoholism and drug addiction
  - illness, treatment, or medical condition arising out of war, service in the armed forces, participation in a felony, suicide, and aviation if a person is a non-fare-paying passenger
  - treatment in a government facility and services available under Medicare and other social insurance programs

- No policy can provide coverage for skilled-nursing care only or provide significantly more coverage for skilled care in a facility than for lower levels of care.
- The definition of preexisting condition can be no more restrictive than to exclude a condition for which treatment was recommended or received within 6 months prior to the effective date of coverage. In addition, coverage can be excluded for a confinement for this condition only if it begins within 6 months of the effective date of coverage.
- Eligibility for benefits cannot be based on a prior hospital requirement or higher level of care.
- Insurance companies must offer the applicant the right to purchase coverage that allows for an increase in the amount of benefits based on reasonable anticipated increases in the cost of services the policy covers. The applicant must specifically reject this inflation protection if he or she does not want it.
- Insurance companies must offer the applicant the right to purchase a nonforfeiture benefit.
- A policy must contain a provision that makes a policy incontestable after 2 years on the grounds of misrepresentation alone. The policy can still be contested on the basis that the applicant knowingly and intentionally misrepresented relevant facts pertaining to the insured's health.

The following provisions of the model legislation pertain to marketing:

- An outline of coverage must be delivered to a prospective applicant at the time of initial solicitation. Among the information this outline must contain is (1) a description of the coverage, (2) a statement of the principal exclusions, reductions, and limitations in the policy, (3) a statement of the terms under which the policy can be continued in force or terminated, (4) a description of the terms under which the policy may be returned and the premium refunded, (5) a brief description of the relationship between cost of care and benefits, and (6) a statement whether the policy is intended to be tax qualified.
- A shopper's guide must be delivered to all prospective applicants. Most insurers use one prepared by the NAIC.
- The policy must allow policyowners to have a 30-day free look after a policy's delivery. Any premium paid is refunded if the insured decides to cancel the policy before the free-look period ends.
- An insurance company must establish procedures to ensure that any comparisons of policies by its agents or other producers are fair and accurate and to prohibit excessive insurance from being sold or issued.
- Applications for insurance must be clear and unambiguous so that an applicant's health condition can be properly ascertained. The application must also contain a conspicuous statement near the place for the

applicant's signature that says the following: "If your answers to this application are incorrect or untrue, the company has the right to deny benefits or rescind your policy." The purpose of these requirements is to control postclaim underwriting—the practice of rescinding a policy or denying a claim based on information obtained at the time a claim is filed that could have been obtained at the time of the application.

- No policy can be issued until the applicant has been given the option to elect a third party to be notified of any pending policy lapse because of nonpayment of premium. The purpose of this provision is to eliminate the problem of policy lapse because a senile or otherwise mentally impaired person fails to pay the premium.

NAIC Model Legislation Concerning Marketing of Long-Term Care Insurance

- Prospective purchasers must be given an outline of the coverage, a shopper's guide, and a 30-day free look at the policy.
- Procedures for fair and accurate policy comparisons must be established.
- Applications must be clear and unambiguous.
- Applicants must have option to name a third party to be notified of pending lapse due to nonpayment of premium.

EFFECT OF HEALTH INSURANCE PORTABILITY AND ACCOUNTABILITY ACT (HIPAA)

The Health Insurance Portability and Accountability Act (HIPAA) made the tax treatment of long-term care insurance more favorable. However, this favorable tax treatment is given only to long-term care insurance policies that meet prescribed standards. The long-term care provisions in the act are primarily changes in the income tax code. States still have the authority to regulate long-term care insurance contracts.

Eligibility for Favorable Tax Treatment

qualified long-term care insurance contract

The act provides favorable tax treatment to a *qualified long-term care insurance contract*. This is defined as any insurance contract that meets all the following requirements:

- The only insurance protection provided under the contract is for *qualified long-term care services.*

- The contract cannot pay for expenses that are reimbursable under Medicare. However, this requirement does not apply to expenses that are reimbursable if (1) Medicare is a secondary payer of benefits or (2) benefits are payable on a per diem basis.
- The contract must be guaranteed renewable.
- The contract does not provide for a cash surrender value or other money that can be borrowed or paid, assigned, or pledged as collateral for a loan.
- All refunds of premiums and policyowner dividends must be applied as future reductions in premiums or to increase future benefits.
- The policy must comply with various consumer protection provisions. For the most part, these are the same provisions contained in the NAIC model legislation and already adopted by most states.

qualified long-term care services

The act defines *qualified long-term care services* as necessary diagnostic, preventive, therapeutic, curing, treating, and rehabilitative services, and maintenance or personal care services that are required by a chronically ill person and provided by a plan of care prescribed by a licensed health care practitioner.

chronically ill individual

A *chronically ill individual* is one who has been certified as meeting one of the following requirements, often referred to as benefit triggers:

activities of daily living (ADLs)

- The person is expected to be unable to perform, without substantial assistance from another person, at least two *activities of daily living (ADLs)* for a period of at least 90 days due to a loss of functional capacity. The act allows six ADLs: eating, bathing, dressing, using the toilet, maintaining continence, and transferring in and out of a bed, chair, or wheelchair. A qualified long-term care insurance contract must contain at least five of the six.
- Substantial supervision is required to protect the individual from threats to health and safety because of severe cognitive impairment.

The act also specifies that any contract issued before January 1, 1997, that met the long-term care requirements in the state where the policy was issued will be considered a tax-qualified long-term care contract. If such a contract undergoes a material change, however, the policy must then conform to the HIPAA requirements to retain this status.

Federal Income Tax Provisions

A qualified long-term care insurance contract, typically referred to as tax qualified, is treated as accident and health insurance. With some exceptions, expenses for long-term care services, including insurance premiums, are treated like other medical expenses. That is, self-employed persons may deduct the premiums paid, and persons who itemize deductions can include the cost of long-term care services, including insurance premiums, for purposes of deducting medical expenses in excess of 7.5 percent of adjusted gross income. However, there is a cap on the amount of personally paid long-term care insurance premiums that a person can claim as medical expenses. These limits, which are based upon a covered individual's age and subject to cost-of-living adjustments, are shown for 2005 in table 15-1. There are no deductions for payments made to a spouse or relative who is not a licensed professional with respect to such services.

TABLE 15-1 **Long-Term Care Deductible Limits**	
Age	**Annual Deductible Limit per Covered Individual**
40 or younger	$ 270
41–50	510
51–60	1,020
61–70	2,720
Older than 70	3,400

Any employer contributions for group contracts are deductible to the employer and do not result in any taxable income to an employee. Coverage cannot be offered through a cafeteria plan on a tax-favored basis. In addition, if an employee has a flexible spending account for unreimbursed medical expenses, any reimbursements for long-term care services must be included in the employee's income.

An employee receives benefits under a qualified long-term care insurance contract tax free with one possible exception. Under contracts written on a per diem basis, proceeds are excludible from income up to $240 per day in 2005. (This figure is indexed annually.) Amounts in excess of $240 are also excludible to the extent that they represent actual costs for long-term care services.

CHARACTERISTICS OF INDIVIDUAL POLICIES

For many types of insurance, policies are relatively standardized. For long-term care insurance, the opposite is true. Significant variations (and therefore differences in cost) exist from one insurance company to another. An applicant also has numerous options with respect to policy provisions.

The discussion in this section of the chapter focuses on issue age, types of care covered, benefit variations, benefit amounts, benefit duration, the ability to restore benefits, the degree of inflation protection, renewability, and cost. The provisions and practices described represent the norm in that most policies fit within the extremes that are described. However, the norm covers a wide spectrum.

Issue Age

Significant variations exist among insurance companies with respect to the age at which they will issue policies. At a minimum, a healthy person between the ages of 40 and 75 is eligible for coverage from most insurance companies. Most companies also have an upper age in the range of 84 to 89, beyond which coverage is not issued. Restrictive policy provisions and very high premiums often accompany coverage written at age 85 or older, when available.

Considerably more variation exists with respect to the youngest age at which coverage is written. Some companies have no minimum age. Most companies sell policies to persons as young as age 18. Still other companies have a higher minimum age, often age 40.

Types of Care Covered

There are many types of care for which a long-term care policy may provide benefits. By broad categories, these can be categorized as nursing home care, assisted-living care, hospice care, care in an Alzheimer's facility, home health care, care coordination, and alternative sources of care. A long-term care policy may provide benefits for one, several, or all of these types of care.

Nursing Home Care

nursing home care

Nursing home care encompasses skilled-nursing care, intermediate care, and custodial care in a licensed facility. *Skilled-nursing* care consists of daily nursing and rehabilitative care that can be performed only by, or under the supervision of, skilled medical personnel and must be based on a doctor's orders. *Intermediate* care involves occasional nursing and rehabilitative care that must be based on a doctor's orders and can be performed only by, or under the supervision of, skilled medical personnel. *Custodial care* is primarily to handle personal needs, such as walking, bathing, dressing, eating, or taking medicine, and can usually be provided by someone without professional medical skills or training.

custodial care

bed reservation benefit

Policies that provide nursing home care often also provide a *bed reservation benefit*, which continues payments to a long-term care facility for a limited time (such as 20 days) if a patient temporarily leaves because of hospitalization or any other reason. Without a continuation of payments, the bed may be assigned to someone else and unavailable upon the patient's release from the hospital.

Assisted-Living Facility Care

assisted-living care

Assisted-living care is provided in facilities that care for the frail elderly who are no longer able to care for themselves but do not need as high a level of care as a nursing home provides.

Hospice Care

Hospice care does not attempt to cure medical conditions but rather is devoted to easing the physical and psychological pain associated with dying. In addition to providing services for the dying patient, a hospice may offer counseling to family members. A hospice may be a separate facility, but this type of care can also be provided on an outpatient basis in the dying person's home. Most long-term care insurance policies that provide benefits for hospice care make no distinction in the setting.

Alzheimer's Facilities

The states require long-term care insurance policies to cover Alzheimer's disease and related forms of degenerative diseases and dementia under the same terms as they cover other conditions that qualify an individual as chronically ill. Therefore, coverage is provided if an individual receives services in a nursing home, in an assisted-living facility, or at home—as long as the policy covers the specific type of care. Most policies, however, have some specific reference to Alzheimer's facilities. In some cases, they are included as part of the definition for assisted-living facilities. In other cases, they are referred to separately but defined as facilities that must meet the policy's definition of either a nursing home or an assisted-living facility.

Home Health Care

Home health care is much broader than just part-time skilled-nursing care, therapy, part-time services from home health aides, and help from homemakers. It may also include benefits for one or more of the following:

- the purchase or rental of needed medical equipment and emergency alert systems
- modifications to the home such as a ramp for a wheelchair or bathroom modifications
- adult day care, which is received at centers specifically designed for the elderly who live at home but whose spouses or families cannot be available during the day
- **respite care**
- *respite care,* which allows occasional full-time care for a person who is receiving home health care. These persons are also often receiving care from a family member or friend. This benefit gives caregivers

needed time off. Respite care can be provided in a person's home or by moving the person to a nursing facility for a short stay.

- caregiver training, which is the training of a family member or friend to provide care so that a person can remain at home
- a homemaker companion who is an employee of a state-licensed home health care agency. The companion may assist with such tasks as cooking, shopping, cleaning, bill paying, or other household chores.
- prescription drugs and laboratory services typically provided in hospitals and nursing homes

Care Coordination

care coordinator

Many policies provide the services of a *care coordinator* who works with an insured, his or her family, and licensed health care practitioners to assess a person's condition, evaluate care options, and develop an individualized plan of care that provides the most appropriate services. The care coordinator may also periodically reevaluate ongoing plans of care and act as an advocate for the insured. Some long-term care policies mandate that the insured use the services of the care coordinator in order to receive benefits.

Alternative Plans of Care

Many policies provide benefits for alternative plans of care, even though the policy might not cover the types of care. For example, a policy covering nursing home care only might provide benefits for care in an assisted-living facility if these benefits are an appropriate and cost-effective alternative to care in a nursing home. As a general rule, the alternative plan must be acceptable to the insurance company, the insured, and the insured's physician.

Benefit Variations

There are almost as many variations among long-term care policies as there are among insurance companies writing the product. Much of this variation is related to the types of care for which benefits are provided. These benefit variations fall into three broad categories: facility-only policies, home-health-care-only policies, and comprehensive policies.

Facility-Only Policies

facility-only policy

Many early long-term care policies were designed to provide benefits only if the insured was in a nursing home. This type of policy was frequently referred to as a nursing home policy. These policies still exist, but they frequently also provide benefits for care in other settings such as assisted-living facilities and hospices. The term *facility-only policy* is often used to describe this broader type of policy, and the term, in its most generic sense, also includes nursing home policies.

Home-Health-Care-Only Policies

home-health-care-only policy

Home-health-care-only policies were originally developed to be used either as an alternative to nursing home policies or to complement such policies if more comprehensive coverage was desired. A *home-health-care-only policy* is designed to provide benefits for care outside an institutional setting. Some home health care policies also provide benefits for care in assisted-living facilities, and this is one area in which they often overlap with facility-only policies.

Although some insurers still write stand-alone home health care policies, many other insurers have exited this market and now write the coverage as part of a broader comprehensive policy.

Comprehensive Policies

comprehensive long-term care insurance policy

Most long-term care policies written today can be described as comprehensive policies. A *comprehensive long-term care insurance policy*, sometimes referred to as an integrated policy, combines benefits for facility care and home health care into a single contract. However, variations exist within this type of policy with respect to what is covered as part of the standard policy and what is an optional benefit that the applicant may select. For example, some policies cover almost all care settings as part of their standard benefits; other policies provide facility-only coverage as a standard benefit with home health care covered as an option for an additional premium.

Some Examples

The following examples of actual long-term care policies in the marketplace illustrate some of the wide variations in benefits.

Example 1:   This policy is advertised as a nursing home policy. The policy provides coverage for

- nursing home care
- hospice-facility care
- a bed reservation benefit
- an alternative plan of care

Example 2:   The policy is advertised as a long-term care insurance policy providing facility benefits only. The policy provides coverage for

- nursing home care
- assisted-living facility care
- hospice-facility care
- a bed reservation benefit
- an alternative plan of care

Example 3: The policy is advertised as a home health care policy and provides coverage for

- home health care
- adult day care
- a care coordinator
- caregiver training
- a homemaker companion
- respite care

Example 4: The policy is advertised as a home health care policy and provides benefits for

- home health care
- adult day care
- a care coordinator
- an alternative plan of care
- caregiver training
- respite care

Example 5: The policy is a comprehensive policy with standard benefits for facility care and optional benefits for home and community-based care. The standard benefits are for

- nursing home care
- assisted-living care
- hospice care
- a bed reservation benefit
- a care coordinator
- an alternative plan of care

Optional coverage includes a rider that provides benefits for

- home health care
- adult day care
- caregiver training
- a homemaker companion

Example 6:   The policy is a comprehensive policy that provides benefits for

- nursing home care
- assisted-living facility care
- hospice care
- a bed reservation benefit
- home health care
- adult day care
- respite care
- an alternative plan of care
- caregiver training
- a home health care coordinator

Benefit Amounts

When purchasing long-term care insurance, the applicant selects the level of benefit he or she desires up to the maximum level the insurance company will provide. Benefits are often sold in increments of $10 per day up to frequently found limits of $200 or $250 or, in a few cases, as much as $400 or $500 per day. Most insurance companies will not offer a daily benefit below $40 or $50. Some policies base benefits on a monthly (rather than daily) amount that can vary from $1,000 to $6,000 or more.

The same level of benefits is usually provided for all types of institutional care. Most comprehensive policies that provide home health care benefits once limited the daily benefit to one-half the amount payable for institutional stays. However, many insurers now allow applicants to select home health care limits that are as high as 75 percent to 100 percent of the benefit for institutional care; a few insurers even offer limits as high as 125 percent or 150 percent. If a policy provides home health care benefits only, the daily amount of that benefit is what the applicant selected.

Policies pay benefits in one of two basic ways: reimbursement or per diem.

Reimbursement Policies

reimbursement basis

The majority of newer policies pay benefits on a *reimbursement basis*. These contracts reimburse the insured for actual expenses up to the specified policy limit. For example, a policy with a daily benefit amount of $200 will pay only $150 if that was the insured's actual charge for care. Tax-qualified policies that provide benefits on a reimbursement basis must be coordinated with Medicare.

Per Diem Policies

per diem basis

Some policies provide benefits on a *per diem basis* once care is actually being received. This means that benefits are paid regardless of the actual cost of care. In this case, a policy with a daily benefit of $200 will pay $200 even if actual long-term care charges for the day are only $150. Per diem contracts are seldom coordinated with any benefits that are payable under Medicare. If home health care benefits are provided, most per diem policies pay benefits regardless of the service provider. In such cases, benefits are paid even if a family member provides care at no charge. Some policies, however, define the type of service provider from whom care must be received.

Example:	Teresa, aged 70, recently entered a nursing home following a lengthy hospitalization. The cost of her care is $200 per day. Because she will need skilled-nursing care for many months, Medicare will pay the cost of the first 20 days of care in full and provide an additional 80 days of benefits with a daily copayment. Teresa also has a tax-qualified long-term care insurance policy that will provide benefits of $150 per day after a 30-day elimination period.
	If Teresa's policy provides benefits on a reimbursement basis, no benefits will be payable as long as Teresa is collecting any benefits from Medicare. When Medicare payments cease after 100 days, Teresa will collect $150 per day as long as her policy counts the days she was receiving Medicare benefits toward the elimination period.
	If Teresa's policy provides benefits on a per diem basis and if the policy is not integrated with Medicare, Teresa will collect a daily benefit of $150 beginning on the 31st day, regardless of any Medicare reimbursement.

Note that per diem policies are sometimes referred to as indemnity policies even though the usual insurance meaning of indemnity implies payment of benefits for actual expenses up to policy limits. In this sense, reimbursement policies, not per diem policies, are actually contracts of indemnity. Per diem policies are valued contracts.

A few insurers offer a variation of the per diem policy that pays benefits as long as the insured satisfies a policy's benefit trigger, even if no long-term care **disability-based policy** is being received. Such a policy is referred to as a *disability-based policy*.

Period of Benefits

To determine the period of benefits under a long-term care insurance policy, it is necessary to look at the elimination period and the maximum duration of benefits.

Elimination Period

The applicant is required to select a period of time that must pass after long-term care commences but before benefit payments begin. The majority of long-term care insurers refer to this period as an elimination period. Some insurers, however, call it a waiting period or a deductible period. Most insurers allow an applicant to select from three to five optional elimination periods. For example, one insurer allows the choice of 20, 60, 100, or 180 days. Choices may be as low as 0 days or as high as 365 days.

In a comprehensive policy, there is generally a single elimination period that can be met by any combination of days during which the insured is in a long-term care facility or receiving home health care services.

There are several ways that home health care services can be counted toward the elimination period. Some policies count only those days when actual services are received for which charges are made and will be covered after the elimination period is satisfied. If an insured receives services 3 days during the week, this counts as 3 days. If the insured's policy has a 60-day elimination period, benefit payments will not begin until the insured has been receiving services for 20 weeks (or 140 days). Some policies count each week as 7 days toward the satisfaction of the elimination period if services were received on any number of days in the week, even one day. In this case, the insured will start receiving benefit payments after 60 days have elapsed from the first service.

Another variation in reimbursement policies is for the insurer to start counting days toward satisfaction of the elimination period as soon as long-term care is certified as being necessary, even if services are received from someone who does not make a charge. Therefore, family members or friends could provide the services until the elimination period is satisfied, and the insurer will then start paying benefits for the services of a paid caregiver.

One final comment about the elimination period concerns its relationship to the requirement that tax-qualified policies cannot pay benefits for the inability to perform ADLs unless this inability is expected to last at least 90 days. Actually, despite what some people think, there is no relationship. If an insured is certified as being unable to perform the requisite number of ADLs for at least 90 days, benefit payments will start after the satisfaction of the elimination period, be it 0, 20, 60, or any other specified number of days. If the insured makes a recovery after the elimination period is satisfied but before the end of the 90-day period, the insured is fully entitled to any benefits received because the period was *expected* to be at least 90 days.

Maximum Duration of Benefits

The applicant is also given a choice as to the maximum period for which benefits are paid, often referred to as the benefit period. This period begins from the time benefit payments start after satisfaction of the elimination period. In addition, the benefit period does not necessarily apply to each separate period for which long-term care services are received. Rather, it is a period that applies to the aggregate time benefits are paid under the policy. When the maximum benefits are paid, the policy will terminate. However, if benefits are only partially exhausted during a course of long-term care, they may be restored under certain circumstances, as explained later. Also as explained later, the length of the benefit period may actually differ from the period chosen if a policy uses a pool-of-money concept.

Most insurers require the applicant to select the benefit period, and they make several options available. For example, one insurer offers durations of 2, 3, and 5 years as well as lifetime benefits. In most cases, a single benefit period applies to long-term care, no matter where it is received. A few policies, however, have separate benefit periods for facility care and home health care. There are also a few policies, usually the per diem type, that specify the maximum benefits as a stated dollar amount such as $100,000.

There are actually two ways that the benefit period is applied in the payment of benefits. Under one approach, benefit payments are made for exactly the benefit period chosen. If the applicant selects a benefit period of 4 years and collects benefits for 4 years, the benefit payments cease. The other approach, most commonly but not exclusively used with reimbursement **pool of money** policies, uses a *pool of money*. Under this concept, there is an amount of money that can be used to make benefit payments as long as the pool of money lasts. The applicant does not select the amount in the pool of money; it is determined by multiplying the daily benefit by the benefit period selected. For example, if the daily benefit is $200 and the benefit period is 1,460 days (or 4 years), then the pool of money is $292,000 ($200 x 1,460). Several important points about this pool of money should be mentioned:

- Daily benefit payments from the pool of money cannot exceed the daily policy benefits.
- Under comprehensive policies, the pool of money is typically determined by using the daily benefit amount for institutional care.
- Adjustments are made to the pool of money during periods of benefit payments to reflect any inflation protection that applies to the policy benefits.

Example:　　Renee has a comprehensive long-term care insurance policy that provides benefits on a reimbursement basis for a benefit period of 4 years. Her daily benefit is $200 for care in a long-term care facility and $100 per day for home health care. The policy makes benefit payments using the pool-of-money concept. Assume that Renee is chronically ill and receives home health care for 2 years at a cost of $80 per day for 5 days each week after she satisfies her elimination period. At that time, her condition deteriorates and she enters a nursing home that has a daily cost of $230.

Under a pool-of-money concept, the amount avail-able for Renee's benefit payments is $292,000, as previously calculated. During the 2 years (104 weeks) that Renee receives home health care, the policy will make benefit payments equal to the full cost of her care because it is less than $100 per day. This totals $41,600 ($80 x 104 x 5). Therefore, the pool of money is reduced by this amount to $250,400 by the time she enters the nursing home. The policy will then pay a daily benefit but only up to the policy limit of $200 per day. (The extra $30 per day is her responsibility.) Consequently, Renee can receive benefits for an additional 1,252 days ($250,400 ÷ $200). The net effect is that Renee will actually receive benefit payments over a period that is equal to almost 5 1/2 years. This period would be somewhat longer if an inflation increase had been assumed for the pool of money.

shared benefit

A few insurers use the concept of a *shared benefit* when a husband and wife are insured under the same policy or with the same insurer. Under this concept, each spouse can access the other spouse's benefits. For example, if each spouse has a 4-year benefit period and one spouse has exhausted his or her benefits, benefit payments can continue by drawing on any unused benefits under the other spouse's policy. In effect, one spouse could have a benefit period of up to 8 years as long as the other spouse receives no benefit payments.

Restoration

Many policies written with less than a lifetime benefit period provide for restoration of full benefits if the insured received less-than-full policy benefits and has not required long-term care for a certain time period, often 180 days. If a policy does not have this provision, maximum benefits for a subsequent claim are reduced by the benefits previously paid.

Inflation Protection

Most states require a long-term care policy to offer some type of automatic inflation protection. The applicant is given the choice to select this option, decline the option, or possibly select an alternative option. If the applicant selects the automatic-increase option, the cost of the option is built into the initial premium, and no additional premium is levied at the time of an annual increase. As a result of the NAIC model act and HIPAA, the standard provision found in almost all policies is a 5 percent benefit increase that is compounded annually over the life of the policy. Under such a provision, the amount of a policy's benefits increases by 5 percent each year over the amount of benefits available in the prior year.

A common alternative that many insurers make available is based on simple interest, whereby each annual automatic increase is 5 percent of the original benefit amount. Other options that are occasionally found are increases (either simple or compound) based on different fixed percentage amounts such as 3 or 4 percent.

The effect of an automatic increase in daily benefits can be dramatic, as table 15-2 indicates. However, such an increase is also accompanied by a significant premium increase.

TABLE 15-2
Effect of Automatic Increase on $100 Per Day Benefit

End of Policy Year	No Increase	5% Simple Interest	5% Compound Interest
5	$100	$125	$128
10	100	150	163
15	100	175	208
20	100	200	265
25	100	225	339
30	100	250	432

If an automatic-increase option is not selected, some insurers allow a policyowner to increase benefits without evidence of insurability on a pay-as-you-go basis at specified intervals such as every one, 2, or 3 years. Each benefit increase is accompanied by a premium increase that is based on attained-age rates for the additional coverage.

The amount of the periodic benefit increase under a pay-as-you-go option may be a fixed dollar amount, such as a daily benefit increase of $20 every third year, or based on a specified percentage or an index such as the CPI. Some insurers have an aggregate limit on the total amount of benefit increases or an age beyond which they are no longer available. Failure to exercise a periodic increase or a series of increases over a specified period typically terminates the right to purchase additional benefits in the future.

It is important to note that increases in benefits are often inadequate to offset actual inflation in the annual cost of long-term care, which has been higher than the general inflation rate over the last decade.

Eligibility for Benefits

Almost all tax-qualified contracts use the same two criteria for determining benefit eligibility; the insured is required to meet only one of the two. The first criterion is that the insured is expected to be unable, without substantial assistance from another person, to perform two of the six ADLs that are acceptable under HIPAA for a period of at least 90 days due to loss of functional capacity. The second criterion is that substantial supervision is required to protect the individual from threats to health and safety because of severe cognitive impairment.

Non-tax-qualified contracts, on the other hand, have more liberal eligibility requirements. Many of these contracts use the same criteria that are in tax-qualified contracts, except there is no time period that applies to the inability to perform the ADLs. A small number of non-tax-qualified contracts require only the inability to perform one ADL and/or use more than the six ADLs allowed by HIPAA. Finally, some non-tax-qualified contracts make benefits available if a third criterion—medical necessity—is satisfied. This generally means that a physician has certified that long-term care is needed, even if neither of the other criteria is satisfied.

Exclusions

Most long-term care policies contain the exclusions permitted under the NAIC model act. One source of controversy is the exclusion for mental and nervous disorders. This is an area that insurers frequently avoid because of the possibility of fraudulent claims and the controversies that often arise over claim settlements. The usual exclusion is stated as follows: "This policy does not provide benefits for the care or treatment of mental illness or emotional disorders without a demonstrable organic cause." Many policies also specifically stipulate that Alzheimer's disease and senile dementia, as diagnosed by a physician, are considered to have demonstrable organic cause, even though state law frequently requires these disorders to be covered.

Underwriting

The underwriting of long-term care policies, like the underwriting of medical expense policies, is based on the health of the insured. However, underwriting for long-term care insurance focuses on situations that will cause claims far into the future. Most underwriting is done on the basis of questionnaires rather than on the use of actual physical examinations. Numerous questions are asked about the health of relatives. For example, if a parent or grandparent had Alzheimer's disease, there is an increased likelihood that the applicant will get this disease in the future. In addition, the insurance company is very interested in medical events, such as temporary amnesia or fainting spells, that might be an indication of future incapacity.

Underwriting tends to become more restrictive as the age of an applicant increases. Not only is a future claim more likely to occur much sooner, but adverse selection can also be more severe.

Many insurers have a single classification for all acceptable applicants for long-term care insurance, but other insurers have three or four categories of insurable classifications, each with a different rate structure.

Some long-term care policies have a preexisting-conditions provision; it specifies that benefits are not paid within the first 6 months for a condition for which treatment was recommended or received within 6 months of policy purchase. Other policies, however, have no such provision or state that the provision does not apply to preexisting conditions that are listed on the policy application. There is little need for such a provision because insurers are required in most states to underwrite at the time coverage is written and are not allowed to use postclaims underwriting. If properly underwritten at the time of application, claims within the usual preexisting-conditions period are unlikely to occur. Elimination periods for benefits often serve a similar purpose.

Renewability

Long-term care policies currently being sold are guaranteed renewable, which means that an individual's coverage cannot be canceled except for nonpayment of premiums. Although premiums cannot be raised on the basis of a particular applicant's claim, they can (and often are) raised by class.

Nonforfeiture Options

Most companies give an applicant for long-term care insurance the right to elect a nonforfeiture benefit, and some states require that such a benefit be offered. With a nonforfeiture benefit, the policyowner will receive some value for a policy if the policy lapses because the required premium is not paid in the future. Few applicants, however, elect this option because of its cost.

The most common type of nonforfeiture option is a shortened benefit period. With this option, coverage is continued as a paid-up policy, but the length of the benefit period (or the amount of the benefit if stated as a maximum dollar amount) is reduced. Under the typical provision, the reduced coverage is available only if the lapse is on or after the policy's third anniversary. The amount of the benefit is equal to the greater of the total premiums paid for the policy prior to lapse or 30 times the policy's daily nursing home benefit.

Some non-tax-qualified policies offer a return-of-premium option, under which a portion of the premium is returned if a policy lapses after a specified number of years. For example, the policy of one insurer pays nothing if a policy lapses before it has been in force for 5 full years. It returns 15 percent of the total premiums paid if the policy was in force for 6 years, 30 percent for 7 years, 45 percent for 8 years, 60 percent for 9 years, and 80 percent for 10 or more years.

In some states that require an insurer to offer a nonforfeiture benefit, a policy must contain a *contingent benefit upon lapse* if the policyowner does not purchase the nonforfeiture benefit. This provision gives the policyowner the right to elect certain options if the premium has increased by a specified percentage since the time of policy issue. The percentage is a sliding scale that is determined by the issue age. For example, the percentage is 110 if the policy was issued when the insured was 50 to 54. The figure drops to 70 percent for an issue age of 60, 40 percent for an issue age of 70, and 20 percent for an issue age of 80. The options are a reduction in benefits to a level sustainable by the current premium or the conversion of the policy to a paid-up status with a shorter benefit period. The policyowner is not required to select either of these options and can continue to pay the higher premium and maintain the current policy benefits.

Premiums

Premium Payment Period

The vast majority of long-term care policies have premiums that are payable for life and determined by the age of the insured at the time of issue. A few insurers, however, offer other modes of payment. Lifetime coverage can sometimes be purchased with a single premium. Some insurers offer policies that have premium payment periods of 10 or 20 years or to age 65, after which time the premium is paid up. These policies are particularly attractive to applicants who do not want continuing premium payments after retirement.

Most long-term care policies have a provision that waives premiums if the insured has been receiving benefits under the policy for a specified period of time, often 60 or 90 days.

Factors Affecting Premiums

Numerous factors affect the premium that a policyowner will pay for a long-term care policy. Even if the provisions of several policies are virtually identical, premiums will vary among companies. For example, the annual premiums for three similar policies from three different companies are shown in table 15-3. Each policy has a daily benefit of $120 per day, a 0-day elimination period, a lifetime benefit period, and coverage for home health care.

Age. Age plays a significant role in the cost of long-term care coverage, as shown by the rates in the table. These figures demonstrate that long-term care coverage can be obtained at a reasonable annual cost if it is purchased at a young age.

TABLE 15-3 Comparison of Annual Long-Term Care Premiums for Similar Policies			
Age	Company A	Company B	Company C
40	$ 391	$ 549	$ 590
50	641	714	832
60	1,104	1,126	1,331
70	2,550	3,157	2,736
75	4,540	5,491	4,763

Types of Benefits. The benefits a policy provides have a significant bearing on the cost. Most policies cover care in a long-term care facility. Many policies also cover home health care and other benefits provided to persons who are still able to reside in their own homes. This broader coverage increases premiums by 60 to 70 percent.

Duration of Benefits. The longer the maximum benefit period, the higher the premium. The longer the elimination period, the lower the premium. With many insurers, a policy with an unlimited benefit period and no elimination period will have a premium about double that of a policy with a 2-year benefit period and a 90-day elimination period.

Inflation Protection. Policies may be written with or without automatic benefit increases for inflation. All other factors being equal, the addition of a 5 percent compound annual increase in benefits can raise premiums by 50 to 100 percent.

Nonforfeiture Benefits. A policy may be written with or without a nonforfeiture benefit. The inclusion of such a benefit can increase a premium by anywhere from 20 to 50 percent or more, depending on type of nonforfeiture benefit and other policy features.

Spousal Coverage. Most insurance companies offer a discount of 10 percent to 15 percent if both spouses purchase long-term care policies from the company.

Nonsmoker Discount. A few insurers offer a discount, such as 10 percent, if the insured is a nonsmoker.

An Example

As the following example shows, an applicant for long-term care insurance must often make several decisions before the final selection of a long-term care insurance policy.

Example: Fred, aged 65, has decided that he needs long-term care insurance. Five years ago, he and his wife sold their small jewelry store and were able to retire comfortably. Their plans of a leisurely life during retirement years were soon shattered when Fred's wife had a serious stroke. For 3 years, Fred was able to care for her at home with the assistance of professional caregivers. After she was totally paralyzed 2 years ago by a second stroke, Fred found it necessary to put her in the nursing home where she recently died.

Having spent almost $250,000 to provide his wife with the best care possible, Fred is fully aware of the effect that long-term care can have on a family's assets. He wants to make sure that any long-term care expenses he might incur will not further deplete the $500,000 in remaining assets that he and his wife spent a lifetime accumulating and intended to leave to their children and grandchildren.

Fred has contacted a well-respected insurance agent whom he has known for several years and asked her to help him find a long-term care insurance policy that meets his objectives. Fred has indicated that he would like a policy that provides these benefits:

- a daily facility benefit of $150. A top-quality nursing home in Fred's town will cost about $250 per day, but Fred feels he can afford to pay $100 from his Social Security and retirement income.
- a home health care benefit of $150 per day
- a lifetime benefit period
- a 20-day elimination period
- 5 percent annual compound inflation protection

Fred's agent calculates that such a policy will have an annual premium of $5,060. Fred feels that this is somewhat more than he can pay without withdrawing funds from his assets and asks her what can be done to reduce the premium to about $4,000 per year. She comes up with the following alternatives:

- If Fred lowers the daily benefit to $130 per day, the premium will drop to $4,380. A further decrease to $120 per day will result in a premium of $4,050. Fred decides to consider this option.

- If Fred decreases the home health care benefit to 50 percent of the facility benefit, the premium will drop to $4,130. Fred realizes how costly home health care can be and doesn't like this option.
- If Fred elects a 5-year benefit period, the premium will drop to $4,135. For a 4-year benefit period, the premium will be $3,800. Fred is aware of some patients in his wife's nursing home who had been there for as long as 10 years and doesn't like this option either.
- If he increases the elimination period to 90 days, the premium will drop to $4,150. The premium for a 180-day elimination period will further decrease the premium to $3,750. Fred is willing to think about a 90-day elimination period, but he feels that 180 days is too long.
- If Fred changes the inflation protection from compound interest to simple interest, the premium will drop to $4,260. Fred hopes to live for many more years and realizes the effect that inflation will have on long-term care costs. This option doesn't appeal to him.

Fred decides to take a day or two to think about his options. He calculates that the longer elimination period will increase his out-of-pocket costs by $10,500 (70 days times $150) over what they would otherwise be if he needs long-term care. He also calculates that the lower benefit amount of $120 will increase his annual out-of-pocket costs by $10,950 (365 days times costs will come from his accumulated assets. He also understands that he could afford the benefits he originally desired if he were willing to reduce his assets by about $1,000 per year to pay the $5,060 premium.

Fred finally decides that the policy with the $5,060 premium is the most appropriate choice. Its benefits will make it more likely that his family will provide the level of care he wants if he is unable to make decisions for himself.

GROUP COVERAGE

Success in the individual marketplace led to interest in group long-term care insurance as an employee benefit. The first group long-term plan was written in 1987, and a growing number of employers, mostly large ones, now make coverage available. The number of insurance companies writing coverage has also grown, but it still remains relatively small and is primarily limited to the largest group insurance carriers. However, over 1 million employees and their family members now have group coverage. In most cases, coverage is voluntary with the employee paying the full cost.

For the most part, group long-term care policies are comparable to the better policies that are being sold in the individual marketplace. There are a few differences, however, mostly because of the characteristics of group coverage:

- Eligibility for coverage generally requires that an employee be full-time and actively at work. At a minimum, coverage can be purchased for an active employee and/or the spouse. Some policies also make coverage available to retirees and to other family members of eligible persons such as minor children, parents, parents-in-law, and possibly adult children.
- The cost of group coverage is usually slightly less than the cost of individual coverage. To some extent, this is a result of the administrative services, such as payroll deduction, being performed by the employer.
- An employee typically has fewer choices with respect to benefit amounts, benefit duration, and the length of the elimination period.
- If a participant leaves employment, the group coverage can usually be continued on a direct-payment basis, under either the group contract or an individual contract.

CHECKLIST FOR EVALUATING AND COMPARING LONG-TERM CARE POLICIES

☐ What is the annual policy premium?

☐ Is the policy qualified to receive favorable tax treatment?

☐ What is the length of the free-look period?

☐ What services are covered?

    ___ Nursing home care
    ___ Assisted-living care
    ___ Custodial care
    ___ Home health care
    ___ Adult day care
    ___ Other

☐ How much does the policy pay per day for the following?

    ___ Facility care
    ___ Home health care
    ___ Other

☐ How long will benefits last?

    ___ For facility care
    ___ At home

☐ Does the policy have a maximum lifetime benefit? If yes, what is it?

☐ Does the policy have a maximum length of coverage for each period of confinement? If yes, what is it?

    ___ For facility care
    ___ For home health care

☐ What is the length of time before preexisting conditions are covered?

☐ What is the elimination period before benefits begin?

    ___ For facility care
    ___ For home health care

☐ What is the age range for enrollment?

☐ Is there a waiver-of-premium provision?

    ___ For facility care
    ___ For home health care

☐ What is the period that an insured must receive benefits before premiums are waived?

☐ Does the policy offer an inflation adjustment feature? If, yes,

    ___ What is the rate of increase?
    ___ How often is it applied?
    ___ For how long?
    ___ Is there an additional cost?

☐ What nonforfeiture options are available?

MINI-CASE: CLARA HARRIS

We first met Clara Harris in the mini-case for chapter 11. She is 75 years old and recently widowed. She is in excellent health, leads an active life, and is financially secure. Her current income is about $47,000 per year, which consists of Social Security, a survivor's pension, proceeds from a life income annuity, and income from savings and investments. She is fortunate in that much of her income is indexed for inflation. Clara also has a home valued at $500,000 and savings and investments of about $100,000.

Clara is concerned about the cost of long-term care. Her assets were diminished by the illness of her husband, who recently died after a long bout with Alzheimer's disease. She also recognizes the amount of care that a frail elderly person needs. Most of her time the last 4 years was taken up with her husband's care. Before that time, she had also devoted considerable time to caring for her elderly parents, both of whom lived well into their 90s. In fact, her mother spent the last 3 years of her life living with Clara and her husband.

Clara knows that her family would take care of her, but she is fiercely independent and does not want to be a burden if her health declines. She lives in the idyllic riverside home that she and her husband built 50 years ago and wants to remain there as long as possible, even if it requires home care. She does not want to live in an assisted-living facility, but she is realistic enough to realize that she might need nursing home care if her health deteriorates significantly. The only nursing home she would like to be in currently charges $5,000 per month.

Clara's four children are all financially secure. They want her to be well taken care of and have told her they do not want any inheritance. However, Clara would like to maintain a significant portion of her net worth so that she can leave something to her 11 grandchildren.

Evaluate Clara's need for long-term care insurance, taking into consideration the cost of both home care and nursing home care.

(See answer section for answers to mini-case.)

SOURCES FOR FURTHER IN-DEPTH STUDY

- Beam, Burton T., Jr., and O'Hare, Thomas P., *Meeting the Financial Need of Long-Term Care,* Bryn Mawr, PA: The American College Press, 2003. Phone 888-263-7265. Web site address www.theamericancollege.edu
- Sadler, Jeff, *How to Sell Long-Term Care Insurance*, Erlanger, KY: The National Underwriter Company, 2001. Phone 800-543-0874. Web site address www.nationalunderwriter.com

- Shilling, Dana, *Financial Planning for the Older Client*, 5th ed., Erlanger, KY: The National Underwriter Company, 2001. Phone 800-543-0874. Web site address www.nationalunderwriter.com

CHAPTER REVIEW

Answers to mini-case, review questions, and self-test questions start on page 793.

Key Terms

look-back period
continuing care retirement
    community
long-term care insurance
qualified long-term care insurance
    contract
qualified long-term care services
chronically ill individual
activities of daily living (ADLs)
nursing home care
custodial care
bed reservation benefit

assisted-living care
respite care
care coordinator
facility-only policy
home-health-care-only policy
comprehensive long-term care
    insurance policy
reimbursement basis
per diem basis
disability-based policy
pool of money
shared benefit

Review Questions

15-1. Why is there a need for long-term care insurance?

15-2. Describe the sources for providing long-term care other than insurance.

15-3. Summarize the criteria for policy provisions in the NAIC model legislation for long-term care insurance.

15-4. What are the requirements that a long-term care insurance contract must meet to be "qualified" under the Health Insurance Portability and Accountability Act (HIPAA)?

15-5. Describe the federal income tax treatment of a qualified long-term care insurance contract.

15-6. What are the usual issue ages for long-term care insurance contracts?

15-7. What are the types of care a long-term care insurance policy might cover?

15-8. Describe the amounts and duration of long-term care benefits.

15-9. Explain how insurance companies determine whether a long-term care policyowner is eligible for benefits.

15-10. Describe the factors that affect the amount of the premium for a long-term care insurance contract.

15-11. Compare group long-term care insurance with the coverage being sold in the individual marketplace. What differences exist between the two types of coverage?

Self-Test Questions

T   F   15-1. Both group and individual medical expense policies typically cover custodial care in a nursing home.

T   F   15-2. The Medicaid program in most states will provide nursing home care to low-income individuals.

T   F   15-3. NAIC model legislation regarding long-term care policies has become federal law and applies retroactively to older policies.

T   F   15-4. NAIC model legislation regarding long-term care policies requires that a shopper's guide must be delivered to all prospective applicants.

T   F   15-5. Under the Health Insurance Portability and Accountability Act (HIPAA), a "qualified long-term care insurance contract" must provide for a cash surrender value that can be borrowed if an insured is seriously ill.

T   F   15-6. Under HIPAA, a "chronically ill person" must be unable to perform at least four activities of daily living (ADLs).

T   F   15-7. Coverage under a group long-term care insurance contract must be offered through a cafeteria plan to receive favorable tax treatment.

T   F   15-8. One of the benefits that may be available under a long-term care insurance contract is adult day care.

T   F   15-9. Long-term care policies written on a per diem basis pay for actual long-term care expenses up to a maximum amount.

T   F   15-10. Variations exist among long-term care insurance policies as to how home health care services are counted toward satisfaction of the elimination period.

T   F   15-11. One advantage to the insured of having a long-term care insurance policy that uses a pool of money concept is that daily benefit payments from the pool of money can exceed the otherwise stated policy benefit.

T   F   15-12. Most states require long-term care policies to offer some type of inflation protection that the applicant can purchase.

T   F   15-13. Most insurance companies offer a discount if both spouses purchase long-term care policies from the same company.

NOTES

1. According to LIMRA International, Inc., the top 10 writers of individual long-term care insurance were Aegon USA, Bankers Life and Casualty, CNA Insurance, Conseco Companies, GE Financial Assurance, IDS Life, John Hancock, Pen Treaty, Thrivent Financial, and UnumProvident.

2. *Projection of Expenditures for Long-Term Care Services for the Elderly,* the Congressional Budget Office, March 1999, pp. 3 and 4 and *Financing Long-Term Care for the Elderly*, the Congressional Budget Office, April 2004, p. 5.

3. *Long-Term Care Insurance: Protection for Your Future*, American Council of Life Insurance, taken from American Council of Life Insurance Web site at www.acli.com; and Centers for Disease Control and Prevention/National Center for Health Statistics, The National Nursing Home Survey: 1997 Survey.

4. *Can Aging Baby Boomers Avoid the Nursing Home?* American Council of Life Insurance, March 2000, Washington, DC, p. 15.

16

Introduction to Property and Liability Insurance

Learning Objectives

An understanding of the material in this chapter should enable the student to

16-1. Describe the types of property and liability loss exposures families and businesses face.

16-2. Explain the policy provisions typically found in property and liability insurance policies.

16-3. Explain the basic types of property and liability policies and coverages available to meet the protection needs of families and businesses.

16-4. Briefly explain the tax treatment of property and liability insurance premiums and loss settlements for individuals and businesses.

16-5. Explain why there is a need for property and liability insurance planning.

Chapter Outline

This is the first of four chapters devoted to property and liability insurance—an area of financial planning that is often overlooked or given less than thorough attention. Financial planners should be equipped to help their clients assess their property and liability risks.

Property and liability insurance is important for many reasons, including but not limited to these:

- Many individuals, especially those with good employee benefits, spend more on property and liability insurance than they spend on all other types of insurance combined.
- Failure to carry appropriate and adequate property and liability insurance can result in a severe uninsured loss that scuttles an otherwise sound plan for capital accumulation and preservation.
- Property and liability insurance is complicated, and exposures and policies must be thoroughly analyzed to determine whether a client is adequately protected.
- Many policy endorsements and other coverage options are available.

A number of financial planning issues involve property and liability exposures and insurance. For example, higher deductibles, or a decision to forgo certain insurance coverages, can reduce insurance costs but increase the need for a sizable emergency fund. The converse is also true. An individual with a substantial emergency fund can often make more efficient use of property and liability insurance by choosing higher deductibles and forgoing some nonessential fringe coverages.

The high premium costs associated with property and liability insurance raise other financial planning issues. For example, because insurance is highly competitive, wise shopping for price and service is advisable. Last but not least, any financial planning that involves property and liability loss financing should recognize the tax implications.

This chapter begins by describing property and liability loss exposures. In connection with property exposures, the chapter explains how the insurable value of property is established and how losses are settled. The liability discussion explains the types of damages covered by liability insurance, how the value of any claim is determined, and how claims are settled. The basic types of policies and their income tax implications are also discussed. The three following chapters examine some specific types of property and liability insurance policies in greater detail, with emphasis on the policies used primarily by individuals and families.

PROPERTY AND LIABILITY LOSS EXPOSURES

A loss exposure is the possibility that a loss could occur. Although property insurance and liability insurance are often provided in the same insurance policy, a clear distinction exists between the loss exposures addressed by each type of coverage.

- A *property loss exposure* is the possibility that a person or organization will sustain a property loss resulting from the damaging, destruction, taking, or loss of use of property in which that person or organization has a financial interest.
- A *liability loss exposure* is the possibility of a claim alleging a person's or organization's legal responsibility for injury or damage suffered by another party. Notice the emphasis on the possibility of a claim rather than on the payment of damages. Many liability claims result in no payment to the claimant because they are successfully defended. However, even then, the defense costs, adverse publicity, and other matters can create a distinct financial loss. Therefore, a liability loss occurs when a responsibility to pay damages is alleged, whether or not damages are ultimately paid to the party making the claim.

PROPERTY INSURANCE

As explained in this section, property insurance deals with property in two broad categories, real property and personal property. However, property insurance does not protect property. It protects property owners and other parties that meet two qualifications. First, they must have an insurable interest in the property at the time of the loss, and second, their interest must be insured under a contract of insurance. The amount any insured party may be entitled to recover from property insurance proceeds depends not only on the extent of that party's insurable interest but also on the method used to determine the value of the property and any financial loss resulting from the fact that the property cannot be used. For example, a driver may need to rent a car while his or her own car is being repaired following an accident.

Likewise, a family may incur expenses to live in a hotel while its house is being repaired, and a business may suffer a loss of income if the place of business has been damaged or destroyed.

Property insurance covers only losses that result from a covered cause, also known as a covered peril. When damage to property by a covered peril occurs, the insurance contract specifies certain duties that the insured party and the insurer must meet. The amount payable under a property insurance policy depends on various provisions in the insurance contract, especially limits, deductibles, and insurance-to-value provisions. These concepts are all summarized in the discussions that follow.

Types of Property

From a legal perspective, all property falls into one of two categories:

- real property
- personal property

real property

Real property, a term closely related to the more familiar term real estate, is defined as land and anything that is growing on it, or affixed to it, and the bundle of rights inherent in the ownership. It includes such items as crops, mineral rights, air rights, buildings, items that are permanently attached to buildings, fences, in-ground swimming pools, driveways, and retaining walls.

The antonym of real property is not imaginary property, but rather personal property. In the context of financial planning, "personal" often means "nonbusiness." The term, "personal property," however, has nothing to do with individuals and families. Personal property is owned and used not only by individuals and families but also by businesses.

personal property

Personal property is defined to include anything that is subject to ownership other than real property. This includes such items as clothes, furniture, dishes, artwork, musical instruments, money, securities, airline tickets, office equipment, business inventory, vehicles, and boats. It also includes intangible property such as copyrights and patents.

For both insurance and financial planning purposes, there is seldom a need to categorize a given item as "real property" or as "personal property." Rather than using these broad legal categories, insurance policies use more specific terms such as building, structure, private passenger auto, or trailer.

Insurable Interests and Insured Parties

Property insurance policies pay only when policyowners or other insured parties have an insurable interest in the property that has suffered a loss. Two persons who jointly own property are likely to both be listed as policyowners and entitled to the policy's protection. In any case, the insurer will not reimburse an insured party for more than that party has lost. Coverage applies to the extent of each insured party's insurable interest in the property at the time of the loss, subject to policy limits and any other relevant provisions.

Lenders have an insurable interest in specific property pledged as collateral for a loan. Therefore, a mortgagee, who has lent money to the purchase of a home or another building, has an insurable interest in the building, and a bank has an insurable interest in an auto pledged as security for an auto loan. The interest of a mortgagee named in the policy's declarations can be protected by a property insurance policy's mortgage clause, and a lender's interest in personal property can be protected by a loss payable clause. In either case, the lender's insurable interest in the property is equal to the unpaid balance on the loan.

Mortgage Clause

mortgage clause

A *mortgage clause* is a standard part of a homeowners policy and many other property insurance policies covering real property. The mortgage clause applies when a mortgagee (lender, mortgage holder) is listed in the policy declarations. The policy gives the mortgagee some rights and imposes on the mortgagee some obligations. The mortgagee has a right to

- receive any loss payments to the extent of its insurable interest in the property. The mortgagee has a right to this payment even if the policyowner's claim is denied, so long as the mortgagee:
  - notifies the insurer of any change in ownership or occupancy or any increase in risks of which the mortgagee is aware
  - pays any premium due if the policyowner fails to do so
  - surrenders any claim it might have against the policyowner to the extent the insurer pays the mortgagee
- receive separate notice of cancellation

A property insurance claim check is issued jointly to the policyowner and the mortgagee. It is up to these parties to determine how the proceeds are split. In most cases, the mortgagee endorses the check to the policyowner so the property can be repaired or replaced. However, in the absence of any provision in the mortgage loan agreement to the contrary, the mortgagee can apply its share of the loss settlement to the loan principal.

Loss Payable Clause

loss payable clause

A *loss payable clause* is added to a policy as an endorsement and is used for autos and other types of personal property that have been financed. A loss payable clause gives the lender more limited rights than those found in the mortgage clause. For example, under the clause that is used for autos, the lender will still be paid if the policyowner is denied coverage but only if coverage was denied because of certain fraudulent acts or omissions. The lender receives notification if the policy is canceled so other provisions can be made to protect its insurable interest. However, the lender cannot pay the premium to keep the coverage in force.

Property Valuation

Property insurance policies invariably include valuation provisions that specify the approach to use to determine the value of covered property. That approach should be used when determining how much insurance to purchase, and it will be used when determining how much the insurer will pay in the event of a property loss.

Traditionally, most property insurance policies provided coverage on an actual cash value basis. Replacement cost valuation, the other dominant approach, is increasingly common, especially for insurance on houses and other buildings. Other variations include coverage on the basis of agreed value, often used with antiques and collectibles; the stated amount approach; and the valued policy laws found in some states.

Actual Cash Value

The concept of actual cash value is based on the principle of indemnity, which means that an insured should not profit from a loss but should be put into approximately the same financial position that existed before a loss.

Policies written on an actual cash value basis (such as auto physical damage and personal property under many homeowners policies) state that losses will be settled at actual cash value at the time of loss but not in an amount greater than the amount required to repair or replace the property.

actual cash value   Although many terms are defined in insurance contracts, *actual cash value* usually is not. As a result, there are varying court interpretations as to its precise meaning. Generally, it is defined as replacement cost less depreciation. As an illustration, assume a 10-year-old refrigerator is destroyed in a fire. It cost $900 when new, but a similar new model now sells for $1,200. The $1,200 amount is the replacement cost. However, according to the principle of indemnity, the insured is not entitled to a new refrigerator because the one that was destroyed was several years old. The issue then becomes the amount of the deduction for depreciation. Insurance companies tend to have depreciation schedules for various items, and refrigerators typically last about 15 years. Therefore, the insurer would probably assume the refrigerator was two-thirds depreciated and offer the insured one-third of $1,200, or $400.

In some cases, market value is used to establish the insurable value of property. The fair market value of property is the amount for which a knowledgeable seller, under no unusual pressure, would sell the property and a knowledgeable buyer, under no unusual pressure, would purchase it. The actual cash value of an auto is usually considered to be its fair market value. It is relatively easy to establish the actual cash value of any auto, because there is an active market for autos, and the price at which comparable used cars have recently sold is readily available

Replacement Cost

replacement cost

When property is valued on a *replacement cost* basis (as the dwelling building is in most homeowners policies), no deduction is made for depreciation. In the past, it was argued that this method of settlement violated the principle of indemnity because the insured was put into a better position after the loss. In many cases, however, there is no way to put the insured into exactly the same position that existed before the loss. For example, if a windstorm blows the shingles off a roof, the insured clearly needs new shingles. However, if the old shingles had already served a portion of their life expectancy, an actual cash value settlement would require the insured to use additional resources to fully repair the roof. Such a result, obviously, would leave the insured feeling less than fully indemnified. To alleviate this situation, replacement-cost coverage is commonly written on homes and commercial buildings.

Replacement cost coverage is also increasingly common with both commercial and residential personal property. If the refrigerator in the previous example had been insured on a replacement cost basis rather than an actual cash value basis, the insurer would pay the $1,200 cost of a similar new model, even though the customer had originally purchased the refrigerator for only $900.

Replacement cost is based on replacement with materials or items of like kind and quality as that lost. For example, if a kitchen were destroyed, the value of the loss would be determined by characteristics of the old kitchen. The insurance company would pay the cost to replace an old Formica countertop with a new countertop of Formica or something similar. The insured would have to assume the extra cost if he or she wanted a new granite countertop. Similarly, the insurance company would not pay to replace low-cost kitchen cabinets with expensive custom-made cabinets.

Agreed Value

With some types of property, it is extremely hard to determine values after an item has been totally destroyed or lost through theft. Examples include fine art and antiques. To avoid this dilemma, the insurer and the insured may agree upon a value at the time a policy is written. In the event of

agreed value

a total loss to the property, the *agreed value* is paid. The insurance company will probably want detailed appraisals before issuing a policy.

Stated Amount

stated amount

The *stated amount* approach is often used in insurance policies on antique autos or other unusual vehicles. The policy lists a stated value for the item. At the time of the loss, the insurer will pay the stated amount, the actual cash value, or the cost to repair or replace the property—whichever is least. In many cases, the insurer therefore pays less than the stated value.

Example: "Smoky" Blaze is a retired fireman. Smoky owns a few cherished memorabilia, including an original painting of The Great Chicago Fire and an old fire truck he purchased when his fire company upgraded its equipment. Smoky displays the painting in his living room. He keeps the fire truck next to his Cadillac in the garage attached to his house and occasionally drives it in a parade.

Smoky's house, which has a replacement cost value of $300,000, is insured for that amount on a homeowners policy, which provides replacement cost coverage on the dwelling building and attached structures and actual cash value on personal property with a $150,000 limit. The painting is insured for $40,000 on a fine arts floater that provides agreed value coverage. The fire truck, which has a great deal of sentimental value for Smoky, is insured for $40,000 on an antique auto policy that provides stated amount coverage. The Cadillac is insured on a personal auto policy that provides actual cash value coverage but does not state a dollar limit.

An electrical fire starts in Smoky's garage and destroys the garage, the fire truck, and the Cadillac. The fire also spreads to the house and does damage to Smoky's personal property, including the painting. It will cost $100,000 to repair the house and another $50,000 to replace Smoky's personal property with equivalent new property. At the time of the loss, the old fire truck has an actual cash value of $30,000, based on its market value.

Smoky's insurer will pay (ignoring deductibles):

- the $100,000 cost of repairing the house
- the $40,000 agreed value of the painting
- the $30,000 actual cash value of the fire truck
- the actual cash value of the Cadillac, which will be established by determining the current market value of similar vehicles
- the actual cash value of Smoky's other personal property, which will be based on its $50,000 replacement cost minus deductions for depreciation

Valued Policy Laws

valued policy law

A few states have *valued policy laws* that can apply to certain types of property losses and/or certain perils. As a rule, this type of law applies to real property only. Under such a law, the full amount of insurance coverage is paid if a total loss occurs. For example, $500,000 is paid for a total loss to a building insured for $500,000 even if the actual cash value or replacement cost of the building is lower. Valued policy laws were introduced to prevent agents and insurance companies from benefiting from premiums and commissions that are too high because a building is insured for an amount greater than what the insurer will pay in the event of a loss. The burden is on the insurance company to either prevent overinsurance or to be bound by the amount of coverage it has sold if a loss occurs.

Today, underinsurance is far more common than overinsurance. Insurers and their agents face the challenge, especially during inflationary periods, of adequately increasing insurance limits at every renewal in order to keep policy limits in line with property values so that the insurer is able to pay for a major property loss. Adequate insurance to value benefits policyowners, and it enables insurers to collect premiums consistent with the values they insure, which, in turn, helps avoid a need for rate increases.

Covered Perils

A peril is a cause of loss. Many different perils can cause a loss to real and personal property. However, few, if any, property insurance policies cover losses from every peril that could occur. Insurance policies take two distinct approaches in describing the causes of loss covered under a given policy:

- named perils, also known as "specified perils"
- open perils, also referred to as "special form" or "all risks"

Named-Perils Policies

named-perils
coverage

Named-perils coverages (also referred to as specified-perils coverages) list the covered perils. If a peril is not listed, losses that result from that peril are not covered by that policy.

Some policies are designed for very specific types of losses and cover few perils. As one might expect, a flood insurance policy, for example, covers only flood-related losses. On the other hand, named-perils policies can be extremely broad. An example is the personal property coverage under a homeowners 3 (HO-3) policy, which is discussed in more detail in a later chapter. The HO-3 policy contains a list of many covered perils for household property, ranging from fire to theft to volcanic eruption.

A mere listing of the covered perils in a named-perils policy can be somewhat misleading because the precise meaning of the terms is often established by either legal precedent or specific policy language. For example, the term *fire* is not usually defined in insurance policies because its meaning has long been established by the courts. A fire consists of a rapid oxidation or combustion that causes a flame or glow. Therefore, an item scorched because it was too close to a burner on a stove would not be covered under the peril of fire. In addition, courts have determined that the peril of fire covers only hostile fires, which are those that are outside normal confines. For example, a fire in a fireplace is a friendly rather than a hostile fire. As a result, an item accidentally thrown into a fireplace would not be covered under a named-perils policy covering fire. Note that a fire that spreads beyond the fireplace has turned from a friendly fire into a hostile fire.

An interesting—and false—urban legend has been in circulation for the past 40 years about the man who submitted a fire insurance claim on the cigars he had smoked. Various versions of this story call it arson and give several differing reasons why the claim was not covered, but we think the best reason of all lies in the fact that the cigars were not burned by a hostile fire.[1]

Unlike the peril of fire, the meanings of most covered perils are clarified to varying degrees in insurance policies. For example, the peril of volcanic eruption in the previously mentioned HO-3 policy is defined to cover volcanic eruptions other than those arising from earthquakes, land shock waves, or tremors.

Open-Perils Coverages

open-perils
coverage

Open-perils coverages (sometimes called all-risks coverages) cover all causes of loss to covered property unless the cause of a given loss is specifically excluded. The dwelling building coverage under the HO-3 policy is an example of a typical open-perils policy in that some potentially significant losses are not covered. The policy has exclusions for earth movement and water damage that are broad enough to eliminate coverage for earthquake and flood. In most cases, such perils can be insured for an extra premium under an HO-3 policy or a separate policy. The policy also contains exclusions for perils that are generally uninsurable such as war and nuclear accidents. Other perils are modified by policy language. For example, although vandalism and malicious mischief to the building are generally covered, this peril is not covered if a building has been vacant for more than 60 days preceding a loss. Similarly, smoke is not a covered peril if it arises from agricultural smudging or industrial operations.

Settling Claims

Settling property insurance claims is usually somewhat more complicated than settling life insurance claims. Property insurance policies therefore need to spell out the post-loss duties of both the insured and the insurer in some detail. Most of these duties are fairly obvious.

Duties of the Insured

A typical property insurance policy requires, for example, that the insured must promptly tell the insurer there has been a property loss, and the insured must cooperate with the insurer in showing that a covered loss occurred within the policy period. If property coverage is on a named-perils basis, the insured also needs to establish that the loss was caused by one of the named perils.

The insured also needs to cooperate with the insurer in establishing the value of covered property that has been lost or damaged. It is much easier to do this when an insured has maintained receipts of major purchases and has a current inventory of personal property supplemented by photographs or video-tapes. Of course, the insured should keep this information at a separate location so that the information itself is not among the property that is destroyed.

Duties of the Insurer

The insurance company has a duty to pay losses fairly and promptly once the coverage and the value of the property loss have been established. The insurance policy and/or state law might specify that losses are payable within a stated period, such as 60 days.

The insurer will usually settle property insurance claims by paying the policyowner unless some other person with an insurable interest is also covered by the policy. As mentioned earlier, a mortgage holder or a lender named as a loss payee is also entitled to be paid to the extent of the lender's interest in the property.

Insurers typically settle property insurance claims by issuing a check or draft to the policyowner and/or other insured parties. However, many policies give the insurer the right to repair or replace the damaged property rather than making a monetary settlement. Thus, for example, an insurer might have a glass shop replace a broken windshield on a car rather than giving the policyowner cash and having the policyowner deal with a repair shop. Auto insurers often do this because they have arrangements with glass shops to provide prompt quality service at a discount that enhances policyowner service and helps keep premiums down.

Other Insurance

other insurance
clause

Most property and liability insurance policies contain detailed *other insurance clauses* that explain how an insurer's obligations are affected when other insurance covers the same loss. Three approaches are common in property insurance policies:

- *pro rata coverage.* If two similar policies provide coverage on the same property, loss payments will be pro-rated based on the limits of insurance. For example, if one policy provides $200,000 of insurance on a building and another similar policy provides $300,000 of coverage, the first insurer will pay two-fifths of any loss, and the second will pay three-fifths.

- *primary and excess coverage.* A common approach with auto insurance is that one policy provides primary coverage and the other covers any losses within the scope of its coverage that have not been covered by the primary policy. For example, Karen, who has a personal auto policy that provides collision coverage on her car with a $1,000 deductible, lends her car to Bob, who has collision coverage under his own policy with a $500 deductible that applies to his use of a nonowned auto. If Bob is involved in an accident, Karen's insurance will pay for the damage to her car after subtracting a $1,000 deductible. Bob's insurance will pay $500—the difference between the coverage provided by the two policies.

- *exclusion for property covered by other insurance.* Some property insurance policies contain a provision relieving the insurer of liability for property that is specifically insured in another policy. For example, homeowners policies generally do not cover losses to personal property that is separately described and specifically covered in a separate policy or an endorsement to the homeowners policy. If, for example, an amateur photographer has a camera worth $1,000 that is specifically insured for $500 in a scheduled personal property endorsement to the homeowners policy, the insurer will pay $500 under the endorsement and nothing additional under the personal property coverage of the homeowners policy. Likewise, if an auto owner purchases a second auto insurance policy while the current policy is still in force, the new policy will replace the old policy; it does not provide duplicate or additional coverage.

Limits, Deductibles, and Insurance to Value Provisions

The amount payable under a policy that provides property insurance coverage is also affected by the policy's limits, deductibles, and insurance-to-value provisions.

Limits

Without adequate policy limits, a client might not be indemnified for a loss that insurance otherwise covers. *Policy limits*, or *limits of insurance* are a dollar amount, stated in the policy, that applies to a specific item, a specific category of property, or a specific type of coverage. Policy limits state the maximum amount payable for most claims covered by the policy. Some property insurance policies do not contain an explicit dollar limit but instead cover the actual cash value of an auto or other property, or cover income lost during a specified period of time.

Policy limits are sometimes called limits of liability. This terminology recognizes the fact that the insurer's obligation or "liability" to provide benefits is limited by the face amount of the policy. It can be confusing, however, to refer to limits of *liability* when dealing with *property* insurance.

A property insurance limit may apply to a specific listed or "scheduled" item, such as a building or a diamond ring. In another policy or coverage, a dollar limit may apply to a broad class of unscheduled property, such as personal property belonging to a family. Sublimits may apply to specific types of property.

Example:	A typical homeowners policy might provide $200,000 in personal property coverage with a $1,500 sublimit that applies to watercraft. Suppose Samantha has a homeowners policy with these limits, and a boat with an actual cash value of $5,000 is stolen from her carport. Although the limit of insurance on Samantha's personal property is $200,000, she cannot collect more than $1,500 for theft of her boat.

Deductibles

Many property insurance policies have deductibles that apply to each loss. In most cases, the deductible is a set dollar amount. Although insurance policies and companies tend to have standard deductibles, such as $250 for collision losses to an auto, deductibles can usually be increased with an accompanying premium reduction. Deductibles can sometimes be decreased for an additional premium.

A few policies—earthquake coverage is a common example—have percentage deductibles. Under such a policy, the deductible is equal to a percentage, such as 5 percent, of the amount of insurance.

While deductibles minimize attitudinal hazard by making the insured bear a portion of any loss, they also lower premium costs by eliminating the relatively high administrative costs of adjusting small claims. Significant discounts are often available for selecting higher deductibles, and an evaluation of this savings should be part of a financial planning analysis.

Insurance-to-Value Provisions

The vast majority of property insurance losses are partial losses. Exceptions occur when property is either totally destroyed or stolen. Anyone who expects to be fully indemnified if a total loss occurs ought to carry property insurance in an amount equal to the full insurable value of the property. As mentioned earlier, the insurable value of the property is usually its replacement cost or its actual cash value.

Property insurance rates are based on an assumption that covered property is insured to value. Insurance to value creates a win-win situation for both the insurer and the insured. If most property an insurer covers is substantially underinsured rather than being insured to value, the insurer would not collect enough premium to cover its exposures without raising its rates per $100 of coverage. Insurance buyers would end up paying higher rates and still having inadequate coverage.

To encourage and maintain this win-win scenario in which insurance buyers carry an amount of insurance that reflects the property's insurable value and pay a fair rate for their coverage, many insurance policies contain provisions designed to encourage insurance to value. This encouragement is in the form of a penalty for underinsurance. Simply stated, a policyowner who is underinsured at the time of a loss will also be underpaid, even for a partial loss.

coinsurance (property insurance)

Coinsurance Provision. A *coinsurance provision* in many commercial property insurance policies serves this purpose. Although the same term is used, it is important to remember that coinsurance in property insurance is not the same as coinsurance in medical expense insurance.

A coinsurance provision requires the policyowner to carry insurance at least equal to a percentage of the property's insurable value in order to receive full payment for losses. The percentage is commonly 80, 90, or 100, and the policy will specify whether this is a percentage of actual cash value, replacement cost, or some other value.

The best way to explain coinsurance is to use an example—in this case, the replacement cost provision that applies to many commercial buildings. It states that if the amount of insurance is 80 percent (or 90 or 100 percent) or more of replacement cost at the time of loss, the loss will be paid on a replacement cost basis up to the limit of coverage. Of course, the insurer will never pay more than the limit of insurance or the insurable value of the loss. If the amount of insurance is less than 80 percent of replacement cost, the insurer will pay the portion of the cost to repair or replace the damage that the limit of insurance bears to 80 percent (or other selected percentage) of the replacement cost at the time of loss. This is explained by the following formula:

$$\text{Loss payment} = \frac{\text{Limit of insurance}}{80\% \text{ of replacement cost}} \text{ x Replacement cost of the loss}$$

Example: Assume a building has a replacement cost of $200,000 but the policyowner carries only $140,000 of coverage on a replacement cost basis. Also assume a windstorm destroys a roof that would cost $8,000 to replace. Using the above formula:

$$\text{Loss payment} = \frac{\$140,000}{80\% \text{ x } \$200,000} \text{ x } \$8,000$$

$$= \frac{\$140,000}{\$160,000} \text{ x } \$8,000 = \$7,000$$

Therefore, the insurer will pay $7,000 (ignoring any deductible).

The same formula is used if losses are settled in an actual cash value basis except that the replacement cost is replaced by the actual cash value, both in determining the insurable value and in determining the amount of the loss.

Homeowners Loss Settlement Provision. Homeowners insurance policies—and also some businessowners policies—include a different type of insurance-to-value provision that bears a slight resemblance to coinsurance. This provision applies only to the dwelling building and other structures; it does not apply to personal property for which it is usually more difficult to establish a value when the policy is written. In essence, the homeowners loss settlement provision works like this:

- If the amount of insurance on the dwelling building equals at least 80 percent of the replacement cost value of the building, the insurer will pay the replacement cost of the loss.

- If the building is slightly underinsured, the insurer will pay an amount somewhere between the actual cash value of the loss and the replacement cost value of the loss. The amount is determined by applying a formula that is essentially the same as the coinsurance clause previously discussed.
- But—and here's the added feature—if the building is more than slightly underinsured, the insurer will still pay at least the actual cash value of the loss.

In any case, the insurer will not pay more than the applicable amount of insurance or the insurable value of the loss, and a deductible will also apply. The example illustrates more specifically how the homeowners loss-settlement provision operates.

Example:	Alex and Sandra own a home with a replacement value of $200,000. A kitchen fire causes a loss to the building with a replacement cost of $10,000 and an actual cash value of $8,000.

If Alex and Sandra's homeowners policy has a policy limit of $160,000 or more that applies to the dwelling building, they will recover the $10,000 replacement cost.

If they are only slightly underinsured and their homeowners policy has a policy limit of $150,000, Alex and Sandra will recover $9,375, determined by applying the coinsurance formula:

$$\$150,000/\$160,000 \times \$10,000 = \$9,375$$

Because $9,375 is more than the actual cash value of the property, the insurer will pay the amount determined by the formula, which is between the actual cash value and the replacement cost value of the loss.

Suppose, instead, that the policy limit is $120,000. Even though they are rather substantially underinsured, Alex and Sandra will still receive the $8,000 actual cash value of the loss.

LIABILITY INSURANCE

The United States' legal climate encourages lawsuits. A client whose momentary carelessness or negligence causes injury or damage to another party can be sued for an amount that equals or exceeds his or her entire life's savings and perhaps future earnings. Even clients with limited assets can face a large liability judgment.

A client who has not been negligent can also be sued by a claimant who *alleges* that the client is responsible for the claimant's injury or damage. In many cases, a strong defense leads to the conclusion that the client is not legally responsible to pay damages, and the suit is dismissed. In other cases, a sound defense reduces the amount of damages the courts award. A sound defense can be expensive, but its importance cannot be underestimated.

Fortunately, liability insurance is available both to cover defense costs and to pay damages awards for many types of claims. The following discussion looks at the types of liability claims that are commonly insured and briefly examines the bases of legal liability.

Types of Liability Losses

Liability claims involve an alleged responsibility to pay damages. Damages fall into two categories:

- *compensatory damages*, designed to financially compensate or reimburse a claimant who has suffered a loss
- *punitive damages*, designed to punish a wrongdoer, or tortfeasor, whose outrageous conduct has caused another party to suffer a loss

Liability insurance policies are designed primarily to cover compensatory damages. Some policies exclude punitive damages, and some state laws prohibit insurers from paying punitive damages. The thinking here is that a wrongdoer is not really punished when the "punishment" is absorbed by his or her insurance.

The types of liability losses property and liability insurance typically cover fall into one of the following categories:

- bodily injury
- property damage
- personal injury
- contractual liability
- wrongful acts

These categories are briefly described below. Other liability insurance coverages might apply to advertising injury, professional liability such as medical malpractice or attorney's errors and omissions, or other consequences.

Bodily Injury

bodily injury

Bodily injury occurs when a person suffers bodily harm, sickness, or disease, and it includes required care, loss of services, and death that results.[2] The injured party may incur tangible losses such as medical bills, lost income, or the need to hire someone to perform services such as cleaning the house or mowing the lawn.

Bodily injury can also result in an award of damages for pain and suffering. In many cases, pain and suffering payments far exceed those paid for medical bills and lost income.

Bodily injury can also result in claims by parties other than the person actively suffering the injury. For example, relatives can sue for wrongful death or loss of companionship.

Property Damage

property damage

Allegedly causing the destruction or damage to someone else's real or personal property can also result in a liability claim. The *property damage* can consist of actual damage to the property, but it can also arise because of lost income or extra expenses that result from the inability to use the property.

Personal Injury

personal injury

Attorneys often consider "personal injury" and "bodily injury" to be synonymous. In the language of liability insurance, however, *personal injury* refers to a group of offenses that generally include libel, slander, invasion of privacy, and other offenses named in the policy such as defamation or malicious prosecution.

Contractual Liability

contractual liability

Legal liability can also arise from the failure of a person or business to meet contractual obligations. This *contractual liability* may result from breach of contract, responsibility for damage to the property of others in one's possession, and implied warranties.

Wrongful Acts

Directors and officers liability policies provide coverage for wrongful acts, defined broadly to include a wide range of acts or omissions, such as "any error, misstatement, misleading statement, act, omission, neglect, or breach of duty committed, attempted, or allegedly committed or attempted by an insured." Coverage applies only to acts or omissions the insured might commit in his or her capacity as a corporate director or officer. A claim by a corporation's stockholders might allege, for example, that a director's or officer's wrongful acts led to a decline in value of the claimants' common stock.

Bases of Legal Liability

A liability claim develops as the result of the alleged invasion of the rights of others. A legal right is more than a mere moral obligation of one person to another; it has the backing of the law to enforce the right. Legal rights impose many specific responsibilities and obligations, such as not invading privacy or property, as well as not harming others.

The invasion of such legal rights is a *legal wrong*. The wrong can be criminal or civil. A *criminal wrong* is an injury that involves the public at large and is punishable by the government, typically by imposing a fine or a jail term.

tort

Civil wrongs are based upon torts and contracts. Contracts can involve legal wrong when implied warranties are violated, bailee responsibilities are not fulfilled, or contractual obligations are breached. *Torts* are wrongs independent of contract (for example, false imprisonment, assault, fraud, libel, slander, and negligence). Although the government takes action with respect to crime, civil injuries are remedied by court action instituted by the injured party in a civil action. The remedy sought is usually the award of monetary damages. The consequences of a crime are not usually insurable, but the liability for damages growing out of a civil wrong can—and often should be—insured.

Figure 16-1 illustrates the legal basis for liability. Although liabilities include criminal wrongs, the emphasis for liability insurance is on civil wrongs and particularly on the many legal wrongs based upon *torts*. Of greatest importance are torts that result from *negligence* (unintentional acts or omissions), which are said to encompass more than nine out of 10 claims for bodily injury or property damage to others.

Liability under Contract Law

Liability under contract law is based on the invasion of another's rights under a contract. It occurs only as a result of a contract between one party and another. In contrast, liability under tort law is based on the breach of one's duty to respect the rights of the general public. It can result from either common law or statute.

Breach of Contract. The nonfulfillment of promises that are made in an agreement, or breach of contract, is the most obvious type of civil wrong based on contracts. The failure to honor a warranty expressly contained in a contract is an example of such a breach.

Implied Warranties. One of the most common extensions of liability under contract law concerns manufacturers and distributors of products. In connection with sales or a contract to sell, the law imposes certain obligations termed *implied warranties*. When a buyer reasonably relies on the skill or judgment of the seller, there is an implied warranty that the goods are reasonably fit for the purpose for which they were sold. A seller can also be held liable if products are supplied to a user without giving proper notice of their dangerous qualities.

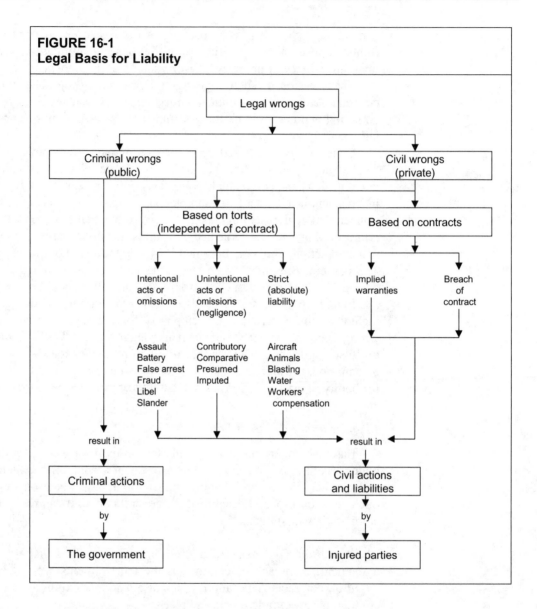

FIGURE 16-1
Legal Basis for Liability

Liability under Tort Law

Torts include all civil wrongs not based on contracts. As such, they are a broad residual classification of many private wrongs against another person or organization. They occur independently of contractual obligations and can result from (1) intentional acts or omissions, (2) strict liability imposed by law, or (3) negligence.

Intentional Acts or Omissions. Lawsuits sometimes occur because of injuries or damage caused by intentional acts or omissions. One example is battery, which is the offensive or harmful touching of another without his or her express or implied consent. Assault is a second example, and this involves threatened battery. Other examples include fraud, trespass (entry on land of another without permission), and false arrest or detention, which results from the unprivileged restriction of another's freedom of movement. In addition, libel (written) and slander (oral) involve false statements made about someone else. All of these acts are based on planned or premeditated acts or omissions, although the harmful results may not have been anticipated.

strict liability

Strict or Absolute Liability. The law in particular situations holds persons responsible for injuries or damage no matter how careful they may have been in trying to avoid losses to others. Under what is called *strict liability* or *absolute liability,* certain persons are held liable for damages, regardless of whether or not fault or negligence can be proved against them. Examples include injury from blasting operations by contractors, injury caused by any type of wild animal kept in captivity, and damage resulting from a release of pressure or weight of water such as a weak dam bursting. Other illustrations of this trend include the absolute liability (up to certain amounts) that airlines have for the safety of their passengers and workers' compensation laws, which hold the employer liable for most employee work-related injuries and diseases.

negligence

Negligence Liability. Negligence is a tort, and most of the liability imposed by law stems from accidents attributable to negligence. If negligence can be shown to be the proximate cause of an injury to another, the negligent party is liable to the injured party for damages. *Negligence* is the failure to exercise the proper degree of care required by circumstances. It can consist of not doing what was required under the circumstances, or of doing something that should not have been done. Behavior in any circumstances that fails to measure up to that expected of a careful, prudent person in like circumstances constitutes negligence. Faulty judgment can result in liability for negligence, even if the motive behind the act was the best.

Negligence requires the existence of four specific elements:

- a legal duty
- a wrong
- injury or damage
- proximate cause

Legal Duty. A *legal duty* to act, or not to act, depends on the circumstances and the persons involved. A bystander has no legal duty to try to prevent a mugging, but a police officer does. Lifeguards have a legal duty to attempt to save a drowning victim, but others usually do not. Whether or not

---

Elements of a Negligent Act

- A certain standard of care is owed to others.
- That standard of care is not met.
- There is injury or damage.
- Failure to meet the standard of care is the proximate cause of the injury or damage.

---

a legal duty is owed to someone else is decided by the courts, and many factors can determine the degree of care required.

Wrong. A *wrong* is a breach of legal duty, based on a standard of conduct that is determined by what a prudent person would have done or not done in similar circumstances. To do a wrong, the act or omission must be voluntary. Thus, if a person in the course of avoiding great danger injures another person without intent, there is held to be no voluntary act and hence no liability. Negligence usually involves injury that is unintentional. On the other hand, it is no defense if the act that injures a party was committed without intent to do an injury or if the motive behind the act was good and praiseworthy.

Injury or Damage. The third requirement for negligence liability is that there is *injury* or *damage.* The guilty person must pay an amount that reasonably compensates the injured party for any losses for which the negligence is the proximate cause.

Proximate Cause. A fourth requisite for fixing liability is found in the rule that the wrongdoer's voluntary act must have been the *proximate cause* of the injury or damage. For the act to be held a proximate cause, there must have been a continuous succession of events from the act to the final event that caused the injury. If there was an independent and intervening cause, the continuous succession of events is broken. Thus, a fire ignited negligently and spread by the winds is one continuous succession of events. If, however, a third party was deliberately pushed into the flames by someone else and injured, there would not have been a continuous sequence. No liability for the injury would attach to the party responsible for the fire.

Several modifications, by court cases or statutes, sometimes change the usual rules pertaining to negligence liability. These include *contributory* and *comparative* negligence laws and the doctrines of *presumed* and *imputed* negligence.

Contributory and Comparative Negligence. Except where statutory enactments have modified the common-law rule, anyone who is so negligent as to contribute to his or her own injuries or damage cannot recover from **contributory negligence** another for these injuries because of *contributory negligence.* Such a person is said to be contributorily negligent and is barred from recovery, no matter how slight the negligence.

The claimant frequently advances the plea that the alleged contributory negligence did not contribute to the injury, and that if the defendant had exercised reasonable care, the accident could have been avoided. There developed a rule, known as the *last clear chance doctrine*, which holds that although the claimant is negligent, there is liability if the defendant had a last clear chance to avoid the accident. Today, the rule is followed by statute in only a few states. It is, however, a concept often used in defense proceedings, sometimes successfully.

last clear chance doctrine

In its strict application, the old common-law doctrine of contributory negligence does not always produce equitable results. A very slight degree of negligence on the part of an injured person would bar recovery. Many states have enacted statutes that provide that contributory negligence does not bar recovery for damages. Such statutes apply the idea of *comparative negligence* and provide that damages be diminished in proportion to the amount of negligence attributable to the person injured or to the owner or person in control of the damaged property.

comparative negligence

At first glance, there seems to be substantial merit to have each person share the cost of an accident in proportion to his or her share of negligence. For example, 80 percent of the damages to others is paid if a person has been held 80 percent negligent. In some states, however, under complete comparative negligence, the person who was primarily responsible for the accident would also receive 20 percent of his or her damages if the other party was deemed 20 percent negligent. The critics of the comparative negligence law used in these states point out this drawback. Other states have partial comparative negligence statutes, under which a plaintiff can recover only if the degree of his or her negligence is less than (or in some states not greater than) the defendant's negligence. In the preceding example, the person who was 20 percent negligent would receive 80 percent of his or her damages, and the other party would receive nothing. In actual practice, slight negligence tends to be disregarded, and suit against the party primarily responsible is permitted. Settlements out of court also frequently ignore slight negligence or take it into consideration in making partial payments.

Presumed Negligence. To establish a case, the claimant in ordinary circumstances must show a failure to exercise reasonable care on the part of the defendant. The burden of proof, therefore, is on the claimant. In certain cases, however, presumed negligence can be assumed from the facts. The legal doctrine that applies is *res ipsa loquitur,* meaning "the thing speaks for itself." Negligence is presumed without the need for the injured person to prove it. The burden of proof is shifted to the defendant, an exception to the common-law rule that a plaintiff must prove the defendant's fault.

The doctrine operates when an accident causes an injury (1) if the instrumentality would not normally cause injury without negligence, (2) if inspection and use of the instrumentality is within exclusive control of the party to be held liable, and (3) if the party to be held liable has superior knowledge of the cause of the accident and the injured party is unable to prove negligence. There must be no contributory negligence, and the accident must be of such nature that injury would not ordinarily occur without negligence.

Modern situations to which this doctrine has been applied include auto injuries in cases where no witnesses are available, railroad or aviation injuries, medical malpractice claims (such as an operation on the wrong part of the body or on the wrong person), and damage caused by defective products.

imputed negligence

Imputed Negligence. Not only is a negligent person liable for his or her acts or omissions that cause injuries or damage to others, but sometimes the responsibility also extends to the negligence of other persons under the concept of *imputed negligence.* Courts and statutes have extended the rules of negligence to apply to employers, landlords, parents, auto owners, and many other parties.

If the negligent party acts in the capacity of employee or agent of another, the wrongdoer and the owner or operator of a property can be held liable. For example, employers can be personally liable for the torts of their employees. Imputed liability is also important in property rentals, where landlords can be held responsible for the actions of their tenants.

Parents, too, although generally not liable for the negligent actions of their children, can be held liable by some state statutes. These statutes usually impose limited liability up to several thousand dollars on the parents for damage caused by their children, but they can extend further for specific types of dangerous instruments (guns, for example) used by minors. A child can also be legally liable for his or her own wrongful acts but is seldom able to pay substantial damages.

Under statutes called *vicarious liability* laws, liability in most states is imputed to auto owners even though they are not driving or riding in their cars when the injuries or damage occurs. In addition, under the *family purpose doctrine,* such liability applies particularly to the car owner whose family members negligently use the car, either under the idea of agency (when the car is used for family purposes) or on the basis of using a dangerous instrumentality.

Several dozen states have passed dram shop or liquor liability laws that make taverns, other businesses, and individuals dispensing liquor liable for injuries that may be caused by their intoxicated patrons such as in an auto accident.

Some states impose liability if children are injured on a premises because they were attracted there by such items as swimming pools, ladders, gasoline, unlocked autos, or other *attractive nuisances*. Other states impose liability for injuries from domestic animals even if it would otherwise be difficult or impossible to prove negligence.

Settling Liability Claims

Liability policies specify the duties of the insured following losses and the obligations of the insurance company.

Duties of the Insured

Most liability insurance policies require the insured to perform duties similar to the following in the case of a covered accident or occurrence:

- Give written notice as soon as practical to the company or its agent. The written notice should include (1) the identity of the policy and the insured, (2) reasonable information on the time, place, and circumstances of the accident or occurrence, and (3) names and addresses of any claimants or witnesses.
- Forward promptly to the insurance company every notice, demand, summons, or other process relating to the accident or occurrence.
- Assist the insurance company, at its request, to do the following:
  - Make settlement.
  - Enforce any of the insured's rights against others who may be liable to the insured.
  - Help with the conduct of suits, and attend hearings and trials.
  - Secure and give evidence, and obtain the evidence of witnesses.

Duties of the Insurer. If a claim is made or a suit brought against an insured because of an occurrence to which coverage applies, the insurance company has two primary obligations.

First, the insurer will provide a defense at its expense by a counsel of its choice, even if a suit is groundless, false, or fraudulent. The company typically has the right to settle any claim or suit as it deems appropriate. The choice of whether a settlement is made is at the insurer's option. In some cases, settlements are made because it is less expensive than going to trial. Even though some insureds may view this as admitting their liability when they are convinced they are not liable, there is usually nothing they can do to prevent a settlement. It once was common to let the insured veto a settlement under professional liability policies, but this right has largely disappeared.

Second, the insurer will pay up to the limit of liability for the damages for which the insured is legally liable. Damages include any prejudgment interest awarded against the insured.

TAX TREATMENT

The tax implications of premium payments for, and loss settlements from, property and liability policies vary by type of loss and type of taxpayer.

Deductibility of Premium

Premiums paid by individual taxpayers for nonbusiness property and liability insurance are not tax deductible. However, premiums paid for business coverage by individuals, partnerships, or corporations are deductible business expenses.

Taxation of Premiums for Employees

Group property and liability insurance as an employee benefit is not widespread, but some group plans exist. These plans typically require an employee to pay the full cost of his or her coverage, and the tax implications are the same as if the employee had purchased an individual policy. If the employer pays any part of an employee's premium, the employer can deduct this cost as a business expense. However, the employer must then report this amount as taxable income to the employee.

Taxation of Benefits

Benefits the insurer pays on behalf of the insured under liability insurance policies do not result in taxable income to the policyowner or insured.

Under property insurance policies, benefits paid for direct loss to real or personal property result in a capital gain to the extent that a taxpayer receives reimbursement in excess of his or her basis in the property. However, the situation is treated as an involuntary conversion and the gain can be postponed to the extent that a taxpayer uses the proceeds to purchase replacement property and the purchase amount exceeds the taxpayer's basis in the lost or damaged property.

Example: Erin purchased a diamond ring for $10,000 many years ago. The ring was stolen and she recovered $25,000, which was the current value of the ring, from her insurer. If she does not purchase a replacement ring, she will have a capital gain of $15,000, just as if she sold the ring for $25,000. If she purchases a replacement ring at a cost of $25,000 or more, she can postpone the entire gain until the future sale of the

> ring. If she purchases a $22,000 replacement ring, $3,000 of the settlement is taxable as a gain in the year the theft was discovered. The ring will continue to have a tax basis of $10,000, and the remaining $12,000 of the gain is taxable if Erin later sells the ring for $22,000 or more.

The situation for certain consequential losses is less clear. To the extent that benefits are paid for actual expenses incurred, there is no taxable income. Business income coverage, however, will result in ordinary income because it insures the policyowner against loss of net profits. Policy proceeds merely replace the net profits that would have been fully taxable if no loss had occurred.

Deductibility of Uninsured Losses

The Internal Revenue Code allows a deduction for certain losses to the extent they are not compensated for by insurance. This involves losses when there is no insurance and losses when the insurance provides less than full protection because there are inadequate limits or deductibles. Those losses must arise from fire, storm, shipwreck, or other casualty, or theft.

Interestingly, the term *casualty* is not defined by the Internal Revenue Code, but IRS and legal interpretations generally consider casualty to be a sudden, unexpected, or unusual event that results in damage, destruction, or loss of property. This definition is very broad and clearly includes losses from such perils as floods, earthquakes, weather-related events, vandalism, fire, motor vehicle accidents, and the like.

Theft is also broadly interpreted to mean loss of money or property resulting from, for example, embezzlement, extortion, larceny, or robbery. Losses from situations caused intentionally by a taxpayer or involving normal wear and tear do not meet the definition.

The maximum amount of the losses for tax purposes is the lesser of (1) the decrease in the fair market value of the property as a result of the casualty or theft or (2) the taxpayer's adjusted basis in the property. Therefore, the amount of the deductible loss for the ring previously discussed would be $10,000 if there were no insurance.

Businesses and individual taxpayers can deduct losses in full if the loss is incurred in a trade or business or any transaction entered into for profit. Other losses of individual taxpayers are deductible only if they itemize income tax deductions and then only to the extent that (1) each separate loss exceeds $100, and (2) the total of all casualty and theft losses for the year exceeds 10 percent of adjusted gross income.

NEED FOR PROPERTY AND LIABILITY INSURANCE PLANNING

Previous chapters demonstrate that many insurance policies include a variety of approaches and coverage options that require choices by the client. Property and liability insurance is no exception. If anything, the range of choices, coverage options, and endorsements is even wider with property and liability insurance than with other lines of insurance discussed in this text.

Property insurance policies can cover buildings and their contents, as well as autos and other personal property. A client should be concerned not only with the possibility that the property itself suffers a loss of value but also with the likelihood of lost income or additional expenses resulting from the fact that lost or damaged property can no longer be used. Property can be valued on the basis of its depreciated actual cash value, its replacement cost, its agreed value, a stated amount, or some other basis. Covered causes of loss may be listed, or the open-perils approach may be used, covering losses by all causes not otherwise excluded. Clients need to consider the potential causes of loss to their specific property, as well as the value of covered property, and they also must select an appropriate limit of insurance. They must also choose deductibles; here, tax effects can be relevant.

Important sources of liability losses involve the ownership, maintenance, or use of the client's auto and other autos, as well as other personal and business exposures. Liability insurance may cover a client's potential liability resulting from bodily injury, property damage, personal injury (definitions vary), contractual liability, wrongful acts, advertising injury, professional liability, errors and omissions, or other sources depending on the policy. Liability losses can be very large, and it is important to ensure that all significant insurable exposures are covered and that limits are set high enough to provide reasonable protection for the client's assets. Many clients purchase liability insurance in layers, as explained in a later chapter, by combining primary insurance coverage with an umbrella policy.

The remaining chapters of this book summarize various types of property and liability insurance and demonstrate the broad set of client needs anticipated and provided for by various standard insurance forms. Although these forms grant broad coverage, they can also provide a false sense of security.

Some clients believe that if they have an auto insurance policy and a homeowners insurance policy, their property and liability exposures are adequately protected. The financial planning process should determine not only whether such policies exist but also where and how they may fall short of providing adequate protection. In many situations, policy endorsements or additional separate policies are available to compensate for shortcomings in the standard unendorsed policies or to accommodate special needs.

Coverage in standard policies is limited for various reasons. Certain perils, such as war, wear and tear, and intentional destruction of covered property by the insured, are considered uninsurable. Other perils are excluded because the cost of coverage tends to be relatively high or because not everyone has a need for the coverage, but those who want coverage can obtain it at a cost. For example, not all policyowners are susceptible to floods and earthquakes, but property insurance coverage is usually available for those who need and want it. Not every policyowner has expensive jewelry or valuable works of art, but those who do may need specialized coverage on those items through a homeowners policy endorsement. Likewise, most policyowners do not have domestic employees or own a large yacht or a motor home, but those who do may need workers' compensation insurance, a yacht policy, or endorsements to their personal auto policy. Standard policies generally limit the dollar amount of coverage for certain property items or for certain liability exposures. Again, those who need higher amounts of coverage can often obtain it for an additional premium.

In the remaining chapters on property and liability insurance, particular attention should be paid to policy limitations and coverage options, so that a client can be properly advised of the need to tailor coverage to specific circumstances.

MINI-CASE: AMY AND JOHN SCHULTZ

Amy and John purchased a homeowners insurance policy when they bought an 80-year-old home for $240,000 with 20 percent down and a 15-year mortgage at an interest rate of 5 percent. Amy and John plan to invest a great deal of time and effort during the next few years in repairing, redecorating, and maintaining it.

Prized possessions that Amy and John keep in their home include a grandfather's clock—a gift appropriately enough from Amy's grandfather—and an antique silver tea service passed along to them by Amy's mother.

Amy and John both own and drive late-model compact cars they purchased before they were married. Both cars are now paid off. They carry separate auto insurance policies, partly because of John's bad driving record, with the minimum coverages required by law.

Amy and John own no individual insurance policies apart from the auto and homeowners insurance policies mentioned above.

    a.   What property exposures do Amy and John face?

    b.   What liability exposures do Amy and John face?

    c.   The bank holding their mortgage requires that Amy and John purchase homeowners insurance in an amount that at least equals the unpaid balance of the mortgage. What protection does the bank receive under Amy and John's homeowners policy?

    d.   What steps should Amy and John take if they have a property loss that might be covered by their homeowners policy?

e. Amy and John's house is covered by their homeowners policy on a replacement cost basis. What advice might you give Amy and John regarding the property insurance limits and deductibles they might select under their homeowners policy?

(See answer section for answers to mini-case.)

SOURCES FOR FURTHER IN-DEPTH STUDY

- Wiening, Eric A., *Foundations of Risk Management and Insurance* Malvern, PA: American Institute for CPCU/Insurance Institute of America, 2002. Phone 800-644-2101. Web site address www.aicpcu.org
- Luthardt, Constance M., Smith, Barry D., and Wiening, Eric A., *Property and Liability Insurance Principles,* 3d ed., Malvern, PA: American Institute for CPCU/Insurance Institute of America, 1999. Phone 800-644-2101. Web site address www.aicpcu.org.

CHAPTER REVIEW

Answers to mini-case, review questions, and self-test questions start on page 793.

Key Terms

real property	coinsurance (property insurance)
personal property	bodily injury
mortgage clause	property damage
loss payable clause	personal injury
actual cash value	contractual liability
replacement cost	tort
agreed value	strict liability
stated amount	negligence
valued policy law	contributory negligence
named-perils coverage	last clear chance doctrine
open-perils coverage	comparative negligence
other insurance clause	imputed negligence

Review Questions

16-1. Describe two broad categories of property and liability loss exposures that families and businesses face.

16-2. Explain to your client the difference between a policy providing specified-perils (named-perils) coverage and an open-perils (all-risks) policy.

16-3. When a property loss occurs,

a.   what duties are typically imposed on the insured?

b.   what obligations does the insurer typically have?

16-4.   Jim Smith has a homeowners policy with replacement cost coverage. After a fire at his home, the damage is estimated at $50,000 on an actual cash value basis and $60,000, ignoring depreciation (that is, on a replacement cost basis). The replacement cost of his home at the time of the loss is $300,000. Ignoring the deductible, how much would Jim recover in each of the following situations:

a.   if Coverage A in his policy is $250,000

b.   if Coverage A in his policy is $220,000

c.   if Coverage A in his policy is $180,000

16-5.   Bill has a property loss of $90,000 and finds that it is covered by two policies—Policy A for $100,000 and Policy B for $80,000. Ignoring deductibles, indicate how much of the loss would be paid by each policy in each of the following situations:

a.   Policy A and Policy B both have pro rata other insurance provisions.

b.   Policy A is written on a primary basis, and Policy B is written on an excess basis.

c.   Policy A excludes property covered by other insurance.

16-6.   Billy, a summer employee at Jones Dry Cleaners, was driving the company truck to pick up dry cleaning in the neighborhood when he failed to see a stop sign, glanced off a car that had the right of way, and hit a phone pole. Indicate the type of liability loss if each of the following resulted from the accident:

a.   the cost of surgery, loss of income, and pain and suffering for the driver of the car that Billy hit

b.   the cost to the phone company to repair its pole

c.   the suit by the driver of the other car that resulted from Billy's slandering her with foul language in front of witnesses at the accident scene

16-7.   What are the four requirements that technically must exist before negligence can be proven?

16-8.   Using the situation in question 6, indicate under what rule of law each of the following can happen:

a.   Billy's employer is found liable for the injuries suffered by others that were caused by Billy.

b.   Neither Billy nor his employer is required to pay the injured driver of the other car because a police officer at a radar trap indicated that the other driver had entered the intersection at an excessive rate of speed and the court held that the other driver was 20 percent at fault.

c.   Billy's employer is required to pay the injured driver of the other car only 80 percent of her damages because a police officer at a radar trap indicated that the other driver had entered the intersection at an excessive rate of speed and the court held that the other driver was 20 percent at fault.

16-9. In the event of a loss under a liability policy, what are the
a. typical duties of the insured
b. obligations of the insurance company

16-10. Explain the basic tax rules that apply to each of the following, and point out where differences exist by type of taxpayer and/or type of loss:
a. deductibility of premium
b. taxation of premiums for employees
c. taxation of benefits
d. deductibility of uninsured losses

Self-Test Questions

T F 16-1. Property losses can occur to either real or personal property.

T F 16-2. Open-perils coverage refers to a policy that contains a very long list of named perils.

T F 16-3. A typical property insurance policy requires that whenever a property loss occurs, the insured must give prompt notice to the insurer.

T F 16-4. The key difference between a settlement on an actual cash value basis and a replacement cost basis is that depreciation is considered in calculating the actual cash value of the loss.

T F 16-5. Deductibles both minimize attitudinal hazard and lower premium costs.

T F 16-6. Most property and liability policies contain a provision that specifies how an insurer's obligation is affected by the existence of other insurance that covers a loss.

T F 16-7. All liability losses involve either bodily injury or property damage.

T F 16-8. Torts can result from negligence or contractual obligations.

T F 16-9. Negligence is the failure to exercise the proper degree of care required by the circumstances.

T F 16-10. If Pete was only 20 percent at fault for an auto accident in a state that relies on the contributory negligence standard, he could collect 80 percent of his damages from the other party.

T F 16-11. People can be held responsible only for their own negligent acts.

T F 16-12. In a liability insurance policy, the insurance company has an obligation to provide a defense at its expense.

T   F   16-13. Property and liability insurance premiums paid for business coverage are generally deductible as a business expense.

T   F   16-14. Standardized property and liability insurance policies largely eliminate the need for consumers to make choices other than policy amounts.

NOTES

1. For details on this urban legend and its critics, see www.snopes.com/crime/ clever/ cigarperson.asp.
2. This is typical of the definitions found in insurance policies.

17

Homeowners and Other Personal Property Coverages

Learning Objectives

An understanding of the material in this chapter should enable the student to

17-1. Briefly describe the nature of a homeowners policy, including who is insured and what property is covered.

17-2. Describe the coverages and exclusions contained in Sections I and II of the HO-3 homeowners policy form.

17-3. Explain the coverages provided by the HO-2, HO-4, HO-5, HO-6, and HO-8 and the key ways they differ from the HO-3.

17-4. Describe the coverage provided by the various endorsements available to tailor a homeowners policy to individual needs.

17-5. Explain why property and liability policies other than a homeowners policy may be required to meet the needs of individuals, and describe the key policies available.

Chapter Outline

Most clients purchase a homeowners policy not only to obtain property insurance coverage against loss or damage to their home but also to obtain insurance protection against the many sources of liability that can arise out of a family's activities. Homeowners insurance is not a single policy, but rather a family of similar policies that provide different degrees of coverage. Two policy forms in the homeowners family are for people who do not literally own homes but rent an apartment or purchase a condominium unit.

Homeowners policies are relatively complex policies. Various exclusions in the policy deal with uninsurable loss exposures. Other limitations and exclusions deal with exposures that can best be handled with a separate policy or an endorsement; these often give the informed financial advisor an opportunity to help a client improve his or her property/liability coverage program.

Without analyzing every detail, this chapter summarizes the coverage of standard homeowners policies and also discusses some coverage options, including flood insurance and title insurance. Readers who need more specific, or more in-depth information on these complex contracts are advised to consult the sources for further in-depth study listed at the end of this chapter. Questions regarding a specific policy can often be resolved by reading the policy itself.

Financial planners should be able to alert their clients to potential property and liability risk exposures. Specific recommendations and implementations are usually handled by a property/liability insurance agent or broker, with one exception. Title insurance, discussed at the end of this chapter, is usually arranged by a real estate firm or a mortgage company.

HOMEOWNERS POLICIES

homeowners policy

ISO (Insurance Services Office)

There is not only one *homeowners policy,* but rather a series of policy forms for different types of situations and with differing degrees of coverages for real and personal property, as well as personal liability. In this book, the discussion centers around the forms of *ISO (Insurance Services Office).* ISO is an advisory organization that provides a wide range of services for insurance companies, including the development and filing of standardized insurance policies. Many property and liability companies purchase the services of ISO, and its policy forms are commonly used. Another, but smaller, advisory organization—the American Association of Insurance Services (AAIS)—also has a series of homeowners forms for its affiliates. In addition, some insurance companies develop and file their own independent forms. Although the AAIS forms and the independent forms are arranged differently and often use different wording, their coverage is very similar to the ISO forms.

Homeowners insurance forms evolve over time, and the discussion in this chapter is based on the current ISO forms.

ISO Forms

There are six standard ISO homeowners forms:

- Homeowners 2—Broad Form
- Homeowners 3—Special Form
- Homeowners 4—Contents Broad Form
- Homeowners 5—Comprehensive Form
- Homeowners 6—Unit-owners Form
- Homeowners 8—Modified Coverage Form

In making reference to these forms, it is common to call them Form 2, Form 3, and so on, or HO-2, HO-3, HO-4, HO-5, HO-6, and HO-8. The latter terminology is used in this book.

The HO-2, HO-3, HO-5, and HO-8 are designed for owner-occupants of one- to four-family dwelling units. Each unit may contain no more than two families or one family and two roomers or boarders. The HO-4 is designed for tenants of residential property and also for the owner of an apartment building who occupies one of its units. The HO-6 is designed for the owners of condominium units.

Each homeowners form has two major sections. Section I provides property coverage, and it is in this section that the forms differ. The liability coverage of Section II is identical in all six forms.

The HO-3 is the most common of the forms and appropriate for most owners of homes. It is analyzed in some detail. Following this analysis, the other forms and their use are briefly discussed.

Sections of a Homeowners Policy

- Section I—Property Coverage (different in each homeowners form)
- Section II—Liability Coverage (same in all homeowners forms)

Definitions

Like many property and liability insurance policies, homeowners policies begin by defining many terms used throughout the policy. When a defined term is used elsewhere in the policy, it usually appears in quotation marks or in boldface type. Terms are used differently in different policies, and to understand their meaning in a specific policy, one must refer to the Definitions in the policy.

The homeowners policy includes two especially important defined terms—"insured" and "insured location"—which also demonstrate the broad scope of coverage these policies provide.

Insured

An insured is a party entitled to protection under the policy. The named insured, as defined, has somewhat more protection than other insureds.

Many persons qualify as insureds under both Section I (property) and Section II (liability) of a homeowners policy. These include

named insured
- the *named insured.* This is the person listed in the policy declarations and the spouse of the named insured, if not also listed, as long as he or she is a resident of the same household.
- residents of the named insured's household who are relatives

- residents of the named insured's household who are under the age of 21 and in the care of any of the persons previously mentioned
- a full-time student (as defined by the school) who was a resident of the insured's household before moving out to attend school, as long as the student is either
  - under 24 and a relative of an insured
  - under 21 and in the care of an insured

Two other categories of persons are considered an insured for the purposes of the Section II (liability) coverage. These categories include

- any person or organization responsible for animals or watercraft owned by anyone on the previous list. However, they are insureds only with respect to animals or watercraft to which the policy applies and only if this possession is with the owner's permission and not in the course of any business. For example, a neighbor while caring for a pet because the named insured is on vacation is an insured, but a veterinarian where the pet is boarded is not.
- any person employed by any one of the insureds in the earlier list with respect to any vehicles insured under the policy and other persons using the vehicles on an insured location with the consent of the named insured

Insured Location

An insured location includes the following:

- the residence premises. This includes the one- to four-family dwelling, other structures, and grounds where the policyowner resides as shown in the declaration.
- that part of other premises, other structures, and grounds used by the named insured or spouse as a residence (for example, a vacation home) if it is shown in the declarations or if it is acquired during the policy year as a residence by the named insured
- other premises not owned by an insured but where an insured is temporarily residing
- vacant land, other than farm land, owned by or rented to an insured
- individual or family cemetery plots or burial vaults of an insured
- any part of a premises occasionally rented to an insured for other than business use

HO-3 Property Coverages

Section I of the HO-3 contains five categories of property coverage:

- Coverage A for the dwelling building
- Coverage B for other structures such as a garage not attached to the house
- Coverage C for household contents and other personal property
- Coverage D for loss of use
- Additional coverages that provide protection for assorted situations

The insurance buyer determines the limit of insurance he or she wishes to purchase for Coverage A (the dwelling itself). In choosing a limit of insurance, it is important to recognize that the insurable value of the house is not directly related to either its purchase price or its market value. Because the HO-3 provides dwelling coverage on a replacement cost basis, the insurable value of the house is the cost to reconstruct the house new, using material of like kind and quality. Also, the value of the land is not relevant in determining the replacement cost of the building, but the land's value has a major effect on the market value of the house. Sometimes the mortgage holder requires an amount of insurance at least equal to the outstanding amount of the mortgage, even though the mortgaged property includes both the building—which is covered property, and the land—which is not covered property. Clients with several acres of valuable land or land at an especially high-priced location, such as ocean-front property, might want to pay special attention to these factors and attempt to convince the lender that there is no point in insuring the property for more than the insurance could possibly pay.

It is, however, sound advice to purchase dwelling insurance in an amount that equals the full replacement cost value of the building itself, for at least two reasons. First, a penalty will be imposed if, at the time of the loss, the house is not insured to at least 80 percent of its replacement cost value. The homeowners loss clause was discussed in the previous chapter. In many cases, the penalty is that the insured receives only the actual cash value of the damaged property, not its full replacement cost. Second, although total losses happen much less frequently than partial losses, they do occur. Moreover, replacement cost values tend to increase as a result of inflation, and a limit of insurance that was adequate last year might be inadequate this year when the policy is renewed.

The standard limits for Coverages B, C, and D are 10, 50, and 30 percent, respectively, of the Coverage A limit, as shown in the following example.

Example: Suppose Henry purchases an HO-3 with a Coverage A limit of $500,000 on the dwelling. Standard limits for his other coverages would then be as follows:

- Coverage B limit: $50,000 (10% of Coverage A)
- Coverage C limit: $250,000 (50% of Coverage A)
- Coverage D limit: $150,000 (30% of Coverage A)

These limits are generally adequate for a typical client. However, they can be increased for an additional premium, and a client who has, for example, an expensive outbuilding or personal property of above average value should consider additional coverage. The Coverage C limit can also be reduced to as little as 40 percent.

The limits on coverages B, C, and D are not part of the Coverage A limit, but rather additional amounts of insurance. So, in the example just given, Henry could collect up to $950,000 if his home is destroyed by a covered peril.

Coverage A for the Dwelling Building

Coverage A provides property insurance for the dwelling building at the address listed in the declarations page of the policy. The land itself is specifically excluded from coverage. Coverage A also applies to structures attached to the dwelling, such as a garage, decks, or fences, and to materials and supplies located on or next to the residence premises for construction, repair, or alteration of the dwelling or other structures on the residence premises.

Excluded Perils and Losses. Coverages A and B of the HO-3 use the open-perils approach, which provides coverage for all losses to covered property unless the cause or circumstances of the loss are excluded. The HO-3 contains a number of exclusions that preclude coverage for certain types of building damage that are somewhat expectable or can be prevented with reasonable care. For example:

- Wear and tear, marring, smog, rust or other corrosion, dry rot, deterioration, and inherent vice (the tendency of something like fabric to deteriorate) are not covered. These types of things normally happen as property ages.
- Mold, fungus, or wet rot is not covered unless it is hidden within or by walls, floors, or ceilings and results from accidental discharge of water or steam from plumbing or appliances. Mold grows where damp conditions are allowed to exist, and serious mold growth can usually be constrained with proper maintenance. In some cases, however, hidden damage occurs, and that hidden damage is covered.
- Pollution damage is not covered unless the pollution results from certain perils.
- Bird, vermin, rodent, or insect damage is not covered.
- Damage by pets or other animals kept by an insured is not covered.
- Loss due to frozen pipes is not covered unless the insured took reasonable care to maintain heat in the building or to drain the pipes. If an insured has taken such precautions and the freezing results from a power outage or a furnace malfunction, then the water damage is covered.

- Theft of construction materials from an uncompleted dwelling is not covered. The insured is expected to safeguard these materials.
- Vandalism and malicious mischief to a dwelling that has been vacant for more than 60 days is not covered.
- Freezing, thawing, ice, and water damage to fences, swimming pools, foundations, retaining walls, and so forth is not covered.

A second set of exclusions in the HO-3 is designed, in effect, to plug a loophole that results from the open-perils approach to coverage. The following example illustrates this point. The standard HO-3 excludes flood coverage because of its catastrophic nature. (Because one flood can simultaneously affect many insureds, flood insurance is best handled by a government insurance program.) However, under the open-perils approach, any peril that is not excluded is covered. So if a policyowner were to say, for example, that the flood was caused by defective planning or zoning, and if defective planning or zoning is not excluded, this claim might be covered under a different, nonexcluded peril. To plug this loophole, a set of exclusions precludes coverage for losses resulting from

- weather conditions
- acts or decisions, including the failure to act or decide by any person, group organization, or government body
- inadequate or defective planning, zoning, development, surveying, siting, design, specifications, workmanship, repair, construction, renovation, grading, or compaction, or defective materials used in repair, construction, renovation, or remodeling, as well as defective maintenance

However, even if one of these excluded perils can be considered the cause of the loss, any "ensuing loss" to covered property is covered if it is not otherwise excluded. Although this seems somewhat involved, a simple example should clarify the intent. As noted, insurers intend to exclude flood coverage but to provide fire coverage. If a flood occurs in a particular area because poor planning did not provide adequate drainage, it is still an excluded flood loss—not covered. But if the same flood causes an electrical short circuit that leads to a fire, the ensuing fire damage is covered.

Another set of exclusions affects not only Coverages A and B but also all other coverages. The standard HO-3, like most property insurance policies covering real property at a fixed location, excludes coverage for war, nuclear reaction, flood, and earthquake losses. The first two are uninsurable. Flood and earthquake coverage are available using separate policies or endorsements.

Also excluded are intentional losses committed by an insured, as well as neglect by the insured to use all reasonable means to protect property at and after the time of loss. The destruction or confiscation of property by a government agency is not a covered cause of loss; however, this exclusion does not apply to acts ordered to prevent the spread of fire. Therefore, if firefighters set a backfire while attempting to contain a brush fire or a forest fire, a house burned by that backfire would be covered.

One of the more noteworthy exclusions, especially from a financial planning perspective, is the ordinance or law exclusion. After a loss, it might not be possible to rebuild a home that is in a historical area, a home in a recently rezoned neighborhood, or simply an old home unless it is modified to comply with current building codes. The extra expenses can be substantial. An Additional Coverage automatically included in the HO-3 provides an additional limit of 10 percent of Coverage A to cover ordinance or law expenses. However, clients who have a recognized exposure might well be advised to purchase additional coverage through an endorsement.

Example:	Here are two clients who should probably carry ordinance or law coverage:

- Holly Wood lives in a California community where, because of brush fires, homeowners who are rebuilding are required to use tile or aggregate roofs, rather than shingles. Tile or aggregate roofs are more likely to resist fire, and they are also more expensive.
- Sandy Shores lives in a coastal community where houses are currently required to be eight feet above the ground to prevent flooding problems. Sandy's house, which is four feet above the ground, met the requirements in effect in 1988 when her house was constructed.

Many situations more subtle than the two in the example above also create significant ordinance or law exposures.

Basis of Loss Settlement. Losses under Coverage A are settled on a replacement cost basis.

Coverage B for Other Structures

Coverage B provides insurance on a replacement cost basis for other structures on the residence premises that are set apart from the dwelling by a clear space. Examples of other structures include swimming pools, detached garages, and garden sheds. If a garage is attached to the house and not separated by a clear space, it is covered as part of the dwelling, and the policy limit for Coverage A—Dwelling should be set high enough to cover both the residence and the garage.

The HO-3 does not cover another structure rented to somebody who is not a tenant of the dwelling, unless it is used only as a private garage. Likewise, a structure is not covered if it is used to store business property unless it is business property an insured or a tenant of the dwelling owns. However, if the business property stored in the garage includes gaseous or liquid fuel (other than fuel in a vehicle's fuel tank), the structure is not covered.

Coverage C for Personal Property

Coverage C provides insurance for personal property owned or used by any insured while it is located anywhere in the world. In addition, if the named insured or spouse so requests it after a loss, coverage is also provided for the property of a guest.

Some people have more than one residence. A client might, for example, have a winter home in the South or a summer home near the ocean. A $1,000 sublimit applies to coverage for personal property usually located at another residence. (If the Coverage C limit is less than $10,000, then the sublimit is 10 percent of the coverage C limit.) Clients who keep personal property in more than one residence should purchase specific insurance for each location rather than relying on the small amount of coverage available under their homeowners policy. Another reason to recommend specific insurance is that the homeowners policy does not cover theft of personal property from another residence of the insured—not even for $1,000—unless the insured is temporarily living there.

This limitation is not intended to limit coverage for homeowners who are in the process of moving from one primary residence to another and have not yet arranged insurance at the new location. Therefore, property in a newly acquired principal residence is not subject to the $1,000 sublimit for 30 days after the move begins.

Perils Covered. Coverage for personal property is written on a named-perils basis in the HO-3. These perils include

- fire or lightning. Neither term is defined in the policy, but, as explained in the previous chapter, it is a well-established principle that coverage is limited to damage by hostile fires. Although fire and lightning are separate perils, property insurance policies traditionally cover them together. If only one of these perils were covered, it would often be impossible to determine where the lightning damage stopped and the fire damage began.

- windstorm or hail. However, losses from rain, snow, sleet, sand, or dust are not covered unless they are a result of direct wind or hail damage to a building. In addition, damage to watercraft is not covered unless the watercraft is in a fully enclosed building.
- explosion
- riot or civil commotion
- aircraft
- vehicles
- smoke other than that from agricultural smudging or industrial operations. Agricultural smudging intentionally creates a dense smoke to prevent plants from frost, and the consequences are both expected and predictable.
- vandalism or malicious mischief
- theft. This also includes mysterious disappearance, which is the loss of property from a known place when it is likely that it has been stolen. However, several exclusions apply to theft, and the following are excluded from Coverage C:
  - theft committed by an insured
  - theft in or to a dwelling under construction, including material and supplies, unless the dwelling is finished or occupied
  - theft from the part of a residence premises rented by an insured to someone other than an insured
  - theft of property from another residence of the insured (such as a vacation home) unless the insured is temporarily living there
  - theft of property belonging to an insured who is a student when the property is at a residence away from home if the student has not been there at any time during the 60 days immediately preceding the loss
  - theft of watercraft, including furnishings and equipment
  - theft of trailers and campers
- falling objects
- weight of ice, snow, or sleet
- accidental discharge or overflow of water or steam
- sudden and accidental tearing apart, cracking, burning, or bulging of a steam, hot water, air conditioning, or automatic fire protective sprinkler system, or appliance for heating water
- freezing of a plumbing, heating, air conditioning, or automatic fire protective sprinkler system, or household appliance
- sudden and accidental damage from an artificially generated electrical current
- volcanic eruption

Sublimits. Coverage C limits the amount of insurance available to certain classes of property. In some cases, this limitation is for all perils; in other cases, it is for theft losses only. Several endorsements are available to increase many of these limits.

The following sublimits apply to the total loss of property from any single category:

- $200 for money, bank notes, bullion, coins, medals, scrip, stored value cards, smart cards, and gold, silver, and platinum other than goldware, silverware, and platinumware
- $1,500 for securities, accounts, deeds, evidences of debt, letters of credit, notes other than bank notes, manuscripts, personal records, passports, tickets, and stamps
- $1,500 for watercraft, including trailers, furnishings, equipment, and motors
- $1,500 for trailers not used with watercraft
- $2,500 for property on the residence premises (and $500 away from the residence premises) used primarily for business purposes
- $1,500 for electronic apparatus and accessories while in a motor vehicle, but only if the apparatus is equipped to be operated by power from the motor vehicle's electrical system while still capable of being operated by other power sources
- $1,500 for electrical apparatus and equipment used primarily for business while away from the insured premises and not in or upon a motor vehicle, but only if the apparatus is equipped to be operated from a motor vehicle's electrical system while still being capable of being operated by other power sources.
- $500 for property away from the residence premises used primarily for business purposes, other than electronic apparatus and equipment as previously described

The following limitations apply to theft but not other perils:

- $1,500 for jewelry, watches, furs, and precious and semiprecious stones
- $2,500 for firearms and related equipment
- $2,500 for silverware, goldware, platinumware, and pewterware

Excluded Property. Some categories and types of property are excluded from coverage under Coverage C:

- articles insured elsewhere
- animals, birds, and fish
- most motor vehicles

- aircraft
- hovercraft
- property of roomers or boarders other than those related to an insured
- property in an apartment rented to others. However, there is some coverage under Additional Coverages.
- property rented or held for rental to others off the residence premises
- business data
- credit cards, electronic fund transfer cards, or access devices used solely for deposit, transfer, or withdrawal of funds. However, there is limited coverage under Additional Coverages.
- water or steam

In a few cases, some limited coverage is provided as an Additional Coverage or under other parts of the policy. In most cases, coverage can also be obtained under separate insurance policies.

Example:	Burglars entered Martine's home and stole $500 in cash and a ring worth $2,000. Martine has an HO-3. Martine will recover $200 for the cash and $1,500 for the jewelry for a total of $1,700.
	A fire in Janelle's home destroyed $500 in cash and a ring worth $2,000. Janelle has an HO-3. Janelle will recover $200 for the cash and $2,000 for the jewelry for a total of $2,200. Janelle recovers more than Martine because the $1,500 sublimit on jewelry applies only to loss by theft.
	A fire in Donna's home destroyed $500 in cash and a ring worth $2,000. Donna has an HO-3 and a separate jewelry policy covering the ring for $1,000. Donna will recover $200 for the cash under her homeowners policy. She will also recover $1,000 for the ring under her jewelry policy. Donna's homeowners policy does not cover her ring at all, because it is specifically insured elsewhere.

Basis of Loss Settlement. Under a standard homeowners policy, Coverage C losses are settled on an actual cash value basis. However, replacement cost coverage is frequently added through the use of an available endorsement. The replacement cost option is usually a wise choice, because it substantially increases the amount a client will recover for an insured loss and covers the extra costs of buying new property to replace existing household property that is several years old or more. The insurance recovery is greater because the replacement cost value of personal property is invariably higher than the actual cash value of the same property. Therefore, most clients who purchase the replacement cost coverage option should also consider purchasing a higher limit of insurance for Coverage C. Many insurers require a limit higher than 50 percent of Coverage A—the usual limit—when this endorsement is used.

Coverage D for Loss of Use

Coverage D covers certain exposures a client is likely to incur when his or her residence cannot be occupied as a result of a covered property loss.

additional living expenses

If the named insured and family must live elsewhere while the portion of the residence that they normally occupy is being repaired or rebuilt, the named insured is entitled to benefits for *additional living expenses*. These benefits pay for any increase in expenses necessary to maintain the family's normal standard of living.

Coverage is also provided for the fair rental value, less any noncontinuing expenses, of the portion of the residence premises that is rented to others. Finally, up to 2 weeks' coverage is provided for the expenses of living elsewhere when civil authorities prohibit the named insured from using the residence premises because neighboring property is damaged by an insured peril. For example, expenses resulting from an evacuation because of a nearby brush fire are covered, but not the same expenses resulting from a threatening flood.

There is no coverage under Coverage D for losses arising out of the cancellation of leases or agreements.

Additional Coverages for Section I (Property)

Section I contains several Additional Coverages that fill in some of the gaps of the other four property coverages. In most cases, these provide amounts of insurance in addition to the limits under Coverages A, B, and C. Some of the more significant additional coverages include

- *ordinance or law.* Ten percent of the Coverage A limit, an additional amount of insurance, may be used to meet the increased costs of complying with an ordinance or law, such as a building code, that increases the expense of restoring property after a covered loss. As mentioned earlier, a higher amount of coverage is available by endorsement, and many clients should consider it.
- *debris removal.* Before property can be repaired or replaced, the damaged property (debris) must be removed. Subject to limitations detailed in the policy, coverage is provided for the expense of removing debris of covered property that has been damaged by a covered peril.

- *fallen trees.* The HO-3 will pay up to $500 per tree or $1,000 per loss for the cost of removing a tree felled by windstorm, hail, ice, snow, or sleet that has damaged a covered structure, blocks a driveway, or blocks a handicap access ramp.
- *trees, shrubs, plants, and lawns.* As detailed in the policy, a limited amount of coverage is available for trees, shrubs, and other plants damaged by certain perils. Weather-related losses are not covered.
- *landlord's furnishings.* Furniture in a furnished apartment that is rented to a tenant is covered for up to $2,500 for other named perils, but not for theft.
- *credit cards, ATM cards, forged checks, and counterfeit money.* The HO-3 provides up to $500 in coverage for losses in this category but does not cover business use or the dishonesty of an insured. Although identity theft is a growing concern, the extent of anyone's financial exposure involving any given credit card is usually limited to $500 or less by law and by the policies of the issuing company. However, this limit can be increased by endorsement.
- *grave markers and mausoleums.* Property in this category does not fit neatly among the types of property covered by homeowners policies. Because they are affixed to the land, grave markers and mausoleums are real property usually located in a cemetery away from the residence premises. Stone monuments do not burn. However, many families have a loss exposure, primarily involving the possibility of vandalism. The homeowners policy covers these real property items for the same named perils as personal property. The policy does not mention whose grave markers are covered; presumably, coverage would apply to those in which the policyowner has an insurable interest.
- *loss assessments.* Many clients today live in housing developments with an association that owns and maintains the common property. For example, homeowners in an over-55 development might belong to an association through which all residents collectively own the clubhouse, the pool, the tennis courts, and the fences and signs at the entrance. If damage occurs to any of this community property, the association can assess association members to recover the loss to the extent it is not covered by the association's property insurance. The coverage in the basic HO-3 provides $1,000 to cover such assessments, charged during the policy period, that are made because association property has been damaged by a peril covered under Coverage A of the policy.

  Unfortunately, many associations are poorly managed by volunteers, have inadequate property insurance, and maintain inadequate cash reserves to handle an emergency without assessing association members. The $1,000 limit can be increased by endorsement. Many clients who live in a condominium or who are members of a homeowners association should seriously consider increasing this limit.

HO-3 Liability Coverages

Section II is the same in all ISO homeowners forms. Like Section I, it contains more than one coverage. These are

- Coverage E for personal liability
- Coverage F for medical payments to others
- Additional coverages that provide some miscellaneous liability and related benefits

Section II provides broad liability coverage against many of the claims that a typical homeowner might face. It is subject to a number of exclusions, however, many of which eliminate homeowners coverage for losses that can be covered by other policies or endorsements.

Coverage E—Personal Liability

In Coverage E, the insurer agrees to defend the insured against any claim alleging that an insured is responsible to pay damages for bodily injury or property damage that would be covered by the policy. The insurer also agrees to pay any covered damages for bodily injury and property damage, up to the policy limit, for which the insured is found to be liable. The insurer pays defense costs in addition to the stated policy limit, and it provides a defense even if a claim is groundless, false, or fraudulent.

The basic limit of liability is typically $100,000, but it can be increased for a relatively small additional premium. A personal umbrella policy, described in chapter 18, is often purchased to provide an additional layer of $1 million or more in addition to the protection provided by the homeowners policy, an auto policy, and possibly other liability policies. In selecting liability limits for a homeowners policy, the usual approach is to purchase homeowners insurance with the minimum limit required to qualify for an umbrella (typically $300,000 or $500,000) and then to purchase an umbrella that adds at least $1 million of additional coverage.

As mentioned, Section II of a homeowners policy provides broad coverage that is more specifically defined by the policy's exclusions. Some exclusions apply only to Coverage E, while others also apply to Coverage F (discussed shortly).

Motor Vehicle Exclusions and Coverage. Homeowners policies include a rather involved motor vehicle liability exclusion. As one might expect, the homeowners policy does not cover vehicles registered for use on public roads. Auto owners are expected to have auto insurance. However, not all motor vehicle-related claims are excluded. Table 17-1 describes various motor vehicle liability exposures that the homeowners policy covers.

TABLE 17-1
Motor Vehicle Exposures Covered by Section II of the HO-3 Policy

Covered Motor Vehicle Liability Exposures	Examples
Motor vehicle in dead storage on an insured location	An unlicensed antique auto is stored in the insured's garage.
Motor vehicle used solely to service an insured's residence	A riding lawn mower is used to maintain the insured's yard.
Motor vehicle designed for assisting people who are handicapped	A motorized wheelchair, or a three- or four-wheeled power scooter, is used by a handicapped person.
Motorized vehicle designed for recreational use off public roads, and *not owned* by an insured	An insured borrows an unlicensed dune buggy for a ride through the sand dunes.
Motorized vehicle designed for recreational use off public roads, and *owned* by an insured and *on an insured location*	An insured owns an unlicensed dirt bike used by the insured's grandchild on the insured's property.
Motorized golf cart, not capable of exceeding 25 miles per hour, owned by an insured and used to play golf on a golf course, or legally used within a private residential association	The insured lives in a gated retirement community and owns a golf cart used for playing golf on the community's golf course, and also for visiting and running errands within the community.
Trailer not towed by, hitched to, or carried on a motor vehicle	An insured has parked the family's travel trailer at campsite for use on a 2-week vacation. Once the trailer is unhitched, the liability exposure is covered under the homeowners policy because it is no longer a "motor vehicle," as defined, and therefore is not subject to the motor vehicle exclusion.

Source: *Personal Insurance,* American Institute for CPCU/Insurance Institute of America, © 2002.

Watercraft Exclusions and Coverage. Another detailed exclusion precludes liability coverage for some, but not all watercraft exposures. Table 17-2 summarizes the exposures that *are* covered. Coverage for excluded exposures is generally available under a policy specifically designed to cover boats or other watercraft.

TABLE 17-2
Watercraft Exposures Covered by Section II of the HO-3 Policy

Covered Watercraft Liability Exposures	Examples
Watercraft that are stored	A 30-foot sailboat stored out of the water at a marina for the winter
Sailboats (with or without auxiliary power) shorter than 26 feet	A 17-foot catamaran owned by the insured
Sailboats (with or without auxiliary power) longer than 26 feet *not owned by or rented to* an insured	A 32-foot sailboat the insured borrowed from her brother for a vacation
Inboard or inboard-outdrive watercraft with engines of 50 horsepower or less that are *not owned* by an insured	A 50-horsepower jet ski rented by an insured
Inboard or inboard-outdrive watercraft of more than 50 horsepower *not owned by or rented to* an insured	A 150-horsepower inboard motor boat borrowed from a neighbor
Watercraft with one or more outboard engines or motors with 25 total horsepower or less	A fishing boat with a 15-horsepower motor, owned by the insured
Watercraft with one or more outboard engines or motors with more than 25 total horsepower that are *not owned* by an insured	A boat with a 75-horsepower outboard motor, borrowed from a friend
Watercraft with outboard engines or motors of more than 25 total horsepower owned by an insured if acquired during the policy period. If the insured acquires such watercraft before the policy period, they are covered only if the insured declares them at the policy inception, or reports the intention to insure them within 45 days of acquiring them.	A new boat with a 100-horsepower outboard motor purchased by the insured after the effective date of the policy

Source: *Personal Insurance,* American Institute for CPCU/Insurance Institute of America, © 2002.

In addition to the motor vehicle and watercraft exclusions, Section II of the homeowners policy contains exclusions for both bodily injury and property damage that

- arises out of aircraft or hovercraft. Most families do not have these exposures.
- arises out of or in connection with a business engaged in by an insured. There are some exceptions to this exclusion, however, and Coverage E applies if
    - a house is occasionally rented to others and used only as a residence
    - part of the residence is rented to others
    - part of the residence is rented and used as an office, school, study, or private garage
    - an insured is under age 21 and involved in part-time or occasional self-employed business (for example, lawn mowing) with no employees

  Several endorsements are available to provide limited coverage for businesses on the residence premises, but in many cases, commercial coverage is needed.
- arises out of the rendering or failure to render professional services. An accountant, a nurse, or another professional should purchase professional liability insurance to address these significant liability exposures.
- arises out of a location owned or rented by an insured that does not meet the policy definition of an insured location. This exclusion precludes coverage for premises claims such as, for example, a claim that somebody was injured by a condition on the property. It does not preclude coverage for claims based on the insured's activities away from home.
- is caused by transmission of a communicable disease. Claims alleging that the insured transmitted to someone else the HIV virus that causes AIDS, or transmitted herpes, or even the common cold are not covered.
- arises out of sexual molestation, corporal punishment, or physical or mental abuse. Providing insurance coverage against some of these claims is considered to be against public policy. Although it is not defined, corporal punishment generally refers to hitting, slapping, spanking, and similar disciplinary actions. Teachers, elder-care workers, or persons providing day care for children can sometimes obtain separate coverage that helps defend against allegations of the types excluded here, which sometimes are false or groundless.
- arises from the use, sale, manufacture, delivery, transfer, or possession of a controlled substance. It is obviously against public policy to provide products liability coverage for a dope dealer.

Another set of exclusions apply only to Coverage E. These preclude liability arising from

- any contract or agreement other than written contracts (1) relating to the ownership, maintenance, or use of an insured location—liability assumed in a lease, for example, is covered—and (2) for liability of others assumed by the insured before an occurrence takes place. People often are asked to sign construction contracts, purchase agreements, tool-rental agreements, and other documents that involve some transfer of liability. Although many people routinely sign contracts without reading them, clients would well be advised to pay attention to any legal obligations of other parties that they agree to assume, whether or not they have contractual liability insurance protection.

Example: Ned hires a contractor to replace the siding on his house. Ned signs a contract that includes wording to the effect that Ned will be responsible if the contractor is sued for negligence in connection with the work on Ned's home. While the contractor is doing the work, a gust of wind blows a siding panel into the street in front of Ned's house and causes an auto accident. The drivers sue the contractor, but the contractor turns the claim over to Ned because of the contract. Ned's homeowners policy will protect him against this contractual liability claim, up to Ned's policy limit. Because of the liability he assumed in the contract, Ned will be personally responsible for any damages that exceed policy limits.

Suppose, instead, that Ned and the contractor had no written agreement before the accident, but after the accident occurred, Ned wrote a letter to the contractor stating that Ned would assume responsibility and would file a claim under his homeowners policy. Under these circumstances, Ned's homeowners policy would provide no protection because he assumed liability after the occurrence had already taken place.

- property damage to property owned by an insured
- damage to property that is rented to, occupied by, or in the care of the insured except for property damage caused by fire, smoke, or explosion

- bodily injury to any person who is eligible to receive benefits or who is provided benefits under a state workers' compensation law, non-occupational disability law, or occupational disease law. Workers' compensation coverage is needed if this loss exposure exists.
- bodily injury arising out of nuclear energy
- bodily injury to any insured. The policy does not provide coverage if one insured injures another insured.

Coverage F—Medical Payments to Others

Coverage F provides up to $1,000 per person of coverage (or more if the basic limit is increased) for the necessary medical expenses of persons other than an insured who are injured while on an insured location with the permission of an insured. Benefits are paid regardless of fault even though this coverage is in the liability section of the policy. Injuries that occur off an insured location are also covered on the same basis if they

- arise out of a condition in an insured location
- are caused by the activities of an insured
- are caused by a resident employee of an insured in the course of employment for an insured
- are caused by an animal owned by or in the care of an insured

To a degree, the medical payments to others coverage overlaps with the bodily injury liability coverage. The key distinction is this:

- Liability coverage applies only when an insured is legally responsible for damages.
- Medical payments claims are often paid because the insured feels a *moral* obligation to another person, even when the insured is not negligent and has no legal responsibility for that person's injuries.

Often, a bodily injury liability claim involves a relatively small amount of money, and the insurer will pay it as a medical payments claim to eliminate any need to determine whether the insured was legally responsible for the other party's injuries.

Example:	Walter Booth held a birthday party at his home for his 6-year-old son. During the festivities, a deck collapsed, and Walter, his son, and six guests were treated for minor injuries. Another guest broke his leg and was unable to work on his job as a bricklayer for the 8 weeks it took to recover.

Walter has a homeowners policy with a $100,000 Coverage E—Liability limit and a $1,000 Coverage F—Medical Payments to Others limit.

The homeowners policy provides no coverage for Walter and his son's medical expenses, because they are insureds under the policy.

The Coverage F—Medical Payments to Others coverage will pay up to $1,000 for each of the six injured guests' injuries. Coverage applies even if the Booths are not legally responsible for the injuries as might, for example, be the case if the deck collapsed because a guest's car had rolled into a pole supporting the deck. In either case, for small claims like this there is no need to determine whether the Booths were liable for this incident, and their insurance addresses the moral obligation they might feel toward their injured guests, even if they have no legal obligation to pay the guests' expenses.

Coverage E—Liability of the homeowners policy addresses the bricklayer's bodily injury claim against the Booths for medical expenses, lost wages, and pain and suffering. The bricklayer may recover damages up to the policy limit of $100,000, provided it is clear that the Booths are legally responsible to pay damages to this guest as a result of the collapse. The insurer will also investigate the claim and defend the Booths if there is reason to believe the deck collapse did not result from their negligence. Any other guest whose damages exceeded $1,000 could also make a bodily injury liability claim against the Booths and attempt to demonstrate that the loss was caused by their negligence.

The liability coverage of the Booths' homeowners policy thus provides protection against sizable claims that involve a legal obligation to pay damages, as well as paying defense costs and other legal expenses associated with the claim. The Medical Payments to Others coverage pays relatively small claims without the need to demonstrate liability or the expense of determining liability; it therefore helps preserve the goodwill of the insureds.

Additional Coverages for Section II

Section II—Liability of homeowners policies includes several additional coverages, including an agreement to pay claims expenses and first aid expenses. Two additional coverages are especially noteworthy:

- damage to property of others
- loss assessment

Damage to Property of Others. This coverage is roughly comparable to the medical payments to others coverage discussed earlier except, of course, that it deals with property damage rather than bodily injury. The homeowners policy covers up to $1,000 per occurrence for property damage to the property of others caused by an insured. However, this additional coverage does not apply to losses when

- the loss is caused intentionally by an insured who is aged 13 or older
- the property is owned by another insured
- the property is owned by or rented to a tenant of an insured or a resident of the named insured's household
- the damage arises out of a business engaged in by an insured
- the damage arises out of any act or omission in connection with premises owned, rented, or controlled by an insured other than the insured location
- the damage arises out of ownership or use of aircraft, hovercraft, watercraft, or motor vehicles other than recreational vehicles that are (1) designed for off-road use, (2) not owned by an insured, and (3) not subject to motor vehicle registration

In addition, there is an offset for any duplicate benefits paid under Section I.

Example:	Liz borrows a neighbor's self-propelled lawn mower because her own push mower is in the shop. While mowing the lawn in her back yard, Liz loses control of the mower, and it self-propels itself into Liz's swimming pool. Liz's homeowners policy provides coverage to damage to the mower for up to $1,000 without having to prove that Liz was actually responsible for the loss. Maybe it really wasn't Liz's fault. Perhaps the mower was defective, or maybe the neighbor failed to instruct Liz in its use. Regardless, Liz's homeowners coverage for damage to

property of others applies, because she did not intentionally damage the mower.

In another incident, Liz's 4-year-old son, Aiden, found a can of spray paint and "decorated" the neighbor's shed. Although the damage was intentional, because Aiden is less than 13 years old, the damage to property of others will provide coverage up to $1,000.

Loss Assessment Coverage. We previously mentioned the $1,000 loss assessment coverage Section I of the homeowners policy provides when a condominium association or homeowners association assesses its members on account of a property loss. A similar provision in Section II of a standard homeowners policy likewise provides up to $1,000 for the insured's share of a loss assessment resulting from a liability claim against a property owners' association. Coverage applies to assessments made as the result of claims alleging (1) liability for bodily injury or property damage or (2) liability of an association's director, officer, or trustee.

Liability claims can be large even when shared with other association members. Suppose, for example, a child drowns in the association's swimming pool while the lifeguard is flirting with another guest, and survivors bring a wrongful death claim against the association and are awarded $5 million in damages. Suppose the association has liability insurance with a limit of $1 million, leaving the association responsible to pay $4 million in damages that it cannot recover from the insurer. The association must assess its members to recover the additional $4 million. If the homeowners association has 80 members, each will be assessed $50,000. Most members will recover only $1,000 under their homeowners policies because they have not purchased additional coverage. Most also will not have an emergency fund that can take a $49,000 hit.

The standard $1,000 limit in homeowners policies can be increased by endorsement, and the additional coverage is relatively inexpensive. Clients who belong to a condominium or homeowners association should seriously consider purchasing additional coverage. Clients in these situations would also be well advised to ensure that their association maintains adequate property and liability insurance. The need seems obvious, but many associations are run by board members who are not well versed in these areas or whose primary goal is to minimize expenses by purchasing minimal insurance coverage.

OTHER HOMEOWNERS FORMS

As previously mentioned, there are other homeowners forms. The ways in which they differ from the HO-3 are discussed below, followed by table 17-1, which provides a side-by-side comparison.

HO-2 Broad Form

The HO-2 is sometimes used when the cost of insurance is the overriding concern. The difference between the HO-2 and the HO-3 is that the HO-2 costs a little less and provides a little less coverage. Rather than providing open-perils coverage on the dwelling building and other structures, the HO-2 covers both buildings and personal property against the specific causes of loss named in the policy. The covered causes of loss were previously discussed in connection with the personal property coverage of the HO-3. Although the list of covered perils is long, it does not include every possible cause of accidental loss to a house.

A subtle difference between open-perils coverage and named-perils coverage involves the burden of proof. When a policy covers loss by named perils, the burden is on the insured to demonstrate that the loss was caused by one of the perils for which coverage is provided. Open-perils coverage, on the other hand, is based on the presumption that any property loss that has occurred is covered unless the insurer can demonstrate that one of the exclusions applies. This subtle distinction is sometimes important when property was obviously damaged, but it is difficult to determine how the damage occurred. Where proof is not readily available, the HO-3, in effect, gives the insured the benefit of the doubt.

HO-4 Contents Broad Form

The HO-4 is called a homeowners policy even though it is intended primarily for people who live in rented quarters and do not own a home. The HO-4 is part of the homeowners policy family, and it is essentially the same thing as an HO-3 without coverage on the building or other structures. The policyowner selects a limit for Coverage C—Personal Property, and Coverage D is set at 30 percent of that amount.

Although the HO-4 is usually written for tenants of an apartment building or a one- or more family dwelling, an HO-4 may also be purchased by the owner of a multi-unit apartment building—too large to be eligible for an HO-3—who also occupies one of the apartment units and wishes to protect his or her personal possessions and personal liability.

A client who owns a home or a condominium unit is usually forced to buy homeowners insurance because he or she is required to do so by the lender that provides the mortgage. Tenants often overlook their insurance needs because nobody requires homeowners insurance, they believe their personal property is not worth insuring, or they fail to recognize the importance of liability insurance. Many have not even checked into the cost of an HO-4 and do not realize that the coverage is relatively inexpensive, which is also why insurers do not aggressively market HO-4 coverage. In light of these factors, a financial advisor whose client is a tenant must often take the initiative to ensure that the client has protected his or her assets with this important coverage.

HO-5 Comprehensive Form

The HO-5 differs from the HO-3 in that Coverage C—Personal Property is written on an open-perils basis. The HO-5 therefore provides the broadest coverage of any standard homeowners policy and, of course, coverage can be expanded even further by endorsement. However, the HO-5 is not as popular as the HO-3, largely because of the added cost.

Both the HO-4 and the HO-6, discussed next, can be endorsed to provide comparable open-perils coverage on personal property.

HO-6 Unit-owners Form

An increasing number of clients have insurance needs that require special attention because they live in condominium or cooperative units. People who own condominium or cooperative units jointly own a building with other co-owners and individually are responsible for their own specific unit. A condominium's ownership deed, also called the "master deed" or "condominium declarations," is a document that establishes unit owners' rights and responsibilities. These documents usually include a section describing insurance requirements. Property not insured by the condominium association is usually the responsibility of the individual unit owner.

Because insurance requirements vary, clients should examine these documents carefully, consulting a legal advisor if necessary to determine the extent of their responsibilities. The association's insurance might provide only "bare walls" coverage for the building structure and the walls that support the structure, leaving the unit owner responsible for other walls and fixtures inside the unit. Or the association's insurance might include coverage for the fixtures, plumbing, wiring, or partitions inside the individual unit.

The HO-6 is designed to cover the unique loss exposures of a condominium or cooperative unit owner. In general, the HO-6 resembles an HO-4 for tenants that, as mentioned, is like an HO-3 without coverage on buildings or other structures. Because unit owners may have an insurable interest in the building, the HO-6 provides $5,000 in named-perils coverage under Coverage A; this amount can be increased when necessary.

The policyowner selects a limit for Coverage C—Personal Property. The Coverage D limit is automatically set at 50 percent of the Coverage C limit. Although the standard HO-6 provides named-perils coverage, Coverages A and C can both be changed by endorsement to apply on an open-perils basis.

HO-8 Modified Coverage Form

The HO-8, not a widely used homeowners form, has been mostly written on older homes where the replacement cost of a dwelling often significantly exceeds its market value. Providing replacement coverage in these cases might create a moral hazard because the policyowner could collect more under an insurance settlement than by selling the house. In addition, the premium for replacement-cost coverage might be beyond the means of many persons who own such homes.

The perils insured against for all coverages are limited to fire, lightning, windstorm or hail, explosion, riot or civil commotion, aircraft, vehicles, smoke, vandalism and malicious mischief, and volcanic eruption. Theft is covered only from the residence premises and up to a limit of $1,000. This limitation reflects the fact that HO-8s are often written in areas where the crime rate is higher.

There are also other limitations. Only 10 percent of Coverage C is provided on property off the insured premises. Additional Coverages are more limited and, for example, do not include collapse or extra expenses because of ordinances or laws.

Loss settlements under Coverages A and B are based on common construction materials and methods that are functionally equivalent to the original construction. Settlements are limited to market value if repairs are not made. (Note, however, that some states require loss settlements to be on an actual cash value basis.)

The issue of functional equivalency is discussed later with respect to the Functional Replacement Cost endorsement.

Comparison of Homeowners Forms

Table 17-3 shows a comparison of the homeowners forms.

HOMEOWNERS ENDORSEMENTS—TAILORING POLICY TO INDIVIDUAL NEEDS

Homeowners policies are designed for the typical needs of a broad range of homeowners. An individual homeowner may need to tailor the policy to meet his or her own special needs. These needs can be met in many instances through the use of appropriate policy endorsements that can add or delete coverage, change definitions, or clarify the intent of the insurance company.

Although an individual company can design almost any type of endorsement, nearly 60 standard endorsements have been prepared by ISO for use with its homeowners forms. Several of these endorsements are briefly described below. The name used is the actual name of the ISO endorsement, and they are listed in alphabetical order. Some endorsements apply to the entire policy; others modify only Section I or Section II.

Note that it is not generally necessary to add an endorsement to increase the limits of insurance for Coverages, C, D, E, or F. This is accomplished by listing the higher amount in the policy declarations and paying the necessary additional premium.

TABLE 17-3
Homeowners Forms

	HO-2 Broad	HO-3 Special	HO-4 Tenants	HO-5 Compre-hensive	HO-6 Unit-owners	HO-8 Modified
Perils insured against	Broad named perils	Open perils for dwelling; broad named perils for personal property	Broad named perils for personal property	Open perils	Broad named perils	Limited named perils
Coverage A—Dwelling	Amount selected	Amount selected	—	Amount selected	$5,000	Amount | selected
Coverage B—Other Structures	10% of A	10% of A	—	10% of A	—	10% of A
Coverage C—Unscheduled Personal Property	50% of A	50% of A	Amount selected	50% of A	Amount selected	50% of A
Coverage D—Loss of Use	30% of A	30% of A	30% of C	30% of A	50% of C	10% of A
Coverage E—Personal Liability	$100,000	$100,000	$100,000	$100,000	$100,000	$100,000
Coverage F—Medical Payments to Others	$1,000 per person	$1,000 per person	$1,000 per person	$1,000 per person	$1,000 per person	$1,000 per person

Endorsements That Modify Section I and Section II

Additional Insured—Residence Premises

In some cases, persons other than the named insured have an interest in residential property. For example, a sister might occupy a house that she and her brother jointly inherited from their parents. This endorsement adds others (such as the brother) as insureds. However, the additional insured's coverage under Section II is only for liability with respect to the residence premises.

Assisted-Living Care Coverage

As the population ages, an increasing number of people live in assisted-living facilities. Many are no longer able to perform the activities of daily living necessary to live on their own. Some are liquidating their life savings in order to meet expenses; others have had the foresight to purchase long-term care insurance that pays for all or part of their care and helps preserve their assets. Still others have spent down their assets and rely on Medicaid for their support. In any case, people whose parents or relatives live in assisted-living facilities often overlook their need for property and liability insurance.

The assisted-living care coverage endorsement provides limited personal property, additional living expenses, and liability coverage for a named relative of a homeowner-insured who lives in these facilities but is not a member of the insured's household. Additional expense coverage is provided for up to $500 per month, and sublimits apply for hearing aids, eyeglasses, contact lenses, false teeth, medical-alert devices, walkers or canes, and wheelchairs.

Home Business Insurance Coverage

This endorsement provides both business property and liability coverage for certain home businesses owned solely by the named insured or jointly by the named insured and resident relatives. Coverage is provided for the following:

- business property, property of others in the insured's care because of the business, and business property leased by the insured if there is a contractual responsibility to insure it
- accounts receivable and valuable papers and records
- business income and extra expense losses
- liability coverage for bodily injury, property damage, personal and advertising injury, products, and completed operations

There is no coverage for liability for the rendering or failure to render professional services.

Home Day-Care Coverage Endorsement

This endorsement is for persons who conduct day-care businesses in their homes for either children or older adults. It provides coverage for personal property used in the day-care business and extends Section II liability coverage to home day-care services. However, liability is excluded for injuries arising out of motor vehicles, watercraft, and saddle animals. Note that Section II excludes liability arising out of sexual molestation and physical or mental abuse inflicted by an insured or an employee. These are obvious liability loss exposures for a day-care center.

Loss Assessment Coverage

The purpose of this endorsement is to increase the $1,000 limits for loss assessments by a homeowners association. Although it can be added to any homeowners form, it is especially common with an HO-6.

Permitted Incidental Occupancies (Residence Premises)

This endorsement deletes many of the homeowners exclusions that pertain to a business conducted on the residence premises. If business is conducted in a separate structure on the premises, it is necessary to list that structure under Coverage B and select a limit of property coverage for the building. The $2,500 limit for business property under Coverage C is deleted and the full limit of Coverage C applies to business and personal property. Liability coverage is still excluded for bodily injury to an employee or to a pupil if the injury is a result of corporal punishment.

This endorsement merely extends the existing homeowners coverage. It does not pick up many of the unique business situations covered by the Home Business Insurance Coverage endorsement.

Residence Held in Trust

For various reasons, clients are sometimes advised to establish a trust that holds the title to their home. When this is done, the residence held in trust endorsement can be used to modify various provisions in Section I and Section II of a homeowners policy to deal with the parties whose interests are insured in a trust situation.

Structures Rented to Others

This endorsement provides both property and liability coverage for structures on an insured premises that are rented to others.

Endorsements That Modify Section I (Property)

Additional Limits of Liability—Coverages A, B, C, and D

For use only with the HO-2 and the HO-3, this endorsement amends the policy to provide coverage for the full replacement cost of the dwelling at the time of loss if the loss exceeds the stated policy limit. Limits for other property coverages are also increased in the same proportion. As a condition for this protection, the policyowner agrees to maintain insurance at full replacement value as determined by the insurer and to report any alterations that increase the dwelling's value by 5 percent or more.

In effect, the endorsement merely guarantees that the insurer has required an adequate amount of coverage. This might seem like a trivial matter, but it can make an important difference, even when a house has been properly appraised. The cost of repairing or replacing houses sometimes increases dramatically following a hurricane, forest fire, or earthquake that damages many homes in the same area and creates a high demand for building materials and contractors' services. This endorsement ensures that enough insurance is available to replace the dwelling even in these situations.

Coverage C—Increased Special Limits of Liability

This endorsement can be used to increase coverage for some of the items where limited amounts of protection are available under Coverage C. The limits can be increased for

- money, bank notes, bullion, coins, medals, scrip, stored value cards, smart cards, and gold, silver, and platinum other than goldware, silverware, or platinumware
- securities, accounts, deeds, evidences of debt, letters of credit, and other valuable papers
- jewelry and watches
- firearms
- electronic apparatus for use in a motor vehicle

An increased amount of coverage is selected for each category. Although this endorsement increases the sublimits that apply to certain types of property, it does not expand coverage to include additional perils, nor does it modify the policy's deductible. When high jewelry values are to be protected, the scheduled personal property endorsement, discussed later, is often a better choice.

Credit Card, Electronic Fund Transfer Card or Access Device, Forgery, and Counterfeit Money Coverage

This endorsement increases the $500 limit for these types of losses.

Earthquake

In most states, this endorsement can be used to add coverage for the peril of earthquake as well as tremors that accompany volcanic eruption. In place of the regular deductible, there is an earthquake deductible equal to 5 percent of the limit of insurance that applies to Coverage A or Coverage C, whichever is greater. The deductible percentage can be increased for a premium credit. Coverage for masonry veneer is optional for an extra premium.

The situation is different in the largest market for earthquake insurance—California. The state requires insurers that sell homeowners policies to offer earthquake coverage. However, because of adverse claims experience and the financial inability of insurers to withstand catastrophic claims from future earthquakes, the market for homeowners policies virtually disappeared in the mid-1990s. At that time, many insurers ceased to write new policies or withdrew from the market altogether. As a result, a state agency was formed to make earthquake coverage available. This coverage is now sold by many insurers along with their homeowners policies, but the insurer of the earthquake coverage is the state agency. Although there is coverage available for the residence, there is no coverage for other structures and a limited amount of coverage for personal property, debris removal, and additional living expenses. A standard deductible of 15 percent of a home's insured value may be reduced to 10 percent.

Some insurers still make earthquake coverage available in California as part of their homeowners policies, and other types of insurers specialize in this market with separate policies. In most cases, more comprehensive coverage and lower deductibles are available from these sources.

Functional Replacement Cost Loss Settlement

Older homes often have replacement values far in excess of their market values. An example would be a 100-year-old Victorian house that might sell for several hundred thousand dollars but that would cost several million dollars to replace. The HO-8 Modified Coverage Form, mentioned earlier, is one approach to dealing with older homes, especially those in a depressed area. The functional replacement cost endorsement to an HO-2, HO-3, or HO-5 provides an alternative that appeals to homeowners who want the broader coverage of these policies without purchasing a limit of insurance equal to the property's full replacement cost value. Some insurance companies are unwilling to insure such dwellings for replacement cost because of the potential moral hazard. In addition, property owners may not desire to pay the premium for replacement-cost coverage.

functional replacement cost

This endorsement replaces the replacement cost provision of an HO-2, HO-3, or HO-5 policy with a provision for *functional replacement cost*. This is defined to mean the cost to repair or replace the damaged dwelling with less costly construction materials and methods that are functionally equivalent to obsolete, antique, or custom construction materials and methods used in the original construction of the dwelling. For example, dry wall would replace plaster walls, composition shingles would replace slate, hollow core doors might replace solid wood interior doors, and wall-to-wall carpeting over plywood might replace hardwood floors. All of this, unfortunately, might result in the loss of a dwelling's unique character.

Some states prohibit loss settlements that are less than the actual cash value of a loss. In these states, a modified endorsement is used so that the insured receives the actual cash value when it exceeds the functional replacement cost.

This endorsement has an 80 percent coinsurance provision based on functional replacement cost, which may be as difficult to determine as regular replacement cost.

Identity Fraud Expense Coverage

Introduced recently, this endorsement provides protection against many of the expenses that can result from identity theft, one of America's fastest-growing white collar crimes. Coverage applies in the event of identity fraud, the unauthorized use of an insured's identity to commit an unlawful activity. Subject to a $250 deductible, up to $15,000 in coverage is provided in each of the following types of expenses:

- costs of notarizing affidavits or related documents to verify the fraud
- costs for certified mail to financial institutions and law enforcement agencies
- lost income (up to $5,000) due to the insured's time off work to complete fraud affidavits and to meet with law enforcement agencies, credit agencies, and attorneys
- loan application fees required to reapply for loans that had been rejected due to inaccurate credit information
- reasonable attorney fees incurred as a result of identity fraud
- long distance phone charges required to report or discuss identity fraud

Clients can also be advised of various measures that can reduce the probability of an identity theft. For example, they should shred documents that contain financial data, including credit card bills, bank statements, mutual fund statements, and so forth. Periodically checking their credit records can reveal inaccurate or unauthorized credit activities. Likewise, clients should minimize the use of their Social Security number or drivers license number and avoid placing important mail in an unlocked mailbox.

Increased Limits on Business Property

The endorsement allows a policyowner to increase the $2,500 limit that applies to business property on the premises. The endorsement is of value to a person who has an office at home but does not conduct a business on the premises.

Increased Limits on Personal Property in Other Residences

Coverage under the homeowners forms for the insured's property usually located at a secondary residence is limited to $1,000. The endorsement can be used to provide increased coverage. The endorsement might, for example, be suitable to protect the property of a college student living in a dormitory, whose computer, stereo, and photographic equipment alone are worth more than $1,000.

Inflation Guard

This popular endorsement provides automatic increases for all Section I coverages by the annual percentage selected. The increase is effective on a pro rata basis during the annual policy period.

Multiple Company Insurance

When an affluent client requires very large amounts of property insurance, the Section I coverage can be divided between two or more insurers if they all agree to such an arrangement. This endorsement specifies the percentage of the total amount of insurance each insurer will pay. Only one of the insurance policies will provide the Section II coverage.

Ordinance or Law—Increased Amount of Coverage

As mentioned earlier, this endorsement can be used to increase the Additional Coverage limit of 10 percent of Coverage A for increased costs of construction because of enforcement of an ordinance or law. These additional costs can be significant when major changes have occurred in building codes such as provisions aimed at minimizing losses due to floods or earthquakes when a structure is rebuilt or undergoes significant repairs.

Other Structures—Increased Limits

When the standard amount of insurance for Coverage B is inadequate, this endorsement is used to provide additional insurance on structures that are described in the endorsement. For example, an insured with $200,000 of coverage on a dwelling would automatically have $20,000 of insurance for Coverage B. If the insured had a separate structure used as an art studio that had a replacement cost of $35,000, this endorsement could provide the additional $15,000 of protection.

Personal Property Replacement Cost Loss Settlement

Most clients should probably consider this popular endorsement, which changes the loss settlement basis for personal property from actual cash value to replacement cost. Some property, such as antiques, fine art, and collectibles, is not eligible for replacement cost coverage.

If the replacement value of a loss is more than $500, repair or replacement must be made before the replacement cost provision is applicable. The insured can make a claim for the actual cash value at the time of loss and amend it to replacement cost with 180 days.

Premises Alarm or Fire Protection System

This endorsement acknowledges that an insurer-acceptable alarm system or automatic sprinkler system is in place. The policyowner agrees to maintain the system in working order and to let the insurer know promptly if any changes are made to the system or if it is removed. In exchange, the policyowner receives a premium reduction.

Refrigerated Property Coverage

This endorsement adds up to $500 coverage (with a $100 deductible) for losses to property in refrigerators or freezers caused by interruption of electrical services (either on or off the premises) or the mechanical failure of the refrigerator or freezer. Some insurers that do not use ISO forms automatically include refrigerated property coverage in their basic homeowners policy forms.

Scheduled Personal Property Endorsement

Clients who have possessions of high value that are subject to the sublimits of the standard homeowners policy commonly use this popular endorsement. It broadens coverage on specific categories of valuable personal property such as jewelry, furs, cameras, musical instruments, silverware, golfer's equipment, fine arts, and stamp and coin collections. Each item is usually listed separately and insured for a specified value, but some coverage can be written on a blanket basis for certain classes of property.

Coverage is open-perils with few exceptions and applies worldwide. There is also coverage for up to 30 days for newly acquired property in a category insured under the endorsement. It is limited, however, to 25 percent of the amount of insurance for that category.

Once property is insured under this endorsement, there is no coverage for it under Coverage C. The Section I deductible does not apply to scheduled items.

Losses are generally settled on an actual cash value basis. However, fine art is written on an agreed value basis, and another available endorsement can provide coverage for other personal property on an agreed value basis.

Sinkhole Collapse

Property is sometimes damaged or destroyed when earth collapses because of voids created under limestone or similar rock formations. This endorsement provides coverage for losses to covered property (not land) from such collapses.

Special Computer Coverage

Designed for homeowners or unit owners who do not have open-perils coverage on their other personal property, this endorsement provides open-perils coverage on computer equipment.

Special Loss Settlement

The loss settlement provision of homeowners policies was discussed in chapter 16. This endorsement lowers the 80 percent insurance-to-value requirement to either 50, 60, or 70 percent. It is used when the replacement cost of a dwelling far exceeds its market value and the insurer is unwilling to write a policy for as much as 80 percent of replacement cost.

Special Personal Property Coverage—HO-4

This endorsement allows tenants to change the named-perils coverage for personal property under an HO-4 to open-perils coverage like the coverage provided by an HO-5.

Unit-owners Coverage A and Unit-owners Coverage C

These endorsements change the named-perils coverage of an HO-6 to open-perils coverage. If both endorsements are purchased, the condominium owner has a policy much like an HO-5.

Endorsements That Modify Section II (Liability)

Additional Residence Rented to Others

Sometimes a policyowner owns a separate rental property. This endorsement can be used to extend the Section II coverages to liability that arises out of such property as long as it is listed in the endorsement and contains no more than four living units.

Business Pursuits

This endorsement provides coverage for liability that arises out of or in connection with a business in which an insured engages. An example is a suit against a salesperson who accidentally injured a customer. The endorsement is most commonly used by persons in sales, clerical, and teaching occupations.

Coverage does not apply with respect to a business owned or financially controlled by an insured or in which an insured is a partner. (A commercial policy is needed for this.) In addition, there is no coverage for liability that arises out of professional services, with the exception of teaching. Bodily injury to fellow employees is also excluded.

Farmers Personal Liability

People whose principal business or occupation is not farming sometimes own some land where farming operations take place. This endorsement provides Section II coverage for this activity at those locations listed in the endorsement. Several exclusions in the endorsement apply to unique farming activities.

Personal Injury

Attorneys and others often use personal injury as a synonym for bodily injury. In the language of liability insurance, the two terms have different meanings. In liability insurance policies, personal injury refers to a group of offenses—such as libel, slander, and invasion of privacy—that are listed in the policy. The homeowners personal injury endorsement modifies the definition of bodily injury to include personal injury, which is defined in this endorsement to include the following offenses:

- false arrest, detention or imprisonment, or malicious prosecution
- libel, slander, or defamation of character
- invasion of privacy, wrongful eviction, or wrongful entry

The coverage does not apply to an insured's violation of criminal law, employment-related injuries, business-related and professional injuries, civic or public activities performed for pay, injury to another insured, or contractual liability other than that relating to the insured's home.

Although the personal injury endorsement can protect against these offenses under a homeowners policy, many clients would best be advised to forgo the homeowners endorsement and instead obtain this protection under a personal umbrella policy, discussed in chapter 18.

Snowmobiles

This endorsement provides coverage for listed snowmobiles when they are used off the insured premises. However, coverage does not apply if the snowmobiles are (1) subject to motor vehicle registration, (2) used to carry paying passengers, (3) used for a business purpose, (4) rented to others, or (5) operated in organized competitions.

Watercraft

This endorsement provides coverage for boats that are longer or more powerful than those covered by the standard homeowners coverage. It does not cover liability arising out of (1) racing or speed competitions except for sailboats, (2) injuries to employees who maintain or use the boats, (3) watercraft used to carry persons for a fee, or (4) watercraft rented to others.

OTHER RESIDENTIAL FORMS

Homeowners policies do not cover all types of residential loss exposures. The following discussion briefly describes three other types of residential coverage:

- dwelling policies
- mobilehome insurance
- insurance for farms and ranches

As with homeowners policies, companies may have their own forms or use those developed by ISO or AAIS. The following discussion is based primarily on the ISO forms.

Dwelling Policies

dwelling policy

A *dwelling policy* is designed primarily for a residence that is ineligible for homeowners coverage for one or more of the following reasons:

- The dwelling is rented to others.
- The dwelling does not meet the insurer's eligibility requirements for homeowners coverage. This may be because of low value, too many living units, the old age of the dwelling, or the poorer than average physical condition of the dwelling.

In addition, a few insureds may elect a more restrictive and less expensive dwelling policy because they do not want all the homeowners coverages or are unwilling or unable to pay the price of a homeowners policy. Under the ISO program, a dwelling policy can also be written for houseboats in some states and for mobile homes, subject to certain restrictions.

Like the homeowners form, ISO has several dwelling forms:

- Dwelling Property 1—Basic Form (DP-1)
- Dwelling Property 2—Broad Form (DP-2)
- Dwelling Property 3—Special Form (DP-3)

The DP-2 and DP-3 are similar to the Section I coverages of the HO-2 and HO-3, respectively. The DP-1 is a more limited policy, and the coverage is slightly less comprehensive. For example, the standard dwelling forms have no coverage for the peril of theft, and off-premises coverage for personal property is limited to 10 percent of Coverage C.

There are five coverages under the forms:

- Coverage A—Dwelling
- Coverage B—Other Structures
- Coverage C—Personal Property
- Coverage D—Fair Rental Value
- Coverage E—Additional Living Expenses (not included with DP-1)

The applicant selects the coverages to purchase and the limits of coverage. Tenants can purchase a policy without Coverages A and B, and landlords can purchase a policy without Coverage C.

The peril of theft can be endorsed to the dwelling forms and, for owner-occupied dwellings, the coverage is then similar to that under the homeowners forms. Tenants are eligible only for more limited coverage.

The dwelling forms do not automatically provide liability coverages as do the homeowners forms. However, these important coverages can be added by endorsement.

Mobilehome Insurance

mobilehome insurance

Insurance on an owner-occupied mobile home, known as *mobilehome insurance,* is very similar to insurance on a conventional dwelling. An endorsement, added to an HO-2 or HO-3, alters a few definitions and amends a few policy provisions to adapt coverage for this type of living unit. For example, because furniture is often built in and part of a mobile home, the Coverage C limit is lowered to 40 percent of the Coverage A limit. Because these homes are mobile, an extra coverage provides up to $500 to cover the cost of moving a mobile home out of harm's way when it is endangered by an insured peril. The $500 limit can be increased by endorsement.

The homeowners forms may be modified to cover a mobile home on an actual cash value basis. The insurer sometimes requires this modification on an older mobile home, because mobile homes depreciate in value as they age.

The owner of a mobile home who does not occupy it can insure the mobile home under a dwelling form. The tenant of a mobile home is eligible for an HO-4 policy.

Farm and Ranch Policies

Many people earn their livelihood by owning farms and ranches, and numerous policies are available to provide them with the necessary property and liability protection. Coverage tends to be written by insurers that use their own forms and often specialize in writing coverage for the persons engaged in this type of occupation.

In addition to coverages for the farm or ranch dwelling and household personal property, coverage is needed for farm structures and farm personal property. Other property loss exposures include food spoilage, damage to private power and light poles, pumps, and loss to animals from numerous perils other than sickness or disease. There are also unique liability loss exposures such as animal boarding, injury or sickness from chemicals, and injury to the public if they are allowed to pick fruits or vegetables.

The available policies tend to look much like homeowners policies with additional coverage for many of these and other farming and ranching loss exposures.

FLOOD INSURANCE

When discussing property insurance with a client, it is all too easy to overlook flood insurance. Many clients do not even consider flood coverage, because they do not think they live in an area susceptible to flooding. Many people in that category lived in North Carolina in 1999 when 55,000 homes were flooded, 15,000 homes became uninhabitable, and 8000 homes were completely destroyed. More than 80 percent of the flooded properties were outside high-risk flood hazard areas.[1] Flood is an individual peril in almost all insurance policies that cover real property and many that cover personal property. At one time, coverage was virtually impossible to obtain, but this changed in the late 1960s when Congress passed legislation that enacted the *National Flood Insurance Program (NFIP)*. This program is currently administered by the Federal Insurance and Mitigation Administration (FIMA). Under the NFIP, the federal government provides limited amounts of flood insurance coverage—often at subsidized rates—for the owners of dwellings, commercial buildings, and the contents of both.

National Flood Insurance Program (NFIP)

Although coverage was once purchased directly from the NFIP, most policies are now written through private insurance companies under the *write-your-own-program*. Under this program, the NFIP reimburses the insurance company for any losses that exceed the sum of premiums collected and any investment income earned on these premiums. Consumers obtain their policies through private insurance agents.

Eligibility

For property owners to be eligible for flood insurance, they must live in a community that participates in the program. These communities must agree to establish and enforce certain land use restrictions to minimize the community's exposure to flood losses. These, for example, might include a prohibition against new construction in flood-prone areas.

Unfortunately, even when flood insurance is available, many consumers do not purchase it, particularly if they live in an area where floods seem unlikely. To minimize uninsured flood losses, the government prohibits the issuance of federal loans or federally assisted or insured loans to persons in highly flood-prone areas (called special hazard flood areas) unless they purchase coverage.

The dollar amount of coverage available for residential property through the flood insurance program is limited to $250,000 on the building and $100,000 on the contents for communities eligible for the "regular program." These limits might be less than the value of the dwelling and personal property in it. However, as explained below, not all types of property are covered. To avoid insuring property when a flood is imminent, the program includes a 30-day waiting period before a flood insurance policy can become effective.

Detailed and current information on the national flood insurance program is available online at www.floodsmart.gov. The following coverage summary is adapted from information there.

Property Covered

The Standard Flood Insurance Policy (SFIP) Forms contain complete definitions of the coverages they provide. Direct physical losses caused by "floods" are covered. Also covered are losses resulting from flood-related erosion caused by waves or currents of water activity exceeding anticipated cyclical levels, or caused by a severe storm, flash flood, abnormal tidal surge, or the like, which result in flooding, as defined. Damage caused by mudslides (that is, mudflows), as specifically defined in the policy forms, is covered.

The NFIP defines a basement as any area of a building with a floor that is below ground level on all sides. Although flood insurance does not cover basement improvements, such as finished walls, floors or ceilings, or personal belongings that may be kept in a basement, such as furniture and other contents, it does cover structural elements, essential equipment and other basic items generally located in a basement. Many of these items are covered under building coverage, and some are covered under contents coverage. The NFIP encourages people to purchase both building and contents coverage for the broadest protection.

The following items are covered under building coverage, as long as they are connected to a power source and installed in their functioning location:

- sump pumps
- well water tanks and pumps, cisterns and the water in them
- oil tanks and the oil in them, natural gas tanks and the gas in them
- pumps and/or tanks used in conjunction with solar energy
- furnaces, hot water heaters, air conditioners, and heat pumps
- electrical junction and circuit breaker boxes, and required utility connections

- foundation elements
- stairways, staircases, elevators, and dumbwaiters
- unpainted drywall and sheet rock walls and ceilings, including fiber-glass insulation
- cleanup

The following items are covered under contents coverage:

- clothes washers
- clothes dryers
- food freezers and the food in them

Increased Cost of Compliance Coverage

Increased Cost of Compliance (ICC) under the NFIP provides for the payment of a claim to help meet the cost to comply with state or community floodplain management laws or ordinances from a flood event in which a building has been declared substantially damaged or repetitively damaged. When an insured building is damaged by a flood and the state or community declares the building to be substantially damaged or repetitively damaged, ICC will help pay for the cost to elevate, floodproof, demolish, or relocate the building up to $30,000. This coverage is in addition to the building coverage for the repair of actual physical damages from flood under the Standard Flood Insurance Policy (SFIP).[2]

HARD-TO-INSURE RESIDENTIAL PROPERTY

Even though most residential property is eligible for coverage in the standard insurance market, some residential property fails to meet most insurers' underwriting guidelines. This can occur for a variety of reasons, including the

- high replacement cost of the property relative to its market value
- physical condition of the property
- environment of the property. For example, the neighborhood is one of high crime or susceptibility to brush fires or severe coastal storms.
- poor reputation of the owner or occupants
- excessiveness of past claims of the applicant
- use of the property. For example, it may be a remote cabin that is seldom occupied and in an area without fire protection.

Policies that are available can be more limited than policies written in the general marketplace. Some companies specialize in the substandard market and write coverage for a variety of properties but at higher-than-normal premiums.

FAIR (Fair Access to Insurance Requirements) plans

Many states have taken actions to make coverage available, often at subsidized rates. More than 30 states have *FAIR (Fair Access to Insurance Requirements) plans*. These plans originally began as a result of urban riots in the 1960s, which made property insurance very difficult to obtain in many major cities. The current plans are state-run programs to provide insurance for buildings and their contents if the property owner is unable to obtain coverage in the standard insurance market, for whatever reason. In most cases, coverage is written by a pool or syndicate of private insurers that are assessed for any losses of the plan if premiums are inadequate.

Each state has its own FAIR plan, and they do differ. Nevertheless, a few generalizations can be made. Some types of property are still largely uninsurable. These may include property that is vacant, poorly maintained, subject to unacceptable hazards (such as the manufacture of fireworks), or not built in accordance with safety and building codes. Coverage is usually written under forms that are more limited than homeowners policies. Often the perils insured against are only fire and a limited number of other perils. Coverage is also subject to maximum limits and mandatory deductibles.

Some states, primarily in the Southeast and on the Gulf Coast, have beachfront and windstorm plans to provide protection that insurers are unwilling to write because of the loss exposure to hurricanes. Some of these plans cover only the perils of windstorm and hail, and property owners obtain protection for other perils in the general insurance market.

HIGH-VALUE RESIDENTIAL PROPERTY

Insurance on expensive homes can present unique and interesting challenges for the financial planner. These challenges result from high property values and unique types of property and liability exposures. They also arise from the demanding nature of people who are accustomed to receiving personal attention and a high level of service tailored to their special needs. Because large values are involved, wealthy clients have a great deal to lose, both in terms of property losses and as the result of high-profile liability suits that may be made against them. Challenges a financial planner might face include

- property values higher than an insurer is willing to write under a standard homeowners program designed for the more typical situation
- old or historic homes
- unique construction that can be difficult or costly to rebuild
- gardens, swimming pools, tennis courts, or stables
- high-risk locations, such as oceanfront or mountainside property
- property in several locations, several states, or several countries with no coordination of insurance
- multiple insurance agents, brokers, or insurance companies

- policies with different, nonconcurrent expiration dates
- high-value jewelry, furs, silver, or fine arts items
- antique or collector cars
- boats, yachts, or aircraft
- collections or other valuable belongings (a wine cellar, for example)
- high-value property outside the home—in transit, on loan to a museum, aboard a yacht, or elsewhere
- full-time or part-time nannies or other domestic employees who may reside on the premises
- frequent use of contractors
- a high-profile lifestyle
- frequent parties and many guests
- potential kidnap and ransom exposure
- lack of personal interest in insurance matters

Insurance programs designed for the typical client cannot properly service clients with significant and unusual exposures. Some insurers, and some insurance agents and brokers, specialize in this market and have developed policies specially designed to address the needs of the well-to-do. Standard HO-3 or HO-5 homeowners policies can also be used in many cases, provided they have been tailored with the endorsements necessary to meet any unique exposures. High deductibles are often advisable both to keep premiums down and to avoid a high frequency of insurance claims for normal maintenance and repair. High-liability limits are especially important, and they are generally provided through a personal umbrella policy, as discussed in the next chapter. Once established, an affluent client's property and liability insurance program should be regularly monitored and reviewed to keep pace with frequently changing property and liability exposures. Of course, the client's business exposures must also be properly insured to protect his or her assets against loss.

FLOATER POLICIES

floater

Several policies are available to provide broad insurance protection on a wide variety of personal property. These policies are commonly referred to as *floaters* because the insured property is often subject to being moved or is "floating around" rather than remaining at a fixed location.

With the broadening of the homeowners forms over the years and the development of endorsements to meet specialized needs, the use of personal floater policies has diminished. However, they are still written for persons who are not eligible for homeowners policies or who, for some reason, prefer to have the property insured separately.

Personal Articles Floater

personal articles floater

A *personal articles floater* is used to provide open-perils coverage for certain scheduled and valuable items of personal property. It is essentially the same as the scheduled personal property endorsement to the homeowners policy that was discussed earlier in the chapter.

Personal Property Floater

personal property floater

A *personal property floater* is designed primarily to provide open-perils coverage for unscheduled personal property on a worldwide basis. The personal property floater essentially provides the same coverage on personal property that is available under an HO-5 policy or under an HO-4 or HO-6 policy that has an endorsement for open-perils coverage on personal property. The floater may be appropriate for persons who are not eligible for a homeowners policy. For example, the floater could be used by a couple who sold their home and stored their personal property with a friend while taking an around-the-world trip for a year. It may also be appropriate for an itinerant person, such as an actor, who does not maintain a permanent home.

Personal Effects Floater

personal effects floater

A *personal effects floater* provides open-perils worldwide coverage on property such as baggage, clothes, cameras, and sports equipment typically worn or carried by tourists. However, it does not provide coverage for such items as money, passports, and tickets. Without any endorsements, most homeowners policies cover this property only on a named-perils basis.

TITLE INSURANCE

title insurance

Title insurance is a unique type of insurance not generally handled by property liability insurers but rather by title insurance companies that specialize in this area. It is designed to protect the purchaser of real estate against defects in title that can result in the loss of ownership or that can be corrected only after certain costs are incurred. These defects can arise from many sources, including forged titles, invalid wills, inaccurate property descriptions, and undisclosed liens and easements. To provide protection against loan defaults, lenders of funds for the purchase of real property usually require that a borrower purchase title insurance.

One method to protect against a defective title is to have an abstract of title prepared (often by an attorney) prior to the purchase of the property. This abstract, based on public records, lists all liens, mortgage loans, easements, and the like. If any previously unknown condition is found, the potential purchaser can have the situation rectified, renegotiate, or withdraw from the transaction. Property is often purchased subject to existing mortgage loans, liens, or easements, and the real purpose of the abstract is to find circumstances about which the purchaser had no knowledge.

Although an abstract of title provides a great deal of protection, there are still sometimes situations in which an existing circumstance that was unknown when the title was prepared arises in the future such as the appearance of a long-lost heir with a legitimate claim to the property. An abstract of title does not provide any indemnification to the property owner, and suits against the attorney or other person preparing the abstract are usually not a recourse unless negligence can be shown. Title insurance, however, is designed to protect against this loss. It is almost always required by lenders who finance property purchases and also frequently obtained when cash purchases are made.

The title insurance company conducts a title search and then issues a policy to provide protection against losses that arise from circumstances other than the items already found in the title search and listed in the policy.

Some characteristics of title insurance include the following:

- The policy provides protection only against unknown title defects that have occurred prior to the effective date of the policy but are discovered after the effective date.
- The policy is written on the assumption that losses will not occur, because most title defects are known and listed in the policy.
- The policy term is indefinite and continues until title to the property is again transferred. At that time, the new owner will need to purchase a new title insurance policy because the existing policy is not assignable.
- The premium is paid only once—when the policy is issued—and either party can cancel the policy.
- The insured is indemnified up to the policy limits if a loss occurs. However, there is no guarantee that possession of the property will be retained.
- The amount of insurance is usually the initial purchase price of the property, and a potential loss in the future can be much higher than the policy limit because of inflation.

CHECKLIST FOR EVALUATING AND COMPARING HOMEOWNERS POLICIES

☐ What is the homeowners form?

___ HO-2
___ HO-3
___ HO-4
___ HO-5

    ___ HO-6
    ___ HO-8

☐ If the policy is not an ISO form, how does it differ?

☐ What is the annual policy premium?

☐ What is the Section I deductible?

☐ Does the policy automatically contain coverages that are optional with other insurers?

☐ What are the limits for the various coverages?

    —— Coverage A—Dwelling
    ___ Coverage B—Other Structures
    ___ Coverage C—Personal Property
    ___ Coverage D—Loss of Use
    ___ Coverage E—Personal Liability
    ___ Coverage F—Medical Payments to Others

☐ Are the coverage limits adequate?

☐ What provisions, if any, are there for increasing policy limits?

☐ Does the insured own personal property subject to sublimits?

☐ Is personal property covered for replacement cost?

☐ Are there, or is there any need for, any of the following endorsements?

    ___ Additional insureds
    ___ Open-perils computer coverage
    ___ Open-perils personal property coverage
    ___ Business pursuits
    ___ Credit card, electronic fund transfer card, forgery, and counterfeit money
    ___ Earthquake
    ___ Higher limits for certain types of personal property
    ___ Home business insurance coverage
    ___ Home day-care coverage
    ___ Identity fraud
    ___ Increased ordinance or law coverage
    ___ Increased loss assessment coverage
    ___ Increased property limits on business property
    ___ Personal injury

___ Premises alarm or fire protection system credits
___ Scheduled personal property coverage
___ Sinkhole collapse
___ Snowmobile
___ Watercraft
___ Other property loss exposures
___ Other liability loss exposures

☐ Is the flood peril adequately covered in another policy?

MINI CASE: EVE AND DON ADAMS

Eve and Don Adams own a two-story house on a one-acre partially wooded lot in the suburbs where they live with their two teenaged children, Bonnie and Claude, and Don's mother, Elizabeth. Don's father, Phillip, suffers from Alzheimer's disease and lives in a nearby nursing home.

Don is employed as a bank officer and also earns a very small income playing his saxophone in a band. Eve is a freelance writer working out of an office in the home.

The Adams family house was new when they made a 10 percent down payment and purchased it 5 years ago at a cost of $400,000. They believe they could sell it today for $475,000. Vacant lots in their area range from $75,000 to $125,000, depending on size and location. The cost to construct a new home similar to the Adams family home on one of these lots is $375,000.

The Adams family house includes an attached garage and an unfinished basement. Don and Eve make regularly monthly mortgage payments to River Bank and also make monthly payments to the Community Homeowners Association, which maintains the community clubhouse, swimming pool, and common grounds.

Apart from an inherited sterling silver service, a diamond cocktail ring, a diamond engagement ring, and two oil paintings, the Adams family owns no unusual property.

What coverages and limits should the Adams family consider?

(See answer section for answers to mini-case.)

SOURCES FOR FURTHER IN-DEPTH STUDY

- *Personal Risk Management and Insurance* (loose-leaf, CD-ROM, or online service periodically updated). Includes unique Personal Exposure Survey (including recommendations) and coverage checklists for personal auto, homeowners, personal umbrella, and personal inland marine. (Access to Word files of the survey and checklists.)

Dallas, TX: International Risk Management Institute, 800-827-4242. Web site address www.irmi.com

- FC&S Bulletins, Personal Lines Volume, (loose-leaf and/or CD-ROM service updated monthly), Erlanger, KY: The National Underwriter Company. Phone 800-543-0874. Web site address www.nuco.com

- Hamilton, Karen L., and Ferguson, Cheryl L., *Personal Risk Management and Property-Liability Insurance,* American Institute for CPCU/Insurance Institute of America, 2002. Phone 800-644-2101. Web site address www.aicpcu.org

- Wiening, Eric A.; Rejda, George E.; Luthardt, Constance M.; and Ferguson, Cheryl L., *Personal Insurance,* Malvern, PA: American Institute for CPCU/Insurance Institute of America, 2002. Phone 800-644-2101. Web site address www.aicpcu.org

CHAPTER REVIEW

Answers to mini-case, review questions, and self-test questions start on page 793.

Key Term

homeowners policy	National Flood Insurance
ISO (Insurance Services	Program (NFIP)
Office)	FAIR (Fair Access to Insurance
named insured	Requirements) plans
additional living expenses	floater
functional replacement	personal articles floater
cost	personal property floater
dwelling policy	personal effects floater
mobilehome insurance	title insurance

Review Questions

17-1. Frank and his wife, Ellen, own a home. Also living in the house is their oldest daughter, Elaine, who returned home after finishing college 8 years ago. Their 21-year-old daughter, Destiny, is currently at college, living in an on-campus dorm room. What members of the family are covered under Frank's homeowners policy?

17-2. What locations are typically listed as insured locations in a homeowners policy?

17-3. Nathan's home is covered for $250,000 (Coverage A) under an HO-3 policy. Which of the following losses are covered under Nathan's HO-3 policy?

a. vandalism to Nathan's home
b. damage to the inside walls and hardwood floors of Nathan's home caused by rain water that blew in when he accidentally left the window open during a storm
c. damage to the family room couch and end tables inside Nathan's home caused by rain water that blew in when he accidentally left the window open during a storm
d. earthquake damage to the walls of Nathan's home
e. stains on the wall-to-wall carpet inside Nathan's home due to housebreaking the new family pet, plus the hole in the outside of Nathan's home cut by a woodpecker
f. theft of the $2,000 cast aluminum porch furniture from the back deck of Nathan's home
g. $1,500 in cash burned in a fire in Nathan's home
h. $2,000 of damage to Nathan's wife's furs as a result of a fire
i. $2,000 of Nathan's wife's jewelry stolen by a burglar
j. $1,000 of additional expense incurred while Nathan's family has to live elsewhere for a day and one-half after a small fire loss
k. $2,000 of windstorm damage to the detached garage at Nathan's home

17-4. Which of the following losses are covered under Sarah's HO-3 policy?
a. Sarah's guests received bodily injuries and the side of her neighbor's house received property damage when a gas grill exploded during a cookout at her house.
b. While running a meeting at work, Sarah accidentally injured a coworker by shining a laser pointer into the co-worker's eye.
c. While at the local mall, Sarah carelessly backed out of a parking space and damaged another shopper's car.
d. Sarah's 3-year-old son Matthew ripped out some of the neighbor's flowers for a Mother's Day gift.
e. Sarah's daughter injured a team member when she tossed a bat into the bat rack and it bounced off and hit the teammate, cutting her head.

17-5. Describe how each of the following homeowners property coverages differs from the HO-3 property coverages:
a. HO-2
b. HO-4
c. HO-5
d. HO-6
e. HO-8

17-6. Describe the nature of the coverages these commonly used endorsements add to the homeowners policy:
a. home day-care coverage
b. increased special limits

    c. earthquake

    d. inflation guard

    e. personal property replacement cost loss settlement

    f. scheduled personal property

    g. business pursuits

17-7. Describe the coverage the National Flood Insurance Program (NFIP) provides, and explain how a client can obtain such coverage if needed.

17-8. Briefly explain the alternatives available for obtaining property coverage for clients who fail to meet the underwriting guidelines of most insurers.

17-9. Describe the characteristics of title insurance.

Self-Test Questions

T F   17-1. Regardless of which of the six property forms is included in a homeowners policy, the liability section is identical for all forms.

T F   17-2. Coverage for children over the age of 21 under their parents' homeowners policy is discontinued, even if the children continue to reside in their parents' household.

T F   17-3. The limits for homeowners Coverages B, C, and D are part of the Coverage A limit.

T F   17-4. Damage to an attached garage is covered under Coverage A in an HO-3 policy, but damage to a detached garage is covered under Coverage B.

T F   17-5. An HO-3 policy covers damage to the insured's residence building against open perils, including earthquake and flood.

T F   17-6. In a homeowners policy, losses under all property coverages are settled on a replacement cost basis.

T F   17-7. In an HO-3 policy, the personal property of any insured is covered while located anywhere in the world.

T F   17-8. In a homeowners policy, the amount payable for the loss of money and securities is limited only for theft.

T F   17-9. A homeowners policy has coverage for additional living expenses incurred while a family lives elsewhere during repairs for a covered property loss.

T F   17-10. The liability coverage contained in an unendorsed homeowners policy provides protection against suits for bodily injury, property damage, and personal injury.

T F   17-11. Liability coverage in an unendorsed homeowners policy excludes coverage for liability arising out of business and professional activities as well as the use of an auto.

T F   17-12. Benefits under the medical payments coverage in the homeowners policy are paid only to persons other than an insured.

T F   17-13. A person who owns and lives in a condominium unit should carry an HO-4 Contents Broad Form, because the association covers the building and detached structures.

T F   17-14. Clients with expensive jewelry and silverware should consider adding a scheduled personal property endorsement to their homeowners policy.

T F   17-15. Most flood insurance policies are now written through private insurance companies.

T F   17-16. Title insurance provides protection against all title defects, regardless of when they occur or are discovered.

NOTES

1. Nbc17.com, Flooding Fact Sheet based on information provided by the National Flood Insurance Program, http://www.nbc17.com/weather/2932395/detail.html accessed 4/29/04.
2. Federal Emergency Management Agency. www.fema.gov, accessed 4/29/04.

18

Personal Auto and Umbrella Liability Insurance

Learning Objectives

An understanding of the material in this chapter should enable the student to

18-1.   Describe the problems associated with auto accidents and the methods of compensating the victims.

18-2.   Describe the basic elements of the Personal Auto Policy.

18-3.   Explain the coverages Parts A, B, C, and D of the Personal Auto Policy provide.

18-4.   Describe the key endorsements available to tailor the Personal Auto Policy to common client needs.

18-5.   Describe the potential sources of auto insurance coverage for hard-to-insure drivers.

18-6.   Explain the key factors for a client to consider in shopping for auto insurance.

18-7.   Briefly describe the policies available for insuring watercraft and aircraft.

18-8.   Describe the need for and general features of personal umbrella liability insurance.

Chapter Outline

Every client—even one who does not own a car—faces the possibility both of serious injury and disability and of a major financial loss resulting from his or her ownership, maintenance, or use of an auto. A significant potential for financial loss exists when a client owns an auto worth $10,000, $30,000, $50,000 or more that could be damaged in an auto accident or by another cause. Even more significant loss exposures lie in the fact that a client could become legally responsible to pay damages to another person who is injured in an auto accident the client causes. Careful drivers are not immune. Although a few statistics are cited in this chapter, they are not necessary to prove that many auto accidents happen every day, and many of them are caused by careful drivers who had a momentary attention lapse or an unfortunate error in judgment. Few would deny the importance of auto insurance in preserving a client's personal assets. Therefore, a financial planner must have at least a basic understanding of the important coverage personal auto policies provide. The chapter also briefly discusses insurance relating to two other modes of transportation: watercraft and aircraft.

Homeowners insurance is usually required by a mortgagee, and auto liability insurance is invariably required by law, as well as by the bank or finance company that helped finance the purchase or lease of an auto. On the other hand, personal umbrella insurance, the other major topic in this chapter, is rarely, if ever, mandatory. Yet, as this chapter demonstrates, umbrella coverage should be recommended to virtually every client with assets to protect, and it is therefore a coverage with which every financial planner should be familiar.

AUTO INSURANCE

The discussion of auto insurance begins with a look at some of the problems associated with auto accidents and auto insurance, and it continues with a history of the methods of compensating auto accident victims. A description of the personal auto policy (PAP) and insurance for high-risk drivers follows.

Problems Associated with Auto Accidents and Auto Insurance

Given the severe financial consequences that can arise from auto accidents, most Americans view auto insurance as a necessity for themselves and for the other drivers who might injure them. Yet there are many problems in providing auto insurance to everyone at an affordable price. These problems center around the

- large number of auto accidents
- high cost of auto accidents
- uninsured and underinsured drivers
- difficulty that some individuals have in obtaining auto insurance

Large Number of Auto Accidents

Auto accidents occur frequently (over 6 million are reported to police every year). Young drivers have a disproportionate number of accidents, and regardless of the driver's age, speeding and/or substance abuse are often involved.

High Cost of Auto Accidents

The costs associated with auto accidents each year in the United States are staggering. The National Highway Transportation Safety Administration (NHTSA) has estimated that highway crashes cost society $230.6 billion a year, about $820 per person. Auto accident estimates released just before this chapter was written indicate that 43,220 people died in auto accidents in 2003. Forty percent of fatalities were alcohol related, and 58 percent of those killed in passenger vehicles were not wearing seat belts.[1]

Uninsured and Underinsured Drivers

Although variations exist from state to state, the number of persons without auto insurance is estimated at between 5 and 30 percent. Even in states with compulsory insurance laws, no perfect mechanism prevents an uninsured, or even unlicensed, driver from getting behind the wheel.

When uninsured drivers are involved in accidents, they can rarely pay for the property damage and bodily injury they cause themselves or others. Another problem is the underinsured driver. The minimum amount of auto liability insurance needed in most states (usually no more than $25,000 for any injured person) is often below the amount necessary to adequately compensate an innocent victim for his or her injuries.

Because of uninsured and underinsured drivers, innocent victims of auto accidents may be inadequately compensated for their injuries, and society must often bear some of the burden. As a result, states have undertaken various actions to minimize these problems.

Difficulty of Some Persons in Obtaining Auto Insurance

Auto insurance can be difficult to obtain. Overregulation of insurance rates in some states has, at times, made it difficult for insurers to collect an adequate premium, forcing them, instead, to withdraw from the market or to limit the number of auto insurance applications they accept. In any state, high-risk drivers (for example, younger persons or drivers with serious or multiple traffic violations) are often unable to find coverage in the standard insurance market. An increasing number of insurers are willing to write these substandard applicants, and all states have established residual market programs, commonly known as assigned risk[2] plans, to ensure the availability of auto insurance.

Affordability is also a problem. U.S. consumers in 2004 paid an estimated average of $871 for each insured vehicle. Many had only minimal coverage. Approximately 80 percent of each auto insurance premium dollar went to pay claims in 2002, the last year for which figures are available. High premiums are therefore a direct result of both high loss frequency and high claims severity. More than $10,000 is paid, on average, for each bodily injury liability claim, over $2,500 for each property damage liability claim, and $3,400 for each claim for physical damage to the policyowner's own vehicle.[3] Some of the auto insurance legislation mentioned later in this chapter attempts to control auto insurance costs and therefore make the insurance more affordable.

Controlling Accidents and Compensating Auto Accident Victims

Since the early days of the motor car, society has been concerned about the number and severity of auto accidents and the methods of compensating auto accident victims.

Numerous laws and regulations have been passed—often with strong support from the insurance industry—to control the number of auto accidents and to lessen the number of injuries and deaths. Among these are

- federal auto design and safety standards
- highway design standards
- seat belt laws
- drunk-driving laws
- tightening of licensing standards for young drivers
- license retesting for older drivers

Appropriate compensation for auto accident victims presents another concern, focused especially on the victims who were not at fault. Historically, accident victims were compensated under the traditional tort liability system discussed in an earlier chapter. Because contributory negligence laws made it difficult for many mostly innocent victims to collect for damages, most states adopted one of the variations of comparative negligence that were previously discussed. In addition, various other methods of ensuring compensation have been developed over the years. These include

- compulsory insurance
- financial responsibility laws
- unsatisfied judgment funds
- uninsured motorists coverage
- underinsured motorists coverage
- no-fault auto insurance

Not every method exists in every state, and none of these methods is exactly the same in all states where it is used. Most of these methods do not alter the concept of tort liability but are aimed at increasing the likelihood that a source of monetary recovery exists for innocent victims.

Compulsory Insurance

Almost all states and the District of Columbia have some type of compulsory insurance law that requires auto owners to have liability insurance before they can legally drive. Unfortunately, such laws are far from perfect for several reasons:

- Victim compensation must come through traditional legal channels and can be delayed by an overburdened legal system.
- Compulsory insurance laws do not guarantee that an innocent victim will be compensated. Some drivers may not license their vehicles; others may drop insurance after a vehicle is licensed. A person may be injured by a hit-and-run driver, an out-of-state driver without insurance, a driver of a stolen car, or a driver of a fraudulently registered auto.
- Required liability limits are relatively low, typically $20,000 or $25,000 for bodily injury to any one person, $40,000 or $50,000 in the aggregate for all bodily injury claims in an accident, and $10,000 or $15,000 for property damage claims.

The "no pay, no play" concept has been considered by lawmakers in many states as a means of encouraging compliance with compulsory insurance laws. No pay, no play statutes limit the rights of uninsured drivers to collect damages from insured drivers. A few states have recently enacted such laws, most of which have not been tested in the courts.

Financial Responsibility Laws

financial responsibility law

All states have some type of *financial responsibility law.* Failure to comply with financial responsibility laws results in the revocation or suspension of a person's driving privileges. These laws require proof of future financial responsibility, generally proof that liability insurance is in force after

- an auto accident involving bodily injury or property damage that exceeds a specified limit
- conviction of a serious offense such as drunk driving or reckless driving
- loss of a driver's license because of repeated motor vehicle violations
- failure to pay a legal judgment that arose from an auto accident

The major criticism of financial responsibility laws is that they become effective only after an accident or serious offense and do not provide any compensation to the innocent victims of that accident. In addition, the same limitations that apply to compulsory auto insurance also apply to financial responsibility laws.

Unsatisfied Judgment Funds

unsatisfied judgment fund

A few states (all of which also have compulsory insurance requirements) have *unsatisfied judgment funds*, which the states established to compensate persons who are unable to collect legal judgments that result from auto accidents. The injured person—in addition to obtaining a legal judgment against the negligent party—must show that the judgment cannot be collected. The maximum amount that can be collected from the fund is usually limited to the state's minimum compulsory insurance requirement and is reduced by collateral sources of recovery such as workers' compensation benefits or insurance.

The negligent driver must repay the fund for payments made to the injured person or lose his or her driver's license until repayment is made.

Collecting from unsatisfied judgment funds involves a slow and cumbersome process. Some funds have had financial problems as a result of inadequate funding, which usually comes from fees levied on insured drivers or insurance companies that write auto insurance in the state.

Uninsured Motorists Coverage

uninsured motorists coverage

In most states, insurers that write auto insurance are required to offer *uninsured motorists coverage.* However, the policyowner can voluntarily waive the coverage in writing. In a few states, uninsured motorists coverage must be included in any auto insurance policy.

Under uninsured motorists coverage, the injured insured is able to collect the amount he or she would have collected from the insurer of an insured driver if that driver had been carrying insurance. In effect, the insured's own company acts as the insurer of the uninsured driver. The term *uninsured motorists* is broadly defined to include not only uninsured drivers, but also the drivers of hit-and-run vehicles and persons whose insurer cannot pay because it has become insolvent. Uninsured motorists coverage, however, does not apply if the negligent party carries insurance that has inadequate limits to fully indemnify the innocent party. Uninsured motorists coverage is analyzed in more detail when the personal auto policy is discussed.

Limitations to uninsured motorists coverage include the following:

- The limits of coverage are equal only to a state's compulsory insurance or financial responsibility limits unless the policyowner has purchased higher limits.
- The insured must establish that the other party was legally liable.
- The coverage usually applies to bodily injury only. States vary as to whether the coverage applies to property damage.
- The innocent victim, not the uninsured driver, bears the cost of the coverage.

Underinsured Motorists Coverage

underinsured motorists coverage

Underinsured motorists coverage provides protection to auto accident victims when a negligent driver has liability insurance but the limits are insufficient to pay the damages for which he or she is responsible. For example, assume a negligent driver causes bodily injury of $30,000 to another person but carries only $25,000 of insurance, which is the minimum state requirement. If the innocent victim has $100,000 of underinsured motorists coverage, he or she can collect the additional $5,000 from his or her own insurance company.

Underinsured motorists coverage is a policy endorsement available in about half the states and can be purchased only if the policyowner also carries uninsured motorists coverage with the same limit. In most other states, underinsured motorists coverage must be included along with uninsured motorists coverage and for the same limits.

No-fault Auto Insurance

The traditional insurance and tort systems for compensating auto accident victims have long been subject to criticism, centering around the following issues:

- Many innocent persons are unable to collect anything for their injuries under the traditional tort system because injuries are caused by uninsured and hit-and-run drivers.
- Injuries from auto accidents are a societal problem for all insured parties whether they are negligent or not.
- It is often difficult or impossible to determine who is at fault in an accident.
- The traditional tort system has resulted in many serious claims being underpaid because of inadequate insurance limits. There is also evidence that many small claims are overpaid for the sake of a quick settlement.
- Under the traditional insurance and tort systems, a large portion of premium dollars is used to pay claims costs and attorneys' fees.
- The traditional tort system is slow. In some states, delays of 3 to 5 years between an accident and a resulting trial are common.

The result of these shortcomings to the traditional systems of compensating auto accident victims led to the passage of some type of no-fault law in many states. The concept of no-fault is not new, having been originally proposed in the 1930s. However, the first such law was enacted in Massachusetts in 1971, and most existing laws date to the 1970s. A few additional states passed laws in the 1980s and early 1990s, but a few others also terminated existing laws. Today 12 states, in addition to Puerto Rico, have no-fault laws.

Despite the appeal of no-fault laws, many arguments against them have been raised such as the following:

- They have not resulted in lower premiums, probably because the right to sue is modified only for relatively minor injuries.
- The traditional systems of compensating auto accident victims work well, with most cases being settled relatively quickly and out of court.
- The inability in some states to sue for pain and suffering has not been popular with plaintiffs' attorneys and many drivers, who feel such suits are their right.
- There are ways to modify the current tort systems such as limiting attorneys' fees and increasing the use of arbitration rather than trials.
- Some of the costs of auto accidents tend to be shifted from negligent parties to innocent victims.
- Widespread fraud exists.

Types of No-fault Laws

The original proposals for no-fault auto insurance were based on the premise that the tort liability system would be abolished for auto accidents. Under such a *pure no-fault* system, each owner of an auto would be required to carry first-party insurance that compensated all persons injured in auto accidents involving that vehicle. The right to sue a negligent party, even for pain and suffering, would not exist. No state has gone as far as adopting a pure no-fault law. The types of laws that do exist fall into three broad categories—modified no-fault laws, add-on plans, and choice no-fault laws.

pure no-fault

Modified No-fault Laws. The most common form of no-fault legislation limits the right of an injured party to recover damages from a negligent party but does not eliminate it. States with *modified no-fault* laws have taken two approaches in allowing suits. Some states have a *dollar threshold*, also referred to as a *monetary threshold,* anywhere from $400 to $5,000 dollars. If a person's injuries are below this amount, he or she must collect from first-party no-fault benefits and cannot sue. However, suits are allowed once the amount reaches the threshold. The injured party can still receive no-fault benefits, but his or her insurer is reimbursed to the extent any amount from a legal judgment duplicates any no-fault benefits received. Other states have a *verbal threshold* and allow suits when there is a fatal injury, serious injury, or serious disfigurement. What constitutes a serious injury or disfigurement varies among these states.

modified no-fault

Add-on Plans. An *add-on plan* has no restriction on the right to sue a negligent party, but first party no-fault type benefits are available. The insurer that pays these benefits has subrogation rights against the negligent party. (Some argue that add-on plans should not be referred to as a type of no-fault because the traditional tort system has not been altered.)

add-on plan

In some add-on states, both liability insurance and no-fault benefits are compulsory; in other states, liability insurance is compulsory, but the no-fault benefits are optional. In still other states, both liability insurance and no-fault benefits are optional.

Types of No-Fault Laws

- Pure no-fault: right to sue negligent party eliminated
- Modified no-fault: right to sue negligent party only if injuries exceed a dollar or verbal threshold
- Add-on no-fault: right to sue negligent party in addition to right to collect first-party no-fault benefits
- Choice no-fault: right to sue negligent party as an alternative to collecting under a modified no-fault plan

choice no-fault

Choice No-fault Laws. A *choice no-fault* law, used in only a few states, gives the insurance buyer two choices: coverage under the traditional tort liability system or coverage under a modified no-fault law at a reduced premium. Depending on the jurisdiction, a person who elects to retain the right to seek damages under the traditional liability system may or may not be able to purchase no-fault-type benefits similar to those in an add-on plan.

Types of No-fault Benefits

No-fault benefits are provided by adding an endorsement to an auto insurance policy. This endorsement varies from state to state to conform to each state's no-fault law. Usually, the endorsement is referred to as a *personal injury protection (PIP) endorsement*.

personal injury protection (PIP) endorsement

Benefits are normally subject to dollar or time limits, and some states require insurers to make optional higher benefits available. Some states also require insurers to offer optional deductibles to reduce or eliminate certain no-fault benefits. The use of these deductibles can make sense to the extent that the no-fault benefits duplicate other medical expense or disability income insurance. No-fault benefits in most states include

- medical expenses
- rehabilitation expenses
- loss of earnings (or some proportion thereof)
- expenses for essential services such as house or yard work that an injured person can no longer perform
- funeral expenses
- survivors' benefits arising from death in an auto accident

No-fault benefits are typically available to the policyowner and relative members of his or her household riding in any vehicle, as well as to other persons riding in the policyowner's vehicle. State law varies as to which policy pays when a person is eligible for benefits as an injured passenger in someone else's auto and also under his or her own auto insurance policy.

Note that the PIP endorsement does not change the liability coverage available under an auto insurance policy. Its existence, however, does result in fewer liability claims being filed.

Coordination of Benefits

No-fault benefits apply to injuries that medical expense insurance, disability insurance, and workers' compensation might also cover. It is therefore logical to consider how benefits are coordinated among these various sources of recovery. The answer depends on what other source of recovery is involved and on the applicable statute.

Federal regulations prohibit Medicare payments to persons injured in auto accidents who have recovered, or are expected to recover, under no-fault coverage. Most state laws require that workers' compensation provides primary coverage and that workers' compensation benefits should be subtracted from the amount due as no-fault benefits. State laws sometimes indicate which coverage is primary in other situations when more than one might apply. Many states make no-fault auto insurance primary over various forms of health insurance.

PERSONAL AUTO POLICY

The discussion of auto insurance focuses on the most common auto policy—ISO's personal auto policy, often referred to as the PAP. Like the homeowners policy, it is a package policy that provides both property and liability insurance for family members. As with homeowners insurance, some insurers use their own auto policy forms. These forms tend to be similar to the PAP.

The following discussion looks at the basic format of the PAP, eligibility, some definitions that apply throughout the policy, and the policy territory. This is followed by an analysis of the various coverages in the policy. Like homeowners policies, the basic PAP does not meet everyone's needs and often must be modified. Finally, some of the more common endorsements are briefly described.

Format of the PAP

Following a declarations and definitions section, the PAP provides four types of insurance coverage:

- Part A—Liability Coverage
- Part B—Medical Payments Coverage
- Part C—Uninsured Motorists Coverage
- Part D—Coverage for Damage to Your Auto

In states with no-fault laws, an endorsement that provides the required no-fault benefits replaces Part B.

The policy also contains two other sections—Part E and Part F—that spell out the duties of an insured following a loss and that contain other policy provisions.

Eligibility

A PAP can be written on eligible vehicles owned or leased by an individual or by a husband or wife residing in the same household. Vehicles with other forms of ownership (such as a father and a son) can also be insured with an endorsement. A vehicle rented to others or used as a public or livery conveyance is not eligible and must be insured under a commercial policy.

Eligible vehicles include private passenger autos, such as cars, vans, and sports utility vehicles, owned by the policy or leased under a written contract of 6 continuous months or longer. Pickups are also eligible vehicles if their gross weight rating is 10,000 pounds or less. However, vans and pickups are ineligible for coverage if they are used for the transportation or delivery of goods and materials except when (1) they are used for farming or ranching, or (2) their use is incidental to the named insured's business of installing, maintaining, or repairing furnishings or equipment. An example of the latter is an electrician's or an appliance repair person's van.

Other vehicles, such as motor homes, motorcycles, golf carts, and snow-mobiles, can also be insured by endorsement in most states.

Finally, the policy can be endorsed to provide auto insurance to a person who does not own any vehicles eligible for coverage under a PAP. Examples include a person who frequently rents a car or has use of a company car on a regular basis.

Definitions

Like a homeowners policy, the PAP contains numerous definitions. One important definition—*insured*—is different for different parts of the policy and is discussed later. However, some definitions are used throughout the policy. These definitions include *covered auto*, *you*, *family member*, and *occupying*.

Covered Auto

covered auto

A *covered auto* (referred to in the PAP as "your covered auto") is any vehicle listed in the policy declarations. In addition, it includes three other categories of vehicles: newly acquired autos, trailers, and temporary substitute vehicles.

newly acquired auto

Newly Acquired Autos. A *newly acquired auto* is one that meets the eligibility requirements previously described but is acquired after the effective date of the policy.

If the new auto replaces an existing vehicle, it is automatically insured for the broadest Parts A, B, and C coverages that apply to any vehicle listed in the declarations. There is no need to notify the insurance company, although it is a good idea to do so. If the new auto is an additional vehicle, the same automatic coverage applies only if the policyowner asks the insurance company to insure the vehicle within 14 days of purchase.

The situation is different for damage to the auto (Part D). The PAP provides automatic insurance for the broadest Part D benefits provided to any vehicle in the declarations only if the insurance company is notified within 14 days of purchase. There is also coverage for newly acquired autos even if Part D is not in effect on any vehicles listed in the declarations, but only if the insurance company is notified within 4 days of purchase that such coverage is wanted. If the 4-day notification is satisfied, any loss prior to insurance company notification is subject to a $500 deductible.

Example:	Tom Howard's car is insured under a PAP for Coverages A, B, C, and D. Tom trades his car in for a new one. Tom's Coverages A, B, and C apply to the new car automatically, with no necessity to notify the insurer.
	Tom's Coverage D also applies to the new car automatically but only if Tom notifies the insurer within 14 days.

Trailers. A *trailer* is a vehicle designed to be pulled by a private passenger auto or van. It also includes a farm wagon or farm implement while it is being towed.

temporary substitute vehicle

Temporary Substitute Vehicles. A *temporary substitute vehicle* is one the insured does not own but is using temporarily in place of a vehicle listed in the Declarations if that vehicle is out of normal use because of breakdown, repair, servicing, loss, or destruction.

You

The terms *you* and *yours* are used throughout the PAP. They refer to the named insured shown in the policy declaration and the spouse of the named insured if a resident of the same household.

If the spouse ceases to be a resident of the same household, the spouse is still a "you" or "your" until the earliest of the following:

- the end of 90 days following the spouse's change of residency
- the effective date of another policy that lists the spouse as a named insured
- the end of the policy period

Family Member

A *family member* is any person related to "you" by blood, marriage, or adoption who is a resident of the same household. This includes a ward or foster child.

Occupying

Occupying means in, upon, or getting in, on, out, or off. Therefore, a person who is injured while getting into or out of an auto is, by definition, occupying that auto.

Policy Territory

The PAP applies only to accidents and losses that occur in the United States, its territories or possessions, Puerto Rico, or Canada. Coverage also applies if a covered auto is being transported between these locations.

PART A—LIABILITY COVERAGE

The discussion of Parts A, B, and C of the PAP focuses on answering four questions:

- What is covered?
- Who are the insureds?
- What exclusions apply?
- What happens when other insurance also covers a claim?

What Is Covered?

Part A of the PAP provides bodily injury and property damage liability protection to any insured who is legally responsible for an auto accident. As with other liability policies, the insurer agrees to pay defense costs until the limit of liability has been exhausted by payment of judgments or settlements.

split limits

The applicant selects the liability limits when he or she purchases insurance, and they apply to each covered accident. The latest version of the PAP is written with split limits, but it can be endorsed to provide single limit coverage. With *split limits*, three separate dollar amounts, such as $25,000/$50,000/$10,000, apply to each accident. The first limit is the maximum amount that will be paid to any one person for bodily injury; the second limit is the maximum that will be paid for all bodily injury claims in one accident; the third limit applies to total property damage claims. With a single limit, there is just one limit that applies in the aggregate to all bodily injury and liability claims arising from an accident. The limits available often range from $50,000 to $500,000 or more.

Example:	Gary Rock's PAP provides split limits under Part A of $500,000/$1,000,000/$50,000. In an auto accident, Gary injures two people in another car. One is awarded

damages of $750,000 and the other is awarded damages of $300,000. Their car, worth $60,000, is totally demolished.

The insurer will pay only $500,000 of the $750,000 award because that is the per person policy limit for bodily injury. The policy will pay the full $300,000 to the other person. The policy will pay only $50,000 for the damage to the car because that is the policy's property damage limit.

Most clients carry the amount needed to satisfy the required underlying limits of an umbrella liability policy (usually in the range of $250,000/$500,000/$50,000). The umbrella liability policy is discussed later in this chapter.

The PAP specifies that the insurer's limit of liability shown in the declarations is the most the company will pay, regardless of the number of insureds, claims made, vehicles or premiums shown in the declarations, or vehicles involved in any accident. For example, if a son has an accident while driving a family car, the son and both parents might be sued. Even though three insureds are sued, the policy limits apply only once to all three claims. An identical provision applies to Part B and Part C of the PAP. In addition, the policy specifies that no one is entitled to receive duplicate payments for the same elements of loss under more than one of Part A, Part B, and Part C of the policy. For example, an injured passenger who sued an insured could not receive a liability payment under Part A for specific medical expenses and medical payments under Part B for the same medical expenses.

The PAP also contains a provision that raises the limits of liability, if necessary, to those required in a state where an accident occurs if the state is not where the insured vehicle is principally garaged. Any other mandatory coverage, such as no-fault benefits, is also provided automatically for out-of-state accidents.

The PAP also provides certain supplementary payments for expenses arising from an accident the policy covers. These payments, like defense costs, are in addition to the stated liability limits. They are

- up to $250 for bail bonds
- premiums on appeal bonds and bonds to release attachments
- interest occurring after a judgment
- up to $200 per day for loss of earnings because of attendance at hearings or trials
- other reasonable expenses incurred at the insurer's request

Who Are the Insureds?

The insureds under Part A include several categories of persons. From the policyowner's standpoint, the most important category is probably the named insured, spouse, and family members for legal liability arising out of the ownership, maintenance, or use of any auto or trailer. There is also coverage for any other person using a covered auto.

In addition, other persons or organizations may have coverage because of their legal liability arising from the actions of any of the parties previously mentioned. For example, if the named insured is driving a vehicle as part of his or her job or while doing work for a charity, it is possible that the employer or charity could also become a party to a legal action. The employer or charity is insured under the policy as long as it does not own or hire the vehicle.

What Exclusions Apply?

The PAP does not provide liability coverage in every situation. One exclusion denies coverage for anyone who intentionally causes an accident. However, other insureds still have coverage if they are sued because of that person's actions. Another exclusion denies coverage to any insured, other than a family member using the covered auto, who uses a vehicle without a reasonable belief that he or she is entitled to do so.

Several exclusions pertain to business situations. Certain types of exposures should be covered under a commercial auto policy rather than the PAP. One of these exclusions denies coverage for the ownership or operation of a vehicle if it is used as a public or livery conveyance, such as a taxicab or limousine hired out to carry persons or property. This exclusion does not preclude coverage where expenses of carpooling or a vacation are shared.

Another exclusion pertains to persons engaged in the business of selling, repairing, servicing, storing, or parking vehicles designed for use mainly on public highways. For example, a named insured who is an auto mechanic would not have coverage when driving customers' cars, nor would the customer's personal auto policy cover the mechanic's liability. A similar exclusion denies liability coverage when the named insured is using certain other vehicles in the course of any business (other than farming or ranching). However, this exclusion does not apply to a private passenger auto, pickup, or van, or to a trailer used with any of the three types of vehicles.

A final business situation exclusion applies to bodily injury to employees of any insured. This exclusion applies to domestic employees, however, only if they either are or should be covered under a workers' compensation policy.

Some exclusions apply to property damage to property being transported by an insured or to property (other than a residence or private garage) rented to, used by, or in the care of any insured. There may be some coverage for these loss exposures under a homeowners policy.

The PAP provides no liability coverage for vehicles with fewer than four wheels or vehicles designed mainly for off-road use except trailers, nonowned golf carts, and vehicles used in a medical emergency. If a policyowner needs to insure such vehicles as motorcycles or mopeds, coverage can be added by an endorsement.

A significant exclusion for many insureds precludes coverage for any vehicle other than a covered auto that is either owned by the named insured or spouse or furnished for his or her regular use. If the vehicle is owned, it should be listed and insured along with other owned vehicles. If a vehicle is furnished for regular use, such as an employer-provided car, it should either be insured by the employer or this exclusion should be modified by endorsement. A similar exclusion applies to vehicles owned by or furnished for the regular use of family members. However, this exclusion does not apply to the named insured or spouse. For example, assume a 22-year-old son living at home owns an uninsured car. He would be insured under his parents' policy for driving other cars, but as a family member, he would not have "free" coverage for driving his own vehicle. However, his parents would have coverage if they drove his car on an occasional basis, as long as it was not available to them for regular use.

Finally, there is no liability coverage for vehicles at a race track competing in, practicing for, or preparing for any type of organized race or speed contest.

Other Insurance

In some cases, more than one PAP might provide coverage. The most common example occurs when a person drives a friend's car. A person remains covered as a named insured under his or her own PAP while driving another auto. He or she is also an insured under the friend's PAP as a person using the covered auto. In situations like these, it is said that the insurance "follows the car." More specifically, the insurance the car owner purchased is primary and the driver's insurance is secondary. The driver's insurance applies, but only after the limits of the insurance policy on the car have been exhausted.

Example:	Sheila, who has a PAP with a single limit of $500,000, borrows a car owned by George, whose PAP has a $50,000 limit. Sheila causes an accident in which a pedestrian is injured, and a judgment for $60,000 in damages is awarded against Sheila. Because insurance follows the car, George's PAP provides primary coverage up to its $50,000 limit, and Sheila's insurance provides excess coverage, paying the remaining $10,000.
	If George had no auto liability insurance, Sheila's policy would pay the entire $60,000 judgment on her behalf.

PART B—MEDICAL PAYMENTS COVERAGE

What Is Covered?

Part B of the PAP provides payment for the reasonable and necessary medical expenses of a covered auto's occupants who are accidentally injured. Only those expenses that result from medical services rendered within 3 years of the date of an accident are covered. Benefits are paid regardless of fault.

The benefit limit, typically in the range of $1,000 to $10,000, is selected by the applicant and applies separately to each person injured in an accident. As previously mentioned, no one can collect for the same expenses more than once under Part A, Part B, and Part C. If an insured incurred $10,000 of medical expenses when struck by a hit-and-run driver, duplicate payments for the same expenses would not be paid under medical payments coverage and uninsured motorists coverage. For example, if the medical payments coverage paid its limit of $5,000, the insured could collect only $5,000 more under Part C for the actual medical expenses.

In most states with no-fault laws, an endorsement that provides the no-fault benefits replaces Part B.

Who Are the Insureds?

As previously mentioned, the medical payments coverage of the PAP protects the occupants of a covered auto who are accidentally injured, regardless of fault. In that sense, it resembles the Medical Payments to Others coverage of homeowners policies. A major difference between these two coverages lies in the fact that the injured persons entitled to PAP medical payments coverage include the named insured, spouse, and other family members. Coverage applies even when a named insured or family member is not occupying a covered auto, so long as he or she is either occupying a motor vehicle designed for use on public roads or a trailer, or is a pedestrian struck by one of these vehicles. For example, a young couple who are injured while riding to their high school prom in a rented limousine are covered under their parents' personal auto policies.

What Exclusions Apply?

With a few minor exceptions, the exclusions that apply to Part B are the same as those for Part A. That is, if liability coverage does not apply to an accident, medical payments coverage is likewise not available.

Other Insurance

The other insurance provision that applies to medical payments coverage is similar to the one for liability coverage. Coverage is excess over other collectible auto insurance on a nonowned auto that provides payments for medical or funeral expenses. Therefore, although the couple on their way to a prom are indeed covered by their parents' PAP, it is excess over any medical payments coverage on the limousine.

PART C—UNINSURED MOTORISTS COVERAGE

What Is Covered?

Part C of the PAP provides uninsured motorists coverage (and underinsured motorists coverage in many states). Under Part C, the insurer agrees to pay compensatory damages that an insured is legally entitled to recover from the owner or operator of an uninsured motor vehicle because of bodily injury (and property damage in a few states) sustained by an insured and caused by an accident. The coverage applies to claims for medical expenses, lost wages, and pain and suffering, but it does not include punitive or exemplary damages.

Typically, an applicant must purchase a minimum amount of coverage in accordance with a state's financial responsibility law. Above that, the applicant can purchase an amount of coverage as high as the liability limits that apply under Part A.

The insurance company has no obligation to pay an uninsured motorists claim unless the owner or operator of the uninsured vehicle is legally responsible for the insured's damages. The insured must file a claim against his or her own insurer and, in the ideal situation, the insured and the insurer will reach a satisfactory settlement. If not, the matter is subject to an arbitration provision. The results of a suit against the uninsured party are not binding on the insurer if it is brought without the insurer's written consent.

For purposes of Part C, an uninsured vehicle is not only one without insurance. The term also includes

- a vehicle that is insured for less than the limits of the financial responsibility laws of the state where the covered auto is principally garaged
- a hit-and-run vehicle whose operator cannot be identified and that hits
  - the named insured, spouse, or family member
  - a vehicle that any of these insureds are occupying
  - a covered auto
- a vehicle to which insurance applies at the time of the accident but the insurance company is insolvent, becomes insolvent, or denies coverage. For example, the insurer of the other driver who caused a collision might have a PAP, but that driver's insurer denies coverage because the other driver-insured intentionally caused the collision.

Part C, however, specifically excludes certain vehicles from the definition of an uninsured vehicle. These are vehicles that are

Uninsured Motor Vehicle

- One with no insurance
- One with liability limits lower than the applicable state law requires
- One driven by a hit-and-run driver
- One whose insurer denies coverage or becomes insolvent

- owned by or furnished for the regular use of any family member
- owned or operated by a self-insurer under an applicable motor vehicle law unless the self-insurer is or becomes insolvent
- owned by any government agency unit
- operated on rails or crawler treads
- designed mainly for use off public roads
- located for use as a residence or premises

Who Are the Insureds?

The insureds under Part C include the named insured, spouse, and any family members. They also include any other persons who occupy a covered auto. In addition, anyone else who is entitled to recover damages because of bodily injury to any of the previously mentioned persons is an insured. This includes, for example, the spouse of a passenger injured while riding in the covered auto if a claim is brought for loss of consortium.

What Exclusions Apply?

The PAP excludes uninsured motorists coverage if an insured is injured while occupying or struck by an auto that is owned by the insured but is not insured under the policy. However, a few state courts have said this exclusion is not enforceable because the intent of the law was to protect injured persons, and a claim must be paid as long as one auto is insured under the policy.

There are also exclusions similar to those previously discussed for use of the covered auto without permission or as a public or livery conveyance.

Other Insurance

As with Part A and Part B, losses are settled on a pro rata basis except that coverage on a nonowned vehicle is primary to coverage on a vehicle that an insured owns. Under Part A and Part B, the insured, in effect, has insurance equal to the combined limit of all policies covering a loss. This is not true under Part C. If more than one policy provides coverage, the recovery for damages under all policies may not exceed the highest limit for any one vehicle under any of the policies.

> *Example:* Assume Policy A provides $25,000 of uninsured motorists coverage and Policy B provides $50,000 of coverage. The maximum amount of coverage is then $50,000. Policy B will pay the entire claim if it is the primary policy. If Policy A is primary, it will pay the first $25,000 of a claim, and Policy B would pay the next $25,000.

PART D—COVERAGE FOR DAMAGE TO YOUR AUTO

Coverage D provides first-party property coverage rather than third-party liability coverage. The focus is on damage to autos rather than on injuries to people.

What Is Covered?

Part D is the portion of the PAP that provides coverage for physical damage to the covered auto and to certain other nonowned autos. There are actually two coverages: (1) *collision* and (2) *other than collision*. Other than collision was formerly called comprehensive, and this terminology is still frequently used colloquially and in commercial policies. The term is no longer used in personal auto policies because of a concern that some consumers might assume anything referred to as "comprehensive" is all-encompassing and covers losses of all kinds. As with virtually every other type of coverage, other-than-collision coverage is subject to some exclusions.

An insurance applicant can elect both other-than-collision and collision coverage or only other-than-collision coverage; he or she cannot purchase collision coverage alone. A client may also choose not to purchase any Part D coverage; this is often a wise decision when purchasing coverage on older vehicles with diminished values small enough to be handled with emergency funds.

The policyowner can select deductibles that apply to each coverage. Frequently, the policyowner purchases a lower deductible for other-than-collision coverage than for collision coverage because of the significant cost savings by selecting a larger deductible for the latter.

Part D also provides an additional coverage, referred to as *transportation expenses*.

Collision

collision

Collision is defined as the upset of the covered auto or any nonowned auto or its impact with another vehicle or object.

Other than Collision

other than collision

The PAP never specifically defines the term *other than collision*. Technically, if a loss is not caused by a collision, it must be a result of other than collision. Together, these two coverages give an insured open-perils coverage on an insured auto, subject to the various policy exclusions.

In some cases, it is difficult to determine when a loss results from collision or other than collision. The PAP has a specific list of sources of loss that are considered other than collision. These are

- missiles and falling objects
- fire
- theft or larceny
- explosion or earthquake
- windstorm
- hail, water, or flood
- malicious mischief or vandalism
- riot or civil commotion
- contact with a bird or animal
- breakage of glass. However, the policyowner may choose to consider this part of the collision loss if it is caused by collision.

For example, a car damaged in a collision by a thief who stole it is a theft loss covered under other than collision. In many cases, this is the most advantageous place for coverage because policyowners sometimes purchase it without collision coverage, and the deductible is often lower. Similarly, if a flood sweeps a car into a tree, the damage is covered as a flood loss under the other-than-collision coverage.

Transportation Expenses

The PAP also pays up to $600, without application of the policy deductible, for temporary transportation expenses because of a loss to a covered auto or because of a loss to a nonowned auto for which the named insured or spouse is legally responsible. However, this benefit is paid for a collision loss only if the policyowner has purchased collision coverage. Similarly, it is paid for an other-than-collision loss only if other-than-collision coverage is in effect.

The amount of the benefit is limited to $20 per day and is payable beginning 48 hours after a theft loss and ending when the vehicle is returned to use or the insurer pays for its loss. For other types of losses, the benefit begins when the vehicle is withdrawn from use for more than 24 hours and is limited to the period of time reasonably required to repair or replace the vehicle.

What Vehicles Are Covered?

Part D applies to both covered autos and nonowned autos. The term *covered auto* was previously defined and applies throughout the PAP. The term *nonowned auto* for purposes of Part D, however, is defined differently and includes either of the following:

- any private passenger auto, pickup, van, or trailer not owned by, furnished to, or available for the regular use of the named insured, spouse or any family member while in the custody of or being operated by the named insured, spouse, or any family member
- any auto or trailer not owned by the named insured or spouse that is used as a temporary substitute for a covered auto that is out of normal use because of breakdown, repair, servicing, loss, or destruction

Example: Assume that a son lives with his parents and owns a car without collision coverage. If one of his parents borrows his car, their collision coverage does not apply to an accident they might have as a result of using the car merely because it was at the end of the driveway. Under their PAP, it does not fit the definition of either a covered auto or a nonowned auto. If, on the other hand, one of the parents borrows the son's car because their car is in the shop for service, the parents' collision coverage applies, because the car now qualifies as a temporary substitute auto.

The coverage for nonowned autos applies to vehicles that are rented on a temporary basis, such as when an insured is on a trip, but the policy deductible applies. If the insured purchases the loss damage waiver from the car rental company, however, the rental company will impose no deductible. In addition, the administrative hassle of resolving the matter might be minimized. These potential advantages of purchasing the rental company's loss damage waiver must be balanced by its relatively high cost—possibly $15 or $20 per day. Note that some credit cards provide a degree of physical damage coverage for certain vehicles if the card is used to pay for the rental.

Coverage for a nonowned auto is the broadest coverage applicable to any covered auto under the policyowner's PAP.

What Exclusions Apply?

Numerous exclusions apply to Part D. Some of these are similar to the exclusions previously discussed in connection with other parts of the PAP. For example, losses to any vehicle are excluded if it was used as a public or livery conveyance or in a racing competition. Losses to nonowned autos are excluded when used without a reasonable belief that an insured is entitled to use them or when the vehicle is used by anyone in the business of selling, repairing, servicing, storing, or parking vehicles designed for use on public highways.

Several exclusions apply to various types of property under certain circumstances. For example, there is no coverage for

- loss to electronic equipment that reproduces, receives, or transmits audio, visual, or data signals unless it is permanently installed in the vehicle. Coverage on permanently installed electronic equipment is limited to $1,000 unless the equipment is in a location used by the auto manufacturer for equipment of that type. For example, after-market speakers mounted in the vehicle's door cutouts to replace OEM speakers are covered in full, but an auxiliary amplifier and subwoofer the owner installs in the trunk of his car are covered for no more than $1,000. Tapes, CDs, and data disks or other media are not covered by the PAP.
- loss to a trailer, camper body, or motor home (including facilities or accessories used with them) not shown in the policy declarations. This exclusion does not apply, however, to nonowned trailers or trailers acquired during the policy period as long as the insurer is asked to insure them within 14 days of acquisition.
- loss to any custom furnishings or equipment in or upon a pickup or van. However, this exclusion does not apply to a cap, cover, or bedliner in or upon a covered auto that is a pickup.
- radar detectors and similar equipment

How Are Losses Settled?

The insurer's limit of liability is generally the lesser of (1) the actual cash value of stolen or damaged property or (2) the amount necessary to repair or replace the property with other property of like kind and quality. However, $1,500 is the maximum payment for loss to a nonowned trailer, and, as mentioned, $1,000 is the maximum payment for equipment designed solely for the reproduction of sound that is installed in locations not used by the auto manufacturer for the installation of such equipment.

The insurance company has the right to pay losses in money or to repair or replace damaged or stolen property. It also has the option of returning stolen property to the named insured and paying any damage that results from the theft, or of keeping all or part of the property and paying the insured an agreed or appraised value. Loss payments in the form of money include applicable sales tax.

The policy contains an appraisal provision that applies to situations when the insurer and insured cannot agree on the amount of a loss.

If there is other insurance, losses are settled on a pro rata basis except that coverage on a nonowned auto is excess over other collectible insurance. In other words, the insurance "follows the car."

PAP ENDORSEMENTS

As with the homeowners policies, various ISO endorsements can be added to personal auto policies to better meet the needs of certain individuals. Some endorsements apply to more than one of the four coverages previously discussed; others apply to one specific coverage only. Several of these endorsements are briefly described.

Extended Nonowned Coverage

With its 2005 revision to the Personal Auto Policy, ISO is introducing two endorsements that may be used to "buy back" certain excluded coverage in the PAP by extending the coverage applicable to nonowned autos. By eliminating exclusions in the standard PAP, both endorsements expand, or "extend" the types of vehicles that qualify as nonowned autos for which coverage may apply. Neither extended nonowned coverage endorsement modifies the other-insurance provision of the PAP. As with other nonowned autos, insurance follows the car, and the auto liability and medical payments insurance purchased by the vehicle owner is primary.

The *extended nonowned coverage—vehicles furnished or available for regular use* endorsement provides liability and medical payments coverage for vehicles not owned by the named insured or a family member that are furnished or available for the regular use of the individual named in the endorsement. An option is available to provide coverage for family members as well, but only for a vehicle regularly furnished to the named individual. A client, for example, who regularly drives a vehicle owned by an employer that carries minimum limits of liability insurance might select this endorsement.

The *extended nonowned coverage—vehicles furnished or available for use as a public or livery conveyance* endorsement provides liability and medical payments coverages for an individual who frequently operates a vehicle as a public or livery conveyance. As with the preceding endorsement, an option is available to extend coverage to include family members. For example, a retired individual with substantial assets to protect, who sometimes helps out as a substitute driver for his son-in-law's limousine service, might purchase this endorsement.

Named Nonowner Coverage

Many clients who do not own an auto do not know that they can purchase an auto insurance policy designed to address their needs.

Example: Bob's only vehicle is a company car. He has absolutely no protection of his own if he borrows or rents another vehicle. Carol lives in New York City where parking costs and public transportation make it impractical to own a car, but she frequently rents a car while on vacation or to make trips outside the city.

This endorsement is for use by people like Bob and Carol, who do not own an auto but want to have protection when they drive nonowned vehicles. Parts A, B, and C of the PAP are available.

If the named insured acquires an auto, there is coverage for 14 days to give the insured time to specifically insure the vehicle. Optional coverages for family members and for regularly furnished autos are also available through this endorsement.

Miscellaneous Type Vehicle Endorsement

This endorsement is used to cover miscellaneous types of owned vehicles such as motor homes, motorcycles and similar type vehicles, all-terrain vehicles, dune buggies, and golf carts. Each vehicle is listed in a schedule, and the policyowner can purchase the same coverages that apply to other autos in the PAP.

Snowmobile Endorsement

An endorsement similar to the Miscellaneous Type Vehicle Endorsement can be used to insure snowmobiles.

Limited Mexico Coverage

Without an endorsement, the PAP does not provide coverage when an insured is driving in Mexico. It is necessary that acceptable coverage be obtained through a licensed Mexican insurance company before driving into Mexico. To drive in Mexico without such coverage is a criminal offense. Coverage can be purchased at the border. Alternatively, it may be possible to add this protection to an existing PAP if an insurance company is a member of a foreign insurance association.

However, this is not the purpose of the Limited Mexico Coverage endorsement. The endorsement is effective only if the insured has also purchased liability insurance through a Mexican insurer, and coverage is excess over that policy. The main advantage of the endorsement is the ability to have higher liability limits than the Mexican insurance provides, as well as other policy coverages. The endorsement is primarily used by people who live near the border and occasionally take brief trips to Mexico. All policy coverages can be purchased for losses that occur in Mexico within 25 miles of the United States' border, and the coverage applies only while the insured is in Mexico for 10 days or less. The insurer will defend the insured under the liability coverage only if the original suit is brought in the United States and if the suit does not involve a Mexican citizen or resident. Repairs to a covered auto are not covered if they are made in Mexico unless the vehicle cannot be driven in its damaged condition.

Coverage for Damage to Your Auto (Maximum Limit of Liability)

Insurers are often reluctant to write Part D coverage on antique or restored vehicles because of the difficulty in determining value when a loss occurs. This endorsement lists a stated amount, which becomes the maximum that the insurer will pay for a loss. This does not mean, however, that the stated amount is automatically paid if a total loss occurs. The insurer's maximum limit of liability is the smallest of the following three amounts (less the applicable deductible):

- the stated amount selected
- the actual cash value of the stolen or damaged property
- the amount necessary to repair or replace the property with property of like kind and quality

Joint Ownership Coverage

This endorsement is used to modify the definition of insured when individuals are not married, reside together, and jointly own one or more vehicles. It can also be used when related persons jointly own a vehicle but do not live together.

Trust Endorsement

Financial planners should be aware of the insurance ramifications when a client's property is retitled in the name of a trust. Many autos are legally owned by a trust, typically a revocable living trust the policyowner establishes for estate planning reasons. Too often, the insurer is not even informed that the vehicle has been retitled in the name of the trust. Traditionally, when the insurer was aware of the situation, a certificate of insurance was used to serve as proof of insurance on vehicles the named insured and a trust owned jointly. However, this approach was not suitable for the most common situations in which the vehicle is titled solely in the name of the trust.

In 2005, ISO is introducing a Trust Endorsement that lists the name of the trust and the trustee, if other than the named insured. The endorsement also adds a statement to the definitions section of the policy to the effect that a vehicle is deemed to be owned by a person if title is transferred to the trust named in the schedule or in the declarations. This is similar to the provision that treats autos under a long-term lease as though they were owned autos.

Auto Loan/Lease Coverage

In some cases, the total loss to a leased vehicle or a financed auto results in the insured's being required to pay the lessor or lending company an amount that exceeds the actual cash value of an insured vehicle. The purpose of this endorsement is to fill that gap.

The endorsement provides indemnification for any unpaid lease or finance amounts other than overdue payments at the time of loss, financial penalties under a lease for excessive use or abnormal wear and tear, security deposits not refunded by a lessor, costs for extended warranties or life and health insurance purchased, and carryover balances from previous leases or loans.

Towing and Labor Costs Coverage

This endorsement pays for towing and labor if a covered auto or nonowned auto is disabled for any reason. The limit of coverage is a stated amount such as $25, $50, or $100 per disablement. The labor costs of repair work (such as changing a flat tire) are covered only at the place of disablement.

The endorsement can be used only for autos that are already covered under Part D of the PAP. It is not unusual for the towing and labor coverage to be a standard part of an insurance company's PAPs if collision coverage is purchased.

Towing and labor costs protection originated as a fringe benefit of auto insurance the auto clubs provided, and other insurers began to offer the coverage to remain competitive. It is a popular coverage addition, partly because it is a low-cost option and partly because it provides a sense of security in the event of an auto breakdown. However, many clients should consider bypassing the towing and labor costs coverage option for at least two reasons. First, the maximum benefit, as mentioned, is usually a nominal amount such as $25, $50, or $100. Most clients could easily handle a cost of this magnitude as a current expense. Second, towing and labor coverage duplicates a benefit available to clients who are members of an auto club. Third, many auto manufacturers provide towing coverage on vehicles that are under warranty; in this situation, towing and labor coverage is redundant at best.

Trip Interruption Coverage

In 2005, ISO is introducing a new trip interruption coverage endorsement that is somewhat related to towing and labor costs coverage. The new endorsement provides coverage up to $600 for reasonable transportation expenses, lodging, and meals when a vehicle is withdrawn from use for 24 hours or more because it is in an accident or breaks down more than 100 miles from home. Coverage is excess over benefits that vehicle warranties, auto clubs, or other sources provide.

Other Endorsements

There are several other endorsements that provide coverage either for property that is excluded under the PAP or where the amount of coverage is limited. These endorsements are very briefly described below:

- Optional Limits Transportation Expense Coverage. The $20 per day and $600 maximums that apply to transportation expenses are increased to $30 and $900, respectively, under this endorsement.
- Customizing Equipment Coverage. This endorsement can be used to insure custom furnishings and/or equipment in a pickup or van.
- Electronic Equipment Coverage. This endorsement can be used to provide coverage in excess of $1,000 on electronic equipment that is permanently installed in locations not used by the auto manufacturer for such equipment.
- Covered Property Coverage. This endorsement provides coverage for awnings, cabanas, and other similar equipment designed for use with insured vehicles such as vans, camping trailers, or motor homes.

HARD-TO-INSURE DRIVERS

Not everybody can readily obtain auto insurance in the standard marketplace. Hard-to-insure drivers include persons with poor driving records and, often, those who are youthful or who have little driving experience. Statistics clearly show that these groups have a high probability of being involved in future accidents.

Another category of hard-to-insure drivers consists of persons with very high-powered and/or expensive autos. Some insurers specialize in this market, particularly for individuals who have good driving records.

The number of hard-to-insure drivers varies significantly from state to state; the number is much higher in states where insurance companies lose money on auto insurance because the state insurance departments are unwilling to grant necessary rate increases.

residual market   Hard-to-insure drivers can usually find some coverage in what is referred to as the *residual market* (sometimes referred to as the *shared market* or *substandard market*). This market consists of specialty insurers and state programs to make insurance available, though not necessarily affordable. A small number of drivers with very poor driving records (for example, several drunk driving convictions) may still be unable to obtain insurance from either of these sources in some states.

Specialty Insurers

A number of insurers specialize in writing coverage for high-risk drivers. They charge substantially higher premiums than in the standard marketplace and often provide more limited coverage. For example, the limits for liability coverage are sometimes only those specified in a state's financial responsibility or compulsory insurance law. However, it is not unusual to have optional higher limits available.

Medical payments coverage can also be limited, and collision coverage, if written, is often subject to a high deductible.

State Programs

State programs for hard-to-insure drivers are commonly referred to as assigned risk plans. This term is no longer formally used, however, because of its negative connotations. State programs for hard-to-insure drivers tend to have higher-than-normal premiums (often much higher) and more limited coverage than in the standard marketplace, but significant variations exist among the states. The state programs usually follow one of three models:

- automobile insurance plans
- joint underwriting associations
- reinsurance facilities

Automobile Insurance Plans

automobile insurance plan

An *automobile insurance plan* is the type of program that exists in most states. To be eligible, an applicant must show that he or she has been unable to obtain coverage within a recent specified period of time. Each auto insurer in the state is assigned its proportionate share of the drivers in the plan based on the total volume of auto insurance written in the state. The company to which the policy is assigned issues and services it. It also receives any profits or absorbs any losses from the policies it writes.

Joint Underwriting Associations

This arrangement involves an association of auto insurers, and all business of the association is placed in a pool. The insurance companies share any underwriting losses in proportion to the auto insurance premiums each company writes in the state. A limited number of companies are designated to issue and service policies on behalf of the association.

Reinsurance Facilities

Under this approach, insurers must accept all applicants who have a valid driver's license, and they issue and service policies for these applicants. However, if an applicant is considered high-risk, the insurer has the option of assigning the premiums for the applicant to the reinsurance facility. All auto insurance companies in the state share underwriting losses from this type of business in proportion to auto insurance premiums written.

Insuring Hard-to-Insure Drivers

- Specialty high-risk auto insurers
- State automobile insurance (assigned risk) plans
- Joint underwriting associations
- Reinsurance facilities

SHOPPING FOR AUTO INSURANCE

The cost of auto insurance varies significantly among insurers in a highly competitive market. In fact, studies by some state insurance departments show that the premium for a hypothetical insured can be two to four times higher if purchased from certain insurance companies rather than others. Therefore, it pays to shop around. Of course, as previously stated, factors such as the financial strength of the insurer and the service from the company and its agents also need to be evaluated.

Many factors affect auto insurance rates, and some of them are not readily within the control of the insured at the time he or she purchases auto insurance. These factors include the age, sex, and marital status of drivers; the use of the insured vehicles (that is, driving to work, pleasure, or business); and the geographic territory where vehicles are normally used and garaged.

Other factors are subject to some control by the insured but not necessarily at the moment he or she purchases a policy. These include driving record and the type and age of vehicles owned. The latter is particularly significant for physical damage coverage where the Part D premium can be several times higher for a new luxury auto than a van that is several years old.

Even though most companies commonly use these previously mentioned factors to determine premiums, companies can apply them differently. For example, premiums are higher if a family has a teenager who drives. If the teenager primarily or solely drives the old family van, many companies will rate this vehicle for the teenager. However, other companies will assign the teenage driver to the highest-rated vehicle even if he or she does not use it.

Other factors can also affect auto insurance premiums for one or more policy coverages. Many companies give discounts for at least some of the following:

- a driver education course for young drivers
- students with good grades
- a defensive driving course
- senior citizens, but the discount may require the periodic attendance of a classroom program on driver education
- nonsmokers
- anti-theft devices in a vehicle
- air bags or automatic seat belts in a vehicle
- reduced use of a vehicle by a student who is away at school over a specified distance from home, provided the student does not have an insured vehicle at school
- no accidents for some period of time such as 3 years
- other policies with the same company. For example, some insurers give a discount if they write both auto insurance and homeowners insurance for a policyowner.

Other important factors in the cost of auto insurance are the coverages selected, their limits, and deductibles. For policyowners with an umbrella liability policy, the limits for liability insurance need only to be those the umbrella policy requires. If a policyowner and family have an adequate medical expense insurance plan, it is probably unnecessary to carry any more Part B coverage for medical payments than a state might require. However, note that this coverage applies to more than just family members and also covers funeral expenses. Similarly, if a policyowner and family members have adequate medical expense and disability income insurance, the need to carry other than minimally required no-fault benefits should be evaluated.

Financial planners often disagree over the appropriate limit of uninsured/underinsured motorists coverage. Some argue that it should be the same as a policy's liability limits. Others argue that this is unnecessary if other insurance exists that will pay for a family's medical expenses and lost wages. However, higher limits do give an insured the right to collect damages for pain and suffering.

Finally, there are ways to lower Part D premiums. Higher deductibles, particularly on collision coverage, can result in significant savings over a period of years. In addition, a policyowner must evaluate the need for coverage on an older vehicle. For example, there are those who argue that it is probably not cost effective to carry physical damage coverage on a vehicle that is worth as little as $3,000 or $4,000. Obviously, this threshold amount varies by factors such as the net worth and risk tolerance of an individual.

INSURING WATERCRAFT AND AIRPLANES

It is common for individuals to own watercraft. For some watercraft, liability coverage is available under a homeowners policy, but that policy provides no protection for larger boats and little physical damage protection for any boat. As a result, many insurers market various types of watercraft policies to meet the insurance needs of boat owners. There is no single common policy such as the ISO forms for homeowners and auto insurance.

Some individuals own private aircraft for their personal or business use. Coverage for aircraft is very specialized and is usually obtained from a small number of aviation pools that underwrite and manage such insurance for their member companies.

Watercraft Policies

There are several types of watercraft policies. Some insurers have policies designed primarily for small boats such as those no longer than 20 or 22 feet. These policies typically provide physical damage coverage on the boat, motor, equipment, and trailer and contain a deductible. They can also be used to provide liability and medical payments coverage.

There are two common types of package policies for boats—boatowners policies and yacht policies. A boatowners policy is typically used for boats under a particular length such as 26 or 30 feet, whereas the yacht policy is used for larger boats. A boatowners policy is generally written by an insurer's personal lines department, while a yacht policy is often written by the insurer's ocean marine department. As a result, the policies tend to use different wording, but the coverage is largely the same.

Boatowners and yacht policies are similar to auto policies in that they contain

- liability coverage, sometimes referred to as protection and indemnity insurance
- medical payments coverage
- uninsured boaters coverage
- physical damage coverage, often referred to as hull insurance. This provides protection not only for the boat but also for equipment, accessories, motors, and trailers. Coverage can usually be written on either a named-perils or an open-perils basis.

As a general rule, the exclusions that apply to these coverages also parallel those found in auto insurance policies.

Other coverages are also available in boatowners and yacht policies. These include coverage for the

- legal obligation of the policyowner to remove a wrecked or sunken vessel
- liability arising out of transportation of the boat on land
- costs of towing and assistance if the boat is disabled
- liability to crew members and other maritime workers covered under various federal acts

Boatowners and yacht policies frequently contain warranties. Failure to comply with these warranties can result in the denial of coverage or higher premiums, depending on the precise policy provision. Common warranties are that the boat will

- be used for pleasure
- not be used during specified seasonal periods unless the policyowner obtains permission from the insurance company and pays any additional premium
- be operated only in the navigational area described in the policy

It is also common to find a warranty that requires at least two occupants in a boat when it is used for waterskiing.

Aviation Policies

Aviation policies for private aircraft are similar to auto insurance with respect to liability insurance in that coverage pays for bodily injury that arises out of the insured's ownership, maintenance, or use of insured aircraft. Coverage also applies to bodily injury liability arising out of the location where the insured aircraft is stored. Exclusions similar to those in auto insurance policies apply. In addition, there are exclusions for damage or injury from noise and pollution.

Medical payments coverage is available to cover passengers. Crew members can also be covered for an additional premium.

The physical damage coverage, also referred to as *hull coverage*, is open-perils and can be written to apply to the following: (1) all losses, (2) only losses that occur while the plane is not in flight, or (3) only losses that occur while the plane is not in motion.

PERSONAL UMBRELLA LIABILITY INSURANCE

umbrella liability policy

Virtually every financial planning client has assets to protect, and virtually every client with assets should be advised to protect those assets with a personal *umbrella liability policy*. Without this coverage, individuals and families face the possibility of losing a lifetime's accumulation of capital and other assets because they are seized to pay a legal judgment. At one time, umbrella liability insurance was viewed as a policy for wealthy people with a large asset base or a high income. In view of the magnitude of today's legal awards, an umbrella policy is appropriate for most middle-income individuals as well.

As explained later in more detail, an umbrella policy protects clients in two ways:

- *high limits over underlying insurance.* Umbrella policies provide high limits of "excess" liability coverage, over and above the "underlying" primary liability coverage that basic auto and homeowners policies provide. For example, a person whose personal auto policy has a single Coverage A liability limit of $500,000 could buy a $1 million umbrella policy to be protected against future auto liability claims up to $1.5 million, the sum of the two policies. If the person also had a homeowners policy with a Coverage E liability limit of $300,000, that policy and the umbrella combined would provide protection up to $1.3 million for liability losses covered by the homeowners policy.
- *broadened drop-down coverage over a self-insured retention.* Many umbrella policies provide not only additional limits but also broader coverage by covering some kinds of claims—such as claims for slander and other personal injury offenses—that an auto policy or a homeowners policy does not cover. The self-insured retention, which works like a deductible, is discussed in the next section of this chapter.

Unlike homeowners insurance and auto insurance, there was historically no standard personal umbrella liability policy, and each insurer that offered this type of insurance developed its own policy. The situation has changed somewhat with the recent development of an ISO policy. Although insurers can now adopt the ISO policy, most continue to use their own policy forms. This results in significant variations among policies. Therefore, the following discussion is general. The appropriate policy for a particular individual is the one that best covers his or her specific loss exposures, and a thorough evaluation of policies is often appropriate.

The following discussion looks at the general nature of personal umbrella liability policies, the underlying coverage requirements, the persons insured, and the exclusions that often exist.

General Nature

A personal umbrella policy is designed primarily to provide liability coverage for catastrophic legal claims or judgments. The smallest limit of coverage available from most insurers is $1 million, and limits up to $5 or $10 million are often available. The policy covers not only bodily injury and property damage liability but also personal injury liability.

A personal umbrella policy requires the policyowner to carry certain underlying liability coverages of specified minimum amounts. These generally include auto liability insurance, watercraft liability insurance if the policyowner owns any watercraft, and personal liability insurance under a homeowners or other policy. If a claim is made under an underlying policy, the umbrella policy will pay only after the limits of the underlying policy are exhausted. The umbrella policy is excess and will pay up to its limits so that the insured effectively has an amount of coverage equal to the sum of the limits of the umbrella policy and the underlying coverage.

Example:	Charlene Smith has a $1 million umbrella policy and an auto liability policy of the required underlying limit of $250,000 per person. If an injured party obtains a legal judgment of $700,000 against her, the underlying auto policy will pay $250,000 and the umbrella policy will pay the remaining $450,000.

self-insured retention

If an underlying policy does not cover a loss that is not excluded from a personal umbrella policy, the umbrella policy is the primary insurer and will cover the loss subject to a *self-insured retention* (SIR). The SIR is like a deductible and requires the policyowner to pay the first portion of the loss—typically $250. However, SIR amounts vary by company and can be $500 or $1,000 or even higher. The SIR is not applicable to losses that underlying policies cover. Note that the term *drop-down coverage* is often used to describe a situation in which an umbrella policy covers a loss that underlying insurance does not cover. In effect, the umbrella drops down to cover the entire loss, other than the SIR, rather than act as excess coverage.

Figure 18-1 shows the relationship of a typical personal umbrella policy to the underlying policies.

In addition to paying liability claims, most personal umbrella policies pay defense costs that are not payable by underlying policies and provide various other supplementary coverages similar to those in the homeowners and PAP policies (premiums on appeal bonds, expenses incurred at the company's request, and so on).

Finally, some states require that the policyowner be given the right to extend coverage under a personal umbrella policy to uninsured and underinsured motorists coverage.

Underlying Coverage Requirements

A requirement of the personal umbrella policy is that the policyowner maintain certain underlying coverages of specified minimum amounts. Some insurers also require that these underlying coverages be purchased from them.

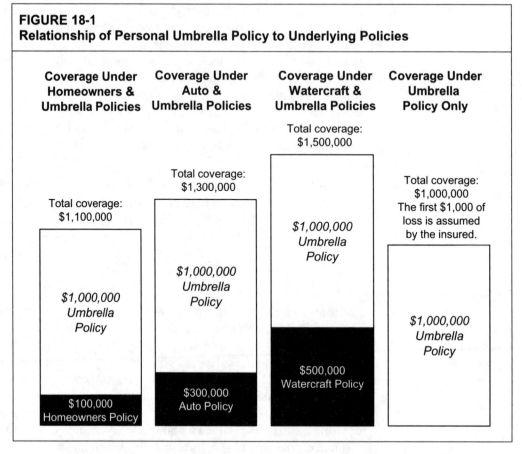

FIGURE 18-1
Relationship of Personal Umbrella Policy to Underlying Policies

At a minimum, the following underlying coverages are required, and the amounts shown, although they vary from company to company, are not unusual:

- auto liability insurance: $250,000/$500,000/$50,000 or $300,000 to $500,000 single limit
- homeowners liability insurance: $100,000 or $300,000
- watercraft liability insurance if the policyowner owns a boat: $300,000 or $500,000

Other underlying coverages for recreational vehicles, aircraft, and employers liability may also be required, particularly if liability from these vehicles or situations is covered under the personal umbrella liability policy.

If the policyowner fails to maintain the required underlying coverages, the insurer will pay only the amount it would have been required to pay if the underlying policies had been in force. In the previous example, if the insured's liability limits had been $50,000, rather than the required $250,000 limit, the umbrella policy would still pay only $450,000 of the $700,000 award. The auto policy would pay $50,000, and the insured would have an uninsured loss of $200,000.

A premium reduction may apply if the underlying limits are greater than those the personal umbrella policy requires.

Who Are the Insureds?

Personal umbrella policies usually provide coverage for the named insured, spouse, and family members living in the household. Other residents of the household who are under the age of 21 and in the care of an insured are usually covered.

Other persons or organizations whose people are driving a named insured's or spouse's auto or are liable because of actions of an insured with respect to an auto are also usually covered in a manner similar to coverage under the PAP. Coverage for these persons or organizations may or may not exist with respect to watercraft and recreational vehicles.

Most policies also extend coverage to persons or organizations who have custody of an insured's animals other than businesses such as kennels, veterinary hospitals, and stables.

What Exclusions Apply?

At one time, personal umbrella policies were relatively inexpensive and contained few of the exclusions found in homeowners and auto policies. Claims experience over the years, however, has led to increased premiums and more numerous exclusions. In fact, some umbrella liability policies now have almost the same exclusions that are in homeowners and auto policies. However, the number and nature of the exclusions vary significantly among companies, and exclusions should be evaluated carefully when selecting a personal umbrella policy.

For example, an individual who is actively involved in recreational boating might frequently operate watercraft that other persons own. Some policies cover damage to such watercraft when an insured is liable; other policies exclude coverage for nonowned watercraft that are in the insured's care, custody, or control.

Some of the exclusions often found in personal umbrella policies include liability that arises from the following:

- intentional injury unless it results from actions to prevent or eliminate danger or to protect persons or property
- government programs such as workers' compensation
- damage to property owned by an insured
- damage to certain types of nonowned property in an insured's care, custody, or control. There is seldom a blanket exclusion for all

property of this type, but damage to certain classes of property (for example, autos, watercraft, and aircraft) is often excluded. In addition, damage to property for which an insured has assumed contractual liability is often excluded. The insured should have some type of property insurance in such situations.

- the use of watercraft, and possibly other recreational vehicles, unless underlying coverage applies
- the use of aircraft
- business pursuits, other than those arising out of a personal auto or when underlying coverage exists
- the rendering or failure to render professional services. A few insurance companies will cover this loss exposure for an additional premium.
- directors' and officers' activities, other than those performed for a not-for-profit organization but only if the insured receives no compensation other than reimbursement of expenses
- transmission of communicable diseases
- sexual molestation, corporal punishment, and physical or mental abuse

As noted earlier, umbrella policies are not all alike. Far from it. Various umbrella policies are available, and it behooves a financial advisor not only to recommend the client have an umbrella policy but also to ensure that the policy in question addresses the client's specific exposures.

CHECKLIST FOR EVALUATING AND COMPARING PERSONAL AUTO INSURANCE POLICIES

☐ What are the limits for each of the following coverages?

    ___ Part A—Liability
    ___ Part B—Medical Payments Coverage or no-fault benefits
    ___ Part C—Uninsured Motorists Coverage
    ___ Part D—Coverage for Damage to Your Auto

☐ Are the coverage limits adequate?

☐ If the policy is not an ISO form, how does it differ?

☐ Does the policy automatically contain coverages or endorsements that are optional with other insurers?

☐ What is the annual policy premium?

☐ Is the policyowner taking advantage of all possible discounts?

☐   What deductible applies to Part D?

☐   Are low-valued vehicles unnecessarily insured under Part D?

☐   Are there, or is there any need for, any endorsements for the following?

  ___   Extended nonowned coverage
  ___   Miscellaneous type vehicles
  ___   Snowmobiles
  ___   Underinsured motorists
  ___   Limited Mexico coverage
  ___   Joint ownership
  ___   Antique or restored vehicles
  ___   Auto loan/lease coverage
  ___   Towing and labor costs
  ___   Customizing equipment
  ___   Trip interruption coverage
  ___   Awnings, cabanas, and the like

CHECKLIST FOR EVALUATING AND COMPARING PERSONAL UMBRELLA LIABILITY INSURANCE POLICIES

☐   What are the policy limits?

☐   What is the self-insured retention?

☐   Does the policy provide uninsured or underinsured motorists coverage?

☐   What is the annual policy premium?

☐   What are the underlying coverage requirements and are they satisfied?

  ___   Auto liability insurance
  ___   Homeowners liability insurance
  ___   Watercraft liability insurance
  ___   Other

☐   What persons are insured?

☐   What types of exclusions apply?

MINI-CASE: AMY AND JOHN SCHULTZ

John, a product manager, frequently travels for SKH, his employer. For shorter trips, he usually drives one of the company-owned cars in SKH's fleet, but he occasionally uses his own car. For longer business trips, he generally flies to an airport near his destination and then rents a car. Amy does little, if any, business travel, but she and John frequently rent a car while they are away from home on vacation.

Amy and John both own late-model compact cars. Amy's car is currently worth about $14,000; John's car has more miles on the odometer and is worth about $8,000. Both cars are paid for. Amy insists that they continue to carry separate auto insurance policies because of John's bad driving record.

Amy purchased her auto insurance from a stock insurance company through an independent agent whose office is near SKH. Her policy has a $100,000 liability limit, a $5,000 medical payments coverage limit, uninsured motorists coverage with a $25,000/$50,000 limit, and other than collision coverage with a $500 deductible.

John purchased insurance through a local agent who represents only one mutual insurance company. Although that company would not accept John's application, the agent was able to obtain coverage in the assigned risk plan. John's policy costs a lot more than Amy's but has only the minimum $25,000/$50,000/$25,000 liability limits and uninsured motorists coverage.

Amy and John own no individual insurance policies apart from their homeowners policy and the auto policies described above. In connection with their homeowners policy, their financial planner recommends they consider a personal umbrella. As part of the financial planning process, they also ask for an evaluation of their auto insurance.

    a.   What changes would Amy and John need to make in their auto insurance before purchasing a personal umbrella policy?

    b.   What coverage do their current personal auto policies provide for each of the following losses?

- Amy's car is stolen.
- John's car is scorched when it is parked next to a car that catches fire.
- An unidentified car backs into Amy's car in a parking lot and damages the rear fender.
- John is absent-mindedly walking across the street and falls into a manhole, breaking his leg and incurring $5,000 in medical bills.

    c.   What advice could be given to John regarding coverage for his business use of an auto owned by the employer or rented by John in the employer's name?

    d.   What advice could be given to Amy and John regarding their use of a rental auto while on vacation?

    e.   What might Amy and John do to minimize the cost of their auto insurance while maintaining adequate coverage?

(See answer section for answers to mini-case.)

SOURCES FOR FURTHER IN-DEPTH STUDY

- Wiening, Eric A.; Rejda, George E.; Luthard, Constance M.; and Ferguson, Cheryl L., *Personal Insurance*, Malvern, PA: American Institute for CPCU/Insurance Institute of America, 2002. Phone 800-644-2101. Web site address www.aicpcu.org
- *Personal Risk Management and Insurance,* (loose-leaf, CD-ROM, or online service periodically updated). Includes unique Personal Exposure Survey (including recommendations) and coverage checklists for personal auto, homeowners, personal umbrella, and personal inland marine. (Access to Word files of the survey and checklists.) Dallas, TX: International Risk Management Institute, 800-827-4242. Web site address www.irmi.com
- Hamilton, Karen L., and Ferguson, Cheryl L., *Personal Risk Management and Property-Liability Insurance*, Malvern, PA: American Institute for CPCU/Insurance Institute of America, 2002. Phone 800-644-2101. Web site address www.aicpcu.org
- *FC&S Bulletins*, Personal Lines Volume, (loose-leaf and/or CD-ROM service updated monthly), Erlanger, KY: The National Underwriter Company. Phone 800-543-0874. Web site address www.nuco.com
- Wiening, Eric, and Thamann, David, *The Personal Auto Coverage Guide,* 2d ed., Erlanger, KY: The National Underwriter Company, 2005. Phone 800-543-0874. Web site address www.nuco.com

CHAPTER REVIEW

Answers to mini-case, review questions, and self-test questions start on page 793.

Key Terms

financial responsibility law
unsatisfied judgment fund
uninsured motorists coverage
underinsured motorists
   coverage
pure no-fault
modified no-fault
add-on plan
choice no-fault
personal injury protection
   (PIP) endorsement

covered auto
newly acquired auto
temporary substitute
   vehicle
split limits
collision
other than collision
residual market
automobile insurance plan
umbrella liability policy
self-insured retention

Review Questions

18-1.   Describe the key problems associated with auto accidents and auto insurance.

18-2.   Explain to your client why he or she should consider purchasing uninsured and underinsured motorists coverage even though the state has a compulsory liability insurance law.

18-3.   Briefly explain the methods of compensating auto accident victims (include the shortcomings of those methods).

18-4.   While driving his car, Jack sustained medical expenses and lost wages due to bodily injury when a drunk teenager driving his own car ran a red light and hit him. Jack in no way contributed to the accident through his own fault. Explain how the settlement would be handled in each of the following situations:
   a.   if Jack's bodily injuries equaled $40,000 and the accident occurred in a state with compulsory liability insurance
   b.   if Jack's bodily injuries equaled $40,000 and the accident occurred in a state with a modified no-fault law containing a $5,000 threshold

18-5.   What vehicles are eligible for coverage under a personal auto policy?

18-6.   Pete pays cash for a new car, and when he drives it off the dealer's lot, he hits another car driving along the street in front of the dealership. The accident is Pete's fault. He injures the driver of the other car and damages both his car and the other driver's car. Pete had $100,000 of liability coverage for bodily injury and property damage (Part A) and collision coverage (Part D) with a $250 deductible on the old car he just traded in as part of the purchase of his new car. What coverage, if any, does Pete have for this accident?

18-7.   Tom falls asleep at the wheel of his car while driving on the interstate, runs across the median, and causes a tractor trailer truck to flip over while trying to avoid a head-on collision with Tom. The truck driver has a claim for $5,000 of bodily injury; damage to his truck and its contents is $150,000. How much will Tom's personal auto policy pay, if Part A—Liability coverage is
   a. $100,000/$300,000/$50,000
   b. $300,000

18-8.   Your client, Betty, mentions that she frequently uses cars in connection with her business and asks whether her personal auto policy provides liability coverage in the following situations:
   a.   when she drives her family car for business purposes
   b.   when she drives the company car furnished to her for her regular use
   c.   when she helps to drive her friend's car to a business meeting in another state

18-9.   A client, who frequently borrows her friend's car, asks whose liability insurance would cover a liability claim that resulted from an accident while she was driving the friend's car.

18-10. A client, whose wife frequently gives rides to several other children attending their daughter's nursery school, asks whether there is any coverage available under their personal auto policy in case the children are injured in an accident that is not his wife's fault.

18-11. On a family vacation, you rent a car and turn down the loss damage waiver the rental company offers. Which coverage in your personal auto policy would provide you with coverage for damage to the rental car (less any deductible) in the following situations:
a.   The rental car is damaged when you hit a phone pole while swerving to avoid another vehicle.
b.   The rental car is scratched by vandals while it is parked in the hotel parking lot.
c.   The rental car is badly dented when you hit a deer while you are driving at night.

18-12. A client asks how he can get liability coverage for his use of his motorcycle, dune buggy, and snowmobile.

18-13. During a meeting to review her financial plan, your client, Celeste, mentions that she and her family plan a vacation driving around Mexico this year. What should you explain to her about auto insurance coverage for the trip?

18-14. Where might auto coverage be obtained for clients who are hard-to-insure drivers?

18-15. What factors should clients consider when shopping for auto insurance?

18-16. Describe the coverages available to meet the needs of clients who own watercraft and/or airplanes.

18-17. A client, who has rather high limits of liability in her personal auto and homeowners policies, asks why she should consider also purchasing a personal umbrella liability policy.

Self-Test Questions

T   F   18-1.   Uninsured and underinsured motorists coverages are unnecessary in states with compulsory liability laws.

T   F   18-2.   Financial responsibility laws require owners of autos to carry liability insurance before a vehicle can be registered.

T   F   18-3.   In uninsured motorists coverage, uninsured motorists include drivers of hit-and-run vehicles.

T   F   18-4.   Under most no-fault laws, the right to sue the negligent party, even for pain and suffering, has been eliminated.

T   F   18-5.   No-fault benefits in most states are limited to medical expenses.

T   F   18-6.   In most states, clients' motorcycles and snowmobiles can be insured under the personal auto policy (PAP) by endorsement.

T   F   18-7.   A 25-year-old woman who lives with her parents is covered under her parents' PAP while she is driving the family car or a friend's car.

T   F   18-8.   If a client has $100,000/$300,000/$50,000 limits of liability in her PAP, she would be fully covered if sued for $150,000 for bodily injury and $20,000 for property damage by the driver of the other car who is injured as a result of an auto accident that was the client's fault.

T   F   18-9.   If a client has a $300,000 single limit of liability in his PAP, he would be fully covered if sued for $150,000 for bodily injury and $20,000 for property damage as a result of an auto accident that was his fault.

T   F   18-10.   If Jim rented a car, damaged it, and was sued by the rental company, he would be covered under the liability coverage of his PAP for the property damage to the rental car.

T   F   18-11.   If Jim has an accident while driving his friend's car and is sued for $250,000 for bodily injury and property damage, the friend's liability insurance would pay first and Jim's liability coverage would be excess and thus pay only if needed.

T   F   18-12.   Medical payments coverage under the PAP applies only to persons other than the named insured.

T   F   18-13.   The insurance company is obligated to pay an uninsured motorists claim only when the owner or operator of the uninsured vehicle is legally responsible for the insured's damages.

T   F   18-14.   If Hank hits a deer, the damage to his car would be paid under the collision coverage.

T   F   18-15.   A client driving to Mexico should be advised to look into purchasing liability coverage from a Mexican insurer.

T   F   18-16.   Most states handle hard-to-insure drivers through joint underwriting associations.

T   F   18-17.   Because of the highly competitive market, the cost of auto insurance differs little from company to company.

T   F   18-18.   Two common package policies for boats are the boatowners policy for smaller boats and the yacht policy for larger boats.

T   F   18-19. Boatowners and yacht policies frequently contain warranties.

T   F   18-20. In addition to covering bodily injury and property damage liability, a typical personal umbrella policy also covers personal injury liability.

T   F   18-21. If Ken has an umbrella policy with a $1 million limit and a $250 self-insured retention, and he is sued for $100,000 for an act covered under the umbrella policy but not under the required underlying coverages, the umbrella policy would pay all but $250 of the judgment.

T   F   18-22. Personal umbrella policies commonly cover situations excluded under the required underlying coverages such as sexual molestation and failure to render professional services.

NOTES

1. "DOT Releases Preliminary Estimates of 2003 Highway Fatalities," NHTSA press release, April 28, 2004, http://www.nhtsa.dot.gov/nhtsa/announce/press/...<long filename> accessed 5/18/04.
2. In this context, the word "risk" refers to the policyowner. The phrase "assigned risk" is used generically by insurance practitioners to refer to all auto residual market plans, although only one type, technically known as "automobile insurance plans," literally assigns risks (policyowners) to specific insurers.
3. Insurance Information Institute, Hot Topics and Insurance Issues, "Auto Insurance," http://www.iii.org/media/facts/statsbyissue/auto/, accessed 5/19/04.

Business Property and Liability Insurance

Learning Objectives
An understanding of the material in this chapter should enable the student to

19-1. Briefly explain the key types of commercial property and liability insurance available to meet the protection needs of businesses.

19-2. Describe the general features of businessowners policies.

Chapter Outline

This final chapter on property and liability insurance is devoted to business insurance. A financial planner may be asked to make specific recommendations about property and liability coverages for a business owner, but the task of implementing this coverage is usually left to a property and liability insurance agent or broker who works in the business market.

A financial planner still needs a general understanding of the types of business insurance described in this chapter for several reasons. Individual clients sometimes need some of the coverages discussed here. For example, anyone with domestic employees may need workers' compensation coverage for household employees. A semi-retired client with a part-time business venture, or a person with a hobby, may also engage in an activity that requires some type of commercial insurance policy to cover his or her business property or liability exposures.

It is especially important for a financial planner to determine whether a client has appropriate liability insurance on his or her business activities to adequately protect personal assets against a claim or judgment. For example, when a client serves on the board of a corporation or a nonprofit organization, it is important to consider the extent to which he or she is protected by organization's directors and officers liability insurance.

The chapter begins by summarizing the more common types of commercial property and liability insurance. It concludes by describing businessowners policies that provide a package of coverages suitable for many small- and medium-sized businesses.

TYPES OF COMMERCIAL PROPERTY AND LIABILITY INSURANCE

Numerous policy forms and endorsements for commercial property and liability insurance are available. A precise breakdown of the types of coverage into categories is somewhat difficult because terminology and insurance company practices are not uniform. In this chapter, the discussion is categorized as follows:

- commercial property insurance
- business income insurance
- crime insurance
- inland marine insurance
- boiler and machinery insurance
- farm insurance
- commercial general liability insurance
- business auto insurance
- workers' compensation and employers liability insurance
- professional liability insurance

- excess and umbrella liability insurance
- surety bonds

Many commercial coverages, such as coverage on ships and commercial aircraft (ocean marine and aviation insurance, respectively), are beyond the scope of this book and are not discussed here.

The focus in most of the following discussion is on the forms used by ISO. Each of these forms can be used as a free-standing "monoline" policy when combined with another form that contains general policy provisions. Often, two or more separate coverage forms are combined into a commercial package policy.

Commercial Property Insurance

commercial property insurance

Broadly speaking, the term commercial property includes business property of all types. ISO has developed a series of so-called *commercial property insurance* policies that deal with property specifically related to buildings and their contents, using those terms rather loosely. The ISO commercial property series of coverages and forms are discussed under this heading.

Covered Property

Commercial property insurance can be used to cover one or more of the following classes of property:

- buildings
- business personal property of the named insured
- personal property of others in the care, custody, or control of the named insured

Each of these classes is specifically defined and subject to various exclusions, some of which can be deleted, or "bought back," by using an endorsement. Other exclusions eliminate coverage for losses that can be covered by other policies.

Various extensions of coverage automatically provide limited coverage for debris removal, pollution cleanup after a loss, newly acquired property, and the cost of research to reconstruct valuable papers and records that have been damaged or destroyed.

Covered Perils

Commercial property can be insured against various perils on either a named-perils basis or a more comprehensive open-perils basis. In all cases, these forms can be expanded with endorsements to cover losses that might arise, for example, from earthquake or the enforcement of ordinances or laws.

Forms for Specific Types of Property

Some commercial property insurance forms have been developed for use in specific situations. These include

- *Builders Risk Coverage Form.* This form provides protection for buildings under construction and covers the unique loss exposures and valuation issues associated with these structures.
- *Condominium Association Coverage Form.* This form covers property for which a residential or commercial condominium association is responsible. It covers not only property owned by the association but also furniture, fixtures, alterations, and appliances of unit owners if the association agreement requires the association to insure them.
- *Condominium Commercial Unit-owners Coverage Form.* This form covers the interest of the owner of a commercial condominium unit. Note that an owner of a residential condominium unit can protect his or her interest under an HO-6 policy.

Loss Settlement

Losses under commercial property forms are settled on an actual cash value basis. However, a replacement cost coverage option is often elected. Losses are subject to a deductible that, depending upon available options, the policyowner can select.

The settlement of losses is subject to a coinsurance provision that is often 80 percent but can also be 90 or 100 percent. To avoid a possible coinsurance penalty, the policyowner has the option to elect an agreed amount of coverage or an inflation guard endorsement that automatically increases coverage limits.

For many businesses, property values, particularly inventory, are subject to wide fluctuations. Various policy forms can be used to address this problem so that premiums charged reflect the varying loss exposures, and, at the time of loss, there is adequate insurance to properly indemnify the policyowner and avoid a coinsurance penalty. These forms include value reporting forms, which require periodic reporting of values, and peak season endorsements that modify policy limits during certain specified periods of the year.

Business Income Insurance

Although business income insurance policy forms are part of ISO's commercial property series, we will discuss them separately. Many businesses will suffer a significant loss of income if direct physical loss or damage to business property forces a suspension of business operations. Others will not be able to suspend operations but will instead incur extra expenses to remain in operation. Policy forms are available to cover these loss exposures, and the protection they provide can make the difference between business success and failure.

Example 1:	Josef Beckmann owns a neighborhood bakery. An overheated oven started a fire that damaged several mixers and a portion of the bakery building. Beckmann's commercial property insurance will pay for the damage to the building, as well as the mixers and other personal property in the bakery. Beckmann will also face a serious cash flow problem, because the bakery will generate no income until the fire damage has been repaired. Business income insurance, if he has purchased the coverage, can provide the needed dough during the period of reconstruction.
Example 2:	Andrea Beckmann is the only veterinarian in a small community. Unlike her father, Josef, Andrea cannot suspend business if her clinic is damaged or destroyed, because the community's pets will continue to get sick or injured and need her services. Andrea would instead rent temporary quarters and equipment so she could set up a temporary clinic to treat sick animals and perform emergency surgery. Extra expense insurance can cover this operation. If Andrea should temporarily suspend routine services until her clinic could be restored, she would also suffer a loss of business income that business income insurance can cover.

business income insurance

   Business income insurance, once known as business interruption insurance, may be purchased not only for profit-seeking commercial businesses but also for nonprofit organizations and governmental entities. Business income coverage applies when property has been damaged by an insured peril. Most policyowners buy business income insurance against the same set of perils as their building and/or personal property, either on a named-perils basis or on an open-perils basis.

   Business income insurance covers the following types of losses:

- reduction in net income—the difference between the net income the business would have earned had no loss occurred and the net income the business did earn after a loss

- extra expenses to minimize or avoid the suspension of operations—rent at a temporary location, for example, and the cost of obtaining services, such as data processing, that can no longer be handled in-house

Policy Forms

ISO forms include two types of business income coverage and an extra expense only form with these names:

- Business Income (and Extra Expense) Coverage Form
- Business Income (without Extra Expense) Coverage Form
- Extra Expense Coverage Form

Both business income forms cover the sum of (1) net profit or loss that would have been earned or incurred during a period of business suspension and (2) normal continuing business expenses, including payroll, during the suspension. Both forms also cover extra expenses to the extent they reduce the loss that would otherwise be payable by the insurer. In addition, the business income (and extra expense) coverage form covers extra expenses to avoid or minimize the suspension of operations even if they do not otherwise reduce the business income loss.

Several endorsements are designed to adapt these forms to policyowners' particular needs. Some of these are

- *Ordinary Payroll Limitation or Exclusion Endorsement.* By laying off certain noncritical employees, organizations can minimize expenses during prolonged periods of business suspension. This endorsement deletes coverage on the amount of the payroll for these employees and results in a premium reduction.
- *Ordinance or Law—Increased Period of Restoration Endorsement.* The business income forms cover losses only for the period of time needed to repair damaged property with reasonable speed and like-quality materials. Ordinances or laws can effectively extend this period, for example, if a damaged frame building must be torn down and replaced with a masonry fire-resistive building. The endorsement provides coverage during this additional period of time.
- *Business Income from Dependent Properties Endorsement.* Some firms are so dependent on a single supplier or customer that a loss at the supplier's or customer's location would result in the suspension of the firm's operations. This endorsement covers the loss of income that results from direct damage at these other locations.
- *Utilities Services—Time Element Endorsement.* This endorsement extends coverage to loss of earnings that results from off-premises interruptions of utilities and communications services.

extra expense insurance

The Extra Expense Coverage Form is designed to provide *extra expense insurance* for organizations that must remain in operation after a property loss. Businesses that might purchase only extra expense insurance include banks, hospitals, newspapers, insurance agencies, and financial planning firms. In most cases, these businesses also have a business income loss exposure, and in such cases the Business Income (and Extra Expense) Coverage Form is the better way to obtain extra expense coverage.

Loss Settlement

Loss settlements for business income insurance are often more complex than settlements for direct property losses, because it is impossible to know precisely what business income might have been. The policy form provides that the amount of the loss is determined by the following:

- the net income of the business before the loss occurred
- the probable net income of the business if no loss had occurred
- the operating expenses that must continue during the period of restoration so the policyowner can resume operations with the quality of service that existed prior to the loss
- other relevant sources of information

As a general rule, the business income forms pay for losses continuing up to 30 days after business is resumed. The revenue of many businesses will not return to normal for longer periods of time, however, and coverage can be extended by endorsement beyond this 30-day period.

Loss payments are subject to a coinsurance provision. However, the variation in length of business suspensions and the difficulty in estimating future net income and expenses make it difficult to select the proper amount of insurance and the coinsurance percentage. Various options can eliminate or suspend the coinsurance provision.

Crime Insurance

Various commercial insurance coverages, especially those that provide coverage on an open-perils basis, cover theft losses to property other than money, securities, and similar financial instruments so long as the person who commits the theft is not an employee of the insured. An ISO commercial crime policy can also be used to cover the theft of personal property, as well as the theft of money, securities, and other property and also various causes of loss that other forms of insurance do not usually cover.

Of the various crime insurance coverages available, one of the most important—employee theft—is all too often overlooked. Perhaps this is because employee theft deals with a cause of loss rather than a specific type of asset. Often, the need for this coverage is overlooked by businessowners who see no need to question the trusted employees who handle cash and accounting records or control the business inventory. Experience demonstrates, however, that the most trusted employees often steal rather large sums of money over a period of several years before the loss is detected. Even religious organizations, civic organizations, and charitable institutions are victims of employee theft.

Covered Property

Commercial crime forms typically cover one or more of three broad classes of property:

- *money,* which includes currency, coins, bank notes, checks, and money orders
- *securities,* which include both negotiable and nonnegotiable instruments, contracts that represent money or other property, tokens, tickets, stamps, and charge slips
- *tangible property other than money or securities,* which includes inventory and office equipment. Intangible property, such as a copyright, is not included in this class of property for purposes of crime insurance. In addition, there are exclusions for certain types of property for which adequate coverage can be obtained under other types of insurance.

Causes of Loss

Crime coverages are written to provide protection from various causes of loss. Crime coverage forms include the following terms, which are not necessarily the same as legal definitions:

- *employee theft*—the unlawful taking of money, securities, or other property by an employee

burglary
- *burglary*—the taking of property from inside an insured premises by a person who enters or leaves the premises unlawfully as evidenced by marks of forcible entry or exit

robbery
- *robbery*—the taking of property from one person by someone else who has either caused harm or threatened to cause harm to the person. It also includes situations in which property is taken in an unlawful act that a person has witnessed.
- *safe burglary*—burglary from a locked safe or vault or the removal of a safe or vault from inside a building

theft
- *theft*—a broad term that includes robbery, burglary, shoplifting, and any other act of stealing

computer fraud

- *computer fraud*—a type of theft of property relating to the use of a computer to fraudulently transfer property from its rightful owner to someone else
- *disappearance and destruction*—a broad term that includes burglary, robbery, and theft, which involve losses from a known location at a known time, and also includes unknown causes of loss
- *extortion*—the surrender of property away from the insured premises as a result of a threat to do bodily harm to someone who is, or allegedly is, being held captive
- *forgery and alteration*—the creation of a document or signature that is not genuine (forgery); changes to a document in a manner that is neither authorized nor intended (alteration)

Policy Forms

ISO currently provides two crime coverage forms; one is written on a loss-sustained basis and the other on a discovery basis. When written on a loss-sustained basis, the only losses covered are those that occur during the policy period and are discovered during that time or within a specified period after the coverage expires. Subsequent policies will respond to losses if the specified discovery period has expired as long as there has been continuous coverage.

When written on a discovery basis, the current coverage pays all losses discovered while the coverage is in force, whether or not there was previous coverage. Insurers may use an endorsement to eliminate coverage for losses that occurred prior to a specified retroactive date.

The new forms contain eight optional insuring agreements. None of the insuring agreements is mandatory, and the insured may select one or more. Coverages that apply are indicated by a limit for each one selected that appears on the declarations page:

- employee theft of money, securities, and other property
- forgery or alteration of an organization's checks (including drafts and promissory notes) by parties other than the organization's owners, employees, directors, or representatives
- theft of money and securities from inside the insured's premises or banking premises. There is also coverage for damage to the premises during the actual or attempted theft and to items on the premises such as locked safes and cash registers.
- robbery and safe burglary of other property inside the insured's premises
- theft, disappearance, or destruction of money outside the insured's premises when in the custody of a messenger, and robbery of other property in the possession of a messenger

- computer fraud to transfer money, securities, or other property from the insured's premises or bank to somewhere else
- funds-transfer fraud for losses resulting from fraudulent instructions to a financial institution to transfer money from the insured's account to someone else
- the acceptance of counterfeit money orders or currency. The acceptance must be in the United States or Canada, but the currency can be that of any country.

Numerous endorsements can be added to the primary forms to provide most additional types of crime coverage that an insured might need. A few examples of these coverages are the following:

- dishonest acts of employees while they are working on a client's property
- extortion payments because of threats to people and threats to damage property
- theft of other property from within the insured's premises
- theft, burglary, robbery, and vandalism of the insured's property while stored in a safe deposit box or vault in a depository premises
- legal liability for losses involving damage to guests' property while in safe deposit boxes or inside the insured's premises

Common Policy Provisions

Some provisions are common to many crime forms:

- There is no coverage for losses caused by the named insured or any of its directors, trustees, or authorized representatives. In addition, there is no coverage for losses caused by employees except under the forms that specifically cover employee theft.
- Coverage is for direct losses only. There is no coverage available for loss of business incurred or other consequential losses that might result from criminal acts.
- Most of the forms require the policyowner to notify the police if there is reason to believe that the loss resulted from a violation of law.
- The forms specify how settlements are valued. Money is valued at its face value. If the money is foreign, the insurer can pay the face value in the foreign currency or at its equivalent value in United States currency. Securities are valued as of the close of the business day a loss is discovered. The insurer can pay the value of the securities or replace them in kind. The insurer also has the option of paying the cost of a bond that is required for the issuance of replacement securities.

Other property is valued at its cash value, and any disputes over value are settled by arbitration.

Inland Marine Insurance

inland marine insurance

Historically, marine insurers wrote insurance on ships and their cargoes, and fire insurance companies wrote insurance on property at fixed locations. As other types of transportation became more common, a hybrid type of insurance—*inland marine insurance*—evolved.

Today, inland marine policies and forms are used to write coverage for the following:

- goods in domestic transit
- property held by bailees
- mobile equipment and property
- property of certain dealers
- instrumentalities of transportation and communication
- difference in conditions (explained later)

Inland marine insurance is largely characterized by coverage for specific situations. It is often written on an open-perils basis but can also be written on a named-perils basis. Commercial property insurance forms often provide some coverage for loss exposures that can also be covered under inland marine forms, usually as additional coverages.

Goods in Transit

Inland marine policies are used to cover domestic goods in transit by mail, rail, truck, or aircraft. It is common for these policies to cover shipments only within and between the continental United States, Alaska, and Canada, but coverage can be endorsed—for example, for shipments to Mexico. Shipments to overseas locations (including Puerto Rico and Hawaii) by either ship or plane are typically insured under ocean marine policies.

Depending on the terms of sale, the responsibility for goods being shipped can fall on the shipper of the goods, the carrier of the goods, or the recipient of the goods. Any of these parties can buy insurance as needed.

The owners of property can purchase transit policies to provide property damage to their goods while in the course of transit by common carriers, contract carriers, or their own vehicles. A trip transit policy covers only the particular shipment specified in the policy. An annual transit policy covers all shipments during an annual period.

There are also policies, called motor truck cargo insurance, that common carriers or contract carriers can use to cover customers' goods when the carrier is legally liable for the damage. These policies do not cover damage for which the carrier is not liable such as those arising from acts of God, war, or neglect of the cargo owner.

Mobile Equipment and Property

Several inland marine forms are designed to insure property that is often moved from one location to another. The floater policies described in chapter 17 are examples of personal forms for this purpose. Examples of property that can be insured under commercial floater forms include the following:

- contractors' mobile equipment
- agricultural equipment
- cameras
- computer equipment
- farm animals
- fine art
- musical instruments
- physicians' and surgeons' equipment
- property on exhibition
- sales samples
- signs
- theatrical property

Property Held by Bailees

Bailees, such as dry cleaners, repair shops, and public warehouses, often have possession of significant amounts of customers' goods. A bailee liability policy can be purchased to cover damage to these goods when the bailee is legally liable. However, many bailees, for the sake of goodwill, purchase a bailees customers policy, which provides coverage whether or not the bailee is legally liable.

Property of Certain Dealers

Certain types of dealers in property have a significant amount of inventory that is likely to be transported. Special policies have been developed for these businesses that pick up not only the transportation loss exposure, but also provide coverage for merchandise in a store, furniture and fixtures of the dealer, and property of others in the dealer's care, custody, or control. These policies, often referred to as *block policies* because they cover a block of unique loss exposures, are often written for dealers in jewelry, furs, fine art, cameras, musical equipment, stamps, coins, and mobile and agricultural equipment.

**difference in
conditions (DIC)
insurance**

Difference in Conditions

A *difference in conditions (DIC) insurance* policy provides open-perils coverage to fill the gaps left by a policyowner's other commercial insurance policies. Traditionally, it was used to provide open-perils coverage to policy-owners whose basic policies provided named-perils protection. Even though open-perils coverage is now relatively common, a DIC policy is still used to provide earthquake and flood coverage. It is also used to cover loss exposures not in basic policies such as property in transit and the consequential losses that result from its damage or destruction. Another use is to provide coverage on overseas property that is broader than is available under the policies that can be purchased in many other countries. A DIC policy can be tailored to meet most of a policyowner's specific property insurance needs.

Instrumentalities of Transportation and Communication

Inland marine forms are used to insure instrumentalities of transportation and communication on either a named-perils or open-perils basis. These types of property include bridges, tunnels, pipelines, television towers, satellite dishes, and power lines.

Equipment Breakdown (Boiler and Machinery) Insurance

Commercial property and business income insurance forms exclude damage caused by steam boiler explosion, electrical breakdown, or mechanical breakdown. The Equipment Breakdown Protection Coverage Form provides insurance for these types of losses. Insurers that write this type of coverage provide extensive inspection and loss control services to prevent losses, and these insurance company inspections are often accepted by governmental organizations that require periodic inspections of boilers and certain types of machinery.

Equipment breakdown coverage (referred to as boiler and machinery coverage by some insurers) agrees to pay for direct damage to covered property as a result of a breakdown to covered equipment. *Covered equipment* includes (1) equipment built to operate under internal pressure or vacuum other than weight of contents, (2) electrical or mechanical equipment that is used in the generation, transmission, or utilization of energy, (3) communication equipment, (4) computer equipment, and (5) equipment of the types previously mentioned that is owned by a utility and used solely to provide utility services to the insured's premises. *Covered property* is not just the covered equipment but also includes any real or personal property that is (1) owned by the named insured or (2) in the named insured's care, custody, or control and for which the named insured is legally liable. A *breakdown* is a direct physical loss to covered equipment that necessitates its repair or replacement and arises from one of the following causes: (1) failure of pressure or vacuum equipment, (2) mechanical failure, including rupture or bursting caused by centrifugal force, or (3) electrical failure, including arcing.

This coverage also agrees to pay the reasonable costs of temporary repairs and expediting repairs or the cost of permanent replacement of damaged property. Equipment breakdown insurance can also provide business income and extra expense coverage as well as coverage for spoilage to raw materials, property in process, or finished products if the spoilage is caused by the lack or excess of power, light, heat, steam, or refrigeration that results from a breakdown to covered equipment.

Farm Insurance

As mentioned in chapter 17, homeowners-type policies are available for small- and medium-size farm operations. Large farms and commercially owned farms are more likely to be insured under commercial forms. In many ways, these forms are similar to other commercial insurance forms except that they are modified to meet farmers' unique loss exposures. Property forms can be written on either a named-perils or open-perils basis for various types of farm property, including livestock. An endorsement is available to cover loss of farm income if real or personal farm property is damaged or destroyed by an insured peril. A farm owner's home and personal property can also be insured under these forms.

A form to cover farmers' liability loss exposures essentially combines commercial general liability insurance, homeowners liability insurance for the farm owner's personal needs, and other insurance coverages unique to farming operations.

A special need of many farm owners is insurance on crops. Insurers offer crop hail insurance, which covers losses due to hail and can sometimes be endorsed to cover additional perils such as windstorm or damage by livestock. These policies may also cover crops while being transported to places of storage. Broader crop insurance is written through the Federal Crop Insurance Corporation, and the federal government subsidizes the cost of this coverage. It provides insurance if a farmer's production of a crop is substantially less than expected for almost any reason, including drought, excessive moisture, and bad weather.

Another special need for some farmers is animal mortality insurance. This is essentially term life insurance and is used for animals such as valuable horses, registered cattle, or breeding stock. This type of coverage can also be purchased on racehorses, circus animals, show cats and dogs, and laboratory animals. These animals are generally covered for death from almost any cause as well as theft.

Commercial General Liability Insurance

Commercial general liability (CGL) insurance is designed to cover a wide variety of liability loss exposures that can face an organization, including

- premises liability. An owner or tenant can be liable if someone is injured or property is damaged because of a condition in or arising out of premises that are owned or occupied.
- business operations liability. A business can be liable if bodily injury, personal injury, or property damage results from the activities of the business owner or an employee. These activities can take place on or away from the business location.
- products liability. Legal liability often arises from bodily injury or property damage caused by a defective product that is manufactured or sold by a business.
- completed operations liability. Similarly, legal liability can arise out of work that has been performed. For example, a fire can start as a result of an improperly installed gas line.
- contractual liability. In many cases, a business, through written or oral contracts, assumes liability for the acts of others.
- contingent liability. This is liability that a business can face because of work performed by independent contractors such as a subcontractor hired by a firm.

CGL forms do not cover all types of business liability. Because of exclusions in policy forms, there is little or no coverage for (1) liability for injury to employees, (2) liability that arises from the rendering or failure to render professional services, or (3) liability that arises from aircraft, auto, or watercraft. Coverage that is available for several of these loss exposures is discussed later in this chapter.

The CGL Coverage Form has three coverages:

- Coverage A—Bodily Injury and Property Damage Liability
- Coverage B—Personal and Advertising Injury Liability
- Coverage C—Medical Payments

Coverage A—Bodily Injury and Property Damage Liability

Coverage A applies to legal liability and defense costs that arise from bodily injury and property damage.

This coverage, therefore, does not apply to claims for damages based on libel, slander, or other personal injury offenses; errors; omissions; or wrongful acts that do not result in bodily injury or property damage, as these terms are defined in the policy. Coverage A of the CGL does not specifically exclude such losses, because it does not cover them in the first place. Personal injury is covered by Coverage B, and directors and officers liability insurance and other professional liability policies provide for other liability coverage needs not met by a CGL.

Exclusions in the policy preclude coverage for losses that can be covered by workers' compensation and employers liability, aircraft, auto, and watercraft insurance. Policyowners must also be aware of other significant exclusions, including those briefly summarized as follows:

- bodily injury or property damage that is expected or intended from the insured's standpoint except when it results from reasonable force to protect persons or property
- certain contractual assumptions of liability. These include contractual assumptions made after bodily injury or property damage has occurred; some contracts with railroads; and some contracts with architects, engineers, and surveyors that involve their errors and omissions in performing professional duties.
- liquor liability of insureds who are in the business of manufacturing, distributing, selling, serving, or furnishing alcoholic beverages. Liquor liability arises from (1) causing or contributing to the intoxication of a person, (2) furnishing alcoholic beverages to underage persons, and (3) statutes pertaining to the sale, gift, distribution, or use of alcoholic beverages. Because this exclusion applies to those in the beverage business, it does not preclude so-called host liability coverage for other businesses that occasionally host a party or event where beverages are served. Firms in the beverage business need liquor liability coverage to protect against this significant loss exposure.
- pollution. The CGL Coverage Form excludes coverage for most pollution liability, including clean-up costs that arise from pollution. Endorsements and other forms can sometimes be used to cover this loss exposure.
- property damage to certain classes of property, including
  - property owned, rented, or occupied by the named insured
  - property loaned to the named insured
  - personal property in the care, custody, or control of the insured
  - premises that have been sold, given away, or abandoned, except property built by the named insured for sale and never occupied, rented, or held for rental
  - the part of real property being worked on by the named insured or a subcontractor if the damage arises from the work

- the part of any property that must be restored, repaired, or replaced because the named insured's work was incorrectly performed on it

   The first three items can be insured under property and inland marine forms.

- damage to the insured's product that arises out of the product. For example, if a generator that the insured sold explodes, the cost to replace it would not be covered, but any damage to other property is covered.

- damage to the insured's work. For example, if the named insured repaired a generator, there would be no coverage for damage to the insured's work if the completed work led to an explosion. However, liability coverage would exist for damage to other property as a result of the explosion.

- damage to impaired property or property not physically injured. This exclusion eliminates coverage to property that has not been physically damaged because of the insured's defective product, poor workmanship, or failure to perform a contractual agreement. For example, if a building cannot be occupied because the electrical work the named insured performed does not meet building code specifications, there is no physical damage to the building, but its owner can suffer a significant loss before the faulty work is corrected.

- product recall. Products are sometimes recalled voluntarily or because of government action. Claims for damages that arise from such actions are excluded. In addition, the manufacturer or distributor of the product can incur significant recall expenses. These loss exposures can be insured through specialty insurers.

- employment-related practices. Most insurers now exclude employment-related practices from CGL coverage. These practices include wrongful termination, discrimination, and sexual harassment. Because coverage is also often limited under other types of liability policies, many employers purchase separate employment practices liability insurance for these loss exposures.

- professional liability. The CGL Coverage Form does not provide coverage for employees for liability that arises out of their providing or failing to provide professional health care services. In addition, insurers frequently exclude the professional liability of certain classes of business by adding an endorsement. Professional liability is discussed in a later section of this chapter.

- liability for damages realized from the loss, or loss of use, of electronic data

Coverage B—Personal and Advertising Injury Liability

Coverage B provides protection for personal injury liability, which has been discussed in earlier chapters. However, the CGL also covers advertising injury liability. Advertising injury can arise out of the following:

- oral or written publication of material that slanders or libels a person or organization or disparages its goods, products, or services
- oral or written publication of material that violates a person's right of privacy
- the use of another's advertising idea in an advertisement
- infringement upon another's copyright, trade dress, or slogan in an advertisement

Among the Coverage B exclusions are liability that arises out of (1) publication of material if the insured knows it is false, (2) willful violation of a penal statute or ordinance, (3) the failure of goods, products, or services to conform with advertised quality or performance, and (4) the wrongful description of the price of goods, products, or services.

Coverage C—Medical Payments

Coverage C is similar to the medical payments coverage of a homeowners policy. It pays medical expenses for bodily injury to persons injured on premises that the named insured owns or rents and because of the named insured's operations.

The coverage does not apply to the following persons:

- any insured other than a volunteer worker
- anyone hired to do work for or on behalf of any insured or a tenant of any insured
- a person injured on that part of a premises that the person normally occupies
- a person entitled to collect workers' compensation or disability benefits for the injury
- a person injured while taking part in athletics

Who Is an Insured?

Several categories of persons are insureds under the CGL Coverage Form: (1) the named insured and others with a family or business relationship to the named insured, (2) employees of the named insured, and (3) certain other persons or organizations.

Policy Provisions

Three specific policy provisions will be mentioned. These pertain to coverage territory, the events that trigger coverage, and policy limits.

Coverage Territory. Claims under the CGL Coverage Form are covered only if they take place in the coverage territory. For most claims, this includes the United States, its territories or possessions, Puerto Rico, and Canada. There is also coverage in international waters or airspace as long as travel is between the above locations. In addition, coverage is worldwide for products made or sold in the previously mentioned locations, for activities of persons who are away from these locations for short periods of time on business trips, and for personal and advertising injury offenses that take place through the Internet or similar electronic means of communication. Firms with broader business territories need to arrange appropriate coverage.

Events That Trigger Coverage. The more commonly used CGL Coverage Form is written on an occurrence basis. This means that a liability claim is covered only for injury or property damage that occurs during the policy period. In other words, the policy that responds to a claim is the one that is in effect when the injury or property damage occurs, even if a claim is made several years later.

The other CGL Coverage Form is written on a claims-made basis. This means that the policy that responds to a claim is the one in force when a claim is made, not the policy in force when the injury or property damage occurred.

The distinction between these two types of triggering events is discussed further in the section on professional liability insurance, for which claims-made coverage is more common.

CGL Coverage Forms

- Occurrence basis: Coverage applies to bodily injury or property damage that occurs during the policy period, regardless of when claims for damages are made.
- Claims-made basis: Coverage applies to claims made while the policy is in force, even when the loss-causing events occur earlier.

Limits of Liability. The CGL Coverage Form has several different limits of liability. Note that defense costs are payable in addition to these limits.

There are two aggregate limits that apply for an annual policy period. Once they are exceeded, the insurer has no further obligations to pay or defend claims. However, the limits are reinstated when a policy is renewed. One of these limits applies to claims that arise out of products or completed operations. The other is a general aggregate limit that applies to all other amounts paid under Coverages A, B, and C.

There are several sublimits. One of these applies to each occurrence for the sum of amounts paid under Coverage A and Coverage B. Another limit applies to personal and advertising liability claims by any one person or organization.

Finally, a Coverage C limit applies to medical payments for any one person during a year, and another limit applies to any damage to a premises that a business rents or temporarily occupies.

Commercial Auto Insurance

Three types of commercial auto policies are as follows:

- Business Auto Coverage Form
- Garage Coverage Form
- Motor Carrier Coverage Form

Business Auto Form

The Business Auto Coverage (BAC) Form provides the most common type of commercial auto insurance and is similar to the Personal Auto Policy with respect to the coverages that can be purchased.

Coverages. Available coverages include liability, medical payments, no-fault benefits, uninsured motorists, underinsured motorists, collision, comprehensive, specified causes of loss, and towing and labor. Comprehensive is equivalent to the personal auto policy's other-than-collision coverage. Specified-causes-of-loss coverage is a more limited named-perils alternative to comprehensive coverage.

The definition of *auto* is very broad and includes any land motor vehicle, trailer, or semitrailer—except mobile equipment—designed for use on public roads.

Covered Auto. Nine classifications of auto can be insured under the BAC Form, and different classifications of auto can be insured for each type of coverage. For example, one classification of auto might be insured for liability, while a different classification might be insured for collision. The nine classifications each have a symbol (numbers 1–9) that is entered in the declarations section of the form by the appropriate coverage. The nine classifications are

- symbol 1—any auto
- symbol 2—owned autos only
- symbol 3—owned private passenger autos only
- symbol 4—owned autos other than private passenger autos
- symbol 5—owned autos subject to no-fault
- symbol 6—owned autos subject to compulsory uninsured motorists law
- symbol 7—specifically designated autos
- symbol 8—hired autos only
- symbol 9—nonowned autos only

A *nonowned auto* is an auto owned by a named insured's employee or a member of his or her household but only while used in the named insured's business or personal affairs. A *hired auto* is an auto, other than a nonowned auto, that is leased, hired, rented, or borrowed by the named insured. Many businesses own no auto but have a loss exposure from accidents that involve nonowned and hired autos.

Temporary substitute autos, other than ones owned by the named insured, are also covered for liability coverage if the autos are used in place of a covered auto because of its breakdown, repair, servicing, loss, or destruction.

Who Is an Insured? The definition of insured includes the named insured, most other persons driving owned autos, and persons or organizations liable because of the acts or omissions of any of the previously mentioned persons. Although the business would have coverage, partners of a partnership, members of a limited liability company, and employees are not insured with respect to an auto owned by that person or a member of his or her household.

Exclusions. Several exclusions in the BAC Form exclude situations that are covered under workers' compensation and employers liability insurance and the CGL Coverage Form. There is no coverage for property that is owned by or is in the care, custody, or control of an insured. However, this property can be insured under the appropriate property and inland marine forms. Claims that arise from pollutants carried by covered autos are also excluded, but separate coverage is available.

Limit of Liability. Liability coverage under the BAC Form is a single limit of insurance that applies to all bodily injury, property damage, and covered pollution costs or expenses that arise from a single accident, and there is no aggregate annual limit. Defense costs are paid in addition to this limit. Split liability limits can be added by endorsement.

Losses for physical damage are limited to the lesser of (1) the actual cash value of the property at the time of loss or (2) the cost of repairing the property with other property of like kind and quality.

Other Commercial Auto Forms

Other commercial auto forms are designed for specific types of businesses.

Garage Coverage Form. The Garage Coverage Form is designed to meet the special needs of auto dealers. It is more than just an auto policy because it also provides liability coverage comparable to what is available under the CGL. It also provides an option for insuring the dealer's autos.

Motor Carrier Coverage Form. The Motor Carrier Coverage Form is designed for businesses that provide transportation by vehicles in the furtherance of commercial enterprise. These include common carriers, contract carriers, and private carriers who transport their own property. The coverage is similar to the BAC Form with modification for motor carriers' unique needs.

Workers' Compensation and Employers Liability Insurance

An employer faces a significant loss exposure for liability that arises from employees' injuries or deaths—either under tort law or because of government statutes. Coverage for this loss exposure is largely excluded under other liability policies and is usually insured under a Workers Compensation and Employers Liability (WC&EL) Insurance Policy. The National Council on Compensation Insurance developed the policy form used in a majority of states.

Some employers operate in states where a monopolistic state fund is the only insurer providing workers' compensation benefits. These employers may still need employers liability insurance, and a variation known as stopgap coverage is available to address this need. Other employers do not purchase workers' compensation insurance because they are large enough to self-fund workers' compensation benefits.

The WC&EL Policy contains three insuring agreements:

- Part One—Workers Compensation Insurance
- Part Two—Employers Liability Insurance
- Part Three—Other States Insurance

Each part is discussed below. The order of the discussion switches the last two parts because Part Three pertains to workers' compensation insurance. Some common endorsements are also described.

Part One—Workers Compensation Insurance

workers' compensation insurance

The states to which Part One applies are listed in the policy declarations. The *workers' compensation insurance* coverage states that the insurer agrees to pay all compensation and benefits required of the insured by the workers' compensation law of any state listed. These benefits vary from state to state and were discussed in chapter 7. The insurer also agrees to pay any defense costs that arise out of a workers' compensation claim and certain other expenses the insured might incur as part of a claim.

The policy explains that the insured is responsible for any penalties under a workers' compensation law because of (1) willful misconduct, (2) illegal employment, (3) failure to comply with health and safety laws and regulations, and (4) discrimination against employees who file claims. If the insurer pays any of these penalties, the policyowner must reimburse the insurer.

The policy does not specify the benefits to be paid except by stating that it will pay what the workers' compensation law requires. If the policy and the law conflict, the policy agrees to conform to the law.

There is no specified dollar limit of liability for Part One. The policy will pay the state-mandated benefits to any and all employees who are injured and to the survivors of any who die.

Part Three—Other States Insurance

This part of the WC&EL Policy provides coverage when an employer expands operations to include other states listed in the policy declarations for which Part Three applies. In many cases, the declarations list all states except those with monopolistic state funds or in which the insurer is not licensed to do business. The policyowner must notify the insurer when operations begin in these states.

Part Two—Employers Liability Insurance

employers liability insurance

Part Two of the WC&EL Policy—*employers liability insurance*—is a traditional form of liability insurance that protects an employer when it is sued because of injuries to employees. These suits occasionally arise for various reasons, including the following:

- An injured employee is not covered under a workers' compensation law.
- A spouse or family member sues for loss of services because of an employee's injury or death.
- An employee sues the employer in a capacity other than as an employer. For example, an employee injured by a faulty product of the employer may be able to bring suit against the employer as a manufacturer rather than as an employer.

- A spouse or family member sues because of bodily injury as a consequence of the injury or death of an employee. For example, a husband may have a heart attack after learning that an enraged coworker has killed his wife.
- The manufacturer of a product that injures one of the employer's workers can be sued by the worker and, in turn, sue the employer for improper maintenance of the product. This is referred to as a *third-party-over suit.*

In the insuring agreement under Part Two, the insurer agrees to pay damages and defend the insured because of bodily injury by accident or disease to an employee. For bodily injury by accident, the policy that covers an injury is the one in effect when the injury occurs. For bodily injury by disease, it is the policy that is in effect on the employee's last day of last exposure to the conditions causing or aggravating the injury.

The Part Two coverage contains three limits of liability, all of which the policyowner can select. One limit of liability applies to bodily injury by accident and is the maximum amount that will be paid for any one accident, regardless of how many employees are injured. There is no annual limit for bodily injury by accident. Two limits of liability apply to bodily injury by disease. One is per employee, and the other is an aggregate limit for the policy period.

Part Two contains several exclusions. Some exclusions eliminate coverage for claims that arise out of state workers' compensation laws and various federal acts. Workers' compensation claims are covered under Part One and endorsements, as described later, can be used to cover liability imposed by federal acts.

There is no coverage outside the United States, its territories or possessions, and Canada except for employees temporarily working in these locations.

Other exclusions eliminate coverage for

- most contractual liability. However, contractual liability is largely covered under the CGL Coverage Form.
- punitive damages for injury or death of illegally employed persons
- bodily injury to employees employed in violation of the law and with the knowledge of the insured or any executive officer
- damages that arise out of employment practices. As discussed later, this can be insured elsewhere.
- fines or penalties imposed for violation of federal or state law

Endorsements

Several endorsements are available to broaden the coverage of the WC&EL Policy.

The Voluntary Compensation and Employers Liability Coverage Endorsement obligates the insurance company to pay an amount equal to what is available under a state's workers' compensation law to employees who are not covered under the law. If an injured employee who is entitled to benefits brings suit, the coverage the endorsement provides reverts to the employer's liability coverage. A few insurers sell an additional endorsement to provide benefits for United States citizens hired to work abroad for indefinite periods. The benefits paid are those of the specific act or state listed in the endorsement.

Several federal acts either require the payment of workers' compensation benefits to certain groups of employees or allow certain groups of employees to sue employers, regardless of state limitations on employee suits. Endorsements are available for employees with loss exposures that might arise out of the following acts:

- United States Longshore and Harbor Workers Compensation Act (for most maritime workers other crew members of vessels)
- Jones Act (for crew members of vessels)
- Defense Base Act (for civilian employees working at foreign military bases or working abroad for agencies of the United States government)
- Outer Continental Shelf Lands Act (for workers engaged in exploration of natural resources)
- Nonappropriated Fund Instrumentalities Act (for civilian employees of certain operations on military facilities)
- Migrant and Seasonal Agricultural Worker Protection Act
- Federal Employers' Liability Act (for employees of interstate railroads)

Professional Liability Insurance

professional liability insurance

Professional liability insurance can best be defined as insurance to protect against liability for the failure to use the degree of skill expected of a person in a particular occupation. Although the terms tend to be used interchangeably, professional liability insurance is often referred to as *malpractice insurance* for those occupations in which professional liability is likely to result from bodily injury and *errors and omissions insurance* for other occupations.

Several other types of insurance are also categorized as professional liability. These are directors and officers liability insurance, employment practices liability insurance, employee benefits liability insurance, and fiduciary liability insurance.

Policies for Various Occupations

Professional liability policies have been developed for many occupations. For some occupations, several insurers write coverage; for other occupations, the number of insurers in the market may be only one or a small number. Businesses and employees both need protection against liability claims; in some cases, the business policy also covers employees. For example, a stockbrokerage firm might have a policy that covers it as well as the representatives it employs. In other cases, however, the employee may need to obtain his or her own coverage. Although coverage is often obtained directly through an insurance agent, professional associations are frequently a source of group coverage or plans of mass-marketed individual insurance.

Although ISO has developed standard policies for some occupations, individual insurers develop many professional liability policies. Policy variations exist among professions and insurers and should be evaluated with respect to limits, covered acts, defense coverage, coverage triggers, exclusions, and coverage territory.

Covered Acts. Professional liability policies differ in the exact wording of their insuring agreements. At a minimum, they cover acts, errors, or omissions that arise out of the rendering of professional services. For many professions, they also cover claims that result from the failure to render appropriate services.

Professional liability policies are not designed to cover routine business activities, such as the maintenance of an office premises, and they do not eliminate the need for a CGL or auto policy to cover the many business activities that do not involve professional services.

Defense Coverage. Professional liability policies cover defense costs. Some policies provide this benefit in addition to the stated policy limits, but most policies include these costs as part of the policy limits. In most policies, the insurer agrees to conduct the defense and has the right to appoint the defense attorney.

Most insurers now reserve the right to defend and settle claims as they see fit, but some policies still require the insurer to obtain the insured's consent before a claim is settled. If the insured does not consent to a settlement that has been recommended by the insurance company, many insurers limit policy benefits to the amount for which the claim could have been settled.

Coverage Triggers. Most professional liability policies are written on a claims-made basis. This means that the policy in force when a claim is made is the policy that covers the claim, not the policy in force when the event that caused the claim occurred. As long as a series of policies remains in force, the professional continues to have coverage for prior acts.

A series of claims-made professional liability policies typically ceases to pay claims if coverage is no longer carried unless the last policy contains an extended reporting period. In most policies, the extended reporting period is not automatic but must be requested and paid for. Some insurers make extended periods of only one to 3 years available, but others offer an unlimited extended period. The latter is of particular importance to someone, such as a retired obstetrician, who might be sued for a birth defect many years after a child is delivered.

Some insurers make extended reporting periods available if either the insurer or the policyowner terminates a policy. Other insurers make coverage available only if the insurer terminates the policy by cancellation or nonrenewal.

A few professional liability policies consider claims to have been made during the policy period as long as the insured, during the policy period, reports any circumstances of an event that might result in a future claim.

Significant gaps in coverage can occur if a policyowner switches from a policy written on a claims-made basis to one written on an occurrence basis and vice versa. Policyowners should make these changes with care and should obtain proper endorsements to eliminate any gaps.

Exclusions. Professional liability policies commonly exclude dishonest, criminal, or malicious acts; contractual liability; and punitive damages. Policies that cover errors and omissions also typically exclude bodily injury and damage to tangible property—which usually are, or should be, covered by a CGL.

Other exclusions may apply to a particular occupation's professional liability insurance.

Coverage Territory. Some professional liability policies cover claims that occur from activities anywhere in the world. Suits may or may not have to be brought in the United States or Canada. Other policies are written for a more restrictive territory such as the United States and Canada.

Directors and Officers Liability Insurance

Clients who sit on a corporation's board of directors or a nonprofit organization's board of trustees sometimes do not realize that they face serious liability exposures. In recent years, especially in light of various corporate scandals, individual board members have increasingly been held accountable for their actions or inactions. Stockholders frequently bring suits alleging that they have been financially harmed by the corporation's negligent management. Other suits are brought against directors and officers by a corporation's employees, customers, and clients. Clients who are aware of these exposures—and their financial planners can help make them aware—are usually unwilling to take the risk of serving on corporate boards unless the corporation protects them against such suits.

directors and officers (D&O) liability insurance

Recognizing that corporate directors and officers face a severe liability exposure directly resulting from their service to the corporation, these corporations usually agree to indemnify their directors and officers for any costs that result from suits against them. Some state laws even require such indemnification.

Directors and officers (D&O) liability insurance is purchased by a corporation, but the corporation (unless it is a nonprofit organization) is often only the policyowner and not an insured; the insureds are the directors and officers.

D&O policies contain at least two insuring agreements. The first agreement covers the directors and officers for their personal liability as directors and officers that results from alleged wrongful acts such as any breach of duty, neglect, errors, misstatements, misleading statements, omissions, and other acts. However, benefits provided under this coverage are usually not paid to the extent that the corporation has indemnified an officer or director.

The second insuring agreement reimburses the policyowner for any sum that it is required or permitted by law to pay to the directors and officers as indemnification.

Some D&O policies have a third insuring agreement that covers the corporation for its liability arising from the acts of officers and directors.

D&O policies commonly exclude coverage for situations that are covered under a firm's other liability policies such as bodily injury or damage to tangible property. Other exclusions often include claims because of

- fraudulent acts
- acts that result in personal gain to which a director or officer is not entitled
- violations of certain securities laws
- failure to maintain adequate insurance for the corporation
- suits that involve one director or officer against another (with some exceptions)
- service on boards not affiliated with the corporation, but this coverage can be obtained if the corporation wants to encourage such service

Because of the high cost of D&O suits, defense costs are often subject to policy limits. In addition, D&O policies may have both an initial deductible and a percentage of participation above the deductible amount. For example, the insured (or the corporation) may be responsible for the first $25,000 of any claim and 5 percent of any remaining amount.

Employment Practices Liability Insurance

employment practices liability insurance

As previously mentioned, coverage for employment-related claims is often excluded under CGL policies. *Employment practices liability insurance* can cover these claims.

An employment practices liability policy covers only those employment practices specified in the policy. These can include discrimination, sexual harassment, wrongful termination, breach of employment contract, failure to employ or promote, and wrongful discipline.

The insured is usually the business, its officers and directors, and some or all of its employees and former employees. Like the D&O policy, there may be both a deductible and percentage participation above the deductible.

Employee Benefits Liability Insurance

employee benefits liability insurance

Employee benefits liability insurance covers claims that arise out of improper advice or other errors or omissions in the administration of employee benefit plans. The insured is usually the business, its directors and stockholders, and officers and directors who are authorized to administer a plan. There is usually a per employee policy limit as well as an aggregate limit for the policy period. Most policies have a deductible. The coverage is typically provided as an endorsement to the CGL policy for little extra premium.

Fiduciary Liability Insurance

fiduciary liability insurance

Fiduciary liability insurance arises from offering employee benefit plans, but it involves claims that result from the breach of fiduciary duties such as pension plan losses because of improper investments. In some cases, employee benefits liability coverage is incorporated into a fiduciary liability policy. Some policies cover all breaches of duties; other policies cover only breaches of duties imposed by ERISA. The insureds usually consist of the employer that sponsors a benefit plan; the plan itself; and past, present, and future directors, officers, and employees in their plan capacities as fiduciaries, administrators, or trustees.

Excess and Umbrella Liability Insurance

The need for individuals to have additional liability insurance coverage under a personal umbrella policy was discussed in chapter 18. This same need exists for businesses. Careful analysis is necessary to determine the appropriate policy in order to avoid unintentional gaps in coverage for at least three reasons. First, the insured has a choice between an excess policy and an umbrella policy. Second, the underlying commercial policies are likely to be less uniform than the underlying personal policies. Third, commercial excess and umbrella policies are not standardized, and each insurer that writes coverage has its own form. As a result, significant variations exist.

The following discussion briefly describes excess liability insurance and then goes into more detail on commercial umbrella liability policies.

Excess Liability Insurance

excess liability
insurance

An *excess liability insurance* policy is written to provide additional liability limits for claims that are covered under specified underlying coverages. There is no drop-down coverage for claims excluded by the underlying coverages. Excess liability insurance is often used to obtain larger limits for loss exposures such as directors and officers liability when a firm's umbrella policy does not cover that particular loss exposure.

There are two basic types of excess liability policies, and a policy can combine these two approaches. Under the first approach—referred to as a *follow form*—the excess policy incorporates the policy provisions and conditions of the underlying policies. Therefore, there are always additional limits available if a claim is covered by the underlying insurance. Under the second approach—referred to as a *self-contained policy*—the excess policy is subject to its own provisions and conditions. This can result in coverage gaps because a claim is paid by the excess policy only if it is covered under the provisions of both the underlying policies *and* the excess policy.

Some excess policies combine these two approaches by incorporating the provisions and conditions of the underlying policies and then making modifications for certain situations.

Commercial Umbrella Liability Insurance

Commercial umbrella policies operate much like the personal umbrella policies discussed in chapter 18. Unlike follow form excess policies, there is often coverage for claims that are excluded by the underlying policies. However, each insurer that sells commercial umbrella policies usually uses its own form, and differences exist. Therefore, it is important to look at several policy provisions, including required underlying limits, insuring agreements, policy limits, events that trigger coverage, exclusions, and coverage territory. Adding to the complexity that can result from analyzing these variations is the terminology insurers use. For example, some insurers that sell umbrella policies refer to them as excess policies.

Required Underlying Limits. The following are typical of required underlying limits:

- CGL
  - $1 million each occurrence
  - $2 million general aggregate
  - $2 million completed operations aggregate
- Business Auto Liability—$1 million single limit
- Employers Liability

- $100,000 bodily injury each accident
- $100,000 bodily injury by disease each employee
- $500,000 disease aggregate

Depending on the insurer, the type of policyowner, and the breadth of the umbrella policy, other underlying limits may be required for loss exposures such as liquor liability, watercraft, and aircraft.

The self-insured retention for claims the underlying policies do not cover may be as low as $500 for small businesses or as high as $25,000 or more for large businesses.

Insuring Agreements. Umbrella policies often have a single insuring agreement that applies to all covered losses. For example, an insurer can agree to pay up to $10 million for any claim in excess of the underlying limits for which the insured is liable for bodily injury, property damage, personal injury, or advertising injury. A policy can have a broader insuring agreement or separate insuring agreements to pick up other specialized loss exposures, such as professional liability, if the insurer is willing to cover them.

Policy Limits. Policy limits are selected by the insured, subject to insurer standards, and can be many millions of dollars. Most policies now have an aggregate limit that applies for the policy period. Defense costs can be included in the policy limit or in addition to it.

Events That Trigger Coverage. Umbrella policies are usually written on an occurrence basis, but some underlying policies can have a claims-made trigger. This can result in coverage gaps. Some insurers write umbrella policies with both types of triggers in the same policy and use the same trigger that applies to a claim under the underlying coverages.

Exclusions. Although commercial umbrella policies provide broader coverage than the underlying policies, they contain exclusions, and it is important to evaluate these exclusions when obtaining coverage. In some cases, the exclusions are like those in the underlying policies such as intentional injury and damage to the insured's product and work. In other cases, exclusions in the underlying policies are omitted from the umbrella policy or made less restrictive. However, the exclusions in an umbrella policy can be more restrictive. For example, it is not unusual to see an exclusion for punitive damages even though they may be covered by the underlying policies.

Coverage Territory. Most umbrella policies provide worldwide coverage. However, some policies require that suits be brought in the United States, its territories or possessions, or Canada.

Surety Bonds

surety bond

Surety bonds are used in situations when an individual or organization wants a guarantee of indemnity if a second party fails to perform a specified act or fulfill an obligation. There are three parties to a surety bond:

- The *principal* is the party who buys the bond and agrees to perform certain acts or fulfill certain obligations.
- The *obligee* is the party who is reimbursed for damages because of the principal's failure to uphold the agreement.
- The *surety* is the party who agrees to indemnify the obligee for damages because of the principal's failure to uphold the agreement. This indemnity can be in the form of cash or the fulfillment of the principal's obligation. The surety can be any person or organization but is usually an insurance company.

Parties to a Surety Bond

- Principal: the one obligated to perform
- Obligee: the one for whom the principal is obligated to perform
- Surety: the one who compensates the obligee for the principal's failure to perform

---

Characteristics of Surety Bonds

Surety bonds have several unique characteristics. These pertain to the liability of the principal, the expected losses, the coverage period, the bond limit, and the statutory nature of some bonds.

Liability of the Principal. Unlike an insured under an insurance contract, a principal who defaults on a bond is liable to the surety to the extent of any expenditure the surety incurs. The surety can require the principal to post collateral to repay the surety if the principal defaults.

Expected Losses. A surety generally expects to pay few losses and underwrites in a strict manner to determine whether the principal is capable of meeting its obligations. The surety will carefully scrutinize the principal's financial resources, character, and ability to perform.

Coverage Period. The coverage period under most surety bonds is indefinite, and the premium for the bond is paid only once. In most cases, neither the surety nor the principal can cancel the bonds.

Bond Limit. A surety bond is written for a dollar limit, and that is the maximum amount of the surety's obligation to the obligee. Some bonds, however, pay court costs and interest on judgments in addition to the bond.

Most surety bonds pay only the obligee's actual loss if it is less than the bond limit, but some bonds are written on a basis that requires the forfeiture of the entire bond limit if the principal defaults.

Statutory versus Nonstatutory Bonds. Governmental ordinances, regulations, or statutes require many bonds, and the provisions of these statutory bonds and the obligations of the parties are established by law. The obligations of the parties under nonstatutory bonds are established by contract between the obligee and the principal.

Types of Surety Bonds

There are several categories of surety bonds, and each is briefly described below.

Contract Bonds. Contract bonds guarantee that the principal will fulfill a commitment according to the provision of a contract. They are most often required of contractors and suppliers.

License and Permit Bonds. State and local governments often require persons who engage in many types of occupations to obtain licenses. They also frequently require permits for various types of activities. Various bonds are often required in connection with these licenses and permits. For example, a license or permit bond might guarantee that the principal will pay required taxes, including remittance of sales taxes collected, or that the principal will provide a means of indemnity for persons injured by its activities.

Public Official Bonds. Statutes often require that persons who are elected or appointed to certain positions be bonded. These bonds guarantee that the principal will uphold the promise made to faithfully and honestly perform the official duties of his or her office. These bonds terminate when a successor takes office.

Judicial Bonds. Numerous bonds are required by courts, and these can be divided into three broad categories—fiduciary bonds, litigation bonds, and bail bonds.

Fiduciary bonds are often required of persons who act as administrators, trustees, and guardians. They guarantee that a person who is responsible for the property of another will faithfully exercise his or her duties, give proper accounting of any property received, and make proper indemnification if the court determines that the principal is responsible for any financial loss that relates to the property.

The purpose of litigation bonds, also referred to as court bonds, is to require a person or organization that is seeking a court remedy to protect other parties from damages if the party seeking the remedy does not prevail.

There are also bonds required in many other legal activities, some of which are garnishment of wages, seizure of a tenant's personal property for back rent, suits to recover property, and removal of mechanic's liens and injunctions.

Finally, a bail bond guarantees that the bonded person will appear in court at the appointed time. Failure to do so can result in the forfeiture of the entire bail amount.

Federal Surety Bonds. Many federal agencies require businesses they regulate to carry bonds. These bonds guarantee that the business will comply with federal standards, including the payment of taxes and duties.

Credit Enhancement Insurance. Also referred to as financial guarantee insurance, this coverage is actually a form of surety bond that guarantees that principal and interest will be paid to the purchasers of debt instruments. The issuer of the debt, such as a municipality or a corporation, purchases the bond to enhance its audit rating.

There has been concern by regulators over the highly catastrophic nature of losses that could occur in case of a major economic downturn, and many states limit the writing of such bonds to specialty companies that are specifically licensed for this type of business.

Miscellaneous Bonds. Numerous other types of bonds do not fit into the previous categories. For example, an employer that self-insures its workers' compensation exposure will need to post a bond to guarantee that statutory benefits will be paid to employees.

Issuers of securities are often required to post a lost instrument bond to replace securities or other valuable papers that have been lost or stolen. The bond guarantees that the principal will reimburse the issuer if the original securities turn up and their holder is able to collect on them.

BUSINESSOWNERS POLICIES

businessowners policy (BPO)

A *businessowners policy* (BOP) is designed to provide property and liability coverage for small- to medium-sized businesses and organizations that meet certain eligibility requirements. A BOP resembles a homeowners policy in the sense that it includes a package of coverages designed to meet most of a typical policyowner's needs. Because it presents a prepackaged set of coverages, a BOP often includes some coverages that might otherwise be overlooked. Where it meets a client's needs, a BOP is usually more convenient and less expensive than purchasing each coverage individually in a commercial package policy.

Despite its breadth, a BOP usually is not the only insurance policy a small business needs. A business with employees generally also needs workers' compensation insurance. A business that owns one or more motor vehicles requires a business auto insurance policy.

ISO has developed a BOP form, but the ISO form does not dominate the market. Many insurers use their own forms, which may be broader or more restrictive than the ISO form. Therefore, rather than specifically examining the ISO form, the discussion here deals with BOPs in general.

Eligibility

BOPs are intended for small- to-medium-sized standard main-street businesses with no unusual features. Every insurer has its own BOP eligibility rules, which typically permit a BOP to be written on the following businesses:

- *retail, wholesale, service, or processing buildings and personal property*. This category includes shoe stores, furniture clothing stores, and so forth subject to a maximum square foot area, typically 15,000 to 25,000 square feet. Not only owner-occupants but also landlords and tenants are typically eligible for a BOP.
- *office buildings*. Eligibility is usually restricted to buildings of a certain height, such as six stories, or a certain total floor area. Tenants occupying offices in a larger building may also be eligible.
- *apartment buildings*. Size restrictions limit eligibility to a certain height, such as six stories, or a certain number of apartments.
- *contractors*. Some insurers will write a BOP on smaller construction contractors that present no unusual risks.
- *restaurants*. BOPs are often available for fast-food restaurants.

Although many types of businesses can be eligible for coverage under a BOP, several are specifically ineligible. These businesses typically include garages, auto dealers, parking lots, bars, restaurants with extensive cooking operations, places of amusement, and banks.

Policy Coverages

The liability coverage of a BOP is essentially the same as that of the commercial general liability (CGL) policy discussed earlier in this chapter.

Most insurers offer a BOP policy that provides property coverage on an open-perils basis, and many also provide a named-perils version. The open-perils version, often referred to as a special-form policy, is by far the more popular. A typical BOP includes several standard features, described below, that differentiate it from the standard coverage a commercial property form provides.

Standard Replacement Cost Coverage

BOPs typically value both buildings and personal property on a replacement cost basis, often with an actual cash value option. In contrast, standard commercial property policies provide actual cash value coverage with a replacement cost option.

Insurance-to-Value Provision

In contrast to commercial property policies that generally include a coinsurance provision, BOPs were traditionally written with neither a coinsurance provision nor any other insurance-to-value provision. Many insurers still have no insurance-to-value provision, but ISO forms and others include a provision similar to the loss clause of the homeowners policy, as discussed in chapter 16. A policyowner who carries insurance to at least 80 percent of the replacement cost value of the property is entitled to have losses settled on a replacement cost basis. Recovery for those who are underinsured is limited to the actual cash value of the lost or damaged property or, for those who are only slightly underinsured, an amount somewhere between the actual cash value and the replacement cost value of the property as determined by applying the coinsurance formula.

Automatic Seasonal Increase Provision on Personal Property

Some BOPs include a provision that automatically adjusts the personal property coverage limit to allow for seasonal changes in inventory values that affect some businesses. If the policyowner carries insurance in an amount equal to at least 100 percent of the monthly average value of the property during the 12 months preceding the loss, the limit is automatically increased by 25 percent.

Example:	Bullina China Shop increases its dinnerware inventory twice a year in preparation for Christmas shopping and June weddings. Bullina's average inventory value over the past 12 months was $60,000, and other store contents are valued at $20,000. When a

windstorm swept through the shop on June 1 and destroyed the entire shop, Bullina's inventory was valued at $80,000. Bullina currently carries personal property coverage under a BOP with a $80,000 limit.

Bullina will recover $100,000—$80,000 for stock and $20,000 for other personal property—under its BOP, which includes the automatic seasonal increase provision.

Business Income and Extra Expense Coverage Automatically Included

Most BOPs automatically include business income and extra expense coverage subject to neither a dollar limit nor a coinsurance requirement. Most do impose a one-year time limit, agreeing to pay lost income and extra expenses during a period of interruption not exceeding 12 months.

Property Coverage Options

Many insurers offer some of the following coverage options under their BOP program, often with relatively low limits or with coverage more restrictive than that available under a commercial property form or in a separate policy. The following coverages may either be included automatically or available by endorsement:

- employee dishonesty
- money and securities
- forgery
- glass breakage
- outdoor signs
- mechanical breakdown
- money orders and counterfeit paper currency
- computer coverage
- accounts receivable coverage
- valuable papers and records coverage

Nonowned and Hired Auto Liability Coverage

Insurance on owned autos is not available in a BOP. However, a business whose only auto liability exposure involves the use of employee-owned autos or borrowed or rented vehicles can often protect itself against these incidental exposures by endorsing nonowned and hired cars liability coverage to a BOP.

MINI-CASE: ARTHUR EACHER

Arthur Eacher, a financial planner's client, recently retired from his college teaching position and opened an art gallery in a small rented main street storefront where he sells his own original paintings as well as those of other artists. He currently uses a room in back of the store to give private lessons to a few high school girls who were referred to him by their teacher, and he hopes to expand both his sales and teaching activities. Arthur has enough income from his 403(b) plan to support himself, and he has also accumulated $200,000 in personal assets, largely from his late wife's life insurance. He also used some additional savings to fund the startup costs of his gallery. Although he would not mind earning a profit on income from the gallery, Arthur's main goal is to keep busy doing what he enjoys. He also serves on the board of the well-endowed Brick Foundation, a nonprofit organization that provides college scholarship money to aspiring artists, and he conducts a summer tour of European art museums for high school students.

When Arthur opened his gallery, he purchased a businessowners policy from the insurance agent that handles his auto and homeowners insurance. Arthur chose a property insurance limit that would cover the estimated value of paintings, supplies, furniture, and fixtures, and a liability limit of $100,000. The agent did not suggest any additional coverages.

What concerns and recommendations might be made with respect to Arthur's insurance program?

(See answer section for answers to mini-case.)

SOURCES FOR FURTHER IN-DEPTH STUDY

- *The CPCU Handbook of Insurance Policies*, 5th ed., Malvern PA: American Institute for CPCU/Insurance Institute of America, 2003. Phone 800-644-2101. Web site address www.aicpcu.org
- *FC&S Bulletins*, Commercial Liability Volume and Commercial Property Volume, (loose-leaf and CD-ROM service updated monthly), Erlanger, KY: The National Underwriter Company, Phone 800-543-0874. Web site address www.nuco.com
- Malecki, Donald S., and Flitner, Arthur L., *Commercial Liability Risk Management and Insurance*, 5th ed., Malvern, PA: American Institute for CPCU/Insurance Institute of America, 2001. Phone 800-644-2101. Web site address www.aicpcu.org
- Trupin, Jerome, and Flitner, Arthur L., *Commercial Property Risk Management and Insurance*, 7th ed., Malvern, PA: American Institute for CPCU/Insurance Institute of America, 2003. Phone 800-644-2101. Web site address www.aicpcu.org

- Flitner, Arthur L., and Trupin, Jerome, *Commercial Insurance*, Malvern, PA: American Institute for CPCU/Insurance Institute of America, 2002. Phone 800-644-2101. Web site address www.aicpcu.org

CHAPTER REVIEW

Answers to mini-case, review questions, and self-test questions start on page 793.

Key Terms

commercial property insurance	employers liability insurance
business income insurance	professional liability insurance
extra expense insurance	directors and officers (D&O)
burglary	liability insurance
robbery	employment practices liability
theft	insurance
computer fraud	employee benefits liability
inland marine insurance	insurance
difference in conditions (DIC)	fiduciary liability insurance
insurance	excess liability insurance
commercial general liability	surety bond
(CGL) insurance	businessowners policy (BOP)
workers' compensation insurance	

Review Questions

19-1. A client has just purchased a building and started a small parts manufacturing business. Without getting into too much detail about the specifics of his business, you recommend that he see an insurance agent who specializes in commercial property and liability coverages. He replies, "I know I need insurance on the building, the equipment, and my inventory, but what other coverages do I need to see an agent about?" What important coverages might he need?

19-2. What are the three common types of business income insurance forms, and what coverage does each provide?

19-3. What are the three broad classes of property covered alone or in various combinations by commercial crime insurance forms?

19-4. Briefly explain the policy provisions common to many crime insurance forms.

19-5. Describe the situations in which inland marine policies and forms are used to provide coverage today.

19-6. Indicate what type of commercial liability coverage you should recommend to a client in each of the following situations:

a.   a client who may be sued if a defective product is manufactured or sold

b.   a client who is concerned about being sued by a person who is injured or whose property is damaged by the client's ongoing business activities at the person's home

c.   a client who is concerned about being sued by a customer who is injured or whose property is damaged because of a condition in the client's store (such as a wet floor)

d.   a client who is concerned about being sued by a person who is injured or whose property is damaged by work the client already performed

e.   a general contractor who is concerned about being sued for poor work done by a subcontractor

f.   a client who is concerned with having to pay a judgment against the railroad if the railroad is sued by the parents of a child who is injured while playing on the side track on the client's business property

g.   a client who is concerned about being held liable for the employees who drive her company's delivery trucks

h.   a client who is concerned about being sued by an injured employee not covered by the workers' compensation law, or by an employee's spouse or family member because of the employee's injury or death

i.   a dentist who is concerned about being sued by one of his patients

j.   an insurance agent who is concerned about being sued by a client for bad advice about the appropriate coverages to purchase

k.   a client who is concerned about members of the board of directors of her corporation being sued for breaches of corporate duty

l.   a client who is concerned about his business being sued for discrimination or sexual harassment

19-7.   What are the similarities and differences between excess liability insurance and commercial umbrella liability insurance?

19-8.   What are the unique characteristics of surety bonds?

19-9.   Describe the key features of the businessowners policies commonly available.

19-10.   After his retirement, Edwin agreed to serve on the boards of directors of a bank and a for-profit hospital. He also agreed to serve on the board of trustees of a local not-for-profit charity. As an afterthought, he asks you, as his financial planner, whether this service involves any special risks to consider in his planning. How would you respond?

Self-Test Questions

T   F   19-1.   Commercial property insurance can cover only buildings and business personal property of the insured.

T   F   19-2.   Commercial property insurance can be written on either a named-perils or open-perils basis.

T   F   19-3. Loss of income, continuing expenses, and extra expenses while a business is closed following a direct physical damage loss can be covered under business income insurance.

T   F   19-4. A client can purchase crime insurance to cover the client's business against losses due to employee theft as well as burglary and robbery.

T   F   19-5. Inland marine insurance provides coverage against a variety of losses, including those to domestic goods in transit by truck, customers' clothes at a dry cleaner, fine art, and television towers.

T   F   19-6. Although the commercial general liability coverage form excludes coverage for most liability from pollution, numerous endorsements and other forms can cover the pollution loss exposure.

T   F   19-7. A Commercial General Liability Coverage Form excludes coverage for advertising injury liability.

T   F   19-8. Most commonly, commercial general liability coverage is written on a claims-made basis.

T   F   19-9. The Commercial General Liability Coverage Form has two aggregate limits that apply for an annual policy period.

T   F   19-10. The most common type of commercial auto insurance is the Business Auto Coverage Form, which is similar to the personal auto policy with respect to the coverages that can be purchased.

T   F   19-11. Due to workers' compensation laws, employers are exempt from suits for injuries to employees.

T   F   19-12. Most professional liability policies are written on an occurrence basis.

T   F   19-13. Although a directors and officers (D&O) liability policy is purchased by a corporation, the insureds are generally the officers and directors and not the corporation.

T   F   19-14. Both excess liability policies and commercial umbrella policies include drop-down coverage for claims the underlying coverages exclude.

T   F   19-15. Surety bonds are three-party contracts in which a principal who defaults on a bond is liable to the surety to the extent of any expenditure the surety incurs.

T   F   19-16. A businessowners policy is designed for small- to medium-size businesses in the sense that it can meet most of the needs of an average policyowner.

a priori reasoning • reasoning with conclusions that are based on self-evident propositions (also known as *deductive reasoning)*. As an example, one can reason deductively, or *a priori*, that the probability of a result of tails in the flip of a balanced coin is one chance in two. *Compare* inductive reasoning

AAIS (American Association of Insurance Services) • an advisory organization that provides various services to its member companies, including the development and filing of standardized property and liability insurance forms

absolute liability • *See* strict liability

accelerated benefits provision • a provision in a life insurance policy that allows death benefits to be paid to the policyowner prior to the insured's death under certain circumstances such as if the insured is terminally ill

accidental death • a death that is caused by an unintentional event that is sudden and unexpected

accidental death benefits • a life insurance rider that increases the death benefit, usually doubling it, if the insured dies accidentally

accumulation period • the period of time in a deferred annuity during which the purchase price is deposited with the insurer and accumulated at interest

accumulation unit • a unit of a variable annuity that is purchased during the annuity's accumulation stage

actively-at-work requirement • a provision in a group insurance master contract specifying that the employee is not eligible for coverage if he or she is not actively on the job on the otherwise effective date of coverage. Coverage commences when the employee returns to work.

activities of daily living (ADLs) • activities such as eating, bathing, and dressing. The inability to perform a specified number of these activities triggers eligibility for benefits in a long-term care insurance contract.

actual cash value • a method of valuing property. Usually, it is defined as replacement cost minus depreciation but in some cases is defined as fair market value.

add-on plan • a no-fault type of auto insurance system that provides first-party benefits but does not restrict the right to sue for damages

additional living expenses • the extra costs of maintaining a family's standard of living while the family's residence is being repaired or rebuilt following a covered loss. Covered by homeowners policies.

adult day care • day care at centers specifically designed for the elderly who live at home but whose spouses or families cannot stay home to care for them during the day

advance-premium mutual • a mutual insurance company that collects the full premium for coverage at the start of the policy period

adverse selection • selection against the insurance company. It is the tendency for those who know that they are highly vulnerable to specific pure risks to be most likely to acquire and to retain insurance to cover related losses.

advertising injury liability • liability that can arise out of (1) oral or written publication of slanderous or libelous material or (2) material that violates a person's rights of privacy. It also includes liability that arises through the misappropriation of advertising ideas or styles of doing business and infringement of copyright, title, or slogan.

advisory organization • an organization that assists insurance companies in such areas as gathering and analyzing statistical information for rate-making purposes and drafting recommended policy language

age set back • an assumption for rating purposes that an annuitant is some years younger than his or her actual age

agent • a legal representative of an insurance company with authority to act on behalf of the insurer

agreed value • a method of valuing property in which value is determined before loss and the agreed value is paid in the event of a total loss

alien insurer • an insurer that is formed in a country other than the United States but that writes business in the United States

all-risks policy • *See* open-perils policy

alteration • the act of making changes to a document in a manner that is neither authorized nor originally intended

Alzheimer's facility • a facility with a high level of staffing and other capabilities to provide the personal assistance individuals with Alzheimer's disease need. It may be a stand-alone facility or part of a nursing home or assisted-living facility.

American Agency System • *See* independent agency system

annual exclusion • the amount of a gift exempt from federal transfer taxation. Currently, it is $11,000 annually for gifts to any one person. This can be increased to $22,000 if the donor is married and the donor's spouse elects to split the gift on a timely filed gift tax return.

annual transit policy • a type of inland marine insurance policy that covers all shipments during an annual period

annuitant • the person whose life governs the duration of benefit payments under a life annuity, usually also the person who received periodic annuity payments

annuity • a periodic payment to begin at a specified or contingent date and to continue for a fixed period or for the duration of a designated life or lives

annuity certain • an annuity with benefit payments that continue for a definite period of time without being linked to the duration of a specified human life

annuity principle • the concept of many persons pooling their funds to provide annuities to all while they live or for some period certain. Each person receives annuity payments consisting of the annuitants' principal, the unliquidated principal of other annuitants who die early, and investment income on these funds.

annuity unit • a measure for valuing a variable annuity during its liquidation stage. The dollar value of each unit fluctuates with the investment performance of the separate account underlying the annuity.

antigag clause rules • legislation that prevents managed care organizations from including provisions in contracts with doctors that prevent them from discussing with patients treatment options that may not be covered under their plans or from referring extremely ill patients for specialized care outside of their plans

any-occupation • a strict definition of disability that requires a person to be so severely disabled that he or she cannot engage in any occupation

apparent authority • authority that, in the absence of contrary action by the principal, appears to a reasonable person to be possessed by the principal's agent

applicant • the person or organization that applies for insurance

Archer MSA • an alternative to first-dollar coverage under a medical expense plan. An employee is given medical expense coverage that has a high deductible, and money is deposited into a medical savings account so that the employee can pay for expenses below the deductible amount. Any monies not used at the end of the year are paid to the employee. Being phased out and replaced with HSAs.

assessment mutual • a mutual company that reserves the right to levy assessments on its policyowners to cover adverse underwriting experience

assignment provision • a clause that specifies the conditions under which a policyowner can transfer some or all of his or her ownership rights in the policy to another

assisted-living care • care provided in facilities that provide care for the frail elderly who are no longer able to care for themselves but who do not need the level of care provided in a nursing home

assumption-of-risk doctrine • a common-law defense formerly available to employers under which a worker could not recover damages for an injury if he or she knowingly assumed the risks inherent in the job

attained-age rate • the insurance rate at the insured's present age, used for attained-age term conversions and sometimes for long-term care insurance upgrades

attitudinal hazard • a condition of carelessness or indifference on the part of an individual as to whether a loss occurs and/or the size of a loss if one does occur

attorney-in-fact • the individual who directs a reciprocal exchange

auto insurance • a property and liability insurance policy that provides (1) liability coverage for losses that arise out of the use, operation, or maintenance of an auto, (2) medical payments benefits, (3) uninsured motorists benefits, and (4) physical damage coverage to owned and certain nonowned vehicles

automatic premium loan option • life insurance policy provision by which a delinquent premium is automatically paid by a policy loan

automatic reinsurance • *See* treaty reinsurance

automobile insurance plan • a state plan that assigns drivers who have been unable to obtain auto insurance to insurance companies in proportion to their volume of business in a state. Formerly called *assigned risk*.

aviation insurance • insurance policies to provide liability, physical damage, and medical payments coverage for the owners of aircraft

backdating • issuance of a life insurance policy as if it had been purchased when the insured was younger in order to obtain a lower periodic premium

bail bond • a bond that guarantees that the bonded person will appear in court at the appointed time

bailee • a person or organization in temporary custody of the property of another for some reason such as for service or repair of the property

bailees customers policy • an insurance policy that covers customers' goods whether or not a bailee is liable for their loss or destruction

bailment • the situation in which a person or business has temporary custody of the property of others

bail-out provision • a clause in an annuity contract that allows the purchaser to surrender the contract without a surrender charge if the interest rate being credited falls below a specified but nonguaranteed minimum

bed reservation benefit • a benefit under a long-term care insurance policy that continues to pay a long-term care facility for a limited time if a patient must temporarily leave because of hospitalization. Without a continuation of benefits, the bed might be rented to someone else and unavailable upon the patient's release from the hospital.

beneficiary • the person or entity designated to receive the death proceeds of a life insurance policy

binder • a written or oral agreement between an agent and an applicant for insurance whereby the principal-insurer is committed to provide the desired insurance on a temporary basis

birthing center • a facility, separate from a hospital, designed to provide a homelike atmosphere for the delivery of babies. Deliveries are performed by nurse-midwives, and mothers and babies are released shortly after birth.

blackout period • the period during which no Social Security benefits are payable for a surviving spouse, extending from the time the youngest child reaches age 16 until the spouse is age 60

block policy • a property insurance policy designed to pick up the exposures of a dealer in such items as jewelry, cameras, fine art, musical equipment, furs, stamps, and coins. The policy covers inventory while at a fixed location or while being transported. There is also coverage for the furniture and fixtures of the dealer and property of others in the dealer's care, custody, or control.

Blue Cross and Blue Shield plans • organizations formed for the purpose of prepaying subscribers' medical care expenses. Blue Cross plans provide coverage primarily for hospital expenses, and Blue Shield plans provide coverage primarily for physicians' services.

boatowners policy • a package policy that provides liability and physical damage coverage for small- and medium-size boats

bodily injury • bodily harm, sickness, or disease. It includes required care, loss of services, and death that results.

boiler and machinery insurance • *See* equipment breakdown insurance

branch manager • an insurance company employee who heads up a branch office for marketing the insurer's products in a given geographic area

branch office system • in life insurance, a marketing system whereby insurers establish branch offices in the areas where they write business. The offices are headed by branch managers.

broker • a marketing intermediary between the insurer and policyowner who represents the policyowner

builders risk insurance • commercial property insurance that provides protection for buildings and construction and the unique exposures associated with these types of structures

burglary • the removal of property from inside a premises by a person who enters or leaves the premises unlawfully as evidenced by marks of forcible entry or exit

business income insurance • insurance that covers business losses after the occurrence of a direct physical damage loss that results in the suspension of business operations. The three basic types of losses covered include net income, normal ongoing business expenses, and extra expenses. Formerly called *business interruption insurance*.

business insurance • the category of insurance used by businesses and other organizations

business interruption insurance • *See* business income insurance

business operations liability • bodily injury, personal injury, or property damage liability that results from the activities of a business owner or employee

business overhead expense insurance • a policy available to cover many of the ongoing costs of operating a business while the business owner is totally disabled

businessowners policy (BOP) • a common type of policy designed to meet the property and liability needs of certain small- and medium-size businesses

buy-sell agreement • a contract binding the owner of a business interest to sell the business interest for a specified or determinable price at his or her death or disability and binding a designated purchaser to buy at that time

buy-up plan • an employee benefit plan under which a covered person can purchase additional coverage (for example, life insurance or disability income insurance) at his or her own expense. Also referred to as a *supplemental plan*

cafeteria plan • an employee benefit plan under which an employee can use a specified amount of employer funds and/or salary reductions to design his or her own benefit package from an array of available benefits

calendar-year deductible • a deductible that applies to medical expenses incurred within a calendar year. A new deductible must be satisfied in a subsequent calendar year.

cancelable • a contract feature that allows the insurance company to terminate the coverage at any time (and perhaps for any reason) during the term of coverage by notifying the insured

capital needs analysis • a system for determining how much life insurance a client needs if the principal sum is to be preserved in the process of meeting the financial objectives for his or her survivors

captive agent system • *See* exclusive agency system

captive insurer • an insurance company owned by a parent corporation and formed primarily to insure the loss exposures of the parent corporation

care coordinator • a licensed health care practitioner who assesses a person's condition, evaluates care options, and develops an individualized plan of care that provides the most appropriate services

carryover provision • a provision in a medical expense plan that allows any expenses applied to the deductible and incurred during the last 3 months of the year to also be applied to the deductible for the following year

carve-out (benefit plan) • the practice of excluding certain classes of employees from a benefit plan and providing benefits to them under an alternative arrangement. Carve-outs are generally used to contain employee costs or provide broader or tax-favored benefits to key employees and executives.

carve-out (medical expense insurance) • coverage under a medical expense plan that has been singled out for individual management by a party other than the employer or the employee's primary health plan provider

cash option • an option that allows an annuitant, at the start of the liquidation period, to withdraw the funds in cash, rather than as an annuity

cash refund annuity • a refund annuity that specifies if the annuitant dies before receiving total benefit payments equal to the purchase price of the annuity, all or a stated percentage of the difference will be refunded in cash

cash value • the savings element that builds up in a permanent life insurance policy, an endowment policy, or an annuity contract

cash value accumulation test • a test to determine whether an insurance policy meets the definition of a life insurance policy for federal income tax purposes. To qualify as such, the cash value must not exceed the net single premium that would be needed to fund the policy's death benefit.

cash value life insurance • a type of life insurance under which premiums are sufficient not only to pay the insurer's death claims and expenses but also to build up a savings fund within the policy

casualty loss • usually considered a loss that is sudden, unexpected, or unusual and which results in damage, destruction, or loss of property

catastrophic benefits rider • a disability income insurance rider that makes additional benefits available if the insured suffers a severe disability that includes cognitive impairment or the inability to perform two or more of six activities of daily living

cede • transfer a portion of the amount of insurance written by a primary or original insurer to a reinsurer

certificate of insurance • a description of the group insurance coverage provided to employees. It is given to the employees, but it is not part of the master contract.

choice no-fault • a modified no-fault law that allows an insurance applicant either to elect traditional tort coverage or to elect no-fault coverage at a reduced premium

chronically ill individual • a person who, for purposes of long-term care insurance, is expected to be unable to perform at least two activities of daily living (ADLs) for at least 90 days or who needs substantial services to protect the individual from threats to health and safety due to substantial cognitive impairment

civil wrong • a legal wrong other than a criminal wrong. It is based upon torts or contracts.

claims adjusting • the basic insurance function of paying covered claims

claims-made policy • a liability insurance policy that covers only claims that are first reported during the policy period as long as the event that caused the claims occurred after a specified retroactive date in the policy

class rate • an average price of insurance that applies to a category or classification of similar insureds

closed-panel plan • a benefit plan under which covered persons must obtain services from practitioners selected by the provider of benefits

COBRA • a provision of the Consolidated Omnibus Budget Reconciliation Act of 1985 that requires group health plans to allow employees and certain beneficiaries to extend their current health insurance coverage at group rates for up to 36 months following a qualifying event that results in the loss of coverage

coinsurance (medical expense insurance) • the percentage of covered expenses under a major medical plan that is paid by the insurance company once a deductible is satisfied. The most common coinsurance is 80 percent.

coinsurance (property insurance) • a provision whereby a property owner must share in a loss if the amount of insurance carried is less than a specified percentage of the property's insurable value

collateral assignment method • the technique used with split-dollar life insurance whereby the employee owns the policy and has the responsibility for paying the premium. The employer's share of the policy proceeds is secured by an assignment.

collision • in auto insurance, the upset of an auto or its impact with another vehicle or object

commercial general liability (CGL) insurance • commercial liability insurance designed to cover a wide variety of liability loss exposures that can face an organization, including premises, business operations, products, completed operations, contractual, and contingent liability

commercial insurance • as contrasted with personal insurance, a category of insurance—particularly of property and liability insurance—that is purchased by businesses and other organizations

commercial package policy • a common type of package policy that covers many of the property and liability loss exposures of a business

commercial property insurance • coverage for losses to real and personal business property. As commonly used, the term applies to policies that cover losses from most perils other than those that relate to crime, transportation, and boiler explosion. There are numerous forms that cover various classifications of property from specified perils or on an open-perils basis.

commingling of funds • an unfair trade practice that occurs when an agent mixes personal funds with the insured's or insurer's funds

common accident provision • a provision in a major medical expense contract whereby if two or more members of the same family are injured in the same accident, the covered medical expenses for all family members will, at most, be subject to a single deductible, usually equal to the individual deductible amount

comparative negligence • the legal principle whereby an injured party can recover a portion of the damages for his or her injuries if he or she was also negligent. In some jurisdictions, a plaintiff can recover only if his or her negligence is less (or not more) than the defendant's negligence.

completed operations liability • bodily injury or property damage liability caused by work that has been performed by an insured

comprehensive coverage • *See* other than collision

comprehensive dental plan • *See* nonscheduled dental plan

comprehensive long-term care insurance policy • a long-term care insurance policy that combines benefits for facility care and benefits for home health care services into a single contract. *Also known as* an integrated policy

compulsory insurance law • a law in most states that requires the owners of autos to carry liability insurance before a vehicle can be registered

computer fraud • the use of a computer to fraudulently transfer property from its rightful owner to someone else

concealment • failure by one party to a contract to affirmatively disclose to the other party all of the important facts that are the exclusive knowledge of the first party. Even if it is not intentional or fraudulent, concealment can make an insurance contract voidable.

condition precedent • a condition in an insurance contract that must be fulfilled by the policyowner before the insurer can be held liable for a loss

condition subsequent • a condition in an insurance contract that must be fulfilled by the policyowner after the insurer has become liable in order to avoid the insurer's release from liability

conditional contract • an agreement in which one party's obligation to perform is subject to meeting specified conditions by the other party to the agreement

conditional receipt • a receipt given to an applicant for life insurance in exchange for the payment of the first premium in which the insurer, through its agent, specifies that the coverage will be effective as of the date of the receipt, subject to the condition that the proposed insured later be found to have been insurable as of the date the receipt was issued

condominium commercial unit-owners coverage • commercial property insurance that covers the interest of the owner of a commercial condominium unit

consequential loss • *See* indirect loss

consideration • a right or something of value (such as money) given to another party in exchange for the assumption of an obligation by the other party. Consideration is a requirement for a valid contract.

consumer-directed medical expense care • an approach to medical expense insurance that gives employees increased choices and responsibilities involving their health care

contingent beneficiary • the person or entity designated to receive the death proceeds of a life insurance policy if the primary beneficiary predeceases the insured

contingent liability • legal liability that arises because of work performed by an independent contractor such as a subcontractor of a business

contingent payee • in life insurance, the person or entity designated to receive the remaining death proceeds if the beneficiary dies after the insured but before the beneficiary has received the full amount of the proceeds payable

continuing care retirement community • a facility that provides lifetime care for older adults. Initial occupancy is in an independent living unit, but a resident must move to an assisted-living or nursing home unit if health deteriorates.

contract of adhesion • a characteristic of a contract that is prepared in all of its details by one party, rather than having its terms bargained over between the parties to the contract. Because insurance policies are generally contracts of adhesion, if ambiguity exists in the terms, the courts are likely to rule in favor of the insured and against the insurer (the party that drew up the contract).

contract of indemnity • contract providing that a policyowner is entitled to payment only to the extent of his or her financial loss or legal liability and should not be permitted to profit from the loss

contractual liability • the assumption of legal liability of others through a written or oral contract

contributory negligence • the legal principle whereby an injured person cannot recover damages for injuries from another negligent party if the injured party was also negligent

contributory plan • a type of employee benefit plan in which the insured pays a portion of the premium cost

conversion • a provision in a group benefit plan that gives an employee whose coverage ceases the right to convert to an individual insurance policy without providing evidence of insurability. The conversion policy may or may not be identical to the prior group coverage.

convertibility • a feature in term life insurance that allows the insured to replace the term coverage with permanent individual life insurance without having to show evidence of insurability. In group insurance, the right is available only at certain times, including termination of the insured from the group or from an eligible class within the group.

coordination-of-benefits provision • a provision in most group medical expense plans under which priorities are established for the payment of benefits if an individual is covered under more than one plan. Coverage as an employee is generally primary to coverage as a dependent. When parents are divorced, the plan of the parent with custody is primary, the plan of the current spouse of the parent with custody is secondary, and the plan of the parent without custody pays last. Other rules apply to other situations.

copayment • a fixed dollar amount that an insured must pay for a covered medical service

cost-of-living adjustment (COLA) rider • increases in benefit levels because of changes in some index such as the CPI. These increases apply to Social Security income benefits and sometimes to benefits under private insurance and retirement programs.

cost shifting • the attempt by employers to control benefit costs by shifting these costs to employees. Examples include the requirement of larger employee contributions and increased deductibles.

counteroffer • an offer made by an offeree to the original offeror in lieu of acceptance of the original offer

covered auto • a vehicle specifically listed in the policy declarations of an auto insurance policy. In the personal auto policy, "your covered auto" includes newly acquired autos, trailers, and temporary substitute vehicles.

credibility • the degree of reliability one can place on past results as an indicator of likely future results

credit, Social Security • the basis on which eligibility for benefits under Social Security is determined. Up to four credits may be earned in any calendar year.

credit enhancement insurance • a form of surety bond that guarantees that the principal and interest will be paid to the purchasers of a debt instrument. Also known as *financial guarantee insurance.*

crime insurance • various insurance coverages for losses that arise from illegal activities such as burglary, robbery, extortion, forgery, employee dishonesty, and theft

criminal wrong • an injury, including to the public at large, that is punishable by the government

critical illness insurance • a form of supplemental medical expense insurance that provides a substantial one-time lump-sum cash benefit for listed critical illnesses

cross-purchase agreement • a business buy-sell agreement in which the surviving co-owners will be the purchasers of the business interest of a deceased owner

current assumption whole life insurance • a nonparticipating whole life insurance policy in which premium rates are redetermined by the insurer periodically, based on its then current assumptions as to mortality, interest, and expenses

currently insured • an insured status under Social Security that requires a person to have at least six credits during the 13 calendar quarters ending with the quarter in which death occurs

custodial care • care given to help with personal needs such as walking, bathing, dressing, eating, or taking medicine. Such care can usually be provided by someone without professional medical skills or training.

declarations • factual statements that are a part of an insurance policy and that identify the specific person, property, or activity being insured; the parties to the insurance transaction; and other descriptive information about the insurance being provided

decreasing term insurance • a form of term life insurance in which the amount of insurance systematically decreases from year to year

deductible • the initial amount or portion of a covered loss that is borne by the insured, rather than by the insurance company

deductive reasoning • *See* a priori reasoning

deferred annuity • an annuity for which benefit payments begin more than one payment interval after the date of purchase

defined-contribution medical expense plan • a plan under which the employer makes a fixed-dollar contribution that an employee can use toward paying the cost of medical expense coverage, regardless of the premium

definitions • explanations of the meaning of key terms in an insurance policy to clarify the coverage

Delta Plans • service plans sponsored by state dental associations for the purpose of providing dental benefits. Also called *Delta Dental Plans.*

demutualization • the process of converting a mutual insurance company into a stock company

dental health maintenance organization (DHMO) • an HMO that provides dental care only

dependent • most commonly defined under a group medical expense plan to include an employee's spouse who is not legally separated from the employee and any other unmarried dependent children (including stepchildren and adopted children) under age 19 or, if full-time students, age 23

difference in conditions (DIC) insurance • a separate insurance policy that provides open-perils coverage to fill in the gaps left by the insured's other commercial property insurance policies

direct loss • the first loss or losses that arise immediately from the occurrence of a peril. For example, the cost to repair a dented fender is a direct loss following an auto accident.

direct recognition • in life insurance, the practice of paying smaller dividends on policies that have outstanding policy loans than on other policies

direct-response marketing • a method of marketing insurance without the intermediary of an agent or broker

directors and officers (D&O) liability insurance • insurance that covers directors and officers of a corporation and that is purchased by a corporation. The policy covers directors and officers for their personal liability as directors and officers that results from wrongful acts, and it also covers reimbursement to the policyowner for any sum that it is required or permitted by law to pay to the directors and officers as indemnification.

disability income insurance • insurance to partially replace income of persons unable to work because of sickness or accident

disability-based policy • a long-term care insurance policy with a per diem basis of payment that provides benefits even if no care is being received as long as the insured satisfies the policy's benefit trigger

disability insured • the insured status under Social Security necessary to receive disability benefits. It requires that a worker (1) be fully insured and (2) have had a minimum amount of work under Social Security within a recent period.

discount plan • a plan that provides discounts to members for products or services. Used for prescription drug, vision, and dental expenses.

dividend options • a set of provisions in a participating life insurance policy that describe how the policyowner can use the dividends, usually to reduce the premium payment, to buy additional paid-up permanent insurance, to accumulate at interest, to buy term insurance, or to make the policy a paid-up policy at an earlier age than originally planned

divisible surplus • that portion of an insurer's surplus that is declared as a dividend to be distributed to policyowners and/or stockholders of the insurer

domestic insurer • an insurer incorporated in the state where it does business

double indemnity provision • *See* accidental death benefit

dram shop laws • laws that impute liability to taverns and other businesses that serve liquor for injuries that may be caused by intoxicated patrons

dread disease insurance • *See* specified disease insurance

dwelling policy • one of a series of policies for the insurance of dwellings. The forms are somewhat less comprehensive than homeowners policies and can be used for dwellings that do not meet certain homeowners standards.

dynamic risk • a possibility of loss that results from changes in society or in the economy. An example of a dynamic risk is the possibility that a retailer's inventory will become obsolete because of a sudden change in consumer tastes.

earnings test • the process for determining whether income benefits of Social Security beneficiaries under age 65 should be reduced because of wages that exceed a specified amount that is subject to annual indexing. Prior to 2000, the test also applied to beneficiaries aged 65–69.

earthquake insurance • a homeowners endorsement or separate policy that covers property for earthquake as well as tremors that accompany volcanic eruption. The coverage has a large deductible such as 5 percent of the limit of insurance.

elimination period • the term usually applied to a waiting period in long-term care insurance. *See* waiting period

employee benefits liability insurance • insurance that covers claims arising out of improper advice or other errors or omissions in the administration of employee benefit plans

employee theft • the unlawful taking of money, securities, or other property by an employee

employers liability insurance • a type of liability insurance that protects an employer when it can be sued because of injuries to employees. Usually accompanies workers' compensation coverage.

employment practices liability insurance • a liability policy that covers specified employment practices such as discrimination, sexual harassment, and wrongful termination

endorsement • a provision added to a property or liability insurance policy, sometimes for an extra or reduced premium charge, by which the scope of the policy's coverage is clarified, restricted, or enlarged

endowment life insurance • a type of life insurance policy that pays the face amount if the insured dies during a specified period of time and also pays the face amount if he or she lives to the end of that period

entire contract provision • in life and health insurance, a provision that specifies that the policy and the attached application constitute the entire agreement between the parties

entity agreement • a business buy-sell agreement in which the business itself is the designated purchaser of the deceased's business interest

equipment breakdown insurance • commercial property and liability insurance that provides coverage for damage caused by steam boiler explosion and electrical or mechanical breakdown; referred to as boiler and machinery coverage by some insurers

equity-indexed annuity • an annuity that guarantees a minimum fixed rate of interest credits but also provides higher credits if a specified common stock index rises sufficiently

errors and omissions insurance • a type of professional liability insurance for those in occupations such as real estate appraising and accounting, where the professional's acts or omissions are unlikely to result in bodily injury

estate tax • a tax imposed upon the transfer of property at a person's death. The federal government and many states levy such taxes.

evidence of insurability • documentation or other evidence submitted to the insurance company regarding the physical condition or other attributes of the applicant for insurance coverage, which is taken into account when the insurer determines whether to accept the risk

excess liability insurance • a policy written to provide additional liability limits for claims that are covered by specified underlying coverage

excess lines broker • a broker who is authorized to place insurance with nonadmitted insurers in certain circumstances. Also known as a *surplus lines broker*

exclusion ratio • the ratio used to determine the portion of the benefit payment from an annuity that is tax free as a return of the investment in the contract. It is the ratio of the total amount invested to the total amount expected to be received.

exclusions • provisions in an insurance contract that indicate what the insurer does not cover. Exclusions can apply to perils, types of losses, types of property, or types of activities.

exclusive agency system • a marketing system in property and liability insurance in which the agent represents only one insurer (or group of affiliated insurers), and the insurer has ownership rights over the business written by the agents

exclusive-provider organization (EPO) • a variation of a preferred-provider organization in which coverage is not provided outside the preferred-provider network except in those infrequent cases where the network does not have an appropriate specialist

exposure unit • the unit of measurement for which an insurance rate is developed. Examples are each $1,000 of life insurance protection or each $100 of property value.

express authority • authority specifically granted by a principal to an agent by means of an agency agreement

extended care facility • a health care facility for a person who no longer requires the full level of medical care provided by a hospital but does need a period of convalescence under supervised medical care. Also known as a *skilled-nursing facility*

extended nonowned coverage • an auto insurance endorsement for persons who have a vehicle that is made available for their regular use

extended term insurance • paid-up term life insurance purchased through the use of a life insurance policy's cash value as a single premium

extension of benefits • a provision in a medical expense plan under which benefits are extended for any covered employee or dependent who is totally disabled at the time coverage would otherwise terminate. The disability must have resulted from an injury or illness that occurred while the person was covered under the group contract. The length of the extension generally ranges from 3 to 12 months.

extortion • the loss of money, securities, or other property surrendered away from the insured premises as a result of the threat of bodily harm to someone who is, or is allegedly, being held captive

extra expense insurance • commercial insurance that provides coverage for expenses to avoid or minimize the suspension of operations following damages to property

extra percentage tables • tables used in treating substandard applicants for life insurance in which separate, higher-than-normal mortality rates are used in calculating the premium for the coverage

facility-only policy • a long-term care insurance policy that provides benefits for care in a nursing home and other settings such as an assisted-living facility and hospice

facultative reinsurance • reinsurance that is optional for both the primary insurer and the reinsurer

FAIR (Fair Access to Insurance Requirements) plan • a state-run program to provide property insurance, within limits, if a property owner is unable to obtain coverage in the standard marketplace. The actual coverage is usually written by a pool or syndicate of private insurers.

family deductible • a provision in a major medical plan that waives future deductibles for all family members once a specified aggregate dollar amount of medical expenses has been incurred or after a specified number of family members have satisfied their individual deductibles

family purpose doctrine • a legal principle that imputes liability to motor vehicle owners for the negligence of family members who use the motor vehicle

federal surety bond • a bond that guarantees that a business will comply with federal standards, including the payment of taxes and duties

fee schedule • a list of covered benefits and the maximum fee that will be paid to the provider of benefits. Such a schedule is found in many surgical expense policies, dental policies, vision care plans, and group legal expense plans.

fellow-servant doctrine • a common-law defense that was available to employers under which a worker could not collect if an injury resulted from a fellow worker's negligence

fiduciary bond • a bond that guarantees that a person who is responsible for the property of another faithfully exercises his or her duties, gives proper accounting of any property received, and makes proper indemnification if the court determines that the principal is responsible for any financial loss that relates to the property. It is often required of persons who act as administrators, trustees, or guardians.

fiduciary liability insurance • insurance that covers claims that result from the breach of fiduciary duties such as pension plan losses because of improper investments

field underwriting • the initial screening of applicants for insurance performed by the agent or broker

fifth dividend option • a provision in cash value life insurance whereby dividends can be used to purchase term insurance

50 percent refund annuity • a refund annuity that pays a benefit to a beneficiary if the annuitant dies before receiving benefits equal to half the cost of the annuity. Installments continue until the total benefits paid equal half the cost of the annuity.

file-and-use law • a law regulating insurance rates that allows insurers to file their rates with the regulatory authority and then begin to use those rates unless/until the regulatory authority disapproves the rates

financial guarantee insurance • *See* credit enhancement insurance

financial institution bond • a bond that is designed to pick up the unique loss exposures faced by financial institutions such as stockbrokerages, investment banks, banks, credit unions, savings and loan associations, and insurance companies

financial needs analysis • a system for determining how much life insurance a client needs if the principal sum is to be liquidated in the process of meeting the client's financial objectives for his or her survivors

financial responsibility law • a law in most states that requires proof of future auto insurance after certain circumstances occur. These can include an auto accident, conviction for certain traffic offenses, or failure to pay a legal judgment that arises from an auto accident.

financial risk • a category of risk for which the possibility of loss involves a decrease or a disappearance of monetary value, usually in an unexpected or relatively unpredictable manner

fire • rapid oxidation or combustion accompanied by a flame or glow

first-to-die policy • *See* joint-life policy

fixed-amount option • a life insurance settlement option under which the death proceeds are distributed in level installments consisting of principal and interest for as long as the proceeds last

fixed annuity • an annuity that provides a stated periodic dollar benefit, regardless of the insurer's investment return

fixed-period option • a life insurance settlement option under which the death proceeds are distributed in installments consisting of principal and interest over a specified period of time

flat extra premium • a method of treating substandard life insurance applicants by charging a specified extra premium per $1,000 of insurance, regardless of age

flexible benefit plan • *See* cafeteria plan

flexible premium life insurance • various types of life insurance in which the premium is flexible, either at the option of the insurer or the policyowner

flexible spending account (FSA) • a cafeteria plan provision that allows an employee to fund certain types of expenses other than insurance premiums on a before-tax basis

flex-rating law • a law regulating insurance rates that requires prior approval of new rates only if they differ from the existing rates by at least some specified percentage such as 5 or 10 percent

floater • a property insurance policy to provide broad insurance protection on property that is subject to being moved

follow form • a basic form of an excess liability policy that incorporates the policy provisions and conditions of an underlying policy, thus providing additional coverage only if a claim is covered by the underlying insurance

foreign insurer • an insurer that writes business in a state but is incorporated in another state

forgery • the creation of a document or signature that is not genuine

formulary • a list of preferred medications for a specific medical condition

fraternal insurer • a nonprofit insuring organization that writes mainly life insurance on members of a fraternal society

fraud • intentional deception or intentional misleading of another person. In order to constitute fraud, intent must be shown, and the information concealed or misrepresented must be relied upon by and injure the other party.

free-look provision • a clause found in some lines of insurance contracts that gives the policyowner a specified period of time, such as 10 days, to return the policy after acceptance and receive a full refund of the premium paid

FSA • *See* flexible spending account (FSA)

full advance funding • a funding method for insurance by which taxes or premiums are set at a level to fund all promised benefits from current service for those making current contributions

full retirement age • the age at which a worker can retire under Social Security and receive nonreduced benefits equal to his or her primary insurance amount (PIA). Also referred to as *normal retirement age*

fully insured • an insured status under Social Security. This status requires either (1) 40 credits or (2) at least as many credits (but a minimum of six) as there are years elapsing after 1950 (or after the year in which age 21 is reached, if later) and before the year in which a person dies, becomes disabled, or reaches age 62, whichever occurs first.

functional replacement cost • the cost to repair or replace damaged real property with less costly construction materials and methods that are functionally equivalent to the old construction

fundamental risk • a loss possibility that can affect a large segment of society at the same time. An example is the possibility of widespread unemployment during an economic downturn.

gambling • the deliberate creation of a speculative risk by betting on an uncertain outcome. Playing poker for money is an example of gambling.

gatekeeper PPO • a preferred-provider organization that requires a participant to select a primary care physician in the manner of an HMO subscriber. However, at the time medical service is needed, the participant can elect to go outside the PPO network.

general agency system • in life insurance marketing, the term used to describe a marketing system whereby a general agent is granted a franchise by an insurer to build an agency force for marketing the insurer's products in a given geographic area

general agent • in the legal sense, an agent who has the authority to bind insurance for a client

gift • for federal gift tax purposes, a completed transfer and acceptance of property for less than full and adequate consideration

gift tax • a tax imposed on transfers of property by gift during the donor's lifetime

grace period • an additional period of time, usually 31 days, granted in some types of insurance for the policyowner to pay the premium after it has become due. During the grace period, the coverage remains in force.

gross estate • for federal estate tax purposes, the property of a decedent that passes by will and by other means

gross rate • an insurance rate that includes loading for profits and contingencies as well as a provision for expected future loss costs

group insurance • in contrast with individual insurance, all types of private insurance that cover many people under one master contract issued to a sponsoring organization such as an employer

group-model HMO • a closed-panel HMO under which physicians and other medical personnel are employees of another legal entity that has a contractual relationship with the HMO to provide medical services for its subscribers

guaranteed purchase (insurability) option • a rider to a life insurance policy that gives the insured the right to buy additional insurance in specified amounts at specified times or ages without having to provide evidence of insurability

guaranteed renewable • a characteristic of an insurance contract in which the insured retains the right to renew the coverage at each policy anniversary date, usually up to a stated age. Also, the insurer is not allowed to cancel the coverage during the period of protection. However, the insurer does retain the right to raise the rates for the coverage for broad classes of insureds.

guaranty fund • a state fund that at least partially protects consumers against the insolvency of insurers. The typical fund assesses solvent insurers to pay the unpaid claims of insolvent companies.

guideline premium and corridor test • a two-pronged test to determine whether an insurance policy meets the definition of a life insurance policy for federal income tax purposes. The test relates to both the size of the total premium paid and the size of the death benefit relative to the cash value.

hazard • an act or condition that increases the likelihood of the occurrence of a loss and/or increases the severity of a loss. The three types of hazards are physical hazards, moral hazards, and attitudinal hazards.

health association • an organization that provides medical expense coverage to members. Examples include HMOs and Blue Cross and Blue Shield plans.

health insurance • protection against the financial consequences of poor health

Health Insurance Portability and Accountability Act (HIPAA) • federal legislation, passed in 1996, that reforms the health care system through numerous provisions. The act's primary purpose is to make insurance more available, particularly when an employed person changes jobs or becomes unemployed.

health maintenance organization (HMO) • a managed system of health care that provides a comprehensive array of medical services on a prepaid basis to voluntarily enrolled persons living within a specific geographic region. HMOs both finance health care and deliver health services. There is an emphasis on preventive care as well as cost control.

Health Maintenance Organization Act • a federal act in 1973 that introduced the concept of the federally qualified HMO

health reimbursement arrangement (HRA) • an account funded with employer dollars from which an employee can withdraw amounts to pay medical expenses that are not covered under a high-deductible medical expense plan

health savings accounts (HSAs) • savings accounts for use with high-deductible medical expense plans and from which certain unreimbursed medical expenses can be paid. Successors to and more attractive than Archer MSAs.

hedging • a procedure by which two compensating or offsetting transactions are used to ensure a position of at least breaking even. An example of hedging is the simultaneous taking of a "long" position and a "short" position in shares of common stock.

high-deductible health plan • medical expense plan with a deductible as high as $5,000 or more. The employer contributes a lower or equal amount to a savings account from which employees can pay medical expenses not covered because of the deductible.

high-risk pool • a state-run insurance pool to provide medical expense coverage for persons who have been rejected in the normal marketplace

HIPAA • *See* Health Insurance Portability and Accountability Act

hired auto • in commercial auto insurance, an auto, other than a nonowned auto, that is leased, hired, rented, or borrowed by the named insured

HMO • *See* health maintenance organization

hold-harmless agreement • an agreement in which one party, such as a tenant, accepts the responsibility of another party, such as a landlord, for losses that would otherwise fall on that other party

home health care • medical care that is received at home. Care is usually part-time and performed under a plan prescribed by a physician.

home health care policy • a long-term care insurance policy designed to provide benefits only for care outside an institutional setting, although some policies may provide benefits for care in assisted-living facilities

homeowners policy • a policy that provides coverage for a family's home, personal possessions, and liability that arises out of the many activities of family members. There are several homeowners forms that provide varying degrees of coverage for different types of homeowners and tenants.

homogeneity • the quality or state of being of the same or a similar kind or nature

hospice care • a health care facility or service that provides benefits to terminally ill persons. The emphasis is on easing the physical and psychological pain associated with dying rather than on curing a medical condition.

hospital indemnity insurance • a medical expense policy that pays a fixed dollar amount for each day a person is hospitalized, regardless of other insurance

hospital-surgical policy • an individual medical expense policy that provides limited coverage for hospital, surgical, and certain other medical expenses. It is less comprehensive than a major medical policy.

HRA • *See* health reimbursement arrangement

hull insurance • the term often applied to physical damage coverage in watercraft and aviation policies

human life value • the present value of that portion of a person's estimated future earnings that will be used to support dependents

immediate annuity • an annuity with benefit payments that begin one payment interval after the date of purchase

impaired risk annuity • an annuity that considers the annuitant's reduced life expectancy in the underwriting process and increases the annuity payments (or lowers the premium) accordingly

implied authority • the authority that an agent has as necessary to carry out acts needed to exercise his or her express authority

implied warranty • an obligation imposed by law on the manufacturer or distributor of products

imputed negligence • legal responsibility extended by the courts to persons other than those who cause injury directly

incident of ownership • an element of ownership or degree of control over a policy such as a life insurance policy

incontestable clause • a provision in life and health insurance that specifies that, except for nonpayment of the premium, the insurer will not contest the policy after it has been in force for a specified period (usually 2 years) during the insured's lifetime

indemnity • a principle underlying most insurance contracts whereby the insurance seeks to reimburse the insured for approximately the amount lost, no more and no less

independent adjuster • a claims adjuster or claims adjusting firm that is not an employee of an insurance company

independent agency system • a marketing system in property and liability insurance in which an agent represents several insurers or groups of insurers and has ownership rights over the business written by the agency

indeterminate premium whole life insurance • *See* interest-sensitive whole life insurance

indirect (consequential) loss • a loss that occurs only as a secondary result following the occurrence of a peril. An example is the additional living expenses a family might incur to pay for substitute living accommodations following fire damage to their home.

individual equity • the principle that each individual's insurance premium payments are based on an actuarial analysis that reflects the insurer's cost of providing benefits for the risks faced by that individual

individual insurance • types of insurance that are normally purchased by individuals and families

individual practice association • an HMO under which participating physicians practice individually or in small groups in their own offices. In many cases, these physicians also accept non-HMO patients on a traditional fee-for-service basis.

inductive reasoning • reasoning in which a generalized conclusion is derived from particular instances. Inductive reasoning is based on statistical analysis. *Compare* a priori reasoning

inflation guard endorsement • a homeowners endorsement that provides an automatic increase for property coverages. The policyowner selects the annual percentage increase.

initial deductible • a deductible that must be satisfied before any benefits are paid under a medical expense plan

inland marine insurance • a specialized type of transportation insurance used for goods in transit, property held by bailees, mobile equipment and property, property of certain dealers, and instrumentalities of transportation and communication

inside build up • the increase in the cash value or investment fund of a permanent life insurance policy

installment refund annuity • a refund annuity specifying that if the annuitant dies before receiving total benefit payments equal to the purchase price of the annuity, the difference will be refunded in the form of continuing benefit payments

insurable interest • a right or relationship with regard to the subject matter of an insurance contract such that the insured will suffer financial loss from damage, loss, or destruction to that subject matter

insurable risk • a risk that substantially meets the following requirements: (1) the amount of the loss must be important, (2) the loss must be of an accidental nature, (3) future loss must be calculable, (4) the loss must be definite, and (5) the risk cannot be excessively catastrophic

insurance • an economic system that reduces financial risks when policyowners transfer risks to an insurer, who combines the potential losses

insurance commissioner • the state official responsible for the regulation of the business of insurance

insurance contract • the agreement that transfers financial risk from a policyowner to an insurer. It may begin with an oral agreement but then is usually converted to written form.

insurance equation • an equation that shows that an insurance company's receipts (premiums, investment earnings, and other income) equal its cost factors (losses, expenses, and profit)

insurance management • the process of determining when, how, how much, and where to insure risks. It is a more narrow term than risk management.

insurance policy • *See* insurance contract

Insurance Services Office • *See* ISO

insured • a person whose life, health, or property is covered under an insurance contract. The policyowner may or may not also be an insured.

insuring agreement • a part of an insurance contract that spells out the basic promise of the insurance company to pay benefits according to the terms of the policy

interest option • a life insurance settlement option under which the death proceeds are retained by the insurer temporarily, with only the interest earnings thereon distributed to the beneficiary

interest-sensitive whole life insurance • a current assumption whole life insurance policy under which a low initial premium is guaranteed for a period of time, often 3 or 5 years. After that time, the premium is recalculated on the basis of current mortality, interest, and expense assumptions.

interinsurance exchange • *See* reciprocal exchange

intermediate care • care that involves occasional nursing and rehabilitative care that must be based on a doctor's orders and can be performed only by or under the supervision of skilled medical personnel

international travel medical insurance • interim medical insurance for international travelers. It is usually folded into a broader policy to cover many non-health-related travel contingencies.

irrevocable beneficiary • a beneficiary that cannot be changed by the policyowner without the beneficiary's permission

ISO (Insurance Services Office) • an advisory organization that provides various services to insurance companies, including the development and filing of standardized insurance forms

joint (joint-life) annuity • an annuity with benefit payments that continue only until the first death among specified lives

joint-and-last-survivor annuity • an annuity with benefit payments that continue until the last death among specified lives

joint-and-two-thirds annuity • a joint-and-survivor annuity with periodic benefit payments that drop to two-thirds of the former amount following the first death among the annuitants

joint-life (first-to-die) policy • a type of life insurance policy covering two or more persons in which the proceeds are payable on the death of the first one to die

joint underwriting association • an association, or pool, of auto insurers that writes hard-to-place drivers in some states

judicial bond • a bond required by courts, including fiduciary bonds and litigation bonds

key employee • a person in an organization whose capital, technical knowledge, skills, experience, business connections, or other attributes make him or her highly valuable to the organization's financial success

key employee life insurance • insurance on the life of a key employee to cover the possibility of an income loss and/or an increase in expenses resulting from the key employee's death

last clear chance doctrine • the legal principle that holds that although a claimant is negligent, the defendant is liable if he or she had the last clear chance to avoid an accident and failed to take advantage of that chance

late remittance offer • an offer made by an insurer to the owner of a lapsed life insurance policy that invites him or her to pay the premium and reinstate the coverage without having to provide evidence of insurability

law of large numbers • a mathematical principle stating that as the number of independent trials or events is increased, the actual results from those trials or events will come closer and closer to the results that one would expect to occur based on the underlying probability

legal reserve • the minimum amount of the reserve, as specified by state law, that a life insurer must maintain to meet its assumed future claim costs under a block of policies. It is discounted for future premium and investment income under those policies.

legal wrong • the invasion of a legal right. It can be either criminal or civil.

less value statute • a state law that prohibits a life insurer from promising something on the face of the policy while taking it away in the fine print, such as by offering a settlement option of less value than the policy's death proceeds

liability risk • a possibility of loss as a result of being held legally responsible for an injury to another, usually for bodily injury or damage to his or her property

license bond • a bond that is often required by state and local governments for persons in many types of occupations that need licensing

lien • a method of treating substandard applicants for life insurance in which the policy is issued as standard except that the death proceeds are reduced if death occurs within the first few years of coverage

life annuity • an annuity whose benefit payments continue for the duration of a designated life

life annuity certain • a life annuity that provides a guaranteed minimum number of benefit payments whether the annuitant lives or dies. It is a combination of an annuity certain and a pure deferred life annuity.

life-care facility • *See* continuing care retirement community

life income option • a life insurance settlement option, and in some insurance policies a nonforfeiture option, under which the proceeds are distributed over the lifetime of the recipient, perhaps subject to some type of minimum guarantee as to the aggregate amount to be paid

life insurance • insurance that provides for payment of a specified amount at the insured's death or, possibly, at a specified date if the insured is still living

limited agent • an agent who does not have the authority to bind the insurance company to provide coverage for an applicant

limited-payment life insurance • a form of whole life insurance for which premiums are based on the assumption that they will be paid for only a specified number of years or until a specified age of the insured

line of insurance • a type of insurance such as life, medical expense, disability income, homeowners, or auto liability

liquidation • the process, overseen by an insurance commissioner, of dissolving a financially troubled insurance company

liquidation period • the period of time during which annuity benefit payments are made

liquidity • an asset characteristic that describes the extent to which the asset can be converted into cash quickly without loss of value

litigation bond • a bond whose purpose is to require a person or organization who is seeking a court remedy to protect other parties from damages if the party seeking the remedy does not prevail

Lloyd's association • an association of individual insurers in which insurance is underwritten by its members rather than by the association itself

Lloyd's of London • a British organization made up of and regulating the activities of members, both individual and corporate, who act as insurers. The organization itself does not write insurance.

loading • that portion of an insurance rate or premium that covers the insurer's expenses and provides a margin for profits and contingencies

long-term care insurance • a form of health insurance that usually provides coverage for custodial care, intermediate care, and skilled-nursing care. Benefits may also be available for home health care, adult day care, and assisted living.

long-term disability income insurance • disability income coverage that provides extended benefits after a person has been disabled for 6 months or longer

look-back period • a specific time period prior to Medicaid eligibility during which Medicaid benefits are reduced (or their onset postponed) if the individual's assets were disposed of at less than their fair market value

loss • a decline in value, usually in an unexpectedly or relatively unpredictable manner

loss assessment coverage • a coverage in many property and liability insurance policies that pays the insured's share of losses levied against members of a homeowners or condominium association

loss exposure • a loss that might occur

loss frequency • the number of losses that occur within a given time period among a given number of units exposed to that loss possibility

loss payable clause • a provision in property insurance policies that protects a lender's insurable interest in personal property. If a loss occurs, the lender receives payment to the extent of its insurable interest.

loss prevention • activities that are designed to reduce loss frequency or the chance that a loss will occur

loss ratio • most commonly, the ratio of losses and loss adjustment expenses to premiums earned

loss ratio method of rate making • a method in which the actual loss ratio is compared to the desired or expected loss ratio to determine the change needed in an existing insurance rate

loss reduction • activities designed to reduce loss severity or the size of a loss if it should occur

loss reserve • in property and liability insurance, an insurer's liability for losses that have already occurred but have not yet been paid or otherwise settled

loss severity • the size of a loss or the average size of a group of losses

lost instrument bond • a bond which guarantees that the principal will reimburse the insurer of lost securities if the original securities turn up and their holder is able to collect on them

major medical insurance • a medical insurance plan designed to provide substantial protection against catastrophic medical expenses. There are few exclusions and limitations, but deductibles and coinsurance are common.

malpractice insurance • a type of professional liability insurance for those in occupations where an act or omission is likely to result in bodily injury

managed care • a process to deliver cost-effective health care without sacrificing quality or access. Common characteristics include controlled access to providers, comprehensive case management, preventive care, risk sharing, and high-quality care.

marital deduction • an unlimited amount that can be taken as a deduction against the federal gift and estate tax for transfers to the donor's spouse

mass • as a characteristic of a statistical group or an insured group, sufficient size within such a group as to allow the true underlying probability to emerge

master contract • a contract issued to someone other than the persons insured that provides benefits to a group of individuals who have a specific relationship to the policyowner

material • so important as to affect whether an insurer will accept an applicant or the terms under which it will accept the applicant

maximum possible loss • the worst loss that could happen

maximum probable loss • the worst loss that is likely to happen

Medicaid • a joint federal and state program to provide medical expense benefits for certain classes of low-income individuals and families

medical expense insurance • protection against financial losses that result from medical bills because of an accident or illness

medical payments coverage • a coverage in many liability policies that pays the medical expenses of persons injured on an insured premises or because of the actions of an insured. Payments are made, regardless of fault, in the hope of reducing liability claims. • in auto insurance, a coverage that pays medical and funeral expenses incurred by a covered person in an auto accident

medical savings account (MSA) • an alternative to first-dollar coverage under a medical expense plan. An employee is given medical expense coverage that has a high deductible, and money is deposited into the medical savings account so that the employee can pay for expenses below the deductible amount. Any monies not used at the end of the year are paid to the employee. Used as part of an Archer MSA or health savings account (HSA).

Medicare • the health insurance portion of the Social Security program that is available to persons aged 65 or older and limited categories of persons under age 65

Medicare Advantage • Part C of Medicare program, previously known as Medicare+Choice, that allows beneficiaries to select HMOs and other alternatives to the traditional Medicare program

Medicare carve-out • an employer-provided medical expense plan for persons over age 65 under which benefits are reduced to the extent that they are payable under Medicare for the same expense

Medicare Part A • part of Medicare program that provides benefits for expenses incurred in hospitals, skilled-nursing facilities, and hospices

Medicare Part B • part of Medicare program that provides benefits for most medical expenses not covered under Part A

Medicare Part C • *See* Medicare Advantage

Medicare Part D • part of Medicare program that provides for prescription drug coverage

Medicare+Choice • *See* Medicare Advantage

Medicare secondary rules • regulations that specify when Medicare will be secondary to an employer's medical expense plan for disabled employees and active employees aged 65 or older

Medicare SELECT policy • a medigap policy that pays benefits for nonemergency services only if care is received from network providers

Medicare supplement • an individual or employer-provided medical expense plan for persons aged 65 or older under which benefits are provided for certain specific expenses not covered under Medicare. These can include a portion of expenses not paid by Medicare because of deductibles, coinsurance, or copayments, and certain expenses excluded by Medicare. In individual insurance, also referred to as a *medigap policy*.

medigap insurance • *See* Medicare supplement

Mental Health Parity Act • federal legislation that requires annual and lifetime dollar limits on mental health benefits to be on par with limits that apply to other medical conditions. The act applies to employers with more than 50 employees.

MIB, Inc. • an organization sponsored by its member life insurance companies to gather and maintain principally medical information disclosed by applicants for life insurance

misappropriation • the unlawful retention of funds that belong to someone else

miscellaneous type vehicle endorsement • an auto insurance endorsement to insure vehicles such as all-terrain vehicles, dune buggies, golf carts, motor homes, motorcycles, and the like

misleading advertising • an unfair trade practice involving confusing, deceptive, false, or otherwise misleading advertising or promotional practices

misrepresentation • a false and material statement made by an applicant for insurance. It is the basis for the insurer to make the contract voidable.

misstatement of age or gender clause • a life insurance policy provision that specifies that if the insured's age or gender has been misstated, the benefits payable under the policy will be adjusted to what the premium paid would have purchased at the correct age or gender

mixed-model HMO • an HMO that has characteristics of two or more of the basic HMO forms. It occurs most often when one HMO purchases a different type of HMO or when an HMO expands its capacity or geographic region by adding other medical care providers under a different type of arrangement.

mobilehome insurance • insurance coverage, similar to homeowners insurance, that provides coverage to owner-occupants of mobile homes

modified cash refund annuity • a refund annuity sometimes used in contributory pension plans that specifies that if the employee dies before receiving total benefit payments equal to his or her share of the purchase price, the difference will be refunded in cash

modified endowment contract (MEC) • a life insurance policy that fails to meet the Internal Revenue Code's 7-pay test. Distributions, therefore, receive less favorable tax treatment than other life insurance contracts receive.

modified no-fault • a no-fault system with the right to sue another party once certain monetary thresholds are exceeded

modified whole life insurance • a form of whole life insurance in which a level premium lower than that for conventional whole life insurance is charged for the first few policy years and a higher level premium is charged thereafter

moral hazard • a dishonest tendency that is likely to increase loss frequency and/or severity

morbidity • the relative incidence of disease

morbidity table • a table showing the number of individuals exposed to the risk of illness, sickness, and disease at each age

mortality • the relative incidence of death

mortality table • a table showing how many people alive at a different ages are expected to die during the coming year

mortgage clause • a provision in property insurance policies that protects a lender's insurable interest in real property. If a loss occurs, the lender receives payments to the extent of its insurable interest, even if a policyowner's claim is denied.

motor carrier insurance • insurance designed for businesses that provide transportation by vehicles in the furtherance of a commercial enterprise

motor truck cargo insurance • a type of inland marine insurance policy used by common carriers or contract carriers to cover customers' goods when the carrier is legally liable for damage

MSA • *See* medical savings account

mutual holding company • a holding company controlled by policyowners that owns a stock insurance company

mutual insurance company • a not-for-profit insurance company owned by its policyowners, who elect its board of directors

NAIC • *See* National Association of Insurance Commissioners

name • a member of Lloyd's of London

named insured • the term often applied to the owner of an insurance policy named in the policy declarations, particularly in property and liability insurance. The term usually includes the spouse if living in the same household.

named nonowner coverage • an auto insurance endorsement for persons who want coverage but do not own an auto

named-perils coverage • an insurance contract that covers only losses that arise from one of a series of listed perils. If the peril is not listed, it is not covered by the policy.

National Association of Insurance Commissioners (NAIC) • a voluntary association of state insurance regulatory officials that is involved in financial examinations of insurers and develops model insurance laws and regulations

National Flood Insurance Program (NFIP) • a federal program that provides subsidized insurance for the peril of flood

negligence • an unintentional tort in the form of an action or omission that leads to the injury of another party

net amount at risk • in a life insurance policy, the difference between the policy's face amount and the reserve at any point in time

net level annual premium • in life insurance, the actuarial spreading of the net single premium on a level basis over a policy's premium-paying period

net payment cost index • a method of estimating the net cost of life insurance on a time-value-adjusted basis, assuming that the policy's death benefit will be paid at the end of a specified time period

net single premium • in life insurance, the amount needed today for all insureds in a classification, together with future investment earnings, to pay all claims within that class of insureds

network-model HMO • an HMO that contracts with two or more independent groups of physicians to provide medical services to its subscribers

newly acquired auto • in personal auto insurance, an auto that otherwise meets the definition of a covered auto but is acquired after the effective date of the policy

no-fault auto insurance • a modification of the traditional tort liability system that provides first-party benefits to injured persons and imposes some restrictions on their rights to sue negligent parties

nonadmitted asset • an asset of an insurer that is not permitted by regulatory authorities to be counted as an asset for Annual Statement purposes

nonadmitted insurer • an insurer that does not have a license to conduct insurance business in a particular state

nonassessable policy • a policy where the initial premium is the final premium (other than reductions for dividends). There can be no assessment of the policyowner if the premium is inadequate.

noncancelable • in an insurance contract, the right of the insured to renew the coverage at each policy anniversary date, usually up to some stated age. The coverage may not be terminated by the insurer during the term of coverage. Also, the rates for the coverage are guaranteed in the contract, although they are not necessarily level.

nonfinancial risk • a category of risk for which the possibility of loss does not represent a reduction in monetary value, although sometimes such losses are compensated by the award of money. An example is pain and suffering.

nonforfeiture options • a set of choices available regarding how a life insurance policyowner can use the policy's cash value. These choices include the options to surrender for cash, buy a reduced amount of paid-up whole life insurance, or buy extended term insurance. For long-term care insurance, an optional benefit provides extended benefits or a cash refund if a policy lapses after it has been in force for a specified number of years.

noninsurance transfer • the contractual transfer of risk by a contract other than an insurance contract. Subcontracting is an example.

nonoccupational disability laws • *See* temporary disability laws

nonowned auto • in personal auto insurance, a vehicle not owned by or furnished for the regular use of the insured or any family member • in commercial auto insurance, an auto owned by a named insured's employee or a member of his or her household, but only while used in the named insured's business

nonparticipating policy • a type of insurance policy that pays no dividends to the policyowner

non-tax-qualified policy • a type of long-term care insurance contract that fails to meet certain standards of the Health Insurance Portability and Accountability Act for favorable tax treatment

notice of loss • the process by which the insurer is notified that a loss has occurred. This begins the loss adjustment process. The actual process of notification is spelled out in a policy and varies by line of insurance.

nursing home care • a term that encompasses skilled-nursing care, intermediate care, and custodial care in a licensed facility

OASDHI • the old age, survivors, disability, and heath insurance program of the federal government. This program consists of Social Security and Medicare.

OASDI • the old-age, survivors, and disability insurance portion of the OASDHI program, commonly referred to as Social Security

obligee • the party to a surety bond who is reimbursed because of the failure of the principal to uphold an agreement

occurrence policy • a liability insurance policy that covers claims that arise out of occurrences that take place during the policy period, regardless of when claims are made

open competition • the reliance mainly on competitive forces in the insurance marketplace to produce acceptable insurance rates

open-ended HMO • an HMO that allows a subscriber to go outside the HMO network of medical care providers

open-panel plan • a benefit plan under which covered persons can obtain services from any practitioner or may have to select one from a limited list of practitioners who have agreed to the plan's terms and conditions

open-perils coverage • an insurance coverage that covers all types of losses except those that are specifically excluded by the policy's terms

opportunity cost • the benefit given up by taking one course of action rather than another—for example, the investment income that is lost when funds are kept as cash rather than invested

optionally renewable • the insurer reserves the right to refuse to renew the coverage at each policy anniversary date, either for specified reasons or for any and all reasons

ordinance or law coverage • insurance for the extra costs to bring damaged property into conformity with current building codes or ordinances

ordinary life insurance • a form of whole life insurance for which premiums are based on the assumption that they will be paid until the insured's death and that provides a guaranteed cash value

original Medicare • the term used to describe the traditional Medicare Parts A and B

other insurance clause • a provision in property and liability insurance policies that specifies how losses are shared if more than one policy covers a loss

other than collision • the term used in auto insurance to refer to physical damage to a vehicle that is not caused by collision. Formerly referred to as *comprehensive.*

ownership provision • in life insurance, a clause that specifies that the insured is the owner of the policy (unless the application states otherwise) and that the owner can change the beneficiary (unless named irrevocably), assign the policy, and exercise other ownership rights

own-occupation • a definition of total disability that requires a disabled person to be unable to perform each and every duty (or material duties) of his or her regular occupation

package policy • an insurance policy that combines two or more types of insurance, often property and liability insurance, in a single contract

paid-up additions • additional amounts of permanent life insurance purchased on a single-premium basis through the use of the policy's dividends

pain and suffering • intangible losses arising from bodily injury

parol evidence rule • a legal principle that specifies that oral contemporaneous evidence is inadmissible to contradict or to vary the terms of a valid written contract

partial advance funding • the funding method used by Social Security and Medicare whereby taxes are more than sufficient to pay current benefits and thus provide some accumulation of assets for the payment of future benefits

partial disability • the inability to perform some stated percentage of job duties or taking a longer-than-normal amount of time in which to complete job duties

participating policy • a type of insurance policy that can pay dividends to the policyowner

participation rate • in an equity-indexed annuity, the percentage (always less than 100 percent) of the increase in the stock index that is used to credit the account of the annuity contract owner

particular risk • a loss possibility that affects only individuals or small groups of individuals at the same time, rather than a large segment of society. An example is the possibility of loss due to the theft of one's wallet.

pay-as-you-go financing • a funding method for insurance whereby taxes are set at a level to provide just enough income to pay future benefits

per diem basis • a method of paying under long-term care insurance policies in which the insured receives a specified daily or weekly benefit amount, regardless of the actual cost of care

percentage participation • the percentage of covered medical expenses that must be paid by a person receiving benefits and that will not be paid by a medical expense plan

peril • a cause of loss. Fire, earthquake, and flood are examples.

permanent life insurance • *See* cash value life insurance

permit bond • a bond often required by state and local governments for persons engaged in various types of activities for which a permit is needed. This guarantee, for example, is in compliance with laws or payment of taxes.

personal articles floater • an open-perils policy for certain scheduled and valuable items of personal property

personal auto policy (PAP) • the most common auto insurance policy for individuals. It is a package policy that can provide liability, medical, no-fault, uninsured motorists, and physical damage coverages.

personal effects floater • a policy to provide open-perils worldwide coverage for baggage, clothes, cameras, and other items commonly worn or carried by tourists

personal injury • a group of legal liability offenses that typically include libel, slander, invasion of privacy, false arrest, and defamation of character

personal injury protection (PIP) endorsement • the usual name for an endorsement that provides a state's no-fault benefits

personal insurance • insurance purchased by individuals and families rather than by businesses and other organizations

personal producing general agent (PPGA) • an agent of a life insurance company who is the insurer's general agent in a given territory but whose primary task is to sell the insurer's products, rather than to build an agency force for the insurer

personal property • an asset, other than real estate, that is subject to ownership

personal property floater • a policy to provide open-perils coverage for unscheduled personal property worldwide

personal risk • a loss possibility associated with death, injury, illness, old age, or unemployment

physical hazard • a physical condition relating to location, structure, occupancy, exposure, and the like

plan change provision • an insurance policy provision that states the parties may agree to change the terms of the contract

point-of-service (POS) plan • a hybrid arrangement that combines aspects of a traditional medical expense plan with an HMO or a PPO. At the time of medical treatment, a participant can elect whether to receive treatment within the plan's network or outside the network.

policy loan • an advance of money available to a life insurance policyowner from the policy's cash value

policyholder • *See* policyowner

policyowner • the person or entity that owns an insurance policy. The policyowner generally has the right to change, renew, or cancel the policy and the obligation to comply with policy conditions such as premium payments.

pool of money • long-term care insurance approach to benefits in which a sum, based on the daily benefit amount times days in the benefit period, can be used to make benefit payments as long as the pool of money lasts, subject to the daily benefit limit

portability • the ability to continue employer-provided or employer-sponsored benefits after termination of employment • the concept of allowing an employee to use evidence of prior medical expense coverage to eliminate or reduce the length of any preexisting-conditions provision when the employee moves to another medical expense plan

POS plan • *See* point-of-service plan

PPO • *See* preferred-provider organization

preadmission certification • a requirement under many medical expense plans that a covered person or his or her physician obtain prior authorization for any nonemergency hospitalization

preexisting-conditions provision • a provision that excludes coverage for a limited period of time for a physical or mental condition for which a covered person in a benefit plan received treatment or medical advice within a specified time period before becoming eligible for coverage

preferred-provider organization (PPO) • benefit plan that contracts with preferred providers to obtain lower-cost care for plan members. Also refers to health care providers that contract with employers or others to provide medical care services at a reduced fee.

premises liability • bodily injury or property damage liability of an owner or tenant because of a condition in or arising out of premises that are owned or occupied

premium • the price charged for a period of coverage provided by an insurance policy and found by multiplying the rate by the number of units of coverage

premium-conversion plan • a cafeteria plan provision that allows employees to elect a before-tax salary reduction to pay for their contributions to an employee-sponsored health plan or certain other types of employee benefits

premium tax • a tax levied by a state on gross insurance premiums

prescription drug expense benefits • medical expense benefits for the cost of prescription drugs. These benefits are often separate from other medical expense coverage because of techniques that can be used to contain costs.

presumed negligence • negligence that can be assumed from the facts of certain situations. It can occur if (1) the action would not normally cause injury without negligence, (2) the action is within the control of the party to be held liable, and (3) the party to be held liable has superior knowledge of the cause of the accident or the injured party is unable to prove negligence.

presumptive-disability provision • a provision in a disability income contract by which an individual is presumed to be totally disabled as long as certain circumstances exist. Examples include loss of sight or one hand. A person with a presumed disability may in fact be able to return to work.

primary beneficiary • the person or organization that is to receive the proceeds of a life insurance policy if he, she, or it survives the insured

primary insurance amount (PIA) • the amount a worker will receive under Social Security if he or she retires at full retirement age or becomes disabled. It is also the amount on which all other Social Security income benefits are based.

principal • the entity for whom an agent acts such as an insurance company • the party to a surety bond who buys the bond and agrees to perform certain acts or to fulfill certain obligations

prior approval law • a law regulating insurance rates that requires proposed rates be approved by the regulatory authority before they may be used by the insurer

probate estate • all property interests possessed by a decedent that pass to others by will or under a law of intestacy

probationary period • in group insurance, a period at the start of a person's employment during which the person is not eligible to participate in the group insurance plan

products liability • bodily injury or property damage liability caused by a defective product that is manufactured or sold by a business

professional liability insurance • insurance that protects against liability for the failure to use the degree of skill expected of a person in a particular occupation

prohibited provisions • certain provisions that states do not allow insurers to include in their contracts

proof of loss • a statement that details the specifics of a loss. It can be a sworn written statement or, in life insurance, a death certificate. The specifics are spelled out in policies and vary by line of insurance.

property damage • destruction or damage to real or personal property, including loss of use

property risk • a loss possibility associated with the loss or destruction of property

prospectus • a highly detailed document accompanying the sale of securities, including variable life insurance, variable universal life insurance, and variable annuity contracts, providing full disclosure of all of the provisions of the contract

protection and indemnity insurance • the term often applied to liability coverage in watercraft policies

proximate cause • one requirement for proving negligence. There must be a continuous succession of events from the negligent act to the final event causing injury.

public adjuster • a person who represents a claimant for a fee in negotiating the settlement of a claim against an insurance company

public official bond • a bond often required of persons who are elected or appointed to certain public positions and that guarantees that the principal will uphold the promise made to faithfully and honestly perform the official duties of his or her office

punitive damages • damages awarded in addition to bodily injury or property damage when a defendant's behavior is so severe that the legal system feels an example should be made of the behavior

pure annuity • a life annuity that provides no guaranteed minimum number of benefit payments or refund of the purchase price. *Also known as* straight life annuity

pure (net) rate • that portion of an insurance rate that is designed to cover future loss costs

pure no-fault • a no-fault system with no right to sue a negligent party. No state has a pure no-fault law.

pure premium method of rate making • a method in which a pure or net rate is calculated, after which a loading is calculated and added to the pure or net rate

pure risk • a possibility of loss that involves only two outcomes, loss or no loss

qualified beneficiary • any employee, spouse, or dependent child who, on the day before a qualifying COBRA event, was covered under the employer's group health plan

qualified long-term care insurance contract • a long-term care contract that meets specified standards and qualifies for favorable tax treatment under the Health Insurance Portability and Accountability Act (HIPAA). *Also called* tax-qualified policy

qualified long-term care services • services that must be provided by a qualified long-term care insurance contract. These include necessary diagnostic, preventive, therapeutic, curative, treatment, and rehabilitative services and maintenance or personal care services that are required by a chronically ill individual and provided by a plan of care prescribed by a licensed health care practitioner.

qualifying event • in life insurance, a condition or event that triggers the payment of accelerated benefits such as an illness that is expected to reduce the insured's life expectancy to 24 months or less • under COBRA, one of the following events that results in loss coverage by a qualified beneficiary: employee's death or termination; reduction of hours making employee ineligible for coverage; legal separation of employee and eligible dependent or spouse; eligibility for Medicare; or child's ceasing to be a dependent

quarters of coverage • *See* credit, Social Security

rate • the price charged for each unit of insurance coverage

rate making • the process of determining insurance rates. It involves the determination of future loss costs and adding the necessary margins for expenses and profit.

rate-up age method • a method of treating a substandard applicant for life insurance that bases the premium rate and policy values on an age older than the actual age

real property • land and anything that is growing on it, erected on it, or affixed to it, and the bundle of rights inherent in the ownership

reasonable-and-customary charge • a charge that falls within the range of fees normally charged for a given procedure by physicians with similar training and experience in a geographic region. It is usually based on some percentile of the range of charges for specific medical procedures.

rebating • the usually illegal practice of returning a part of the premium paid to the policyowner (except as a dividend) as a price-cutting sales inducement

reciprocal exchange • a not-for-profit unincorporated mutual association managed by an attorney-in-fact. Each member of the reciprocal is both an insured and an insurer of the other members.

reentry term insurance • a form of renewable term life insurance under which one rate schedule is used if the insured can prove continuing insurability. A higher schedule is used if the insured cannot prove continuing insurability.

refund annuity • a life annuity that promises to return in some manner a portion or all of the purchase price

rehabilitation • the process, overseen by an insurance commissioner, of restoring an insurance company to financial stability

rehabilitation benefit • a benefit under workers' compensation laws or disability income plans that provides rehabilitative services for disabled workers. Benefits may be given for medical rehabilitation and for vocational rehabilitation, including training, counseling, and job placement.

rehabilitation provision • a provision in a disability income contract that allows a person to receive reduced benefits during trial work periods in rehabilitative employment. The original benefit is resumed if the person is unable to perform the rehabilitative employment.

reimbursement basis • the method of paying long-term care insurance benefits that reimburses the insured for actual expenses incurred up to the specified policy limit

reinstatement provision • in life insurance, a clause giving the owner of a lapsed policy the right to reacquire the coverage under certain conditions

reinsurance • an arrangement in which an insurance company transfers to another insurance company some or all of the risks it has taken on through the writing of primary insurance

reinsurance facility • a system of providing auto insurance to high-risk drivers. Insurers write coverage but assign premiums to a statewide reinsurance pool. All insurers in the state share the pool's losses and expenses.

renewability • a feature frequently found in individual term life insurance that allows the policyowner to renew the policy for another period of protection, up to a stated point in time, without having to show evidence of insurability

replacement • replacing one life insurance policy with another. To prevent financial harm to the policyowner, agents and insurers must follow prescribed procedures.

replacement cost • the method of valuing property where no deduction is made for depreciation

representation • a statement in an insurance application that is substantially true to the best of the applicant's knowledge and belief. A false representation of a material fact is a misrepresentation.

reserve • an amount that must be maintained by an insurance company to meet definite future obligations. *See also* legal reserve, loss reserve, unearned premium reserve

residual-disability benefits • a provision for the replacement of lost earnings due to less-than-total disability. The benefit is based on a person's reduction in earnings rather than his or her physical condition.

residual market • specialty insurers and government programs that provide insurance for hard-to-insure drivers or property

respite care • occasional full-time care at home for a person who is receiving home health care. Coverage for such care under a long-term care insurance policy enables family members (or other persons) who are providing much of the home care to take a needed break.

restoration of benefits • a provision in long-term care insurance that provides for a restoration of used benefits after a period without claims

return-of-premium option • a provision in disability insurance that provides for the return of some portion of premiums at specified intervals, such as 5 years or 10 years, if no claims have been made during that period

revocable beneficiary • a beneficiary that can be changed by the policyowner without the beneficiary's permission

rider • the term used in life insurance in place of the term endorsement

risk • the possibility of loss

risk and insurance survey form • a questionnaire or checklist used to identify the risks that confront a family or organization

risk avoidance • a risk control method that involves avoiding situations that include certain types of risks

risk control • a program to minimize losses through such activities as avoidance, loss prevention, loss reduction, and noninsurance transfers

risk financing • a program to pay for losses through such means as risk retention in various ways and risk transfer, including insurance

risk identification • the process that involves the careful and systematic discovery of all the risks that confront a household or organization

risk management • a coordinated program for treating risks based on risk identification, risk measurement, choice and use of methods of treatment, and administration

risk retention • a method of risk financing that involves assuming the financial consequences associated with risk

risk-tolerance level • the degree to which an individual is attracted to or averse to the possibility of loss

risk transfer • a method of risk financing that involves shifting the financial consequences of risk to someone else

robbery • the removal of property from one person by someone else who has either caused harm or threatened to cause harm to the person. It also includes situations in which property is taken in an unlawful act that a person has witnessed.

salary continuation plan • *See* sick-leave plan

savings bank life insurance • life insurance allowed to be written by mutual savings banks in Connecticut, Massachusetts, and New York on residents of, and persons regularly employed in, those three states

second surgical opinion • a cost-containment strategy under which covered persons are encouraged or required to obtain the opinion of another physician after certain categories of surgery have been recommended. If a second opinion is mandatory, benefits are reduced if the second opinion is not obtained. Benefits are usually provided for the cost of a third opinion if the opinions of the first two physicians are in disagreement.

second-to-die policy • *See* survivorship life policy

Sec. 79 plan • a group term life insurance plan that qualifies for favorable federal income tax treatment under Sec. 79 of the Internal Revenue Code

self-insurance • a formal program of risk retention usually characterized by factors necessary for a sound insurance enterprise, including funding based on actuarial calculations

self-insured retention • the initial portion of a loss under an umbrella policy that must be assumed by the policyowner when there is no underlying policy to cover the loss

settlement options • ways in which a life insurance policy's death proceeds can be taken, typically in cash, under an interest option, under a fixed-period or fixed-amount option, or under a life-income option

7-pay test • a test to determine if a particular life insurance contract is or is not a modified endowment contract. If the total premium paid into the policy in the first 7 years or in the 7 years following a material change in it exceeds the sum of the net level premiums that would be needed to pay up the policy in 7 years, the policy is an MEC.

shared benefit • long-term care insurance approach to benefits in which a husband and wife are insured under the same policy or with the same insurer and can access each other's unused benefits

shared market • *See* residual market

shopper's guide • a state-approved booklet that must be provided to potential purchasers of certain types of insurance to enable them to better evaluate the benefits and costs of the insurance

short-term disability income plans • insured or uninsured disability income benefit with a typical duration of 6 months or less

sick-leave plan • an uninsured arrangement to replace lost income for a limited time period, often starting on the first day of disability

single premium annuity • an annuity paid with a single premium rather than with installment payments

skilled-nursing care • daily nursing and rehabilitative care that can be performed only by or under the supervision of skilled medical personnel and that must be based on doctors' orders

skilled-nursing facility • *See* extended care facility

social adequacy • a principle emphasized by social insurance programs in which benefits are designed to provide a minimum floor of benefits to all beneficiaries, regardless of their economic status. Social adequacy also is reflected in the provision of disproportionately large benefits relative to contributions for some groups of beneficiaries, particularly lower-income groups.

social insurance • government-run or government-regulated insurance programs designed primarily to solve major social problems that affect a large portion of society. Distinguishing characteristics are compulsory employment-related coverage, partial or total employer financing, benefits prescribed by law, benefits as a matter of right, and emphasis on social adequacy.

Social Security • the term commonly used to identify the old-age, survivors, and disability (OASDI) program of the federal government

Social Security rider • a disability income policy amendment to provide additional disability income benefits payable when an individual is disabled but does not qualify for Social Security disability benefits

Social Security Statement • a statement issued by the Social Security Administration that enables an employee to verify his or her contributions to the Social Security and Medicare programs. The statement also contains an estimate of benefits that will be available because of retirement, disability, or death.

specific rate • property rates for a particular building developed by applying a schedule that measures the relative quantity of fire hazard to the particular loss exposure

specific (schedule) rate • a rate that is created for an individual insured based on that insured's particular risk characteristics

specified disease insurance • a type of medical expense coverage that provides benefits for persons who have certain specified diseases or medical events, such as cancer or heart attacks. The policy may pay for actual medical expenses or, more likely, pay a specified dollar amount, regardless of actual medical expenses and without regard to other coverages.

specified-perils policy • *See* named-perils policy

speculative risk • a possibility of loss with three possible outcomes: loss, no loss/no gain, or gain

split-dollar carve-out arrangement • a plan whereby life insurance is provided to selected employees under a split-dollar arrangement that is superimposed on a group life insurance plan for employees in general

split-dollar life insurance • a plan under which two parties, usually an employer and an insured employee, share the premium costs, death proceeds, and perhaps the cash value of a life insurance policy pursuant to a prearranged agreement

split limits • in liability insurance, separate limits that apply to any one person for bodily injury, to the aggregate for all bodily injury claims in an accident, and to property damage

staff adjuster • an employee of an insurance company whose full-time job is adjusting claims for that insurer

staff-model HMO • an HMO that owns its own facilities and hires its own physicians. It may also own hospitals, laboratories, or pharmacies, or it may contract for these services.

standard policy provisions laws • state laws that require life and health insurance policies to include certain provisions but allow insurers to select the actual wording as long as it is at least as favorable to the policyowner as the statutory language

stated amount • an approach to valuing property found in some property insurance policies. At the time of the loss, the insurer will pay the least of the stated amount, the actual cash value, or the cost to repair or replace the property.

static risk • in contrast with dynamic risk, a possibility of loss that exists even in the absence of changes in society. Hurricanes are an example.

step-rate annuity • an annuity for which future benefits increase, possibly at a compound annual rate. Step-rate annuities are often used in structured settlements.

stock insurance company • a profit-seeking insurance company owned by its stockholders

stop-loss limit • the maximum amount of out-of-pocket medical expenses that a covered person must pay in a given period (usually one year). After this limit is reached, future copayments and deductibles are waived for the remainder of the period.

straight life annuity • *See* pure annuity

strict compliance rule • a legal principle that specifies that a written contract will normally be enforced on the basis of strict conformity with the terms contained in that contract

strict liability • liability under law, regardless of whether fault or negligence can be proved

structured settlement • an agreement to pay a specified set of periodic benefits in lieu of (or in addition to) a single lump-sum amount

subrogation • a process by which an insurer takes over the legal rights its insured has against a responsible third party

substandard annuity • an annuity whose benefit payments are larger per dollar of purchase price than those of a standard annuity because of the annuitant's impaired health

substandard market • *See* residual market

suicide provision • an optional life insurance policy provision that specifies that if the insured, whether sane or insane, commits suicide during the first one or 2 years of the policy, the insurer will be liable only for a return of the premium

supplemental plan • *See* buy-up plan

surety • the party to a surety bond who agrees to indemnify the obligee for damages because of the principal's failure to uphold an agreement

surety bond • an agreement in which a surety provides a guarantee of indemnity if a second party, the principal, fails to perform a specified act or fulfill an obligation to the obligee

surplus lines broker • *See* excess lines broker

surrender charge • a fee imposed on the owners of certain types of life insurance policies and annuities at the time they surrender their contracts

surrender cost index • a method of estimating the net cost of life insurance on a time-value-adjusted basis, assuming the policy will be surrendered at the end of a specified time period

survivorship (second-to-die) life policy • a type of life insurance policy that covers two or more persons in which the proceeds are payable on the death of the last person to die

target premium • the level renewal premium that the insurer suggests be paid for a universal life insurance policy

tax-qualified policy • a long-term care insurance contract that meets the requirements of the Health Insurance Portability and Accountability Act for favorable income tax treatment

temporary disability law • a law in a few states that requires employers to provide short-term disability income benefits to employees for non-work-related disabilities. Often referred to as a *nonoccupational disability law.*

temporary life annuity • an annuity whose benefit payments continue until the earlier of the death of a designated person or the end of a specified period of time

temporary medical insurance • short-term medical insurance that generally provides coverage for periods between 30 days and one year while a person is between medical expense plans

temporary substitute vehicle • in personal auto insurance, a vehicle not owned by the insured while it is used temporarily in place of a covered auto that is out of normal use because of breakdown, repair, servicing, loss, or destruction

term life insurance • a form of life insurance in which the death proceeds are payable in the event of the insured's death during a specified period and nothing is paid if the insured survives to the end of that period

theft • a broad term that encompasses robbery, burglary, shoplifting, and any other act of stealing

third-party-over suit • a suit that can result when the manufacturer of a product that injures one of the employer's workers is sued by the worker who, in turn, sues the employer for improper maintenance of the product

title insurance • protection for the purchaser of real estate against defects in title that occurred prior to the effective date of coverage but are discovered after the effective date

tort • a civil wrong other than breach of contract

transfer-for-value rule • a rule that specifies that, subject to certain exceptions, if a life insurance policy is transferred from one owner to another for valuable consideration, the death proceeds will be subject to federal income taxation

transfer tax • a tax on gifts, estates, or generation-skipping transfers

treaty reinsurance • reinsurance that is obligatory for the original or primary insurer and the reinsurer with respect to every loss exposure covered by the treaty or agreement

trip transit policy • a type of inland marine insurance policy that covers only the particular shipment specified in the policy

twisting • the illegal practice in life insurance of using misrepresentation to induce a policyowner, to his or her disadvantage, to replace a life insurance policy with a new one

umbrella liability policy • a personal or business liability policy that provides high limits for a broad range of liability situations. The policyowner is required to have underlying liability coverage of specified amounts. Claims not covered by the underlying insurance are subject to a self-insured retention.

unauthorized entity • an insurance company (or other organization, either real or fictitious) that has not gained approval to place insurance business from a department of insurance in the jurisdiction where it or a producer wants to sell insurance

uncertainty • a state of mind that arises from the presence of risk and is characterized by not being sure about something. Uncertainty often is characterized by worry and fear.

underinsured motorists coverage • an auto insurance coverage that enables an insured to collect from his or her own insurance company for bodily injuries (and property damage in a few states) that are caused by a legally liable but underinsured driver. Covers the difference between the limit of the underinsured motorists coverage and the amount of the auto liability insurance carried by the underinsured driver.

underlying coverage • the primary policies and limits required by an insurer that provides umbrella liability insurance. If these policies and limits are not carried, the insured must absorb this amount of any claim before the umbrella policy pays.

underwriting • the selection (or rejection) and pricing of applicants for insurance

unearned premium reserve • in property and liability insurance, an insurer's liability for future claims or premium refunds, as measured by the proportion of the written premiums for those policies that the insurer has not yet earned by providing protection for the full policy period

unemployment insurance • joint federal and state programs to provide income benefits to unemployed workers who meet the specific program requirements. In most states, these programs are financed entirely by employer contributions.

Uniform Premium Table I • an IRS table used to determine the amount of taxable income from group term life insurance

unilateral contract • a contract in which only one of the parties to it makes a binding promise that, if broken, gives rise to an action against that party for breach of contract

uninsured motorists coverage • an auto insurance coverage that enables an insured to collect from his or her own insurance company for bodily injuries (and property damage in a few states) that are caused by a legally liable but uninsured driver

universal life insurance • a type of life insurance policy characterized by flexible premiums, a shift of some investment risk to the policyowner even though the policyowner is not allowed to direct the investment portfolio, and a choice of death benefit designs

unsatisfied judgment fund • a fund in some states to compensate victims who are unable to collect a legal judgment that results from an auto accident. The maximum amount that can be received is usually equal to a state's financial responsibility limits.

use-and-file law • a rating law with which rates are filed with the insurance commissioner within a specified time after the rates are first used. The insurance commissioner may, however, disapprove the rates.

utilization review • the process of reviewing the appropriateness and quality of medical care provided to patients. It can be conducted on a prospective, concurrent, or retroactive basis.

valued contract • a contract in which the amount of recovery does not depend on the financial amount of the loss but rather on the limit specified in the contract

valued policy law • a law in a few states that makes valued policies mandatory for property insurance on homes or other real estate property. Most valued policy laws apply only when property is totally destroyed and only by certain perils.

vanishing premium whole life insurance • a type of current assumption whole life insurance designed so that if experience is favorable, the accumulation account equals or exceeds the net single premium necessary to pay up the contract

variable annuity • an annuity with benefit payments that vary depending on the performance of selected blocks of the insurer's invested assets

variable life insurance • a type of life insurance policy in which the policyowner directs how the cash value will be invested and bears the investment risk, and in which the death benefit is linked to the investment performance of the policy

variable universal life insurance • a type of life insurance policy that combines the premium flexibility features of universal life insurance with the policyowner-directed investment aspects of variable life insurance

viatical settlement • the sale of a terminally ill insured's life insurance policy in exchange for a percentage of the face amount

viatical settlement provider • the party that purchases a policy from a viator under a viatical settlement purchase agreement

viatical settlement purchase agreement • contract arranging for the sale of a life insurance policy by a viator to a viatical settlement provider

viator • the policyowner who sells a life insurance policy to a third party

vicarious liability • imputed liability to, for example, owners of vehicles

vision care expense benefits • benefits for vision care expenses that are not usually covered under other medical expense plans. Benefits are provided for the cost of eye examinations and eyeglasses or contact lenses.

void contract • a contract that is entirely without legal effect and, therefore, unenforceable by either party. In essence, a void contract never was a contract.

voidable contract • a contract that can be affirmed or rejected at the option of one of the parties but is binding on the other party

voluntary benefits • a plan offered to employees under which they may purchase insurance coverages with premiums paid through payroll deductions. The employer does not share in the premium cost.

voluntary compensation and employers liability coverage endorsement • an insurance policy endorsement that obligates the insurance company to pay an amount equal to what is available under a state's workers' compensation law to employees who are not covered under the law

waiting period (elimination period) • a period of time that an employee must be disabled before benefits commence under an employee benefit plan, such as disability income insurance, Social Security, workers' compensation insurance, and long-term care insurance

waiver-of-premium rider • a rider under which, if the insured becomes totally disabled, the insurer will waive the premiums on the policy during the continuance of the disability. It is commonly used in life and health insurance.

warranty • a statement that becomes a part of an insurance contract and that must be strictly complied with. A warranty, if false, makes the policy voidable, even if the false statement is not material.

watercraft insurance • insurance policies to provide liability, physical damage, and medical payments coverage for boat owners

whole life insurance • a form of life insurance that provides death benefits upon the death of the insured, no matter when that occurs, if the policy is kept in force by the policyowner

withdrawal • the right, in some life insurance policies, to take part of the cash value without its being treated as a loan. It is commonly found in forms of universal life insurance.

workers' compensation insurance • insurance under which the insurer agrees to pay all compensation required by workers' compensation laws

workers' compensation law • a type of law enacted in all states under which employers are required to provide benefits to employees for losses that result from work-related accidents or diseases. Benefits include medical care, disability income, income for survivors, and rehabilitative services.

yacht policy • a package policy that provides liability and physical damage coverage for large boats

yearly renewable term insurance • a plan that provides a level amount of insurance for one year, renewable for a stated number of years, with the premium at each renewal date rising at an increasing rate consistent with the rise in the mortality rate over time

Answers to Mini-Cases, Review Questions, and Self-Test Questions

Chapter 1

Answers to Mini-Case

    a. Amy and John's house could be damaged by the peril of fire. A physical hazard relates to the age of the house, which also appears to need repairs.

    b. Amy and John face the following risks:
- financial—Amy's car could be totaled in an auto accident, requiring them to pay for a replacement vehicle.
- nonfinancial—Amy and John might find that they are unable to have children.
- particular—Amy and John could both lose their jobs at the same time if SKH reorganizes.
- fundamental—The value of their house could decline if real estate values drop because of problems in the economy.
- static—The house could be struck by lightning.
- dynamic—Changes in the educational system might make it impossible for Amy and John's future children to attend the school conveniently located across the street from their house.
- pure—John's car might be damaged in an auto accident.
- speculative—The house they just purchased might increase or decrease in value.
- insurable—Physical damage to their cars would be insurable.
- uninsurable—Property losses resulting from war are uninsurable due to their catastrophic nature.

    c. John and Amy seem to be inconsistent in their tolerance for risk. Their investments are extremely conservative and avoid risk. It appears they buy only the minimum amounts of insurance required, so their approach to insurance leaves them exposed to risk. It is not clear whether this is the result of a high tolerance for risk or a lack of sufficient understanding regarding the benefits of insurance. At the other extreme, they took the risk of buying an old home with plans of fixing it.

    d. John and Amy have these types of insurance:
- life and health insurance—life insurance, medical expense insurance, and disability income insurance provided through SKH
- property and liability insurance—auto and homeowners insurance
- individual insurance—auto and homeowners insurance
- group insurance—life insurance, medical expense insurance, and disability income insurance provided through SKH

    e. Amy and John's current insurance program provides assurance of payment for losses arising from sickness, death, disability, liability claims from an auto accident, and damage to their home. These assurances give them peace of mind. Their homeowners insurance also enabled them to borrow the money to buy their house.

    f. While paying for the benefits of auto and homeowners insurance, Amy and John are also paying money that contributes to the insurer's operating costs and profits.

Answers to Review Questions

1-1.   For purposes of this book, *risk* is defined as the *possibility of loss*. Uncertainty is the state of mind of being unsure. As a consequence, uncertainty can vary significantly from one person to another, even when each is confronted with the same set of facts, the same objective reality, or the same risk.

1-2.   A fire can cause direct and indirect losses. The damage to the printing equipment and paper are examples of direct losses. The loss of income from having to close temporarily and the extra expense of having to rent other premises at a higher cost are examples of indirect loss. If the fire was a result of Jim's negligence, any damages awarded for bodily injury or property damage to others are direct losses; any income Jim lost while attending court proceedings is an indirect loss.

1-3.   These factors represent the following to Sally:
   a.   risk—the possibility of Sally's children losing her financial support
   b.   peril—Sally's death
   c.   hazard—her high blood pressure, which increases the chance of loss

1-4.   The types of hazards are as follows:
   a.   physical hazards
   b.   attitudinal hazard (carelessness)
   c.   moral hazard

1-5.   a.   Although the probability of death for a woman aged 29 is quite small, she is only one person, and knowledge of the probability is no help in measuring the risk (possibility of loss) she alone faces. If she dies, her family will suffer a loss of her future income that would have been available for their support. The financial loss to her family would be severe even though the chance of loss is small. This situation of low probability but high severity is where insurance works most effectively and efficiently.
   b.   Life insurance companies measure their probabilities by observing large numbers (mass) of similar (homogeneous) exposures (females aged 29 insured in the past) in the statistical group from which they make their estimate of the probability of a female dying at age 29. They also apply this estimate to a large number (mass) of (homogeneous) exposures (females aged 29 insured at present) in estimating the percentage of the currently insured females aged 29 who will die during the year. However, the insurer cannot determine any better than Janet whether she or any particular individual in the group will or will not die this year.

1-6.   a.   Particular risks are loss possibilities that affect only individuals or small groups of individuals at the same time, rather than a large segment of society. Fundamental risks, in contrast, are loss possibilities that can affect large segments of society at the same time.
   b.   Dealing with particular risks is generally thought to be the responsibility of the individuals who are exposed to them. However, some social insurance programs also deal with particular risks. Fundamental risks, on the other hand, are not the fault of any specific individual, and dealing with them is generally thought to be the responsibility of society as a whole through government action.

1-7.   Homeownership can give rise to
   a.   pure risk by providing a possibility of loss from fire, windstorm, theft, and many other property-related perils as well as from legal liability (for example, the possibility of someone's falling down your shaky stairs to the basement).
   b.   speculative risk by providing a possibility of a gain or a loss when the home is sold

1-8.   Insurance is concerned mainly with the economic problems created by pure risks where there is only the potential for loss or no loss. The pure risks confronting individuals and businesses are ordinarily divided into three categories: risks involving the person, risks involving loss of or damage to property, and risks involving liability for injury or damage to persons or the property of others.

1-9.   Gambling creates risk, while insurance transfers or reduces a risk that already exists.

1-10.   A risk must substantially meet the following five requirements:
   •   The amount of the loss must be important.
   •   The loss must be accidental in nature.
   •   Future losses must be calculable.
   •   The loss must be definite.
   •   The loss cannot be excessively catastrophic.
   Many insurance risks do not meet each of the requirements perfectly, but when considered as a whole, they may meet the requisites adequately.

1-11.   Risk-tolerance levels vary from person to person, situation to situation, and risk to risk. Based on research on the risk tolerance of individuals, we know that:
   •   Most people are more risk averse than they are risk tolerant.
   •   Risk taking in physical or social activities does not necessarily correlate with high risk tolerance in financial matters.
   •   The way in which questions about a risk are worded or posed to a person can influence the person's attitude toward that risk.
   •   Emotions can severely limit a person's ability to make rational decisions about a risk.

- People tend to overestimate low-probability risks and underestimate higher-probability risks.
- People are more likely to be risk averse if the major impact of a possible loss will fall on them or their loved ones, rather than mainly on strangers.
- Most people have a greater fear of risks with which they are inexperienced than of risks with which they are familiar.

1-12. Because pure risks generally produce either losses or no losses, they represent a cost to society with little or no offsetting benefit. Losses could cripple a business or cause an individual or family great financial hardship. Direct physical loss, such as fire damage, results in several billion dollars of property loss each year in the United States. Indirect loss, such as lost profits following a direct loss, is also considerable. Billions of dollars are lost, too, because of the loss of human life values due to such perils as death and disability. Even if no losses ever occur as anticipated, at least three factors add to the costs of risks: (1) fear and worry, (2) inadequate preparation, and (3) expenses of managing risks.

1-13. Insurance can be defined from the following viewpoints:
  a. economics. Insurance reduces risk by transferring them to an insurer who combines policyowners' potential losses.
  b. legal. Insurance transfers risk by the terms of a contract.
  c. business. Insurance is a financial institution specializing in the treatment of risk.
  d. social. Insurance pools losses by using group members' contributions to pay losses suffered by some group members.
  e. mathematical. Insurance predicts and distributes losses using actuarial estimates based on principles of probability.

1-14. Benefits include the following: Insurance pays for losses, provides a basis for credit, encourages peace of mind, stimulates saving, offers the advantages of specialization, and fosters loss prevention. Costs of insurance include operating costs, insurer profits, opportunity costs, possible increased losses, and adverse selection.

1-15. Social insurance programs tend to have the following characteristics: compulsory employment-related coverage, partial or total employer financing, benefits prescribed by law but not uniform for everyone, benefits as a matter of right, and emphasis on social adequacy rather than individual equity.

1-16. Individual insurance is usually owned by the person or entity that is insured or who owns the property. Group insurance is issued as a single contract to someone other than the person insured and provides coverage to a number of persons.

   Coverage under individual insurance normally begins with the inception of the contract and ceases with its termination. Under group insurance, individual members may become eligible for coverage long after the inception of the contract or lose their eligibility status long before the contract terminates.

   Individual insurance underwriting typically requires the individual to show evidence of insurability. Under group insurance, underwriting is focused on the characteristics of the group, and individual members are usually not required to show evidence of insurability when initially eligible for coverage.

   Individual insurance rates are based on characteristics of the insured person, entity, or property; under group insurance, the group as a whole may be experience rated.

Answers to Self-Test Questions

1-1. True.

1-2. False. Risk is the possibility, not the probability or chance, of loss.

1-3. False. This is an *indirect* loss.

1-4. True.

1-5. False. Perils are causes of loss. Hazards are acts or conditions that increase the chance or amount of loss caused by a peril.

1-6. False. Attitudinal hazards are evidenced by carelessness or indifference. Moral hazards are evidenced by dishonest tendencies.

1-7. True.

1-8. False. An individual cannot use the probability of a loss to measure the risk he or she faces—the individual either will or will not suffer a loss. Statistical probabilities have no relevance in this case. To use a probability to measure risk, a large number of similar exposures would be needed.

1-9. False. This is most likely if the number of insureds is also large.

1-10. True.

1-11. False. Because pure risks involve only loss or no loss, they cannot be handled effectively with hedging. Because speculative risks involve *gain* as well as loss, they *can* be handled effectively with hedging.

1-12. False. The fact that risk is an existing condition is what removes insurance from the category of a gambling risk. Insurance does not create risk—gambling does.

1-13. True.

1-14. False. In addition to the actual loss that takes place, the costs associated with pure risk include fear and worry, less-than-optimal use of resources, and the expenses of treating risks.

1-15. True.

1-16. False. Adverse selection is the natural tendency for those who know they are highly vulnerable to loss from a specific risk to be most inclined to acquire and retain insurance to cover that loss. Adverse selection by applicants and policyowners is counterbalanced by the care insurers exercise in underwriting, a matter discussed further in chapter 4.

1-17. True.

1-18. True.

1-19. False. Social insurance emphasizes social adequacy rather than individual equity.

1-20. True.

Chapter 2

Answers to Mini-Case

a. Amy and John could identify their risks by using a survey form or questionnaire, reviewing their balance sheet, and conducting a personal inspection of their house and cars.

b. Amy and John could use risk management techniques in the following ways:

- risk avoidance—Amy and John briefly consider taking a trip to a third-world country but, worried about their safety, instead take a trip to Disney's Epcot Center.
- loss prevention—Keeping their sidewalk clear of snow helps prevent the possibility that John, Amy, or a guest or member of the public will slip and fall on their property.
- loss reduction—Using seat belts whenever they drive will not prevent John and Amy from having auto accidents, but it can make the resulting injuries less severe.
- noninsurance transfer—A contract with any contractor working on their house might shift responsibility for injury or damage, resulting from his or her work, to the contractor.
- risk retention—With no collision insurance on either car, they are currently practicing risk retention.

c. Amy and John's risks can be categorized as follows:

- Because John has a bad driving record, it would appear that accident damage to his car is a high-frequency, high-severity exposure. Loss prevention—improving his driving habits—is advisable.
- Liability claims from an injured guest would probably be rare (low frequency), but a serious injury could result in a large claim (high severity). The liability coverage of their homeowners policy is important.
- Surgery is usually a low-frequency, high-severity exposure, but it is one of many good reasons to have medical expense insurance.
- Dental cavities occur with some frequency, but dental fillings are usually relatively inexpensive. The Schultzes could retain this high-frequency, low-severity exposure.

Answers to Review Questions

2-1. The four steps in the risk management process are identification, measurement, choice and use of methods to treat each identified risk, and administration.

2-2. Many risk managers might say that the objective is to "preserve the assets and income of my organization or household by providing protection against the possibility of accidental loss." More specific risk management goals might include (1) survival, (2) peace of mind, (3) lower costs (or higher net income), (4) stable earnings, (5) minimal interruption of business operations or personal life, (6) continued growth, and (7) satisfaction of social responsibility with a good public image.

2-3. The risk manager's responsibilities and authority in a large organization are quite broad and cut across many of the organization's activities. The risk manager of a larger firm has, in a majority of cases, full responsibility in the property and liability area for (1) identifying and evaluating risks, (2) selecting insurers, (3) approving insurance renewals and amounts, (4) negotiating insurance rates, (5) seeking competitive insurance bids, (6) keeping insurance records, (7) choosing deductibles, and (8) handling insurance claims. The risk manager usually shares authority for (1) deciding whether or not to insure or retain (including self-insuring) financial risks, (2) selecting insurance agents and brokers, (3) instituting safety programs, and (4) reviewing contracts other than insurance. In some organizations, the risk manager also has some responsibility for life and health insurance programs, while in others, these programs fall within the scope of the human resources or personnel department.

Sometimes, particularly in small- and medium-size firms, an insurance agent, broker, or consultant serves as the risk manager, because the organization has no one person assigned to these responsibilities. Larger agencies and brokerages, especially, offer to serve in this capacity. Care must be taken to see (1) that the services are much broader than mere insurance coverages and include loss prevention and other risk treatment alternatives, and (2) that the insurance agency or brokerage representative or consultant knows the firm's special individual needs.

2-4. Risk control methods attempt to reduce the probability or severity of losses, focusing on minimizing losses that might occur to assets and income. Risk financing methods facilitate paying for losses that do occur.

2-5. Although some unusual risks with a high chance of loss can be avoided, realistically, risk avoidance is an alternative for only a limited number of risks. Some risks may be impossible to avoid; others may not be economically desirable to avoid because of the high costs of doing so or because avoiding one risk may create another.

2-6. Unplanned risk retention is the result of lack of planning, or lack of knowledge concerning the exposure. Unplanned risk retention can also result from unintentional or irrational actions or from passive behavior due to lack of thought, laziness, or lack of interest in discovering possibilities of loss.

2-7. Deductibles lower insurance premiums by eliminating the relatively high claims costs associated with small losses. From the insurer's perspective, deductibles also minimize moral hazards by making an insured responsible for a portion of any loss.

2-8. Retention through the use of deductibles generally provides a more cost-effective method of handling high-frequency, low-severity losses than the purchase of first-dollar insurance for those losses. With insurance, not only would Sam's premium contain a charge for expected losses (close or equal to actual losses in the case of high-frequency, low-severity losses), but he would also be charged for insurance company expenses and profit. Instead, by using a deductible and keeping the freed-up premium dollars invested, Sam can save the charge for insurance company expenses and profit, and he also can earn a return on his money until it is needed to pay the high-frequency, low-severity losses.

2-9. Family or business retained risks are commonly financed by (1) absorption in current operating expenses or family budgets, (2) funding and reserves, (3) self-insurance through a formal program of risk retention, and (4) captive insurers, which are separate subsidiary insurance companies established to write the parent company's insurance.

2-10. a. The insurance equation shows that the receipts taken in equal what is paid out. The receipts include (1) premiums (or insurance payments from policyowners), (2) investment earnings, and (3) other income. The factors that enter into what is paid out are (1) the cost of losses, (2) the cost of doing business, or expenses, and (3) the cost of capital, or profits.

b. Probability measures the chance of occurrence of a particular event. In the field of insurance, the theory of probability has proved to be of great importance in measuring (predicting) losses. The probability of loss is expressed algebraically in a fraction whose numerator is the number of unfavorable outcomes and whose denominator is the total number of all possible outcomes. The insurer can reduce the total of all the uncertainties to within a reasonable degree of certainty. Within calculable limits, the insurer can foresee the normal losses and estimate losses from catastrophes to compute the premium necessary to pay all losses, as well as to cover expenses and profits.

c. As the number of independent events increases, the likelihood increases that the actual results will be close to the expected results. Insurance is concerned with the number of times an event, or loss, can be expected to happen over a series of occasions. Certain events occur with surprising regularity when a large number of instances is observed. The regularity of the events increases as the observed instances become more numerous.

d. Use of the mathematical laws of probability and large numbers requires adequate statistical data. Unless accurate statistical information is available, predictions in the form of probabilities will be defective. In each of the lines of insurance, carefully compiled statistics are assembled to accumulate experience as a basis for rate making.

The goal is to reduce judgment factors to a minimum and to set rates scientifically, based on the use of statistical data in applying known laws of probability, variability, and large numbers. Insurance applies mathematical tools to statistical data on groups to achieve better predictions than individuals can make.

2-11.   Four methods of risk identification are as follows:

- *survey forms.* Although most often used in business situations, survey forms are also appropriate for nonprofit organizations, as well as for individuals and families. In the business sector, small- and medium-sized businesses need good risk and insurance surveys as much as larger firms do. The smaller businesses, in fact, are particularly vulnerable to financial ruin as the result of a mistake or omission regarding insurance protection. Risk and insurance survey forms focus on risk detection, identification, and classification. Sometimes they also include estimates of the possible loss values, which are part of risk measurement.

- *financial statement analysis.* In financial statement analysis, each account in the balance sheet, the profit and loss statement, and other financial statements is listed separately and analyzed to determine the potential perils that might cause losses. A comprehensive analysis of a firm's financial statements thus becomes a very useful method for identifying both direct and indirect losses. Similarly, for a family, financial records can reveal many of the risks confronting a household.

- *personal inspections.* Personal inspections of a business a household by insurance consultants or agents are a significant source of information about possible losses.

- *contract analysis.* Hold-harmless agreements can mean liability exposures are transferred to or by the client. Other relevant contracts involve short-term auto rental agreements, auto lease agreements, apartment rental agreements, agreements for the purchase or sale of a house, and the master deed or declarations of a condominium complex.

2-12.   At the level of the household or small business organization, the choice of the best technique or combination of techniques is likely to be determined by such hard-to-quantify factors as the following:

- maximum probable loss associated with a particular risk in comparison with the household's or firm's financial and other capacities for bearing risk

- legal restrictions that may force or preclude the use of one or more of the available techniques

- extent to which the household or firm is able to exert control over the loss frequency or severity associated with the risk

- loading fees (expense charges) associated with the available risk management techniques

- value of ancillary services that may be provided as part of the risk treatment technique, especially the insurance technique

- time value of investable funds that may be gained or lost by using certain of the available techniques

- federal income tax treatment of losses under the various techniques

- possible unavailability of certain techniques for dealing with some pure risks

2-13.   A review of insurance priorities first assumes that, for each of the pure risks that have been identified and measured in the risk management process, insurance will be used if it is available. The most suitable policy and its cost are listed for each risk as a benchmark against which to evaluate other possible techniques. Listing insurance policies also clarifies which risks must be treated by means other than insurance—that is, the risks for which no insurance policy is available.

Next, insurance coverages are grouped into priority categories such as

- essential (for example, insurance required by law or losses of possibly disastrous results for the household or business)

- desirable (for example, losses that would seriously impair but not totally wipe out the financial position of the household or business)

- available (all other types of insurance coverage)

Finally, each insurance coverage is compared with the other available techniques for treating the particular risk.

A different approach to selecting the most appropriate technique is to group the most logical techniques based on the probable frequency and severity of the losses associated with each pure risk confronting the family or organization.

2-14.   The three building blocks in an insurance program are

- *social insurance.* The first building block is several social insurance programs, each of which is designed to provide a floor of protection against certain perils. For example, Social Security (OASDI) covers the perils of old age, death, and disability.

- *employer-sponsored insurance.* The second building block is various insurance programs made available at work. Group insurance programs can provide specified types of coverage such as group life insurance, group medical expense insurance, and a pension plan.

- *individual insurance.* The third building block—individual insurance—should fill in coverage gaps left by social insurance and employer-sponsored insurance and increase total coverage amounts to the necessary levels.

2-15.   Norma and Sidney's approach to risk management should follow a four-step process:

(1)   Norma and Sidney should begin with risk identification, using a combination of tools such as survey forms, checklists, and questionnaires; financial statement analysis; personal inspection of their premises; and analysis of any contracts, especially the master deed or declarations on their condominium and the lease agreement on their car.

(2)   Norma and Sidney should attempt to measure the risks associated with the various loss exposures they identify, taking into account both loss frequency and loss severity. Among other factors, they should consider both the maximum possible loss and the maximum probable loss associated with their various exposures. For example, the maximum possible loss resulting from fire or hurricane damage to their condominium is likely to be limited to the value of the condominium unit, its contents, and any additional living expenses that result from the damage; they can set insurance limits accordingly. On the other hand, potential liability losses can be very high; to preserve the assets on which their retirement depends they must be sure to have high limits of liability insurance.

(3)   The third step in the risk management process is to evaluate both the suitability and the cost of various methods of treating their pure risks. Property insurance and liability insurance were briefly mentioned in connection with risk measurement, but insurance is not the only option for dealing with risks. Safe driving and periodic physical exams are among many risk control measures Norma and Sidney should consider. In deciding which risks to insure and which to retain, Norma and Sidney can determine whether insurance is essential, desirable, or available, and they can group their various exposures by their frequency and severity characteristics.

(4)   Last but not least, Norma and Sidney need to put their risk management plan into action by purchasing insurance, scheduling physical exams with their doctors, and taking other measures to administer their risk management program. They should also engage in a periodic review to address any changes that might be necessary.

Answers to Self-Test Questions

2-1.   True.

2-2.   False. The risk management process considers all the alternatives for treating risks.

2-3.   True.

2-4.   True.

2-5.   False. Self-insurance is generally appropriate only for large businesses that can act like an insurance company for their own risks.

2-6.   False. Other noninsurance risk transfer methods also can be used to handle pure risks—for example, extended warranties and hold-harmless agreements.

2-7.   False. Premiums plus investment earnings plus other income must equal losses, expenses, and profits.

2-8.   True.

2-9.   False. The first step is risk identification.

2-10. True.

2-11. True.

Chapter 3

Answers to Review Questions

3-1.   Both stock and mutual insurance companies are corporations. The stock company is owned by stockholders who elect the board of directors and who typically receive any dividends. The mutual company is owned by policyowners who elect the board of directors and who typically receive any dividends.

3-2.   a.   Probably the most important reason for demutualization is to enable the insurer to raise capital quickly. A second and often related reason is to enable the insurance company to diversify its activities by acquiring other insurers or other types of financial institutions through the issuance or exchange of stock. A third reason for demutualization is to facilitate payment of certain types of noncash compensation to the insurance company's key executives and board members. A fourth reason is to gain federal income tax savings.

b. One disadvantage of demutualization is that the time, cost, and complexity may be enormous due to the difficult regulatory, tax, legal, and accounting problems that must be overcome. Of particular importance is the regulatory requirement that the policyowners of the company that seeks to demutualize be compensated adequately for loss of their ownership rights. A second disadvantage of demutualization is that, as a stock company, the insurer might become vulnerable to a hostile takeover. Third, as a stock insurer, the company would have to meet SEC and state rules relating to its equity securities. Fourth, demutualization represents a major change in corporate philosophy by introducing an explicit profit motive, a change that may be difficult for senior executives and other long-standing employees of the former mutual company to accept.

3-3. Reciprocal exchanges are not mutual insurers in the legal sense because the individual subscribers assume liability as individuals, not as a group as a whole. Another basic difference from mutual insurers is that reciprocal exchanges are not incorporated but are formed under separate laws as associations under the direction of an attorney-in-fact.

3-4. Lloyd's itself does not directly issue insurance policies; rather, insurance is written by underwriting members who sign "each for himself and not for another." The insurer, then, is not Lloyd's but the underwriters at Lloyd's. A policyowner insures *at* Lloyd's but not *with* Lloyd's.

3-5. Both stock and mutual insurance companies attempt to operate at a profit in a very competitive marketplace, and profits account for only a small component of the insurance premium. Factors other than the insurer's organizational structure have a greater bearing on the ultimate cost of insurance to the consumer.

3-6. First, financial planners must understand insurance marketing because they are, in many cases, active participants in the marketing process, deriving some of their compensation from being participants. Second, working with consumers of insurance, financial planners need to understand the choices among insurers and agents that clients must make in buying insurance. Finally, the methods companies use to sell and service insurance contracts are significant in determining their costs and usefulness.

3-7. The agent's powers are defined by his or her agency contract with the insurer. The agency contract spells out the agent's express authority. The agent also has implied or incidental authority to carry out those acts needed to exercise his or her express authority. An agent's acts may bind the principal even if those acts are outside the scope of the agent's express or implied authority, or if the acts are within the agent's apparent authority. This type of authority arises when the agent, without contrary action by the principal, performs an act that appears to a reasonable person to be within the agent's express or implied authority.

Among the legal duties an agent owes to his or her principal are the duty to be loyal to the principal, not to be negligent, and to obey instructions given by the principal. Duties the principal owes to the agent include the duty to give the agent an opportunity to work, to compensate the agent, to keep accounts of amounts owed to the agent, and to reimburse the agent for authorized payments the agent makes and liabilities he or she incurs while working for the principal.

3-8. a. Life insurance companies customarily limit the authority to issue or modify life insurance contracts to salaried company officers. Life insurance agents, even those called general agents, are thus limited agents. Generally, life insurance agents are authorized to solicit, receive, and forward applications for the contracts written by their companies. Agents are authorized to receive the first premiums due on applications but not subsequent premiums. The life insurance agent's authority is also limited in the ability to accept business or bind the coverage. The life insurer issues the contract after receiving the written, signed application and, often, a medical examination report. The agent may not cover the policyowner immediately, nor may contract modifications be made later without the insurance company's approval.

b. Agents appointed to represent property and liability insurers are often granted the powers of a general agent. The limitations on their authority are set forth in the agency agreement. General agents may bind their companies for a client's coverage in certain cases. This is done by an oral or written binder, which is temporary evidence of coverage until the full insurance policy is issued by the insurance company. Among their other responsibilities, these agents inspect and collect initial (and sometimes renewal) premiums. Some general agents even issue contracts in their own offices for auto or homeowners policies. Contracts for other lines of insurance may have to be issued by the insurer in the home office or a branch office.

3-9. a. Tom would be covered immediately by XYZ Insurance Company under the homeowners policy. Property and liability agents typically have express authority to bind their companies for most cases involving a homeowners policy. However, even if the agent didn't have express authority to bind the company in this case, the company would be bound by the agent's apparent authority exercised when the agent told Tom he was covered.

b. Tom would not be covered immediately by ABC Life. A life insurance agent does not have the authority to cover the applicant immediately.

3-10. a. The agent (often referred to as a producer) is a representative of the insurance company (called the principal in agency law). The broker acts on behalf of the applicant for insurance or the policyowner after the insurance goes into effect.

      b. The insurance agent is acting under specific and delegated authority from the insurer and is sometimes authorized to bind coverage within specific limits. The broker, on the other hand, has no such authority. In fact, because the broker represents the applicant or policyowner, the applicant or policyowner is bound by the broker's acts.

3-11. a. Historically, a general agent was an individual entrepreneur granted a franchise by an insurer to market the insurer's products in a specified geographic area. The general agent represented only that one insurer, and he or she was responsible for hiring, training, motivating, and supervising agents. The general agent was compensated solely by commissions on business the agency produced and was fully responsible for all expenses of operating the agency. In more recent times, however, insurance companies have typically given some form of financial assistance to the general agent, perhaps paying some of the costs involved in hiring and training new agents and/or providing an allowance to cover some of the operating agency's expenses.

      b. In the branch office or managerial system, the insurer establishes branch offices in the areas where it writes business, with each branch headed by a manager who is a salaried employee of the insurance company. Again, the manager is responsible for hiring, training, motivating, and supervising agents for the company, but the insurer bears all costs of operating the branch. The branch manager may also receive a bonus as part of his or her compensation, depending on the quantity and quality of business the branch writes. Payment of bonuses to branch managers, together with coverage of some general agency operating expenses, has tended to blur somewhat the historical distinctions between the two agency systems.

      c. A variation of the general agency system that has become significant in some life insurance companies is the personal producing general agent (PPGA) system. In this system, the insurer hires an experienced agent with a proven record of sales success as its general agent in a given territory. Unlike a traditional general agent, however, the PPGA's main responsibility is to sell the insurer's products, rather than to build an agency force for the company. The PPGA often receives higher commissions than other agents to help cover his or her own operating expenses. The PPGA may be expected to meet certain sales quotas for the company, but he or she may also be allowed to represent other insurers.

3-12. a. Under the independent agency system, an agency represents several companies or groups of companies, while under the exclusive agency system, only one company is represented.

      b. Under the independent system, the agency is an independent business organization and pays its own operating expenses; under the exclusive system, the insurer may cover the agent's operating expenses, particularly for new agents.

      c. Agents in the independent system are compensated mainly through commissions on business written by the agency; also, these agents may receive fees for other services provided. Under the exclusive agency system, compensation is mainly from commissions on the sale of new business.

      d. In the independent agency system, commission rates are generally the same for renewing policies as for the sale of new policies, while in the exclusive agency system, lower commission rates are paid for renewals than for new business.

      e. The independent agent generally has ownership, use, and control of policy and expiration data; under the exclusive system, the insurer has these rights.

      f. The independent agent generally collects premiums and settles small claims (although the trend is toward the insurer performing these functions). Under the exclusive system, the insurer generally performs these duties, although the agent may collect initial premiums and settle some small claims.

3-13. Neither type is inherently better. An independent agency can "shop" among the coverages available from more than one insurance company, but an exclusive agency might be able to provide sound and competitively priced coverage from the single company he or she represents. It is more important for the client to consider the coverage, the price, and the character of the agent than to consider the type of marketing system involved behind the scenes.

3-14. a. The insurance company headquartered in their state is referred to as a domestic insurance company; the insurance company based in another state is technically known as a foreign insurance company. Assuming both companies are licensed to do business in their state, the difference should have no effect on the Olsons.

         The mutual insurance company that provides their life insurance is a company owned by its policyowners. As part-owners of the company, the Olsons can vote to elect the company's board of directors, and they may receive dividends in the form of a check or a premium discount.

The stock insurance company that provides their homeowners insurance is owned by corporate stock-holders who have purchased shares of stock. The stockholders elect the company's board of directors. Stockholders who may receive dividends.

The reciprocal exchange that provides their auto insurance is an unincorporated association through which each policyowner insures other policyowners. The reciprocal exchange is managed by an attorney-in-fact rather than a board of directors.

Blue Cross and Blue Shield, which provide the Olsons' group medical expense protection, traditionally operated by providing physician and hospital services rather than reimbursing for such services. Today, most such plans operate much like insurance companies, but they may benefit from favorable state taxation, and their underwriting and rating flexibility might be limited.

The differences in these different organizations' corporate structures have little, if any, practical effect on the Olsons.

b. The insurance salesperson who represented many different insurance companies apparently worked for an independent agency—an independent business that has a contract with the various insurance companies it represents. The salesperson representing only one insurer was probably an exclusive agent who is contractually bound to sell insurance for one insurance company or group of related companies.

Answers to Self-Test Questions

3-1. False. Foreign insurers are organized in another state; alien insurers are incorporated in another country.

3-2. False. Although stock insurers are owned by stockholders who elect the board of directors, mutuals are owned by their policyowners who elect the board of directors.

3-3. True.

3-4. False. Neither stocks nor mutuals are inherently superior from a consumer's standpoint. The real issue for the insurance consumer is which specific insurer and coverages to select, not which type to select.

3-5. False. The trend is for mutual companies to demutualize.

3-6. False. Insurance is written by the underwriters at Lloyd's. The corporation of Lloyd's is purely to supervise transactions and to guard the reputation of the institution.

3-7. True.

3-8. True.

3-9. True.

3-10. False. An insurance agent has implied and apparent authority, as well as the express authority spelled out in the agency contract.

3-11. False. From a legal standpoint, nearly all life insurance agents, even those called general agents, are granted the powers of a limited agent.

3-12. True.

3-13. True.

3-14. True.

3-15. False. Independent agents traditionally receive the same commission rate for renewing a policy as for initially selling the policy, whereas exclusive agents generally receive renewal commissions that are considerably smaller than their initial commissions.

Chapter 4

Answers to Mini-Case

a. The process involved in John's life insurance application is known as underwriting, a term that refers to the selection and pricing of insurance applications. The insurance company underwriter wants to ascertain John's physical condition because it can price his coverage appropriately if the company knows that John's life insurance risk is comparable to the risks of the pool of applicants on whom its class rates are based. An insurer that does not underwrite its life insurance applicants would be the victim of "adverse selection," meaning that people in poor health, who on average die at a younger age, would take advantage of the insurer's competitive rates designed for people with average mortality. Underwriting is especially important with individual life insurance, because the policy is likely to be in force for many years.

John's and Amy's auto insurance companies had already decided to accept them as policyowners and apparently did not need to underwrite their applications all over again to process a relatively minor change in coverage.

b. Amy and John's duties as policyowners who have suffered a loss are spelled out in their homeowners policy, along with the duties of the insurance company. The Schultzes should report the claim either to the agent who sold them the policy or to the insurance company's claims department. The insurer will probably send a staff adjuster (an employee of the insurance company) to examine the damage, determine whether a loss occurred while the policy was in force at a covered location, confirm that the loss was caused by a covered peril under circumstances where no exclusion applied, make sure the policyowners have fulfilled all relevant conditions, and ascertain that there is no evidence of fraud. After determining that the Schultzes are entitled to recover under the policy, the adjuster will determine the value of the damage and pay the claim.

It is possible the insurer will instead pay an independent adjuster to settle the claim rather than assigning a staff adjuster. Chances are, the Schultzes and their insurer will settle the claim with no problems, but if the situation becomes sticky, the Schultzes could also hire a public adjuster, for a fee paid by them, to represent their interests.

Answers to Review Questions

4-1. a. With adverse selection, the insurer's actual losses and expenses on insurance written would far exceed the expected losses and expenses built into its premium rates, and its underwriting losses would tend to be substantial. Through underwriting selection, insurers attempt to choose applicants for insurance so that the insurer's actual losses and expenses on insurance written would approximate the expected losses and expenses built into its premium rates. This would leave an acceptable margin for profit (or at least a small enough loss so that it could be offset by investment income).

b. Applicants who are not rejected in the selection phase of underwriting are assigned to the class that best fits their hazards and are charged the rate for that class. Therefore, an applicant with greater hazards is likely to be assigned to a class with a higher rate than an applicant who brings fewer hazards to the insurance company.

4-2. The applicant for an insurance contract often makes both written and oral statements. Signed written statements are normal procedures in life and health insurance, and the application becomes a part of the contract. Auto and business insurance applicants also frequently prepare written statements as a means of giving the insurance company basic underwriting details. Agents in many kinds of insurance give their companies reports, opinions, and recommendations that are valuable aids to the insurers in selecting or rejecting applications. Many insurers maintain separate inspection departments to provide the underwriters with physical inspection and engineering reports on applicants' properties. The insurer's claims department, too, can be a source of important underwriting data for renewal decisions.

Insurers also combine efforts to maintain bureau or association lists of insurance applicants—for example, MIB, Inc., formerly the Medical Information Bureau. In many kinds of insurance, companies use outside agencies to supplement the information gathered from the applicants, agents, and other insurer representatives. Sources include physicians, financial rating services, credit investigators, motor vehicle reports, court orders, and inspection agencies.

4-3. The primary purpose of reinsurance is to enable the insurer to spread or diversify losses. Reinsurance also reduces the ceding company's reserve requirements, which drain surplus and restrict growth. In addition, reinsurers offer many technical advisory services to new insurers or those expanding to new types of insurance or territories.

4-4. Facultative reinsurance is optional for both the insurer and the reinsurer. Each facultative reinsurance contract is written on its own merits and is a matter of individual bargaining between the primary insurer and the reinsurer. In treaty, or automatic, reinsurance, the primary insurer agrees in advance to transfer some types of loss exposures, and the reinsurer agrees to accept them.

4-5. The objective of insurers and claims departments is to pay covered claims in an amount that reflects a fair and equitable measure of the loss, or subject to policy terms.

4-6. In property insurance, some agents have their companies' authority to settle a claim with the policyowner immediately. The authority can extend to actually issuing checks in the name of the company. In life insurance, the agent is often involved in loss payment as an intermediary but not as an adjuster. The life insurance agent usually forwards the death notice and certificate to the insurer, and the check is issued by the company for delivery by the agent to the policyowner's beneficiary. For larger policies, the agent may need to explain various installment payment options in place of a lump-sum cash payment.

4-7. The four steps in the claims adjustment process are as follows:

- The insurer must be notified as spelled out in the policy. Often, the time frame is specified as "immediately," "promptly," or "as soon as practicable," and a few types of policies may be more specific. This step must occur with all types of insurance.

- The claim is investigated to determine whether a loss occurred and, if so, whether it is covered by the policy. In life insurance, this process is usually quite simple, but complicating factors occasionally arise.
- The third step in the process of adjusting a claim is filing a proof of loss. In life insurance, proof of loss may be in the form of a death certificate. In other lines, a written and sworn statement may be required that details all the specifics of the loss.
- Finally, the amount to be paid must be determined in one of three ways: denial of the claim, payment of the claim in full, or payment of a lesser amount than the claimant seeks. Life insurance claims are usually simpler because there are no partial losses. There can, however, be some complicating factors that affect the amount to be paid, including an accidental death benefit provision, a misstatement-of-age-or-sex clause, or a settlement option selected by the policyowner or by the beneficiary.

  In other lines of insurance, the amount to be paid, if any, can be more difficult to determine. Numerous policy provisions may deal with other insurance covering the same loss, provide for a deductible, specify that recovery will be affected by the amount of insurance carried relative to the value of the covered property, give the insurer the choice of two or three methods to calculate the amount of the loss, stipulate the use of appraisers to establish the amount of the loss, and impose a specific limit on the insurer's liability for certain types of losses.

4-8. a. The insurance rate is the *unit* cost for the coverage; the insurance premium is the price charged for the *total* coverage provided by the policy. The insurance premium is determined by multiplying the rate by the number of exposure units (number of units of coverage).

  b. An insurance rate is typically developed using the pure premium method, which first requires an estimate for the future loss costs per unit of coverage during the policy period. This portion of the rate is called the pure or net rate and entails a statistical analysis of past loss data with a projection of that experience into the future policy period. Added to the pure rate is a loading factor, which covers the insurer's anticipated expenses and provides a margin for profit and contingencies. The sum of the pure rate and the loading is called the gross rate, which is the rate applied to an insured.

Answers to Self-Test Questions

4-1. False. The general purpose of underwriting is to select insureds who, on average, will produce actual loss experience comparable to the expected loss experience incorporated into the premium rates.

4-2. True.

4-3. False. Under treaty reinsurance, the insurer agrees in advance to transfer some types of risks, and the reinsurer agrees to accept those risks. With facultative reinsurance, the insurer is under no obligation to offer the risk to the reinsurer, and the reinsurer is under no obligation to accept.

4-4. True.

4-5. False. A life insurance agent may become involved as an intermediary, delivering a death proceeds check to a beneficiary, but not as an adjuster with authority to settle a claim.

4-6. False. As with staff adjusters, independent adjusters represent insurers. Public adjusters represent the public.

4-7. False. In calculating the insurance premium, the gross rate (composed of the pure rate plus a loading for expenses, profit, and contingencies) is multiplied by the number of units of coverage.

4-8. True.

4-9. True.

Chapter 5

Answers to Review Questions

5-1. The general purpose of insurance regulation is to protect the public against insolvency or unfair treatment by insurers. From the state's viewpoint, regulation is also important as a revenue producer through state taxes on insurance premiums. The insurance business is among the types of private enterprise subject to considerable government regulation because it is generally classed as a business that is "affected with a public interest." Although competition is an effective regulator for some businesses, uncontrolled competition in insurance could work a hardship on the buyers of insurance, most of whom do not understand insurance contracts.

5-2. Insurers engage in self-regulation through a variety of collaborative activities. Two examples are the American Council of Life Insurers (ACLI), which promotes better public relations and legislation, and The American College, which strives to improve insurance education and set standards for professional courses and designations.

5-3. Three basic methods of providing insurance regulation that the government uses are (1) legislative action, (2) administrative action, and (3) court action. Legislation is the foundation of insurance regulation because it creates the insurance laws. The insurance laws of each state are often combined in an insurance code. Administrative action refers to the application and enforcement of insurance laws, which is the responsibility of the insurance commissioner in each state. Court action provides detailed interpretations of troublesome parts of the law.

5-4. The regulation of insurers falls into the following three categories:

- *formation and licensing of insurers.* Insurance companies must meet specific standards of organization that are often higher than those set for general business organizations. Standards are necessary to ensure the solvency, competence, and integrity of the insuring organization. The first step is incorporation, which is an introductory process in which the state recognizes and approves the existence of a new legal identity.

  The next step, licensing, is a check on the insurer's financial condition to ascertain that it has the required initial capital and surplus for the kinds of insurance permitted in the license. The objective of licensing is to provide a preliminary method of lessening the chance of the insurer's financial insolvency, particularly during the difficult formative years.

- *insurer operations.* The states exercise some control over many phases of the operations of insurers. Most obligations of insurers extend years into the future, so the state provides supervision to see that the promises in the contracts are fulfilled. The ways in which insurer operations are supervised are strikingly different among the states and among the various kinds of insurance. Most states provide some regulation of the following types: contracts and forms, rates, reserves, asset and surplus values, investments, agents' licensing and trade practices, claims practices, and taxation.

- *rehabilitation and liquidation of insurers.* The insurance commissioner of a state presides over the insurance company's liquidation. Some liquidations occur due to financial insolvency; others are voluntary in order to effect a corporate reorganization or merger. All outstanding liabilities and contracts may be reinsured so that no loss results to policyowners.

5-5. a. *contracts and forms.* Because insurance policies are complex legal documents that are often not fully understood by consumers, they could be used to mislead or unfairly treat policyowners. Consequently, in many lines of insurance, policy forms must be approved by, or at least filed with, the insurance commissioner.

  Life and health insurance contracts are not standard contracts in the sense that similar forms or benefits are required. Most states do, however, provide some uniformity by requiring a number of standard provisions in life and health contracts pertaining to such items as the grace period, loan and surrender values, and the like. Examples of little regulation over contracts are found in the transportation insurance field. Except for a few required provisions, these contracts are among the most nonuniform of insurance contracts and should be carefully studied by policyowners to determine what benefits, conditions, and exclusions they contain.

  b. *rates.* The price of insurance contracts is controlled to a varying degree in the different lines of insurance. In some lines of insurance, such as aviation insurance, practically no regulation exists in the states. In life insurance, regulation involves maintaining minimum reserves, rather than setting the prices that must be charged. Most other major kinds of insurance are subject to some direct rate regulation.

  The statutory standards are set forth in an insurance rating law. Basic standards recognized by rating laws usually require that (1) rates be reasonable and adequate for the class of business to which they apply, (2) no rate be unfairly discriminatory, and (3) consideration be given to the past and prospective loss experience and a reasonable underwriting profit. Rates are considered reasonable (not too high) and adequate (not too low) when, along with investment income, they can be expected to produce sufficient revenue to pay all losses and expenses of doing business, and to produce a reasonable profit.

  Instead of direct regulation of insurance prices by required rate approval, some state laws supervise the cost of life insurance by limiting the portion of the premium that can be used for expenses rather than claims.

  c. *reserves.* The states require insurers to maintain (as a liability) a minimum reserve considered adequate to meet policy obligations as policies mature. In life insurance, the legal reserve is an amount that, augmented by premium payments under outstanding contracts and interest earnings, is sufficient to enable the life insurer to meet its assumed policy obligations. Minimum reserve requirements are also thought to indirectly regulate life insurance rates, at least by reducing the likelihood of inadequate rates.

  In the field of property insurance, the unearned premium reserve must at all times be adequate to pay a return premium to policyowners in the event of cancellation of a policy before it expires.

  A second type of reserve required of property and liability insurers is the loss reserve. Because many contracts do not involve immediate payment of all losses that have occurred, a reserve must be set up to ensure their payment.

d. *asset and surplus values.* The value of assets appearing in the balance sheets of insurers must be correct and conservative in order that liabilities, reserves, and residual surplus items have true meaning. Securities held by insurers are valued according to practices adopted by a committee of the NAIC. Stocks are usually given year-end market values, while most bonds are carried at amortized values. Some assets of insurance companies are not allowed to be carried on balance sheets as assets. These *nonadmitted assets* are thought to be of marginal quality or of little liquidity for policyowners if their insurers should get into financial difficulty.

e. *investments.* To protect the solvency of insurers, most states have laws governing the types of securities that may be purchased for investment. The strictest regulations apply to life insurers, which are subject to vigorous supervision of their investment portfolios. Bonds and common stocks are the prime investments in the portfolios of life insurers, although most states grant some limited permission for certain other investments such as stocks as a percentage of assets or of surplus. Real estate holdings, especially commercial properties, are also limited to a maximum in various states.

    The investment of assets by property and liability insurers is also supervised, although the laws are more lenient and vary greatly among the states. The general practice aims at requiring the safest types of investments for all assets held as reserves (unearned premium and loss reserves) and other liabilities. Cash, bonds of high grade and specified experience, and perhaps preferred stocks of proven quality may be permitted for such assets. The remainder of assets (representing capital and surplus) may be invested in a wider range of securities, including common stocks meeting certain standards. Limitations on real estate holdings, the size of single investments in relation to total assets or surplus, and investments in foreign companies, as well as many other restrictions, are also common.

f. *agents' licensing and trade practices.* An important control of insurer operations is through laws in all states that require licensing for insurance agents and brokers. The insurance departments usually administer these laws; the objective is to permit insurers to use only competent and trustworthy representatives. The standards vary tremendously, from little more than payment of a license fee to a comprehensive written examination following required attendance in insurance courses approved by the department. The examinations are often divided into separate tests for different lines of insurance. The examinations for insurance brokers are usually more difficult and extensive than those given to agents. Some adjusters and consultants also must be licensed in a few states. Almost all states now require continuing education as a condition for license renewal.

    Unfair trade practices in insurance are made illegal in all states under laws similar to the Federal Trade Commission Act. These laws aim at retaining jurisdiction for the states (under the provisions of Public Law 15) in preventing fraudulent and unethical acts of agents and brokers. They provide fines and, more important, suspension or revocation of licenses as penalties for violations.

    The insurance commissioner has broad powers to prevent unfair practices and exercises this authority by investigating complaints, as well as by initiating investigations of any questionable acts of insurers or their representatives.

g. *claims practices.* Most states now have enacted laws patterned after the NAIC's model acts and regulations pertaining to unfair claim settlement practices. Some of the practices that are regarded as unfair are the following:

    - failing to investigate claims promptly
    - failing to communicate with or acknowledge communications from clients on a timely basis
    - failing to provide a reasonable explanation as to why a claim has been denied
    - failing to maintain procedures for complaint handling about claims
    - misrepresenting pertinent policy provisions affecting claims
    - failing to try to settle a claim once the insurer's liability has become clear
    - attempting to settle a claim for far less than a reasonable person would expect to receive based on the insurer's advertising material

5-6. In recent years, all 50 states have adopted insurance guaranty fund plans to at least partially protect consumers against the insolvency of insurers. The plans are administered on a state-by-state basis, but usually they assess solvent insurers in order to pay the unpaid claims of an insolvent company and to return unearned premiums to its policyowners. Insurers each pay a proportional share of the losses, based on their premium volume in the state.

    The guaranty funds appear to protect the consumer reasonably well. In some states, several improvements have been adopted concerning (1) giving the guaranty funds immediate access to assets of the insolvent insurer (rather than waiting until liquidation proceedings are completed), (2) giving the guaranty funds priority before general creditors to obtain assets of the insolvent insurer, and (3) permitting a tax offset against premium taxes to solvent insurers for money paid into the guaranty funds. Even with these improvements, however, problems remain in the areas of lengthy delays before consumers receive their money and dollar limits on some types of claims that will be paid.

5-7. Advocates of state regulation of insurance have pointed out such reasons as (1) the local nature of many insurance transactions, for which any difficulties can best be resolved on a state basis, (2) the reasonable success of state regulation for many years, during which insurance has become an important and sound business, (3) the value of regulation on a state-by-state basis, which permits gradual changes and innovations in regulation without applying them to the entire country all at once, and (4) the help of the NAIC in recommending model legislation to the states to achieve some uniformity in insurance regulation. While recognizing that state regulation is not perfect, its supporters claim that federal regulation would be cumbersome, expensive, less effective, and fragmented among dozens of agencies.

Proponents of federal regulation of insurance have criticized state regulation on many points, emphasizing (1) inconsistencies and lack of uniformity in regulation of insurers, (2) inadequate funding for the important tasks of the insurance commissioners, and the short-term and political aspects of their term of office, (3) the need for greater standardization in insurance contracts to cover many interstate exposures, and (4) the desire for increased competition to ensure availability and lower and fairer prices for insurance. Implicit in these criticisms of the present state of insurance regulation is the idea that federal regulation would be better.

5-8. Probably the single most important criterion a client should use to select an insurance company is the insurer's financial strength. Selection of an insurer should also be based on its willingness to pay claims.

Another criterion that clients should use to evaluate insurers is service. The insurer's ability to provide proper protection for the applicant is essential. As part of the evaluation of an insurer's service, the applicant is interested in knowing whether or not the insurer is liberal with respect to underwriting. The insurer's facilities for loss-prevention recommendations that may reduce insurance costs are also important to the consumer.

Another important criterion in the evaluation of an insurer, of course, is the cost of the products it offers. Initial costs are only part of the necessary analysis; final costs over a longer period of protection must be considered, including possible rate changes, dividends, assessments, or premium adjustments under some types of rating plans.

5-9. The criteria to help clients choose an agent or broker include
- *knowledge and ability.* The agent or broker must have the background and experience necessary to identify, analyze, and treat risk properly.
- *willingness.* If qualified, can and will the agent or broker also take the time to apply his or her knowledge conscientiously to fully appraise all the client's needs and alternatives? The producer must be able and willing to see that services (including those of the producer's staff and insurance companies) are performed in the most effective way possible.
- *integrity and character.* Agents or brokers must be able to command the confidence and trust of the policyowner.
- *representation.* Good agents or brokers generally do not deal with weak insurers. They must represent or have contacts with one or many insurers that can provide the required protection and services for the policyowner. All the necessary coverages, including even special or unusual ones, must be available through the agent(s) in a prompt and efficient manner and at a reasonable cost. The insurer or insurers represented should be capable of writing many different kinds of insurance with a progressive attitude toward newer coverages and forms designed to meet the particular needs of individual buyers.

Answers to Self-Test Questions
5-1. True.
5-2. True.
5-3. True.
5-4. False. Insurance regulations prohibit *unfair* discrimination. Many insurance rates are based on fair discrimination. Life insurance rates, for example, vary by age and reflect different mortality rates for people of different ages.
5-5. False. Life insurance is not subject to direct rate regulation. Instead, some states supervise the cost of life insurance by limiting the portion of the premium that can be used for expenses rather than claims. Also, life insurance rates are indirectly regulated through the minimum reserve requirements.
5-6. True.
5-7. False. Most states prohibit rebating and twisting as unfair trade practices.

5-8.   False. Most premium taxes paid by insurers to the states are used for revenue purposes rather than to pay for the cost of insurance regulation.

5-9.   False. Financial strength is determined by the insurer's ability to pay claims.

5-10.   True.

5-11.   False. Some of the criteria for evaluating an agent are knowledge and ability, willingness, integrity and character, and representation.

Chapter 6

Answers to Mini-Case

    a.   If the insurer determines that Amy's and John's applications are acceptable without physical exams, Amy's and John's life insurance policies will become effective as of the date of the application because they paid the premiums with the application. Therefore, they would be covered if either of them dies during the vacation— even if their application is not approved until later—but only if the insurer determines that they meet the insurer's underwriting standards. If they do not, the insurer may make a counteroffer such as offering coverage at a higher premium or in a more limited amount.

    b.   Because the application specifically asked about depression and Amy provided a false answer to that question, Amy is guilty of misrepresentation. If the insurer accepts the application based on the false information, and she dies while on vacation, her survivors would not be able to enforce the contract. As we will see in chapter 9, a life insurance policy also contains an incontestable clause that will prohibit the insurer from disputing the validity of the policy after it has been in force for a specified period of time such as 2 years.

Answers to Review Questions

6-1.   Unlike most of the physical goods—like a car—that are purchased for immediate use, insurance provides *future* benefits when loss payments are made. However, the relief from anxiety and freedom from worry about financial losses are immediate and continual benefits throughout the period of protection.

         Insurance has a *contingent* nature, in that benefits are paid based on particular events. Policyowners buy insurance against many perils, despite feeling that such perils will not really cause losses to them. Insurance can be considered a service contract or a bundle of services, rather than a single physical product.

         Financial *risk* is a final characteristic that differentiates insurance from other goods and services. The basis of the insurance contract is uncertainty about many perils that may cause accidental loss. Insurance transfers the financial risk of such losses to the insurer, a professional risk bearer. Other service contracts may be future and contingent, but they do not involve payment for the occurrence of such unexpected perils as fire, windstorm, disability, and death.

6-2.   a.   *offer and acceptance.* A legally binding agreement, or contract, requires both an offer by one party and an acceptance by another party. In insurance, the offer is usually made in a request for coverage by the prospect, or applicant.

           Before a contract is effective, acceptance of the offer is necessary. In property and liability insurance, the agent often has authority to bind, or accept, the offer even without receiving any payment from the applicant. In life insurance, a written application with the first premium payment is usually considered the offer to the insurer. Most courts hold that acceptance occurs if the applicant meets the normal underwriting standards of the insurer, and coverage becomes effective as of the time of the application and premium payment. If the premium was not paid with the application, the offer to insure is made by the insurer. The insurance is accepted when the contract is delivered to the applicant while the applicant is in good health, and the premium is paid. If the applicant does not meet the underwriting standards of the insurer, the insurer may make a counteroffer with a different contract, which the prospect may accept or reject upon delivery by the agent.

    b.   *legal purpose.* A legally binding contract must have a legal purpose or object. The courts will not enforce a contract that has an illegal purpose or is contrary to public policy.

    c.   *competent parties.* Valid contracts require that the party making the offer and the one accepting the offer be legally competent to make the agreement. In insurance, the most common problem arises in connection with applicants who are under the age of legal majority. Some insurance contracts are voidable by applicants who are minors, and these applicants will receive a full return of the premiums paid if they later decide to make the contract void. Some states have made exceptions for life, health, and auto insurance contracts by establishing special age limits of 14 or 16; beyond this age, minors are considered to have the legal capacity to insure themselves, and a contract is binding on them.

A similar problem may occur in insurance written for insane or intoxicated persons. They cannot make legal contracts because they fail to understand the agreement.

Insurers, too, must be competent to enter into a legal contract by meeting charter and license requirements of the states. In cases where such legal capacity is lacking, many courts have nevertheless held the contracts binding on the insurer, or on its corporate officers personally, rather than penalizing a good-faith purchaser of the coverage.

d. *consideration.* The final requirement for a valid contract is some consideration exchanged by both parties to the agreement—a right or something of value given up, or an obligation assumed. In insurance, the applicant typically makes a premium payment, or the contract may become effective on the basis of the applicant's promise to pay and to meet other conditions of the contract. The insurer's consideration is its promise to pay for specified losses or to provide other services to the policyowner.

6-3. a. *unilateral nature.* The insurance contract is a unilateral one because only one party, the insurer, makes a legally enforceable promise. If the company fails to fulfill the promises it makes, such as to pay the specified benefits at the death of the insured, the insurer may be held legally liable for breach of contract. The insured makes no such promises after the contract comes into force (although, of course, failure to live up to policy conditions like paying the premiums may release the insurer from the contract).

b. *personal nature.* The insurance contract is personal and covers the person rather than the property. Insurance provides repayment of a loss arising out of an undesired happening by indemnifying the person who has incurred the loss.

c. *conditional nature.* The obligation to perform on the part of one of the parties to an agreement may be conditioned upon the performance of the second party. A clause in an insurance contract requiring such performance is usually referred to as a *condition.* Failure of one party to perform relieves the other party of his or her obligation.

6-4. a. As a general rule, the benefit of doubt in an insurance contract goes to the insured if the terms are unclear.

b. Sue is bound by the contract whether she read it or not. A planner should take great care to explain the contract to his or her client because the chances are good that the client will not read and/or understand it.

c. Under the parol evidence rule, oral evidence cannot be used to modify the contract.

6-5. As a contract of indemnity, insurance provides compensation for a covered loss but only to the extent of that financial loss. Insurance will not buy a new car. However, it will pay an amount of money that reflects the cost of repairing or replacing the vehicle that was damaged or destroyed, subject to any deductible that might apply.

6-6. The purposes of requiring an insurable interest in insurance contracts are to prevent gambling, to decrease moral hazard, and to help measure the actual loss. Without an insurable interest, a contract is a wager or gambling contract. It also could be an undesirable incentive for some persons to cause losses or injuries on purpose. When an insurable interest exists, no profit results because policyowners merely receive repayment for the loss they have suffered.

6-7. a. An insurable interest exists because your client may suffer a financial loss if his debtor friend dies before repaying the loan.

b. An insurable interest exists because an auto owner or driver can sustain losses to his or her car by collision, theft, or other perils.

c. No insurable interest exists because your client did not own the precious stone at the time it was destroyed. For property to be insurable, an insurable interest must exist at the time of the loss.

6-8. The common law doctrine of subrogation gives the insurer whatever rights the insured possessed against responsible third parties. It is basically a process of substitution, the other driver's insurer taking over the legal rights of its insured to recover from Cheryl.

In common law, it is a matter of equity that, on paying the insured the amount of the loss, the insurer has a right of action against any other person who may have caused the loss.

The right of the insurer against other negligent persons usually does not rest on any contractual relationship, but arises out of the nature of the contract of insurance as one of indemnity. If the insured is indemnified, it would be inequitable for him or her also to try to collect from the party responsible for the loss. If the insured were permitted to do this, a double collection of the loss from both the insurer and the party responsible might result in a profit to the insured. Subrogation also holds wrongdoers responsible for the results of their wrongful actions, instead of permitting them not to pay only because an insurance contract bought by someone else was in force. The overall cost of the insurance to policyowners is also reduced in this manner.

6-9. The difference between concealment and misrepresentation is that the applicant conceals if a silence is maintained when there is an obligation to speak; he or she misrepresents if a statement is made that is not true.

6-10. a. *Declarations* are factual statements that identify the specific person, property, or activity being insured and the parties to the insurance transactions; they also provide descriptive information about the insurance being provided.

    b. The *definitions* section carefully defines terms used in the policy. Because ambiguities in the contract are likely to be construed against the insurer, this section of the policy is a substantial help in making the insurer's intentions precise.

    c. The *insuring agreements* spell out the basic promises of the insurance company.

    d. Every insurance policy has *exclusions*—situations that the insurer does not cover. The exclusions usually apply to certain perils, types of losses, types of property, or types of activities.

    e. The insuring agreement is not an absolute promise by the insurer with "no strings attached." Instead, the promise is a qualified one, enforceable only if the policyowner fulfills a number of *conditions* that are spelled out in the policy.

6-11. Both noncancelable and guaranteed renewable policies give the policyowner the right to renew the coverage at each policy anniversary date, although possibly only to some stated age such as 65. These policies may not be terminated by the insurer during the period of coverage. A truly noncancelable policy guarantees future rates for the coverage in the contract itself. In a guaranteed renewable policy, the insurer does not guarantee future rates for the coverage. Instead, the insurer retains the right to raise the rates for broad classes of insureds, but not just for individual insureds with poor claims experience.

6-12. As a general legal principle, whenever the wording in an endorsement or rider conflicts with the terms of the policy to which it is attached, the endorsement or rider takes precedence. The assumption underlying this principle is that an alteration of the basic agreement between the policyowner and insurer more accurately reflects the true intent of the parties than does the basic agreement itself.

Answers to Self-Test Questions

6-1. False. Policyowners realize the immediate benefits of relief from anxiety and freedom from worry about financial losses.

6-2. True.

6-3. False. A written application and the first premium payment are usually submitted by the applicant as the offer to the insurer through the agent, who issues a conditional receipt.

6-4. False. Clients under the age of 21 (18 in some states) are considered minors and can void many types of insurance contracts and get a full refund of premiums paid. However, state laws may hold legal capacity for 16-year-olds who enter into auto insurance contracts.

6-5. False. An insurance contract is a unilateral contract.

6-6. False. Property and liability insurance policies are not freely assignable by policyowners. They have to obtain the insured's approval to effectuate a transfer. Life insurance policies, however, are freely assignable by policyowners.

6-7. False. This is an example of a condition subsequent.

6-8. True.

6-9. True.

6-10. True.

6-11. False. Life insurance contracts are valued contracts and are not contracts of indemnity.

6-12. True.

6-13. False. The misrepresentation or concealment of a material fact by an applicant for insurance will not void the contract but will make it voidable by the insurer.

6-14. False. Fraud involves an active *intent* to deceive. The applicant making the statement must know that it is false or make the statement in reckless disregard of whether it is true or false.

6-15. True.

6-16. True.

6-17. False. Under an initial deductible, the insurer will pay for losses only after they exceed a specified amount. The insured must absorb all losses up to that specified amount.

6-18. True.

Chapter 7

Answers to Review Questions

7-1. Part A of Medicare and all the benefits of the Social Security program are financed through a system of payroll and self-employment taxes paid by all persons covered under the programs. In addition, employers of covered persons are also taxed. (These taxes are often referred to as FICA taxes because they are imposed under the Federal Insurance Contributions Act.)

In 2005, an employee and his or her employer pay a tax of 6.2 percent each on the first $90,000 of the employee's wages for Social Security. The employee and employer also pay the Medicare tax rate of 1.45 percent on employee wages. The tax rates are currently scheduled to remain the same after 2005, but the wage bases are adjusted annually for changes in the national level of wages.

Part B of Medicare is financed by a combination of monthly premiums paid by persons eligible for benefits and contributions from the federal government.

7-2. a. Evelyn does not meet the first test to determine if a person is fully insured under Social Security, as she has not earned 40 credits. However, she does qualify as fully insured under the second test. Evelyn is 38 this year, 2005, so she was born in 1967. She was age 21 in 1988, so she would require 15 credits from 1989 to 2004 to be fully insured, and she has 28.

b. Because Evelyn is fully insured, she is also currently insured.

c. Although Evelyn is fully insured, she is not disability insured because she does not have the minimum number of credits within a recent time period. She would need 20 credits during the last 40 calendar quarters, and she only has four.

7-3. A worker who is fully insured under Social Security is eligible to receive monthly retirement income benefits as early as age 62. However, the election to receive benefits prior to the full retirement age results in a permanently reduced benefit. Beginning in 2003, the age at which full benefits are payable started to increase in gradual steps from age 65 to age 67. Workers born in 1960 or later will wait until age 67 for their full retirement benefits. Additional benefits are also available to certain dependents of the retired worker. These dependents include a spouse aged 62 or older, a spouse caring for a worker's child, and dependent, unmarried children under age 18.

7-4. If a deceased worker was either fully or currently insured at the time of death, the following categories of persons are eligible for benefits:

- dependent, unmarried children under age 18. This child's benefit will continue until age 19 as long as he or she is a full-time student in elementary or secondary school. In addition, disabled children of any age are eligible for benefits as long as they were disabled before reaching age 22.
- a spouse caring for at least one child of the retired worker who is (1) under age 16 or (2) disabled and entitled to a child's benefit

   If the deceased worker was fully insured, the following categories of persons are also eligible for benefits:

   - a widow or widower aged 60 or older. However, benefits are reduced if taken prior to full retirement age. This benefit is also payable to a divorced spouse if the marriage lasted at least 10 years. The widow's or widower's benefit is payable to a disabled spouse at age 50 as long as the disability commenced no more than 7 years after the (1) worker's death or (2) end of the year in which entitlement to a mother's or father's benefit ceased.
   - a parent aged 62 or over who was a dependent of the deceased worker at the time of death

7-5. a. The definition of disability requires a mental or physical impairment that prevents the worker from engaging in any substantial gainful employment. The disability must also have lasted (or be expected to last) at least 12 months or be expected to result in death. A more liberal definition of disability applies to blind workers who are aged 55 or older. They are considered disabled if they are unable to perform work that requires skills or abilities comparable to those required by the work they regularly performed before reaching age 55 or becoming blind, if later.

b. Certain family members not otherwise eligible for Social Security benefits may be eligible if they are disabled. Disabled children are subject to the same definition of disability as workers. Disabled widows or widowers must be unable to engage in any gainful (rather than substantial gainful) employment.

7-6. a. The primary insurance amount (PIA) is the amount a worker receives if he or she retires at full retirement age or becomes disabled; it is the amount on which benefits for family members are based. If a worker is retired or disabled, benefits are paid to family members, as follows: The spouse at full retirement age, or a spouse at any age caring for a disabled child or a child under 16 receives 50 percent of the worker's PIA. Each child under 18 or disabled also receives 50 percent of the worker's PIA. If a worker dies, benefits are paid to family members, as follows: The spouse at full retirement age receives 100 percent of the worker's PIA. A spouse at any age caring for a disabled child or a child under 16 receives 75 percent of the worker's PIA. Each child under 18 or disabled also receives 75 percent of the worker's PIA. Additionally, a worker's sole dependent parent receives 82.5 percent, while two dependent parents receive 75 percent each. However, the full benefits described above may not be payable because of a limitation imposed on the total benefits that may be paid to a family.

    b.   If the total amount of benefits payable to family members exceeds the family maximum, the worker's benefit (in the case of retirement and disability) is not affected, but the benefits of other family members are reduced proportionately.

7-7.   If a worker elects to receive retirement benefits prior to full retirement age, benefits are permanently reduced by 5/9 of one percent for each of the first 36 months that the early retirement precedes full retirement age and 5/12 of one percent for each month in excess of 36. A worker who delays applying for benefits until after full retirement age is eligible for an increased benefit for each month of late retirement until age 70. The size of the increased benefit depends on the worker's date of birth.

7-8.   Beneficiaries under full retirement age are allowed earnings of up to $12,000 in 2005, and this figure is subject to annual indexing for later years. If a beneficiary earns more than this amount, then his or her Social Security benefit is reduced by $1 for each $2 of excess earnings. There is one exception to the test: The reduction is $1 for every $3 of earnings in excess of $31,800 (in 2005) in the calendar year a worker attains full retirement age, for earnings in months prior to reaching that age.

7-9.   Social Security benefits are increased automatically each January if there was an increase in the CPI for the one-year period ending in the third quarter of the prior year. The increase is the same as the increase in the CPI since the last cost-of-living adjustment, rounded to the nearest 0.1 percent.

7-10.   a.   The types of benefits available under Medicare Part A are as follows:

- *hospital benefits.* Part A pays for inpatient hospital services for up to 90 days in each benefit period (also referred to as a spell of illness). A benefit period begins the first time a Medicare recipient is hospitalized and ends only after the recipient has been out of a hospital or skilled-nursing facility for 60 consecutive days. A subsequent hospitalization then begins a new benefit period.
- *skilled-nursing facility benefits.* In many cases, a patient may no longer require continuous hospital care but may not be well enough to go home. Consequently, Part A provides benefits for care in a skilled-nursing facility if a physician certifies that skilled-nursing care or rehabilitative services are needed for a condition that was treated in a hospital within the last 30 days. In addition, the prior hospitalization must have lasted at least 3 days. Benefits are paid in full for 20 days in each benefit period and for an additional 80 days with a daily copayment charge.
- *home health care benefits.* If a patient can be treated at home for a medical condition, Medicare Part A will pay the full cost for an unlimited number of home visits by a home health agency. To receive these benefits, a person must be confined at home and be treated under a home health plan set up by a physician.
- *hospice benefits.* Hospice benefits are available under Part A of Medicare for beneficiaries who are certified as being terminally ill with a life expectancy of 6 months or less.

    b.   The following deductibles and copayment are required:

- *hospital benefits.* In each benefit period, covered hospital expenses are paid in full for 60 days, subject to an initial deductible ($912 in 2005). This deductible is adjusted annually to reflect increasing hospital costs. Benefits for an additional 30 days of hospitalization are also provided in each benefit period, but the patient must pay a daily copayment ($228 in 2005) equal to 25 percent of the initial deductible amount. Each recipient also has a lifetime reserve of 60 additional days that may be used if the regular 90 days of benefits have been exhausted. However, once a reserve day is used, it cannot be restored for use in future benefit periods. When using reserve days, patients must pay a daily copayment ($456 in 2005) equal to 50 percent of the initial deductible amount.
- *skilled-nursing facility benefits.* Benefits are paid in full for 20 days in each benefit period and for an additional 80 days with a daily copayment ($114 in 2005) that is equal to 12.5 percent of the initial hospital deductible.
- *home health care benefits.* There is no charge for these benefits other than a required 20 percent copayment for the cost of such durable medical equipment as oxygen tanks and hospital beds.
- *hospice benefits.* There are modest copayments for some services.

    c.   Exclusions under Part A of Medicare include the following:

- services outside the United States and its territories or possessions. However, there are a few exceptions to this rule for qualified Mexican and Canadian hospitals. Benefits will be paid if an emergency occurs in the United States and the closest hospital is in one of these countries. Persons living closer to a hospital in one of these countries than to a hospital in the United States may also use the foreign hospital even if an emergency does not exist. Finally, there is coverage for Canadian hospitals if a person needs hospitalization while traveling the most direct route between Alaska and another state in the United States. However, this latter provision does not apply to persons vacationing in Canada.
- elective luxury services such as private rooms or televisions
- hospitalization for services not necessary for the treatment of an illness or injury such as custodial care or elective cosmetic surgery
  In addition to the exclusions, there are times when Medicare will act as the secondary payer of benefits.

7-11. a. Part B of Medicare provides benefits for most medical expenses not covered under Part A. These can include physicians' and surgeons' fees, diagnostic tests, physical therapy, drugs and biologicals that cannot be self-administered, radiation therapy, medical supplies, rental of medical equipment, prosthetic devices, ambulance service, mammograms and Pap smears, diabetes glucose monitoring and education, diabetic screening for persons at risk of diabetes, screening blood test for detection of heart disease, colorectal cancer screening, bone mass measurement, prostate cancer screening, pneumococcal vaccination and flu shots, and home health care services as described for Part A when a person does not have Part A coverage or when Part A benefits are not applicable.

      b. With some exceptions, Part B pays 80 percent of the approved charges for covered medical expenses after the satisfaction of a $110 annual deductible (in 2005). A lower level of benefits is paid for mental health care. A few charges are paid in full without any cost sharing. These include (1) home health services, (2) pneumococcal vaccinations and flu shorts, (3) certain surgical procedures that are performed on an outpatient basis in lieu of hospitalization, (4) diagnostic preadmission tests performed on an outpatient basis within 7 days prior to hospitalization, (5) mammograms, and (6) Pap smears.

      c. Exclusions include most drugs and biologicals that can be self-administered, most routine examinations, routine foot care, most immunizations, most cosmetic surgery, most dental care, custodial care, eyeglasses, hearing aids, and orthopedic shoes.

7-12. Medicare Advantage plans include HMOs, PPOs, PSOs, private fee-for-service plans, and private contracts with physicians. These plans must provide all benefits available under Parts A and B. They may include additional benefits as part of the basic plan or for an additional fee.

7-13. a. Medicare Part D is available (beginning in 2006) to all Medicare beneficiaries entitled to Part A and enrolled in Part B. There is be a monthly premium that averages about $35 per month. However, the premium is partially or totally waived for persons with very low incomes.

      b. Medicare prescription drug plans do not have to cover every prescription drug, but they must cover at least two in every prescription category. It is expected that each plan will develop a formulary, which lists the drugs it will cover.

      c. After an annual deducible ($250 in 2006) is met, the plan pays 75 percent of the next $2,000 of covered drug costs, then payment ceases until the beneficiary's out-of-pocket costs reach $5,100. Subsequently, the plan pays 95 percent of covered drug costs.

      d. To discourage employers or unions from dropping their previously offered coverage for retirees, the government subsidizes the cost of continuing prescription drug coverage.

7-14. a. All payroll taxes and other sources of funds for Social Security and Medicare are deposited into four trust funds: an old-age and survivors fund, a disability fund, and two Medicare funds. Benefits and administrative expenses are paid out of the appropriate trust fund from contributions to that fund and any interest earnings on accumulated assets. The trust funds have limited reserves to serve as emergency funds in periods when benefits exceed contributions such as in times of high unemployment.

      b. The solution to ensuring the adequacy of these funds lies in doing one or both of the following: increasing revenue into the trust funds or decreasing benefit costs. There are numerous ways to do each. These ways include raising the tax rate, increasing the wage base for Social Security, subjecting a greater portion of income benefits to taxation, raising the age for benefits, lowering cost-of-living increases, increasing Medicare deductibles and copayments, and establishing some degree of privatization of Social Security.

7-15. Benefits received in the form of monthly income under Social Security are partially subject to income taxation for some Social Security recipients. If the modified adjusted gross income is $25,000 or less for a single taxpayer

($32,000 or less for married taxpayers filing jointly), Social Security benefits are not taxable. If the modified adjusted gross income is between $25,001 and $34,000 ($44,000 for married taxpayers filing jointly), up to 50 percent of the Social Security benefit is includible in taxable income. If the modified adjusted gross income exceeds $34,000 ($44,000 for married taxpayers filing jointly), up to 85 percent of the Social Security benefit is includible in taxable income. The exact amount of the taxable Social Security benefit is determined by complex formulas that are beyond the scope of this discussion. Medicare benefits and any lump-sum Social Security benefits are received tax free.

7-16.   a.   The objectives of unemployment insurance are to provide periodic cash income to workers during periods of involuntary unemployment and to help the unemployed find jobs.

      b.   Unemployment insurance programs are financed primarily by unemployment taxes levied by both the federal and state governments.

      c.   The right to benefits depends on the worker's attachment to the labor force within a prior base period. During this base period, the worker must have earned a minimum amount of wages or worked a minimum period of time, or both. The right to benefits is also contingent on an unemployed worker's being available for work, and being both physically and mentally capable of working.

7-17.   Temporary disability laws enable employees to collect disability income benefits regardless of whether their disability begins while they are employed or unemployed. These laws are generally patterned after the state unemployment insurance law and provide similar benefits.

7-18.   a.   Workers' compensation laws were enacted to require employers to provide benefits to employees for losses resulting from work-related accidents or diseases.

      b.   Medical care benefits for medical expenses are usually provided without any limitations on time or amount. Disability income benefits are a function of an employee's average weekly wage over some time period. Death benefits provide burial allowances in a flat amount, varying by state; death benefit cash income payments to survivors are a function of the worker's average wage prior to the injury resulting in death. Rehabilitation benefits are payable for medical rehabilitation and vocational rehabilitation.

7-19.   Unemployment insurance benefits and benefits received under temporary disability laws are included in a recipient's gross income. Workers' compensation benefits are received free of income taxation.

Answers to Self-Test Questions

7-1.   True.

7-2.   False. A person born in 1962 will be eligible to receive full Social Security benefits when he or she reaches age 67.

7-3.   True.

7-4.   True.

7-5.   True.

7-6.   True.

7-7.   False. There is no earnings test reduction for a worker older than his or her full retirement age.

7-8.   True.

7-9.   False. Part A of Medicare pays for inpatient hospital services for an uninterrupted stay of up to 90 days plus another 60 lifetime reserve days.

7-10.   False. A new 90-day benefit period begins after an individual has been out of a hospital or skilled-nursing facility for 60 consecutive days.

7-11.   True.

7-12.   True.

7-13.   False. Benefits for eyeglasses, hearing aids, and orthopedic shoes are excluded.

7-14.   True.

7-15.   False. Participation in Medicare Part D is voluntary.

7-16.   False. Medicare Part D pays 75 percent of the next $2,000 of prescription drug costs after an annual deductible of $250 (in 2006) has been met. Benefits then cease until a beneficiary's total drug cost equals $5,100 (in 2006). Subsequently, the plan pays 95 percent of covered drug costs. These dollar figures are subject to indexing.

7-17.   True.

7-18.   True.

7-19.   True.

7-20. False. In almost all cases, the full cost of providing workers' compensation benefits is borne by the employers, not the employees.

7-21. False. Workers' compensation benefits are received free of income taxation.

Chapter 8

Answers to Mini-Case

a. Paying off Amy and John's 15-year mortgage would be considered a temporary need. The need for money to pay the children's college expenses if one or both parents should die would also be considered a temporary need that expires when all the children finish college. (As noted later, permanent insurance could also build cash values that help pay college expenses if both parents are still alive.) The desire to provide an inheritance is a permanent life insurance need.

b. In all likelihood, the group benefit provided by Amy and John's employer involves term insurance, a temporary form of insurance. If this is a typical group program, they may have a right to convert this group insurance to individual permanent insurance if either of them ceases to be employed by SKH.

c. During the mortgage's 15-year span, the amount of money required to pay if off decreases every year. Decreasing term insurance on John's life is ideally suited for this specific need.

d. Guaranteed renewable term life insurance on John and Amy would provide funds to substitute for the income that might otherwise be earned if either parent should die. However, whole life insurance would not only meet this need but also provide for an inheritance if Amy and John die after their children finish college. Additionally, whole life insurance will build cash values that can be tapped to help provide college funding. To provide increased flexibility if they need to access the policies' cash values or modify their premium payments at some point, John and Amy might consider universal life insurance. Universal life insurance will also provide some benefits that reflect the impact of inflation.

Two important comments: First, although temporary insurance would meet the mortgage redemption need itself, a more detailed needs analysis *might* reveal that permanent insurance is more appropriate for concurrently meeting all Amy's and John's various needs. Second, although life insurance cash values can help pay college expenses, a variety of other financial planning measures should also be considered.

Answers to Review Questions

8-1. When an income producer's family is completely dependent on his or her personal earnings for subsistence and the amenities of life and the income earner dies, the unrealized portion of his or her total earnings potential is lost. Life insurance can enable the family to retain the same economic position that they would have enjoyed had the income earner lived. At this point, term life insurance will provide the most protection at the lowest cost. Marty will probably want to consider term insurance that is renewable, to preserve his insurability, and also convertible, so he can change it to permanent insurance when the Gibsons' financial situation improves.

8-2. The annual premium under the yearly renewable term plan must (along with interest earned during the year) pay the policy's share of death claims each year for the group (class) to which the insured has been assigned. The death rate rises at an increasing rate as age increases for the class from year to year, so the overall premium also rises at an increasing rate.

Premiums under the level premium plan are constant throughout the premium-paying period. In the early years, the level premium is larger than the policy's share of the death claims. In the years when the level premiums are more than sufficient to meet the policy's share of the death claims, the excess premiums are accumulated at interest in a reserve to help pay the policy's share of the death claims in later years when (in most cases) the policy's share of the death claims is larger than the policy's level premium. With cash value insurance, the reserve increases over the years and equals the face amount of the policy at the maturity of the policy.

The term plan provides protection for the face amount of the policy; the level premium plan provides protection for the net amount at risk, equal to the face amount of the policy minus the reserve. The term plan provides no cash value; the level premium plan builds cash value (except for short-term level premium term policies, where the reserve is very small).

8-3. a. (1) Term insurance provides temporary death protection for the policy period. With whole life insurance, there is permanent death protection as long as the policy remains in force.

    (2) If the insured lives beyond the end of the policy period with term insurance, no benefit is paid. For a whole life policy, if the insured is still alive at maturity age (usually age 100), the policy matures, and the face amount (for tax purposes, the cash value) is paid.

    (3) With yearly renewable term insurance, the full gross premium is used to pay mortality costs, expenses, contingencies, and profit. With level premium policies, whether term or whole life, the early year premiums are greater than needed (along with interest) to pay mortality costs, expenses, contingencies, and profit. The excess premium is accumulated at an assumed rate of interest in a reserve.

  b. If the client buys a 10-year *renewable* term policy, he or she may extend it at the end of 10 years without proof of insurability. The client will pay the new higher level premium that reflects the higher death rates in the next 10 years. If the client's policy was not renewable term, he or she would have to reapply for insurance and prove insurability again.

  c. If the client buys a 10-year *convertible* term policy and then needs a more permanent form of insurance, he or she can switch it to whole life insurance or another form of permanent insurance sold by the insurer in the future without proof of insurability.

  d. A decreasing term policy is appropriate for funding the balance of the client's mortgage when he or she dies.

  e. (1) There is no difference in permanence of protection.

    (2) With an ordinary life policy, the premium is paid as long as the insured lives (up to the assumed mortality age 99), and premium outlay will be smaller per year than that for limited-payment whole life policies of the same face amount. With limited-payment whole life policies, the shorter the premium payment period, the larger the amount of premium outlay per year.

    (3) Because limited-payment whole life policies have higher premiums for the same death benefit as ordinary life policies, their reserves and cash values are larger than for ordinary life policies.

8-4. Participating (par) policies provide for the payment of dividends to the policyowner. These policies anticipate charging a small extra margin in the premium with the intent to return part of the premium as policyowner dividends, depending on the extent to which the insurer has favorable experience from interest, mortality, and/or expenses. Nonparticipating policies do *not* provide for the payment of policyowner dividends, and policyowners share in the insurer's experience via changes in premiums and/or cash values.

8-5. a. An endowment policy pays the death benefit at the death of the insured or at the end of the policy period, whichever comes first. The endowment policy requires a much higher premium than whole life and has a savings element much larger relative to the protection element for whole life insurance.

  b. A 1984 tax law change eliminated the tax-free buildup of cash values for most newly sold endowment policies, so endowment purchases do not make sense today.

8-6. a. A variable life insurance policy provides no interest rate guarantee and no minimum cash value.

  b. The SEC requires variable life policies to be registered and all sales to be subject to the requirements applicable to other registered securities. Policy sales may be made only after the prospective purchaser has had a chance to read the policy prospectus. The SEC also requires that the insurance company be registered as an investment company and that all sales agents be registered with the SEC for the specific purpose of variable life insurance policy sales. Agents who sell variable life insurance policies must be licensed as both life insurance agents and securities agents.

  c. Variable life insurance policies give the purchaser several investment options into which the funds can be directed. The policyowner is free to put all of the funds into one of these choices or to distribute the funds among the options in whatever proportions he or she desires. Some insurance companies have more than a dozen funds to choose from in their current product offering.

  d. Variable life insurance contracts include mortality charges for the death benefits they provide. Consequently, the return on the invested funds within a variable life insurance contract will never equal that of a separate investment fund that does not provide death benefits but invests in assets of a similar type and quality.

  e. There are two basic ways used to link a policy's death benefit to the associated portfolio's investment performance—the level additions method or the constant ratio method. Regardless of the linkage design, a minimum death benefit is guaranteed. The purchaser selects a target level of investment performance as a benchmark against which actual investment performance will be measured. Performance in excess of the target level is used to fund incremental increases in the death benefit; performance below the target amount requires downward adjustments in the death benefits to make up for the deficit.

  f. After administrative charges, the balance of the premium payment goes into the cash value account. Cash value accounts are further diminished by mortality charges to support the death benefits. The actual value of the cash component is determined by the net asset value of the separate account funds that make up the policy portfolio. The cash value of a variable life policy fluctuates daily. Each day's net asset value is based on the closing price for the issues in the portfolio on that trading day. Variable life insurance policies usually limit maximum policy loans to a slightly smaller percentage of the total cash value than is traditionally available in whole life policies.

    g. The prospectus must contain a full disclosure of all the contract provisions, including expenses, investment options, benefit provisions, and policyowner rights under the contract. Other information explains the expense charges levied by the insurance company against variable life insurance contracts, surrender charges, and investment portfolio information.

8-7.   a. Premiums are flexible after the first year—the only time that a minimum level of payment is required.

    b. The higher the amount or proportion of prefunding through premium payments, the more investment earnings will be credited to the policy and utilized to cover mortality and administrative costs. All premium suggestions are based on some assumed level of investment earnings, and the policyowner accepts the possibility that actual investment earnings will be less than necessary to support the suggested premium. Even though investment earnings cannot go below the guaranteed rate, a long-term shortfall may necessitate either an increase in premiums or a reduction in coverage at some future point. The accumulations from prefunding are credited to the policy's cash value and are quite visible to the policyowner. The earnings rates applied to those accumulations are also clearly visible as they fluctuate with current economic conditions.

    c. The policyowner can make partial withdrawals from the policy's cash value without incurring indebtedness. There is no obligation to repay those funds, nor is there any interest incurred on the amount withdrawn. Withdrawals do affect the policy's future earnings, because the fund still intact to earn interest for future crediting periods is reduced by the amount of the withdrawal. The effect on the death benefit depends on the type of death benefit in force.

    d. The target premium amount is the suggested premium to be paid on a level basis throughout the contract's duration, or for a shorter period of time if a limited-payment approach was originally intended to fund the policy. The target premium amount is a suggestion and carries no liability to the insurer if it is inadequate to maintain the contract.

    e. (1) The level death benefit design is much like the traditional whole life design. The death benefit stays constant, the cash value increases over time, and the net amount at risk decreases.

       (2) Under the increasing death benefit design, a constant net amount at risk is superimposed over the policy's cash value. As the cash value increases, the total death benefit also increases. A reduction in the cash value will reduce the death benefit. At the insured's death, the policy's stated face amount plus its cash value are paid.

    f. Most insurance companies credit current interest rates on the universal life cash value as long as there are no policy loans outstanding. Once the policyowner borrows funds from the cash value, the insurance company usually credits a lower interest rate or earnings rate to the portion of the cash value associated with the policy loan.

    g. From each premium dollar paid for universal life insurance, deductions are made for expenses and mortality. In addition, the universal life cash value account is increased at the current crediting rate to reflect investment earnings on that cash value. These dollars help to reduce the policyowner's current and future out-of-pocket premium expenses. The actual rate is credited at the insurer's discretion and tends to fluctuate, reflecting current economic conditions.

8-8. If just enough premium is paid annually to cover policy expense and mortality charges for the year, the universal life policy will essentially be the equivalent of yearly renewable term insurance, providing pure protection for the year with no cash value (savings). As the amount of premium paid in each year increases (with the policy death benefit unchanged), the universal life policy will provide protection and savings *comparable* to that available with longer and longer term insurance, then comparable to an ordinary life policy, and finally comparable to limited-payment whole life insurance with a shorter and shorter premium-payment period.

8-9.   a. Federal income tax law requires that to meet the tax law definition of life insurance, a specified proportion of the death benefit must be derived from the amount at risk (for tax purposes, that is the death benefit minus the cash value). Whenever the cash value in the contract becomes high enough that the proportion is no longer satisfied, the death benefit of the universal life policy starts to increase, even though the contract has a level death benefit design.

    b. With the increasing benefit design, a constant amount at risk is superimposed over the policy's cash value. Thus, the total death benefit payable equals the policy's stated face amount plus its cash value. If the cash value decreases (for example, because premium payments were skipped), the death benefit will likewise decrease.

8-10. a. Variable universal life insurance is similar to variable life insurance in that it gives policyowners several options for directing the investments. The policyowner can reposition the portfolio at any time. Like variable life, variable universal life has no interest rate or cash value guarantee. Variable universal life, like variable life, is technically classified as a security and is subject to regulation by the SEC. In addition, sales of both variable universal life and variable life policies require a prospectus.

    b. Variable universal life insurance and universal life policies incorporate similar premium flexibility, death benefit design, and partial withdrawal features. Like universal life policies, variable universal life policies have no guarantee that once the cash value is large enough to carry the policy, it will always be able to do so.

8-11. a. A joint-life or first-to-die policy is written on the lives of two or more persons and is payable on the death of the first person to die. These policies are common for funding business buy-sell agreements. However, they could also be used in this situation to provide the money to hire an assistant for the surviving spouse.

    b. A survivorship or second-to-die policy is written on two or more lives and payable on the death of the last insured to die. These policies are used to fund federal estate taxes of wealthy couples whose wills provide for maximum tax deferral at the first death. However, they could also be used to fund a specific need such as in this situation where funds are necessary upon the death of the second spouse.

      Join-life insurance is usually written on either a first-to-die or a second-to-die basis. Because the Millers have specific needs for both first-to-die and second-to-die funding, a combination of whole life insurance on each spouse and second-to-die coverage might meet their needs.

8-12. a. To be eligible for a group insurance plan, an employee must be in a covered classification of workers, work on a full-time basis, and be actively at work. He or she may be required to fulfill a probationary period and, in some cases, to show insurability and meet premium contribution requirements.

    b. Most group life coverage is provided without individual evidence of insurability. However, this evidence is required in some cases such as when an employee decides after the expiration of the eligibility period that he or she wants the coverage after all.

    c. The amount of group life insurance on each covered worker is normally set according to a schedule, most commonly based on earnings or position. In an earnings schedule, the amount of insurance is often equal to some multiple of earnings, such as two times the employee's annual earnings, rounded up to the next $1,000 and subject to a maximum benefit. In a position schedule, differing benefit amounts are provided based on each employee's position within the firm.

    d. Any employee whose group life insurance ceases has the right, according to the master contract, to convert to an individual insurance policy. Conversion does not require proof of insurability and must occur within the first 31 days of eligibility to convert. The individual policy may be any type the insurer offers except term insurance, and the face amount may not exceed the amount of group life insurance. The premium for the individual policy is based on the employee's attained age at the time of conversion.

    e. Additional amounts of insurance may be made available to some or all classes of employees. Proof of insurability is usually required to obtain the additional amount, except when the amount of coverage is small, and the employer does not usually pay any part of the premium for the additional insurance.

      Dependent life insurance also may be available. Coverage is usually optional, with the employee paying the entire cost. The amount of insurance is usually modest, and the employee typically is not allowed to select which of his or her eligible dependents will be covered but must decide on an all-or-none basis.

Self-Test Questions

8-1.   True.

8-2.   False. Yearly renewable term insurance pays benefits only if the insured dies during the protection period.

8-3.   True.

8-4.   True.

8-5.   False. Insurers offering term insurance on an individual basis often place a limit on the period during which the insurance can be renewed, in order to protect against adverse selection.

8-6.   True.

8-7.   True.

8-8.   False. Decreasing term represents a substantial portion of the term insurance used for financial planning purposes, especially mortgage coverage.

8-9.   True.

8-10.   False. Both of these policies provide protection for the lifetime of the insured (until the assumed mortality age).

8-11.   True.

8-12.   False. Federal income tax reform in 1984 eliminated the tax-free buildup of cash values in most endowment policies, so few endowment policies are sold today.

8-13.   True.

8-14.   False. Both the cash value and the level of death benefits reflect investment performance.

8-15.   False. Variable life insurance can be sold only with an accompanying prospectus.

8-16.   True.

8-17.   False. Under the level death benefit design, death benefits are level unless the cash value gets too close to the death benefit to comply with the federal income tax law, in which case the death benefit will start increasing. However, under the increasing death benefit design, the death benefit will increase or decrease with the policy's cash value.

8-18.   True.

8-19.   False. A joint-life policy is payable on the death of the first of two or more lives insured under the single contract. A survivorship or second-to-die policy is payable on the death of the last of two or more lives insured under the single contract.

8-20.   True.

Chapter 9

Answers to Mini-Case

a. Amy and John have the option of taking dividends in cash, using them to reduce premiums, allowing them to accumulate at interest, using them to purchase paid-up additions, or electing a fifth-dividend option. The cash option and the reduced-premium option would both reduce Amy and John's bottom-line out-of-pocket costs for the life insurance. The accumulation-at-interest option would not reduce their immediate costs but would instead use accumulated dividends to increase the cash value of the policy and return a guaranteed minimum rate of interest, which might or might not be competitive with the return on other investments. The accumulated dividends could be withdrawn at any time or, if not withdrawn, would increase death proceeds or the policy's nonforfeiture value. Purchasing paid-up additional insurance would help address their concerns about inflation by gradually increasing the face value of the policy by adding small amounts of paid-up whole life insurance. The fifth-dividend option would more substantially increase the policy's death benefit but only for one year.

b. (1) An accidental death benefits rider, also known as a double indemnity provision, would double the standard death benefit if Amy or John should die because of an accident. The main advantage of this rider is that its premium is relatively low. This reflects the low likelihood of an accidental death. A disadvantage, in many cases, is that the money might better be spent on additional life insurance covering death from any cause.

(2) The guaranteed purchase option rider, in effect, guarantees that Amy and John have a right to buy additional life insurance at certain specified times in the future without proving that they are currently in good health. Because of the needs they are addressing and their concerns about inflation, this is probably something Amy and John should consider.

(3) The waiver-of-premium provision would enable Amy and John to continue insurance in force without having to pay premiums if the insured becomes totally disabled. Doing so would help them maintain this important coverage even under conditions when the family income might be limited. However, Amy and John need to factor into their evaluation that they currently have group long-term disability coverage, which addresses essentially the same issue and might provide the funding necessary to continue paying life insurance premiums even if they become disabled. They should, however, recognize that the long-term disability coverage is provided through their current employer, it replaces only a portion of their income, and the benefit might no longer be available if either of them drops out of the workforce or changes jobs.

Answers to Review Questions

9-1.   The declarations page of most life insurance contracts contains the name of the insurance company; the identities of the insured, the policyowner and the beneficiary; specific policy details; a general description of the type of insurance provided by the policy contract; a statement about the policy's free-look provision; and the insurer's promise to pay.

9-2. Frank should review these policy provisions to answer his questions:

a. *grace period.* Life insurance policies include a grace period, during which an overdue premium may be paid without a lapse in coverage. The standard length of the grace period is 30 or 31 days. Frank's coverage is still in force.

b. *policy loan provision.* The policy loan provision gives the policyowner access to the cash value that accumulates inside the policy without terminating the policy. The policyowner requests a loan, and the life insurer lends the funds confidentially. The loan provisions in the policy specify the portion of the cash value that is available for loans and how interest will be determined. In most policies, over 90 percent of the cash value is available for loans.

c. *incontestable clause.* The incontestable clause provides that once the policy has been in force for 2 years during Frank's lifetime, the insurer cannot deny payment to the beneficiary because of concealment or misrepresentation in the application.

d. *dividend options.* In addition to a reduction in premiums (and cash), participating whole life policies generally offer

- *accumulation at interest.* The insurer retains the dividends in the equivalent of a savings account with a minimum guaranteed rate of interest, although a higher rate may be credited if conditions warrant. The accumulated dividends may be withdrawn at any time. If not withdrawn, they are added to the death proceeds or to the nonforfeiture value if the policy is surrendered.

- *purchase of paid-up additions.* Each dividend purchases a small amount of additional fully paid whole life insurance on an attained-age basis. The purchase premium does not contain expense loading, and no evidence of insurability is required.

- *purchase of term insurance ("fifth dividend").* Some insurers use a portion of the dividend to buy one-year term insurance equal to the policy's then cash value, with the remainder used to buy paid-up additions or to accumulate at interest. Alternatively, other insurers use the entire dividend to buy one-year term insurance. In either case, the term insurance is purchased on the basis of the insured's attained age.

e. *misstatement of age.* The insurer will adjust the death benefits payable to the beneficiary to the amount that the premium paid would have purchased at the correct age.

9-3. The policyowner has the option of taking a reduced amount of paid-up whole life insurance, payable upon the same conditions as the original policy. The amount of the paid-up insurance is the amount that can be purchased at the insured's attained age by the net cash value (cash value, less any policy indebtedness, plus any dividend accumulations) applied as a net single premium. The paid-up insurance is purchased at net rates.

The other option provides extended term insurance in an amount equal to the original face amount of the policy, increased by any dividend additions or deposits and decreased by any policy indebtedness. The length of the term is that which can be purchased at the insured's attained age with the net cash value applied as a single premium. If the insured fails to elect an option within a specified period after default of premiums, this option is usually the one that automatically goes into effect.

9-4. The types of settlement options, in addition to the lump-sum or cash option, most commonly found in life insurance policies are as follows:

- *interest option.* Death proceeds are retained temporarily by the insurer, and only the interest is paid to the beneficiary periodically. A minimum interest rate is guaranteed in the policy, although insurers frequently pay a higher rate if investment earnings warrant. Death proceeds are paid at a specified later date at the request of the beneficiary, or on the occurrence of a specified event such as the death of the beneficiary.

- *fixed-period option.* Installment payments consisting of both the death proceeds and interest are made to the beneficiary over a specified period of time. A minimum interest rate is guaranteed. If the insurer pays a higher rate than the guaranteed rate, the amount of the installment payment is increased accordingly.

- *fixed-amount option.* Level periodic installments of a specified amount are paid to the beneficiary. The payments consist of a portion of the death proceeds and interest, and they continue for as long as the funds held by the insurer last. Unlike the fixed-period option, excess interest earnings under the fixed-amount option do not increase the size of the periodic payments but instead extend the length of time during which the payments will continue.

- *life income options.* Death proceeds are applied as a single premium to purchase an annuity for the beneficiary. Various forms of annuities may be available, most commonly straight life income, a life income with a period certain, a life income with some type of refund feature, and a joint-and-survivor life income.

9-5.   a.   The primary beneficiary is the person or organization that is to receive the proceeds if he, she, or it survives the insured. The estate of the insured may be named primary beneficiary, although this is usually unwise because it subjects the proceeds to transfer taxes and costs that can be avoided.

A contingent beneficiary is a person or organization that is to receive the proceeds only if the primary beneficiary predeceases the insured or loses entitlement to any of the proceeds for some other reason. If the primary beneficiary is eligible to receive the policy proceeds, the rights of the contingent beneficiary to the proceeds are extinguished.

   b.   If a beneficiary is named revocably, the policyowner can change the designation at any time prior to the insured's death without the beneficiary's consent. If the beneficiary is named irrevocably, the policyowner must obtain the beneficiary's consent before changing the beneficiary. Normally, an irrevocable designation requires the beneficiary's consent to the exercise of various other ownership rights in the policy such as surrendering for cash or borrowing against the nonforfeiture value.

9-6.   Yes, Bill's beneficiary would receive the death benefit. Although most insurance contracts do not provide coverage for a death by suicide within the first one or 2 years after the policy is issued, they do cover suicide after the exclusion period has expired.

9-7.   Some insurers permit the insured to withdraw policy death benefits under certain circumstances. These accelerated benefits, or living benefits provisions, state that if the insured develops a medical condition that renders the insured terminally ill, then he or she may withdraw a portion of the policy's death benefit. According to the NAIC Accelerated Benefits Model Regulation, the condition that permits the payment of the accelerated benefits must be a medical condition that drastically limits the insured's normal life span expectation (for example, to 2 years or less). Therefore, Harold may be able to withdraw his policy's death benefits due to his poor prognosis.

9-8.   Double indemnity may give the illusion of "double coverage." However, certain conditions must be satisfied in order for the insurer to pay double the face amount. One requirement is that death must occur as a result of an accident.

9-9.   The guaranteed purchase option, also called the guaranteed insurability option, helps policyowners protect themselves against the possibility that the insured might become uninsurable. Under the typical option, the owner may purchase additional insurance in specified amounts at specified times or ages of the insured. Typically, this provision allows additional purchases every 3 years, upon marriage, and after the birth of a child, provided the events occur before the insured reaches a specified maximum age (often age 45). No evidence of insurability is required to exercise the option. Also, the new coverage is normally not subject to a new suicide provision or a new incontestability clause.

9-10.   Susan could use the policy's cash surrender value to purchase an annuity that would provide her with a stream of income, but that does not seem to be what she needs. Rather than using the policy's cash value to fund a trust, Susan should seriously consider the reduced paid-up insurance option or the extended term insurance option. The extended term option would provide $250,000, to be split among the three grandchildren, if Susan dies before the end of the extended term. The reduced paid-up option would provide a smaller payment, but coverage would not expire.

In deciding among these options, Susan should first consider her health. If poor health has reduced her life expectancy, insurance might be a better choice than the cash option—and vice versa. In choosing between paid-up whole life insurance and the extended term option, Susan needs to recognize that college expenses are a temporary need that no longer exists after her grandchildren have completed college (unless they are paying off college loans). She should therefore consider the ages of the children, which, in turn, relate to how soon they will need money for college. Next, she needs to consider the period of extended term insurance that would be available under her policy.

Self-Test Questions

9-1.   False. Although certain provisions must be included, insurers can select the actual wording as long as it is at least as favorable to the policyowner as the statutory language.

9-2.   False. If the insured dies 2 weeks after the premium was due but not paid, the policy remains in force under the grace period provision, and the life insurance company must pay the beneficiary an amount equal to the full death benefit (possibly minus one month's premium).

9-3.   True.

9-4.   True.

9-5.   True.

9-6.   False. The company would lower the death benefit to the amount that the premium paid would have purchased at the correct age. The incontestable clause does not apply to a misstatement of age.

9-7.   False. If the premium for a whole life insurance policy is not paid by the end of the grace period, the policy will lapse and automatically go under a nonforfeiture option, usually extended term. The policyowner then has a period of time to decide to keep the policy under the automatic option, surrender it for its cash value, or switch to the paid-up whole life option.

9-8.   False. The death proceeds from Sarah's policy will be paid to her children as contingent beneficiaries. Upon her husband's death, the right to receive the death proceeds from Sarah's policy transfers to the children as contingent beneficiaries.

9-9.   True.

9-10. False. This person is the policyowner.

9-11. False. Accidental death benefit riders do not pay for deaths caused by disease.

9-12. True.

Chapter 10

Answers to Mini-Case

a.   Based on the information below, Jean does not have adequate life insurance. Therefore, recommendation for $75,000 additional life insurance (using a round number, because all figures are based on estimates) would seem appropriate.

Resources available	$820,000		
Lump-sum needs	282,000		
Difference	538,000		

Income needs Year	Need	Steve's Salary	Gap
1	$120,000	$40,000	$80,000
2	100,000	40,000	60,000
3	100,000	40,000	60,000
4	100,000	40,000	60,000
5	100,000	40,000	60,000
6	100,000	40,000	60,000
7	100,000	40,000	60,000
8	100,000	40,000	60,000
9	100,000	40,000	60,000
10	100,000	40,000	60,000
11	100,000	40,000	60,000
12	100,000	40,000	60,000
13	100,000	40,000	60,000
14	100,000	40,000	60,000
Need (based on NPV calculation)			$611,161
Resources minus lump-sum needs			–$538,000
Additional life insurance needed			$ 73,161

b.   Although this financial needs analysis provides a reasonable starting point for examining Jean's life insurance needs, it has a number of shortcomings that include the following:

- No inflationary increase in Steve's annual income needs is taken into account.
- Steve's goal of living on Social Security and pension income might be unrealistic.
- Steve's rate-of-return assumption might be invalid.
- Insurance on Steve's life might also be needed.

A complete financial plan would also consider many additional factors.

Answers to Review Questions

10-1. Life insurance planning includes a determination of how much insurance is needed and an evaluation of the proper type of insurance. The first of these tasks is usually based on an analysis of the client's needs. The second task begins with a decision between temporary versus permanent coverage and proceeds to the selection of a particular type of policy.

10-2. The first step in the financial needs analysis is to estimate the family's financial needs in the event of the client's death, both lump-sum needs and ongoing needs. Lump-sum needs encompass, for example, final medical expenses not covered by insurance, repayment of debt, estate taxes, final expenses, probate costs, attorneys' fees, ongoing short-term household operational expenses, and an emergency fund. Information needed to determine the lump-sum needs includes the spending habits of the surviving dependents, as well as the level of liquid or near-liquid assets available at the death of the client.

Ongoing income needs also must be estimated for four time periods: (1) the readjustment period immediately after the client's death, (2) the period following the readjustment period and continuing until the youngest child becomes self-sufficient, (3) the blackout period between the time that the youngest child becomes self-sufficient and the surviving spouse becomes eligible again for Social Security, and (4) the period after the surviving spouse becomes eligible again for Social Security and for any other pension benefits. Sources of income are identified that can offset the ongoing income needs. Information needed to determine the sources of income includes determining the Social Security retirement benefit, identifying other employer-provided plan benefits, and estimating the surviving spouse's earnings. Then the present value of the income shortfall is calculated and added to the lump-sum needs at death that are not covered by liquid or near-liquid assets.

10-3. The financial needs analysis approach, which involves the liquidation of principal, calculates the amount of additional life insurance needed by computing the gap between the needs of the client's dependents and the resources available to meet those needs in the event of the client's death. In this case, $50,000 of additional life insurance would be needed to meet the lump-sum needs ($300,000 minus $250,000 from existing insurance and savings). Another $200,000 of life insurance would be needed to meet the children's income support needs after taking into account their Social Security benefits after their mother's death. Thus, Sophie would need an additional $250,000 ($50,000 plus $200,000) of life insurance to meet her family's needs in the event of her death.

10-4. Unlike the capital liquidation approach in financial needs analysis, which assumes that policy proceeds will provide a life income through orderly consumption of available funds, the capital needs analysis approach assumes that the income benefits can be provided from investment income only. First, family financial needs are determined in the same manner as in the capital liquidation approach. Then the client's personal balance sheet is prepared. All the liabilities, immediate cash needs, and all assets that do not produce income are subtracted from the total assets. The remainder is the client's present income-producing capital. Finally, the additional capital needed to achieve the desired income objective, net of all other income sources, is computed. The amount of additional capital needed to meet the desired objective is calculated by dividing additional income needed by the applicable interest rate that represents the after-tax rate of investment return anticipated on the capital sum.

10-5. The use of permanent life insurance meets these three key objectives of an investment program:

- *safety of principal.* The life insurance industry has compiled a solvency record over the years that is unmatched by any other type of business organization. It has survived war, depression, and inflation; losses to policyowners have been relatively rare. Even the few companies seized by the regulators in recent years have been able to honor most of their policyowners' contracts.
- *yield.* Life insurance companies unquestionably obtain the highest possible yield commensurate with the standard of safety they have set for themselves and the regulatory constraints within which they operate. It is highly questionable that the typical life insurance policyowner can, over a long period, earn a consistently higher yield than a life insurance company without taking on a greater degree of speculative investment risk. Annual increases in cash values are not subject to federal income taxes as they accrue, while the earnings from a separate investment program are often taxed as ordinary income.
- *liquidity.* The liquidity of a life insurance contract is unsurpassed. The policyowner's cash value can be taken out at any time with no loss of principal. This can be accomplished through surrender for cash, through policy loans, or through partial withdrawals (in many newer life insurance products). In traditional products, the insured virtually never faces the possibility of liquidating his or her assets in an unfavorable market; nor can the insured's policy loans be called because of inadequate collateral.

10-6. Among the distinguishing characteristics that may make one type of permanent life insurance preferable over another for a particular client are the following:

- length of the planned premium-paying period
- emphasis on saving versus protection. If the client places heavy emphasis on the savings element, he or she should consider a very short premium-paying period (perhaps even single-premium whole life) or an endowment (though some of the advantage of the tax-deferred buildup of the savings element can be lost).

- time when death benefits are needed. If the principal need for funds is at the death of the main income-earner, a single-life policy is appropriate. However, if the principal need for funds is to provide estate liquidity when the surviving spouse dies, the client should consider a joint or survivorship life (second-to-die) policy.
- desire for inflation protection. Variable life, universal life, or variable universal life insurance can provide increasing amounts of death benefit protection.
- importance of yield versus safety in the savings component. If the client's risk-tolerance permits, variable, universal, or variable universal life may be appropriate as a way to achieve a higher yield.
- unbundling of cost components. If the client wants to know where his or her premium dollars go, he or she should consider variable, universal, or variable universal life insurance.
- premium-payment flexibility. If this is an important consideration, universal life or variable universal life can be appropriate recommendations.

10-7.   a.   The surrender cost index indicates the cost of surrendering the policy and withdrawing the cash value at some future point in time such as 20 years. The result is the average amount of each annual premium—in this case, $7.35 per $1,000 of coverage—that is not returned if the policy is surrendered for its cash value.

To compute the surrender cost index, the usual steps are as follows:

(1) Assume that each annual premium is placed in an account to accumulate at 5 percent interest until the end of a 20-year period.

(2) Assume that each annual dividend is placed in an account to accumulate at 5 percent interest until the end of the 20-year period.

(3) Subtract the 20th year cash value and the result of step (2) from the result of step (1).

(4) Divide the result of step (3) by the future-value-of-an-annuity-due factor for 20 years and 5 percent. The result represents the estimated level annual cost of the policy.

(5) Divide the result of step (4) by the number of thousands of dollars in the policy's death benefit. The result is the estimated level annual cost per $1,000 of coverage.

b.   The net payment cost index is useful when the main concern is the death benefit, rather than the cash value to be paid at some future point in time such as the end of the 20th year. The procedure for calculating this index is identical to that for the surrender cost index, except that in step (3) there is no subtraction of the 20th year cash value.

c.   The calculations must take into account the time value of money. The future value of all premium payments is compared to the eventual cash value plus the future value of dividends accumulated. The net shortfall, or future value of net costs, is then annuitized across the payment period.

10-8.   a.   In recent years, with sometimes higher interest rates and improved mortality experience, a policyowner may be able to substantially improve his or her situation by replacing an existing policy in either the same or a different company.

b.   The Unfair Trade Practices Act contains prohibitions against misrepresentation, including misrepresentations to induce the lapse, forfeiture, exchange, conversion, or surrender of any life insurance policy.

c.   The replacing agent must state whether the policy is a replacement at the time of application. For a replacement, the agent must give the applicant a prescribed notice alerting the applicant to the need to compare the existing and the proposed benefits carefully and to seek information from the agent or insurer from whom he or she purchased the original policy.

The replacing insurer must advise the other insurer of the proposed replacement and provide accurate information on the new policy. The replacing insurer must also give the applicant at least a 20-day free look at the new policy, during which time he or she has an unconditional right to a full refund of all premiums paid if he or she decides not to retain the policy.

The existing insurer or agent has 20 days to furnish the policyowner with accurate information on the existing policy, including its premium, cash values, death benefits, and dividends.

10-9.   A group that is rated as substandard by an insurer is expected to produce a higher mortality rate than a group of normal lives. If 1,000 persons, each of whom is engaged in a hazardous occupation, are granted insurance, it is certain that the death rate among them will be greater than the death rate among a group of people the same age who are not engaged in a hazardous occupation. To allow for the higher death rates (called extra mortality) that will certainly occur within the substandard group, the company must collect an extra premium from—or impose special terms on—all who are subject to the extra mortality, because it is not known which of the members of the group will be responsible for it. Every member of the group is not expected to survive for a shorter period than the normal life expectancy. In fact, it is a certainty that this will not be the case; it is known merely that a larger proportion of the people in a standard group will attain normal life expectancy.

10-10.   The methods life insurers use for handling substandard risks include the following:

- *increase in age.* Under this method, the applicant is assumed to be a number of years older than his or her real age, and the policy is written accordingly. This method of dealing with substandard applicants is often used when the extra mortality is markedly increasing and will continue to increase indefinitely.

- *extra percentage tables.* If an applicant presents an increasing hazard, the life insurer may charge premiums that reflect the appropriate increase in mortality. Depending on company practice and state law, surrender values may be based on the special mortality table or may be the same as surrender values under policies issued to standard applicants.

- *flat extra premium.* Under this method, the life insurer increases the standard premium by a specified number of dollars per $1,000 of insurance. The flat extra premium method is normally used when the hazard is thought to be constant (deafness or partial blindness, for example) or decreasing (as with a family history of tuberculosis or the aftermath of a serious illness or surgical operation, in which case the flat extra premium is usually temporary). The flat extra premium is widely used to cover the extra mortality associated with certain occupations and avocations. It is not reflected in policy values and dividends.

- *liens.* When the extra mortality to be expected from an impairment is of a distinctly decreasing and temporary nature, such as that associated with convalescence from a serious illness, an insurer might agree to create a lien against the policy for a number of years; the amount and term of the lien depend on the extent of the impairment. If such a method is utilized, the policy is issued at standard rates and is standard in all respects except that, should death occur before the end of the period specified, the amount of the lien is deducted from the proceeds otherwise payable.

- *other methods.* When the degree of extra mortality is small, or when its nature is not well known, the life insurer may make no extra charge but, if the policy is participating, may place all of the members of the group in a special class for dividend purposes, adjusting the dividends in accordance with the actual experience. Another approach is to deal with the impairment by merely limiting the plan of insurance to one with a high savings component.

10-11.   The major benefit of viaticating a policy is that cash will be available to the policyowner to fund the insured's final needs. However, the surviving family will no longer be provided for by the policy. Other pitfalls include potential loss of social benefits based on need and the lack of regulation regarding privacy. Furthermore, state regulation is not uniform (and may be nonexistent), information regarding the provider's financial strength may be unavailable, and fraudulent practices taint the industry.

10-12.   a.   The business can purchase life insurance on Betty, a key employee, to cover the possibility of an income loss and/or increase in expenses resulting from her death. Term insurance can be purchased if the primary concern is the key employee's dollar value to the business. Decreasing term might be appropriate because the key employee loss exposure decreases as the insured approaches retirement. Key employee insurance, however, is usually coupled with some other purpose such as providing a retirement benefit for the key employee. Permanent life insurance is typically purchased to meet this objective.

b.   Suzie can set up a buy-sell agreement with the two minor shareholders so that upon Suzie's death, her shares will be sold to the surviving owners of the business. The agreement may be funded with life insurance and should indicate how that life insurance will be structured and paid for. If an entity arrangement is used, the firm itself enters into an agreement with each owner specifying that, on the death of an owner, the firm will buy and the deceased's estate will sell the business interest of the deceased. The firm carries life insurance on each owner, with the firm as beneficiary, to provide the money to fund the agreement. If a cross-purchase approach is used, each stockholder is both a seller and a purchaser. On the death of one owner, the decedent's estate will sell, and the other owners will buy, the deceased's interest. To fund this type of agreement, each owner should carry and be the beneficiary of insurance on the lives of the other owners.

c.   The company can provide group term life insurance to participating employees under a Sec. 79 benefit plan. This plan allows the employer a tax deduction for premium payments on behalf of a participant unless the premium amounts cause the tax code's reasonable compensation test to be exceeded (an unlikely event). If the coverage provided by the plan is nondiscriminatory, the first $50,000 of coverage is provided tax free to all plan participants.

10-13.   Federal tax treatment of life insurance is as follows:

a.   Subject to some exceptions, lump-sum proceeds paid under a life insurance contract by reason of the insured's death are excludible from gross income for federal income tax purposes. The basic requirement for the income tax exclusion for life insurance proceeds is that they be paid by reason of the death of the insured. Current law also extends the exclusion to certain accelerated death benefits made on behalf of an insured who is terminally ill and expected to die within 24 months. The most important exception to the general rule of excluding life insurance death proceeds from federal income taxation is the transfer-for-value rule, which provides that if a policy is transferred from one owner to another for valuable consideration, the income tax exclusion is lost. (There are some exceptions to the transfer-for-value rule.)

b.   Death proceeds distributed as a series of payments under a settlement option generally include an element of interest earned, which is taxable. However, the portion of a settlement option payment that represents principal (the policy's face amount) still qualifies for the income tax exclusion.

c.   Policy dividends are treated as a nontaxable return of premium and reduce the policyowner's basis. If total dividends paid exceed total premiums, dividends are taxable to that extent. If dividends are used to reduce premiums or otherwise paid back into the policy (for example, to buy paid-up additions), the basis reduction caused by the payment of the dividend is offset by a corresponding basis increase when the dividend is reinvested in the policy because it is then treated as an additional premium payment.

d.   The inside buildup (increase in the cash value or investment fund) of a permanent life insurance policy is not subject to taxation as long as it is left inside the policy.

e.   If a policyowner withdraws funds from a policy's cash value, the general rule is that the withdrawal is first treated as a nontaxable return of basis. The excess, if any, of the amount of the withdrawal over the policyowner's current basis is taxable in the year of withdrawal. However, there are important exceptions, including certain withdrawals from universal life policies and withdrawals from policies classified as modified endowment contracts.

   One exception typically occurs in a universal life contract. If a cash value withdrawal results in a reduction in the policy's death benefit during the first 15 years of the policy, the withdrawal may first be taxed as income to the extent of income earned within the contract. This income first, or LIFO (last in, first out), method of taxation is the reverse of the general rule of basis first, or FIFO (first in, first out), taxation that life insurance typically enjoys.

f.   Loans from a policy are not taxable unless the policy is a modified endowment contract (MEC).

g.   Any life insurance policy that falls under the definition of a MEC is subject to an income first tax treatment with respect to loans and most distributions from the policy. A 10 percent penalty tax also generally applies to the taxable portion of any loan or withdrawal from a MEC unless the taxpayer has reached age 59½. With respect to loans (not withdrawals) from a MEC, the policyowner receives an increase in basis in the policy equal to the amount of the loan that is taxable. However, the nontaxable portion of a loan from a MEC will not affect the policyowner's basis. A nontaxable portion of a withdrawal, on the other hand, will reduce basis.

h.   The general rule is that premium payments for individual life insurance policies are not deductible for federal income tax purposes. This rule applies, regardless of who owns the policy and whether it is used for personal or business purposes. However, in certain situations, life insurance premiums can be deductible because they also fit the definition of some other type of deductible expense, not because they are premium payments—for example, because they are for a policy written for the benefit of a charitable organization or because the premium is a corporate expense or part of an alimony payment.

10-14.   Three aspects of federal gift taxation can be briefly described as follows:

a.   The federal gift tax applies only if there has been a completed transfer and acceptance of property and the transfer was for less than full and adequate consideration.

b.   Qualifying gifts of $11,000—the annual exclusion—or less may be made by a donor to any number of donees without gift tax consequences. The annual exclusion amount is indexed to inflation, and it will increase in $1,000 increments. To qualify for an annual exclusion, the gift must provide the donee with a present interest.

c.   Two types of gifts are fully deductible from the gift tax base. First, the marital deduction provides that unlimited qualifying transfers made by a donor to his or her spouse are fully deductible from the gift tax base. Second, qualifying gifts to a legitimate charity are deductible.

10-15.   The starting point in the federal estate tax calculation is determining the property in the decedent's gross estate. This includes all property that passes under the deceased's will or, in the absence of a valid will, under the state intestacy law, as well as property transferable by other means by the decedent at death. Certain items are deductible from the gross estate for estate tax calculation purposes such as legitimate debts of the decedent, reasonable funeral and other death costs of the decedent, and the reasonable cost of estate settlement, such as the executor's commission and attorney fees. Qualifying transfers to a surviving spouse and transfers to qualifying charities are also deductible from the estate tax base. Then the unified credit, if it has not been exhausted to shelter lifetime gifts, is applied against transfers made at death. The estate may also take a deduction on the federal estate tax return for state death taxes paid.

10-16. a. Life insurance proceeds payable to or for the benefit of the insured's estate are includible in the estate, regardless of who owned the contract or who paid the premium.

   b. When insurance proceeds are paid to a named beneficiary other than the insured's estate, incidents of ownership in the policy at the time of death are the key criteria for determining inclusion. As in this case, because the insured held an incident of ownership at the time of his or her death—the right to change the beneficiary—the policy is included in his gross estate.

   c. Although the decedent had transferred all rights to the policy to his wife, the transfer occurred within 3 years of his death. Under the 3-year rule, life insurance transferred to a third party for less than full consideration within 3 years of the insured's death is automatically includible in the insured's gross estate.

10-17. Life insurance can serve as an estate enhancement in order to provide for the basic needs of the decedent's heirs. This is particularly true for young clients, clients with family members dependent on their income, and/or clients with small to moderate-sized estates. Also, insurance can provide estate liquidity/wealth replacement for older clients or clients with large estates, providing coverage for probate expenses, death taxes, and estate liquidity needs.

Answers to Self-Test Questions

10-1. True.

10-2. True.

10-3. False. With the capital needs analysis approach, the amount of additional life insurance needed is determined by subtracting the resources already available from the resources needed by the survivor's dependents if the client should die today, assuming that future income payments can be composed solely of investment earnings on a capital sum. With the financial needs analysis approach, the amount of additional life insurance needed is determined by subtracting the resources already available from the resources needed by the survivor's dependents if the client should die today, assuming that future income payments can be composed of a combination of investment earnings and liquidation of the capital sum.

10-4. False. A major advantage of the financial needs analysis approach is that it does take into account factors that would be available in the event of the insured's death such as Social Security benefits and future earnings by a spouse.

10-5. False. In addition to a number of needs that can and should be met with term insurance, various types of permanent insurance, not just whole life, should be considered in determining how to best meet a client's life insurance needs.

10-6. True.

10-7. True.

10-8. False. Only those life insurance policy replacements involving agent or insurer distortion or misrepresentation of facts constitute twisting. Sometimes a policyowner can substantially improve his or her situation by replacing an existing policy in either the same or a different company.

10-9. True.

10-10. False. The most common method of dealing with risks that present an increasing hazard is to use extra percentage tables. A flat extra premium is normally used when the hazard is thought to be constant or decreasing.

10-11. True.

10-12. False. Viaticals are not deemed securities and are not subject to SEC regulation.

10-13. False. There are no federal privacy laws regarding viatical agreements.

10-14. False. One of the common uses of life insurance in business is to serve as a method of funding, not of replacing, a properly designed buy-sell agreement.

10-15. False. In a traditional split-dollar plan, the corporation contributed an amount equal to the annual increase in the policy's cash surrender value, while the executive paid the remainder of the annual premium.

10-16. False. In general, and subject to some exceptions, proceeds paid under a life insurance contract by reason of the insured's death are excludible from gross income for federal income tax purposes.

10-17. False. The inside buildup in a permanent life insurance policy is not subject to taxation as long as it is left inside the policy.

10-18. True.

10-19. False. The gift tax applies only to gifts during the donor's lifetime.

10-20. True.

10-21. False. Life insurance can provide estate enhancement for young clients as well as estate liquidity/wealth replacement for older clients.

Chapter 11

Answers to Mini-Case

a. To meet her income objective, Clara needs to generate between $12,000 and $17,000 of additional income. She currently has the $200,000 in insurance proceeds that can be used for this purpose. Note that Clara also has $100,000 in savings and investments that yield about 4 percent annually. Clara might want to explore ways to increase this yield. However, her return does not seem unreasonable in light of today's environment and the fact that she needs to maintain an emergency fund of up to 6 months' income. This fund should be invested with safety and liquidity in mind.

If Clara were to annuitize the $200,000 of proceeds from her husband's life insurance policy, she should be able to generate an annual income of between $18,000 and $20,000 with a life annuity from a reputable provider of annuities. (These amounts are based on figures obtained from various Internet sites and include rates for annuities obtained as life insurance settlement options.) If she elected to have the annuity paid for 10-years certain, these figures would drop to between $16,000 and $18,000. In either case, Clara could use traditional annuities to meet her need for lifetime income at the currently desired level.

b. Even with modest rates of inflation, Clara's income will lose its purchasing power as she ages. Her Social Security income has a cost-of living adjustment. The income from her husband's pension probably does not, although some private pensions do have cost-of-living adjustments. Her annuity income will remain the same unless she purchases an annuity that provides annual adjustments. For example, one mutual fund company has an annuity that will increase with changes in the consumer price index. For a $200,000 premium, its initial annual annuity payment is $13,000. As another example, one insurer allows the annuitant to select annual payment increases up to 5 percent. At 3 percent, the annuity payment begins at $14,000. At 5 percent, the amount is $12,200. These amounts are all at the low end of Clara's desired income needs, but they address her concerns about inflation.

Answers to Review Questions

11-1. a. The primary function of life insurance is to create an estate or principal sum; the primary function of an annuity is to liquidate a principal sum, regardless of how it was created.

b. Life insurance and annuities are based on the same fundamental pooling, mortality, and investment principles. First, both insurance and annuities use the pooling technique. In insurance, all make contributions so that the dependents of those who die prematurely are partially compensated for loss of income. In annuities, those who die prematurely contribute on behalf of those who live beyond their life expectancy and would otherwise outlive their income. Second, both life insurance and annuity costs are based on probabilities of death and survival as reflected in a mortality table. Finally, under both arrangements, premiums are discounted for the compound interest that the insurance company will earn.

11-2. If the annuitant is willing to pool savings with those of other annuity owners, the administering agency can provide all the participants with an income of a specified amount as long as they live—regardless of longevity. This arrangement implies the willingness of participants to have all or a portion of their unliquidated principal at the time of death used to supplement the principal of those who live beyond their life expectancy. Therefore, each payment under an annuity is composed partly of the annuitant's principal, partly of the unliquidated principal of other annuitants who die early, and partly of investment income on these funds.

11-3. Annuities can be classified as follows:

a. The annuity can be distributed on a *pure annuity* basis, which provides periodic income payments that continue as long as the annuitant lives but terminate at that person's death. A *refund annuity* is any type that promises to return, in one manner or another, a portion or all of the purchase price of the annuity.

b. The annuity may be a *single life annuity,* or it may cover two or more lives. A *joint annuity* provides that the income ceases at the first death among the lives covered. A *joint-and-last-survivor annuity* provides that the income ceases only at the last death among the lives covered.

c. An *immediate annuity* makes the first benefit payment one payment interval after the date of purchase. Under a *deferred annuity,* more than one payment interval will elapse after purchase before the first benefit payment is due.

d. A deferred annuity can be purchased with either a *single premium* or *periodic premiums.*

e. Annuity payments may be *fixed,* providing a fixed number of dollars for each benefit payment, or they may be *variable,* providing payments based on the investment performance of the assets underlying the annuity.

11-4. Immediate and deferred annuities differ as follows:

a. Although deferred annuities can be purchased with either single premiums or periodic premiums, immediate annuities can be purchased only with single premiums because the first benefit payment is made at the end of one payment period from the purchase date of the annuity.

b. Although all annuities have a liquidation period, deferred annuities also have an accumulation period when funds are accumulated with the insurance company to provide the annuity income benefits during the liquidation period.

11-5. Jim should purchase a deferred annuity on a periodic premium basis (flexible premiums in case he wants to contribute more or less in some periods). To protect against loss of purchasing power, he should use a variable annuity product. When he reaches retirement, he can choose a joint-and-last-survivor option to guarantee an income to him and his wife as long as either is living. At that time, he can also decide whether he wishes to keep the annuity in a variable mode or switch to fixed payments during the liquidation period. He can also decide at retirement whether he wants any additional guarantees (for example, 10-years certain).

11-6. The following would occur after Ann's death:

a. The annuity payments would cease under a pure annuity.

b. Annuity payments would continue to Ann's beneficiary for the remainder of the 20 years—in this case, for 19 years and 10 months—if Ann had purchased a life annuity with 20-years certain.

c. Under an installment refund annuity, payments would continue to Ann's beneficiary until the insurer had paid out the purchase price of $300,000.

11-7. During the accumulation period of a deferred variable annuity, premium deposits are applied to the purchase of accumulation units. The accumulation unit is assigned an arbitrary value, such as $10, at the inception of the plan, and the initial premiums purchase accumulation units at that price. Thereafter, the units are revalued each month to reflect changes in the market value of the common stock that constitutes the company's variable annuity portfolio. On any valuation date, the value of each accumulation unit is determined by dividing the market value of the common stock underlying the accumulation units by the aggregate number of units. Dividends are usually allocated periodically and applied to the purchase of additional accumulation units, although they may simply be reinvested without allocation and used to increase the value of each existing accumulation unit. Capital appreciation or depreciation, both realized and unrealized, is always reflected in the value of the accumulation units, rather than in the number of units. A portion of each premium payment is deducted for expenses, and the remainder is invested in accumulation units at their current market value.

At the beginning of the liquidation period, the accumulation units are exchanged for annuity units. The number of annuity units that the annuitant will acquire depends on the company's assumptions as to mortality, dividend rates, and expenses, and on the market value of the assets underlying the annuity units. In essence, the number of annuity units is determined by dividing the dollar value of the accumulation units by the present value of a life annuity at the participant's attained age in an amount equal to the current value of one annuity unit. The number of annuity units remains constant throughout the liquidation period, but units are revalued each year, reflecting the current market price of the common stock and the mortality, investment, and expense experience for the preceding year. The dollar income payable to the annuitant each month is determined by multiplying the number of annuity units the annuitant owns by the current value of one unit.

11-8. Key features of equity-indexed annuities include the following:

- *participation rate formula.* This formula defines the potential return of the annuity, based on increases in the value of a stock index.

- *term period.* Most contracts anticipate a series of terms of uniform length; however, some contracts reserve the insurer's right to modify the term period available for continuation at the expiration of any existing term.

- *participation rate.* The participation rate is used in the participation rate formula to determine the amount of the index gain that can be applied (if any) to produce more than the guaranteed yield. Higher participation rates may be available from some insurers if the purchaser accepts a lower guaranteed interest rate.
- *cap on the crediting rate.* Some contracts cap the crediting rate that is applied to the accumulated value of the contract, preventing full formula participation in times of very rapid index increases.
- *minimum crediting rate.* Most contracts specify a floor of zero percent as the minimum extra interest crediting rate applicable to the accumulated value. This prevents the application of a negative percentage in the formula to reflect plunges in the index value, and it ensures that the fixed-interest-rate guarantee is the worst possible outcome.
- *no SEC regulation.* Equity-indexed annuities currently are regarded as fixed annuities and may be sold by agents who are not licensed to sell variable products.
- *minimum guarantees.* The minimum guarantees under equity-indexed annuities are lower than those for traditional fixed-interest annuities, and the rates actually guaranteed apply to less than the full amount paid as a premium. The specified interest rate applied each year to the contract value is set forth in the contract and remains fixed unless a negotiated change is later agreed to by both the contract owner and the insurance company.

11-9. Life insurance companies cope with problems of adjusting annuity prices for anticipated future increases in life expectancy in three ways:
- computing annuity premiums on the basis of mortality tables that reflect annuitants' lower mortality. This current approach has replaced an earlier technique of using age setbacks.
- using a low-interest assumption in the premium formula. Intensified competition among insurance companies and between insurance companies and investment media, however, has caused companies to adopt interest assumptions closer to the level of their actual investment earnings.
- calculating the premiums and/or benefits on a participating basis, which enables the insurance company to use conservative assumptions

11-10. Under a gift annuity agreement, Lynn would donate cash or other assets to the institution. In exchange for the gift, the institution would provide Lynn with fixed payments for life.

Because Lynn's donation is an irrevocable gift, she would be entitled to an immediate income tax deduction based, in part, on the value of the donated asset. A further benefit is that assets used to fund the gift annuity are generally removed from Lynn's taxable estate.

Besides realizing immediate tax benefits, Lynn would receive a periodic annuity payment. The payment may be annual, monthly, or at some other interval. Only part of these payments is taxable income, because a portion of the payments is deemed to be a tax-free return of the donor's gift during the donor's expected lifetime under federal tax regulations.

Benefits to the institution are any difference between its earnings and its costs of providing periodic payments. The institution also benefits from the residual value of the donated property, if any, after Lynn's death.

11-11. The usual structured settlement uses an annuity to provide periodic payments that meet the recipient's financial needs as much as possible. The periodic payments of income are received tax free by the claimant during his or her life and by the claimant's beneficiaries thereafter for the balance of any guarantee period. All timing decisions, as well as the exact amount of money, are predetermined by the defendant and its insurer, who are the legal owners of the annuity. Structured settlements might be more useful than a lump sum in replacing a lost income stream and addressing specific needs, such as the ongoing expense of medical treatments or household help, that require a continual and ongoing source of funding.

11-12. Advantages of structured settlements include the following:
- *for the injured party.* The structured settlement provides financial security for the lifetime of the injured party. The use of periodic payments reduces the possibility of dissipation of funds through mismanagement, imprudent investment, unwise expenditures, misuse, or neglect by claimants and their families or guardians. Payments represent personal bodily injury damages, which are excluded from income tax.
- *for the plaintiff's attorney.* Attorneys are assured that the settlement is guaranteed and will not be subject to dissipation as is a lump-sum settlement. Some attorneys believe that recommending a structured settlement insulates them from exposure to legal malpractice because attorneys do not take a sizable portion of the total value of the benefit payable as a lump sum at the time of settlement.
- *for the judge.* Guaranteed lifetime periodic payments assure the plaintiff of financial security, regardless of when he or she dies. Unlike the lump-sum settlement, the judge or jury does not need to determine how much money the plaintiff will need for the rest of his or her life.

- *for the public.* The injured party does not become a ward of the state and is assured of a guaranteed income and proper care. The delay of prolonged litigation is avoided, reducing court costs and placing fewer burdens on an overloaded judicial system.
- *for the defendant's liability insurer.* The offer of additional, tax-free income may make the settlement more attractive to the claimant, who will receive more money in total than with a lump-some payment.

    Disadvantages of structured settlements can arise from the insurer's insolvency, resulting in delayed and/or reduced benefits. Also, the annuitant must absorb losses in excess of any state guaranty fund limitations. Moreover, the annuitant cannot accelerate or decelerate future payments, so problems can occur if more immediate cash is needed than the stream of payments provides.

11-13. A client with a reduced life expectancy is likely to qualify for an impaired risk annuity. Because the applicant's health is considered in the underwriting process, annuity payments are increased (or the premium lowered) in relation to the shorter life expectancy.

Answers to Self-Test Questions

11-1. True.
11-2. False. Annuities serve the function of liquidation of a principal sum, regardless of how it was created. Life insurance creates an estate or principal sum.
11-3. False. Jack should purchase a deferred annuity with periodic premiums. Immediate annuities do not provide for accumulation and cannot be purchased with periodic premiums.
11-4. False. If Rachel is still alive at the end of 20 years, her annuity benefit payments would continue until her death.
11-5. False. An installment refund annuity makes payments for the life of the annuitant. If the annuitant dies before receiving monthly payments equal to the purchase price of the annuity, the annuity also pays installment benefits to the annuitant's estate and/or beneficiary until the total equals the purchase price of the annuity.
11-6. True.
11-7. False. During liquidation, a variable annuity pays a fixed number of annuity units of variable value in each payment period.
11-8. True.
11-9. False. Annuity considerations are not calculated using the same mortality rates as those used in calculating life insurance premiums.
11-10. False. It is very important to evaluate the charity's long-term solvency. If a charity goes bankrupt or faces financial difficulty, the annuitant is merely a general creditor.
11-11. True.
11-12. False. When a client's life expectancy is reduced, the insurer is most likely to provide annuity payments for a shorter period of time. Consequently, the premium to provide a given level of benefits is lower than the premium charged to an annuitant with a normal life expectancy.

Chapter 12

Answers to Mini-Case

There are several factors that Amy and John should evaluate.

First, they should look at cost, even though they have very good incomes and can afford any of these plans. Cost includes their monthly premium as well as any anticipated out-of-pocket expenses. Although the premiums for two of the alternatives are higher than John and Amy currently pay, their out-of-pocket expenses are likely to be less under a managed care plan as long as network providers are used. They should, however, also evaluate the potential cost of visiting nonnetwork providers.

Second, they need to determine whether current physicians are in the networks of the alternative plans. This is particularly important to Amy. Note, however, that there is no reason why Amy and John have to select the same managed care option as long as they each have separate employee-only coverage.

Third, they need to determine their ability to see specialists. This will probably be very restricted under the HMO alternative and thus will eliminate it as a viable option. Although they will have much more flexibility under the other options, they should look at the extent to which specialists are available in their community as network providers. Going outside the preferred-provider network can often require significant out-of-pocket costs.

Fourth, Amy and John need to look at the benefits available and any plan limitations and exclusions. For example, couples sometimes have trouble concerning children. Treatment for infertility is expensive and covered to varying degrees under medical expense plans.

Fifth, they should look at the reputation of the managed care plans. Talking to friends and colleagues who have coverage under each plan may give them some insight into member satisfaction.

Last, but not least, they should consider which plan will provide the best coverage for Amy when she gets pregnant. Are the obstetrician and hospital she would like to use within the plan's network? Amy and John also should consider that one of them will need to add coverage for dependents when they have a child. As a result, they should evaluate the benefits available for children under each option.

Answers to Review Questions

12-1. Renewal rates for employer-provided medical expense plans are increasing at a high percentage, and large increases are predicted to continue. A great majority of Americans are satisfied with their own health care plan; dissatisfaction is higher among plans with the greatest degree of managed care. Surveys indicate that Americans are becoming less satisfied with and less confident about the health care system in general, despite satisfaction with their own coverage. Federal legislation continues to change the character of medical expense plans, as witnessed by new Medicare drug benefits and favorable tax treatment of HSAs.

12-2. a. She is covered. Hospital expense benefits are typically payable for a period of from 31 to 365 days.

    b. She is not covered. Cosmetic surgery is generally not covered unless it is needed to correct a condition resulting from an accidental injury.

    c. She is covered. Extended care facility benefits typically are provided to people who have been hospitalized for a period of at least 3 days. Confinement in the extended care facility must usually be for the same or a related condition for which the covered person was hospitalized. An extended care facility typically furnishes room and board and 24-hour-a-day skilled-nursing care under the supervision of a physician or a registered professional nurse.

    d. She is not covered. Home health care benefits are not designed for custodial or rest care. They are designed for those situations when the necessary part-time nursing care ordered by a physician following hospitalization can be provided in the patient's home.

    e. Major medical plans give broad coverage for necessary expenses incurred for medical services and supplies that a physician has ordered or prescribed, including prescription drugs.

12-3. The exclusion for preexisting conditions in many major medical plans differs from the other exclusions in major medical plans in that it applies only for a limited time, after which the condition will no longer be considered preexisting and will be covered in full, subject to any other contract limitations or exclusions.

A preexisting condition is typically defined as any illness or injury for which a covered person received medical care during a 3-month period prior to the person's effective date of coverage. Usually, the condition is no longer considered preexisting after the earlier of (1) a period of 3 consecutive months during which no medical care is received for the condition or (2) 12 months of coverage under the contract by the individual.

Some insurers provide limited coverage rather than exclude coverage for preexisting conditions.

12-4. a. The initial deductible is the amount that a covered person must pay for covered expenses before the plan will pay any insurance benefits.

    b. The family deductible is a provision that waives future deductibles for all family members once a specified aggregate dollar amount of medical expenses has been incurred or after a specified number of family members have satisfied their individual deductibles.

12-5. Peggy's out-of-pocket expenses are calculated as follows:

    $1,500 of covered medical expenses
    <u>− 250</u> deductible (out-of-pocket expense)
    $1,250
    <u>x   .20</u> (percentage Peggy is required to pay)
     $250 (out-of-pocket expense)

Therefore, Peggy will have to pay $500 of her medical expenses out-of-pocket, and the insurance company will pay the remaining $1,000.

12-6. A true managed care plan should have five basic characteristics: controlled access to specialists and hospitals, emphasis on case management, encouragement of preventive care and healthy lifestyles, sharing by medical care providers in the financial consequences of medical decisions, and careful selection and monitoring of medical providers.

12-7. HMOs act like insurance companies and the Blues in that they finance health care. However, unlike insurance companies and the Blues, they also deliver medical services. HMOs offer their subscribers a comprehensive package of health care services, generally including benefits for outpatient services as well as for hospitalization. Subscribers usually get these services at no cost except the periodically required premium and, in some cases, a copayment. HMOs emphasize preventive care and provide such services as routine physicals and immunizations. HMOs provide for the delivery of medical services, which, in some cases, are performed by salaried physicians and other personnel employed by the HMO. Although this approach is in contrast to the usual fee-for-service delivery system of medical care, some HMOs do contract with providers on a fee-for-service basis. Subscribers are required to obtain their care from providers of medical services who are affiliated with the HMO.

12-8. PPOs typically differ from HMOs in several respects. First, the preferred providers are generally paid on a fee-for-service basis as their services are used. However, fees are usually subject to a schedule that is the same for all similar providers within the PPO contracts, and providers may have an incentive to control utilization through bonus arrangements. Second, employees and their dependents are not required to use the practitioners or facilities that contract with the PPO; rather, a choice can be made each time medical care is needed, and benefits are also paid for care provided by nonnetwork providers. However, employees are offered incentives to use network providers; these incentives include lower or reduced deductibles and copayments, as well as increased benefits such as preventive health care. Third, most PPOs do not use a primary care physician as a gatekeeper, so employees do not need referrals to see specialists.

12-9. A POS plan is a hybrid arrangement that combines aspects of a traditional HMO and a PPO. With a POS plan, participants in the plan elect, at the time medical treatment is needed, whether to receive treatment within the plan's tightly managed network, usually an HMO, or outside the network. Expenses incurred outside the network are reimbursed in the same manner as expenses for nonnetwork services under PPO plans. One type of POS plan, the open-ended HMO, consists of traditional HMO coverage with an endorsement for nonnetwork coverage. The other type of POS plan, the gatekeeper PPO, requires the PPO participant to elect a primary care physician in the manner of an HMO participant. This physician acts as a gatekeeper to control utilization and refer members to specialists within the PPO network. However, at any time care is needed, a covered person can elect to go outside the network.

12-10. Benefit carve-outs can be used to contain costs via managed care techniques. A well-managed specialty provider may also provide a higher quality of care.

12-11. The first approach to consumer-directed plans is the defined-contribution medical expense plan. Under this approach, the employer generally pays a fixed-dollar amount toward the cost of coverage. This amount is often pegged to a fixed percentage of the cost of the least expensive plan available, usually an HMO. An employee who elects a more expensive plan must make a greater contribution to the cost of his or her coverage.

The second approach is the use of savings accounts. Typically, an employer will provide employees with a high-deductible medical expense plan. The employer then puts dollars into a savings account from which an employee can make tax-free withdrawals to pay medical expenses that are not covered because of the deductible.

12-12. Three types of benefit carve-outs can be described as follows:

a. *prescription drugs.* The typical prescription drug plan covers the cost of drugs (except those dispensed in a hospital or in an extended care facility) that are required by law to be dispensed by prescription. Drugs for which prescriptions are not required by law are usually not covered even if a physician orders them on a prescription form; a frequent exception is injectable insulin, which is generally covered. Most plans have a copayment, which may vary depending on whether the drug is generic or brand-name; other plans have a three-tier structure for generic drugs, formulary drugs, and brand-name nonformulary drugs.

b. *vision benefits.* Normally, a benefit schedule is used that specifies the type and amounts of benefits and the frequency with which they will be provided. If the plan is written by a provider of vision services, a discount for costs incurred with the provider that are not covered by the schedule of benefits may be available. Benefits are generally provided for eye examinations by either an optometrist or an ophthalmologist, and larger benefits are sometimes provided if the latter is used.

c. *behavioral health.* Behavioral health programs offer treatment for mental health, alcoholism, and drug addiction. These programs should use case management to design and coordinate treatment plans and to monitor the follow-up needs, have a referral mechanism, have a provider network, and provide patient access to care on a 24-hour basis.

12-13. Eligible dependents usually include an employee's spouse who is not legally separated from the employee and any unmarried dependent children (including stepchildren, adopted children, and children born out of wedlock) under the age of 19. However, coverage may be provided for children to age 23 or 26 if they are full-time students. In addition, coverage may also continue (and is required to be continued in some states) for children who are incapable of earning their own living because of a physical or mental infirmity. If an employee has dependent coverage, all newly acquired dependents (by birth, marriage, or adoption) are automatically covered.

12-14. HIPAA's provisions put limitations on preexisting-conditions exclusions and allow an employee to use evidence of prior insurance coverage to reduce or eliminate the length of any preexisting-conditions exclusion when the employee moves to another employer-provided medical expense plan.

12-15. The plan of the stepparent who is the spouse of the parent with custody takes priority over the father's plan.

12-16. Unless an employee elects otherwise, the employer's plan is primary and Medicare is secondary. Except in plans that require large employee contributions, it is doubtful that employees will elect Medicare to be primary because employers are prohibited from offering active employees or their spouses a Medicare carve-out, a Medicare supplement, or some other incentive not to enroll in the employer's plan.

Medicare is the secondary payer of benefits when persons who are eligible for Medicare benefits receive treatment for end-stage renal disease with dialysis or kidney transplants. Medicare provides these benefits to any insured workers (either active or retired) and to their spouses and dependent children, but the employer's plan is primary during the first 30 months of treatment only; after that time Medicare is primary and the employer's plan is secondary.

Medicare is also the secondary payer of benefits to disabled employees (or the disabled dependents of employees) under age 65 who are eligible for Medicare and who are covered under the medical expense plan of large employers (defined as plans with 100 or more employees). Medicare, however, does not pay anything until a person has been eligible for Social Security disability income benefits for 2 years. The rule applies only if an employer continues medical expense coverage for disabled persons; there is no requirement for such a continuation.

12-17. a. A strong likelihood. One characteristic of dental insurance seldom found in medical expense plans is the inclusion of benefits for routine diagnostic procedures, including X rays.

b. A strong likelihood. Treatment for diseases of the dental pulp within teeth, such as root canals, is covered under the category of endodontics.

c. Almost no likelihood. A common exclusion in dental plans is the replacement of lost, missing, or stolen dentures.

d. Almost no likelihood. A common exclusion in dental plans is services that are purely cosmetic, which includes teeth whitening.

e. Some likelihood. Some dental plans include benefits for orthodontics, which involves the prevention and correction of dental and oral anomalies through the use of corrective devices such as braces.

12-18. Additional medical and dental benefits for executives may include reimbursement for deductibles and coinsurance under the employer's plan; coverage for annual physicals and the extra cost of private hospital rooms; and extra coverage for mental or emotional treatment, hearing care, vision care, and dental work.

12-19. A portion of an employee's contribution for coverage may be tax deductible as a medical expense if that individual itemizes his or her income tax deductions. Under the Internal Revenue Code, individuals are allowed to deduct certain medical care expenses (including dental expenses) for which no reimbursement was received. This deduction is limited to expenses (including amounts paid for insurance) that exceed 7.5 percent of the person's adjusted gross income.

12-20. Premium conversion plans and FSAs are funded with salary reductions that lower an employee's taxable income for federal tax purposes. Therefore, federal taxes (and often state income taxes) are also reduced. In addition, the amount of the salary reduction is not subject to any Social Security and Medicare taxes that would otherwise be payable.

Answers to Self-Test Questions

12-1. True.

12-2. False. The Pregnancy Discrimination Act requires that benefit plans of employers with 15 or more employees treat pregnancy, childbirth, and related conditions the same as other illnesses.

12-3. True.

12-4. True.

12-5. True.

12-6. False. Basic extended care facility benefits do not cover rest or domiciliary care for the aged. These benefits are for people who require convalescence under supervised skilled nursing.

12-7. False. Hospice care does not attempt to cure medical conditions but tries to ease terminally ill patients' physical and psychological pain associated with dying.

12-8.   True.

12-9.   False. HMOs may operate in a geographic area no larger than a single metropolitan area, and most HMOs offer out-of-area coverage only in the case of medical emergencies.

12-10. False. By providing and encouraging preventive care, HMOs attempt to detect and treat medical conditions at an early stage, thereby avoiding expensive medical treatment in the future.

12-11. True.

12-12. False. For the most part, PPOs pay benefits for the same medical procedures, whether they are performed by a network or nonnetwork provider. However, a few procedures may be covered only if they are received from network providers.

12-13. False. The EPO does not provide coverage outside the preferred-provider network, except in those infrequent cases when the network does not contain an appropriate specialist.

12-14. True.

12-15. True.

12-16. True.

12-17. True.

12-18. False. Drugs for which prescriptions are not required by law are usually not covered, even if a physician orders them on a prescription form.

12-19. True.

12-20. False. Any unmarried dependent children who are full-time students are usually covered only up to age 23 or 26.

12-21. True.

12-22. False. Employers with 20 or more employees must make coverage available under their medical expense plans to active employees aged 65 or older. Unless the employee elects otherwise, the employer's plan is primary and Medicare is secondary.

12-23. True.

12-24. False. Premium contributions by an employer to group medical and dental coverage for an employee do not create any income tax liability for the employee.

12-25. False. FSAs result in lower taxable income. The reduction in taxes, therefore, increases the spendable income of employees.

Chapter 13

Answers to Mini-Case

a. Sam and Mary can look into continuing the employer coverage. If Sam's employer is subject to COBRA, they can elect COBRA continuation. This will probably be the most cost-effective alternative for people their ages. Whether or not COBRA coverage is an available option, the group plan may have a conversion privilege.

Sam and Mary can also explore coverage in the individual marketplace. Because of HIPAA, there are alternatives available to them for obtaining coverage without having to provide evidence of insurability. The exact nature of these alternatives, and the scope of coverage available, varies from state to state.

b. After Sam is eligible for Medicare, he needs some type of supplemental coverage. He will be able to purchase a Medicare supplement policy without evidence of insurability. As an alternative, he might want to explore enrolling in a Medicare Advantage plan.

Mary, however, still needs coverage until her eligibility for Medicare. If Sam and Mary had obtained an individual policy after Sam's retirement, this coverage can continue for Mary. If they had elected COBRA continuation, that coverage ceases after 18 months. Mary then needs to obtain coverage through conversion of the employer-provided coverage or purchase of a policy in the individual marketplace. Again, coverage will be available because of the HIPAA rules.

c. After Mary is eligible for Medicare, she, too, can obtain a Medicare supplement policy without evidence of insurability or enroll in a Medicare Advantage plan.

Answers to Review Questions

13-1. a. The term *group health plan* as used by COBRA is broad enough to include medical expense plans, dental plans, vision care plans, and prescription drug plans, regardless of whether benefits are self-funded or provided through other entities such as insurance companies or HMOs. Long-term care coverage is not subject to COBRA rules.

b. Under COBRA, each of the following is a *qualifying event* if it results in the loss of coverage by a qualified beneficiary:

- the death of the covered employee
- the termination of the employee for any reason except gross misconduct
- a reduction of the employee's hours so that the employee or dependent is ineligible for coverage
- the divorce or legal separation of the covered employee and his or her spouse
- for spouses and children, the employee's eligibility for Medicare
- a child's ceasing to be an eligible dependent under the plan

   c. A *qualified beneficiary* is defined as any employee, or the spouse or dependent child of the employee, who on the day before a qualifying event was covered under the employee's group health plan. In addition, the definition includes any child who is born to or placed for adoption with the employee during the period of COBRA coverage.

13-2. The Health Insurance Portability and Accountability Act (HIPAA) encourages states to adopt mechanisms for helping individuals find alternative coverage. If the state does not have its own plan, the state alternative must provide a choice of health insurance coverage to all eligible individuals, impose no preexisting-conditions restrictions, and include at least one form of coverage that is either comparable to comprehensive health coverage offered in the individual marketplace or comparable to (or a standard option of) coverage available under the group or individual laws of the state.

     If a state fails to adopt an alternative to federal regulation, then insurance companies, HMOs, and other health plan providers in the individual marketplace must make coverage available on a guaranteed-issue basis to individuals with 18 or more months of creditable coverage and whose most recent coverage was under a group health plan, although coverage does not have to be provided to an individual who has other health insurance or is eligible for COBRA coverage, Medicare, or Medicaid. No preexisting-conditions exclusions can be imposed.

13-3. The basic benefits that must be included in all Medicare supplement policies consist of the following:

- *hospitalization.* This is the coinsurance or cost sharing of Part A benefits for the 61st through the 90th day of hospitalization and the 60-day lifetime reserve. In addition, coverage is extended for 365 additional days after Medicare benefits end.
- *medical expenses.* This is the Part B insurance for Medicare-approved charges for physicians' and medical services.
- *blood.* This is the payment for the first three pints of blood each year.

13-4. Persons aged 65 or older may buy any available Medicare supplement policy, regardless of health status, at any time during the 6-month period after initial enrollment for Medicare Part B benefits. If a person initially elects a managed care option in lieu of regular Medicare benefits, the person will be eligible to purchase a Medicare supplement policy, without evidence of insurability, if he or she leaves the managed care option during the first 12 months of coverage and returns to regular Medicare benefits. Similarly, a person who drops Medicare supplement coverage and elects a managed care option can regain Medicare supplement coverage if he or she decides to drop the managed care option during the first 12 months of coverage. Also, a person can obtain a medigap policy on a guaranteed-issue basis because an employer-provided plan that supplements Medicare terminates, because a Medicare Advantage plan no longer provides coverage, or because the person loses eligibility by moving out of the plan's service area.

13-5. a. *Temporary medical insurance* provides coverage for periods between 30 days and one year to under-age-65 individuals and their dependents who are between permanent medical plans. The plans are similar to individual major medical policies; applicants usually have a choice of deductibles and coinsurance percentages.

   b. *International travel medical insurance* provides coverage ranging from a minimum of 15 days to a maximum of one year, with optional renewal of some policies for up to 5 years. Benefits cover the expenses of inpatient and outpatient hospitalizations, as well as medical and related services. Deductibles are selected, and coinsurance levels are frequently available at 80 percent up to a specific dollar amount; 100 percent is payable thereafter to the policy maximum. Coverage typically ceases when a person returns to his or her home country.

   c. *Hospital-surgical policies* typically provide coverage for a limited number of days of hospitalization, and the daily benefit can be less than the cost of semiprivate accommodations. Surgical benefits are usually paid on a fee-schedule basis. Depending on the policy, benefits may be available for expenses associated with physician's visits, maternity, and extended care facilities. These policies are typically inadequate for prolonged sicknesses, serious accidents, or the significant medical expenses that can arise outside a hospital setting that normally a major medical policy would cover.

   d. *Hospital indemnity insurance* provides the insured with a fixed daily cash benefit during a covered hospitalization. A spouse or dependent child is usually eligible for coverage, although benefits may be reduced. The policy provides daily benefits in the event of hospital confinement in a specified dollar amount for a defined period, and additional benefits are available as a standard feature or as a rider.

 e. *Specified disease insurance* provides benefits to insured individuals and covered family members upon the diagnosis of or medical events related to the treatment of a disease named in the policy. Benefits vary, and provisions may utilize a combination of three payment structures: per-day or per-service, expense-incurred, or a lump-sum payment. Benefits are contingent on a diagnosis of the specified disease, but payments will cover the first day of care or confinement even though the diagnosis is made at some later date.

 f. *Critical illness insurance* provides a substantial one-time lump-sum cash benefit for listed critical illnesses. Some of these conditions result from injury, as well as disease, and include specified major surgeries. The policyowner selects a maximum benefit amount, which can range from $10,000 to several hundred thousand dollars. The maximum benefit is payable only once—upon the first diagnosis of a condition or specified surgical treatment that is covered.

13-6. Two types of individuals are eligible:

- an employee (or spouse) of a small employer that maintains an individual or family high-deductible health plan that covers the individual. These persons will establish their Archer MSAs under an employer-sponsored plan.
- a self-employed person (or spouse) who maintains an individual or family high-deductible health plan that covers himself or herself. These persons will need to seek out a custodian or trustee for their Archer MSAs.

13-7. The following rules apply to Archer MSAs:

 a. Either the account holder or the account holder's employer, but not both, may contribute to an Archer MSA. Contributions by an employer are tax deductible to the employer and are not included in an employee's gross income or subject to Social Security and other employment taxes. Employee contributions are deductible in computing adjusted gross income. The amount of the annual deductible contribution to an employee's account is limited to 65 percent of the deductible for the health coverage if the MSA is for an individual, to 75 percent if the MSA covers a family. Employee contributions must generally be made by April 15 of the year following the year for which the contributions are made.

 b. An individual can take any part or all of the account balance from an MSA at any time. Subject to some exceptions, distributions of both contributions and earnings are excludible from an account holder's gross income if used to pay medical expenses of the account holder and the account holder's family, as long as these expenses are not paid by other sources of insurance. For the most part, the eligible medical expenses are the same ones that would be deductible, ignoring the 7.5 percent of adjusted gross income limitation, if the account holder itemized his or her tax deductions. Tax-free withdrawals are also permitted for the purchase of long-term care insurance, COBRA continuation coverage, or health insurance coverage while an individual receives unemployment compensation. Distributions for reasons other than paying eligible medical expenses are included in an account holder's gross income and are subject to a 15 percent penalty tax unless certain circumstances exist.

13-8. HSAs can be established by employees, the self-employed, and anyone else who meets the following rules for qualification:

- The individual must be covered by a high-deductible health plan. That plan may be insured or self-insured if offered by an employer, as long as it meets the criteria for a qualifying high-deductible plan.
- The individual is not eligible to be claimed as a dependent on another person's federal income tax return.
- With certain exceptions, the individual must not be covered by other health insurance. These exceptions are the same as those for Archer MSAs and include policies that provide coverage for specified disease or illness, a fixed payment for a period of hospitalization, accidents, disability, dental care, vision care, or long-term care. An employer can establish HSAs for its employees, or an individual may establish his or her own HSA.

13-9. In many ways, Archer MSAs and HSAs are similar. In other ways they differ. These differences include the following:

- HSAs can be established by a wider variety of individuals (as explained in previous answers).
- The deductible and out-of-pocket limits for high-deductible health plans (HDHPs) are different from those for Archer MSAs.
- HDHPs used with HSAs can waive the deductible for certain preventive care services. This is not allowed for HDHPs used with Archer MSAs.
- Contributions to an HSA can be shared by an employee and employer. Contributions to an Archer MSA cannot be shared.

- Contributions to an HSA can be made under a cafeteria plan. This is not permitted with Archer MSAs.
- HSAs can be established after retirement, whereas Archer MSAs cannot.

13-10. Noncancelable policies are rare because of the uncertain nature and cost of future medical claims.

Answers to Self-Test Questions

13-1.   False. The term group health plan as used for COBRA purposes is broad enough to include dental plans and vision care plans, but not long-term care plans. Long-term care coverage is not subject to the COBRA rules.

13-2.   True.

13-3.   False. COBRA coverage is not automatic but must be elected.

13-4.   True.

13-5.   True.

13-6.   True.

13-7.   True.

13-8.   False. ERISA exempts noninsured plans from state insurance mandates. This exemption includes a self-funded, employer-provided medical expense plan.

13-9.   False. Because of the emphasis on first-dollar coverage and preventive medicine, HMO coverage for individuals is typically more expensive than an individual major medical policy.

13-10. False. Estimates indicate that about two-thirds of Medicare recipients have some type of coverage to supplement Medicare.

13-11. True.

13-12. False. Insurance companies are allowed to exclude benefits for no more than 6 months because of preexisting conditions. In fact, some policies immediately provide benefits for preexisting conditions or have an exclusion period shorter than 6 months.

13-13. False. Most specified disease insurance policies cover cancer as well as other diseases.

13-14. True.

13-15. True.

13-16. False. Either the account holder or the account holder's employer, but not both, may make a contribution to an Archer MSA.

13-17. False. A high-deductible health plan used with an HSA is permitted to waive any deductible requirements for preventive care.

13-18. True.

13-19. False. Individuals who itemize deductions for income tax purposes are allowed to deduct most unreimbursed medical expenses to the extent that the total of such expenses exceeds the threshold of 7.5 percent of adjusted gross income.

Chapter 14

Answers to Review Questions

14-1.   At all working ages, the probability of being disabled for at least 90 consecutive days is much greater than the chance of dying. About half of all employees will have a disability that lasts at least 90 days during their working years, and one out of every 10 persons can expect to be permanently disabled prior to age 65. In terms of its financial effect on the family, long-term disability is more severe than death. In both cases, income ceases. In the case of long-term disability, however, family expenses—instead of decreasing because the family has one fewer member—may actually increase due to the cost of providing care for the disabled person.

14-2.   The sources of coverage that may protect your client against financial trouble in case of disability include the Social Security program, workers' compensation, state temporary disability laws, unemployment compensation, employer-provided short-term disability plans, employer-provided long-term disability plans, individual disability income insurance, and sick-leave plans.

14-3.   Sick-leave plans (often called salary continuation plans) are usually uninsured and generally fully replace lost income for a limited period of time, starting on the first day of disability. Almost all sick-leave plans are limited to permanent full-time employees. Most sick-leave plans are designed to provide benefits equal to 100 percent of an employee's regular pay. Most plans, however, provide a reduced level of benefits after an initial period of full pay.

The most traditional approach used in determining the duration of benefits credits eligible employees with a certain amount of sick leave each year such as 10 days.

14-4.   In addition to being in a covered classification, an employee must usually work full-time and be actively at work before coverage under a group disability plan commences. Any requirements concerning probationary periods, insurability, and premium contributions must also be satisfied. Long-term disability plans often limit benefits to salaried employees; some long-term plans also exclude employees below a certain salary level. Long-term plans sometimes require that the employee be on the job for an extended probationary period (such as 30 days) without illness or injury before coverage becomes effective.

14-5.   Group short-term disability plans typically define disability as the total inability of the employee to perform each and every duty of his or her regular occupation (an "own occupation" definition). In contrast, group long-term disability plans contain a dual definition under which benefits will be paid for 24 (or 36) months "as long as an employee is unable to perform his or her regular occupation." After that time, benefits will be paid only if the employee is unable to engage in any occupation for which he or she is qualified by reason of training, education, or experience. The purpose of this dual definition is to require and encourage a disabled employee who becomes able after a period of time to adjust his or her lifestyle and earn a livelihood in another occupation. Under the short-term disability plan, coverage for nonoccupational disabilities and having different definitions of disabilities for different classes of employees are unlikely; those characteristics are more likely under the long-term disability plan.

14-6.   Common exclusions under both short-term and long-term disability income contracts specify that no benefits will be paid for any period during which the employee is not under the care of a physician, for any disability caused by an intentionally self-inflicted injury, and for any disability that commenced while the employee was not covered under the contract. Additionally, employers with fewer than 15 employees may exclude disabilities arising from pregnancy unless they are subject to state laws to the contrary.

Long-term disability contracts commonly deny benefits for disabilities resulting from

- war, whether declared or undeclared
- participation in an assault or felony (some insurers have expanded this to include the commission of any crime)
- mental disease, alcoholism, or drug addiction
- preexisting conditions

14-7.   Benefit schedules classify employees and, for each class of employee, specify the amount of disability income to be provided, indicate the length of time that benefits are payable, and coordinate benefits with other available types of disability income. Benefits may be expressed as either flat-dollar amounts, varying dollar amounts by classification, or a percentage of earnings. Short-term disability income contracts commonly contain a waiting, or elimination, period. The typical short-term contract has no waiting period for disabilities resulting from accidents, but a one- to 7-day waiting period for disabilities resulting from sickness. Long-term disability income plans have waiting periods of 3 to 6 months. The waiting periods for sicknesses and accidents are the same under the long-term contract. Long-term disability income benefits may be paid for as short a period as 2 years or as long as the lifetime of the disabled employee.

14-8.   To minimize the possibility of an employee's receiving total benefits higher than his or her predisability earnings, disability income plans commonly stipulate that benefits be integrated with other sources of disability income. Benefits under short-term plans are generally integrated with (1) workers' compensation benefits if the plan covers occupational disabilities, (2) temporary disability laws if they are applicable, and (3) Social Security benefits if the maximum benefit period is longer than 5 months.

Long-term disability income benefits are usually integrated with benefits provided under the following:

- Social Security
- workers' compensation laws
- temporary disability laws
- other insurance plans for which the employer makes a contribution or payroll deduction
- pension plans for which the employer has made a contribution or payroll deduction to the extent that the employee elects to receive retirement benefits because of disability
- sick-leave plans
- earnings from employment, either with the employer or from other sources

To prevent the integration with other benefits from totally eliminating a long-term disability benefit, many plans provide (and some states require) that a minimum benefit be paid. Most plans also contain a provision freezing the amount of any Social Security reduction at the initial level that was established when the claim began.

14-9.   The following additional benefits are sometimes included in group long-term disability income contracts:
   a.   A disability income plan may have a COLA to prevent inflation from eroding the purchasing power of disability income benefits being received. Under the typical COLA formula, benefits increase annually along with changes in the consumer price index.
   b.   A firm may treat disabled employees as if they were still working and accruing pension benefits. Such a provision requires that contributions on behalf of disabled employees be made to the pension plan, usually from the employer's current revenues. However, some disability income contracts stipulate that the contributions necessary to fund a disabled employee's accruing pension benefits will be paid from the disability income contract.
   c.   Some long-term contracts continue payments to survivors after the death of a disabled employee. The disability income payments are continued, possibly at a reduced amount, for periods ranging up to 24 months to eligible survivors, who commonly are the spouse and unmarried children under age 21.

14-10.   The tax consequences are as follows:
   a.   The benefits are received by Kevin free of income taxation.
   b.   The benefits are included in Patty's income for tax purposes.
   c.   Benefits attributable to contributions by Julie are received free of income taxation. Benefits attributable to employer contributions are includible in Julie's income for tax purposes.

14-11.   Residual-disability benefits replace lost earnings due to less-than-total disability. The focus of the benefit is on the income reduction rather than on the physical dimensions of the disability. Policies providing residual-disability benefits usually specify a fraction (representing the proportion of lost income) that is multiplied by the stated monthly benefit for total disability to derive the residual benefit payable. The numerator of that fraction is usually income prior to disability minus earned income during disability; the denominator of the fraction is income prior to disability. The definitions of each form of income differ from one insurance company to another, and persons subject to income fluctuation should insist on a definition allowing the greater of two different base periods so that they are not unduly penalized as a result of a single base period applied during a slump in income. Most of the definitions either explicitly or implicitly include not only income earned from work activities but also pension or profit-sharing contributions made on behalf of the individual. Additionally, a minimum benefit clause specifies that the minimum benefit payable for residual-disability periods is at least 50 percent of the benefit payable for total disability.

14-12.   In advising clients, planners might explain the following aspects in individual disability income policies:
   a.   Guaranteed renewable contracts, which are high-quality contracts, give the policyowner the right to continue the coverage in force by paying the premium due. The premium may be increased on a class basis for all guaranteed-renewable policies in the classification, but it cannot be increased on an individual basis. The highest quality contracts, noncancelable disability contracts, guarantee that the individual can keep the policy in force by paying the premium and that the premium will not increase. Low-quality cancelable disability insurance contracts offer very questionable protection for the insured because the insurance company can refuse renewal or can increase the premium.
   b.   Disability income policies generally have a waiting period before benefit payments begin. When selecting the waiting period for a disability income policy, the insured should consider his or her ability to pay living costs and other expenses during the waiting period, and whether the insured has other sources of funds available during short-term disabilities. Residual-disability benefits specify a qualification period, which indicates the number of days of total disability that must be sustained before residual-disability benefits are payable.
   c.   Most disability policies define a specified period of recovery (usually measured by return to work) that automatically separates one disability from another. For disability policies with a limited benefit period, it can be advantageous to have each relapse classified as a new disability, which then starts with a full benefit period.
   d.   Disability income policies differ according to the duration of benefits that they provide once the individual becomes disabled. Disability contracts often provide choices such as 2 years, 3 years, 5 years, to age 65, or even for the insured's lifetime. Policies with short benefit durations do not provide comprehensive protection against disability, but their main appeal is the premium savings associated with the relatively short maximum benefit period. Some policies differentiate between disabilities caused by injury and disabilities caused by illness. These policies may provide lifetime benefits if the disability results from injury but limit benefits to age 65 if the disability stems from illness.

Even policies purporting to provide lifetime benefits for disability include limitations on disabilities occurring after specified ages such as 50, 55, or 60. Disabilities with their first onset after the specified age are often limited to benefit periods of 2 or 5 years or may terminate at a specified age such as 65, 68, or 70.

Insurance companies are more restrictive in writing longer benefit duration policies than they are in writing policies of short benefit duration. Fewer occupations qualify for policies with long benefit durations than for policies of short benefit durations. Policies with long benefit durations are rarely available to any occupation that involves physical labor or direct involvement in dangerous processes.

e. Disability income policies specify the amount of monthly benefits payable during periods of total disability after the waiting period has been satisfied. At the time of policy issuance, the stated monthly benefit amount should be in line with the insured's income and provide fairly complete protection. However, over time, the stated benefit amount is likely to become inadequate as the insured's income increases because of inflation and job promotions. Disability income policies are available with provisions to counteract such erosion in benefit levels.

f. Premiums for disability income policies are based on the policyowner's age at the time of policy issuance and remain level for the duration of the coverage. Consequently, an individual can lock in lower premiums by buying a policy at a younger age and keeping it in force. Premiums must be paid on a timely basis to keep the coverage in force, but the policies do contain a 31-day grace period for late premium payments.

14-13. Increased predisability benefits consist of provisions aimed at increasing the benefit level while the coverage is in force, but the insured is not disabled. There are basically three approaches to keeping disability income benefits in step with increased income for insured individuals who are not disabled:

- Purchase new policies to supplement the in-force policies incrementally as income increases. This is the oldest and least attractive method. The drawback is that evidence of insurability is required every time incremental amounts of coverage are obtained. If the individual's health deteriorates, additional coverage may not be available at any price.

- Adjust predisability benefit levels through a rider that guarantees the right to purchase additional coverage at specified future intervals up to some stipulated maximum age such as 45, 50, or 55. This approach is similar to the first one in that additional coverage must be purchased every time an adjustment is needed, but the additional amounts can be acquired at the specified intervals regardless of the health of the insured. However, these incremental purchases are subject to underwriting requirements regarding the individual's current income.

- Use riders that automatically increase the base benefit amount on a formula basis such as a stated flat-percentage amount at each policy anniversary. This is the most attractive way to adjust benefits upward for inflation while the insured is not disabled. But even this approach requires purchasing additional coverage, and the premium will increase appropriately. As with the second approach, the additional increment of coverage is purchased at premium rates based on the insured's attained age at the time it is added to the policy. The real advantage to this approach is that the changes are automatic unless they are refused by the policyowner.

14-14. Some insurance companies offer, on an optional basis, a policy provision that returns some portion of premiums at specified intervals such as 5 or 10 years. For example, one company has an option that returns 60 percent of premiums paid at the end of each 5-year interval if no claims have been made during that period. This particular option can increase premiums by more than 40 percent over the base premium level. Other companies offer variations in the percentage of premium to be returned, such as 70 percent or 80 percent of the premiums paid, and in the duration of the interval over which the coverage must be without claims in order to collect the return of premium.

14-15. Many insurance companies offer an optional provision that requires a separate extra premium to cover additional benefits payable when the individual is disabled under the base policy but does not qualify for Social Security disability benefits. The supplemental benefit is paid over and above the base disability benefit of the underlying policy. The maximum benefit available in the base policy can be supplemented under this rider so that the total benefits collected from the insurance company are essentially the same as would have been collected if the individual qualified for Social Security disability benefits.

14-16. To minimize the motivation for fraudulent claims as well as padding of legitimate claims by malingering, insurance companies limit the amount of coverage they will issue to any individual in relation to that individual's income. Generally speaking, disability income coverage is not available for benefit amounts that exceed 60 or 66 2/3 percent of the individual's gross earned income. In fact, as the level of income increases, the percentage of income replacement that insurance companies will issue decreases. High-income professionals are often limited to less than 50 percent of their income level in setting the maximum benefit level for their disability policies. Some experts advise that, for individuals providing full disclosure to the insurance company, the appropriate amount of disability income protection to purchase is the maximum amount available from an insurance company that provides quality coverage.

14-17.   A business can use individual disability income policies in the following ways:

a.   Overhead expense policies cover many of the ongoing costs of operating a business while the business owner is totally disabled. These policies tend to be limited to benefit durations of one or 2 years and have relatively short waiting periods. The intent is to keep the necessary staff and premises available for the resumption of business if the business owner recovers from the disability. The application must be accompanied by supporting financial statements to verify the stability of the business and to establish the appropriate level of insurable expenses. Actual expenses are reimbursed at the time of disability up to a maximum monthly indemnity selected at the time of policy issue.

b.   Benefits from key employee disability policies are payable to the business entity when the insured key employee is disabled. Proceeds from key person disability policies can be used to replace lost revenue directly attributable to the key person's disability. Proceeds can also be used to fund the search for individuals to replace the insured person, the extra cost of hiring specialized individuals to replace the multiple talents of the insured, and the training costs that may be incurred to prepare replacements to carry out the duties the insured performed. The costs of training, hiring, and compensating are usually rather easy to ascertain, whereas estimating lost revenue is a very difficult and complex task. These policies are not designed to provide continuance of salary for the key employee.

c.   Individual disability income policies can be purchased by the business entity to fund formal plans to continue the salary for the disabled owner or key employees. Formal plans can be set up in two different ways. The corporation can own the policy and be the beneficiary under the policy, or the corporation can pay the premiums on a policy owned by the employee to whom benefits will be paid. In some informal plans to continue salary, the corporation pays a large enough bonus to the employee for the employee to buy an individual disability income policy.

d.   Buy-sell agreements triggered by the disability of an owner can be funded with disability insurance specifically designed for this purpose. These policies can fund either an installment purchase or a lump-sum buyout. The disability definition in the policy should be the same definition as that specified in the buy-sell agreement. The waiting period for a buy-sell policy is typically one year or longer to avoid triggering the buyout for disabilities that last less than one year. Most buy-sell policies pay the benefit in one lump sum.

Answers to Self-Test Questions

14-1.   True.

14-2.   False. Although most employed persons are potentially eligible for disability benefits under the Social Security program, its definition of disability is more restrictive than that in most individual or group contracts.

14-3.   True.

14-4.   False. Insurance companies that offer disability income policies are very concerned about overinsurance and the accompanying moral hazard and, consequently, limit the amount of benefits relative to the individual's income. As a result, many individuals with coverage through other sources are ineligible for additional disability income protection.

14-5.   False. Most employers do not provide long-term disability income insurance.

14-6.   True.

14-7.   False. Almost all sick-leave plans are limited to permanent full-time employees.

14-8.   True.

14-9.   True.

14-10.   False. The majority of short-term disability contracts limit coverage to nonoccupational disabilities because employees have workers' compensation benefits for occupational disabilities.

14-11.   True.

14-12.   False. Most group disability income contracts cover disabilities that result from pregnancy because it is illegal under federal law for an employer with 15 or more employees to exclude these disabilities. Employers with ewer than 15 employees may still exclude pregnancy disabilities unless the employers are subject to state laws to the contrary.

14-13.   True.

14-14.   False. Group short-term disability income contracts typically have no waiting period for disabilities that result from accidents, but a waiting period of one to 7 days for disabilities that result from sickness.

14-15.   False. Most insurers include a rehabilitation provision in their long-term disability income contracts as an incentive to encourage disabled employees to return to active employment as soon as possible. This provision permits employees to enter a trial work period. If the trial work period indicates that the employees are unable to work, the full benefits will be reinstated without the employees having to satisfy a new waiting period.

14-16. False. Some disability income plans have COLAs to prevent inflation from eroding the purchasing power of disability income benefits received. Under the typical COLA formula, benefits increase annually along with changes in the consumer price index.

14-17. False. Any-occupation policies are too restrictive and generally should not be purchased. Most individual policies use a dual definition of disability under which benefits are first paid accordingly to an own-occupation definition of disability, and then under a definition that looks to the individual's training, education, or experience.

14-18. True.

14-19. True.

14-20. True.

14-21. True.

14-22. False. The most attractive way to adjust benefits upward for inflation while the insured is not disabled is to use riders that automatically increase the base benefit amount on a formula basis.

14-23. True.

14-24. False. The laws of all states require that disability income policies contain incontestability provisions.

14-25. False. Benefits under the Social Security rider terminate when the insured elects early retirement benefits under Social Security.

14-26. True.

14-27. True.

14-28. False. Benefits from key employee disability policies are payable to the business entity when the insured key employee is disabled. These policies are not designed to provide continuance of salary for the key employee.

14-29. True.

Chapter 15

Answers to Mini-Case

Evaluating the need for long-term care insurance involves analyzing the cost of long-term care and the resources already available to meet these costs. In Clara's case, significant resources already exist.

If and when Clara needs nursing home care, the cost of the care will be $60,000 per year in current dollars. However, at that time she should be able to pay a significant portion of this amount from her current income. Her personal expenses will diminish significantly. Of her $47,000 in income, it would not be unreasonable to assume that at least $25,000 to $30,000 or more could be devoted to the cost of care in the nursing home. Presumably, her home would be sold and she would then have total assets of between $500,000 and $600,000 that could be invested. With a modest investment return, she should have adequate income to pay the remaining nursing home cost while retaining all or most of the principal amount for a legacy to her grandchildren.

The situation is somewhat different if Clara needs home care. In that situation, the costs of maintaining her home still exist. However, many expenses, such as maintaining a car and taking cruises with friends, will probably cease. Let's assume that she will be able to devote about $20,000 per year to her care. The cost of home care will vary, depending on the degree of care needed. Costs in the range of $25,000 to $50,000 per year and maybe higher are not unrealistic. Therefore, Clara needs to determine the source of the additional funds needed. One possibility is to exhaust her savings and investments and tap her home equity if necessary. However, this alternative will lower her net worth and the amount she can bequeath to her grandchildren. Another alternative is to purchase a long-term care insurance policy that provides home care only. A policy with a waiting period of 60 days that provides a $100 per day ($36,500 per year) lifetime benefit with a 5 percent compound annual inflation increase will have an annual premium of about $4,000 if purchased at her current age of 75. With a daily benefit of $75 ($27,375 per year), the premium will be about $3,000. Although Clara may need to limit her other expenses somewhat, she would seem to be able to pay this premium from her current income.

Two final comments need to be made. First, the previous discussion is based on current dollars, and future inflation needs to be considered. Although some of Clara's income will increase with inflation and her primary asset (her home) will probably also increase in value over time, nursing home costs have continued to increase much faster than the general inflation rate. Therefore, if Clara enters a nursing home many years from now, she may have to decrease her net worth to pay the full cost of care. On one hand, she might want to consider a long-term care insurance policy that has a small facility benefit. On the other hand, the length of nursing home stays that begin at old ages very seldom last longer than one year, and the depletion of her net worth is unlikely to be large.

The situation is different for home care. This type of care (which usually uses less skilled caregivers than nursing homes) tends to increase at about the general level of inflation. So although costs will rise, she should have corresponding increases in income and benefits from a home care only policy.

Second, at some point, Clara may be unable to make decisions about her care. Therefore, she needs to make her family aware of her wishes.

Answers to Review Questions

15-1.   Some of the reasons there is a need for long-term care insurance include the following:
   - *demographics.* The population aged 65 and over is the fastest-growing age group.
   - *increasing costs.* Annual nursing home costs are over $60,000 on the average and may be much higher in some locations.
   - *inability of families to provide care.* Geographic dispersion, women in the workforce, and fewer children are just some of the reasons why it is increasingly difficult for families to provide full care.
   - *inadequacies of Medicare and medical expense insurance.* Custodial care is not covered well, if at all, under Medicare and Medicaid expense insurance.

15-2.   There are several other sources for providing long-term care other than insurance:
   - *personal savings.* Unless a person has substantial resources, this approach may force an individual and his or her dependents into poverty. It may also mean that the person will not meet the financial objective of leaving assets to heirs.
   - *relatives and friends.* These individuals may provide caregiving themselves or furnish financial support to purchase care.
   - *welfare.* The Medicaid program in most states will provide benefits, which usually include nursing home care, to the "medically needy." However, a person is not eligible unless he or she is either poor or has a low income and has exhausted most other assets (including those of a spouse).
   - *state programs.* These programs have attempted to encourage better coverage for long-term care. One aspect of these experiments has been to waive or modify certain Medicaid requirements if a person carries a state-approved long-term care policy. These programs increase the assets that a person can retain and still collect Medicaid benefits; the increase in the allowable asset threshold is related to the amount of long-term care coverage carried and exhausted.
   - *continuing care retirement communities.* These facilities require an "entrance fee" that enables residents to occupy a dwelling unit but usually does not give them actual ownership rights. Residents pay a monthly fee that includes meals, some housecleaning services, and varying degrees of health care. If a person needs long-term care, he or she must give up the independent living unit and move to the nursing home portion of the facility, but the monthly fee normally remains the same. The disadvantages of this option are that the cost of a continuing care retirement community is beyond the reach of many persons, and a resident must be in reasonably good health and able to live independently at the time he or she enters the facility.
   - *long-term care benefits in cash value life insurance policies.* Some companies provide this benefit, which enables an insured to use a portion of death benefits while he or she is still living. However, any benefits received reduce the future death benefit. The benefit acceleration may result in the reduction of the death benefit to a level inadequate for accomplishing the purpose of life insurance—the protection of family members after a wage earner's death. In addition, the availability of an accelerated benefit may give the insured a false sense of security that long-term care needs are being met when, in fact, the potential benefit may be inadequate to cover extended nursing home stays.

15-3.   Highlights of the criteria for policy provisions include the following:
   - Many words or terms cannot be used in a policy unless they are specifically defined in accordance with the legislation—for example, adult day care, home health care services, personal care, and skilled-nursing care.
   - Renewal provisions must be either guaranteed renewable or noncancelable.
   - Limitations and exclusions are prohibited except in the cases of preexisting conditions; mental or nervous disorders (but Alzheimer's disease cannot be excluded); alcoholism and drug addiction; illness, treatment, or medical condition arising out of war, participation in a felony, service in the armed forces, suicide, and aviation if a person is a non-fare-paying passenger; and treatment in a government facility and services available under Medicare and other social insurance programs.
   - No policy can provide coverage for skilled-nursing care only or provide significantly more coverage for skilled care in a facility than for lower levels of care.

- The definition of preexisting condition can be no more restrictive than to exclude a condition for which treatment was recommended or received within 6 months prior to the effective date of coverage. In addition, coverage can be excluded for a confinement for this condition only if it begins within 6 months of the effective date of coverage.
- Eligibility for benefits cannot be based on a prior hospital requirement or higher level of care.
- Insurance companies must offer the applicant the right to purchase coverage that allows for an increase in the amount of benefits based on reasonable anticipated increases in the cost of services covered by the policy. The applicant must specifically reject this inflation protection if he or she does not want it.
- Insurance companies must offer the applicant the right to purchase a nonforfeiture benefit. If the applicant declines the nonforfeiture benefit, the insurer must provide a contingent benefit upon lapse that is available for a specified period of time following a substantial increase in premiums.
- A policy must contain a provision that makes a policy incontestable after 2 years on the grounds of misrepresentation. The policy can be contested on the basis that the applicant knowingly and intentionally misrepresented relevant facts pertaining to the insured's health.

15-4. The act provides favorable tax treatment to tax-qualified long-term care insurance contracts, which are defined as insurance contracts that meet all the following requirements:
- The only insurance protection provided under the contract is for qualified long-term care services.
- The contract cannot pay for expenses that are reimbursable under Medicare.
- The contract must be guaranteed renewable.
- The contract does not provide for a cash surrender value or other money that can be borrowed or paid, assigned, or pledged as collateral for a loan.
- All refunds of premiums and policyowner dividends must be applied as future reductions in premiums or to increase future benefits.
- The policy must comply with various consumer protection provisions. For the most part, these are the same provisions in the NAIC model act and already adopted by most states.

15-5. With some exceptions, expenses for long-term care services, including insurance premiums, are treated like other medical expenses. Self-employed persons may deduct the premiums paid. Persons who itemize deductions can include long-term care insurance premiums, up to an annual limit, for purposes of deducting medical expenses in excess of 7.5 percent of adjusted gross income. Limits are based on a covered individual's age and subject to cost-of-living adjustments. Employer contributions for group contracts are deductible to the employer and do not result in taxable income to an employee. Benefits received under a qualified long-term care insurance contract written on a reimbursement basis are received tax free by an employee. Under contracts written on a per diem basis, proceeds are excludible from income up to $240 per day in 2005. (This figure is indexed annually.) Amounts in excess of $240 are also excludible to the extent that they represent actual costs for long-term care services.

15-6. Most companies have an upper age in the range of 84 to 89, beyond which coverage is not issued. Some companies have no minimum age, while others have a minimum age such as age 40.

15-7. A long-term care insurance policy can cover one, several, or more types of care. The types of care include nursing home care, assisted-living facility care, hospice care, care in an Alzheimer's facility, home health care, care coordination, and alternative plans of care.

15-8. The amount of benefits is usually limited to a specified amount per day. The same level of benefits is usually provided for all levels of institutional care. The applicant can select home health care limits from 50 to 150 percent of the benefit amount payable for institutional stays. The policyowner is usually given a choice regarding the maximum duration of benefits, which can range from one year to the insured's lifetime.

15-9. Under a tax-qualified plan, the insured must be chronically ill, which means that one of the following criteria must be met:
- The insured is unable, without substantial assistance from others, to perform two of the six ADLs acceptable under HIPAA for at least 90 days due to loss of functional capacity.
- Substantial services are required to protect the individual from threats to health and safety due to severe cognitive impairment.

    Many non-tax-qualified plans use the same criteria that are in tax-qualified contracts, except no time period applies to the inability to perform ADLs. Some non-tax-qualified plans require the inability to perform only one ADL or extend the definition of ADLs beyond the six allowed by HIPAA. Finally, some non-tax-qualified plans make benefits available when a physician certifies medical necessity, regardless of whether other criteria are satisfied.

15-10. Factors that affect the premium include age, types of benefits, duration of benefits, inflation protection, waiver-of-premium, spousal coverage, and nonsmoker discounts.

15-11. Differences between individually purchased long-term care insurance and group long-term care insurance include the following:
- Eligibility for group coverage generally requires that an employee be full-time and actively at work. At a minimum, coverage can be purchased for an active employee and/or the spouse. Some policies also make coverage available to retirees and to other family members of eligible persons such as minor children, parents, parents-in-law, and possibly adult children. There may be a maximum age for eligibility, but it is often age 80 or 85.
- The cost of group coverage is usually slightly less than the cost of individual coverage.
- An employee typically has less choice in benefit levels and the duration of benefits under a group policy. The amounts and duration of benefits are selected by the employer and normally apply to all employees. However, some policies do allow choice but to a lesser extent than is allowed under individual policies.
- If a participant leaves employment, the group coverage usually can be continued on a direct-payment basis, under either the group contract or an individual contract.

Answers to Self-Test Questions
15-1. False. Both group and individual medical expense policies exclude custodial care.
15-2. True.
15-3. False. The NAIC model legislation establishes guidelines that have been adopted by several states (not federally). Furthermore, older policies that are still in existence and were written prior to the adoption of the model legislation or one of the later revisions may be unaffected.
15-4. True.
15-5. False. A long-term care insurance contract cannot provide for a cash surrender value or other money that can be borrowed or paid, assigned, or pledged as collateral for a loan.
15-6. False. Under HIPAA, a chronically ill person must be unable to perform only two activities of daily living.
15-7. False. Coverage under a group long-term care insurance contract cannot be offered through a cafeteria plan on a tax-favored basis.
15-8. True.
15-9. False. Benefits paid are a specified amount per day that is independent of the actual charge for long-term care.
15-10. True.
15-11. False. Daily benefits from a pool of money cannot exceed the daily policy benefits stated in the policy.
15-12. True.
15-13. True.

Chapter 16

Answers to Mini-Case
a. Amy and John face many property loss exposures. Examples include the possibility of fire damage to their house or theft of its contents—including the grandfather's clock and the silver service—the possibility of collision damage to their cars, and the possibility that they would incur extra expenses if they are unable to occupy their house because it has been damaged by a windstorm.
b. Amy and John also face many liability loss exposures. Examples include the possibility that they might become responsible for collision damage to somebody else's car in an auto accident, the possibility that a guest would be injured in their home, and the possibility that they could be sued for libel or slander.
c. Assuming the mortgagee is named in Amy and John's homeowners policy, the mortgagee will be protected to the extent of its interests, which equal the unpaid balance on the mortgage loan. Any check for damage to that property will probably be payable not only to Amy and John but also to the mortgagee. The insurer will also notify the mortgagee if the policy is canceled, and the mortgagee has a right to pay the premium if Amy and John do not. Under some circumstances, such as fraud on the part of Amy or John, the mortgagee will be able to recover for a covered property loss even if Amy and John's claim is denied.
d. Amy and John's insurance policy spells out their specific duties after a loss. In general, they should promptly report the loss to the insurer or its representative and cooperate with the insurer.

e. Amy and John should be advised that the replacement cost value of their house is neither its market value (which includes the land) nor its $240,000 purchase price but, rather, what it would cost to build the house today with materials of like kind and quality. The mortgagee requires insurance in the amount of the mortgage (which is 80 percent of the purchase price), and the homeowners policy limits their recovery if the limit of insurance does not equal at least 80 percent of the replacement cost value of the house. Generally, the best advice is to insure to 100 percent of the home's replacement cost value (not including land). Amy and John plan to spend quite a bit of money repairing, redecorating, and maintaining the house. Renovations will increase its market value, but unless the building is expanded, they will not generally increase the home's replacement cost value. However, Amy and John should periodically review insurance limits to be sure they remain consistent with the insurable value of the property.

With regard to deductibles, Amy and John should determine how much their premiums would be reduced by electing an optional higher deductible and weigh that against the probability of having a loss. Homeowners losses are relatively uncommon, and they should be able to absorb an insured loss of at least $1,000 since they have $60,000 in a money market fund.

Answers to Review Questions

16-1. Property loss exposures involve the possibility that a person or organization will sustain a property loss resulting from the damaging, destruction, taking, or loss of use of property in which that person or organization has a financial interest. A liability loss exposure involves the possibility of a claim alleging a person's or organization's legal responsibility for injury or damage suffered by another party.

16-2. Named-perils policies contain a list of the covered perils. If a peril is not listed, losses resulting from that peril are not covered. In contrast, open-perils policies cover all losses to covered property unless the loss is specifically excluded.

16-3. The duties of the insured and insurer when a property loss occurs are as follows:

a. A typical property insurance policy requires that the insured must promptly tell the insurer there has been a property loss, and the insured must cooperate with the insurer in showing that a covered loss occurred within the policy period. If property coverage is on a named-perils basis, the insured needs to establish that the loss was caused by one of the named perils. The insured also needs to cooperate with the insurer in establishing the value of covered property that has been lost or damaged.

b. The insurance company has a duty to pay losses fairly and promptly once the coverage and the value of the property loss have been established. The insurance policy and/or state law might specify that losses are payable within a stated period such as 60 days. The insurer will settle property insurance claims by paying the policyowner unless some other person with an insurable interest is also covered by the policy.

16-4. Jim would recover as follows:

a. If Coverage A in his policy is $250,000 and Jim has the house repaired, Jim would receive $60,000, the replacement cost of the loss, because he carries insurance greater than 80 percent of the replacement cost of his home at the time of the loss (.80 x $300,000 = $240,000).

b. If Coverage A in his policy is $220,000 and Jim has the house repaired, he would be paid only $55,000 because his amount of insurance is less than the 80 percent required ($240,000) but the amount calculated by the following formula is greater than the actual cash value of the loss:

$$\frac{\text{Insurance carried}}{80\% \text{ of replacement cost of the house}} \times \frac{\text{Replacement cost}}{\text{of the loss}} = \frac{\$220,000}{\$240,000} \times \$60,000 = \$55,000$$

c. If Coverage A in his policy is $180,000, Jim would receive the actual cash value of the loss, $50,000, because it is larger than the amount produced by the underinsurance formula:

$$\frac{\text{Insurance carried}}{80\% \text{ of replacement cost of the house}} \times \frac{\text{Replacement cost}}{\text{of the loss}} = \frac{\$180,000}{\$240,000} \times \$60,000 = \$45,000$$

16-5. The insurers would make these payments:

a. If Policy A and Policy B both have pro rata other insurance provisions, Policy A would pay 55.56 percent ($100,000/$180,000) of the loss, or $50,000, and Policy B would pay 44.44 percent ($80,000/$180,000) of the loss, or $40,000.

b. If Policy A is written on a primary basis and Policy B is written on an excess basis, Policy A would pay first up to a maximum of its limit and then Policy B would pay any unpaid loss up to a maximum of its limit. In this case, Policy A would pay $90,000 (the entire loss) and Policy B would not be required to pay.

c. Policy B would pay $80,000 (its limit) and Policy A would pay nothing.

16-6.   The types of liability losses are as follows:

    a. The cost of surgery, loss of income, and pain and suffering for the driver of the car that Billy hit are bodily injury liability losses.

    b. The cost to the phone company to repair its pole is a property damage liability loss.

    c. The suit by the driver of the other car that resulted from Billy slandering her with foul language in front of the witnesses at the accident scene is under personal injury liability.

16-7.   For negligence to be proven, there must be (1) a legal duty to act, or not to act, depending on the circumstances and the persons involved, (2) a wrong, or voluntary breach of legal duty, based on a "prudent person" standard of conduct, (3) an injury or damage, and (4) a proximate relationship between the wrong and an injury or damage, where a continuous succession of events occurred, from the act to the final event that caused the injury.

16-8.   The following are the applicable rules of law:

    a. Under imputed negligence, legal responsibility for injuries or damage is extended to other persons such as employers. In this case, because the negligent party, Billy, acted in the capacity of employee or agent of Jones Dry Cleaners, both the wrongdoer and the owner of the property can be held liable.

    b. Under contributory negligence, anyone who is so negligent as to contribute to his or her own injuries or damage cannot recover from another for these injuries.

    c. Under comparative negligence, damages are diminished in proportion to the amount of negligence attributable to the person injured or to the owner or person in control of the damaged property.

16-9.   The duties of the insured and obligations of the insurer are summarized below.

    a. Duties imposed on the insured typically include the following:

        • to give written notice as soon as practical to the company or its agent

        • to forward promptly to the insurance company every notice, demand, summons, or other process relating to the accident or occurrence

        • to assist the insurance company, at its request, to (1) make settlement, (2) enforce the insured's rights against others who may be liable to the insured, (3) help with the conduct of suits and attend hearings and trials, (4) secure and give evidence, and (5) obtain the evidence of witnesses

    b. First, the insurer will provide a defense at its expense by a counsel of its choice, even if a suit is groundless, false, or fraudulent. Second, the insurer will pay up to the limit of liability for the damages for which the insured is legally liable.

16-10.   The basic tax rules are as follows:

    a. *deductibility of premium.* Premiums paid by individual taxpayers for personal property and liability insurance are not deductible. However, premiums paid for business coverage by an individual, partnership, or corporation are a deductible business expense.

    b. *taxation of premiums for employees.* Group property and liability insurance as an employee benefit typically requires that an employee pays the full cost of his or her coverage, and the tax implications are the same as if the employee had purchased an individual policy. If the employer pays any part of an employee's premium, for either individual or group coverage, the employer can deduct this cost as a business expense. However, the employer must report this amount as taxable income.

    c. *taxation of benefits.* Benefits paid under liability insurance policies do not result in taxable income to the policyowner or insured even if they are paid on their behalf. Under property insurance policies, benefits paid for direct loss to real or personal property result in a capital gain to the extent that a taxpayer receives reimbursement in excess of his or her basis in the property. However, the situation is treated as an involuntary conversion, and the gain can be postponed to the extent that a taxpayer uses the proceeds to purchase replacement property, and the purchase amount exceeds the taxpayer's basis in the lost or damaged property.

       The situation for certain consequential losses is less clear. To the extent that benefits are paid for actual expenses incurred, there is no taxable income. Business interruption coverage, however, will result in ordinary income if it is written on a basis that insures the policyowner against loss of net profits.

    d. *deductibility of uninsured losses.* The Internal Revenue Code allows a deduction for certain losses to the extent that they are not compensated for by insurance. Those losses must arise from fire, storm, shipwreck, or other casualty, or from theft. The maximum amount of the losses for tax purposes is the lesser of (1) the decrease in the fair market value of the property as a result of the casualty or theft or (2) the taxpayer's adjusted basis in the property. Losses can be deducted in full by businesses and by individual taxpayers if the loss is incurred in a trade or business or any transaction entered into for profit. Other losses of individual taxpayers are deductible only if the taxpayer itemizes income tax deductions and then only to the extent that (1) each separate loss exceeds $100 and (2) the total of all casualty and theft losses for the year exceeds 10 percent of adjusted gross income.

Answers to Self-Test Questions

16-1.   True.

16-2.   False. Open-perils coverage refers to a policy that covers all losses to covered property unless the loss is specifically excluded. Some named-peril policies contain a very long list of named perils.

16-3.   True.

16-4.   True.

16-5.   True.

16-6.   True.

16-7.   False. Liability losses can involve bodily injury, property damage, personal injury, contractual liability, wrongful acts, or other offenses.

16-8.   False. Torts can result from negligence, intentional acts or omissions, and strict or absolute liability.

16-9.   True.

16-10. False. If Pete was only 20 percent at fault for an auto accident in a state that relies on the contributory negligence standard, he could collect none of his damages from the other party.

16-11. False. People can be responsible not only for their own negligent acts but also for those of others. For example, employers can be personally liable for the torts of their employees. In states with vicarious liability laws, the owner of an auto can be liable for the acts of another person driving the car.

16-12. True.

16-13. True.

16-14. False. Many additional choices must be made. With property insurance, consumers often need to decide which causes of loss will be covered and to select a deductible. Because most policies contain exclusions and limitations, consumers also need to ensure that their policy or policies cover all significant property that is exposed to loss. Endorsements or additional policies may be needed to provide some necessary coverages. With liability insurance, it is important to recognize that large claims or judgments can consume a client's financial resources, and to make sure that all relevant sources of liability loss are recognized and covered, using additional policies or endorsements as necessary.

Chapter 17

Answers to Mini-Case

The basic needs for property insurance on the Adams family house can be met with a homeowners HO-3 policy with a Coverage A limit of $375,000 (the current replacement cost value) and an inflation guard endorsement to provide inflationary increases. The homeowners policy will name River Bank as mortgagee, and a $375,000 limit will be more than adequate to protect the bank's interest in the unpaid value of the mortgage. The property limit for Coverage C will automatically be set at 50 percent of Coverage A, or $187,500. However, the Adams family would well be advised to purchase the optional personal property replacement cost loss settlement endorsement, and their insurer will probably require then that they increase the Coverage C limit.

The Adamses should purchase a Coverage E liability insurance limit that meets the underlying insurance requirement of their umbrella liability policy (discussed in chapter 18). The standard $1,000 medical payments to others coverage limit can be increased, but this is not as important as some of the other coverage options.

Even if it is not required by their lender, the Adamses should consider flood insurance if there is any possibility of flood damage to their home and should also consider earthquake insurance, depending on their location.

A scheduled personal property endorsement should be considered to provide broader coverage on Don's saxophone, the silver service, Eve's diamond rings, and the oil paintings if they are valued art objects.

In light of Eve's home business activities, she should investigate the need for home business insurance coverage, increased limits on business property, or other options to address the property and liability exposures created by her business.

An assisted-living care coverage endorsement should be added to protect Phillip's property and liability exposures.

As members of a homeowners association, the Adams family could face an assessment if the association incurs a property loss or a liability loss that is not adequately covered by the association's insurance policy. The association's swimming pool could result in a large liability claim. Although the HO-3 policy provides $1,000 in loss assessment coverage for both property and liability claims, this amount can be increased by endorsement, and the Adamses should seriously consider doing so.

In addition to adding endorsements that improve their coverage, the Adamses can do some things to reduce their insurance costs. A larger property deductible, for example, might substantially reduce their premium costs by eliminating coverage for small claims while still providing coverage against major losses. If their home has an alarm system, a premium discount might be available if the policy is properly endorsed.

Other endorsements discussed in chapter 17 could also be considered. For example, because the house is only 5 years old, it probably does not face a significant ordinance or law exposure, but it is possible a recent ordinance would affect their house, and this possibility should be considered.

Answers to Review Questions

17-1. Frank and Ellen are covered, as the named insured and spouse. Elaine is covered as a relative residing in the named insured's household. Destiny, who is temporarily residing at college, is also a covered person.

17-2. An insured location includes

- the residence premises. This includes a one- to four-family dwelling, other structures, and grounds where the policyowner resides as shown in the declaration.

- that part of other premises, other structures, and grounds used by the named insured or spouse as a residence if it is shown in the declarations or if it is acquired during the policy year as a residence by the named insured

- other premises not owned by an insured but where an insured is temporarily residing

- vacant land, other than farm land, owned by or rented to an insured

- individual or family cemetery plots or burial vaults of an insured

- any part of a premises occasionally rented to an insured for other than business use

17-3. Nathan's HO-3 policy provides the following:

   a. Damage to Nathan's home done by vandals is covered under the open-perils Coverage A (as long as the house has not been vacant for more than 60 consecutive days preceding the loss).

   b. Damage to the inside walls and hardwood floors caused by rain water that blew in when Nathan accidentally left the window open during a storm is covered under the open-perils Coverage A because it is not excluded.

   c. Damage to the family room couch and end tables caused by rain water that blew in when Nathan accidentally left the window open during a storm is not covered under the named-perils Coverage C, because the windstorm peril does not cover the damage from rain that was not a result of direct wind or hail damage to the building.

   d. Damage to the walls of the house caused by an earthquake is excluded under Coverage A. Nathan would have to obtain coverage via a policy endorsement or a separate policy.

   e. Stains on the wall-to-wall carpet due to housebreaking the new family pet and the hole in the outside of the house cut by a woodpecker are excluded under Coverage A.

   f. Theft of the $2,000 cast aluminum porch furniture from the deck off the back of Nathan's home is covered under Coverage C, which includes the peril of theft.

   g. Only $200 of the $1,500 in cash burned in a fire in Nathan's home is covered under the typical HO-3 policy due to the special limits of liability for Coverage C.

   h. The damage to Nathan's wife's furs as a result of a fire is covered under Coverage C.

   i. Jewelry is covered property and theft is a covered peril under Coverage C, but recovery for the burglary claim is limited to $1,500 by special sublimit for theft of jewelry.

   j. The $1,000 of additional expense incurred while Nathan's family had to live elsewhere for a day and one-half after a small fire loss is covered under Coverage D. The limit for Coverage D is 30 percent of Coverage A (or $75,000 for Nathan).

   k. The $2,000 loss is included under Coverage B, which provides insurance for other structures on the residence premises that are set apart from the dwelling by a clear space such as Nathan's detached garage. Coverage B is open-perils and windstorm damage is not among the exclusions.

17-4. Sarah's coverage under her HO-3 policy is as follows:

   a. Assuming Sarah is legally liable for the explosion, the bodily injuries to Sarah's guests and the property damage to the side of the neighbor's house when Sarah's gas grill exploded during a cookout at her house would be covered up to the limit of Coverage E. The policy would also pay Sarah's defense costs in addition to the stated limit of liability.

b. There was no coverage when Sarah accidentally injured a coworker when running to a meeting at work, because both bodily injury and property damage arising out of or in connection with a business engaged in by the insured are excluded under Coverage E and Coverage F.

c. There was no coverage when Sarah damaged another shopper's car at the mall while carelessly backing out of a parking space, because there is an exclusion for this type of loss that would be covered by auto liability insurance.

d. Although intentional acts by an insured are excluded under Coverage E, there would be limited coverage under the additional coverages for Section II when Sarah's 3-year-old son, Matthew, ripped out some of the neighbor's flowers to make a Mother's Day gift.

e. Without regard to fault, there was medical expense coverage under Coverage F for the injury to a team member when Sarah's daughter tossed a bat into the bat rack and it bounced and hit the teammate, cutting her head. Coverage E would also apply if a lawsuit were involved.

17-5. Differences from the HO-3 coverages can be summarized as follows:

a. HO-2 differs from HO-3 in that HO-2 Coverages A and B are written on the same named-perils basis as Coverage C. HO-2 is less comprehensive and therefore a little less expensive.

b. HO-4 is often referred to as tenants homeowners insurance or renters insurance and is identical to HO-3 except that there is no Coverage A or Coverage B. The policyowner selects a limit for Coverage C, and Coverage D is 30 percent of this amount.

c. HO-5 coverage, unlike HO-3 coverage, is written on an open-perils basis.

d. HO-6 is designed to cover the loss exposures of a policyowner who lives in a condominium or cooperative unit. It is like HO-3 in that Coverage C is on a named-perils basis. This is also the amount of insurance selected by the policyowner. Coverage D is 50 percent of this amount. HO-6 provides $5,000 for Coverage A on a named-perils basis. This amount also applies to other structures and can be increased if needed. There is no Coverage B.

e. HO-8 has been written mostly on older homes where the replacement cost of a dwelling often significantly exceeds its market value. Providing replacement coverage might create a moral hazard because the policyowner could collect more under an insurance settlement than by selling the house. Perils insured against for all coverages are limited to fire, lightning, windstorm or hail, explosion, riot or civil commotion, aircraft, vehicles, smoke, vandalism and malicious mischief, and volcanic eruption. Theft is covered only from the residence premises and up to a limit of $1,000. There are also other limitations. Loss settlements under Coverages A and B are based on common construction materials and methods that are functionally equivalent to the original construction. Settlements are limited to market value if repairs are not made, although some states require loss settlements to be on an actual cash value basis.

17-6. The endorsements provide the following:

a. *Home day-care coverage* is for persons who conduct day-care businesses in their homes either for children or older adults. The endorsement provides coverage for personal property used in the day-care business and extends Section II liability coverage to home day-care services. However, liability is excluded for injuries arising out of motor vehicles, watercraft, and saddle animals and for liability arising out of sexual molestation and physical or mental abuse inflicted by an insured or an employee.

b. The *increased special limits* of liability endorsement can be used to increase coverage for some of the items where limited amounts of protection are available under Coverage C. Examples of items for which coverage can be increased include currency, securities, jewelry and watches, firearms, and electronic apparatus for use in a motor vehicle.

c. An *earthquake* endorsement can be used in most states to provide coverage for earthquakes and tremors that accompany volcanic eruption. In place of the regular deductible, there is an earthquake deductible equal to 5 percent of the limit of insurance that applies to Coverage A or Coverage C, whichever is greater. In California, earthquake coverage is sold by many insurers along with homeowners policies, but the insurer is a state agency established to make earthquake coverage available to homeowners.

d. The *inflation guard* endorsement provides automatic increases for all Section I coverages by the percentage selected.

e. The *personal property replacement cost loss* endorsement changes the loss settlement basis for personal property from actual cash value to replacement cost. Certain property, such as antiques, fine art and collectibles, is not eligible for replacement cost coverage.

    f.   The *scheduled personal property* endorsement broadens coverage on specific categories of valuable personal property. Coverage is open-perils with few exceptions and applies worldwide except for fine art that is covered only in the United States and Canada. There is also limited coverage for up to 30 days for newly acquired property in a category insured under the endorsement. Losses, except for fine art, are generally settled on an actual cash value basis.

    g.   The *business pursuits* endorsement provides coverage for liability that arises out of or in connection with a business engaged in by an insured, and it is most commonly used by persons in sales, clerical, and teaching occupations. Coverage does not apply with respect to a business owned or financially controlled by an insured or in which an insured is a partner. There is no coverage for liability that arises out of professional services, with the exception of teaching.

17-7.   For property owners to be eligible for flood insurance, they must live in a community that participates in the NFIP. These communities must agree to establish and enforce certain land use restrictions to minimize the community's exposure to flood losses.

    A homeowner can purchase insurance on the dwelling, its contents, or both. Coverage is similar to that provided for other perils under the homeowners policy, with some additional exceptions. Losses on the dwelling are settled on an actual cash value basis, but replacement cost coverage can be endorsed under some circumstances. Contents coverage applies only on the residence premises except when property is removed to protect it from flood, and there is an extensive list of property that is not covered under the policy.

17-8.   Several alternatives for coverage are available, but policies can be more limited than those written in the normal marketplace. Some companies specialize in the substandard market and write coverage for a variety of properties but at higher-than-normal premiums.

    Many states have taken a variety of actions to make coverage available, often at subsidized rates. State-run FAIR programs provide insurance for buildings and their contents if the property owner is unable to obtain coverage in the standard insurance market, for whatever reason. In most cases, coverage is written by a pool or syndicate of private insurers who are assessed for any losses of the plan if premiums are inadequate. Each state has its own FAIR plan, and the plans differ.

    Some states, primarily in the Southeast and on the Gulf Coast, have beachfront and windstorm plans to provide protection that insurers are unwilling to write because of the loss exposure to hurricanes. Some of these plans cover only the perils of windstorm and hail, and property owners obtain protection for other perils in the normal insurance market.

    Finally, the amount of insurance needed on an expensive home may exceed the limit an insurer is willing to write. In other cases, replacement cost substantially exceeds market value. Some insurers specialize in this market and have their own policies to meet the needs of the well-to-do. Other insurers tailor standard homeowners forms (such as the HO-3 with endorsements that were previously described).

17-9.   Some characteristics of title insurance include the following:

- The policy provides protection only against unknown title defects that have occurred prior to the effective date of the policy but are discovered after the effective date.
- The policy is written on the assumption that losses will not occur because most title defects are known and listed in the policy.
- The policy term is indefinite and continues until title to the property is again transferred. At that time, the new owner will need to purchase a new title insurance policy because the existing policy is not assignable.
- The premium is paid only once—when the policy is issued—and the policy cannot be canceled by either party.
- The insured is indemnified up to the policy limits if a loss occurs. However, there is no guarantee that possession of the property will be retained.
- The amount of insurance is usually the initial purchase price of the property, and a potential loss in the future can be much higher than the policy limit because of inflation.

Answers to Self-Test Questions

17-1.   True.

17-2.   False. Regardless of age, children are covered under their parents' homeowners policy as long as they continue to reside in their parents' household.

17-3.   False. The limits for homeowners Coverages B, C, and D are additional amounts of insurance and do not affect the amount of coverage (Coverage A) on the dwelling.

17-4.   True.

17-5.   False. An HO-3 policy covers damage to the insured's residence against open perils but excludes, among other things, earthquake and flood.

17-6.   False. In a homeowners policy, losses to the dwelling under Coverage A are settled on a replacement cost basis, while losses under personal property Coverage C are settled on an actual cash value basis (unless an endorsement is added for replacement cost).

17-7.   True.

17-8.   False. In a homeowners policy, the amount payable for the loss of money and securities is limited for all perils.

17-9.   True.

17-10. False. The liability coverage contained in an unendorsed homeowners policy provides protection against suits for bodily injury and property damage, but it excludes intentional acts (personal injury). However, the policy can be endorsed to provide coverage for personal injury liability as well.

17-11. True.

17-12. True.

17-13. False. A person who lives in a condominium should carry an HO-6 Unit-owners Form because the association covers the building and detached structures. A renter should buy an HO-4 Contents Broad Form.

17-14. True.

17-15. False. Flood insurance is now available only to property owners who live in a community that participates in the National Flood Insurance Program. It is not available to other property owners.

17-16. False. Title insurance provides protection only against unknown title defects that have occurred prior to the effective date of the policy but were discovered after the effective date.

Chapter 18

Answers to Mini-Case

a. The umbrella policy would provide Amy and John with $1 million or more in coverage over and above the liability insurance limits of their auto policies and their homeowners policy. However, the umbrella would require underlying auto liability limits higher than the limits they are now carrying, and they should increase their auto liability limits to meet the umbrella requirements. For John, this might mean he needs to buy insurance from a specialty insurer if one will accept his driving record, rather than purchasing insurance under the assigned-risk plan in his state.

b. (1) If Amy's car is stolen, the other-than-collision coverage of her policy will apply.

    (2) If John's car sustains fire damage, other-than-collision coverage *would* apply if he had purchased that coverage. However, he has no coverage for this loss.

    (3) Amy has no coverage for collision damage because she has not purchased collision coverage. (Uninsured motorists coverage applies only to bodily injury in most states.)

    (4) A personal auto policy provides coverage for pedestrians struck by an auto. It would not cover this incident unless John was injured while getting into or out of a motor vehicle.

c. John should be sure SKH has adequate limits of auto liability insurance that would protect him if he causes an accident while driving a car owned by SKH or rented on behalf of SKH. If John does not believe SKH has adequate limits, he can purchase an extended non-owned coverage—vehicles furnished or available for regular use endorsement to his personal auto policy.

d. Because a personal auto policy provides essentially the same coverage on a car rented to the insured as it provides on their own car(s), many people find it unnecessary to pay for extra coverage when they rent a car. Amy and John do not currently have collision coverage on their owned cars. Because any vehicle they rent is probably worth more than their own cars, they should be advised to purchase the collision damage waiver available from the car rental company (unless they are certain coverage is provided by the firm issuing the credit card they use to rent the car).

e. First, John's auto insurance premiums are high because of his driving record. It would behoove him to change his driving habits so that he qualifies for a better rate in the future, when his driving record improves. Second, it pays to shop around, because auto insurance is very competitive in most areas. Last but not least, auto insurance rates are often based on the vehicle involved, and Amy and John should consider safety features and insurance costs when buying or replacing a car.

Answers to Review Questions

18-1.   Key problems include the large number of auto accidents, the high cost of auto accidents, uninsured and underinsured drivers, the difficulty of some persons in obtaining auto insurance, and the affordability of that insurance.

18-2.   Your client should consider purchasing uninsured and underinsured motorists coverage, because even in states with compulsory insurance laws:

   • The compensation must come through traditional legal channels and can be delayed by an overburdened legal system.

   • Some drivers may not register their vehicles; others may drop insurance after a vehicle is registered.

   • A person may be injured by a hit-and-run driver, an out-of-state driver without insurance, a driver of a stolen car, or a driver of a fraudulently registered auto.

   • The required liability limits are relatively low, leaving some motorists underinsured.

18-3.   Compulsory insurance requires the owners of autos to carry liability insurance (or to post a cash deposit, bond, or other security) before a vehicle can be registered. Shortcomings of this system were discussed in question 18-2.

   Financial responsibility laws require proof of future financial responsibility by carrying insurance (or posting a cash deposit, bond, or other security) but only after some triggering event. Financial responsibility laws have the same shortcomings as compulsory insurance. In addition, they become effective only after an accident or serious offense and do not provide any compensation to the innocent victims of that accident.

   Unsatisfied judgment funds are established by the state to compensate persons who are unable to collect a legal judgment resulting from an auto accident. The injured person must obtain a legal judgment against the negligent party and show that the judgment cannot be collected. The maximum claim is usually limited to the state's minimum compulsory insurance requirement and is reduced by collateral sources of recovery. The collection process is slow and cumbersome, and some states' funds are inadequately funded.

   Uninsured motorists coverage provides the insured with the amount he or she would have collected from the insurer of an uninsured driver had that driver been carrying insurance. Uninsured motorists coverage does not apply if the negligent party carries insurance that has inadequate limits to fully indemnify the innocent party. The limits of coverage are equal only to the state's compulsory insurance or financial responsibility benefit unless the policyowner has purchased higher limits, and the insured must establish that the other party was legally liable. The coverage usually applies to bodily injury only. The cost of the coverage is borne by the innocent victim, not the uninsured driver.

   Underinsured motorists coverage provides protection to auto accident victims when a negligent driver has insufficient insurance limits to pay for the damages for which he or she is responsible. Shortcomings are similar to those of the uninsured motorists coverage.

   No-fault auto insurance provides first-party benefits to injured persons and imposes some restrictions on their rights to sue negligent parties. No-fault has not necessarily resulted in lower premiums. In addition, it restricts the right in some states to sue for pain and suffering, and it shifts some costs of auto accidents from negligent parties to innocent victims.

18-4.   In each situation, the settlement would be handled as follows:

   a. In a state with compulsory liability insurance, John would sue the driver of the other car and, given the assumptions with regard to fault, receive payment for the $40,000 in bodily injury plus any pain and suffering to the extent of the liability coverage on the other car. If the teenager had no liability coverage or less than the amount of John's uninsured and underinsured motorists coverages, those coverages in John's own policy would respond.

   b. If the accident occurred in a state with a modified no-fault law containing a $5,000 threshold, John's own insurer would pay for lost wages and medical expenses from benefits available under his no-fault coverage. (Even if he is from a state without no-fault, his PAP will automatically provide no-fault coverage when he is driving in a no-fault state.) Because his bodily injuries exceed the $5,000 threshold, he can sue the other driver for bodily injury losses, including pain and suffering. His insurance company would be reimbursed to the extent that any of the amount from the legal judgment duplicates the no-fault benefits received. If the teenager had no liability coverage or less than the amount of John's uninsured and underinsured motorists coverages, those coverages in John's own policy would respond for the amount unpaid in excess of the no-fault benefits.

18-5.   A PAP can be written on eligible vehicles owned or leased by an individual or by a husband or wife residing in the same household. Vehicles with other forms of ownership can be insured with an endorsement. Eligible vehicles include private passenger autos, such as cars, vans, and sports utility vehicles, owned by the policyowner or leased under a written contract of six continuous months or longer. Also eligible are newly acquired autos, trailers, temporary substitute vehicles, and pickups with a gross weight of 10,000 pounds or less. Vans and pickups are ineligible for coverage under some circumstances when used for the transportation or delivery of goods and materials. Other vehicles, such as motor homes, motorcycles, golf carts, and snowmobiles, can be insured by endorsement in most states.

18-6.   Pete would be covered up to a total of $100,000 for bodily injury to the other driver and property damage to the other driver's car. Pete's own car would be covered by the collision coverage subject to the deductible as long as he notifies his company that he wants collision coverage on the new car within 14 days of purchase.

18-7.   Tom's personal auto policy would pay these amounts:
   a.   With split limits, Tom's policy would pay the claim for $5,000 of bodily injury but only $50,000 of the property damage to the truck and its contents. Tom would have to pay the remaining $100,000 out of his pocket unless he has an umbrella liability policy.
   b.   With a single limit of $300,000, all $155,000 of claims for bodily injury and property damage would be paid by Tom's personal auto policy.

18-8.   Betty's policy provides coverage as follows:
   a.   Unless Betty's business involves use of the vehicle as a public or livery conveyance hired out to carry persons or property, her liability coverage applies.
   b.   Betty has liability coverage under her PAP only if she has added an endorsement to include liability coverage on this car.
   c.   The friend's policy is primary because it covers an "owned vehicle," and Betty's insurance is secondary or excess because she is driving a "nonowned vehicle." Betty's policy will pay only on an excess basis after the limits of the owner's policy are exhausted.

18-9.   If the friend's car is furnished for the client's regular use, the client's PAP provides no coverage; a court might need to determine whether the facts of this situation involve a car furnished for the client's regular use. Assuming coverage applies, when a person drives a friend's car, the first person is a named insured under his or her own PAP while driving another auto. He or she is also an insured under the friend's PAP as a person using the covered auto. In this situation, the friend's policy is primary because it covers an "owned vehicle," and the driver's insurance is secondary or excess because he or she is driving a "nonowned vehicle." The driver's policy will pay only on an excess basis after the limits of the owner's policy are exhausted.

18-10.   Part B of the PAP provides payment for the reasonable and necessary medical expenses of an insured as a result of an auto accident. Benefits are paid regardless of fault. The insureds under Part B include the named insured, spouse, and any family members (1) while occupying either a motor vehicle designed for use on public roads or a trailer or (2) when struck as a pedestrian by such a vehicle or trailer. Any other person, such as a child being transported, who is injured while occupying a covered auto is also an insured. The answer to this question might be different in a state with a no-fault law.

18-11.   The following coverages apply:
   a.   Coverage under Part D, Coverage for Damage to Your Auto, applies to nonowned vehicles that are rented on a temporary basis such as when an insured is on a trip. Damage to the nonowned auto caused by the impact of that auto with an object is covered under Part D's collision coverage.
   b.   Damage to the nonowned auto caused by malicious mischief or vandalism is covered under Part D's other-than-collision coverage.
   c.   Damage to the nonowned auto caused by the contact of that auto with an animal is covered under Part D's other-than-collision coverage.

18-12.   A miscellaneous type vehicle endorsement is used to cover miscellaneous types of owned vehicles, including motorcycles and dune buggies. Each vehicle is listed in a schedule, and the same coverages that apply to autos in the PAP can be purchased. Likewise, a snowmobile endorsement can be used to insure snowmobiles.

18-13.   Without an endorsement, the PAP does not provide coverage when an insured is driving in Mexico. Acceptable coverage must be obtained through a licensed Mexican insurance company prior to the trip. Driving in Mexico without such coverage is a criminal offense. Coverage can be purchased at the border. Alternatively, it may be possible to add this protection to an existing PAP if an insurance company is a member of a foreign insurance association; however, this endorsement is primarily used by people who live near the border and occasionally take brief trips to Mexico. The endorsement is effective only if the insured has also purchased liability insurance through a Mexican insurer and coverage is excess over that policy. The main advantage of the endorsement is the ability to have higher liability limits than the Mexican insurance, as well as other policy coverages.

18-14.   Hard-to-insure drivers can usually find some coverage in the residual market, which consists of specialty insurers and state programs to make insurance available, though not necessarily affordable. State programs usually follow one of three models: auto insurance plans, joint underwriting associations, or reinsurance facilities. A small number of drivers with very poor driving records may still be unable to obtain insurance from any of these sources in some states.

18-15.   Clients should evaluate the cost of coverage, the financial strength of the insurer, and the service from the company and its agents.

18-16.   For some watercraft, liability coverage is available under a homeowners policy, which provides no protection for larger boats and little physical damage protection for any boat. Boatowners policies, for smaller boats, and yacht policies, for larger boats, contain liability coverage, medical payments coverage, uninsured boaters coverage, and physical damage coverage. Also available are coverages for the legal obligation of the policyowner to remove a wrecked or sunken vessel, for liability arising out of transportation of the boat on land, for costs of towing and assistance if the boat is disabled, and for liability to crew members and other maritime workers.

   Aviation policies for private aircraft pay for bodily injury liability that arises out of the insured's ownership, maintenance, or use of insured aircraft. Coverage also applies to bodily injury liability arising out of the location where the insured aircraft is stored. Medical payments coverage is available to cover passengers, and crew members can be covered for an additional premium. Physical damage coverage is open-perils.

18-17.   A personal umbrella policy is designed to provide liability coverage for catastrophic legal claims or judgments. Without broad liability insurance of sufficiently high limits, individuals face the possibility of having assets and/or income seized to pay a legal judgment. The umbrella policy covers bodily injury and property damage liability, as well as personal injury liability. Most personal umbrella policies also pay defense costs not payable by underlying policies, and they provide other supplementary coverages similar to those in the homeowners and PAP policies (premiums on appeal bonds, expenses incurred at the company's request, and so forth).

Answers to Self-Test Questions

18-1.   False. Even in compulsory liability states, there are uninsured and even unlicensed drivers. Also, many drivers carry only the limits required by law and thus are underinsured. Therefore, uninsured and underinsured motorists coverages are necessary even in states with compulsory liability laws.

18-2.   False. Compulsory insurance laws require owners of autos to carry liability insurance before a vehicle can be registered. Financial responsibility laws only require proof of future financial responsibility under certain circumstances.

18-3.   True.

18-4.   False. Under most no-fault laws, the right to sue the negligent party exists once a dollar or verbal threshold has been met. No state has adopted a pure no-fault law.

18-5.   False. No-fault benefits in most states include rehabilitation expenses, loss of earnings, expenses for essential services, funeral expenses, and survivors' benefits, as well as medical expenses.

18-6.   True.

18-7.   True.

18-8.   False. If a client has $100,000/$300,000/$50,000 limits of liability in her PAP, she would be fully covered for the $20,000 of property damage, but she would be covered only to the extent of $100,000 of the other driver's bodily injury claim.

18-9.   True.

18-10.   False. If Jim rented a car, damaged it, and was sued by the rental company, he would be covered under the collision or other-than-collision coverages of his PAP for the property damage to the rental car. Liability coverage excludes damage to property rented to the insured.

18-11.   True.

18-12.   False. Medical payments under the PAP cover the insureds as well as other people riding in the insured's car. Insureds are covered while occupying a motor vehicle designed for use on public roads or when struck as a pedestrian.

18-13.   True.

18-14.   False. If a client hits a deer, the damage to his car would be paid under the other-than-collision coverage.

18-15.   True.

18-16.   False. Most states handle hard-to-insure drivers through automobile insurance plans.

18-17.   False. Despite the highly competitive market, the cost of auto insurance differs significantly from company to company in most states.

18-18.   True.
18-19.   True.
18-20.   True.
18-21.   True.
18-22.   False. Personal umbrella policies commonly exclude sexual molestation and failure to render professional services.

Chapter 19

Answers to Mini-Case

Issues regarding Arthur's insurance program include the following:

- Arthur should carry much higher liability limits to protect the assets accumulated over his lifetime against the possibility of loss in a lawsuit related to the business. The planner should recommend that Arthur buy a commercial umbrella policy with limits at least as high as Arthur's personal umbrella policy and increase the liability limits of the BOP to meet the umbrella's underlying requirements.
- Arthur's private tutoring introduces a special concern, especially because it involves high school girls. If he examines his BOP and umbrella policy carefully, he should not be surprised to find that he has no coverage to pay the cost of defending against claims of inappropriate conduct. Arthur should be advised to pursue the possibility of professional liability insurance with a property-liability insurance professional and also to be very careful in his conduct.
- If Arthur accepts other artists' paintings on consignment, Arthur's BOP might not provide adequate property coverage to respond to any damage to this property of others. Additionally, it is difficult to place a value on works of art, and the standard replacement cost valuation of the BOP might not be adequately suited to the needs of an art gallery. Arthur should be advised to pursue this issue.
- Arthur's service on the Brick Foundation Board also exposes him to liability, especially since the Foundation might be held responsible for the safety of children traveling abroad. It is strongly recommended that Arthur verify that the Brick Foundation has directors and officers liability protection with limits high enough to provide a level of comfort.

Answers to Review Questions

19-1.   In addition to commercial property insurance on the building, the equipment, and inventory, the client is likely to need, or at least should consider the need for, the following:

- business income insurance to cover lost profits, continuing expenses, and/or extra expenses to minimize the suspension of business after the occurrence of a direct physical damage loss to business property
- crime insurance, especially to cover employee dishonesty
- inland marine insurance to cover goods in transit
- equipment breakdown insurance to cover repairs or replacement of machinery that breaks down
- commercial general liability insurance to cover premises and operations liability and products liability
- business auto insurance for company vehicles
- workers' compensation and employers liability insurance to provide protection for injuries to employees
- directors and officers liability insurance (if the business is incorporated)
- employment practices liability insurance

19-2.   The Business Income (without Extra Expense) Coverage Form covers the sum of (1) net profit or loss that would have been earned or incurred during a period of business suspension and (2) normal continuing business expenses, including payroll, during the suspension. The Business Income (and Extra Expense) Coverage Form provides for the same expenses, as well as expenses incurred to avoid or minimize the suspension of operations, even if they do not otherwise reduce the business income loss. The Extra Expense Coverage Form provides extra expense insurance for organizations that must remain in operation after a property loss and, therefore, are unlikely to have a significant decrease in revenue. However, the extra expenses of remaining open can be significant.

19-3.   First, commercial crime forms typically cover money, which includes currency, coins, bank notes, checks, and money orders. Second, these forms also typically cover securities, which include both negotiable and nonnegotiable instruments, contracts that represent money or other property, tokens, tickets, stamps, and charge slips. Finally, these forms also typically cover tangible property other than money or securities; however, there are exclusions for certain types of property for which adequate coverage can be obtained under other types of insurance.

19-4. The following provisions are common to many crime forms:
- There is no coverage for losses caused by the named insured or any of its directors, trustees, or authorized representatives. In addition, there is no coverage for losses caused by employees except under the forms that specifically cover employee dishonesty.
- Coverage is for direct losses only. There is no coverage available for consequential losses that might result from criminal acts.
- Most of the forms require the policyowner to notify the police if there is a reason to believe that a loss results from a violation of law.
- The forms specify how settlements are valued. Currency is valued at its face value. If the currency is foreign, the insurer can pay the face value in the foreign currency or at its equivalent value in United States currency. Securities are valued as of the close of the business day a loss is discovered. The insurer can pay the value of the securities or replace them in kind. The insurer also has the option of paying the cost of a bond that is required for the issuance of replacement securities. Other property is valued at its actual cash value, and any disputes over value are settled by arbitration.

19-5. Today, inland marine policies and forms are used to write coverage for
- goods in domestic transit, by mail, rail, truck, or aircraft. Commonly, these policies cover shipments within and between the continental United States, Alaska, and Canada, but coverage can be endorsed, for example, for shipments to Mexico. Depending on the terms of sale, the responsibility for goods being shipped can fall on the shipper, the carrier, or the recipient. Any of these parties can buy insurance as needed. Owners of property can purchase transit policies to cover property damage to their goods while in the course of transit by common carriers, contract carriers, or their own vehicles. Certain policies, such as motor truck cargo insurance, are used by common carriers or contract carriers to cover customers' goods when the carrier is legally liable for the damage. These policies do not cover damage for which the carrier is not liable such as those arising from acts of God.
- mobile equipment and property that is often moved from one location to another
- property held by bailees, such as dry cleaners, repair shops, and public warehouses, who often have possession of significant amounts of customers' goods. A bailee liability policy can be purchased to cover damage to these goods when the bailee is legally liable. Many bailees purchase a bailees customers policy, which provides coverage regardless of whether the bailee is legally liable.
- property of certain dealers who own a significant amount of inventory that is likely to be transported such as jewelry, furs, fine art, cameras, musical equipment, stamps, coins, and mobile and agricultural equipment
- instrumentalities of transportation and communication, which include bridges, tunnels, pipelines, television towers, satellite dishes, and power lines
- gaps left by a policyowner's other commercial insurance policies. The differences in conditions (DIC) insurance has open-perils coverage that can be used to provide earthquake and flood coverage, to provide higher limits than are otherwise obtainable, or to cover loss exposures not in basic policies.

19-6. The types of commercial liability coverage to recommend are as follows:
a. commercial general liability insurance (products liability)
b. commercial general liability insurance (business operations liability)
c. commercial general liability insurance (premises liability)
d. commercial general liability insurance (completed operations liability)
e. commercial general liability insurance (contingent liability)
f. commercial general liability insurance (premises liability)
g. commercial auto coverage (liability)
h. workers' compensation and employer liability policy (employer liability under part 2)
i. professional liability insurance, also known as malpractice insurance
j. professional liability insurance, also known as errors and omissions insurance
k. directors and officers liability insurance
l. employment practices liability insurance

19-7. Both excess liability insurance and commercial umbrella liability insurance provide additional liability limits for claims that are covered under specified underlying coverages. Under the excess liability policy, there is no drop-down coverage for claims excluded by the underlying coverages. Unlike excess policies, commercial umbrella liability insurance often covers claims excluded by the underlying policies.

19-8. Unique characteristics of surety bonds include

- *liability of the principal*. Unlike an insured under an insurance contract, a principal who defaults on a bond is liable to the surety to the extent of any expenditure the surety incurs. The surety can require the principal to post collateral to repay the surety if the principal defaults.
- *expected losses*. A surety generally expects to pay few losses and underwrites in a strict manner to determine whether the principal is capable of meeting any obligations.
- *coverage period*. The coverage period under most surety bonds is indefinite, and the premium for the bond is paid only once. In most cases, neither the surety nor the principal can cancel the bond.
- *bond limit*. A surety bond is written for a dollar limit, and that is the maximum amount of the surety's obligation to the obligee. Some bonds, however, pay court costs and interest on judgments in addition to the bond limit.
- *statutory versus nonstatutory bonds*. Governmental ordinances, regulations, or statutes require many bonds, and the provisions of these statutory bonds and the obligations of the parties are established by law. The obligation of the parties under nonstatutory bonds is established by contract between the obligee and the principal.

19-9. A businessowners policy is designed to provide property and liability coverage for small- to medium-size businesses and organizations that meet certain eligibility requirements. Two property forms are available—named-perils coverage and open-perils coverage. Losses are paid on a replacement cost basis, and there is no coinsurance provision.

19-10. Edwin's major concern would involve any claim made directly against him in his role as a corporate director. This is a matter of increasing concern in light of many financial scandals, accompanied by claims and suits, that have come to light in recent years. In addition to performing his duties diligently, Edwin should be sure the for-profit corporations have adequate directors and officers D&O liability insurance that would protect him against such claims. If adequate D&O coverage is not available, Edwin should seriously consider declining the positions.

If the not-for-profit charity does not have D&O coverage, Edwin's personal umbrella policy might protect him if he receives no compensation for his service on the board. Umbrella policies vary, and he should check his policy carefully to determine what coverage it provides. If his current policy does not provide the necessary coverage, he might be able to obtain an umbrella from another insurer that includes this protection.

Answers to Self-Test Questions

19-1. False. Commercial property insurance can cover personal property of others in the care, custody, or control of the insured, as well as buildings and business personal property of the insured.

19-2. True.

19-3. True.

19-4. True.

19-5. True.

19-6. True.

19-7. False. Advertising injury liability is covered under Coverage B of a commercial general liability coverage form.

19-8. False. Most commonly, commercial general liability coverage is written on an occurrence basis.

19-9. True.

19-10. True.

19-11. False. Even with workers' compensation laws, employers can be sued for injuries to employees.

19-12. False. Most professional liability policies are written on a claims-made basis.

19-13. True.

19-14. False. Excess liability policies do not include drop-down coverage for claims excluded by the underlying coverages, but commercial umbrella policies often do provide such coverage.

19-15. True.

19-16. True.

Index